Contents

Articles

References

Article Licenses

Operational risk management

The term **Operational Risk Management** (ORM) is defined as a continual cyclic process which includes risk assessment, risk decision making, and implementation of risk controls, which results in acceptance, mitigation, or avoidance of risk. ORM is the oversight of operational risk, including the risk of loss resulting from inadequate or failed internal processes and systems; human factors; or external events.

Four Principles of ORM

The U.S. Department of Defense summarizes the principles of ORM as follows:[1]

- Accept risk when benefits outweigh the cost.
- Accept no unnecessary risk.
- Anticipate and manage risk by planning.
- Make risk decisions at the right level.

Three Levels of ORM

In Depth

> In depth risk management is used before a project is implemented, when there is plenty of time to plan and prepare. Examples of in depth methods include training, drafting instructions and requirements, and acquiring personal protective equipment.

Deliberate

> Deliberate risk management is used at routine periods through the implementation of a project or process. Examples include quality assurance, on-the-job training, safety briefs, performance reviews, and safety checks.

Time Critical

> Time critical risk management is used during operational exercises or execution of tasks. It is defined as the effective use of all available resources by individuals, crews, and teams to safely and effectively accomplish the mission or task using risk management concepts when time and resources are limited. Examples of tools used includes execution check-lists and change management. This requires a high degree of situational awareness.[1]

ORM Process

In Depth

The International Organization for Standardization defines the risk management process in a four-step model:[2]

1. Establish context
2. Risk assessment
   - Risk identification
   - Risk analysis
   - Risk evaluation
3. Risk treatment
4. Monitor and review

This process is cyclic as any changes to the situation (such as operating environment or needs of the unit) requires re-evaluation per step one.

Deliberate

The U.S. Department of Defense summarizes the deliberate level of ORM process in a five-step model:[1]

1. Identify hazards
2. Assess hazards
3. Make risk decisions
4. Implement controls
5. Supervise (and watch for changes)

Time Critical

The U.S. Navy summarizes the time critical risk management process in a four-step model:[3]

The Link Between Time Critical and Deliberate

Time Critical Process and Mnemonic	5-Step Deliberate Process
A – Assess the situation (your potential for error)	1. Identify Hazards
B – Balance your resources (to prevent and trap errors)	2. Assess Hazards
C – Communicate (risks and intentions)	3. Make Risk Decisions
D – Do and Debrief (take action and monitor for change)	4. Implement Controls
	5. Supervise (watch for changes)

1. **A**ssess the situation.

The three conditions of the Assess step are task loading, additive conditions, and human factors.

- Task loading refers to the negative effect of increased tasking on performance of the tasks.
- Additive factors refers to having a situational awareness of the cumulative effect of variables (conditions, etc.).
- Human factors refers to the limitations of the ability of the human body and mind to adapt to the work environment (e.g. stress, fatigue, impairment, lapses of attention, confusion, and willful violations of regulations).

2. **B**alance your resources.

This refers to balancing resources in three different ways:

- Balancing resources and options available. This means evaluating and leveraging all the informational, labor, equipment, and material resources available.
- Balancing Resources verses hazards. This means estimating how well prepared you are to safely accomplish a task and making a judgement call.
- Balancing individual verses team effort. This means observing individual risk warning signs. It also means observing how well the team is communicating, knows the roles that each member is supposed to play, and the stress level and participation level of each team member.

3. **C**ommunicate risks and intentions.

- Communicate hazards and intentions.
- Communicate to the right people.
- Use the right communication style. Asking questions is a technique to opening the lines of communication. A direct and forceful style of communication gets a specific result from a specific situation.

4. **D**o and debrief. (Take action and monitor for change.)

This is accomplished in three different phases:

- Mission Completion is a point where the exercise can be evaluated and reviewed in full.
- Execute and Gauge Risk involves managing change and risk while an exercise is in progess.
- Future Performance Improvements refers to preparing a "lessons learned" for the next team that plans or executes a task.

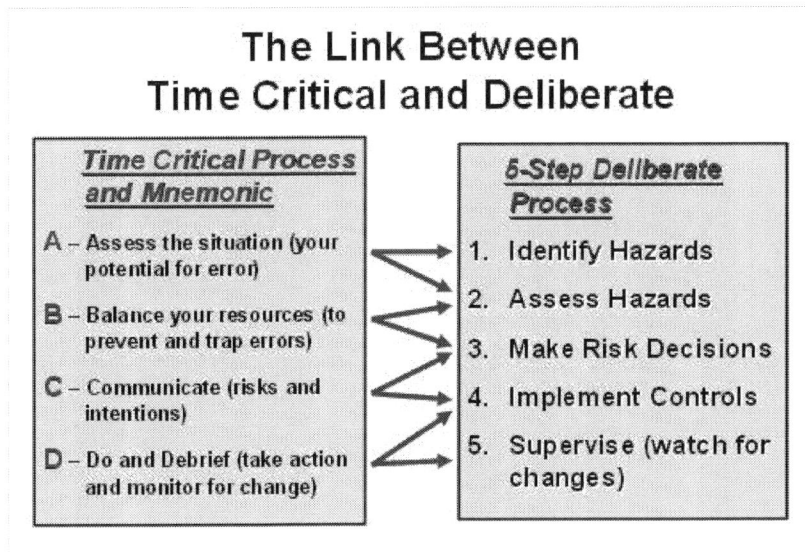

Benefits of ORM

1. Reduction of operational loss.
2. Lower compliance/auditing costs.
3. Early detection of unlawful activities.
4. Reduced exposure to future risks.

Chief Operational Risk Officer

The role of the Chief Operational Risk Officer (CORO) continues to evolve and gain importance. In addition to being responsible for setting up a robust Operational Risk Management function at companies, the role also plays an important part in increasing awareness of the benefits of sound operational risk management.

Most complex financial institutions have a Chief Operational Risk Officer. The position is also required for Banks that fall into the Basel II Advanced Measurement Approach "mandatory" category.

ORM Software

The impact of the Enron failure and the implementation of the Sarbanes-Oxley Act has caused several software development companies to create enterprise-wide software packages to manage risk. These software systems allow the financial audit to be executed at lower cost.

Forrester Research has identified 115 Governance, Risk and Compliance vendors that cover operational risk management projects. Active Agenda is an open source project dedicated to operational risk management.

References

General

- OPNAVINST 3500.39B OPERATIONAL RISK MANAGEMENT (ORM) [4]
- MARINE CORPS ORDER 3500.27B OPERATIONAL RISK MANAGEMENT (ORM) [5]

Cited

[1] "Naval Safety Center ORM" (http://www.safetycenter.navy.mil/orm/index.asp). . Retrieved November 4, 2008.
[2] "Committee Draft of ISO 31000 Risk management" (http://www.nsai.ie/uploads/file/N047_Committee_Draft_of_ISO_31000.pdf). International Organization for Standardization. 2007-06-15. .
[3] "Operational Risk Management - Time-Critical Risk Management" (https://ile-deers.nko.navy.mil/ELIAAS/logon/Welcome.jsf). U.S. Navy. . Retrieved 12 July 2009.
[4] http://doni.daps.dla.mil/Directives/03000%20Naval%20Operations%20and%20Readiness/ 03-500%20Training%20and%20Readiness%20Services/3500.39B.pdf
[5] http://safetycenter.navy.mil/instructions/orm/MCO203500.27B.pdf

External links

- The Institute of Operational Risk (http://www.ior-institute.org/) The institute provides professional recognition and enables members to maintain competency in the discipline of operational risk.

Risk management

Risk management is the identification, assessment, and prioritization of risks (defined in ISO 31000 as *the effect of uncertainty on objectives*, whether positive or negative) followed by coordinated and economical application of resources to minimize, monitor, and control the probability and/or impact of unfortunate events[1] or to maximize the realization of opportunities. Risks can come from uncertainty in financial markets, project failures, legal liabilities, credit risk, accidents, natural causes and disasters as well as deliberate attacks from an adversary. Several risk management standards have been developed including the Project Management Institute, the National Institute of Science and

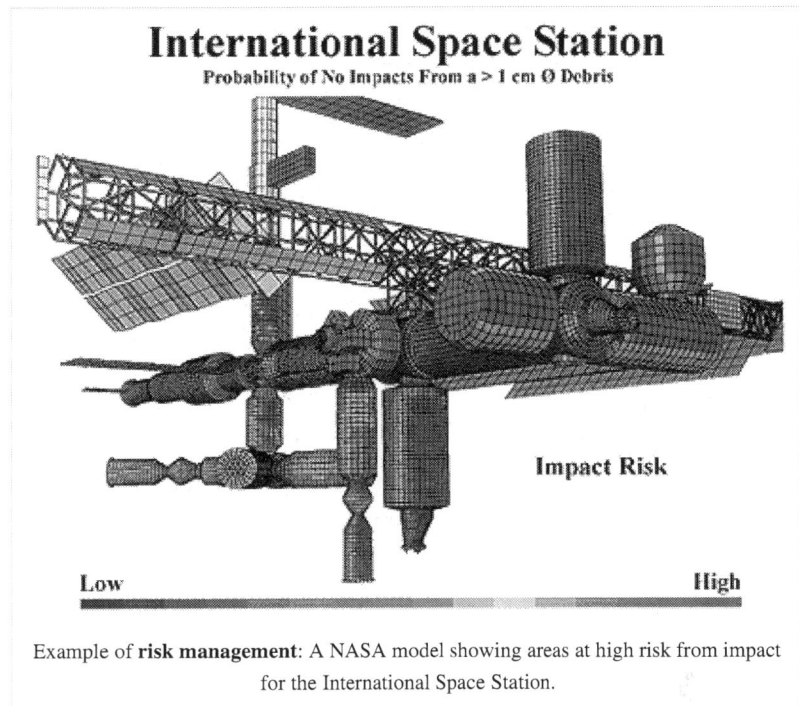

Example of **risk management**: A NASA model showing areas at high risk from impact for the International Space Station.

Technology, actuarial societies, and ISO standards.[2] [3] Methods, definitions and goals vary widely according to whether the risk management method is in the context of project management, security, engineering, industrial processes, financial portfolios, actuarial assessments, or public health and safety.

The strategies to manage risk include transferring the risk to another party, avoiding the risk, reducing the negative effect of the risk, and accepting some or all of the consequences of a particular risk.

Certain aspects of many of the risk management standards have come under criticism for having no measurable improvement on risk even though the confidence in estimates and decisions increase.[1]

Introduction

This section provides an introduction to the principles of risk management. The vocabulary of risk management is defined in ISO Guide 73, "Risk management. Vocabulary."[2]

In ideal risk management, a prioritization process is followed whereby the risks with the greatest loss and the greatest probability of occurring are handled first, and risks with lower probability of occurrence and lower loss are handled in descending order. In practice the process can be very difficult, and balancing between risks with a high probability of occurrence but lower loss versus a risk with high loss but lower probability of occurrence can often be mishandled.

Intangible risk management identifies a new type of a risk that has a 100% probability of occurring but is ignored by the organization due to a lack of identification ability. For example, when deficient knowledge is applied to a situation, a knowledge risk materializes. Relationship risk appears when ineffective collaboration occurs. Process-engagement risk may be an issue when ineffective operational procedures are applied. These risks directly reduce the productivity of knowledge workers, decrease cost effectiveness, profitability, service, quality, reputation, brand value, and earnings quality. Intangible risk management allows risk management to create immediate value from the identification and reduction of risks that reduce productivity.

Risk management also faces difficulties in allocating resources. This is the idea of opportunity cost. Resources spent on risk management could have been spent on more profitable activities. Again, ideal risk management minimizes spending and minimizes the negative effects of risks.

Method

For the most part, these methods consist of the following elements, performed, more or less, in the following order.

1. identify, characterize, and assess threats
2. assess the vulnerability of critical assets to specific threats
3. determine the risk (i.e. the expected consequences of specific types of attacks on specific assets)
4. identify ways to reduce those risks
5. prioritize risk reduction measures based on a strategy

Principles of risk management

The International Organization for Standardization (ISO) identifies the following principles of risk management:[4]

Risk management should:

- create value
- be an integral part of organizational processes
- be part of decision making
- explicitly address uncertainty
- be systematic and structured
- be based on the best available information
- be tailored
- take into account human factors
- be transparent and inclusive
- be dynamic, iterative and responsive to change
- be capable of continual improvement and enhancement

Process

According to the standard ISO 31000 "Risk management -- Principles and guidelines on implementation,"[3] the process of risk management consists of several steps as follows:

Establishing the context

Establishing the context involves:

1. **Identification** of risk in a selected domain of interest
2. **Planning** the remainder of the process.
3. **Mapping out** the following:
   - the social scope of risk management
   - the identity and objectives of stakeholders
   - the basis upon which risks will be evaluated, constraints.
4. **Defining a framework** for the activity and an agenda for identification.
5. **Developing an analysis** of risks involved in the process.
6. **Mitigation or Solution** of risks using available technological, human and organizational resources.

Identification

After establishing the context, the next step in the process of managing risk is to identify potential risks. Risks are about events that, when triggered, cause problems. Hence, risk identification can start with the source of problems, or with the problem itself.

- **Source analysis** Risk sources may be internal or external to the system that is the target of risk management.

Examples of risk sources are: stakeholders of a project, employees of a company or the weather over an airport.

- **Problem analysis** Risks are related to identified threats. For example: the threat of losing money, the threat of abuse of privacy information or the threat of accidents and casualties. The threats may exist with various entities, most important with shareholders, customers and legislative bodies such as the government.

When either source or problem is known, the events that a source may trigger or the events that can lead to a problem can be investigated. For example: stakeholders withdrawing during a project may endanger funding of the project; privacy information may be stolen by employees even within a closed network; lightning striking an aircraft during takeoff may make all people on board immediate casualties.

The chosen method of identifying risks may depend on culture, industry practice and compliance. The identification methods are formed by templates or the development of templates for identifying source, problem or event. Common risk identification methods are:

- **Objectives-based risk identification** Organizations and project teams have objectives. Any event that may endanger achieving an objective partly or completely is identified as risk.
- **Scenario-based risk identification** In scenario analysis different scenarios are created. The scenarios may be the alternative ways to achieve an objective, or an analysis of the interaction of forces in, for example, a market or battle. Any event that triggers an undesired scenario alternative is identified as risk - see Futures Studies for methodology used by Futurists.
- **Taxonomy-based risk identification** The taxonomy in taxonomy-based risk identification is a breakdown of possible risk sources. Based on the taxonomy and knowledge of best practices, a questionnaire is compiled. The answers to the questions reveal risks.[5]
- **Common-risk checking** In several industries, lists with known risks are available. Each risk in the list can be checked for application to a particular situation.[6]
- **Risk charting**[7] This method combines the above approaches by listing resources at risk, threats to those resources, modifying factors which may increase or decrease the risk and consequences it is wished to avoid. Creating a matrix under these headings enables a variety of approaches. One can begin with resources and consider the threats they are exposed to and the consequences of each. Alternatively one can start with the threats and examine which resources they would affect, or one can begin with the consequences and determine which combination of threats and resources would be involved to bring them about.

Assessment

Once risks have been identified, they must then be assessed as to their potential severity of loss and to the probability of occurrence. These quantities can be either simple to measure, in the case of the value of a lost building, or impossible to know for sure in the case of the probability of an unlikely event occurring. Therefore, in the assessment process it is critical to make the best educated guesses possible in order to properly prioritize the implementation of the risk management plan.

The fundamental difficulty in risk assessment is determining the rate of occurrence since statistical information is not available on all kinds of past incidents. Furthermore, evaluating the severity of the consequences (impact) is often quite difficult for intangible assets. Asset valuation is another question that needs to be addressed. Thus, best educated opinions and available statistics are the primary sources of information. Nevertheless, risk assessment should produce such information for the management of the organization that the primary risks are easy to understand and that the risk management decisions may be prioritized. Thus, there have been several theories and attempts to quantify risks. Numerous different risk formulae exist, but perhaps the most widely accepted formula for risk quantification is:

Rate of occurrence multiplied by the **impact of the event** equals **risk**

Composite Risk Index

The above formula can also be re-written in terms of a Composite Risk Index, as follows:

Composite Risk Index = Impact of Risk event x Probability of Occurrence

The impact of the risk event is assessed on a scale of 1 to 5, where 1 and 5 represent the minimum and maximum possible impact of an occurrence of a risk (usually in terms of financial losses).

The probability of occurrence is likewise assessed on a scale from 1 to 5, where 1 represents a very low probability of the risk event actually occurring while 5 represents a very high probability of occurrence. This axis may be expressed in either mathematical terms (event occurs once a year, once in ten years, once in 100 years etc) or may be expressed in "plain english" - event has occured here very often; event has been known to occur here; event has been known to occur in the industry etc).

The Composite Index thus can take values ranging from 1 through 25, and this range is usually arbitrarily divided into three sub-ranges. The overall risk assessment is then Low, Medium or High, depending on the sub-range containing the calculated value of the Composite Index. For instance, the three sub-ranges could be defined as 1 to 8, 9 to 16 and 17 to 25.

Note that the probability of risk occurrence is difficult to estimate since the past data on frequencies are not readily available, as mentioned above.

Likewise, the impact of the risk is not easy to estimate since it is often difficult to estimate the potential financial loss in the event of risk occurrence.

Further, both the above factors can change in magnitude depending on the adequacy of risk avoidance and prevention measures taken and due to changes in the external business environment. Hence it is absolutely necessary to periodically re-assess risks and intensify/relax mitigation measures as necessary.

Risk Options

Risk mitigation measures are usually formulated according to one or more of the following major risk options, which are:

1. Design a new business process with adequate built-in risk control and containment measures from the start.

2. Periodically re-assess risks that are accepted in ongoing processes as a normal feature of business operations and modify mitigation measures.

3. Transfer risks to an external agency (e.g. an insurance company)

4. Avoid risks altogether (e.g. by closing down a particular high-risk business area)

Later research has shown that the financial benefits of risk management are less dependent on the formula used but are more dependent on the frequency and how risk assessment is performed.

In business it is imperative to be able to present the findings of risk assessments in financial terms. Robert Courtney Jr. (IBM, 1970) proposed a formula for presenting risks in financial terms.[8] The Courtney formula was accepted as the official risk analysis method for the US governmental agencies. The formula proposes calculation of ALE (annualised loss expectancy) and compares the expected loss value to the security control implementation costs (cost-benefit analysis).

Potential risk treatments

Once risks have been identified and assessed, all techniques to manage the risk fall into one or more of these four major categories:[9]

- **Avoidance** (eliminate, withdraw from or not become involved)
- **Reduction** (optimize - mitigate)
- **Sharing** (transfer - outsource or insure)
- **Retention** (accept and budget)

Ideal use of these strategies may not be possible. Some of them may involve trade-offs that are not acceptable to the organization or person making the risk management decisions. Another source, from the US Department of Defense, Defense Acquisition University, calls these categories **ACAT**, for Avoid, Control, Accept, or Transfer. This use of the ACAT acronym is reminiscent of another ACAT (for Acquisition Category) used in US Defense industry procurements, in which Risk Management figures prominently in decision making and planning.

Risk avoidance

This includes not performing an activity that could carry risk. An example would be not buying a property or business in order to not take on the legal liability that comes with it. Another would be not flying in order not to take the risk that the airplane were to be hijacked. Avoidance may seem the answer to all risks, but avoiding risks also means losing out on the potential gain that accepting (retaining) the risk may have allowed. Not entering a business to avoid the risk of loss also avoids the possibility of earning profits.

Hazard Prevention

Hazard prevention refers to the prevention of risks in an emergency. The first and most effective stage of hazard prevention is the elimination of hazards. If this takes too long, is too costly, or is otherwise impractical, the second stage is mitigation.

Risk reduction

Risk reduction or "optimization" involves reducing the severity of the loss or the likelihood of the loss from occurring. For example, sprinklers are designed to put out a fire to reduce the risk of loss by fire. This method may cause a greater loss by water damage and therefore may not be suitable. Halon fire suppression systems may mitigate that risk, but the cost may be prohibitive as a strategy.

Acknowledging that risks can be positive or negative, optimising risks means finding a balance between negative risk and the benefit of the operation or activity; and between risk reduction and effort applied. By an offshore drilling contractor effectively applying HSE Management in its organisation, it can optimise risk to achieve levels of residual risk that are tolerable.[10]

Modern software development methodologies reduce risk by developing and delivering software incrementally. Early methodologies suffered from the fact that they only delivered software in the final phase of development; any problems encountered in earlier phases meant costly rework and often jeopardized the whole project. By developing in iterations, software projects can limit effort wasted to a single iteration.

Outsourcing could be an example of risk reduction if the outsourcer can demonstrate higher capability at managing or reducing risks.[11] For example, a company may outsource only its software development, the manufacturing of hard goods, or customer support needs to another company, while handling the business management itself. This way, the company can concentrate more on business development without having to worry as much about the manufacturing process, managing the development team, or finding a physical location for a call center.

Risk sharing

Briefly defined as "sharing with another party the burden of loss or the benefit of gain, from a risk, and the measures to reduce a risk."

The term of 'risk transfer' is often used in place of risk sharing in the mistaken belief that you can transfer a risk to a third party through insurance or outsourcing. In practice if the insurance company or contractor go bankrupt or end up in court, the original risk is likely to still revert to the first party. As such in the terminology of practitioners and scholars alike, the purchase of an insurance contract is often described as a "transfer of risk." However, technically speaking, the buyer of the contract generally retains legal responsibility for the losses "transferred", meaning that insurance may be described more accurately as a post-event compensatory mechanism. For example, a personal injuries insurance policy does not transfer the risk of a car accident to the insurance company. The risk still lies with the policy holder namely the person who has been in the accident. The insurance policy simply provides that if an accident (the event) occurs involving the policy holder then some compensation may be payable to the policy holder that is commensurate to the suffering/damage.

Some ways of managing risk fall into multiple categories. Risk retention pools are technically retaining the risk for the group, but spreading it over the whole group involves transfer among individual members of the group. This is different from traditional insurance, in that no premium is exchanged between members of the group up front, but instead losses are assessed to all members of the group.

Risk retention

Involves accepting the loss, or benefit of gain, from a risk when it occurs. True self insurance falls in this category. Risk retention is a viable strategy for small risks where the cost of insuring against the risk would be greater over time than the total losses sustained. All risks that are not avoided or transferred are retained by default. This includes risks that are so large or catastrophic that they either cannot be insured against or the premiums would be infeasible. War is an example since most property and risks are not insured against war, so the loss attributed by war is retained by the insured. Also any amounts of potential loss (risk) over the amount insured is retained risk. This may also be acceptable if the chance of a very large loss is small or if the cost to insure for greater coverage amounts is so great it would hinder the goals of the organization too much.

Create a risk management plan

Select appropriate controls or countermeasures to measure each risk. Risk mitigation needs to be approved by the appropriate level of management. For instance, a risk concerning the image of the organization should have top management decision behind it whereas IT management would have the authority to decide on computer virus risks.

The risk management plan should propose applicable and effective security controls for managing the risks. For example, an observed high risk of computer viruses could be mitigated by acquiring and implementing antivirus software. A good risk management plan should contain a schedule for control implementation and responsible persons for those actions.

According to ISO/IEC 27001, the stage immediately after completion of the risk assessment phase consists of preparing a Risk Treatment Plan, which should document the decisions about how each of the identified risks should be handled. Mitigation of risks often means selection of security controls, which should be documented in a Statement of Applicability, which identifies which particular control objectives and controls from the standard have been selected, and why.

Implementation

Implementation follows all of the planned methods for mitigating the effect of the risks. Purchase insurance policies for the risks that have been decided to be transferred to an insurer, avoid all risks that can be avoided without sacrificing the entity's goals, reduce others, and retain the rest.

Review and evaluation of the plan

Initial risk management plans will never be perfect. Practice, experience, and actual loss results will necessitate changes in the plan and contribute information to allow possible different decisions to be made in dealing with the risks being faced.

Risk analysis results and management plans should be updated periodically. There are two primary reasons for this:

1. to evaluate whether the previously selected security controls are still applicable and effective, and
2. to evaluate the possible risk level changes in the business environment. For example, information risks are a good example of rapidly changing business environment.

Limitations

If risks are improperly assessed and prioritized, time can be wasted in dealing with risk of losses that are not likely to occur. Spending too much time assessing and managing unlikely risks can divert resources that could be used more profitably. Unlikely events do occur but if the risk is unlikely enough to occur it may be better to simply retain the risk and deal with the result if the loss does in fact occur. Qualitative risk assessment is subjective and lacks consistency. The primary justification for a formal risk assessment process is legal and bureaucratic.

Prioritizing the *risk management processes* too highly could keep an organization from ever completing a project or even getting started. This is especially true if other work is suspended until the risk management process is considered complete.

It is also important to keep in mind the distinction between risk and uncertainty. Risk can be measured by impacts x probability.

Areas of risk management

As applied to corporate finance, **risk management** is the technique for measuring, monitoring and controlling the financial or operational risk on a firm's balance sheet. See value at risk.

The Basel II framework breaks risks into market risk (price risk), credit risk and operational risk and also specifies methods for calculating capital requirements for each of these components.

Enterprise risk management

In enterprise risk management, a risk is defined as a possible event or circumstance that can have negative influences on the enterprise in question. Its impact can be on the very existence, the resources (human and capital), the products and services, or the customers of the enterprise, as well as external impacts on society, markets, or the environment. In a financial institution, enterprise risk management is normally thought of as the combination of credit risk, interest rate risk or asset liability management, market risk, and operational risk.

In the more general case, every probable risk can have a pre-formulated plan to deal with its possible consequences (to ensure *contingency* if the risk becomes a *liability*).

From the information above and the average cost per employee over time, or cost accrual ratio, a project manager can estimate:

*   the cost associated with the risk if it arises, estimated by multiplying employee costs per unit time by the estimated time lost (*cost impact, C* where *C = cost accrual ratio * S*).

- the probable increase in time associated with a risk (*schedule variance due to risk, Rs* where $Rs = P * S$):
  - Sorting on this value puts the highest risks to the schedule first. This is intended to cause the greatest risks to the project to be attempted first so that risk is minimized as quickly as possible.
  - This is slightly misleading as *schedule variances* with a large P and small S and vice versa are not equivalent. (The risk of the RMS *Titanic* sinking vs. the passengers' meals being served at slightly the wrong time).
- the probable increase in cost associated with a risk (*cost variance due to risk, Rc* where $Rc = P*C = P*CAR*S = P*S*CAR$)
  - sorting on this value puts the highest risks to the budget first.
  - see concerns about *schedule variance* as this is a function of it, as illustrated in the equation above.

Risk in a project or process can be due either to Special Cause Variation or Common Cause Variation and requires appropriate treatment. That is to re-iterate the concern about extremal cases not being equivalent in the list immediately above.

Risk management activities as applied to project management

In project management, risk management includes the following activities:

- Planning how risk will be managed in the particular project. Plans should include risk management tasks, responsibilities, activities and budget.
- Assigning a risk officer - a team member other than a project manager who is responsible for foreseeing potential project problems. Typical characteristic of risk officer is a healthy skepticism.
- Maintaining live project risk database. Each risk should have the following attributes: opening date, title, short description, probability and importance. Optionally a risk may have an assigned person responsible for its resolution and a date by which the risk must be resolved.
- Creating anonymous risk reporting channel. Each team member should have possibility to report risk that he/she foresees in the project.
- Preparing mitigation plans for risks that are chosen to be mitigated. The purpose of the mitigation plan is to describe how this particular risk will be handled – what, when, by who and how will it be done to avoid it or minimize consequences if it becomes a liability.
- Summarizing planned and faced risks, effectiveness of mitigation activities, and effort spent for the risk management.

Risk management for megaprojects

Megaprojects (sometimes also called "major programs") are extremely large-scale investment projects, typically costing more than US$1 billion per project. Megaprojects include bridges, tunnels, highways, railways, airports, seaports, power plants, dams, wastewater projects, coastal flood protection schemes, oil and natural gas extraction projects, public buildings, information technology systems, aerospace projects, and defence systems. Megaprojects have been shown to be particularly risky in terms of finance, safety, and social and environmental impacts. Risk management is therefore particularly pertinent for megaprojects and special methods and special education have been developed for such risk management.[12] [13]

Risk management of Information Technology

Information technology is increasing pervasive in modern life in every sector.[14] [15] [16]

IT risk is a risk related to information technology. This relatively new term due to an increasing awareness that information security is simply one facet of a multitude of risks that are relevant to IT and the real world processes it supports.

A number of methodologies have been developed to deal with this kind of risk.

ISACA's Risk IT framework ties IT risk to Enterprise risk management.

Risk management techniques in petroleum and natural gas

For the offshore oil and gas industry, operational risk management is regulated by the safety case regime in many countries. Hazard identification and risk assessment tools and techniques are described in the international standard ISO 17776:2000, and organisations such as the IADC (International Association of Drilling Contractors) publish guidelines for HSE Case development which are based on the ISO standard. Further, diagrammatic representations of hazardous events are often expected by governmental regulators as part of risk management in safety case submissions; these are known as **bow-tie** diagrams. The technique is also used by organisations and regulators in mining, aviation, health, defence, industrial and finance.[17]

Risk management and business continuity

Risk management is simply a practice of systematically selecting cost effective approaches for minimising the effect of threat realization to the organization. All risks can never be fully avoided or mitigated simply because of financial and practical limitations. Therefore all organizations have to accept some level of residual risks.

Whereas risk management tends to be preemptive, business continuity planning (BCP) was invented to deal with the consequences of realised residual risks. The necessity to have BCP in place arises because even very unlikely events will occur if given enough time. Risk management and BCP are often mistakenly seen as rivals or overlapping practices. In fact these processes are so tightly tied together that such separation seems artificial. For example, the risk management process creates important inputs for the BCP (assets, impact assessments, cost estimates etc.). Risk management also proposes applicable controls for the observed risks. Therefore, risk management covers several areas that are vital for the BCP process. However, the BCP process goes beyond risk management's preemptive approach and assumes that the disaster **will** happen at some point.

Risk communication

Risk communication is a complex cross-disciplinary academic field. Problems for risk communicators involve how to reach the intended audience, to make the risk comprehensible and relatable to other risks, how to pay appropriate respect to the audience's values related to the risk, how to predict the audience's response to the communication, etc. A main goal of risk communication is to improve collective and individual decision making. Risk communication is somewhat related to crisis communication.

Bow tie diagrams

A popular solution to the quest to communicate risks and their treatments effectively is to use **bow tie** diagrams. These have been effective, for example, in a public forum to model perceived risks and communicate precautions, during the planning stage of offshore oil and gas facilities in Scotland. Equally, the technique is used for HAZID (Hazard Identification) workshops of all types, and results in a high level of engagement. For this reason (amongst others) an increasing number of government regulators for major hazard facilities (MHFs), offshore oil & gas, aviation, etc. welcome safety case submissions which use diagrammatic representation of risks at their core.

Communication advantages of bow tie diagrams: [17]

- Visual illustration of the hazard, its causes, consequences, controls, and how controls fail.
- The bow tie diagram can be readily understood at all personnel levels.
- "A picture paints a thousand words."

Seven cardinal rules for the practice of risk communication

(as first expressed by the U.S. Environmental Protection Agency and several of the field's founders[18])

- Accept and involve the public/other consumers as legitimate partners.
- Plan carefully and evaluate your efforts with a focus on your strengths, weaknesses, opportunities, and threats.
- Listen to the public's specific concerns.
- Be honest, frank, and open.
- Coordinate and collaborate with other credible sources.
- Meet the needs of the media.
- Speak clearly and with compassion.

References

[1] Hubbard, Douglas (2009). *The Failure of Risk Management: Why It's Broken and How to Fix It.* John Wiley & Sons. p. 46.

[2] ISO/IEC Guide 73:2009 (2009). *Risk management — Vocabulary* (http://www.iso.org/iso/iso_catalogue/catalogue_ics/catalogue_detail_ics.htm?csnumber=44651). International Organization for Standardization. .

[3] ISO/DIS 31000 (2009). *Risk management — Principles and guidelines on implementation* (http://www.iso.org/iso/iso_catalogue/catalogue_tc/catalogue_detail.htm?csnumber=43170). International Organization for Standardization. .

[4] "Committee Draft of ISO 31000 Risk management" (http://www.nsai.ie/uploads/file/N047_Committee_Draft_of_ISO_31000.pdf) (PDF). International Organization for Standardization. .

[5] CMU/SEI-93-TR-6 Taxonomy-based risk identification in software industry (http://www.sei.cmu.edu/library/abstracts/reports/93tr006.cfm)

[6] Common Vulnerability and Exposures list (http://cve.mitre.org)

[7] Crockford, Neil (1986). *An Introduction to Risk Management* (2 ed.). Cambridge, UK: Woodhead-Faulkner. p. 18. ISBN 0859413322.

[8] Disaster Recovery Journal (http://www.drj.com/index.php?option=com_content&task=view&id=605&Itemid=450)

[9] Dorfman, Mark S. (2007). *Introduction to Risk Management and Insurance* (9 ed.). Englewood Cliffs, N.J: Prentice Hall. ISBN 0-13-224227-3.

[10] IADC HSE Case Guidelines for MODUs 3.2, section 4.7

[11] Roehrig, P (2006). "Bet On Governance To Manage Outsourcing Risk" (http://www.btquarterly.com/?mc=bet-governance&page=ss-viewresearch). *Business Trends Quarterly*. .

[12] [Bent Flyvbjerg, Nils Bruzelius, and Werner Rothengatter, 2003, Megaprojects and Risk: An Anatomy of Ambition (Cambridge University Press).]

[13] *Oxford BT Centre for Major Programme Management

[14] Cortada, James W. (2003-12-04) *The Digital Hand: How Computers Changed the Work of American Manufacturing, Transportation, and Retail Industries* USA: Oxford University Press pp. 512 ISBN 0195165888

[15] Cortada, James W. (2005-11-03) *The Digital Hand: Volume II: How Computers Changed the Work of American Financial, Telecommunicati ons, Media, and Entertainment Industries* USA: Oxford University Press ISBN 978-0195165876

[16] Cortada, James W. (2007-11-06) *The Digital Hand, Vol 3: How Computers Changed the Work of American Public Sector Industries* USA: Oxford University Press pp. 496 ISBN 978-0195165869

[17] http://www.bowtiexp.com.au/bowtiexp.asp#aboutBowTies

[18] Covello, Vincent T.; Allen., Frederick H. (April 1988). *Seven Cardinal Rules of Risk Communication.* Washington, DC: U.S. Environmental Protection Agency. OPA-87-020.

Further reading

- Alberts, Christopher; Audrey Dorofee, Lisa Marino (March 2008). *Mission Diagnostic Protocol, Version 1.0: A Risk-Based Approach for Assessing the Potential for Success* (http://www.sei.cmu.edu/library/abstracts/ reports/08tr005.cfm). Software Engineering Institute. Retrieved 2008-05-26.
- Alexander, Carol and Sheedy, Elizabeth (2005). *The Professional Risk Managers' Handbook: A Comprehensive Guide to Current Theory and Best Practices*. PRMIA Publications. ISBN 0-9766097-0-3.
- Altemeyer, Lynn (2004). *An Assessment of Texas State Government: Implementation of Enterprise Risk Management, Applied Research Project* (http://ecommons.txstate.edu/arp/14/). Texas State University.
- Borodzicz, Edward (2005). *Risk, Crisis and Security Management*. New York: Wiley. ISBN 0-470-86704-3.
- Flyvbjerg, Bent (August 2006). "From Nobel Prize to Project Management: Getting Risks Right" (http:// flyvbjerg.plan.aau.dk/Publications2006/Nobel-PMJ2006.pdf) (PDF). *Project Management Journal* (Project Management Institute) **37** (3): 5–15. Retrieved 2008-05-26.
- Gorrod, Martin (2004). *Risk Management Systems : Technology Trends (Finance and Capital Markets)*. Basingstoke: Palgrave Macmillan. ISBN 1-4039-1617-9.
- Hutto, John (2009). *Risk Management in Law Enforcement, Applied Research Project* (http://ecommons.txstate. edu/arp/301/). Texas State University.
- Institute of Risk Management/AIRMIC/ALARM (2002). *A Risk Management Standard* (http://www.theirm. org/publications/PUstandard.html). London: Institute of Risk Management.
- Moteff, John (2005) Risk Management and Critical Infrastructure Protection: Assessing, Integrating, and Managing Threats, Vulnerabilities and Consequences (http://opencrs.com/document/RL32561/2005-02-04). Washington DC: Congressional Research Service. (Report).
- Standards Association of Australia (1999). *Risk management*. North Sydney, N.S.W: Standards Association of Australia. ISBN 0-7337-2647-X.
- Stoneburner, Gary; Goguen, Alice and Feringa, Alexis (July 2002) (PDF). *Risk Management Guide for Information Technology Systems* (http://csrc.nist.gov/publications/nistpubs/800-30/sp800-30.pdf). Gaithersburg, MD: National Institute of Standards and Technology.
- United States Environmental Protection Agency (April 2004). *General Risk Management Program Guidance* (http://www.epa.gov/OEM/content/rmp/rmp_guidance.htm#General). United State Environmental Protection Agency.
- Ward, Dan; Quaid, Chris (March/April 2007). "The Pursuit of Courage, Judgment and Luck" (http://web. archive.org/web/20080408205443/http://www.dau.mil/pubs/dam/03_04_2007/war_ma07.pdf) (PDF). *Defense AT&L* (Defense Acquisition University): 28–30. Archived from the original (http://www.dau.mil/ pubs/dam/03_04_2007/war_ma07.pdf) on 2008-04-08. Retrieved 2008-05-26.
- Airmic / Alarm / IRM (2010) "A structured approach to Enterprise Risk Management (ERM) and the requirements of ISO 31000" http://www.theirm.org/documents/SARM_FINAL.pdf
- Hopkin, Paul "Fundamentals of Risk Management" Kogan-Page (2010) ISBN 978 0 7494 5942 0

External links

- Risk management (http://www.dmoz.org/Business/Financial_Services/Insurance/Risk_Management/) at the Open Directory Project

Association of Management Consulting Firms

Association of Management Consulting Firms

AMCF Association of Management Consulting Firms	
Type	Not-for-profit[1]
Founded	1929
Headquarters	New York, NY
Area served	Worldwide
Key people	**John Furth**, President & CEO **Peggy Vaughan**, Chairman of the Board
Services	Management consulting
Website	amcf.org [2]

The Association of Management Consulting Firms (AMCF) is an international not-for-profit[3] membership association of firms which are engaged in the practice of consulting to management. Founded in 1929 as ACME (Association of Management Consulting Engineers)[4] , AMCF is now an integral part of the management consulting industry.[5]

Headquartered in New York, NY, the Association of Management Consulting Firms serves the industry as a resource for information on the management of a consulting practice. It provides a forum for the exchange of ideas, helping consultants to better understand developments within the profession and to capitalize on new opportunities. Just as consultants help clients manage change within their industries, AMCF helps its members cope with the rapid changes affecting their practices today.

AMCF promotes knowledge exchange and professional standards for the community of management consulting firms around the world. It does this by helping members strengthen their senior management teams through value-driven programs, research, and communications. The association also promotes a better understanding of the profession among the business community, government, academia, and the public. It also serves as the voice of the industry on major issues, representing the profession before government and regulatory bodies, working to improve standards and practices and enabling firms to work smarter.[6]

AMCF represents leading management consulting firms worldwide. Its membership is diverse: large and small firms, traditional management consultants as well as providers of professional services, generalists and specialists, single-office firms along with large multinational organizations.

History

The Association of Management Consulting Firms (AMCF) was founded in 1929 as ACME, the Association of Management Consulting Engineers. The founders of the association included the following:

- *Edwin G. Booz, founder of both Booz Allen & Hamilton and Booz & Company*[7]
- *Marvin Bower, named the "father of modern management consulting" by Harvard Business School; a leader with McKinsey & Company*[8]
- *H.B. Maynard, founder of H.B. Maynard & Company*[9] *, now owned by Accenture*[10]
- *Richard M. Paget, Cresap McCormick & Paget, Towers Perrin*
- *Kurt Salmon, founder of KSA, Kurt Salmon Associates, a firm owned by Management Consulting Group*[11]

Members

According to the AMCF bylaws, any firm which engages in the practice of management consulting may be considered for membership, and in turn enjoy the rights and privileges of an AMCF member. Some of the most recognized members of AMCF include:

- *Capgemini*
- *Deloitte Consulting*
- *Ernst & Young*
- *FTI Consulting*
- *IBM Business Consulting Services*
- *Management Consulting Group PLC*
- *Navigant Consulting, Inc.*
- *The Saint Consulting Group*
- *Tata Consultancy Services*
- *Towers Watson*[12]

Code of Ethics

The association is well-known for its strong Code of Ethics [13]. According to their website, AMCF's Code of Ethics [13] conforms with recent regulatory and legislative initiatives and assures the users of consulting services that AMCF members are publicly committed to providing the highest quality work. Member firms and their staffs subscribe to this Code of Ethics [13], [14]

References

[1] "AMCF Bylaws" (http://www.amcf.org/memBylaws.asp). .

[2] http://www.amcf.org/

[3] "AMCF Bylaws" (http://www.amcf.org/memBylaws.asp). .

[4] "New York Times: February, 1997" (http://www.sree.net/stories/consult.html). .

[5] "PR Newswire: January, 2003" (http://www.encyclopedia.com/doc/1G1-96956293.html). .

[6] "The Business of AMCF" (http://amcf.org/amcf/index.php?option=com_content&view=article&id=4&Itemid=6). .

[7] "Booz Allen Article" (http://www.boozallen.com/about/article/981170). .

[8] "BusinessWeek: January, 2003" (http://www.businessweek.com/bwdaily/dnflash/jan2003/nf20030124_5912.htm). .

[9] "AMCF Historical Information" (http://amcf.org/amcf/index.php?option=com_content&view=article&id=4&Itemid=6). .

[10] "AllBusiness: January, 2008" (http://www.allbusiness.com/company-activities-management/company-structures-ownership/6621079-1.html). .

[11] "AMCF Historical Information" (http://amcf.org/amcf/index.php?option=com_content&view=article&id=4&Itemid=6). .

[12] "Member Firms of AMCF, 2009" (http://amcf.org/amcf/index.php?option=com_content&view=article&id=8&Itemid=19). .

[13] http://amcf.org/amcf/index.php?option=com_content&view=article&id=14&Itemid=25

[14] "Bylaws and Code of Ethics" (http://amcf.org/amcf/index.php?option=com_content&view=article&id=14&Itemid=25). .

External links

- Association of Management Consulting Firms (AMCF) (http://www.amcf.org/)

Peter L. Bernstein

Peter Lewyn Bernstein (January 22, 1919 – June 5, 2009) was an American financial historian, economist and educator whose development and refinement of the efficient-market hypothesis made him one of the country's best known authorities in popularizing and presenting investment economics to the general public.

Education and military service during World War II

A native of New York City, Peter Bernstein was the son of financial consultant Allen Bernstein and his wife, Irma Lewyn. His primary education was at the Ethical Culture School where, in first grade, he became a lifelong friend of another renowned economics historian, Robert Heilbroner, with whom he later attended Horace Mann School and Harvard College, from which both received, in 1940, bachelors degrees in economics. Following Harvard, where he was elected to Phi Beta Kappa and graduated magna cum laude, came service as a member of the research staff at the Federal Reserve Bank of New York and, in a civilian capacity, at the Office of Strategic Services in Washington. In the aftermath of the December 7, 1941 Pearl Harbor attack, he joined the Air Force and rose to the rank of captain, assigned to the Office of Strategic Services in the European theater.

As investment manager

In 1951, after teaching economics at Williams College and a five-year stint in commercial banking, Bernstein took over, at family insistence, the management of his late father's wealth management firm, Bernstein-Macaulay Inc., where he personally managed billions of dollars of individual and institutional portfolios. The assets under his management had grown more than tenfold by the time the firm was sold in 1967 and he resigned in 1973 to launch Peter L. Bernstein, Inc. and, a year later, to become the first editor of the *Journal of Portfolio Management*, a widely-read scholarly financial publication for investment managers and academics. He continued as consulting editor of the *Journal* and served on the advisory panel of Robert D. Arnott's investment management firm, Research Affiliates.

Career as educator and lecturer

Bernstein served for many years on the Visiting Committee to the Economics Department at Harvard University, as a Trustee and member of the Finance Committee of the College Retirement Equities Fund (CREF), and as a Trustee of the Investment Management Workshop sponsored by the Association for Investment Management & Research (AIMR), and had been lecturing widely throughout the United States and abroad on risk management, asset allocation, portfolio strategy, and market history.

A longtime resident of Manhattan, Peter Bernstein was 90 years old when he died of pneumonia at NewYork-Presbyterian/Weill Cornell Hospital, after having broken a hip. His first wife, Shirley, died in 1971 and he is survived by his second wife, Barbara, whom he married in 1972.

Works

Bernstein was the author of ten books in economics and finance as well as countless articles in professional journals such as *Harvard Business Review, Financial Analysts Journal* and, in the popular press, *The New York Times, The Wall Street Journal, Worth magazine* and Bloomberg, among others, and has contributed to collections of articles published by Perseus and FT Mastering, among others.

Against The Gods: The Remarkable Story of Risk, was published by John Wiley & Sons in September 1996 and won the Edwin G. Booz Prize for the most insightful, innovative management book published in 1996. In 1998, it was awarded the Clarence Arthur Kelp/Elizur Wright Memorial Award from The American Risk and Insurance Association (ARIA) as an outstanding original contribution to the literature of risk and insurance. The book has sold over 500,000 copies worldwide.

In 1992 *Capital Ideas: The Improbable Origins of Modern Wall Street* was published by The Free Press in Canada and Maxwell Macmillan Internationaland in USA since become a worldwide guide to modern investment theories and practices. *Capital Ideas Evolving*, the follow-up to this seminal work, was published in May 2007 by John Wiley and Sons.

Streetwise: The Best of The Journal of Portfolio Management, edited by Peter L. Bernstein and Frank J. Fabozzi, was published in 1997 by Princeton University Press:

Earlier books include *A Primer on Money, Banking and Gold* (Random House 1965), as well as *Economist on Wall Street* (Macmillan 1970), and *The Price of Prosperity* (Doubleday, 1962), in addition to two books on government finance co-authored with Robert Heilbroner.

Bernstein's other books are *The Power of Gold: The History of an Obsession*, published in the fall of 2000 by John Wiley and Sons, *Wedding of the Waters: The Erie Canal and the Making of a Great Nation*, published in 2005 by W.W. Norton & Co.

Bibliography

- Bernstein, Peter L. (2007). *Capital Ideas Evolving*. Hoboken, NJ: John Wiley & Sons. ISBN 0-471-73173-0.
- Bernstein, Peter L. (2005). *Special Real Estate Issue*. New York: Institutional Investor Systems.
- Bernstein, Peter L. (2005). *Wedding of the Waters: The Erie Canal and the Making of a Great Nation*. New York: W.W. Norton & Co.. ISBN 0-393-05233-8.
- Bernstein, Peter L. (2000). *The Power of Gold: The History of an Obsession*. New York: John Wiley & Sons. ISBN 0-471-25210-7.
- Bernstein, Peter L.; Aswath Damodaran (1998). *Investment Management*. New York: John Wiley & Sons. ISBN 0-471-19716-5.
- Bernstein, Peter L.; Frank J. Fabozzi (1997). *Streetwise: The Best of The Journal of Portfolio Management*. Princeton, NJ: Princeton University Press. ISBN 0-691-01129-X.
- Bernstein, Peter L. (1996). *Against The Gods: The Remarkable Story of Risk*. New York: John Wiley & Sons. ISBN 0-471-12104-5.
- Bernstein, Peter L. (1995). *The Portable MBA in Investment*. New York: John Wiley & Sons. ISBN 0-471-10661-5.
- Bernstein, Peter L. (1992). *Capital Ideas: The Improbable Origins of Modern Wall Street*. New York: Maxwell Macmillan International. ISBN 0-029-03011-0.
- Heilbroner, Robert L.; Peter L. Bernstein (1989). *The Debt and the Deficit: False Alarms/Real Possibilities*. New York: W.W. Norton & Co.. ISBN 0-393-02752-X.
- Bernstein, Peter L. (1983). *International Investing*. New York: Institutional Investor Books.
- Bernstein, Peter L. (1978). *Security Selection and Active Portfolio Management*. New York: Institutional Investor Books.

- Bernstein, Peter L. (1977). *The Theory and Practice of Bond Portfolio Management.* New York: Institutional Investor Books.
- Bernstein, Peter L. (1977). *Portfolio Management and Efficient Markets: Theoretical Relevance and Practical Applications.* New York: Institutional Investor Books.
- Bernstein, Peter L. (1970). *Economist on Wall Street: Notes on the Sanctity of Gold, the Value of Money, the Security of Investments, and Other Delusions.* New York: Macmillan.
- Bernstein, Peter L. (1965). *A Primer on Money, Banking, and Gold.* New York: Random House.
- Heilbroner, Robert L.; Peter L. Bernstein (1963). *A Primer on Government Spending.* New York: Random House.
- Bernstein, Peter L. (1962). *The Price of Prosperity: A Realistic Appraisal of the Future of our National Economy.* Garden City, NY: Doubleday.

Awards

Peter Bernstein received three major awards from the Association for Investment Management & Research (AIMR), the key organization for investment managers and analysts:

- The Award for Professional Excellence, AIMR's highest award,
- The Graham & Dodd Award, given annually for the outstanding article in the Financial Analysts Journal for the previous year, and
- The James R. Vertin Award, recognizing individuals who have produced a body of research notable for its relevance and enduring value to investment professionals.

References

- Peter L Bernstein's Homepage. Retrieved January 25, 2005 [1]
- Uchitelle, Louis. "Peter L. Bernstein, Explainer of Risks of Stocks, Dies at 90" (*The New York Times* obituary {with photograph}, June 8, 2009) [2]

External links

- Book Reviews: Peter Bernstein [3]

References

[1] http://www.peterlbernsteininc.com/
[2] http://www.nytimes.com/2009/06/08/business/08bernstein.html?_r=1&scp=2&sq=Peter%20L.%20Bernstein&st=cse
[3] http://www.marketthoughts.com/peter_bernstein_capital_ideas.html

Building Safer Communities. Risk Governance, Spatial Planning and Responses to Natural Hazards

Building Safer Communities. Risk Governance, Spatial Planning and Responses to Natural Hazards	
Author(s)	Urbano Fra Paleo (editor)
Country	Netherlands
Language	English
Series	Human and Societal Dynamics
Subject(s)	Natural hazards, Risk management
Genre(s)	Essay
Publisher	IOS Press
Publication date	2009
Pages	278 pages
ISBN	ISBN 978-1-60750-046-9
OCLC Number	441170952 [1]
LC Classification	2009932645

Building Safer Communities. Risk Governance, Spatial Planning and Responses to Natural Hazards is a 2009 book edited by Urbano Fra Paleo, published by IOS Press.

This textbook examines the central principles of enhanced risk governance, whose implementation might help to mitigate the increasing losses caused by natural hazards. It promotes the adoption of proactive, preventive approaches in public policies, particularly through land use planning, by influencing on the occupation of hazard-prone areas. It serves both as a comprehensive introduction to the formulation and implementation at the strategic level of policies that address risk, and as an advancement in the integration of current practices, including emergency management, environmental management, community development and spatial planning. The authors study and construe solutions that review integrated strategies of the various levels of government considering:

- The central role of local government in planning for mitigation,
- The integration of mitigation with other social, economic and environmental goals,
- The engagement of all stakeholders in mitigation planning,
- The avoidance of disruption of environmental functions,
- The need of integrating mandates of higher level government with cooperative planning in order to both secure local government participation and make planning sustainable,
- Participatory decision-making processes need to be improved by differentiating among their types and applications, in order to effectively respond in risk management,
- People perception of and response to risk must be part of the planning process,
- Processes of human exposure to natural hazards should be fully understood in order to prevent further exposure,
- The precautionary principle needs to be integrated in risk management, although under comprehensible regulation in order to promote action,
- Urban risk governance can only be understood within the framework of regional and biophysical systems,
- Social impact assessment is a tool that helps to better identify the social and community dimensions of risk,

- Planning should be considered more as a process than as a result, and
- Post-disaster recovery also provides opportunities for mitigation and community improvement.[2] [3]

Urbano Fra Paleo is a geographer, and an Associate Professor of Human Geography at the University of Santiago de Compostela, Spain.

References

[1] http://worldcat.org/oclc/441170952

[2] Building Safer Communities. Risk Governance, Spatial Planning and Responses to Natural Hazards (http://www.iospress.nl/loadtop/load.php?isbn=9781607500469)

[3] Building Safer Communities. Risk Governance, Spatial Planning and Responses to Natural Hazards (http://www.booksonline.iospress.nl/Content/View.aspx?piid=14130)

Burn pit

A **burn pit** is an area devoted to open-air combustion of trash. Modern waste contains significant amounts of plastic and other material which may emit toxic aerial compounds and particulates when burned. In Iraq and Afghanistan the U.S. military, or its contractors such as KBR operated large burn pits for long periods of time burning many tons of assorted waste. Active duty personnel reported respiratory difficulties and headaches in some cases and some veterans have made disability claims based on respiratory system symptoms.[1]

Materials burned and combustion products

It has been reported that every type of waste was burned including: plastics, batteries, appliances, medicine, dead animals, even human body parts with jet fuel being used as an accelerant. Clouds of black smoke resulted.[1] According to an Air Force fact sheet, "Burning solid wastes in an open pit generates numerous pollutants. These pollutants include dioxins, particulate matter, polycyclic aromatic hydrocarbons, volatile organic compounds, carbon monoxide, hexachlorobenzene, and ash. Highly toxic dioxins, produced in small amounts in almost all burning processes, can be produced in elevated levels with increased combustion of plastic waste (such as discarded drinking water bottles) and if the combustion is not at high incinerator temperatures. Inefficient combustion of medical or latrine wastes can emit disease-laden aerosols."[2]

Locations

Joint Base Balad, the largest U.S. base in Iraq had a burn pit operation as late as the summer of 2008 burning 147 tons of waste per day when the *Army Times* published a major story about it and about health concerns. An Air Force spokesman speaking for the 609th Combined Air and Space Operations Center Southwest Asia vigorously contested allegations of heath affects and emphasized mitigation efforts.[3]

Duration

Burn pits were adopted as a temporary measure but remained open long after alternative methods of disposal such as incineration were available. After some years the American military did adopt other methods. [1]

Defense Department position

A statement was made August 6, 2008 by the Defense Department Office of Force Health Protection and Readiness:

> While exposure to burn pit smoke may cause temporary coughing and redness or stinging of the eyes, extensive environmental monitoring indicates that smoke exposures not interfering with breathing or requiring medical treatment at the time of exposure usually do not cause any lasting health effects or medical follow-up.[3]

Health effects

At the request of the Veteran's Administration (VA)and the Department of Defense The Board on the Health of Select Populations of the Institute of Medicine formed the Committee on Long-term Health Consequences of Exposure to Burn Pits in Iraq and Afghanistan which held its first meeting February 23, 2010 - February 24, 2010 in Washington, D.C.[4] If there is sufficient evidence of a connection between exposure to burn pits and subsequent illness and disability it might serve as the basis for congressional enactment of a "presumption of service connection" similar to that in place for exposure to Agent Orange.[5]

In November 2009, at the request of VA, the National Academy of Sciences Institute of Medicine (IOM) had begun an 18-month study to determine the long-term health effects of exposure to burn pits in Iraq and Afghanistan. The report for the study should be completed and available by summer 2011.[6]

Notes

[1] "Veterans Sound Alarm Over Burn-Pit Exposure" (http://www.nytimes.com/2010/08/07/us/07burn.html) article by James Risen in *The New York Times* August 6, 2010, accessed August 7, 2010

[2] "Open Pit Burning (http://deploymenthealthlibrary.fhp.osd.mil/products/Open Pit Burning (55).pdf): U.S. Air Force fact sheet. Copied text is in the public domain as the work of an employee of the United States government while in the performance of their duties, accessed August 7, 2010

[3] "Burn pit at Balad raises health concerns (http://www.armytimes.com/news/2008/10/military_burnpit_102708w/): Troops say chemicals and medical waste burned at base are making them sick, but officials deny risk" article by Kelly Kennedy in *Army Times* Oct 29, 2008, accessed August 7, 2010

[4] First Meeting of the Committee on the Long-Term Health Consequences of Exposure to Burn Pits in Iraq and Afghanistan Keck Center of the National Academies (http://www8.nationalacademies.org/cp/meetingview.aspx?MeetingID=4206&MeetingNo=1), accessed August 8, 2010

[5] "VA, DoD seek better data on burn-pit exposure" (http://www.armytimes.com/news/2010/02/military_burn_pits_022310w/) article by Kelly Kennedy in the *Army Times* Feb 24, 2010, accessed August 8, 2010

[6] Department of Veterans Affairs, accessed August 19 2010 (http://www.publichealth.va.gov/exposures/burnpits/index.asp)

External links and further reading

- "Open Pit Burning (http://deploymenthealthlibrary.fhp.osd.mil/products/Open Pit Burning (55).pdf): U.S. Air Force fact sheet
- "Report: Army making toxic mess in war zones" (http://www.militarytimes.com/news/2008/10/military_toxiciraq_100208w/) article by Kelly Kennedy in *Military Times* Oct 3, 2008
- David E. Mosher, Beth E. Lachman, Michael D. Greenberg, Tiffany Nichols, Brian Rosen, Henry H. Willis, *Green Warriors: Army Environmental Considerations for Contingency Operations from Planning through Post-Conflict*, Rand Corporation (2008), trade paperback, 252 pages, ISBN-13: 9780833043184
  - About *Green Warriors* on Rand website (http://www.rand.org/pubs/monographs/MG632/)

Cascading Discontinuity Sets

A **Cascading Discontinuity Set** is a term related to Wild Cards and applied in foresight and risk management areas. It attempts to define a series of smaller, seemingly disconnected events that merge over time leading to a Wild Card like result.

References

- Barber MP (2004, 2006) 'Wildcards - Signals from a Future near You'; Journal of future Studies Vol 11 No1; Tamkang University

Dangerous Goods Safety Advisor

A **Dangerous Goods Safety Advisor (DGSA)** is a consultant or an owner or employee of an organization appointed by an organization that transports, loads, or unloads dangerous goods in the European Union.

Rules

The rules involving the transport of dangerous goods are complex and each mode of transport, i.e. road, rail or inland waterway, has its own set of regulations. There are also separate sets of regulations for sea and air transportation. For many elements of transportation the regulations from each mode are similar or identical. All the various sets of regulations are based upon "Recommendations on the transport of Dangerous Goods - Model Regulations", known as "The Orange Book," issued by the United Nations Committee of Experts on the Transportation of Dangerous Goods and the Globally Harmonized System of Classification and Labeling.

Duties

The duties of the DGSA include providing advice to the appointing organization, preparing accident reports, monitoring the activities of the organisation which involve dangerous goods and preparing an annual report.

To become a DGSA, it is usual for a candidate to be trained by a specialist training organization, then to sit various examinations. The qualification lasts five years. The examining body in the UK is the Scottish Qualifications Authority.[1]

Notes

[1] UK Department for Transport page on Dangerous Goods Safety Advisors (http://www.dft.gov.uk/pgr/freight/dgt1/training/dangerousgoodssafetyadvisors)

External links

- "Dangerous Goods-HazMat Group" (http://tech.groups.yahoo.com/group/DangerousGoods), a Yahoo-hosted global network for discussion of dangerous goods and hazardous materials storage and handling issues.

Defensive driving

The standard *Safe Practices for Motor Vehicle Operations*, ANSI/ASSE Z15.1, defines **defensive driving** as "driving to save lives, time, and money, in spite of the conditions around you and the actions of others."[1] This definition is taken from the National Safety Council's Defensive Driving Course. It is a form of training for motor vehicle drivers that goes beyond mastery of the rules of the road and the basic mechanics of driving. Its aim is to reduce the risk of driving by anticipating dangerous situations, despite adverse conditions

The two-second rule tells a defensive driver the *minimum* distance to avoid collision in ideal driving conditions. The red car's driver picks a tree to judge a two-second safety buffer.

or the mistakes of others. This can be achieved through adherence to a variety of general rules, as well as the practice of specific driving techniques.

Training and Courses

Several government agencies, non profit organizations, and private schools have launched specialty courses that improve the public's driving skills. In the United States a few of the familiar courses in defensive driving include Alive at 25, DDC or Defensive Driving Course, Coaching the Mature Driver, Attitudinal Dynamics of Driving, Professional Truck Driving, and DDC for Instructors. In relation to this, the government has launched active Air Bag and seat Belt safety campaigns that encourage High Visibility Enforcement.

Courses can often be taken both online and in the classroom. There are advantages to each. When you take the course online, you can take it on your own time and in the comfort of your own home. Classroom courses help you take it all at one time and allow you to discuss and ask questions. Classroom courses last only 6 hours. While online courses also are supposed to take six hours, many times because of pages loading, it takes closer to eight hours to complete a course. With faster Internet connections, many online courses can be completed in fewer hours than a classroom course.

Defensive driving courses offer several benefits to those who choose to take them. In many states, a defensive driving course can be taken as a way to dismiss traffic tickets. Courses may also qualify the student for a discount on car insurance.[2]

References

[1] American National Standard Safe Practices for Motor Vehicle Operation, American Society of Safety Engineers, Des Plaines, IL, 2006

[2] http://driversafetycourses.net/

External links

- "WHO (World Health Organization)| World report on road traffic injury prevention" (http://www.who.int/violence_injury_prevention/publications/road_traffic/world_report/en/index.html)

David Eager

<table>
<tr><td colspan="2" align="center">David Eager</td></tr>
<tr><td colspan="2" align="center"></td></tr>
<tr><td>Nationality</td><td>Australian</td></tr>
<tr><td>Occupation</td><td>Associate Professor, Faculty of Engineering and Information Technology, University of Technology Sydney</td></tr>
</table>

Dr **David Eager**, an Australian, a Professional Engineer, an expert in Risk Management and Childhood Injury Prevention and an Engineering Professor at the University of Technology, Sydney, Australia.[1] [2] [3] [4] [5] [6] [7]

Eager is notable for his tireless volunteer work assisting Standards Australia writing safety Standards. For fifteen years he represented Engineers Australia, the peak Professional Engineering body in Australia on Technical Committees assisting Standards Australia with the drafting of numerous safety standards. He has been the Chairperson for several Standards Committees including: Children's Playground Equipment and Surfacing CS-005, Trampolines CS-100[8] , Contained Play Facilities ME-051-03, and Artificial Climbing Structures and Challenge Course Equipment SF-047.

Eager assisted the NSW Government Department of Fair Trading with the drafting of the Portable Soccer Goal Regulation and the Trampoline Product Safety inquiry.

Eager represents Australia on a number of ASTM International Safety Standards Committees including: ASTM F08 Sports Equipment and Facilities, ASTM F15 Consumer Products, and ASTM F24 Amusement Rides and Devices. He is also an invited observer on the European Standards Committee CEN/TG 136 SC 1 Children's Playground Equipment. He is also an Honorary Playground Safety Adviser, Royal Society for the Prevention of Accidents (RoSPA).

Eager regularly conducts accredited playground safety training courses[9] for Local Government Authorities and other organizations around Australia.[10]

References

[1] http://www.smh.com.au/articles/2004/06/05/1086377188056.html
[2] http://datasearch2.uts.edu.au/feit/staff/listing/details.cfm?StaffId=5785&CFID=1
[3] http://datasearch2.uts.edu.au/research/strengths/imes/member-detail.cfm?StaffID=5785
[4] http://ims.uts.edu.au/people/david.html
[5] http://www.abc.net.au/science/articles/2009/12/15/2771117.htm
[6] http://www.kidsafensw.org/docs/newsletters/PAU/2008/newsletter%2028%20Spring%202008%20Final.pdf
[7] http://www.healthpromotion.org.au/journal/journal-downloads/article/1-hpja/
     108-falls-from-playground-equipment-will-the-new-australian-playground-safety-standard-make-a-difference-and-how-will-we-tell
[8] https://www.springfreetrampoline.com.au/blog/tag/dr-david-eager/
[9] http://www.playgroundinspections.com.au/index_files/Page909.htm
[10] http://www.eng.uts.edu.au/courses/short/playground/index.html

Exposure Factor

Exposure Factor is the subjective, potential percentage of loss to a specific asset if a specific threat is realized. The exposure factor (EF) is a subjective value that the person assessing risk must define.

Michael Featherstone

Michael "Mick" Featherstone is a risk management consultant and private investigator. Featherstone is also an author, his book "Bullet Proof Your Business" was released in 2006 by Wilkinson Publishing.[1] [2] Featherstone lives, and his offices are located, on the Gold Coast, Queensland, Australia.

Early career

Featherstone served 16 years with The Queensland Police Service until resigning from the police in the mid-1990s. Featherstone spent 13 of his 16 years with the Queensland Police as a detective. During his career with the Queensland Police he held positions as Officer in Charge of the Whitsunday Criminal Investigation Branch, Officer in Charge of the Gold Coast Juvenile Aid Bureau, Officer in Charge of the Surfers Paradise Criminal Investigation Branch, and the Gold Coast District Crime Manager. Featherstone was also a member of the Queensland Major Fraud Investigation Group.[3]

Investigation career

Featherstone left The Queensland Police Service in the mid-1990s and began work as a private investigator. He founded what would eventually become Phoenix Global [4] [5]

References

[1] (http://www.wilkinsonpublishing.com.au/index.html) Publisher of Bullet Proof Your Business
[2] (http://www.retailbooks.com.au/shopexd.asp?id=208) Bullet Proof Your Business sales website
[3] (http://www.brisbanetimes.com.au/articles/2008/06/08/1212863418295.html) Brisbane times Article
[4] (http://www.brisbanetimes.com.au/articles/2008/06/08/1212863418295.html) Brisbane Times Article
[5] (http://www.phoenixglobal.com.au) Phoenix Global Website

Financial risk management

Financial risk management is the practice of creating economic value in a firm by using financial instruments to manage exposure to risk, particularly credit risk and market risk. Other types include Foreign exchange, Shape, Volatility, Sector, Liquidity, Inflation risks, etc. Similar to general risk management, financial risk management requires identifying its sources, measuring it, and plans to address them.

Financial risk management can be qualitative and quantitative. As a specialization of risk management, financial risk management focuses on when and how to hedge using financial instruments to manage costly exposures to risk.

In the banking sector worldwide, the Basel Accords are generally adopted by internationally active banks for tracking, reporting and exposing operational, credit and market risks.

When to use financial risk management

Finance theory (i.e., financial economics) prescribes that a firm should take on a project when it increases shareholder value. Finance theory also shows that firm managers cannot create value for shareholders, also called its investors, by taking on projects that shareholders could do for themselves at the same cost.

When applied to financial risk management, this implies that firm managers should not hedge risks that investors can hedge for themselves at the same cost. This notion was captured by the hedging irrelevance proposition: *In a perfect market, the firm cannot create value by hedging a risk when the price of bearing that risk within the firm is the same as the price of bearing it outside of the firm.* In practice, financial markets are not likely to be perfect markets.

This suggests that firm managers likely have many opportunities to create value for shareholders using financial risk management. The trick is to determine which risks are cheaper for the firm to manage than the shareholders. A general rule of thumb, however, is that market risks that result in unique risks for the firm are the best candidates for financial risk management.

The concepts of financial risk management change dramatically in the international realm. Multinational Corporations are faced with many different obstacles in overcoming these challenges. There has been some research on the risks firms must consider when operating in many countries, such as the three kinds of foreign exchange exposure for various future time horizons: transactions exposure,[1] accounting exposure,[2] and economic exposure.[3]

Megaprojects (sometimes also called "major programs") have been shown to be particularly risky in terms of finance. Financial risk management is therefore particularly pertinent for megaprojects and special methods have been developed for such risk management.[4] [5]

References

- Crockford, Neil (1986). *An Introduction to Risk Management (2nd ed.)*. Woodhead-Faulkner. ISBN 0-85941-332-2.
- Charles, Tapiero (2004). *Risk and Financial Management: Mathematical and Computational Methods*. John Wiley & Son. ISBN 0-470-84908-8.
- Lam, James (2003). *Enterprise Risk Management: From Incentives to Controls*. John Wiley. ISBN 978-0-471-43000-1.
- van Deventer, Donald R., Kenji Imai and Mark Mesler (2004). *Advanced Financial Risk Management: Tools and Techniques for Integrated Credit Risk and Interest Rate Risk Management*. John Wiley. ISBN 978-0-470-82126-8.

References

[1] http://www.emeraldinsight.com/Insight/viewContentItem.
do;jsessionid=EFA8D4FB63329F2C94F48279646551BF?contentType=Article&contentId=1649008 (contrary to conventional wisdom it
may be rational to hedge translation exposure. Empirical evidence of agency costs and the managerial tendency to report higher levels of
translated income, based on the early adoption of Financial Accounting Standard No. 52).

[2] Aggarwal, Raj, "The Translation Problem in International Accounting: Insights for Financial Management." Management International
Review 15 (Nos. 2-3, 1975): 67-79. (Proposed accounting framework for evaluating and developing translation procedures for multinational
corporations).

[3] http://www.iijournals.com/doi/abs/10.3905/jpm.1997.409611 (Discusses the benefits for hedging in foreign currencies for MNCs).

[4] Bent Flyvbjerg, Nils Bruzelius, and Werner Rothengatter, 2003, *Megaprojects and Risk: An Anatomy of Ambition* (Cambridge University
Press).

[5] *Oxford BT Centre for Major Programme Management

External links

- CERA - The Chartered Enterprise Risk Analyst Credential - Society of Actuaries (SOA) (http://www.
  ceranalyst.org/)
- Financial Risk Manager Certification Program - Global Association of Risk Professional (GARP) (http://www.
  garp.com)
- Professional Risk Manager Certification Program - Professional Risk Managers' International Association
  (PRMIA) (http://www.primia.org/)
- Managing a portfolio of stock and risk-free investments: a tutorial for risk-sensitive investors (http://www.
  sigmadewe.com/portfoliomanagement.html?&L=1)

Fish & Richardson

Fish & Richardson	
FR FISH & RICHARDSON P.C.	
No. of offices	11
No. of attorneys	350+
Major practice areas	Patent, Trademark, Copyright, IP Litigation, Commercial Litigation, Regulatory
Key people	Peter Devlin (President)
Date founded	1878
Company type	Professional Corporation
Website	
www.fr.com [1]	

Fish & Richardson P.C. is a national law firm practicing intellectual property law. Fish is the 109th largest firm in the United States.[2] Fish has over 350 attorneys, of which 96 percent are dedicated to intellectual property law.[3] Fish is one of the most sought-after firms for both patent prosecution and patent litigation services among Fortune 100 companies.[4] From 2004 to 2009, IP Law & Business has ranked Fish as the nation's top patent litigation firm.[5] In January 2010, Fish was a finalist for American Lawyer's "Top IP Litigation Department of the Year".[6] Fish's patent prosecution practice received a top "Tier 1" U.S. ranking by Managing Intellectual Property magazine.[7] The firm's growing regulatory group advises clients seeking to market products subject to United States Federal Communications Commission and the Food and Drug Administration regulation.

Layoffs

In 2009 Fish & Richardson closed its corporate practice and laid off 100 employees.[8] Despite managing partner Tim French's statement that "It was a painful year for everyone," Fish saw a revenue increase of 4.7% in 2009, and an increase in profits per partner of nearly 20%. (Legal blog AbovetheLaw.com reported different layoff numbers, with the amount at 120, citing an internal communication which stated 35 attorneys and 85 staff were laid off).[9]

Recognition

- Fish & Richardson named Top "Tier 1" National Rankings in Patent Prosecution, Patent Litigation, Litigation, Life Sciences, and International Trade Commission (January, 2011 Managing Intellectual Property) [10]
- Fish & Richardson named International Trade Group of the Year (January, 2011 Law360) [11]
- Fish & Richardson named Top 30 Game Law Firm (January 2011 Interactive Age) [12]
- Fish & Richardson named Top Patent Prosecution Firm (February 2010, Managing Intellectual Property Magazine)[13]
- Fish & Richardson named IP Firm of the Year (January 2010, Law 360)[14]
- Fish & Richardson Named Finalist – Litigation Department of the Year(January 2010, The American Lawyer)[15]

Notable alumni

- Frederick Perry Fish, Founder of the firm and president of American Telephone & Telegraph Corporation from 1901 to 1907.[16]

Offices

- Atlanta
- Boston
- Dallas
- Delaware
- Houston
- Munich
- New York
- Silicon Valley
- Southern California
- Twin Cities
- Washington, D.C.

Focus Areas

Practice Areas: Copyright, Litigation, Patent, Regulatory, Trademark

Industry Sectors: Academic Research and Medical Centers, Aerospace/Defense, Biotech/Pharma, Chemicals, Cleantech, Consumer Products, Electrical/Computer Technology, Energy, Financial/Business Services, Internet, Manufacturing, Medical Devices, Nanotechnology, New Media and Entertainment, Start-up/Emerging Growth, Telecommunications, Transportation

References

[1] http://www.fr.com/

[2] List of largest U.S. law firms by number of lawyers

[3] "IP Attorneys Dominate At Fish & Richardson" (http://www.law360.com/registrations/user_registration?article_id=135576& concurrency_check=false). 2009. . Retrieved 2010-08-19. "...Fish & Richardson dedicates 96 percent of its attorneys to IP work and stands far above runner-up Howrey LLP, which devotes..."'

[4] "Who Protects Innovation in America 2009: The Guardians" (http://www.law.com/jsp/cc/PubArticleCC.jsp?id=1202437199898). 2009. . Retrieved 2010-08-17. "...With eight and six mentions, respectively, two of the top litigation firms—Fish & Richardson and IP Litigation Department of the Year winner Quinn Emanuel Urquhart Oliver & Hedges (see "What Rhymes with Win?" page 26) had four clients between the tech and telecom sectors. ..."'

[5] "Patent Litigation Survey 2009: A Little Less Buzz" (http://www.law.com/jsp/cc/PubArticleCC.jsp?id=1202433129756). 2009. . Retrieved 2010-08-17. "...By any measure, Fish & Richardson comes out on top. While the firm's 77-case workload in 2008 represented a 21 percent dip from the previous year, it was down just 3 percent from the 79 cases it handled while claiming the number one spot in 2007...."'

[6] "Winners & Finalists" (http://www.law.com/jsp/tal/PubArticleTAL.jsp?id=1202437074860&Winners__Finalists&slreturn=1& hbxlogin=1). 2010. . Retrieved 2010-08-19. "...Finalists - Fish & Richardson...."'

[7] "Managing Intellectual Property World IP Survey" (http://www.fr.com/files/News/4ec64103-d9c4-410e-b385-38ccc267b01a/ Presentation/NewsAttachment/56d1daaf-cf09-468b-85f3-0681af4eca0f/MIPWorldIPSurvey.pdf). 2010. . Retrieved 2010-08-19.

[8] Chellel, Kit (2010-02-05). "Profits soar for law partners" (http://www.boston.com/business/articles/2010/02/05/ profits_soar_for_boston_law_partners/). *The Boston Globe*. .

[9] Abovethelaw.com (http://abovethelaw.com/2009/05/nationwide-layoff-watch-fish-richardson-throws-associatesstaff-back/)

[10] Managing Intellectual Property. "Patent Survey: Americas" (http://www.managingip.com/Article/2757164/Search/ Patent-survey-Americas.html?Home=true&Keywords=Fish+&+Richardson+2011&Brand=Site). .

[11] Law360. "International Trade Group of the Year: Fish & Richardson" (http://www.law360.com/web/articles/222940). .

[12] Morning Star. "Fish & Richardson Named "Top 30 Game Law Firm" by Interactive Age" (http://news.morningstar.com/all/market-wire/ 11713006/fish-richardson-named-top-30-game-law-firm-by-interactive-age.aspx). .

[13] Managing Intellectual Property. "Survey 2010: 2010 World IP Survey Rankings" (http://www.fr.com/files/News/
4ec64103-d9c4-410e-b385-38ccc267b01a/Presentation/NewsAttachment/56d1daaf-cf09-468b-85f3-0681af4eca0f/MIPWorldIPSurvey.
pdf). . Retrieved 28 June 2010.

[14] "IP Firms of The Year" (http://www.law360.com/registrations/user_registration?article_id=140383&concurrency_check=false). *Law
360*. 01 January 2010. .

[15] "Winners and Finalists" (http://www.law.com/jsp/tal/PubArticleTAL.jsp?id=1202437074860&Winners__Finalists). *All the results in
our fifth biennial Litigation Department of the Year competition.*. 2010. . Retrieved 2010-06-28. "... Finalists Fish & Richardson, Weil,
Gotshal & Manges, Winston & Strawn...'"

[16] Staff report (November 7, 1930). Frederick P. Fish, Noted Lawyer, Dies; Was President of American Telephone and Telegraph Co. for
Many Years. An Overseer of Harvard. Also a Leading Member of Massachusetts "Tech's" Board and a Bank Director. *New York Times*

External links

- Fish & Richardson web site (http://www.fr.com)
- Fish & Richardson on Twitter (http://twitter.com/FishRichardson)
- Fish & Richardson on Facebook (http://www.facebook.com/fishrichardson)
- Fish & Richardson LinkedIn Profile (http://www.linkedin.com/company/fish-&-richardson-p.c.)
- Profile (http://www.martindale.com/Fish-Richardson-PC/654088-law-firm-office.htm) from LexisNexis
  Martindale-Hubbell
- LawPeriscope Profile (http://www.lawperiscope.com/profiles/090.html)
- Hoover's Profile (http://www.hoovers.com/free//co/factsheet.xhtml?ID=119899)
- Vault Profile (http://www.vault.com/wps/portal/usa/companies/company-profile/Fish-&-Richardson-P.C.
  ?companyId=6600)

Flood Forecasting Centre

The **Flood Forecasting Centre** (FFC) is a joint venture between the Environment Agency and the Met Office to provide warnings of flooding which may affect England and Wales. The FFC is based in the Operations Centre at the Met Office headquarters in Exeter.

Background

Following severe flooding across the UK in 2007 a review was commissioned by the government to see what lessons could be learned. Chaired by Sir Michael Pitt the review produced a number of recommendations which were published in June 2008, among them was the recommendation that the different agencies work more closely together to improve warnings services.[1]

Formation and role

The FFC was officially opened on 21 April 2009 in London by Environment Minister Hilary Benn.[2] The centre combines the work of meteorologists from the Met Office and hydrologists from the Environment Agency. Its role is to provide better warnings advice to the government, local authorities, emergency responders and the general public. It faced its first major test in November 2009 when severe flooding affected Northern England, in particular Cumbria and the town of Cockermouth, the Pitt Review progress report highlighted the accuracy of the warnings issued ahead of this event.[1] In April 2011 the FFC moved from its location in central London and is now located within Ops Centre at the Met Office HQ in Exeter.[1]

Scottish Flood Forecasting Service

In March 2011 the **Scottish Flood Forecasting Service** (SFFS) was formed, a partnership between the Scottish Environment Protection Agency (SEPA) and the Met Office with £750,000 of funding from the Scottish Government.[3] It will fulfil much of the same role as the FFC, though it is a virtual centre with meteorologists based at the Operations Centre in Aberdeen and hydrologists based at SEPA in Perth.[4]

References

[1] "Flood Forecasting Centre moves to Exeter" (http://www.exeterscience.org/news/33/129/Flood-Forecasting-Centre-moves-to-Exeter. html). Exeter Science. . Retrieved 4 June 2011.

[2] "New Flood Forecasting Centre oficially opened" (http://www.metoffice.gov.uk/news/releases/archive/2009/flood-forecasting-centre). MetOffice.gov.uk. .

[3] "Commercial insurance news: Flood forecasting service launched" (http://www.premierlinedirect.co.uk/knowledge/insurance-news/ Commercial_insurance_news_Flood_forecasting_service_launched). Premierlinedirect.co.uk. . Retrieved 4 June 2011.

[4] "Scottish Flood Forecasting Service" (http://www.sepa.org.uk/flooding/flood_forecasting_service.aspx). Sepa.org.uk. . Retrieved 4 June 2011.

External links

- Official FFC website (http://www.ffc-environment-agency.metoffice.gov.uk/)
- Official Environment Agency website (http://www.environment-agency.gov.uk/)
- Official Met Ofice website (http://www.metoffice.gov.uk/)
- Scottish Flood Forecasting Service (http://www.sepa.org.uk/flooding/flood_forecasting_service.aspx)
- The Pitt Review (http://webarchive.nationalarchives.gov.uk/20100807034701/http:/archive.cabinetoffice. gov.uk/pittreview/thepittreview.html)

Hazard prevention

Hazard prevention refers to the prevention of risks. The first and most effective stage of hazard prevention and emergency management is the elimination of hazards. If this is too timely or impractical, comes the more costly stage in emergency management: disaster mitigation.

Accident Chain

Every accident as a result of a hazard is preventable by breaking the accident chain before the last link. [1] Breaking the chain is known as intervention, which is *reactive*, whereas reducing the potential for an accident chain at all is mitigation, which is *proactive*. An example of a reactive step is the creation of a collapse zone at a structure fire. An example of a proactive step is wearing personal protective equipment at a fire call.

The accident chain:

- The environment *such as weather or lighting*
- Human factors *such as training or attitude*
- Equipment *such as proper use and maintenance*
- Event *the unsafe junction of the previous three links*
- Accident *the actual injury or property damage*

Safety Standards and Regulations

The United States Congress passed the William Stieger Act in 1970 with the signature of Richard Nixon. This established the Occupational Safety and Health Administration (OSHA). OSHA enforces safety-related regulations, known as Codes of Federal Regulation (CFRs) in the workplace.

References

[1] Firefighters Handbook (New York Edition). 2004.

Institute of Risk Management

Institute of Risk Management (IRM) is a risk management professional education and training body. It was established in 1986, as a not-for-profit company limited by guarantee, and is governed by a Board of Directors elected from members with specialist non-member support. It has around 3000 members in more than 50 countries.

The Institute provides both taught and distance learning education, training and professional development in risk management at a range of levels. IRM Membership (MIRM) is recognised worldwide as the sign of a risk management professional and is achieved through examination and relevant experience. Fellowship (FIRM) follows through accredited practical experience.

The Institute is the only organisation currently offering vocational post-graduate level qualifications designed from the ground-up to meet the challenge of Enterprise Risk Management (ERM). Many other bodies run courses focussed on individual areas of risk (e.g. insurable risk, risk in banks, health and safety, project risk, disaster recovery etc) and in some cases there is the option to take an additional ERM paper. Only IRM offers dedicated ERM qualifications.

Membership Grades

- Fellow (FIRM) – Open to members who can demonstrate accredited practical experience, a record of personal professional development and proven contribution and support to the Institution
- Member (MIRM) – Requires completion of Institute's Diploma programme or equivalent qualification and a minimum of three years work experience
- Graduate (GradIRM) - Requires completion of Institute's Diploma programme or equivalent qualification recognised by the IRM
- Specialist (SIRM) - Requires formal qualification of the applicant in a risk specialism - e.g. audit, health and safety, risk financing, environment, project management, business continuity etc
- Certificant (CIRM) – Completion of the Institute's Certificate programme
- Student – Open to all candidates registered for the Institute's examinations
- Affiliate – Open to anyone with an interest in risk management. Discounted rates are available to groups of 10 or more. Affiliate membership is free to university students on IRM approved courses

IRM Courses

- The International Diploma in Risk Management – A challenging post graduate professional qualification, usually taken over a few years and completed via distance learning. It is recognised worldwide as the sign of a risk management professional.

- The International Certificate in Risk Management – This practitioner-level qualification provides a sound foundation in risk management theory and practice. It can be taken as a stand-alone course or as an introduction to the IRM Diploma.

- Fundamentals of Risk Management – This one to three day training programme provides a broad introduction to the subject of risk management. It aims to improve knowledge and practical skills in the identification, assessment and control of business risk, and provides an introduction to ERM and ISO 31000.

These qualifications are moderated by a panel of leading educationalists drawn from universities and business schools across the world.

Risk Management Standard

The IRM is responsible for the Risk Management Standard [1] in conjunction with The Association of Insurance and Risk Managers (AIRMIC) and ALARM, the National Forum for Risk Management in the Public Sector. The standard is available free of charge in 17 world languages.

IRM has also issued a free guidance note on the implementation of ISO 31000.

Address

Institute of Risk Management, 6 Lloyd's Avenue, London, EC3N 3AX, UK

IRM Website

IRM [2]

References

[1] http://www.theirm.org/publications/PUstandard.html
[2] http://www.theirm.org

Insurance Certificate Tracking

Managing and validation of incoming certificates of insurance (COI's) is a time consuming and a costly exercise for most organizations. Be it real estate / property management companies who in order to mitigate their risk, require their tenants to carry specific insurance coverage and make these as terms of their lease agreement or Construction Companies wherein the requirement varies from location to location.

How It Works

Process 1: Certificates are received via fax, email or postal service and scanned into the system and stored as an image along with any other key contractual information.

Process 2: Certificate Tracking:-

   a) Measures certificates and endorsements to the custom requirements (Coverages, AI wording[1] , A. M. Best Rating etc.)

   b) Certificate override for special exceptions (typically approved by customers)

   c) Documented history of certificate status and review process

Process 3: Certificate Monitoring:-

   a) Reporting on certificate expirations, carrier rating downgrade, expired status and cancellations

Process 4: Correspondence:-

   a) Unique correspondence letters are sent through email, mailers or fax

   b) Receive certificates and other required documents through email, mailers or fax

While many systems have the flexibility to manage insurance for virtually any organization in any industry, there are just few companies who have developed specific functionality geared towards industry specific requirements. These companies maintain a devoted team of employees in their centers who work exclusively with industry specific customers. Insurance requirements enclosed in real estate/property management lease agreements have an inclination to have a larger degree of divergence than requirements contained in other types of agreements because lease terms tend to get negotiated on case to case basis more than other types of agreements or industries. In addition, many real estate managers will frequently inherit lease agreements through property acquisitions. These agreements in general contain requirements that are exclusive to each property location. To accommodate this, these systems needs to have the ability to establish and implement a distinct coverage requirement for every tenant record and successfully manage all other types of agreement that property management organizations enter into such as vendor service agreements and construction contracts and ensure proper parties are shown as additional insureds for each agreement. It is not unusual for different approaches to exist within a single customer application as well. Similar kind of uniqueness exist for other industries as well be it Construction Practice or Retail but the basic approach remains the same.[2]

Two separate solutions for managing COI's

1) **Full service outsourcing**: The service provider assumes the accountability for soliciting and validating evidence of coverage and managing the customer service phone calls associated with this effort.

2) **ASP/Self Service approach**: In this approach the customer utilizes a web based tracking system. Using this approach, the customer retains responsibility for managing all of the day-to-day tracking functions (e.g. sending out requests for evidence of renewal coverage, sending out deficiency notices, responding to customer services inquires etc.) while the service provider provides the software and data storage.

Data Interface Competence

Sometimes a customer organization may ask for data interface of the insurance coverage info and/or compliance status created by the service providers system to its own internal systems like Accounts Payable, CRM etc. There are systems which can accommodate this easily with custom interfaces with the customers application.

Notable vendors and their total experience in Certificate Tracking

- Insurance Tracking Services, Inc. (ITS) [3]
- SOFTSERVD® [4] - Intelligent Certificate of Insurance Tracking Software
- InsureTrack [5] - Web Based Insurance Tracking System
- Ebix BPO [6] (15 Years)
- JW Software, Inc. [7] - JW Software, Inc. - since 1989
- CertsOnline [8] (Same as/DBA Ebix -15 Years)
- ConfirmNet [9] (Same as/DBA Ebix -15 Years)
- RISKworks [10]
- CMS: Certificate Management Solutions [11] - since 1998
- I-RAVS ISNetworld [12] ISNetworld
- Data Trac Plus
- EXIGIS rm.Compliance [13]
- Ebix Inc. (Ebix BPO)[14]
- CS Stars (Marsh Product)
- LTS (Lease Tracking Services)
- Business Credentialing Services (BCS) [15]
- CertTracker (Australia) [16]
- ISNetworld [17]
- Insurance Certificate Administrators [18] - since 1994
- Succeed Management Solutions, LLC Succeed Management Solutions: COI Track [19]
- InsureGUARD http://picsauditing.com

References

1. http://www.softservd.com
2. http://www.insurancetrackingservices.com
3. http://www.insuretrack.com
4. http://www.thefreelibrary.com/Insurance+Certificate+Tracking-a01073975687
5. http://www.willis.com/Documents/publications/Industries/Real_Estate/Views_Mar_09_Real_Estate_Newsletter.pdf
6. http://www.linkedin.com/groups?gid=73683
7. http://www.certsonline.com/
8. http://www.confirmnet.com/
9. http://www.ebix.com/channel_bpo.aspx
10. http://www.datatracplus.com
11. http://www.jwsoftware.com
12. http://www.isnetworld.com/ProcurementRavs.asp
13. http://www.insuranceandtechguide.com/Ebix-BPO-cp550386.htm?c=7073
14. http://www.ltsinc.com
15. http://www.ggonesoftware.com/
16. http://www.exigis.net

17. http://bcsaudit.com
18. http://www.certtracker.com.au
19. http://www.certaincert.com
20. http://www.cmstrack.com
21. http://www.riskworks.com
22. http://www.exigis.com/solutions.php
23. http://www.picsauditing.com

Direct References

[1] "Additional insured" (http://en.wikipedia.org/wiki/Additional_insured). Wikipedia. .
[2] "Willis Real Estate Newsletter" (http://www.willis.com/Documents/publications/Industries/Real_Estate/
     Views_Mar_09_Real_Estate_Newsletter.pdf). Willis. .
[3] http://www.insurancetrackingservices.com
[4] http://www.softservd.com
[5] http://www.insuretrack.com
[6] http://www.ebixbpo.com
[7] http://jwsoftware.com/certificatehandler.asp
[8] http://www.certsonline.com
[9] http://www.confirmnet.com
[10] http://www.riskworks.com
[11] http://www.cmstrack.com
[12] http://www.isnetworld.com/ProcurementRavs.asp
[13] http://www.exigis.com/solutions/rmCompliance.php
[14] "Ebix BPO" (http://www.ebix.com/channel_bpo.aspx). Ebix. .
[15] http://bcsaudit.com
[16] http://www.certtracker.com.au
[17] http://www.isnetworld.com
[18] http://www.icaprogram.com
[19] http://www.succeedmanagementsolutions.com/COI-certificate-of-insurance-software.html

Investment Controlling

Definition

Investment controlling[1] is a monitoring function within the asset management, portfolio management or investment management. It is concerned with independently supervising and monitoring the quality of asset management accounts with the aim of ensuring performance and quality in order to provide the required benefit for the asset management client. Dependent on setup, investment controlling not only encompasses controlling activities but also can include areas from compliance to performance review. Besides, investment controlling aspects can also be taken into consideration by asset management clients or investment advisers/consultants and consequently it is likely that these stakeholders also run certain investment controlling activities.

Introduction and overview

Efficient and appropriate management information on the quality of their discretionary managed portfolios is very important for an asset management company. Without decision-oriented information on the quality or performance of its products and/or asset managers for an asset management company it is very difficult to stand the increasing challenges of the asset management industry (increasing regulations, need for sophisticated risk management, etc.). Clients and consultants have similar needs where these often correspond to the asset manager ones some years ago. Investment controlling deals with such needs and helps to overcome the information gaps within asset management.

Investment controlling is an area of activity that is part of the overall controlling process within the asset management and is an important component of the recurring investment decision making process. From an asset management company point of view, in general investment controlling is defined as information management that gathers, processes, checks and distributes information necessary to meet the overall objectives of the asset management company. In this respect the investment controlling objective consists in configuring the infrastructure – particularly within the framework of the investment decision making process – in such a way that the processes (e.g. forecasting, decision making and implementation), the quality and the results (e.g. returns), the risks (e.g. of using derivatives) and the costs become more transparent and comprehensible. Considering the client perspective, in the following investment controlling is in general defined as independent monitoring of the performance of asset management products and/or accounts with the aim of ensuring that the client gets what was promised in the first place with respect to quality and performance.

As part of the overall investment decision making process investment controlling intents to visualise the contributions of the individual decisions of the investment process, especially with respect to return and risk, and to allocate the contributions to the responsible decision makers. The results and conclusions of the different investment controlling activities are important feedback and input into the investment process to enhance the quality or performance of the specific asset management product.

Objectives

Form a general point of view investment controlling adds to the visibility, transparency and credibility of any asset management company. In detail investment controlling helps

- implementing best practice in performance measurement and performance presentation, for example by implementing the GIPS Standards[2] ,
- producing an independent performance analysis of the asset management accounts and/or products,
- enabling deep level analysis which is necessary to identify the real drivers of the account return and account risk and this from an ex-post as well as from an ex-ante point of view,
- monitoring risk and return of accounts and/or products against their designated benchmark and objectives, capturing performance dispersion,
- reducing unnecessary discussions by using more objective and less subjective information during the performance review,
- creating of or increasing the transparency and comparability of the asset management products and/or accounts,
- addressing performance issues on an regular basis and not leaving them running,
- creating a basis not only for ongoing analyses but also for structural changes in the investment process,
- reducing of unintended business risks through early addressing of potential performance issues,
- and others.

Investment controlling activities

Investment controlling is very manifold and encompasses a lot of different activities like:

- performance attribution or more precisely return attribution and/or risk attribution and this ex-post as well as ex-ante,
- market index and benchmark comparisons, composite dispersion analysis and peer group analysis with respect to the return and/or risk but also to characteristics like asset class or sector weights, duration, exposure to specific risk factors and so on,
- calculation of performance figures and statistics representing manager skills or the investment style and running style analysis,
- review of the set up of the specific asset management account with respect to benchmark, investment guidelines, transaction costs and management fees, etc.,
- product review against client expectations and best practice,
- identifying of actual and potential performance issues and highlighting the serious ones to senior management,
- suggesting remedial action to solve performance issues,
- risk decomposition and risk budgeting,
- analyzing and identifying all steps of the investment process,
- review of the investment guidelines and benchmarks,
- checking whether risk levels and limits are appropriate and
- aggregated performance reporting to senior management.

Articles on investment controlling

There are no text books on investment controlling available. Therefore general literature on controlling, risk management and compliance may be a good starting-point for a deeper study of investment controlling.

Articles on investment controlling:

- Philippe Grégoire (2010): Performance Attribution as a Management Control System,
- Stefan Illmer (1997): Controlling im Portfolio Management (in German),
- Stefan Illmer (2000): Controlling – Eine grosse Herausforderung für das Real Estate Management (in German).

Further reading on aspects of investment controlling

On performance measurement and attribution:

- Carl Bacon: Practical Portfolio Performance Measurement and Attribution,
- Andreas Bickel: Moderne Performance-Analyse und Performance Presentation Standards (in German),
- Bruce J. Feibel: Investment Performance Measurement,
- Bernd Fischer: Performanceanalyse in der Praxis (in German),
- Todd Jankowski and Philip Lawton: Investment Performance Measurement: Evaluating and Presenting Results,
- David Spaulding: Investment Performance Attribution.

External links

- Welcome to Investment Controlling [3],
- GIPS Standards [4],
- Real Estate Information Standard [5],
- CIPM Program [6].

References and footnotes

[1] for more information on investment controlling (http://www.paforum.ch/)
[2] for more information on GIPS Standards (http://www.gipsstandards.org/)
[3] http://www.paforum.ch/
[4] http://www.gipsstandards.org/
[5] http://www.reisus.org/
[6] http://www.cfainstitute.org/cipm/pages/index.aspx/

ISO 31000

ISO 31000 is intended to be a family of standards relating to risk management codified by the International Organization for Standardization. The purpose of ISO 31000:2009 is to provide principles and generic guidelines on risk management. ISO 31000 seeks to provide a universally recognised paradigm for practitioners and companies employing risk management processes to replace the myriad of existing standards, methodologies and paradigms that differed between industries, subject matters and regions.

Currently, the ISO 31000 family is expected to include:

*   ISO 31000:2009 _ Principles and Guidelines on Implementation[1]
*   ISO/IEC 31010:2009 - Risk Management - Risk Assessment Techniques
*   ISO Guide 73:2009 - Risk Management - Vocabulary

Introduction

ISO 31000 was published as a standard on the 13th of November 2009, and provides a standard on the implementation of risk management. A revised and harmonised ISO/IEC Guide 73 was published at the same time. The purpose of ISO 31000:2009 is to be applicable and adaptable for "any public, private or community enterprise, association, group or individual."[2] Accordingly, the general scope of ISO 31000 - as a family of risk management standards - is not developed for a particular industry group, management system or subject matter field in mind, rather to provide best practice structure and guidance to all operations concerned with risk management.

Scope

ISO 31000:2009 provides generic guidelines for the design, implementation and maintenance of risk management processes throughout an organization. This approach to formalizing risk management practices will facilitate broader adoption by companies who require an enterprise risk management standard that accommodates multiple 'silo-centric' management systems.[3]

The scope of this approach to risk management is to enable all strategic, management and operational tasks of an organization throughout projects, functions, and processes to be aligned to a common set of risk management objectives.

Accordingly, ISO 31000:2009 is intended for a broad stakeholder group including:

*   executive level stakeholders
*   appointment holders in the enterprise risk management group
*   risk analysts and management officers
*   line managers and project managers
*   compliance and internal auditors
*   independent practitioners.

Risk Conceptualisation

One of the key paradigm shifts in ISO 31000 is how risk is conceptualised, under the ISO 31000:2009 and a consequential major revision of the terminology in ISO Guide 73, risk with respect to the "effect of uncertainty on objectives". [4]

ISO 31000 Framework approach

ISO 31000:2009 has been received as a replacement to the existing standard on risk management, AS/NZS 4360:2004 (In the form of AS/NZS ISO 31000:2009). Whereas the Standards Australia approach provided a process by which risk management could be undertaken, ISO 31000:2009 addresses the entire management system that supports the design, implementation, maintenance and improvement of risk management processes.

Implementation

The intent of ISO 31000 is to be applied within existing management systems to formalise and improve risk management processes as opposed to wholesale substitution of legacy management practices. Subsequently, when implementing ISO 31000, attention is to be given to integrating existing risk management processes in the new paradigm addressed in the standard.

The focus of many ISO 31000 'Harmonisation' programmes[5] have centred on:

- Transferring accountability gaps in enterprise risk management
- Aligning objectives of the governance frameworks with ISO 31000
- Embedding management system reporting mechanisms
- Creating uniform risk criteria and evaluation metrics

Implications

Most implications for adopting the new standard concern the re-engineering of existing management practices to conform with the documentation, communication and socialisation of the new risk management operating paradigm; as opposed to wholesale re-orientation of management practice throughout an organisation. Accordingly, most senior position holders in an enterprise risk management organisation will need to be cognisant of the implication for adopting the standard and be able to develop effective strategies for implementing the standard across supply chains and commercial operations.[6]

Certain aspects of top management accountability, strategic policy implementation and effective governance frameworks, will require more consideration by organisations that have previously used now redundant risk management methodologies.

In some domains that concern risk management, particular security and corporate social responsibility, which may operate using relatively unsophisticated risk management processes, more material change will be required, particularly regarding a clearly articulated risk management policy, formalising risk ownership processes, structuring framework processes and adopting continuous improvement programmes.

Accreditation

ISO 31000 has not been developed with the intention for certification.

References

[1] National Standards Authority of Ireland (http://www.nsai.ie/index.cfm/area/news/action/article/information/ISO31000)

[2] ISO 31000 catalogue http://www.iso.org/iso/catalogue_detail.htm?csnumber=43170

[3] ISO 31000 Update (http://www.optaresystems.com/index.php/optare/news_articles/iso_31000_update/)

[4] ISO Guide 73: Risk Management - Vocabulary

[5] ISO 31000 update: What it means to C-Suite Risk Owners (http://www.optaresystems.com/index.php/optare/publication_detail/iso_31000_update_what_it_means_to_a_c-suite_risk_owner/)

[6] Implications for ISO adoption http://www.optaresystems.com/index.php/optare/publication_detail/iso_31000_update_what_it_will_mean_for_a_cso/

External links

- International Organization for Standardization (http://www.iso.org/iso/catalogue_detail.htm?csnumber=43170)
- AS/NZS ISO 31000:2009 Risk management - Principles and guidelines (http://infostore.saiglobal.com/store/Details.aspx?ProductID=1378670)
- Discussion forum on ISO 31000:2009 Risk management - Principles and guidelines (http://www.linkedin.com/groups/ISO-31000-2009-Risk-Management-1834592?mostPopular=&gid=1834592)

List of books about risk

This is a **list of books about risk** issues.

Title	Author(s)	Year
Acceptable risk	Baruch Fischhoff, Sarah Lichtenstein, Paul Slovic, Steven L. Derby, and Ralph Keeney	1984
American hazardscapes: The regionalization of hazards and disasters	Susan L. Cutter	2001
At risk: Natural hazards, people's vulnerability and disasters	Piers Blaikie, Terry Cannon, Ian Davis, and Ben Wisner	1994
Big dam foolishness; the problem of modern flood control and water storage	Elmer Theodore Peterson	1954
Building Safer Communities. Risk Governance, Spatial Planning and Responses to Natural Hazards	Urbano Fra Paleo	2009
Catastropic coastal storms: Hazard mitigation and development management	David R. Godschalk, David J. Brower, and Timothy Beatley	1989
Cities on the beach: management issues of developed coastal barriers	Rutherford H. Platt, Sheila G. Pelczarski, and Barbara K. Burbank	1987
Cooperating with nature: Confronting natural hazards with land-use planning for sustainable communities	Raymond J. Burby	1998
Dangerous earth: An introduction to geologic hazards	Barbara W. Murck, Brian J. Skinner, Stephen C. Porter	1998
Disasters and democracy	Rutherford H. Platt	1999
Disasters by design: A reassessment of natural hazards in the United States	Dennis Mileti	1999
Disasters: The anatomy of environmental hazards	John Whittow	1980
Divine wind: The history and science of hurricanes	Kerry Emanuel	2005

Earth shock: Hurricanes, volcanoes, earthquakes, tornadoes and other forces of nature	Andrew Robinson	1993
Earthquakes: A primer	Bruce A. Bolt	1976
Environmental hazards: Assessing risk and reducing disaster	Keith Smith	1992
Facing the unexpected: Disaster preparedness and response in the United States	Kathleen J. Tierney, Michael K. Lindell, and Ronald W. Perry	2001
Floods	Dennis J. Parker	2000
Human adjustment to floods	Gilbert F. White	1942
Human System Response to Disaster: An Inventory of Sociological Findings	Thomas E. Drabek	1986
Hurricanes : their nature and impacts on society.	Roger A. Pielke, Jr. and Roger Pielke, Sr.	1997
Judgment under uncertainty: heuristics and biases	Daniel Kahneman, Paul Slovic, and Amos Tversky	1982
Mapping vulnerability: disasters, development, and people	Greg Bankoff, Georg Frerks, and Dorothea Hilhorst	2004
Mitigation of hazardous comets and asteroids	Michael J.S. Belton, Thomas H. Morgan, Nalin H. Samarasinha, Donald K. Yeomans	2005
Mountains of fire: The nature of volcanoes	Robert W. Decker, Barbara B. Decker	1991
Natural disasters	David Alexander	1993
Natural disasters	Patrick L. Abbott	1991
Natural disasters: Protecting vulnerable communities	Paul A. Merriman, and C.W. A. Browitt	1993
Natural disaster hotspots: a global risk analysis	Maxx Dilley	2005
Natural hazard mitigation: Recasting disaster policy and planning	David Godschalk, Timothy Beatley, Philip Berke, David Brower, and Edward J. Kaiser	1999
Natural hazards	Edward Bryant	1991
Natural hazards: Earth's proceses as hazards, disasters, and catastrophes	Edward A. Keller, and Robert H. Blodgett	2006
Natural hazards: Explanation and integration	Graham A. Tobin, and Burrell E. Montz	1997
Natural hazards: Local, national, global	Gilbert F. White	1974
Normal accidents. Living with high-risk technologies	Charles Perrow	1984
On borrowed land: Public policies for floodplains	Faber Scott	1993
Paying the price: The status and role of insurance against natural disasters in the United States	Howard Kunreuther, and Richard J. Roth	1998
Planning for earthquakes: Risks, politics, and policy	Philip R. Berke, and Timothy Beatley	1992
Recontruction Following Disaster	J. Eugene Haas, Robert Kates, and Martyn J. Bowden	1977
Recovery from Natural Disasters: Insurance or Federal Aid?	Howard Kunreuther	1973
Reduction and predictability of natural disasters	John B. Rundle, William Klein, Don L. Turcotte	1996
Regions of risk: A geographical introduction to disasters	Kenneth Hewitt	1997
Risk and culture: An essay on the selection of technical and environmental dangers	Mary Douglas, and Aaron Wildavsky	1982
Risk communication: A handbook for communicating environmental, safety, and health risks	Regina E. Lundgren, and Andrea H. McMakin	1994
Risk society: Towards a new modernity	Ulrich Beck	1992
Risk, environment and modernity: towards a new ecology	Scott Lash, Bronislaw Szerszynski and Brian W. Sage	1996
Terra non firma: Understanding and preparing for earthquakes	James M. Gere and Haresh M. Shah	1984

The angry earth: Disaster in anthropological perspective	Anthony Oliver-Smith, and Susanna Hoffman	1999
The Control of Nature	John McPhee	1989
The hurricane and its impact	Robert H. Simpson, and Herbert Riehl	1981
The environment as hazard	Ian Burton, Robert Kates, and Gilbert F. White	1978
The perception of risk	Paul Slovic	2000
The social amplification of risk	Nick Pidgeon, Roger E. Kasperson, and Paul Slovic	2003
There is no such thing as a natural disaster : race, class, and Hurricane Katrina	Chester W. Hartman, and Gregory D. Squires	2006
Understanding catastrophe: It's impact on life on earth	Janine Bourrian	1992
What is a disaster? New answers to old questions	Ronald W. Perry, and Enrico Quarantelli	2005
What is a disaster? Perspectives on the question	Enrico Quarantelli	1998

Master of Science in Risk Management Program for Executives

The **Master of Science in Risk Management Program for Executives**[1] is a joint-venture with NYU's Stern School of Business and the Amsterdam Institute of Finance.[2] This program, which was given provisional accreditation by PRMIA, spans 12 months and takes place in Amsterdam and New York City, aided by the use of distance learning techniques. Further program details are provided through MasterStudies.com [3] [4]

Overview

This pioneer program incorporates traditional and innovative modeling techniques, but aims to situate this knowledge within the larger context of business strategy and risk management. The field of risk management has evolved rapidly and significantly, post the financial crisis of 2007-2010, and will help prepare for those risk management discussions that arise.

Academic

The Master of Science in Risk Management Program [5] is a one year, executive friendly, part time schedule with a June start date. It consists of five modules held over one year, rotating between New York City and Amsterdam.

Students receive a Master of Science degree, issued by New York University Stern School of Business[6] .

Students

The student profile of the most recent Class of 2010 consists of global executives, whose average age is 38 and who have 15 years of work experience. The students represent 13 nationalities and work in a broad range of industries.

Professors

Professors who teach and have taught in the Master of Science in Risk Management Program:

* Theo Vermaelen
* Ingo Walter
* Viral Acharya
* Edward Altman
* Rohit Deo
* Robert Engle
* Richard Levich
* Holger Mueller
* Marti Murray
* Anthony Saunders
* Zur Shapira
* Stijn Van Nieuwerburgh

References

[1] Master of Science in Risk Management - Official Site (http://w4.stern.nyu.edu/academic/global/riskmanagement/)

[2] Reuters.com (http://www.reuters.com/article/pressRelease/idUS161971+03-Sep-2008+BW20080903)

[3] http://www.masterstudies.com/MBA-MSc-Masters-Degree/Business-Economics-and-Administration/Executive-Programs/
Executive-MS-in-Finance/Netherlands/New-York-University-Leonard-N.-Stern-School-of-Business/
Master-of-Science-in-Risk-Management-for-Executives/

[4] MasterStudies.com (http://www.masterstudies.com/MBA-MSc-Masters-Degree/Business-Economics-and-Administration/
Executive-Programs/Executive-MS-in-Finance/Netherlands/New-York-University-Leonard-N.-Stern-School-of-Business/
Master-of-Science-in-Risk-Management-for-Executives/)

[5] http://w4.stern.nyu.edu/academic/global/riskmanagement/

[6] NYU Stern School of Business (http://www.stern.nyu.edu/)

External links

* Reuters.com Article, "Amsterdam Institute of Finance & NYU Stern School of Business Partner to Launch..." (http://www.reuters.com/article/idUS161971+03-Sep-2008+BW20080903)
* MastersStudies.com, Listed under "Best Masters Degree" (http://www.masterstudies.com/ MBA-MSc-Masters-Degree/Business-Economics-and-Administration/Executive-Programs/ Executive-MS-in-Finance/Netherlands/New-York-University-Leonard-N.-Stern-School-of-Business/ Master-of-Science-in-Risk-Management-for-Executives/)
* Master of Science in Risk Management Program for Executives - Official Site (http://w4.stern.nyu.edu/ academic/global/riskmanagement/)
* Stern Global Programs
* NYU Stern School of Business (http://www.stern.nyu.edu/)
* Amsterdam Institute of Finance (http://www.aif.nl/)

Moody's Analytics

Moody's Analytics

Headquarters	New York City
Employees	1,600
Website	www.moodysanalytics.com [1]

Moody's Analytics provides capital markets and risk management professionals with credit analysis, economic research, financial risk management software, and advisory services. The firm, a global organization with offices in New York City, San Francisco, London, Paris, Brazil, Canada, Japan, Hong Kong, Australia, and China, has approximately USD 600 million in annual revenue.[2]

History

The firm was formed as a subsidiary of Moody's Corporation in 2007, when the company split into two operating divisions. Moody's Investors Service, the rating agency, and Moody's Analytics, with all of its other products.[3]

In 2002 , the parent Moody's Corporation had acquired **KMV**, which provides quantitative credit risk management tools including KMV's flagship solution, the EDF™ (Expected Default Frequency). KMV, formerly known as Kealhofer, McQuown and Vasicek, was headquartered in San Francisco, CA.[4] In 2005, **Economy.com**, based in West Chester, Pennsylvania was added to the portfolio. This expansion, added economic, financial, country and industry research and data services.[5] In 2006, the firm acquired **Wall Street Analytics,** a developer of structured finance analysis and monitoring software.— an addition enhancing the firm's collateralized debt obligations (CDO) product suite and added mortgage-backed securities (MBS) and asset-backed securities (ABS) analytic software capabilities.[6]

In 2008, the now separate Moody's Analytics acquired **Fermat International**, a Paris, France based provider of risk and performance management software to the global banking sector.[7] Also in 2008, it acquired **Enb Consulting**, a provider of training services for the financial markets, including technical and soft skills programs for banking and capital markets professionals. That company had been founded in 2000 in the United Kingdom.[8]

In 2010, the firm acquired Canadian Securities Institute Global Education Inc. (CSI). That company had a 40 year history as Canada's leading provider of financial learning, credentials, and certification, serving in excess of 700,000 professionals.[9]

Executive officers

- Mark Almeida - President
- Geoff Fite - Executive Director and Chief Operating Officer [10]

Awards

Publications and organizations have recognized the firm in 2010 with the following awards:

- Risk Technology Rankings 2010 - #1 in Basel II Compliance, Regulatory Risk Capital [11]
- Risk Technology Rankings 2010 - #3 in Economic Risk Calculation [11]
- Risk Technology Rankings 2010 - #3 in Asset and Liability Management [11]
- Asia Risk Technology Survey 2010 - #1 in Liquidity Management [12]
- Chartis RiskTech100 2010 - #1 in Credit Risk overall [13]

- Waters Rankings 2010 – "Best Credit Risk Solutions Provider" [14]

References

[1] http://www.moodysanalytics.com

[2] Moody's Corporation Investor Relations (http://ir.moodys.com/overview.cfm)

[3] Moody's Corporation Announces New Business Unit Structure August 7, 2007 (http://www.allbusiness.com/services/business-services/4540649-1.html)

[4] Moody's Corporation Completes Acquisition of KMV April 15, 2002 (http://ir.moodys.com/releasedetail.cfm?ReleaseID=288619)

[5] Moody's Acquires Economy.com December 1, 2005 (http://www.allbusiness.com/legal/856708-1.html)

[6] Moody's Corporation Acquires Wall Street Analytics December 18, 2006 (http://www.allbusiness.com/finance/business-loans-business-credit/4020182-1.html)

[7] Moody's Analytics to Acquire Fermat International September 15, 2008 (http://www.streetinsider.com/Mergers+and+Acquisitions/Moodyâs+(MCO)+to+Acquire+Fermat+International+for+$189+Million+Plus+Considerations;+Sees+Deal+Dilutive+Through+2009/3987962.html)

[8] Moody's Analytics Acquires Enb Consulting December 18, 2009 (http://www.businesswire.com/news/home/20081218005238/en/Moodys-Analytics-Acquires-Enb-Consulting)

[9] Moody's Corporation Acquires CSI Global Education November 22, 2010 (http://www.businesswire.com/news/home/20101122005446/en/Moodyâs-Corporation-Acquires-CSI-Global-Education)

[10] Officers and Directors from Moody's Analytics Website (http://moodysanalytics.com/About_Us/Leadership_Team.aspx)

[11] Risk Technology Rankings 2010 (http://www.risk.net/risk-magazine/research/1899406/risk-technology-rankings-2010)

[12] Asia Risk Technology Survey 2010 (http://www.risk.net/asia-risk/research/1732252/competition-intensifies-risk-technology-vendors-asia)

[13] Chartis Research (http://chartis-research.com/research/reports/risktech100-2010)

[14] Waters Rankings 2010 (http://www.waterstechnology.com/waters/news/1724170/waters-rankings-2010-all-winners)

External links

- Moody's Analytics (http://www.moodysanalytics.com)

Occupational safety and health

Occupational health and safety is a cross-disciplinary area concerned with protecting the safety, health and welfare of people engaged in work or employment. The goal of all occupational health and safety programs is to foster a safe work environment.[1] As a secondary effect, it may also protect co-workers, family members, employers, customers, suppliers, nearby communities, and other members of the public who are impacted by the workplace environment. It may involve interactions among many subject areas, including occupational medicine, occupational (or industrial) hygiene, public health, safety engineering, chemistry, health physics.

Definition

Since 1950, the International Labour Organization (ILO) and the World Health Organization (WHO) have shared a common definition of occupational health. It was adopted by the Joint ILO/WHO Committee on Occupational Health at its first session in 1950 and revised at its twelfth session in 1995. The definition reads: "Occupational health should aim at: the promotion and maintenance of the highest degree of physical, mental and social well-being of workers in all occupations; the prevention amongst workers of departures from health caused by their working conditions; the protection of workers in their employment from risks resulting from factors adverse to health; the placing and maintenance of the worker in an occupational environment adapted to his physiological and psychological capabilities; and, to summarize, the adaptation of work to man and of each man to his job". This standard is based on the methodology known as *Plan-Do-Check-Act (PDCA)*

Relationship to occupational health psychology

Occupational health psychology (OHP), a related discipline, is a relatively new field that combines elements of occupational health and safety, industrial/organizational psychology, and health psychology.[2] The field is concerned with identifying work-related psychosocial factors that adversely affect the health of people who work. OHP is also concerned with developing ways to effect change in workplaces for the purpose of improving the health of people who work. For more detail on OHP, see the section on occupational health psychology....

Reasons for Occupational health and safety

The event of an incident at work (such as legal fees, fines, compensatory damages, investigation time, lost production, lost goodwill from the workforce, from customers and from the wider community).

- Legal - Occupational requirements may be reinforced in civil law and/or criminal law; it is accepted that without the extra "encouragement" of potential regulatory action or litigation, many organizations would not act upon their implied moral obligations.

Occupational health and safety officers promote health and safety procedures in an organisation. They recognize hazards and measure health and safety risks, set suitable safety controls in place, and give recommendations on avoiding accidents to management and employees in an organisation. This paper looks at the main tasks undertaken by OHS practitioners in Europe, Australia and the USA, and the main knowledge and skills that are required of them. "Like it or not, organisations have a duty to provide health and safety training. But it could involve much more than you think." (Damon, Nadia. 2008. 'Reducing The Risks', Training and Coaching Today, United Kingdom, pg.14)

An effective training program can reduce the number of injuries and deaths, property damage, legal liability, illnesses, workers' compensation claims, and missed time from work. A safety training program can also help a trainer keep the required OSHA-mandated safety training courses organized and up-to-date.

Safety training classes help establish a safety culture in which employees themselves help promote proper safety procedures while on the job. It is important that new employees be properly trained and embrace the importance of workplace safety as it is easy for seasoned workers to negatively influence the new hires. That negative influence however, can be purged with the establishment of new, hands-on, innovative effective safety training which will ultimately lead to an effective safety culture. A 1998 NIOSH study concluded that the role of training in developing and maintaining effective hazard control activities is a proven and successful method of intervention.[3]

Safety Professionals in Europe

In Norway, the main required tasks of an Occupational Health and Safety Practitioner include:

• Systematic evaluations of the working environment
• Endorsing preventative measures which eliminate reasons for illnesses in the work place
• Giving information in the subject of employees' health
• Giving information on occupational hygiene, ergonomics and also environmental and safety risks in the work place (Hale A, Ytehus I, 2004, 'Changing requirements for the safety profession: roles and tasks', Journal of Occupational Health & Safety – Australia and New Zealand)

In the Netherlands, required tasks for health and safety staff are only summarily defined, and include:

• Voluntary medical examinations
• A consulting room on the work environment for the workers
• Health check assessments (if needed for the job concerned) (Hale, A et alia. 2004)

'The main influence on the Dutch law on the job of the safety professional is through the requirement on each employer to use the services of a certified working conditions service to advise them on health and safety' (Hale, A et alia. 2004). A 'certified service' must employ sufficient numbers of four types of certified experts to cover the risks in the organisations which use the service:

• A safety professional
• An occupational hygienist
• An occupational physician
• A work and organisation specialist. (Hale, A et alia. 2004)

It shows in Table 1 (based on the European Network of Safety and Health Practitioner Organisations [ENHSPO] survey to) that in Norway, 37 % of Health and Safety practitioners had a MSc education level, and 14% in the Netherlands; 44% were BSc graduates and 63% in the Netherlands; and 19% were of a Technician level and 23% in the Netherlands (Hale, A et alia. 2004).

Safety Professionals in the USA

The main tasks undertaken by the OHS practitioner in the USA include:

• Develop processes, procedures, criteria, requirements, and methods to attain the best possible management of the hazards and exposures that can cause injury to people, and damage property, or the environment;

• Apply good business practices and economic principles for efficient use of resources to add to the importance of the safety processes;

• Promote other members of the company to contribute by exchanging ideas and other different approaches to make sure that every one in the corporation possess OHS knowledge and have functional roles in the development and execution of safety procedures;

• Assess services, outcomes, methods, equipment, workstations, and procedures by using qualitative and quantitative methods to recognise the hazards and measure the related risks;

• Examine all possibilities, effectiveness, reliability, and expenditure to attain the best results for the company concerned

(Board of Certified Safety Professionals, 2006, "Examination Guide" accessed 20 April at http://www.bcsp.org/bcsp/media/exam_guide.pdf)

Knowledge required by the OHS professional in USA include:

• Constitutional and case law controlling safety, health, and the environment

• Operational procedures to plan/ develop safe work practices

• Safety, health and environmental sciences

• Design of hazard control systems (i.e. fall protection, scaffoldings)

• Design of recordkeeping systems that take collection into account, as well as storage, interpretation, and dissemination

• Mathematics and statistics

• Processes and systems for attaining safety through design

(Board of Certified Safety Professionals, 2006)

Some skills required by the OHS professional in the USA include (but are not limited to):

• Understanding and relating to systems, policies and rules

• Holding checks and having control methods for possible hazardous exposures

• Mathematical and statistical analysis

• Examining manufacturing hazards

• Planning safe work practices for systems, facilities, and equipment

• Understanding and using safety, health, and environmental science information for the improvement of procedures

• Interpersonal communication skills

(Board of Certified Safety Professionals, 2006)

The differences in each location

Similar to the findings of the ENHSPO survey conducted in Australia, the Institute of Occupational Medicine found that in the UK, there is a need to put a greater emphasis on work-related illness (Anonymous. 2008. 'Occupational Health', Health and Safety News: In Brief, Vol 60, Iss. 3; UK. pg. 6). Its been shown that in Australia and the USA that a major responsibility of the OHS professional is to keep company directors and managers aware of the issues that they face in regards to Occupational Health and Safety principles and legislation. However, in Europe, it has been shown that this is where they are lacking. "Nearly half of senior managers and company directors do not have an up-to-date understanding of their health and safety-related duties and responsibilities." (Paton, Nic. 2008. 'Senior Managers Fail to Show Competence in Health and Safety' Occupational Health, Vol. 60, Iss. 3; pg. 6)

National implementing legislation

Different states take different approaches to legislation, regulation, and enforcement.

In the European Union, member states have enforcing authorities to ensure that the basic legal requirements relating to occupational health and safety are met. In many EU countries, there is strong cooperation between employer and worker organisations (e.g. Unions) to ensure good OSH performance as it is recognized this has benefits for both the worker (through maintenance of health) and the enterprise (through improved productivity and quality). In 1996 the European Agency for Safety and Health at Work was founded.

Member states of the European Union have all transposed into their national legislation a series of directives that establish minimum standards on occupational health and safety. These directives (of which there are about 20 on a variety of topics) follow a similar structure requiring the employer to assess the workplace risks and put in place preventive measures based on a hierarchy of control. This hierarchy starts with elimination of the hazard and ends with personal protective equipment.

In the UK, health and safety legislation is drawn up and enforced by the Health and Safety Executive and local authorities (the local council) under the Health and Safety at Work etc. Act 1974. Increasingly in the UK the regulatory trend is away from prescriptive rules, and towards risk assessment. Recent major changes to the laws governing asbestos and fire safety management embrace the concept of risk assessment.

In the United States, the Occupational Safety and Health Act of 1970 created both the National Institute for Occupational Safety and Health (NIOSH) and the Occupational Safety and Health Administration (OSHA).[4] OSHA, in the U.S. Department of Labor, is responsible for developing and enforcing workplace safety and health regulations. NIOSH, in the U.S. Department of Health and Human Services, is focused on research, information, education, and training in occupational safety and health.[5]

OSHA have been regulating occupational safety and health since 1971. Occupational safety and health regulation of a limited number of specifically defined industries was in place for several decades before that, and broad regulations by some individual states was in place for many years prior to the establishment of OSHA.

In Canada, workers are covered by provincial or federal labour codes depending on the sector in which they work. Workers covered by federal legislation (including those in mining, transportation, and federal employment) are covered by the Canada Labour Code; all other workers are covered by the health and safety legislation of the province they work in. The Canadian Centre for Occupational Health and Safety (CCOHS), an agency of the Government of Canada, was created in 1978 by an Act of Parliament. The act was based on the belief that all Canadians had "...a fundamental right to a healthy and safe working environment." CCOHS is mandated to promote safe and healthy workplaces to help prevent work-related injuries and illnesses.

In Malaysia, the Department of Occupational Safety and Health (DOSH) under the Ministry of Human Resource is responsible to ensure that the safety, health and welfare of workers in both the public and private sector is upheld. DOSH is responsible to enforce the Factory and Machinery Act 1969 and the Occupational Safety and Health Act 1994.

In the People's Republic of China, the Ministry of Health is responsible for occupational disease prevention and the State Administration of Work Safety for safety issues at work. On the provincial and municipal level, there are Health Supervisions for occupational health and local bureaus of Work Safety for safety. The "Occupational Disease Control Act of PRC" came into force on May 1, 2002.[6] and Work safety Act of PRC on November 1, 2002.[7] The Occupational Disease Control Act is under revising. The prevention of occupational disease is still in its initial stage compared with industried countries such as the US or UK.

Identifying Safety and Health Hazards

Hazards, risks, outcomes

The terminology used in OSH varies between states, but generally speaking:

- A hazard is something that can cause harm if not controlled.
- The outcome is the harm that results from an uncontrolled hazard.
- A risk is a combination of the probability that a particular outcome will occur and the severity of the harm involved.

"Hazard", "risk", and "outcome" are used in other fields to describe e.g. environmental damage, or damage to equipment. However, in the context of OSH, "harm" generally describes the direct or indirect degradation, temporary or permanent, of the physical, mental, or social well-being of workers. For example, repetitively carrying out manual handling of heavy objects is a hazard. The outcome could be a musculoskeletal disorder (MSD) or an acute back or joint injury. The risk can be expressed numerically (e.g. a 0.5 or 50/50 chance of the outcome occurring during a year), in relative terms (e.g. "high/medium/low"), or with a multi-dimensional classification scheme (e.g. situation-specific risks).

Hazard Assessment

Hazard analysis or hazard assessment is a process in which individual hazards of the workplace are identified, assessed and controlled/eliminated as close to source (location of the hazard) as reasonable and possible. As technology, resources, social expectation or regulatory requirements change, hazard analysis focuses controls more closely toward the source of the hazard. Thus hazard control is a dynamic program of prevention. Hazard-based programs also have the advantage of not assigning or implying there are "acceptable risks" in the workplace. A hazard-based program may not be able to eliminate all risks, but neither does it accept "satisfactory" -- but still risky—outcomes. And as those who calculate and manage the risk are usually managers while those exposed to the risks are a different group, workers, a hazard-based approach can by-pass conflict inherent in a risk-based approach.

Risk assessment

Modern occupational safety and health legislation usually demands that a risk assessment be carried out prior to making an intervention. It should be kept in mind that risk management requires risk to be managed to a level which is as low as is reasonably practical.

This assessment should:

- Identify the hazards
- Identify all affected by the hazard and how
- Evaluate the risk
- Identify and prioritize appropriate control measures

The calculation of risk is based on the likelihood or probability of the harm being realized and the severity of the consequences. This can be expressed mathematically as a quantitative assessment (by assigning low, medium and high likelihood and severity with integers and multiplying them to obtain a risk factor), or qualitatively as a description of the circumstances by which the harm could arise.

The assessment should be recorded and reviewed periodically and whenever there is a significant change to work practices. The assessment should include practical recommendations to control the risk. Once recommended controls are implemented, the risk should be re-calculated to determine of it has been lowered to an acceptable level. Generally speaking, newly introduced controls should lower risk by one level, i.e., from high to medium or from medium to low.

Common workplace hazard groups

- **Mechanical hazards** include:

  By type of agent:

  - Impact force
    - Collisions
    - Falls from height
  - Struck by objects
  - Confined space
  - Slips and trips
  - Falling on a pointed object
  - Compressed air/high pressure fluids (such as cutting fluid)
  - Entanglement
  - Equipment-related injury

  By type of damage:

  - Crushing
  - Cutting
  - Friction and abrasion
  - Shearing
  - Stabbing and puncture

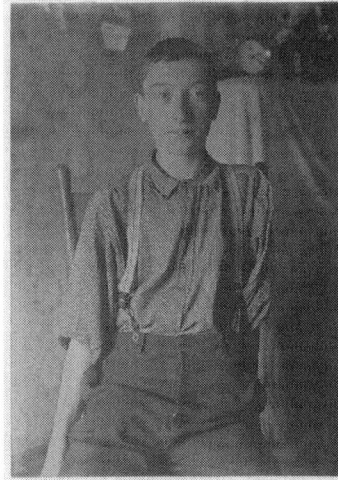

Harry McShane, age 16, 1908. Pulled into machinery in a factory in Cincinnati. His arm was ripped off at the shoulder and his leg broken. No compensation paid. Photograph by Lewis Hine.

- Other **physical hazards**:
  - Noise
  - Vibration
  - Lighting
  - Barotrauma (hypobaric/hyperbaric pressure)
  - Ionizing radiation
  - Electricity
  - Asphyxiation
  - Cold stress (hypothermia)
  - Heat stress (hyperthermia)
    - Dehydration (due to sweating)
- **Biological hazards** include:
  - Bacteria
  - Virus
  - Fungi
    - Mold
  - Blood-borne pathogens
  - Tuberculosis

- **Chemical hazards** include:
  - Acids
  - Bases
  - Heavy metals
    - Lead
  - Solvents
    - Petroleum
  - Particulates
    - Asbestos and other fine dust/fibrous materials
    - Silica
  - Fumes (noxious gases/vapors)
  - Highly-reactive chemicals
  - Fire, conflagration and explosion hazards:
    - Explosion
    - Deflagration
    - Detonation
    - Conflagration
- **Psychosocial issues** include:
  - Work-related stress, whose causal factors include excessive working time and overwork
  - Violence from outside the organisation
  - Bullying, which may include emotional and verbal abuse
  - Sexual harassment
  - Mobbing
  - Burnout
  - Exposure to unhealthy elements during meetings with business associates, e.g. tobacco, uncontrolled alcohol
- **Musculoskeletal disorders**, avoided by the employment of good ergonomic design

Fire prevention (fire protection/fire safety) often comes within the remit of health and safety professionals as well.

Canadian Classification

In Canada, Hazards are typically categorized into one of six groups:

1. Safety (moving machinery, working at heights, slippery surfaces, mobile equipment, etc.)
2. Ergonomic (material handling, environment, work organization, etc.)
3. Chemical Agents
4. Biological Agents
5. Physical Agents(noise, lighting, radiation, etc.)
6. Psychosocial(stress, violence, etc.)

Future developments

Occupational health and safety has come a long way from its beginnings in the heavy industry sector. It now has an impact on every worker, in every work place, and those charged with managing health and safety are having more and more tasks added to their portfolio. The most significant responsibility is environmental protection. The skills required to manage occupational health and safety are compatible with environmental protection, which is why these responsibilities are so often bolted onto the workplace health and safety professional.

References

[1] Oak Ridge National Lab Safety Document http://www.ornl.gov
[2] Everly, G. S., Jr. (1986). An introduction to occupational health psychology. P. A. Keller & L. G. Ritt (Eds.), *Innovations in clinical practice: A source book, Vol. 5* (pp. 331-338). Sarasota, FL: Professional Resource Exchange.
[3] OSHA Outreach Resources (http://www.easysafetyschool.com/courses/osha-outreach/)
[4] Occupational Safety and Health Act of 1970 (http://www.osha.gov/pls/oshaweb/owasrch.search_form?p_doc_type=OSHACT). Occupational Safety and Health Administration.
[5] About NIOSH (http://www.cdc.gov/niosh/about.html). National Institute of Occupational Safety and Health.
[6] "Occupational Disease Control Act of the People's Republic of China" http://www.gov.cn/banshi/2005-08/01/content_19003.htm
[7] "The Work Safety Act of the People's Republic of China" http://www.gov.cn/ztzl/2006-05/27/content_292725.htm

Further reading

- Koester, Frank (April 1912). "Our Stupendous Yearly Waste: The Death Toll of Industry" (http://books.google.com/books?id=Vv--PfedzLAC&pg=PA713). *The World's Work: A History of Our Time* **XXIII**: 713–715. Retrieved 2009-07-10.
- Ladou, Joseph (2006). *Current Occupational & Environmental Medicine* (4th ed.). McGraw-Hill Professional. ISBN 0-07-144313-4.
- Roughton, James (2002). *Developing an Effective Safety Culture: A Leadership Approach* (1st ed.). Butterworth-Heinemann. ISBN 0-7506-7411-3.
- OHSAS 18000 series: (derived from a British Standard, OHSAS is intended to be compatible with ISO 9000 and 14000 series standards, but is not itself an ISO standard)

External links

- CDC page on Workplace Safety & Health (http://www.cdc.gov/Workplace/)
- European Academy of Occupational Health Psychology (http://eaohp.org/default.aspx/)
- ILO International Occupational Safety and Health Information Centre (http://www.ilo.org/public/english/protection/safework/cis/)
- Society for Occupational Health Psychology (http://www.sohp-online.org/)
- UK Health & Safety Executive - Getting started for Small Business (http://www.hse.gov.uk/smallbusinesses/gettingstarted.htm)
- IOSH Occupational Health Toolkit (http://www.iosh.co.uk/information_and_resources/our_oh_toolkit.aspx)

Opasnet

Opasnet is a web-workspace for making open assessments,[1] which are impact assessments where anyone can freely participate and contribute. Opasnet is a wiki website and it is built on Mediawiki platform. It is currently maintained and developed by the National Institute for Health and Welfare in Finland.[2] Opasnet has won the World Summit Award Finland competition, the eGovernment and Institutions category.[3]

References

[1] Jouni T. Tuomisto, Mikko Pohjola: Open Risk Assessment - A new way of providing scientific information for decision-making. Publications of the National Public Health Institute 2007:B18 ISBN 978-951-740-736-6 (http://www.ktl.fi/attachments/suomi/julkaisut/julkaisusarja_b/2007/2007b18.pdf)

[2] About Opasnet (http://en.opasnet.org/w/Opasnet:About), accessed Jan 12, 2011.

[3] World Summit Award Finland (http://www.mindtrek.org/2010/wsa), accessed Jan 12, 2011.

External links

- Official website (http://en.opasnet.org)

Open assessment

Open assessment is a method for making impact assessments where anyone can participate and contribute.[1] Most open assessments have been made in Opasnet, which is a wiki-based web-workspace specifically designed for this purpose. The open assessment method has been developed in the National Institute for Health and Welfare in Finland originally for providing guidance in complex environmental health problems. So far, it has been applied on e.g. air pollution[2] and pollutants in fish.[3] Opasnet has won the World Summit Award Finland competition, the eGovernment and Institutions category.[4]

References

[1] Jouni T. Tuomisto, Mikko Pohjola: Open Risk Assessment - A new way of providing scientific information for decision-making. Publications of the National Public Health Institute 2007:B18 ISBN 978-951-740-736-6 (http://www.ktl.fi/attachments/suomi/julkaisut/julkaisusarja_b/2007/2007b18.pdf)

[2] Marko Tainio: Methods and Uncertainties in the Assessment of the Health Effects of Fine Particulate Matter (PM2.5) Air Pollution. National Institute for Health and Welfare, 2009:18. ISBN 978-952-245-102-6 (http://www.thl.fi/thl-client/pdfs/2af475e8-6b79-47a6-8553-2d96cb5a2d96)

[3] (http://en.opasnet.org/w/Benefit-risk_assessment_on_farmed_salmon), accessed Jan 12, 2011.

[4] World Summit Award Finland (http://www.mindtrek.org/2010/wsa), accessed Jan 12, 2011.

External links

- Description of open assessment (http://en.opasnet.org/w/Open_assessment) in Opasnet

Profit risk

Categories of financial risk
Credit risk
Concentration risk
Market risk
Interest rate risk
Currency risk
Equity risk
Commodity risk
Liquidity risk
Refinancing risk
Operational risk
Legal risk
Political risk
Reputational risk
Volatility risk
Settlement risk
Profit risk
Systemic risk

Profit risk is a risk management tool that focuses on understanding concentrations within the income statement and assessing the risk associated with those concentrations from a net income perspective.[1]

Alternate definitions

Profit risk is a risk measurement methodology most appropriate for the financial services industry, in that it complements other risk management methodologies commonly used in the financial services industry: credit risk management and asset liability management (ALM).[2] Profit risk is the concentration of the structure of a company's income statement where the income statement lacks income diversification and income variability, so that the income statement's high concentration in a limited number of customer accounts, products, markets, delivery channels, and salespeople puts the company at risk levels that project the company's inability to grow earnings with high potential for future earnings losses.[3] Profit risk can exist even when a company is growing in earnings, which can cause earnings growth to decline when levels of concentration become excessive.

Description of profit risk

When a company's earnings are derived from a limited number of customer accounts, products, markets, delivery channels (e.g., branches/stores/other delivery points), and/or salespeople, these concentrations result in significant net income risk that can be quantified. A loss of just a handful of customer accounts, a loss of a limited number of products, a loss of a select market, a loss of a small number of delivery channels, and/or a loss of a few salespeople can result in significant net income volatility.[4] At this stage, income loss risk is present and the company has reached a level of profit risk that is unhealthy for sustaining net income. The method for quantifying and assessing this potential income loss risk and the volatility that it creates to the company's income statement is profit risk measurement and management.[5] For financial institutions, profit risk management is similar to the diversification strategies[6] commonly used for investment asset allocations, real estate diversification, and other portfolio risk management techniques.

Basis of profit risk

The concept of profit risk is loosely akin to the well known "80-20" rule or the Pareto principle, which states that approximately 20% of a company's customers drive 80% of the business.[7] This rule and principle may be appropriate for some industries, but not for the financial services industry.[8] According to Rich Weissman, [9] it is true that this small group of customer/member dominates the income statement, but the old "80/20" rule ~ it does not longer applied. "There are real-life examples where financial institutions have seen profit risk ratios as high as 300 percent. Their top 10 percent of customer/member relationships accounted for three times net earnings - a "300/10" rule!"

Measuring profit risk

To measure these concentrations and manage profit risk, the most important tools for financial institutions may be their MCIF, CRM, or profitability systems that they use to keep track of their customer/member relationship activities. The data in these systems can be analyzed and grouped to gain insights into profitability contribution of each customer/member, product, market, delivery channels, and salespeople.[10] Reports illustrating the concentrations of net income are used by senior management to show (1) the location of the concentrations in the income statement, (2) the levels of the concentrations, and (3) the predictions for future earning losses to be drawn from the concentrations.[11] Often, these reports examine earnings contributions by deciles (groupings of customers or other units of analysis by 10% increments), illustrating concentrations for each 10% group.[12]

References

[1] Weissman, Rich " Managing Profit Risk to Avoid a Meltdown (http://www.dmacorporation.com/dmarecognized/AvoidAMeltdown.pdf)", California Banker Magazine, August 2008 Retrieved 05/06/2010

[2] Weissman, Rich " Profit Risk – The Third Leg of Risk Management (http://www.dmacorporation.com/dmarecognized/MortgagePress. pdf)", The Mortgage Press, December 2004 Retrieved 05/06/2010

[3] Weissman, Rich " Bank Marketers Measure Profit Risk in Changing Times (http://www.mibankers.com/publications/mbabanking.asp)", Michigan Bankers Magazine, March/April 2009, p 12-14, Retrieved 05/06/2010

[4] Coffey, John and Palm, Gene " Profit Decile Report: An Eye-Opener (http://findarticles.com/p/articles/mi_hb4838/is_1_38/ ai_n29289502/)", ABA Bank Marketing, Jan-Feb, 2006 Retrieved 05/06/2010

[5] Weissman, Rich " Profit in the Drink (http://www.thefreelibrary.com/Profit+in+the+Drink:+in+today's+recessionary+environment,+ more+than...-a0221749129)", ABA Bank Marketing, March 2010 Retrieved 05/06/2010

[6] Investopedia, " Diversification Strategies (http://www.investopedia.com/terms/d/diversification.asp)" Retrieved 05/06/2010

[7] Website Magazine, " Pareto Principle and the Infinite Value of CRM (http://www.websitemagazine.com/content/blogs/posts/articles/ Pareto_CRM.aspx)" Retrieved 05/06/2010

[8] Wang, Hongjie " For Bank Marketing, Re-Focus the Pareto Principle on Customer Profitability (http://www.banktech.com/blog/archives/ 2009/11/for_bank_market.html)", Bank Systems and Technology, November 2009 Retrieved 05/06/2010

[9] Reprinted with permission from The Mortgage Press; Profit Risk: The third leg of risk management

[10] Totty, Patrick " Pinpointing Preferences with MCIF (http://www.cunaopsscouncil.org/news/477.html)", CUNA Operations and Sales/Services Council, August, 2005

[11] Duclaux, Denise " Are You Getting the Most from Your MCIF? (http://www.allbusiness.com/marketing/direct-marketing/512324-1. html)", ABA Banking Journal, June 1995

[12] Retail Profit Management, " Decile Report (http://home.earthlink.net/~rpminfonet/decile.html)"

External links

- " Profit Risk: The Third Critical Piece of Risk Management (http://webcache.googleusercontent.com/ search?q=cache:IHpL-muUhnUJ:www.dmacorporation.com/dmarecognized/ PROFIT%20RISK%20WHITE%20PAPER%208-2009.htm+profit+risk+site:http://www.dmacorporation. com/&hl=en&gl=us&strip=1)"

Project risk management

Project risk management is an important aspect of project management. Risk Management is one of the nine knowledge areas defined in PMBOK. Project Risk can be defined as unforeseen event or activity that can impact the project progress, result or outcome in a positive or negative way. A risk can be assesed using two factors: impact and probability.

If the probability is 1, it is an issue. This means that risk is already materialized. if the probability is zero, this means that risk will not happen and should be removed from the risk register.

Ready Georgia

Ready Georgia

Type	Public Awareness
Founded	January 2008
Location	Atlanta, Georgia
Key people	Charley English, Director of Homeland Security for GEMA
Area served	The State of Georgia
Focus	Disaster Preparedness
Motto	Prepare. Plan. Stay Informed.
Website	Ready Georgia [1]

Ready Georgia is a statewide emergency preparedness campaign in the U.S. state of Georgia instituted by the Georgia Emergency Management Agency (GEMA) and Governor Sonny Perdue in conjunction with the national *Ready America* campaign sponsored by the Federal Emergency Management Agency (FEMA). *Ready Georgia* is supported by The Ad Council, local volunteer organizations, and corporate partnerships.

Mission

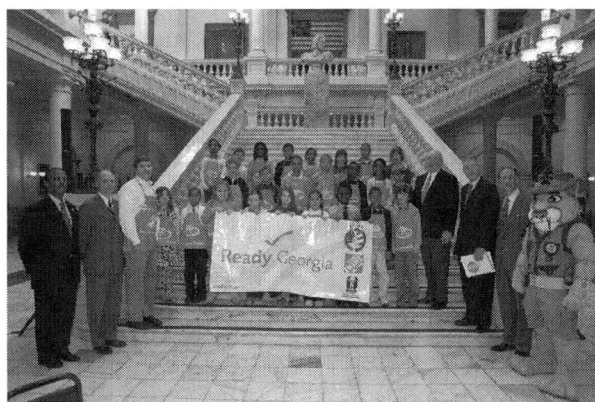

Governor Sonny Perdue, GEMA/OHS director Charley English, Ready Kids mascot Rex the mountain lion, and Georgia elementary school students pose during Ready Georgia's official launch at the state capital building.

GEMA created the *Ready Georgia* campaign in response to survey data revealing that nearly 80 percent of Georgia residents had not taken even the most basic steps towards being prepared for the wide range of natural and man-made disasters that threaten the state.[2] *Ready Georgia* intends to "promote a preparedness and prevention culture" in Georgia through public education and outreach.[3] The campaign specifically encourages residents to be prepared so they can safely oversee their own evacuation and maintain self-sufficiency for a full three days after an emergency.[4]

Education and outreach

One of *Ready Georgia's* primary concerns is ensuring that individuals and households have an adequately stocked ready kit, which is essential in maintaining awareness and self-sufficiency in the wake of a disaster. Through a partnership with the Home Depot corporation, *Ready Georgia* has been able to put on state-wide workshops that teach children about disaster preparedness.[5] Utilizing its Web site, *Ready Georgia* has also been able to provide a tool that can assist users in calculating exactly how much food and water they will need for their own kits.[6] Notable Georgians such as Atlanta Falcons fullback Ovie Mughelli, NASCAR Sprint Cup driver David Ragan, and former

Atlanta Braves outfielder Jeff Francoeur participated by creating profiles on *Ready Georgia's* Web site letting Georgians know what is in their ready kits.

Georgia's 5th graders were able to enter a *Ready Georgia* art and essay contest, for which they were asked to submit work demonstrating how they are their families would prepare for a variety of disasters. The winners received their own ready kits from Home Depot, as well as personal and school recognition on *Ready Georgia's* Web site.[7]

In 2009, *Ready Georgia* was able to provide Georgia residents with 200 NOAA weather radio receivers at no cost and many more at a reduced price, in an effort to acknowledge and address the fact that economically disadvantaged citizens face greater challenges in the face of a disaster and are often unprepared.[8]

Ready Georgia has additionally sought to address the economic impact of disasters through the development of materials stressing the importance of proper business continuity planning to Georgia based businesses. This is especially critical in the Atlanta metro area, which is home to the fourth most Fortune 500 company headquarters among all cities in America.[9]

Emergencies addressed since inception

In September 2009, Georgia experienced significant flooding, resulting in a state of emergency being declared for 17 counties.[10] Awareness and preparation are critical elements of an effective response to flooding, which often necessitates evacuation and cuts off access to supplies of food and clean water. The importance of flood insurance in mitigating the social and economic damage caused by flooding is another awareness and preparedness issue for anyone facing the prospect of flooding; *Ready Georgia* has sought to address all of these issues.[11]

H1N1 influenza, known commonly as "swine flu", has been a health issue of public concern since early 2009, and was declared a pandemic by the World Health Organization.[12] The Georgia Department of Community Health Division of Public Health and the Georgia Emergency Management Agency have used the *Ready Georgia* campaign to disseminate preparedness information to Georgians.[13]

References

[1] http://ready.ga.gov/

[2] *Ready Georgia finds Georgians aren't ready* (http://www.effinghamherald.net/news/archive/7466/), The Effingham Herald, June 15, 2009,

[3] Lisa Janak Newman (November 10, 2008), *Ready Georgia Campaign Provides Tools for Residents to Be Prepared* (http://www.piersystem. com/go/doc/759/239955/), The Georgia Emergency Management Agency,

[4] *"Severe Weather Awareness Week" Proclaimed By Governor Purdue* (http://www.ready.gov/america/about/testimonials/story7.html), Ready Georgia, November 10, 2008,

[5] *The Home Depot Partners with GEMA's Ready Georgia to Teach Thousands of Kids about Emergency Preparedness* (http://www. fayettefrontpage.com/public-safety/09/8-10-09_home-depot-gema.html), The Fayette Front Page, August 10, 2009,

[6] *Georgia wants you to spend week getting ready for disaster* (http://www.gainesvilletimes.com/news/archive/14323/), The Gainesville Times, February 2, 2009,

[7] "Congratulations to our "Get Ready Georgia" Art and Essay Contest Winners!" (http://www.example.org/). Ready Georgia. . Retrieved 3 November 2009.

[8] *WSB-TV Teams With Ready Georgia To Save Lives* (http://www.wsbtv.com/weather/15139439/detail.html), WSB-TV Online, March 20, 2009,

[9] *The Fortune 500, 2009* (http://money.cnn.com/magazines/fortune/fortune500/2009/cities/), CNN Money, November 2, 2009,

[10] *Gov. Sonny Perdue issues state of emergency for 17 Georgia counties* (http://savannahnow.com/latest-news/2009-09-21/ gov-sonny-perdue-issues-state-emergency-17-georgia-counties), Savannah Now, September 21, 2009,

[11] "Get Ready for Floods and Flash Floods" (http://www.ready.ga.gov/Stay-Informed/Floods-and-Flash-Floods). Ready Georgia. . Retrieved 3 November 2009.

[12] *World Health Organization* (http://www.who.int/mediacentre/news/statements/2009/h1n1_pandemic_phase6_20090611/en/index. html), June 11, 2009,

[13] *Good Day Atlanta* (http://www.myfoxatlanta.com/dpp/good_day_atl/Ready_Kit_to_Fight_H1N1_091109), Fox 5 TV Atlanta, September 11, 2009,

External links

* The Georgia Emergency Management Agency (http://www.gema.state.ga.us/)

Risk assessment

Risk assessment is a step in a risk management procedure. Risk assessment is the determination of quantitative or qualitative value of risk related to a concrete situation and a recognized threat (also called hazard). *Quantitative risk assessment* requires calculations of two components of risk: R, the magnitude of the potential loss L, and the probability p, that the loss will occur.

Methods may differ whether it is about general financial decisions or environmental, ecological, or public health risk assessment.

Explanation

Risk assessment consists in an objective evaluation of risk in which assumptions and uncertainties are clearly considered and presented. Part of the difficulty of risk management is that measurement of both of the quantities in which risk assessment is concerned - potential loss and probability of occurrence - can be very difficult to measure. The chance of error in the measurement of these two concepts is large. A risk with a large potential loss and a low probability of occurring is often treated differently from one with a low potential loss and a high likelihood of occurring. In theory, both are of nearly equal priority in dealing with first, but in practice it can be very difficult to manage when faced with the scarcity of resources, especially time, in which to conduct the risk management process. Expressed mathematically,

$$R_i = L_i p(L_i)$$

$$R_{total} = \sum_i L_i p(L_i)$$

Financial decisions, such as insurance, express loss in terms of dollar amounts. When risk assessment is used for public health or environmental decisions, loss can be quantified in a common metric,such as a country's currency, or some numerical measure of a location's quality of life. For public health and environmental decisions, loss is simply a verbal description of the outcome, such as increased cancer incidence or incidence of birth defects. In that case, the "risk" is expressed as:

$$R_i = p(L_i)$$

If the risk estimate takes into account information on the number of individuals exposed, it is termed a "population risk" and is in units of expected increased cases per a time period. If the risk estimate does not

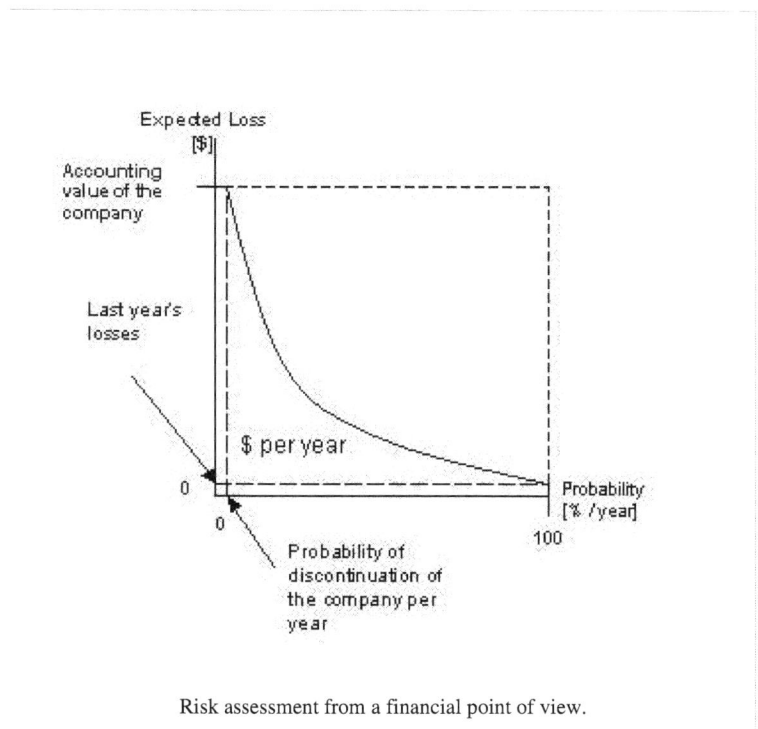

Risk assessment from a financial point of view.

take into account the number of individuals exposed, it is termed an "individual risk" and is in units of incidence rate per a time period. Population risks are of more use for cost/benefit analysis; individual risks are of more use for evaluating whether risks to individuals are "acceptable"....

Risk assessment in public health

In the context of public health, risk assessment is the process of quantifying the probability of a harmful effect to individuals or populations from certain human activities. In most countries, the use of specific chemicals, or the operations of specific facilities (e.g. power plants, manufacturing plants) is not allowed unless it can be shown that they do not increase the risk of death or illness above a specific threshold. For example, the American Food and Drug Administration (FDA) regulates food safety through risk assessment.[1] The FDA required in 1973 that cancer-causing compounds must not be present in meat at concentrations that would cause a cancer risk greater than 1 in a million lifetimes. The US Environmental Protection Agency provides basic information about environmental risk assessments for the public via its risk assessment portal.[2]

How the risk is determined

In the estimation of the risks, three or more steps are involved, requiring the inputs of different disciplines:

1. *Hazard Identification*, aims to determine the qualitative nature of the potential adverse consequences of the contaminant (chemical, radiation, noise, etc.) and the strength of the evidence it can have that effect. This is done, for chemical hazards, by drawing from the results of the sciences of toxicology and epidemiology. For other kinds of hazard, engineering or other disciplines are involved.

2. *Dose-Response Analysis*, is determining the relationship between dose and the probability or the incidence of effect (dose-response assessment). The complexity of this step in many contexts derives mainly from the need to extrapolate results from experimental animals (e.g. mouse, rat) to humans, and/or from high to lower doses. In addition, the differences between individuals due to genetics or other factors mean that the hazard may be higher for particular groups, called susceptible populations. An alternative to dose-response estimation is to determine an effect unlikely to yield observable effects, that is, a no effect concentration. In developing such a dose, to account for the largely unknown effects of animal to human extrapolations, increased variability in humans, or missing data, a prudent approach is often adopted by including safety factors in the estimate of the "safe" dose, typically a factor of 10 for each unknown step.

3. *Exposure Quantification*, aims to determine the amount of a contaminant (dose) that individuals and populations will receive. This is done by examining the results of the discipline of exposure assessment. As different location, lifestyles and other factors likely influence the amount of contaminant that is received, a range or distribution of possible values is generated in this step. Particular care is taken to determine the exposure of the susceptible population(s).

Finally, the results of the three steps above are then combined to produce an estimate of risk. Because of the different susceptibilities and exposures, this risk will vary within a population.

Small subpopulations

When risks apply mainly to small subpopulations, there is uncertainty at which point intervention is necessary. What if a risk is very low for everyone but 0.1% of the population? A difference exists whether this 0.1% is represented by *all infants younger than X days or *recreational users of a particular product. If the risk is higher for a particular sub-population because of abnormal exposure rather than susceptibility, there is a potential to consider strategies to further reduce the exposure of that subgroup. If an identifiable sub-population is more susceptible due to inherent genetic or other factors, there is a policy choice whether to set policies for protecting the general population that are protective of such groups (as is currently done for children when data exists, or is done under the Clean Air Act for populations such as asthmatics) or whether if the group is too small, or the costs to high. Sometimes, a more specific calculation can be applied whether it is more important to analyze each method specifically the changes of the risk assessment method in containing all problems that each of us people could replace.

Acceptable risk increase

The idea of not increasing lifetime risk by more than one in a million has become common place in public health discourse and policy. How consensus settled on this particular figure is unclear. In some respects, this figure has the characteristics of a mythical number. In another sense, the figure provides a numerical basis for what to consider a negligible increase in risk. Some current environmental decision making allows some discretion to deem individual risks potentially "acceptable" if below one in ten thousand increased lifetime risk. Low risk criteria such as these do provide some protection for the case that individuals may be exposed to multiple chemicals (whether pollutants or food additives, or other chemicals). But both of these benchmarks are clearly small relative to the typical one in four lifetime risk of death by cancer (due to all causes combined) in developed countries. On the other hand, adoption of a zero-risk policy could be motivated by the fact that the 1 in a million policy still would cause the death of hundreds or thousands of people in a large enough population. In practice however, a true zero-risk is possible only with the suppression of the risk-causing activity.

More stringent requirements, or even the 1 in a million one, may not be technologically feasible at a given time, or so expensive as to render the risk-causing activity unsustainable, resulting in the optimal degree of intervention being a balance between risks vs. benefit. For example, it might well be that the emissions from hospital incinerators result in a certain number of deaths per year. However, this risk must be balanced against the available alternatives. In some unusual cases, there are significant public health risks, as well as economic costs, associated with all options. For example, there are risks associated with no incineration (with the potential risk for spread of infectious diseases) or even no hospitals. But, often further investigation identifies further options, such as separating noninfectious from infectious wastes, or air pollution controls on a medical incinerator, that provide a broad range of options of acceptable risk - though with varying practical implications and varying economic costs. Intelligent thought about a reasonably full set of options is essential. Thus, it is not unusual for there to be an iterative process between analysis, consideration of options, and then further analysis.

Risk assessment in auditing

In auditing, risk assessment is a very crucial stage before accepting an audit engagement. According to ISA315 *Understanding the Entity and its Environment and Assessing the Risks of Material Misstatement*, "the auditor should perform risk assessment procedures to obtain an understanding of the entity and its environment, including its internal control."<evidence relating to the auditor's risk assessment of a material misstatement in the client's financial statements. Then, auditor obtains initial evidence regarding the classes of transactions at the client and the operating effectiveness of the client's internal controls.In auditing, audit risk includes inherent risk, control risk and detection risk.

Risk assessment and human health

There are many resources that provide health risk information. The National Library of Medicine provides risk assessment and regulation information tools for a varied audience.[3] These include TOXNET (databases on hazardous chemicals, environmental health, and toxic releases),[4] the Household Products Database (potential health effects of chemicals in over 10,000 common household products),[5] and TOXMAP (maps of US Environmental Agency Superfund and Toxics Release Inventory data). The United States Environmental Protection Agency provides basic information about environmental risk assessments for the public.[6]

Risk assessment in information security

IT risk assessment can be performed by a qualitative or quantitative approach, following different methodologies.

Risk assessment in project management

In project management, risk assessment is an integral part of the risk management plan, studying the probability, the impact, and the effect of every known risk on the project, as well as the corrective action to take should that risk occur.[7]

Risk assessment for megaprojects

Megaprojects (sometimes also called "major programs") are extremely large-scale investment projects, typically costing more than US$1 billion per project. Megaprojects include bridges, tunnels, highways, railways, airports, seaports, power plants, dams, wastewater projects, coastal flood protection, oil and natural gas extraction projects, public buildings, information technology systems, aerospace projects, and defence systems. Megaprojects have been shown to be particularly risky in terms of finance, safety, and social and environmental impacts. Risk assessment is therefore particularly pertinent for megaprojects and special methods and special education have been developed for such risk assessment.[8] [9]

Quantitative risk assessment

Quantitative risk assessments include a calculation of the single loss expectancy (SLE) of an asset. The single loss expectancy can be defined as the loss of value to asset based on a single security incident. The team then calculates the Annualized Rate of Occurrence (ARO) of the threat to the asset. The ARO is an estimate based on the data of how often a threat would be successful in exploiting a vulnerability. From this information, the Annualized Loss Expectancy (ALE) can be calculated. The annualized loss expectancy is a calculation of the single loss expectancy multiplied by the annual rate of occurrence, or how much an organization could estimate to lose from an asset based on the risks, threats, and vulnerabilities. It then becomes possible from a financial perspective to justify expenditures to implement countermeasures to protect the asset.

Risk assessment in software evolution

Studies have shown that early parts of the system development cycle such as requirements and design specifications are especially prone to error. This effect is particularly notorious in projects involving multiple stakeholders with different points of view. Evolutionary software processes offer an iterative approach to requirement engineering to alleviate the problems of uncertainty, ambiguity and inconsistency inherent in software developments.

Criticisms of quantitative risk assessment

Barry Commoner, Brian Wynne and other critics have expressed concerns that risk assessment tends to be overly quantitative and reductive. For example, they argue that risk assessments ignore qualitative differences among risks. Some charge that assessments may drop out important non-quantifiable or inaccessible information, such as variations among the classes of people exposed to hazards. Furthermore, Commoner and O'Brien claim that quantitative approaches divert attention from precautionary or preventative measures.[10] Others, like Nassim Nicholas Taleb consider risk managers little more than "blind users" of statistical tools and methods.[11]

References

Footnotes

[1] Merrill, Richard A. "Food Safety Regulation: Reforming the Delaney Clause" in *Annual Review of Public Health*, 1997, 18:313-40. This source includes a useful historical survey of prior food safety regulation.

[2] EPA.gov (http://www.epa.gov/risk/)

[3] SIS.nlm.nih.gov (http://sis.nlm.nih.gov/enviro/riskinformation.html)

[4] Toxnet.nlm.nih.gov (http://toxnet.nlm.nih.gov)

[5] HPD.nlm.nih.gov (http://hpd.nlm.nih.gov/)

[6] EPA.gov (http://www.epa.gov/risk/)

[7] Managing Project Risks (http://www.pmhut.com/managing-project-risks) - Retrieved May 20th, 2010

[8] Bent Flyvbjerg, Nils Bruzelius, and Werner Rothengatter, 2003, *Megaprojects and Risk: An Anatomy of Ambition* (Cambridge University Press).

[9] Oxford BT Centre for Major Programme Management

[10] Commoner, Barry. O'Brien, Mary. Shrader-Frechette and Westra 1997.

[11] The fourth quadrant: a map of the limits of statistics [9.15.08] Nassim Nicholas Taleb An Edge Original Essay

General references

- Committee on Risk Assessment of Hazardous Air Pollutants, Board on Environmental Studies and Toxicology, Commission on Life Sciences, National Research Council (1994), *Science and judgment in risk assessment* (http://books.google.com/books?id=k9mKUyfHakcC&printsec=frontcover&dq=Science+and+judgment+in+risk+assessment&hl=en&ei=VzagTJK4HIyuvgPZw4SADQ&sa=X&oi=book_result&ct=result&resnum=1&ved=0CC8Q6AEwAA#v=onepage&q&f=false), Washington, D.C: National Academy Press, ISBN 0-309-04894-X, retrieved 27 September 2010

- Barry Commoner. "Comparing apples to oranges: Risk of cost/benefit analysis" from *Contemporary moral controversies in technology*, A. P. Iannone, ed., pp. 64–65.

- Flyvbjerg, Bent, "From Nobel Prize to Project Management: Getting Risks Right." *Project Management Journal*, vol. 37, no. 3, August 2006, pp. 5-15. (http://flyvbjerg.plan.aau.dk/Publications2006/Nobel-PMJ2006.pdf)

- Hallenbeck, William H. *Quantitative risk assessment for environmental and occupational health.* Chelsea, Mich.: Lewis Publishers, 1986

- Harremoës, Poul, ed. *Late lessons from early warnings: the precautionary principle 1896–2000.*

- John M. Lachin. *Biostatistical methods: the assessment of relative risks.*

- Lerche, Ian; Glaesser, Walter (2006), *Environmental risk assessment : quantitative measures, anthropogenic influences, human impact.* (http://books.google.com/books?id=qB54qgpA_fEC&printsec=frontcover&dq=Environmental+risk+assessment&hl=en&ei=9jSgTO-OK5CKvgPb55SzDQ&sa=X&oi=book_result&ct=result&resnum=1&ved=0CDUQ6AEwAA#v=onepage&q&f=false), Berlin: Springer, ISBN 3-540-26249-0, retrieved 27 September 2010

- Kluger, Jeffrey (November 26, 2006), "How Americans Are Living Dangerously" (http://www.time.com/time/magazine/article/0,9171,1562978,00.html), *Time*, retrieved 27 September 2010 Also published as December 4 cover title: "Why We Worry About the Wrong Things: The Psychology of Risk" (http://www.time.com/time/magazine/0,9263,7601061204,00.html)

- Library of Congress. Congressional Research Service. & United States. Congress. House. Committee on Science and Technology. Subcommittee on Science, Research, and Technology (1983), *A Review of risk assessment methodologies*, Washington: U.S: report / prepared by the Congressional Research Service, Library of Congress for the Subcommittee on Science, Research, and Technology; transmitted to the Committee on Science and Technology, U.S. House of Representatives, Ninety-eighth Congress, first session

- Deborah G. Mayo. "Sociological versus metascientific views of technological risk assessment" in Shrader-Frechette and Westra.

- Nyholm, J, 2009 " Persistency, bioaccumulation and toxicity assessment of selected brominated flame retardants (http://umu.diva-portal.org/smash/get/diva2:216812/FULLTEXT01)"
- O'Brien, Mary (2002), *Making better environmental decisions: an alternative to risk assessment* (http://books. google.com/books?id=LtCOEN9HWIcC&printsec=frontcover&dq=Making+better+environmental&hl=en& ei=kzmgTL_UJY_0vQPxtLSADQ&sa=X&oi=book_result&ct=result&resnum=1& ved=0CCwQ6AEwAA#v=onepage&q&f=false), Cambridge, Massachusetts: MIT Press, ISBN 0-262-15051-4, retrieved 27 September 2010 Paperback ISBN 0-262-65053-3
- Shrader-Frechette, Kristin; Westra, Laura, eds. (1997), *Technology and values* (http://books.google.com/ books?id=y5BfvU6uMQMC&printsec=frontcover&dq=Technology+and+values&hl=en& ei=qjKgTPmwL4yiuQPZrez_DA&sa=X&oi=book_result&ct=result&resnum=1& ved=0CC0Q6AEwAA#v=onepage&q&f=false), Lanham, Maryland: Rowman & Littlefield, ISBN 0-8476-8631-0, retrieved 27 September 2010

External links

- Risk Assessment Worksheet and Management Plan (http://www.pmhut.com/wp-content/uploads/2008/01/ risk_management.pdf) A comprehensive guide to risk assessment in project management, includes template - *By John Filicetti*

Risk governance

Risk governance is a systemic approach to decision making processes associated to natural and technological risks, based on the principles of cooperation, participation, mitigation and sustainability, adopted to achieve more effective risk management, that is convergent with other public and private policies. It seeks to reduce risk exposure and vulnerability by filling gaps in risk policy, in order to avoid or reduce human and economic costs caused by disasters.[1] [2] [3]

References

[1] Ortwin Renn. Risk Governance: Coping with Uncertainty in a Complex World. Earthscan, London. 2008. (http://www.springerlink.com/ content/e80726q73j67q0l7/)

[2] Ortwin Renn. Risk Governance. Towards an integrative approach. International Risk Governance Council, Geneva. 2005. (http://www. google.com/url?sa=t&source=web&cd=17&ved=0CC0QFjAGOAo&url=http://www.irgc.org/IMG/pdf/ IRGC_WP_No_1_Risk_Governance__reprinted_version_.pdf&rct=j&q=ortwin renn risk governance&ei=vhCqTLv6IdTNjAfGuuXkDA& usg=AFQjCNFeQx8da_-WsT5q_-qUbWNLgH0YHg&cad=rja)

[3] Urbano Fra Paleo (ed.). Building Safer Communities. Risk Governance, Spatial Planning and Responses to Natural Hazards. IOS Press, Amsterdam. 2009.

Risk International

Risk International

Type	Private
Industry	Management Consulting
Founded	Houston, TX, U.S. (1986)
Founder(s)	Del Jones
Headquarters	Fairlawn, Ohio, USA
Area served	Worldwide
Key people	Michael Davis (CEO)[1] Doug Talley (Chairman of the Board)[2] Kirk Walsh (CFO)[3]
Employees	30+
Website	www.riskinternational.com [4]

Company Overview

Founded in 1986, **Risk International** is a risk management consulting firm.[5] [6] It services clients in the areas of outsourced risk management, claims recovery, insurance archaeology, loss prevention and mitigation.[5] Headquartered in Fairlawn, Ohio, the company also has offices in Charlotte, North Carolina and opened its first international office in London in 2010.[7] [8]

In 2010 the firm received the Silver Circle Award for the Best Risk Management Consultant in Business Insurance's 2010 Readers Choice Awards for the fourth consecutive year.[9] In 2011 the firm was ranked as the third largest independent U.S. risk management consultant by Business Insurance magazine.[10] This marked the fifth consecutive time that Risk International was recognized in the top five largest risk management consultants.

Also in 2010, Risk International was recognized as one of the fastest growing companies in Northeast Ohio as a member of the Weatherhead 100 presented by Case Western Reserve University's Weatherhead School of Management with Ohio's Council of Smaller Enterprises (COSE). The firm was #66 on the 2010 Weatherhead 100 list.[11] [12]

History

Risk International's parent company was formed in 1985 when Zapata Corporation, an offshore drilling and marine services company, spun off its risk management department.[13] Under the direction of Del R. Jones, Risk International was organized and gained its first client in 1986 when BFGoodrich, now Goodrich Corporation, outsourced its entire risk management department to Risk International.[14] [15] [16] Because of its roots in the petrochemical industry Risk International's core competency was asset risk management and insurance claims resolution.[14] As Risk International continued to hire experienced legal and insurance industry executives, it expanded its capabilities to include insurance archaeology, loss prevention and enterprise risk management.[5] Throughout the 1990s Risk International developed expertise in long-tail claims resolution with Fortune 500 companies.[17] During that period Risk International also did extensive research related to Holocaust survivor insurance claims culminating in testimony before the U.S. House of Representatives and the New York State Senate.[18] [19] [20]

Risk International is headquartered in Fairlawn, Ohio where BFGoodrich, now Goodrich Corporation, maintained its worldwide headquarters.[17] Risk International opened another office in Charlotte, North Carolina to support the growth in that region of the US marketplace.[7] In 2002 Del R. Jones retired from the business and Douglas L. Talley was named chairman and CEO of Risk international.[2] After seven years, Michael D. Davis was named CEO while Talley retained his title of chairman.[1] [21] In 2010 Risk International opened its first international office in London to expand its capabilities in the European marketplace.[6] [8]

Services

Risk International has five primary service offerings including:[5] [22]

- Risk Consultation[23]
- Outsourcing risk management for major corporations[24]
- Insurance Archaeology, finding historical insurance policies[25]
- Claim Recovery [26]
- Claims Mitigation[27]

Awards and Rankings

2011

- 3rd Largest Independent U.S. Risk Management Firm[10]
- Best's Recommended Expert Service Provider[28]

2010

- Business Insurance Readers Choice Silver Award[9]
- 3rd Largest Independent U.S. Risk Management Firm[29] [30]
- Weatherhead 100 Recipient[11]

2009

- Business Insurance Readers Choice Silver Award[31] [32]
- 3rd Largest Independent U.S. Risk Management Firm[33]

2008

- Business Insurance Readers Choice Silver Award[34]
- 5th Largest Independent U.S. Risk Management Firm[35]

2007

- Business Insurance Readers Choice Second Runner-up[36]

2006

- 3rd Largest Independent U.S. Risk Management Firm[37]

In the News

Holocaust and Kristallnacht Victims

In 1998 Risk International's then Vice-President Douglas L. Talley provided expert testimony and evidence before the New York State Senate and evidence before the U.S. House of Representatives related to the discovery and examination of historical documents related to Holocaust victims insurance policies.[2] [19] Based on this evidence, he asserted that the victims of the Holocaust were the target of a Nazi scheme to confiscate insurance benefits, and beginning with Kristallnacht, insurance companies conspired to deny claims to German Jews.[20] [38] Upon conclusion of its investigations the United States Congress, New York Senate and other states passed legislation that paved the way for victims to recover monetary damages from still-existing companies and organizations.[39] [40] [41] [42]

Expansion to Europe

In March, 2010, Risk International announced the opening of its first international office in London.[8] The UK-based team will serve its European clients and pave the way for growth within the E.U. market.[43]

Further reading

- *Proof Emerges of Insurer-Nazi Complicity*, Amy S. Friedman, June 1, 1998, National Underwriter[44]
- *Insurance Archaeologists* , Gene Linn, April 16, 1998, The Journal of Commerce[45]
- *Archaeologists unearth coverage for past liabilities*, Mark A. Hofman, June 9, 1997, Business Insurance[46]
- *Environmental research helps clients see green*, April 24, 1997, The Journal of Commerce[47]

References

[1] "Michael Davis" (http://www.riskinternational.com/bios/michael-davis-bio.htm). *Risk International.* . Retrieved 2010-09-15.

[2] "Doug Talley" (http://www.riskinternational.com/bios/doug-talley-bio.htm). *Risk International.* . Retrieved 2010-09-15.

[3] "Kirk Walsh" (http://www.riskinternational.com/bios/kirk-walsh-bio.htm). *Risk International.* . Retrieved 2010-09-15.

[4] http://www.riskinternational.com/

[5] May 8, 1987, The Brownfields Report, Buried Treasure: Insurance Archaeology, Claims Recovery, Vol. 2 No. 9, p.1

[6] March 29, 2010, Business Insurance, Risk International Services enters European Market, p. 17

[7] Howard, J. Lee (1999-08-13). "REIT picks up 10 area buildings for portfolio" (http://bizjournals.com/charlotte/stories/1999/08/16/newscolumn1.html). *Charlotte Business Journal.* . Retrieved 2010-11-23.

[8] "Risk International Announces Expansion to Europe, Offering Risk Management Services Closer to Home for Clients with European Holdings" (http://www.prweb.com/releases/risk-management/insurance-archaeology/prweb3732014.htm). *PR Web.* 2010-03-16. . Retrieved 2010-09-01.

[9] "Risk International Awarded Silver Circle by Business Insurance" (http://www.prweb.com/releases/risk-management/insurance-archeology/prweb4860884.htm). *Risk International.* 2010-12-02. . Retrieved 2011-01-07.

[10] "Largest Independent U.S. risk management consultant" (http://www.businessinsurance.com/apps/pbcs.dll/article?AID=/20110509/NEWS/110509915). *Business Insurance.* 2011-05. . Retrieved 2011-05-11.

[11] "Risk International Named 'Fastest Growing Company' by Weatherhead 100" (http://www.prweb.com/releases/insurance-archaeology/risk-management/prweb4864494.htm). *Risk International.* 2010-12-07. . Retrieved 2011-01-07.

[12] "No. 66 – Risk International" (http://www.weatherhead2010.com/?p=90). *Smart Business.* 2010-12-08. . Retrieved 2011-01-07.

[13] February 6, 1998, Houston Business Journal, Insurance archeologists find billions in old policy limits: Environmental cleanups financed with forgotten insurance policy coverage, Vol. 27, No. 38, p. 27A.

[14] Pybus, Kenneth R. (1996-06-14). "Marine Casualty Services moves back to Houston" (http://houston.bizjournals.com/houston/stories/1996/06/17/story8.html). *Houston Business Journal.* . Retrieved 2010-09-01.

[15] Elizabeth Kirschner, June 9, 1997, Chemical and Engineering News, Digging for Environmental Insurance, Vol. 75, p. 18

[16] Lynn J. Cook, February 6, 1998, Houston Business Journal, Insurance archeologists find billions in old policy limits: Environmental cleanups financed with forgotten insurance policy coverage, Vol. 27, No. 38, p. 27A.

[17] Tom Vander Neut, August, 1997, Risk & Insurance, Out of the Past.

[18] Turner, Missy (2000-05-05). "Compelling Claims" (http://houston.bizjournals.com/houston/stories/2000/05/08/focus1.html). *Houston Business Journal.* . Retrieved 2010-09-01.

[19] "Archives Yield Aid for Claims on Holocaust: Insurance is linked to Funds for Nazis" (http://www.nytimes.com/1998/01/11/world/archives-yield-aid-for-claims-on-holocaust.html?scp=2&sq=Archives Yield Aid for Claims on Holocaust: Insurance is linked to Funds for Nazis, &st=cse). *New York Times.* 1998-01-011. . Retrieved 2010-09-03.

[20] Wren, Christopher S. (1998-05-18). "Documents Indicate German Insurers Stole From Jews" (http://www.nytimes.com/1998/05/18/world/insurers-swindled-jews-nazi-files-show.html?scp=1&sq= Documents Indicate German Insurers Stole From Jews&st=cs). *New York Times.* . Retrieved 2010-09-03.

[21] "Risk International Announces New President and CEO" (http://www.riskinternational.com/news/2009-11-02-michael-davis-ceo-risk-international.htm). *Risk International.* 2009-11-0216. . Retrieved 2010-09-01.

[22] "services" (http://www.riskinternational.com/services.htm). *Risk International.* . Retrieved 2010-09-14.

[23] "Risk management" (http://www.riskinternational.com/risk-management.htm). *Risk International.* . Retrieved 2010-09-14.

[24] "Outsourced risk management" (http://www.riskinternational.com/outsourced-risk-management.htm). *Risk International.* . Retrieved 2010-09-14.

[25] "Insurance archaeology" (http://www.riskinternational.com/insurance-archaeology.htm). *Risk International.* . Retrieved 2010-09-14.

[26] "Claims recovery" (http://www.riskinternational.com/claims-recovery.htm). *Risk International.* . Retrieved 2010-09-14.

[27] "Claims mitigation" (http://www.riskinternational.com/claims-mitigation.htm). *Risk International.* . Retrieved 2010-09-14.

[28] "Best's Directories of Insurance Professionals" (http://www3.ambest.com/DPSDirectorySearch/CompanyDisplay.aspx?dpid=38851& nid=6). *A.M. Best.* 2009-11-16. . Retrieved 2011-05-12.

[29] December 20, 2010, Business Insurance, Largest Independent U.S. Risk Management Consultants, p.24

[30] October 18, 2010, Business Insurance, Largest Independent U.S. Risk Management Consultants, p.12

[31] "Risk International Again Receives Prestigious Industry Award" (http://www.riskinternational.com/news/2009-11-16-risk-international-2009-business-insurance-silver-award.htm). *Risk International.* 2009-11-16. . Retrieved 2010-09-07.

[32] November 16, 2009, Business Insurance, Readers Choice Awards 2009

[33] September 21, 2009, Business Insurance, Largest Independent U.S. risk management consultants, p.12

[34] "RMI Ascends on Teamwork" (http://www.businessinsurance.com/article/20080817/ISSUE03/100025658). *Business Insurance.* 2008-08-17. . Retrieved 2010-09-04.

[35] "Largest Independent U.S. risk management consultant" (http://www.businessinsurance.com/article/99999999/PAGES/1237). *Business Insurance.* 2008-11. . Retrieved 2010-09-04.

[36] "RMI wins top pick by acting as risk manager for clients" (http://www.businessinsurance.com/article/99999999/PAGES/676). *Business Insurance.* 2007. . Retrieved 2010-09-04.

[37] "Largest Independent U.S. risk management consultants" (http://www.businessinsurance.com/article/20061203/ISSUE03/100020505). *Business Insurance.* 2006-12-03. . Retrieved 2010-09-04.

[38] "Holocaust-Era Insurance Claims: Background and Issues" (http://www.jewishvirtuallibrary.org/jsource/Holocaust/crs5.html). *Jewish Virtual Library.* 1999-11-24. . Retrieved 2010-09-01.

[39] "William J. Clinton, Statement on Signing of Holocaust Victims Redress Act" (http://www.presidency.ucsb.edu/ws/index. php?pid=55479). *White House.* 1998-02-13. . Retrieved 2010-09-03.

[40] "Article 27, Holocaust Victims Insurance Act of 1998" (http://public.leginfo.state.ny.us/LAWSSEAF.cgi?QUERYTYPE=LAWS+& QUERYDATA=@PLISC0A27+&LIST=SEA5+&BROWSER=BROWSER+&TOKEN=56219587+&TARGET=VIEW). *NY State Senate.* 1998-06-15. . Retrieved 2010-09-03.

[41] "Circular Letter No. 17 State of New York Insurance Department, Regarding Holocaust Insurance Act of 1998" (http://www.ins.state.ny. us/circltr/1998/cl98_17.htm). *NY State Department of Insurance.* 1998-07-23. . Retrieved 2010-09-01.

[42] "Federal and State Laws Regarding Holocaust Restitution" (http://govinfo.library.unt.edu/pcha/lawsinfo.htm). *University of North Texas.* 2010-09-01. . Retrieved 2010-09-01.

[43] "RI Opens European Office" (http://www.riskinternational.com/news/2010-03-16-risk-international-european-expansion.htm). *Risk International.* 2010-03-16. . Retrieved 2010-09-01.

[44] "Proof Emerges of Insurer-Nazi Complicity" (http://www.allbusiness.com/insurance/insurance-policies-claims-insurance/9215629-1. html). *National Underwriter.* . Retrieved 2010-09-24.

[45] "Insurance Archaeologists" (http://www.joc.com/insurance-archaeologists). *The Journal of Commerce.* . Retrieved 2010-09-24.

[46] "Archaeologists unearth coverage for past liabilities" (http://www.businessinsurance.com/apps/pbcs.dll/article?AID=/19970608/ISSUE01/10008639). *Business Insurance.* . Retrieved 2010-09-24.

[47] "Environmental research helps clients see green" (http://www.joc.com/environmental-research-helps-clients-see-green). *The Journal of Commerce.* . Retrieved 2010-09-24.

External links

- Official Corporate Site (http://www.riskinternational.com/)
- Weatherhead 100 Site (http://www.weatherhead100.org/default.asp/)

Risk management framework

NIST Special Publication 800-37, "Guide for Applying the Risk Management Framework to Federal Information Systems," developed by the Joint Task Force Transformation Initiative Working Group, transforms the traditional Certification and Accreditation (C&A) process into the six-step Risk Management Framework (RMF).

The Risk Management Framework (RMF), illustrated at right, provides a disciplined and structured process that integrates information security and risk management activities into the system development life cycle.[1]

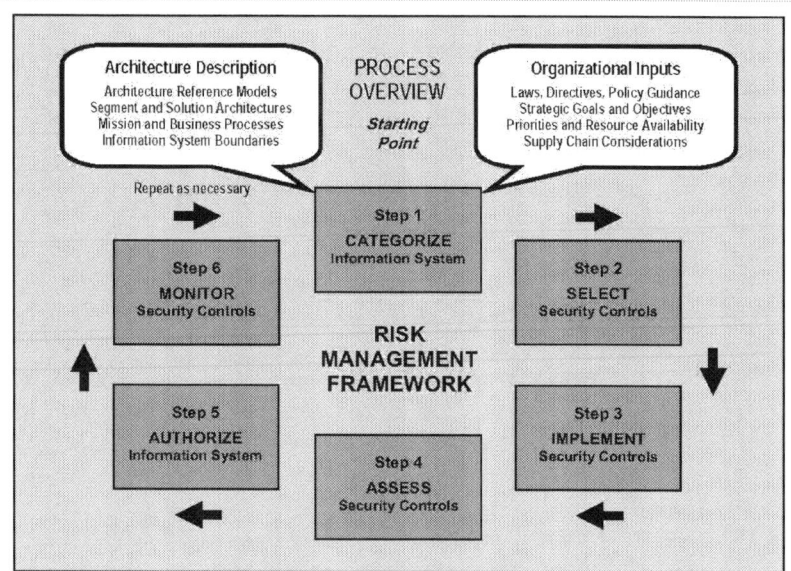

FIGURE 2-2: RISK MANAGEMENT FRAMEWORK

The Risk Management Framework (NIST Special Publication 800-37).

The RMF steps include:

- **Categorize** the information system and the information processed, stored, and transmitted by that system based on an impact analysis.
- **Select** an initial set of baseline security controls for the information system based on the security categorization; tailoring and supplementing the security control baseline as needed based on an organizational assessment of risk and local conditions.
- **Implement** the security controls and describe how the controls are employed within the information system and its environment of operation.
- **Assess** the security controls using appropriate assessment procedures to determine the extent to which the controls are implemented correctly, operating as intended, and producing the desired outcome with respect to meeting the security requirements for the system.
- **Authorize** information system operation based on a determination of the risk to organizational operations and assets, individuals, other organizations, and the Nation resulting from the operation of the information system and the decision that this risk is acceptable.
- **Monitor** the security controls in the information system on an ongoing basis including assessing control effectiveness, documenting changes to the system or its environment of operation, conducting security impact analyses of the associated changes, and reporting the security state of the system to designated organizational officials.

References

[1] Guide for Applying the Risk Management Framework to Federal Information Systems

External links

- NIST Special Publication 800-37 Guide for Applying the Risk Management Framework to Federal Information Systems (http://nistdocs.com)
- Content of the framework proposed in the ISO 31000 Risk Management Standard (http://www.linkedin.com/groups?mostPopular=&gid=3813799)

Risk management tools

Risk Management is a non-intuitive field of study, where the most simple of models consist of a probability multiplied by an impact. Even understanding individual risks is difficult as multiple probabilities can contribute to Risk total probability, and impacts can be "units" of cost, time, events (for example, a catastrophe), market states, etc. This is further complicated by there being no straightforward approach to consider how multiple risks will influence one another or increase the overall risk of the subject of analysis.

Risk management tools allow planners to explicitly address uncertainty by identifying and generating metrics, parameterizing, prioritizing, and developing mitigations, and tracking risk. These capabilities are very difficult to track without some form of documentation or, with the advent of information technology, software application. Simple risk management tools allow documentation. More sophisticated tools provide a visual display of risks, while the most cutting edge, such as those developed by Air Force Research Laboratory Headquarters, are able to aggregate risks into a coherent picture. A few tools have predictive capability, which, through collaboration between partners allow fair partition of risks and improvement of business relations.[1]

The following is a list of risk management tools.

@Risk - performs risk analysis using Monte Carlo simulation to show many possible outcomes in Microsoft Excel spreadsheet—and predicts how likely they are to occur.

The Aggregate Risk Tool - (ART), generates predictive financial data from any probability-impact model.[2]

Bow tie diagrams - a fault identifying visual tool.

Capital asset pricing model - (CAPM) is used to determine the appropriate required rate of return of an asset, if that asset be added to an already well diversified portfolio, based on non-diversifiable risk.[3]

Control Estratégico de Riesgo (CERO) - Software tool with specific tools for each activity of the risk management process. With clients mostly in Latin America. [4]

Cost/Risk Identification & Management System (CRIMS) - Integrated Probabilistic risk assessment model with cost and other variables.[5]

Crystal Ball - performs risk analysis using Monte Carlo simulation, analyzes time series and creates statistical forecasts, and determines the best values of decision variables based on stochastic optimization, all in a Microsoft Excel spreadsheet.

Cura Enterprise - Cura's GRC platform is a highly configurable solution that meets organizational requirements, and provides a balance between qualified and quantified data, all of which can be normalized and reported on across the entire organization.

Cura Quants - Is a quantitative modeling solution designed to integrate with the existing Enterprise GRC Platform. Cura Quants enables customers to quickly and easily quantify the impact of capital and project related risks as well as the effects of accompanying treatment strategies.

Dymonda - Dymonda is a software tool that enables Dynamic Flowgraph Methodology (DFM) modelling and analysis. The model explicitly identifies the cause-and-effect and timing relationships between parameters and states that are best suited to describe a particular system behavior.

Resolve by RPM'" - Cloud software toolbox to manage, track and audit processes associated with risk and safety areas within corporations.

IBM OpenPages GRC Platform - Integrated enterprise governance, risk and compliance solution that includes modules for operational risk management, policy and compliance management, financial controls management, IT governance, and internal audit management

Methodware - Methodware's ERA is a GRC solution that is a scalable,and flexible tool to automate,identify and track risk across departments, regions, and business units effectively.transparency

Operational risk management - The continual cyclic process which includes risk assessment, risk decision making, and implementation of risk controls, which results in acceptance, mitigation, or avoidance of risk.[6]

PIMS Risk - Is a complete risk framework for identifying, analysing and evaluate threats and opportunities. Created for and used by major companies in oil and energy sector.

Probabilistic risk assessment (PRA), **Probability Consequence (P/C)** or **Probability Impact Model** - Simple model where estimates of probability of occurrence are multiplied by the consequence (cost, schedule delay, etc.). This is the most common tool, examples are RiskNav and RiskMatrix.

Reference class forecasting – Predicts the outcome of a planned, risky action based on actual outcomes in a reference class of similar actions to that being forecast.[7]

RiskAid products - collaborative web/intranet-based risk management software environments for projects, operations and Enterprise Risk Management (ERM), developed by Risk Reasoning.

RiskAoA – A predictive tool used to discriminate between proposals, choices or alternatives, by expressing risk for each as a single number, so a proposal's trade-space between cost, scheduled time and risk from its desired characteristics can be compared instantly.[8] RiskAoA and variations of PRA are the only approved tools for United States Department of Defense Military Acquisition.

RiskComplete - Tracks project risk from planning approached to measuring tasks, from concept to manufacture.

RiskIssue.com - An online risk management tool for business, projects, teams and processes. [9]

RiskLike'Con - A free probabilistic risk assessment tool. Displays risks in the industry-standard matrix; Probability vs. Consequence.

Risk register - A project planning and organizational risk assessment tool. It is often referred to as a Risk Log.

RiskPath - An improvement of RiskAoA, available to the public, where forecasts are quantified for each alternative.

Safety case - An assessment of the potential risks in a project and of the measures to be taken to minimize them.

SAPHIRE - A probabilistic risk and reliability assessment software tool. SAPHIRE stands for Systems Analysis Programs for Hands-on Integrated Reliability Evaluations.

SCHRAM - The Schedule Risk Assessment Manager; allows the generation of risk-adjusted schedules; the time of least risk, consequence of rushed/broken schedules. Allows realistic planning based on operational realities.

TRIMS - Provides insight as a knowledge-based tool that measures technical risk management rather than cost and schedule.[10]

Unified Risk Assessment and Regulatory Compliance - A standards based end-to-end comprehensive cloud service from Unisys that performs model based risk assessment and also provides a real time dashboard for Regulatory & Policy Compliance traceability and transparency.

Xero Risk - Web based enterprise risk governance tool to identify, track and balance risks across an organization using user definable assessment and impact criteria.

References

[1] ART, RiskAoA, RiskPath, SCHRAM

[2] http://www.hotfrog.com/Companies/Gesicc/Risk-Management-269782, Also; RiskComplete, RiskLike'Con, RiskPath, and SCHRAM

[3] http://papers.ssrn.com/sol3/papers.cfm?abstract_id=447580

[4] http://www.riesgoscero.com/

[5] http://www.crims.org/

[6] http://www.uscg.mil/directives/ci/3000-3999/Ci_3500_3.pdf

[7] Flyvbjerg, B., 2006, ""From Nobel Prize to Project Management: Getting Risks Right." Project Management Journal, vol. 37, no. 3, August 2006, pp. 5-15. (http://flyvbjerg.plan.aau.dk/Publications2006/Nobel-PMJ2006.pdf)

[8] https://acc.dau.mil/CommunityBrowser.aspx?id=126070

[9] https://riskissue.com

[10] https://acc.dau.mil/CommunityBrowser.aspx?id=19151

Risk pool

A **risk pool** is one of the forms of risk management mostly practiced by insurance companies. Under this system, insurance companies come together to form a pool, which can provide protection to insurance companies against catastrophic risks such as floods, earthquakes etc. The term is also used to describe the pooling of similar risks that underlies the concept of insurance. While risk pooling is necessary for insurance to work, not all risks can be effectively pooled. In particular, it is difficult to pool dissimilar risks in a voluntary insurance market, unless there is a subsidy available to encourage participation. [1]

Risk pooling is an important concept in supply chain management.[2] Risk pooling suggests that demand variability is reduced if one aggregates demand across locations because as demand is aggregated across different locations, it becomes more likely that high demand from one customer will be offset by low demand from another. This reduction in variability allows a decrease in safety stock and therefore reduces average inventory.

For example: in the centralized distribution system, the warehouse serves all customers, which leads to a reduction in variability measured by either the standard deviation or the coefficient of variation.

The three critical points to risk pooling are:

1. Centralized inventory saves safety stock and average inventory in the system.
2. When demands from markets are negatively correlated, the higher the coefficient of variation, the greater the benefit obtained from centralized systems; that is, the greater the benefit from risk pooling.
3. The benefits from risk pooling depend directly on the relative market behavior. This is explained as follows: If we compare two markets and when demand from both markets are more or less than the average demand, we say that the demands from the market are positively correlated. Thus the benefits derived from risk pooling decreases as the correlation between demands from the two markets becomes more positive.

In government

Intergovernmental risk pools (IRPs) operate under the same general principle, except that they are made up of public entities, such as government agencies. Thus, IRPs provide alternative risk financing and transfer mechanisms to their members, through which particular types of risk are underwritten with contributions (premiums), with losses and expenses shared in agreed ratios. In other words, Intergovernmental Risk Pools are a cooperative group of governmental entities joining together to finance an exposure, liability or risk.

Intergovernmental risk pools may include, but are not limited to, authorities, joint power authorities, associations, agencies, trusts, and other risk pools.

References

[1] "Wading Through Medical Insurance Pools: A Primer," American Academy of Actuaries September 2006 http://www.actuary.org/pdf/health/pools_sep06.pdf

[2] D.S.Levi,P.Kaminsky,E. Simchi-Levi."Chapter 3: Inventory Management and Risk Pooling"; "Designing & Managing the Supply Chain-Second Edition"(p-66)

RiskAoA

RiskAoA is the name of a United States Department of Defense (USDoD) project Risk Management tool, allowing the instantaneous review of portfolio (see Project Portfolio Management), proposal or alternative Risk. It was designed by Air Force Research Laboratory (AFRL) Headquarters to perform predictive risk analysis for the Analysis of Alternatives (AoA) process. The prototype, "RiskHammer" was approved by the US Air Force Electronic Systems Center-Acquisition Center of Excellence (ESC/ACE) in 2002 (see Hanscom Air Force Base). RiskAoA is proprietary to the United States Government, but is available from Air Force Materiel Command (AFMC) Headquarters, the office of AFMC/A5, in accordance with Distribution B.

RiskAoA is a simple to use Excel and Visual Basic -based program that allows the predictive and quantitative assessment of Risk. The results are statistically-based values of the relative risk associated with the evaluated alternatives. The capability and algorithms for the program are unprecedented; making RiskAoA the most advanced alternatives management technology employed institutionally.

RiskAoA fulfills a unique role among risk management tools-transforming qualitative statements of an alternative or option risk into a single quantitative value as useful as the cost and schedule. An aim of the USDoD acquisition process is to maximize "value" or return on investment, using the fundamental properties of Cost, Schedule, Performance (CSP) and Risk (or CSPR) as metrics. Just as the cost of one proposal can be higher than another, or one schedule take longer, so risk can be prioritized with RiskAoA. It is further unique in being the only technology ever produced by AFRL Headquarters.

RiskAoA is also well suited for the Evaluation of Alternatives (EoA) process.

The Program Objectives are:

1. Support US Government program managers and decision makers in the assessment of risks and events for any selection of alternatives for Capability-Based Planning or Joint Capabilities Integration Development System (JCIDS), the military equivalent of Enterprise Resource Planning (ERP). This application provides a predictive 'at-a-glance' assessment of the number and magnitude of difficulties expected from different alternatives, necessary for Enterprise Risk Management, supported by RiskAoA.

2. Provide easily reviewable documentation for support or defense of acquisition decisions. RiskAoA helps justify risk vs. return propositions from alternatives and proposals.

3. Provide the Risk Adjusted Life Cycle Costs (LCC) estimates required by the General Services Administration (GSA) for the Analysis of Alternatives.[1]

The USDoD uses a "Probability-Consequence Model" (also known as "Probability-Impact" as one of its key risk metrics[2] . A difficulty with this metric is the constructive "adding" of risk. Probabilities add as

$P1 + P2(1- P1) + P1(1- P1) (1- P2) +...$; P1 is probability of event 1, P2 event 2, etc..

Multiplying these by a consequence that can be cost, time or action, makes the addition and summary of these risks challenging. Further complicating matters is the Probability Consequence Models inability to adjust for compound effects from the same risk. An example from network security: If a network of 10 computers comes under network attack, the risk depends on the defense mechanism. If only one of the computers succumbs to the attack and infects the entire network, then this situation is different than if each computer must be attacked and infected individually.

RiskAoA solves these issues by developing a function which uniquely identifies each probability series as a value relative to one another, utilizing the property from probability theory that the order of occurrences does not affect the result.

The program is easy to use requiring only a few entries:

1. Name and save the analysis.

2. Determine the number of interacting systems, enter this number.

3. Identify each risk.

3a. Name the risk

3b. Describe the risk

3c. Mitigation plan (if any)

3d. Determine the number of compounding effects from each risk-for the network attack example above, enter 10 for one attack being successful, 1/10 if all need to succumb.

3e. Assess the risk, High (H), Medium (M), Low (L), Negligible (N) or use a quantitative numbered assessment (1-99%)

3f. Determine if this risk impacts the entire program (critical path, key performance characteristic, etc..) and rate H,M,L.

4. Repeat step 3 for each risk for each alternative.

RiskAoA includes a forecasting tool, allowing users to determine the level of confidence in the results. The forecasting tool is based on two elements; the worst-case confidence in each of the alternative's risks, and the number of these risks. This is the equivalent of a shot-gun approach to risk management-the more germane data, the more likely the result is to be correct. If well understood data is input this function is unnecessary.

Because of the nature of the RiskAoA approach, errors tend to cancel and be moderated. This makes the forecasting tool itself a worst-case model. If the confidence in the individual risks is greater than 50%, this approach remains accurate.

Since it first release in 2002, it has been validated by other DoD organizations: Air Force Material Command (AFMC) Reporting Units; Validated, Verified and Accredited (VV&A) by AFRL[3] and reviewed by AFMC/EN. It was endorsed DoD wide by the Office of the Under Secretary of Defense for Acquisition, Technology and Logistics[4] in 2007 and by the Defense Acquisition University [5].

RiskAoA is available to all members of the US DoD, and Federal Government employees, in accordance with Distribution B, by contacting AFMC/A5.

References

[1] U.S. General Services Administration. IT Budget Submission Instructions: Guide for Major IT Initiatives (BY2009 Exhibit 300 & Exhibit 53). Washington, DC: Office of the Chief Information Officer, 2007

[2] Risk Management Guide for DoD Acquisition, Aug 2006

[3] http://www.dtic.mil/cgi-bin/GetTRDoc?AD=ADA463123&Location=U2&doc=GetTRDoc.pdf AFRL Alternatives Planning Technology Aids Decision Makers

[4] Defense ATL, Quantifying Risk across the Department of Defense, Jan-Feb 2007

[5] https://dap.dau.mil/aphome/das/Lists/Software%20Tools/DispForm.aspx?ID=57>

Security risk

Security Risk describes employing the concept of risk to the security risk management paradigm to make a particular determination of security orientated events.

According to CNSS Instruction No. 4009 dated 26 April 2010 by Committee on National Security Systems of United States of America[1] a risk is:

> *A measure of the extent to which an entity is threatened by a potential circumstance or event, and typically a function of 1) the adverse impacts that would arise if the circumstance or event occurs; and 2) the likelihood of occurrence.Note: Information system-related security risks are those risks that arise from the loss of confidentiality, integrity, or availability of information or information systems and reflect the potential adverse impacts to organizational operations (including mission, functions, image, or reputation), organizational assets, individuals, other organizations, and the Nation.*

IETF RFC 2828 [2] define risk as:

> *An expectation of loss expressed as the probability that a particular threat will exploit a particular vulnerability with a particular harmful result.*

Introduction

Security risk is the demarcation of risk, into the security silo, from the broader enterprise risk management framework for the purposes of isolating and analysing unique events, outcomes and consequences.[3]

Security risk is often, quantitatively, represented as any event that compromises the assets, operations and objectives of an organisation. **'Event'**, in the security paradigm, comprises those undertaken by actors intentionally for purposes that adversely affect the organisation.

The role of the 'actors' and the intentionality of the 'events', provides the differentiation of security risk from other risk management silos, particularly those of safety, environment, quality, operational and financial.

Common Approaches to Analysing Security Risk

Risk = Threat × Harm

Risk = Consequence × Threat × Vulnerability

Risk = Consequence × Likelihood

Risk = Consequence × Likelihood × Vulnerability Factor Analysis of Information Risk deeply analyze different risk factors and measure security risk.

There are a number of methodologies to analyse and manage security risk: see Category:Risk analysis methodologies

Usually after a cost benefit analysis a countermeasure is set to decrease the likelihood or the consequence of the threat. Security service is the name of countermeasure while transmitting the information.

Psychological Factors relating to Security Risk

Main article: Risk - Risk in Psychology

Given the strong influence affective states can play in the conducting of security risk assessment, many papers have considered the roles of affect heuristic[4] and biases in skewing findings of the process.[5]

References

[1] CNSS Instruction No. 4009 (http://www.cnss.gov/Assets/pdf/cnssi_4009.pdf) dated 26 April 2010

[2] RFC 2828 Internet Security Glossary

[3] Function of security risk assessments to ERM (http://www.optaresystems.com/index.php/optare/publication_detail/security_risk_assessment_enterprise_risk_management/)

[4] Keller, C., Siegrist, M., & Gutscher, H. *The Role of the Affect and Availability Heuristics in Risk Communication.* Risk Analysis, Vol. 26, No. 3, 2006

[5] Heuristics and risk perception – Risk assessments pitfalls (http://www.optaresystems.com/index.php/optare/publication_detail/heuristics_risk_perception_risk_assessment_pitfalls/)

External links

- 800-30 NIST Risk Management Guide (http://csrc.nist.gov/publications/nistpubs/800-30/sp800-30.pdf)
- 800-39 NIST DRAFT Managing Risk from Information Systems: An Organizational Perspective (http://csrc.nist.gov/publications/PubsDrafts.html#SP-800-39)
- FIPS Publication 199, Standards for Security Categorization of Federal Information and Information (http://csrc.nist.gov/publications/fips/fips199/FIPS-PUB-199-final.pdf)
- FIPS Publication 200 Minimum Security Requirements for Federal Information and Information Systems (http://csrc.nist.gov/publications/fips/fips200/FIPS-200-final-march.pdf)
- 800-37 NIST Guide for Applying the Risk Management Framework to Federal Information Systems: A Security Life Cycle Approach (http://csrc.nist.gov/publications/nistpubs/800-37-rev1/sp800-37-rev1-final.pdf)
- FISMApedia is a collection of documents and discussions focused on USA Federal IT security (http://fismapedia.org/index.php?title=Main_Page)
- Internet2 Information Security Guide: Effective Practices and Solutions for Higher Education (https://wiki.internet2.edu/confluence/display/itsg2/Home)
- The Institute of Risk Management (IRM) (http://www.theirm.org/index.html) is risk management's leading international professional education and training body

Singapore Mercantile Exchange

Singapore Mercantile Exchange Pte. Ltd. (SMX)

Type	Private Limited
Industry	Financial Services Business Services
Headquarters	1 Temasek Avenue, #23-02, Millenia Tower, Singapore 039192
Key people	Chairman Ang Swee Tian, Vice Chairman Jignesh Shah, Executive Director Framroze Pochara, Chief Executive Officer Thomas J. McMahon
Products	Exchange-cleared futures and options contracts on precious metals, base metals, agriculture commodities, energy, currencies and commodity indices.
Website	www.smx.com.sg [1]

The **Singapore Mercantile Exchange** (SMX) is a pan-Asian multi-product commodity and currency derivatives exchange situated in Singapore. SMX offers a comprehensive platform for trading a diversified basket of commodities including futures and options contracts on precious metals, base metals, agriculture commodities, energy, currencies and commodity indices. In August 2010 the Singapore Mercantile Exchange was granted 'Approved Exchange' (AE) status, the final approval needed to operate as a regulated and licensed exchange.[2]

Notes

[1] http://www.smx.com.sg
[2] http://www.smx.com.sg/Uploads/PressReleases/2010/August/English/PR_12_AUG_10.pdf

Singapore Workplace Safety and Health Conference

The **Singapore Workplace Safety and Health Conference** (SWSHC) is a platform for the promotion of workplace safety and health (WSH, OH&S) thought and practice in Singapore and the region.

Organised by the Workplace Safety & Health Council (WSH Council) in partnership with Singapore's Ministry of Manpower, the conference aims to bring together regulators, industry leaders and safety professionals to identify problems, formulate recommendations and develop and implement best practices to ensure the improvement and advancement of safety standards in the workplace.

Embracing Challenges, Pushing WSH Frontiers

The inaugural conference will be held on 15 to 16 September 2010 at Suntec Singapore International Convention and Exhibition Centre.

The theme for the two day conference, "Embracing Challenges, Pushing WSH Frontiers", is aimed at creating awareness for the legal, moral and economic reasons behind WSH legislation, changing opinions of WSH practices, and creating a framework for the sustained promotion of WSH thought.

Speakers at the 2010 conference include local and international WSH thought leaders and Captains of Industry, including Professor Harri Vainio from the Finnish Institute of Occupational Health, Mr. John Spanswick from the United Kingdom's Health and Safety Executive Board and Mr. Choo Chiau Beng, CEO of Keppel Corporation.

External links

- www.singaporewshconference.sg [1]

References

[1] http://www.singaporewshconference.sg

Student Investment Advisory Service (SIAS Fund)

Student Investment Advisory Service (SIAS Fund) is type of Student managed investments fund and part of Simon Fraser University (SFU) Endowment Portfolio managed by Financial risk management (FRM) program candidates at SFU business school.

The fund follows a value investing mandate, set by the client (the SFU Treasurer, Mr. Michael Murdock) through a conservative Investment Policy Statement (IPS). The SIAS portfolio is composed of four actively managed asset classes: Cash, Canadian Equity, Global Equity and Fixed Income[1] . At the beginning of the program (academic year), candidates (investment managers) go through extensive training via three sources: (1) the previous SIAS cohort, (2) faculty members and most importantly, (3) a group of elite industry professionals, before they are handed down the power. Additionally, the new investment managers are immediately grouped into six managing teams, namely Economics and Strategy, Canadian Equity, Global Equity, Fixed Income, and Risk Metrics. The activities of each team are closely monitored by the sixth team; compliance and performance, in accordance to the IPS. This team generates monthly compliance and performance reports for the fund which is sent to the clients and the faculty advisors. The fund also holds quarterly performance review presentations before a panel of industry advisors; a few of B.C's preeminent portfolio managers, which are open to the public[2]

As one of the largest student managed funds in North America, SIAS was awarded the best student-run value investment fund in North America in 2007 based on performance by RISE (recognized by Businessweek)[3] . SFU's endowment portfolio is among the top 25% largest endowments in North America. As active contributors to managing SIAS; $10 million of SFU's large endowment portfolio, FRM candidates also provide mentorship to a number of well qualified and trained SFU finance undergraduate students in their role as associate analyst for the fund.

References

[1] http://business.sfu.ca/files/PDF/SIAS/About_SIAS.pdf
[2] http://beedie.sfu.ca/sias/reports.php
[3] http://www.financeclub.ca/usias.htm

External links

- SFU Business (http://business.sfu.ca/sias/sias/)
- Financial Risk Management Financial risk management
- Student Managed Investment Student managed investments

Julian Talbot (risk management)

Julian Talbot (born 1961) is an Australian writer, speaker and consultant on risk management.

Security Risk Management Body of Knowledge

In 2009 Talbot co-authored the *Security Risk Management Body of Knowledge*, a large and comprehensive repository of knowledge, including the best practices, recent innovations and evolving research, in the area of security risk management.[1] [2]

Education

Talbot graduated with a Master in Risk Management degree from Monash University, Melbourne, Australia, in 2006. He is a Certified Protection Professional, the security industry's highest level of professional achievement.[3]

Security Career

In the period 1995-2001, Talbot served as head of security for Woodside Energy's North West Shelf Venture, Australia's largest natural resources project. He then worked as head of risk and security for the Malaysia Smelting Corporation's Indonesian operations, as senior risk adviser for the Australian Department of Health and Ageing, and as head of security for the Australian Trade Commission (Austrade).

In 2007 he was chairman of the Citadel Group Limited [4] and in 2008 was a member of its Audit Review Committee.[5]

Currently, he is risk management practice leader for Jakeman Business Solutions (JBS), one of Australia's leading consulting firms.[6]

Public Service

Talbot served as director of the Risk Management Institution of Australasia (2006-09)[7] and as director of the Australian Institute of Professional Intelligence Officers (2008-09).

He is currently a director of the Security Analysis and Risk Management Association,[8] based in Washington, DC.

References

[1] Mickelberg, Graeme (24 September 2008). "Body of Knowledge a valuable tool for industry" (http://www.Securitymanagement.com.au/articles/body-of-knowledge-a-valuable-tool-for-industry-63.html). Securitymanagement.com.au. . Retrieved 18 April 2011.

[2] "Book Review: Security Risk Management - Body of Knowledge" (http://www.husdal.com/2010/10/13/book-review-security-risk-management/). Husdal.com. 13 October 2010. . Retrieved 19 April 2011.

[3] "Certified Protection Professional" (http://www.asisonline.org/certification/cpp/index.xml). Asisonline.org. 2011. . Retrieved 19 April 2011.

[4] Citadel Group Limited. *Annual report for the year ended 30 June 2008.* Page 6.

[5] "CGL Board Members Overview" (http://replay.web.archive.org/20080723235437/http://www.citadelgroup.com.au/CGL Board Members Overview - 2008.pdf). Citadel Group Limited. 2008. . Retrieved 25 April 2011.

[6] Thistleton, John (14 February 2011). "Canberra firm lands $45m Defence deal" (http://www.canberratimes.com.au/news/local/news/general/canberra-firm-lands-45m-defence-deal/2075931.aspx). Canberratimes.com.au. . Retrieved 28 April 2011.

[7] "Annual Report 2009" (http://www.rmia.org.au/LinkClick.aspx?fileticket=8xwPhDTE5fA=&tabid=72&mid=432). Risk Management Institution of Australasia. 2010. . Retrieved 20 April 2011.

[8] "SARMA Organization and Leadership" (http://sarma.org/about/organizationandgov/). Security Analysis and Risk Management Association. 2010. . Retrieved 23 April 2011.

External links

- Julian Talbot's official website (http://www.juliantalbot.com/)

Tsunami

A **tsunami** (plural: tsunamis or tsunami; from Japanese: 津波, lit. "harbor wave";[1] English pronunciation: English pronunciation: /suːˈnɑːmi/ *soo-**nah**-mee* or English pronunciation: /tsuːˈnɑːmi/ *tsoo-**nah**-mee*[2]), also called a **tsunami wave train**,[3] and at one time referred to as a **tidal wave**, is a series of water waves caused by the displacement of a large volume of a body of water, usually an ocean, though it can occur in large lakes. Tsunamis are a frequent occurrence in Japan; approximately 195 events have been recorded.[4] Owing to the immense volumes of water and the high energy involved, tsunamis can devastate coastal regions.

A destroyed town in Sumatra after being hit by a tsunami, caused by the 2004 Indian Ocean earthquake

Earthquakes, volcanic eruptions and other underwater explosions (including detonations of underwater nuclear devices), landslides glacier calvings[5] and other mass movements, meteorite ocean impacts or similar impact events, and other disturbances above or below water all have the potential to generate a tsunami.

The Greek historian Thucydides was the first to relate tsunami to submarine earthquakes,[6] [7] but the understanding of a tsunami's nature remained slim until the 20th century and is the subject of ongoing research. Many early geological, geographical, and oceanographic texts refer to tsunamis as "**seismic sea waves.**"

Some meteorological conditions, such as deep depressions that cause tropical cyclones, can generate a storm surge, called a meteotsunami, which can raise tides several metres above normal levels. The displacement comes from low atmospheric pressure within the centre of the depression. As these storm surges reach shore, they may resemble (though are not) tsunamis, inundating vast areas of land.

Etymology and history

The term *tsunami* comes from the Japanese 津波, composed of the two kanji 津 (*tsu*) meaning "**harbor**" and 波 (*nami*), meaning "**wave**". (For the plural, one can either follow ordinary English practice and add an *s*, or use an invariable plural as in the Japanese.[8])

Tsunami are sometimes referred to as **tidal waves**. In recent years, this term has fallen out of favor, especially in the scientific community, because tsunami actually have nothing to do with tides. The once-popular term derives from their most common appearance, which is that of an extraordinarily high tidal bore. Tsunami and tides both

Lisbon earthquake and tsunami in 1755

produce waves of water that move inland, but in the case of tsunami the inland movement of water is much greater and lasts for a longer period, giving the impression of an incredibly high tide. Although the meanings of "tidal" include "resembling"[9] or "having the form or character of"[10] the tides, and the term *tsunami* is no more accurate because tsunami are not limited to harbours, use of the term *tidal wave* is discouraged by geologists and oceanographers.

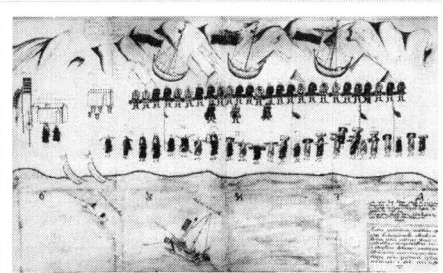

The Russians of Pavel Lebedev-Lastochkin in Japan, with their ships tossed inland by a tsunami, meeting some Japanese in 1779

There are only a few other languages that have an equivalent native word. In the Tamil language, the word is *aazhi peralai*. In the Acehnese language, it is *ië beuna* or *alôn buluëk*[11] (Depending on the dialect. Note that in the fellow Austronesian language of Tagalog, a major language in the Philippines, *alon* means "wave".) On Simeulue island, off the western coast of Sumatra in Indonesia, in the Defayan language the word is *smong*, while in the Sigulai language it is *emong*.[12]

As early as 426 B.C. the Greek historian Thucydides inquired in his book *History of the Peloponnesian War* about the causes of tsunami, and was the first to argue that ocean earthquakes must be the cause.[6] [7]

> The cause, in my opinion, of this phenomenon must be sought in the earthquake. At the point where its shock has been the most violent the sea is driven back, and suddenly recoiling with redoubled force, causes the inundation. Without an earthquake I do not see how such an accident could happen.[13]

The Roman historian Ammianus Marcellinus (*Res Gestae* 26.10.15-19) described the typical sequence of a tsunami, including an incipient earthquake, the sudden retreat of the sea and a following gigantic wave, after the 365 A.D. tsunami devastated Alexandria.[14] [15]

While Japan may have the longest recorded history of tsunamis, the sheer destruction caused by the 2004 earthquake and tsunami event mark it as the most devastating of its kind in modern times, killing around 230,000 people. The Sumatran region is not unused to tsunamis either, with earthquakes of varying magnitudes regularly occurring off the coast of the island.[16]

Generation mechanisms

The principal generation mechanism (or cause) of a tsunami is the displacement of a substantial volume of water or perturbation of the sea.[17] This displacement of water is usually attributed to either earthquakes, landslides, volcanic eruptions,glacier calvings or more rarely by meteorites and nuclear tests.[18] [19] The waves formed in this way are then sustained by gravity. Tides do not play any part in the generation of tsunamis.

Tsunami generated by seismicity

Tsunami can be generated when the sea floor abruptly deforms and vertically displaces the overlying water. Tectonic earthquakes are a particular kind of earthquake that are associated with the Earth's crustal deformation; when these earthquakes occur beneath the sea, the water above the deformed area is displaced from its equilibrium position.[20] More specifically, a tsunami can be generated when thrust faults associated with convergent or destructive plate boundaries move abruptly, resulting in water displacement, owing to the vertical component of movement involved. Movement on normal faults will also cause displacement of the seabed, but the size of the largest of such events is normally too small to give rise to a significant tsunami.

Drawing of tectonic plate boundary before earthquake

Overriding plate bulges under strain, causing tectonic uplift.

Plate slips, causing subsidence and releasing energy into water.

The energy released produces tsunami waves.

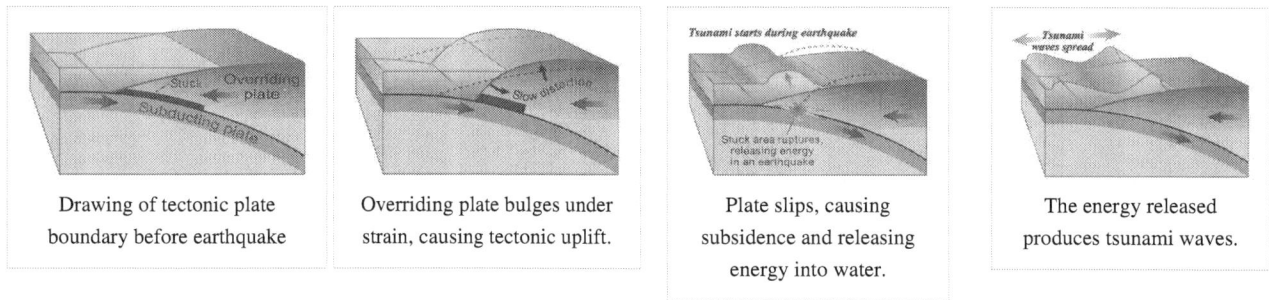

Tsunamis have a small amplitude (wave height) offshore, and a very long wavelength (often hundreds of kilometers long, whereas normal ocean waves have a wavelength of only 30 or 40 metres),[21] which is why they generally pass unnoticed at sea, forming only a slight swell usually about 300 millimetres (12 in) above the normal sea surface. They grow in height when they reach shallower water, in a wave shoaling process described below. A tsunami can occur in any tidal state and even at low tide can still inundate coastal areas.

On April 1, 1946, a magnitude-7.8 (Richter Scale) earthquake occurred near the Aleutian Islands, Alaska. It generated a tsunami which inundated Hilo on the island of Hawai'i with a 14 metres (46 ft) high surge. The area where the earthquake occurred is where the Pacific Ocean floor is subducting (or being pushed downwards) under Alaska.

Examples of tsunami originating at locations away from convergent boundaries include Storegga about 8,000 years ago, Grand Banks 1929, Papua New Guinea 1998 (Tappin, 2001). The Grand Banks and Papua New Guinea tsunamis came from earthquakes which destabilized sediments, causing them to flow into the ocean and generate a tsunami. They dissipated before traveling transoceanic distances.

The cause of the Storegga sediment failure is unknown. Possibilities include an overloading of the sediments, an earthquake or a release of gas hydrates (methane etc.)

The 1960 Valdivia earthquake (M_{w} 9.5) (19:11 hrs UTC), 1964 Alaska earthquake (M_{w} 9.2), 2004 Indian Ocean earthquake (M_{w} 9.2) (00:58:53 UTC) and 2011 Tōhoku earthquake (M_{w}9.0) are recent examples of powerful megathrust earthquakes that generated tsunamis (known as teletsunamis) that can cross entire oceans. Smaller (M_{w} 4.2) earthquakes in Japan can trigger tsunamis (called **local** and **regional tsunamis**) that can only devastate nearby coasts, but can do so in only a few minutes.

In the 1950s, it was discovered that larger tsunamis than had previously been believed possible could be caused by giant landslides. These phenomena rapidly displace large water volumes, as energy from falling debris or expansion transfers to the water at a rate faster than the water can absorb. Their existence was confirmed in 1958, when a giant landslide in Lituya Bay, Alaska, caused the highest wave ever recorded, which had a height of 524 metres (over 1700 feet). The wave didn't travel far, as it struck land almost immediately. Two people fishing in the bay were killed, but another boat amazingly managed to ride the wave. Scientists named these waves megatsunami.

Scientists discovered that extremely large landslides from volcanic island collapses can generate megatsunamis that can cross oceans.

Characteristics

Tsunamis cause damage by two mechanisms: the smashing force of a wall of water travelling at high speed, and the destructive power of a large volume of water draining off the land and carrying all with it, even if the wave did not look large.

While everyday wind waves have a wavelength (from crest to crest) of about 100 metres (330 ft) and a height of roughly 2 metres (6.6 ft), a tsunami in the deep ocean has a wavelength of about 200 kilometres (120 mi). Such a wave travels at well over 800 kilometres per hour (500 mph), but owing to the enormous wavelength the wave oscillation at any given point takes 20 or 30 minutes to complete a cycle and has an amplitude of only about 1 metre (3.3 ft).[22] This makes tsunamis difficult to detect over deep water. Ships rarely notice their passage.

When the wave enters shallow water, it slows down and its amplitude (height) increases.

As the tsunami approaches the coast and the waters become shallow, wave shoaling compresses the wave and its velocity slows below 80 kilometres per hour (50 mph). Its wavelength diminishes to less than 20 kilometres (12 mi) and its amplitude grows enormously. Since the wave still has the same very long period, the tsunami may take

The wave further slows and amplifies as it hits land. Only the largest waves crest.

minutes to reach full height. Except for the very largest tsunamis, the approaching wave does not break, but rather appears like a fast-moving tidal bore.[23] Open bays and coastlines adjacent to very deep water may shape the tsunami further into a step-like wave with a steep-breaking front.

When the tsunami's wave peak reaches the shore, the resulting temporary rise in sea level is termed *run up*. Run up is measured in metres above a reference sea level.[23] A large tsunami may feature multiple waves arriving over a period of hours, with significant time between the wave crests. The first wave to reach the shore may not have the highest run up.[24]

About 80% of tsunamis occur in the Pacific Ocean, but they are possible wherever there are large bodies of water, including lakes. They are caused by earthquakes, landslides, volcanic explosions glacier calvings, and bolides.

Drawback

If the first part of a tsunami to reach land is a trough—called a **drawback**—rather than a wave crest, the water along the shoreline recedes dramatically, exposing normally submerged areas.

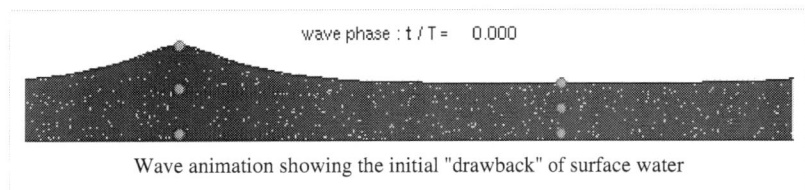

Wave animation showing the initial "drawback" of surface water

A drawback occurs because the water propagates outwards with the trough of the wave at its front. Drawback begins before the wave arrives at an interval equal to half of the wave's period. Drawback can exceed hundreds of metres, and people unaware of the danger sometimes remain near the shore to satisfy their curiosity or to collect fish from the exposed seabed.

Scales of intensity and magnitude

As with earthquakes, several attempts have been made to set up scales of tsunami intensity or magnitude to allow comparison between different events.[25]

Intensity scales

The first scales used routinely to measure the intensity of tsunami were the *Sieberg-Ambraseys scale*, used in the Mediterranean Sea and the *Imamura-Iida intensity scale*, used in the Pacific Ocean. The latter scale was modified by Soloviev, who calculated the Tsunami intensity I according to the formula

$$I = \frac{1}{2} + \log_2 H_{av}$$

where H_{av} is the average wave height along the nearest coast. This scale, known as the *Soloviev-Imamura tsunami intensity scale*, is used in the global tsunami catalogues compiled by the NGDC/NOAA and the Novosibirsk Tsunami Laboratory as the main parameter for the size of the tsunami.

Magnitude scales

The first scale that genuinely calculated a magnitude for a tsunami, rather than an intensity at a particular location was the ML scale proposed by Murty & Loomis based on the potential energy.[25] Difficulties in calculating the potential energy of the tsunami mean that this scale is rarely used. Abe introduced the *tsunami magnitude scale* M_t, calculated from,

$$M_t = a \log h + b \log R = D$$

where h is the maximum tsunami-wave amplitude (in m) measured by a tide gauge at a distance R from the epicenter, a, b & D are constants used to make the M_t scale match as closely as possible with the moment magnitude scale.[26]

Warnings and predictions

Drawbacks can serve as a brief warning. People who observe drawback (many survivors report an accompanying sucking sound), can survive only if they immediately run for high ground or seek the upper floors of nearby buildings. In 2004, ten-year old Tilly Smith of Surrey, England, was on Maikhao beach in Phuket, Thailand with her parents and sister, and having learned about tsunamis recently in school, told her family that a tsunami might be imminent. Her parents warned others minutes before the wave arrived, saving dozens of lives. She credited her geography teacher, Andrew Kearney.

Tsunami warning sign

In the 2004 Indian Ocean tsunami drawback was not reported on the African coast or any other eastern coasts it reached. This was because the wave moved downwards on the eastern side of the fault line and upwards on the western side. The western pulse hit coastal Africa and other western areas.

A tsunami cannot be precisely predicted, even if the magnitude and location of an earthquake is known. Geologists, oceanographers, and seismologists analyse each earthquake and based on many factors may or may not issue a tsunami warning. However, there are some warning signs of an impending tsunami, and automated systems can provide warnings immediately after an earthquake in time to save lives. One of the most successful systems uses bottom pressure sensors that are attached to buoys. The sensors constantly monitor the pressure of the overlying water column. This is deduced through the calculation:

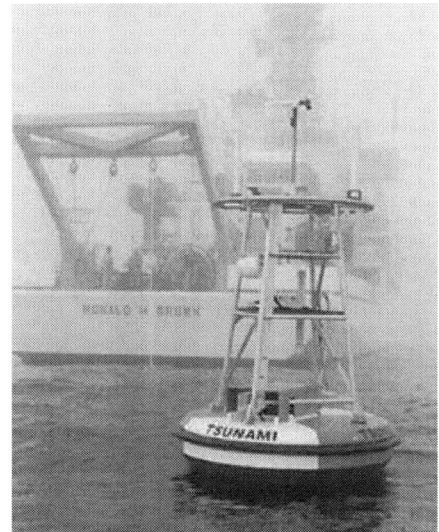

One of the deep water buoys used in the DART tsunami warning system

$$P = \rho g h$$

where

P = the overlying pressure in newtons per metre square,

ρ = the density of the seawater= 1.1 x 10^3 kg/m^3,

g = the acceleration due to gravity= 9.8 m/s^2 and

h = the height of the water column in metres.

Hence for a water column of 5,000 m depth the overlying pressure is equal to

$$P = \rho g h = \left(1.1 \times 10^3 \ \frac{\text{kg}}{\text{m}^3}\right)\left(9.8 \ \frac{\text{m}}{\text{s}^2}\right)\left(5.0 \times 10^3 \ \text{m}\right) = 5.4 \times 10^7 \ \frac{\text{N}}{\text{m}^2} = 54\,\text{MPa}$$

or about 5500 tonnes-force per square metre.

Regions with a high tsunami risk typically use tsunami warning systems to warn the population before the wave reaches land. On the west coast of the United States, which is prone to Pacific Ocean tsunami, warning signs indicate evacuation routes. In Japan, the community is well-educated about earthquakes and tsunamis, and along the Japanese shorelines the tsunami warning signs are reminders of the natural hazards together with a network of warning sirens, typically at the top of the cliff of surroundings hills.[27]

The Pacific Tsunami Warning System is based in Honolulu, Hawai'i. It monitors Pacific Ocean seismic activity. A sufficiently large earthquake magnitude and other information triggers a tsunami warning. While the subduction zones around the Pacific are seismically active, not all earthquakes generate tsunami. Computers assist in analysing the tsunami risk of every earthquake that occurs in the Pacific Ocean and the adjoining land masses.

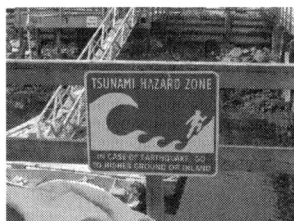

Tsunami hazard sign at Bamfield, British Columbia

A tsunami warning sign on a seawall in Kamakura, Japan, 2004

The monument to the victims of tsunami at Laupahoehoe, Hawaii

Tsunami memorial in Kanyakumari beach

As a direct result of the Indian Ocean tsunami, a re-appraisal of the tsunami threat for all coastal areas is being undertaken by national governments and the United Nations Disaster Mitigation Committee. A tsunami warning system is being installed in the Indian Ocean.

Computer models can predict tsunami arrival, usually within minutes of the arrival time. Bottom pressure sensors relay information in real time. Based on these pressure readings and other seismic information and the seafloor's shape (bathymetry) and coastal topography, the models estimate the amplitude and surge height of the approaching tsunami. All Pacific Rim countries collaborate in the Tsunami Warning System and most regularly practice evacuation and other procedures. In Japan, such preparation is mandatory for government, local authorities, emergency services and the population.

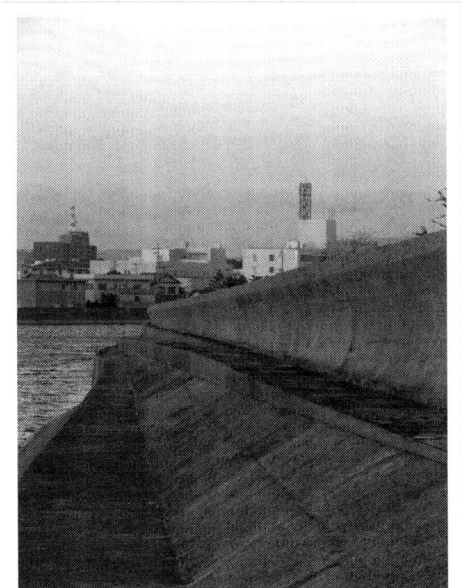

A seawall at Tsu, Japan

Some zoologists hypothesise that some animal species have an ability to sense subsonic Rayleigh waves from an earthquake or a tsunami. If correct, monitoring their behavior could provide advance warning of earthquakes, tsunami etc. However, the evidence is controversial and is not widely accepted. There are unsubstantiated claims about the Lisbon quake that some animals escaped to higher ground, while many other animals in the same areas drowned. The phenomenon was also noted by media sources in Sri Lanka in the 2004 Indian Ocean earthquake.[28] [29] It is possible that certain animals (e.g., elephants) may have heard the sounds of the tsunami as it approached the coast. The elephants' reaction was to move away from the approaching noise. By contrast, some humans went to the shore to investigate and many drowned as a result.

Along the United States west coast, in addition to sirens, warnings are sent on television & radio via the National Weather Service, using the Emergency Alert System.

Tsunami Evacuation Route signage along U.S. Route 101, in Washington

Forecast of tsunami attack probability

Kunihiko Shimazaki (University of Tokyo), a member of Earthquake Research committee of The Headquarters for Earthquake Research Promotion of Japanese government, mentioned the plan to public announcement of tsunami attack probability forecast at Japan National Press Club on 12 May 2011. The forecast includes tsunami height, attack area and occurrence probability within 100 years ahead. The forecast would integrate the scientific knowledge of recent interdisciplinarity and aftermath of the 2011 Tōhoku earthquake and tsunami. As the plan, announcement will be available from 2014.[30] [31] [32]

Mitigation

In some tsunami-prone countries earthquake engineering measures have been taken to reduce the damage caused onshore. Japan, where tsunami science and response measures first began following a disaster in 1896, has produced ever-more elaborate countermeasures and response plans.[33] That country has built many tsunami walls of up to 4.5 metres (15 ft) to protect populated coastal areas. Other localities have built floodgates and channels to redirect the water from incoming tsunami. However, their effectiveness has been questioned, as tsunami often overtop the barriers. For instance, the Okushiri, Hokkaidō tsunami which struck Okushiri Island of Hokkaidō within two to five minutes of the earthquake on July 12, 1993 created waves as much as 30 metres (100 ft) tall—as high as a 10-story building. The port town of Aonae was completely surrounded by a tsunami wall, but the waves washed right over the wall and destroyed all the wood-framed structures in the area. The wall may have succeeded in slowing down and moderating the height of the tsunami, but it did not prevent major destruction and loss of life.[34]

As a weapon

There have been studies and at least one attempt to create tsunami waves as a weapon. In World War II, the New Zealand Military Forces initiated Project Seal, which attempted to create small tsunamis with explosives in the area of today's Shakespear Regional Park; the attempt failed.[35]

Footnotes

[1] "Tsunami Terminology" (http://nthmp-history.pmel.noaa.gov/terms.html). NOAA. . Retrieved 2010-07-15.

[2] Wells, John C. (1990). *Longman pronunciation dictionary*. Harlow, England: Longman. p. 736. ISBN 0582053838. Entry: "tsunami"

[3] Fradin, Judith Bloom and Dennis Brindell (2008). *Witness to Disaster: Tsunamis* (http://shop.nationalgeographic.com/product/977/4389/971.html). Witness to Disaster. Washington, D.C.: National Geographic Society. pp. 42, 43. .

[4] "Answers.com" (http://www.answers.com/topic/tsunami). Answers.com. . Retrieved 2010-08-24.

[5] Barbara Ferreira (April 17, 2011). "When icebergs capsize, tsunamis may ensue" (http://blogs.nature.com/barbaraferreira/2011/04/17/when-icebergs-capsize). *Nature*. . Retrieved 2011-04-27.

[6] Thucydides: "A History of the Peloponnesian War", 3.89.1–4 (http://www.perseus.tufts.edu/cgi-bin/ptext?lookup=Thuc.+3.89.1)

[7] Smid, T. C. (Apr., 1970). *'Tsunamis' in Greek Literature*. **17** (2nd ed.). pp. 100–104.

[8] [a. Jap. tsunami, tunami, f. tsu harbour + nami waves.— *Oxford English Dictionary*]

[9] "Tidal", The American Heritage Stedman's Medical Dictionary. Houghton Mifflin Company. 11 November 2008. Dictionary.reference.com (http://dictionary.reference.com/browse/tidal)

[10] -al. (n.d.). Dictionary.com Unabridged (v 1.1). Retrieved November 11, 2008, Dictionary.reference.com (http://dictionary.reference.com/browse/-al)

[11] "Acehrecoveryforum.org" (http://www.acehrecoveryforum.org/en/index.php?action=ARFNews&no=73). Acehrecoveryforum.org. 2007-11-06. . Retrieved 2010-08-24.

[12] JTIC.org (http://www.jtic.org/en/jtic/images/dlPDF/Lipi_CBDP/reports/SMGChapter3.pdf)

[13] Thucydides: "A History of the Peloponnesian War", 3.89.5 (http://www.perseus.tufts.edu/cgi-bin/ptext?lookup=Thuc.+3.89.1)

[14] Kelly, Gavin (2004). "Ammianus and the Great Tsunami". *The Journal of Roman Studies* **94** (141): 141–167. doi:10.2307/4135013. JSTOR 4135013.

[15] Stanley, Jean-Daniel & Jorstad, Thomas F. (2005), " The 365 A.D. Tsunami Destruction of Alexandria, Egypt: Erosion, Deformation of Strata and Introduction of Allochthonous Material (http://gsa.confex.com/gsa/2005AM/finalprogram/abstract_96386.htm)"

[16] The 10 most destructive tsunamis in history (http://www.australiangeographic.com.au/journal/the-10-biggest-tsunamis-in-history.htm/), Australian Geographic, March 16, 2011.

[17] Haugen K, Løvholt F, Harbitz C, K; Lovholt, F; Harbitz, C (2005). "Fundamental mechanisms for tsunami generation by submarine mass flows in idealised geometries". *Marine and Petroleum Geology* **22** (1-2): 209–217. doi:10.1016/j.marpetgeo.2004.10.016.

[18] Margaritondo, G (2005). "Explaining the physics of tsunamis to undergraduate and non-physics students". *European Journal of Physics* **26** (3).

[19] Voit, S.S (1987). "Tsunamis". *Annual Review of Fluid Mechanics* **19** (1): 217–236. Bibcode 1987AnRFM..19..217V. doi:10.1146/annurev.fl.19.010187.001245.

[20] "How do earthquakes generate tsunamis?" (http://www.geophys.washington.edu/tsunami/general/physics/earthquake.html). University of Washington. .

[21] Facts and figures: how tsunamis form (http://www.australiangeographic.com.au/journal/facts-and-figures-how-tsunamis-form.htm/), Australian Geographic, March 18, 2011.

[22] Earthsci.org (http://earthsci.org/education/teacher/basicgeol/tsumami/tsunami.html), Tsunamis

[23] "Life of a Tsunami" (http://walrus.wr.usgs.gov/tsunami/basics.html). *Western Coastal & Marine Geology*. United States Geographical Survey. 22 October 2008. . Retrieved 2009-09-09.

[24] Prof. Stephen A. Nelson (28-Jan-2009). "Tsunami" (http://www.tulane.edu/~sanelson/geol204/tsunami.htm). Tulane University. . Retrieved 2009-09-09.

[25] Gusiakov V.. "Tsunami Quantification: how we measure the overall size of tsunami (Review of tsunami intensity and magnitude scales)" (http://www.ngdc.noaa.gov/hazard/data/presentations/jtc/gusiakov.pdf). . Retrieved 2009-10-18.

[26] Abe K. (1995). *Estimate of Tsunami Run-up Heights from Earthquake Magnitudes* (http://books.google.com/?id=5YjaGdQOJIwC&pg=PA21&dq=abe+magnitude+scale+tsunami+1981&q=abe magnitude scale tsunami 1981). ISBN 9780792334835. . Retrieved 2009-10-18.

[27] Chanson, H. (2010). *Tsunami Warning Signs on the Enshu Coast of Japan* (http://espace.library.uq.edu.au/view/UQ:203103). Shore & Beach, Vol. 78, No. 1, pp. 52-54. ISSN 0037 4237.

[28] Lambourne, Helen (2005-03-27). "Tsunami: Anatomy of a disaster" (http://news.bbc.co.uk/1/hi/world/south_asia/4269847.stm). BBC. .

[29] Kenneally, Christine (2004-12-30). "Surviving the Tsunami: What Sri Lanka's animals knew that humans didn't" (http://www.slate.com/id/2111608). Slate Magazine. .

[30] Forecast of earthquake probability is within 30 years ahead, however Tsunami attack probability is much lower than earthquake so that the plan is set to be within 100 years ahead. Yomiuri Shimbun 2011-05-13 ver.13S page 2, "津波の襲来確率、初の公表へ…地震調査委員会 [Newly public announce of Tsunami attack probability...Earthquake Research committee of Japan]" (http://www.yomiuri.co.jp/science/news/20110512-OYT1T00947.htm) (in Japanese). *Yomiuri Shimbun*. 2011-05-12. . Retrieved 2011-05-13.

[31] IndiaTimes (http://oneclick.indiatimes.com/photo/03XDbnv4J99vW?q=Tokyo) Kunihiko Shimazaki speaks during a press conference in Tokyo Thursday, May 12, 2011

[32] "Experts: Early warnings mitigated Japan disaster" (http://www.miamiherald.com/2011/05/12/2213495/experts-early-warnings-mitigated.html). *The Miami Herald*. 2011-05-12. . Retrieved 2011-05-14.

[33] http://content.hks.harvard.edu/journalistsresource/pa/society/health/tsunami-japan/

[34] "1993年7月12日 北海道南西沖地震" (http://library.skr.jp/19930712_nanseioki.htm) (in Japanese). .

[35] "The Hauraki Gulf Marine Park, Part 2". *Inset to The New Zealand Herald*: p. 9. 3 March 2010.

References

- IOC Tsunami Glossary (http://ioc3.unesco.org/itic/contents.php?id=19) by the Intergovernmental Oceanographic Commission (IOC) at the International Tsunami Information Centre (http://ioc3.unesco.org/itic/) (ITIC) of UNESCO

- Tsunami Terminology (http://nthmp-history.pmel.noaa.gov/terms.html) at NOAA

- abelard.org. (http://www.abelard.org/briefings/tsunami.php) *tsunamis: tsunamis travel fast but not at infinite speed*. retrieved March 29, 2005.

- Dudley, Walter C. & Lee, Min (1988: 1st edition) *Tsunami!* ISBN 0-8248-1125-9 website (http://www.tsunami.org/references.htm#Books)

- Iwan, W.D., *editor*, 2006, Summary report of the Great Sumatra Earthquakes and Indian Ocean tsunamis of December 26, 2004 and March 28, 2005: Earthquake Engineering Research Institute, EERI Publication #2006-06, 11 chapters, 100 page summary, plus CD-ROM with complete text and supplementary photographs, EERI Report 2006-06. ISBN 1-932884-19-X website (http://www.eeri.org/)

- Kenneally, Christine (December 30, 2004). "Surviving the Tsunami." *Slate*. website (http://www.slate.com/id/2111608/)

- Lambourne, Helen (March 27, 2005). "Tsunami: Anatomy of a disaster." *BBC News*. website (http://news.bbc.co.uk/1/hi/sci/tech/4381395.stm)

- Macey, Richard (January 1, 2005). "The Big Bang that Triggered A Tragedy," *The Sydney Morning Herald*, p 11—quoting Dr Mark Leonard, seismologist at Geoscience Australia.

- The NOAA's page on the 2004 Indian Ocean earthquake and tsunami (http://www.ngdc.noaa.gov/spotlight/tsunami/tsunami.html)

- Tappin, D; 2001. Local tsunamis. Geoscientist. 11–8, 4–7.

- Girl, 10, used geography lesson to save lives (http://www.telegraph.co.uk/news/1480192/Girl-10-used-geography-lesson-to-save-lives.html), *Telegraph.co.uk*

- Philippines warned to prepare for Japan's tsunami (http://www.noypi.ph/index.php/nation/3283-key-locations-in-philippines-warned-to-prepare-for-tsunami.html), *Noypi.ph*

External links

- Animation of DART tsunami detection system (http://nctr.pmel.noaa.gov/Mov/DART_04.swf)
- Can HF Radar detect Tsunamis? (http://ifmaxp1.ifm.uni-hamburg.de/tsunami.shtml) − University of Hamburg HF-Radar.
- Envirtech Tsunami Warning System (http://www.envirtech.org/envirtech_tsunameter.htm) − Based on seabed seismics and sea level gauges.
- Geology.com (http://geology.com/records/biggest-tsunami.shtml) *The highest tsunami was caused by rockfall*
- IOC Tsunami Glossary (http://ioc3.unesco.org/itic/contents.php?id=19) by the Intergovernmental Oceanographic Commission (IOC) at the International Tsunami Information Centre (http://ioc3.unesco.org/itic/) (ITIC) of UNESCO
- How to survive a tsunami (http://www.edu4hazards.org/tsunami.html) − Guide for children and youth
- International Centre for Geohazards (ICG) (http://www.geohazards.no/)
- ITSU (http://ioc.unesco.org/itsu/) − Coordination Group for the Pacific Tsunami Warning System.
- Jakarta Tsunami Information Centre (http://www.jtic.org/)
- National Tsunami Hazard Mitigation Program (http://nthmp.tsunami.gov/) *Coordinated U.S. Federal/State effort*
- NOAA Center for Tsunami Research (NCTR) (http://nctr.pmel.noaa.gov/)
- NOAA Tsunami (http://www.tsunami.noaa.gov/) − General description of tsunamis and the United States agency NOAA's role
- NOVA: Wave That Shook The World (http://www.pbs.org/nova/tsunami/) − Site and special report shot within days of the 2004 Indian Ocean tsunami.
- Pacific Tsunami Museum (http://www.tsunami.org/)
- *Science of Tsunami Hazards* journal (http://www.sthjournal.org/)
- Tsunami scientific publications list (http://nctr.pmel.noaa.gov/pubs.html)
- Scientific American Magazine (January 2006 Issue) Tsunami: Wave of Change (http://sciam.com/article.cfm?chanID=sa006&articleID=000CDB86-32E0-13A8-B2E083414B7F0000) What we can learn from the Indian Ocean tsunami of December 2004.
- Social & Economic Costs of Tsunamis in the United States (http://www.ncdc.noaa.gov/oa/esb/?goal=weather&file=events/tsunami/) from "NOAA Socioeconomics" website initiative
- Tsunami Centers (http://tsunami.gov/) − United States National Weather Service.
- Tsunami database with detailed statistics (http://tsunami.name/)
- Interactive map of recent and historical tsunami events (http://nctr.pmel.noaa.gov/database_devel.html) *with links to graphics, animations and data*
- Tsunami Warning (http://tsunami-warning.org/) − Tsunami warnings via mobile phone.
- Tsunamis and Earthquakes (http://walrus.wr.usgs.gov/tsunami/)
- USGS: Surviving a tsunami (http://pubs.usgs.gov/circ/c1187/) (United States)
- Impact of Tsunami on groundwater resources (http://www.igrac.net/publications/134) IGRAC International Groundwater Resources Assessment Centre
- Tsunami Surges on Dry Coastal Plains: Application of Dam Break Wave Equations (http://espace.library.uq.edu.au/view.php?pid=UQ:7781), Coastal Engineering Journal, 48 4: 355-370

Images, video, and animations

- **Tsunami videos on YouTube** (http://www.youtube.com/noaapmel#p/c/3BDBAAAA7D4EB2DA/8/ 4rWDrZIucAQ) from the NOAA Center for Tsunami Research (http://nctr.pmel.noaa.gov)
- Amateur Camcorder Video Streams of the December 26, 2004 tsunami that hit Sri Lanka, Thailand and Indonesia (search on tsunamis) (http://www.archive.org/details/opensource_movies)
- Animation of 1960 tsunami originating outside coast of Chile (http://www.geophys.washington.edu/tsunami/ general/physics/characteristics.html)
- Animations of actual and simulated tsunami events (http://nctr.pmel.noaa.gov/animate.html) from the NOAA Center for Tsunami Research
- CBC Digital Archives – Canada's Earthquakes and Tsunamis (http://archives.cbc.ca/IDD-1-75-1561/ science_technology/earthquakes_and_tsunamis/)
- Computer-generated animation of a tsunami (http://www.geophys.washington.edu/tsunami/general/physics/ runup.html)
- Origin of a Tsunami – animation showing how the shifting of continental plates in the Indian Ocean created the catastrophe of December 26, 2004. (http://www.forskning.no/Artikler/2006/juni/1149444923.73)
- Photos (http://www.mindef.gov.sg/tsunami/photos1.asp) and Videos (http://www.mindef.gov.sg/tsunami/ videos.asp) of Humanitarian Assistance to Tsunami-hit areas by the Singapore Armed Forces
- Tsunami Aftermath in Penang (http://thanks4supporting.us/tsunami-aftermath-penang-island-malaysia.html) and Kuala Muda, Kedah (http://thanks4supporting.us/visit-to-kota-kuala-muda.html).
- Satellite Images of Tsunami Affected Areas (http://www.crisp.nus.edu.sg/tsunami/tsunami.html) High resolution satellite images showing the effects of the 2004 tsunami on the affected areas in Indonesia, Thailand and Nicobar island of India.
- The Survivors – A moving travelogue full of stunning images along the tsunami ravaged South-Western Coast of India (http://www.riveroflife.be/tsunami/index.html) (Unavailable)
- Animations of tsunami propagation model results (http://nctr.pmel.noaa.gov/animate.html) *for actual tsunami events*
- 2004 Boxing Day Tsunami (http://www.youtube.com/watch?v=RDOuwMj7Xzo&feature=PlayList& p=F78585C6FE0C11CA&playnext=1&playnext_from=PL&index=81) at YouTube
- Raw Video: Tsunami Slams Northeast Japan (http://www.youtube.com/watch?v=k4w27IczOTk), a video of the 2011 Tōhoku (Japan) earthquake tsunami by Associated Press at YouTube, showing the wave from a tsunami engulfing a town and farmlands.

Tsunamis in lakes

A tsunami is defined as a series of water waves caused by the displacement of a large volume of a body of water, such as an ocean. This is misleading as destructive water waves are not restricted to the ocean, in the case of this article the body of water being investigated will be a lake rather than an ocean. **Tsunamis in lakes** are becoming increasingly important to investigate as a hazard, due to the increasing popularity for recreational uses, and increasing populations that inhabit the shores of lakes. Tsunamis generated in lakes and reservoirs are of high concern because it is associated with a near field source region which means a decrease in warning times to minutes or hours.

Causes

Inland tsunami hazards can be generated by many different types of earth movement, these are earthquakes in or around lake systems, landslides, debris flow, rock avalanches glacier calving and volcanogenic processes such as gas or mass flow characteristics, these are discussed in more detail below.

Earthquakes

Tsunamis in lakes can be generated by fault displacement beneath or around lake systems. Faulting shifts the ground in a vertical motion through reverse, normal or oblique strike slip faulting processes, this displaces the water above causing a tsunami (Figure 1). The reason strike-slip faulting does not cause tsunamis is because there is no vertical displacement within the fault movement, only lateral movement resulting in no displacement of the water. In an enclosed basin such as a lake, tsunamis are referred to as the initial wave produced by coseismic displacement from an earthquake, and the seiche as the harmonic resonance within the lake.[1]

In order for a tsunami to be generated certain criteria is required:

- Needs to occur just below the lake bottom.
- Earthquake is of high or moderate magnitude typically over magnitude four.
- Displaces a large enough volume of water to generate a tsunami.

These tsunamis are of high damage potential due to being within a lake, making them of a near field source. This means a vast decrease in warning times, resulting in organised emergency evacuations after the generation of the tsunami being virtually impossible, and due to low lying shores even small waves lead to substantial flooding.[2] Planning and education of residents needs to be done beforehand, so that when an earthquake is felt they know to head to higher ground and what routes to take to get there.

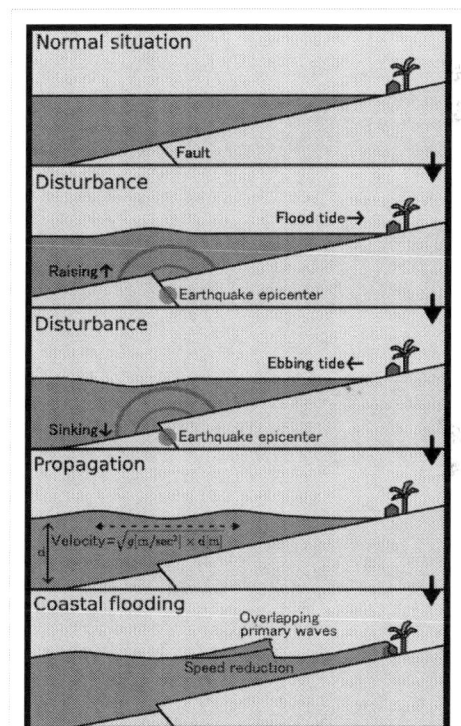

Figure 1: Diagram showing how earthquakes can generate a tsunami.

Lake Tahoe

Lake Tahoe is an example of a lake that is in danger of having a tsunami due to faulting processes. Lake Tahoe in California and Nevada USA lies within an intermountain basin bounded by faults, with most of these faults at the lake bottom or hidden in glaicofluvial deposits. Lake Tahoe has had many prehistoric eruptions and in studies of the lake bottom sediments, a 10m high scarp has displaced the lake bottom sediments, indicating that the water was displaced by the same magnitude, as well as generating a tsunami. A tsunami and seiche in Lake Tahoe can be treated as shallow-water long waves as the maximum water depth is much smaller than the wavelength. This demonstrates the interesting impact that lakes have on the tsunami wave characteristics, as it is very different to ocean tsunami wave characteristics due to the ocean being deeper, and lakes being relatively shallow in comparison. With ocean tsunami waves amplitudes only increase when the tsunami gets close to shore, in lake tsunami waves are generated and stay in a shallow environment.

This would have a major impact on the 34,000 permanent residences along the lake, not to mention the impact on tourism in the area. Tsunami run-ups would leave areas near the lake inundated due to permanent ground subsidence attributed to the earthquake, with the highest run-ups and amplitudes being attributed to the seiches rather than the actual tsunami. The reason seiches cause so much damage is due to resonance within the bays reflecting the waves were they combine to make larger standing waves. For more information see seiches.[3]

Sub-aerial mass flows

Sub aerial mass flows happen when a large amount of sediment becomes unstable, this can happen for example from the shaking from an earthquake, or saturation of the sediment initiating a sliding layer. This volume of sediment then flows into the lake giving a sudden large displacement of water. Tsunamis generated by sub aerial mass flows are defined in terms of the first initial wave being the tsunami wave and any tsunamis in terms of sub aerial mass flows are characterised into three zones. A splash zone or wave generation zone, this is the region were landslides and water motion are coupled and it extends as far as the landslide travels. Near field area, were the concern is based on the characteristics of the tsunami wave such as amplitude and wave length which are crucial for predictive purposes. Far field area, the process is influenced mainly by dispersion characteristics and is not often used when investigating tsunamis in lakes, as most lake tsunamis are related only to near field processes.[4]

New Zealand example

In the event of the Alpine fault in New Zealand rupturing in the South Island, it is predicted that there would be shaking of approximately magnitude eight in the lake side towns of Queenstown (Lake Wakatipu) and Wanaka (Lake Wanaka). These could possibly cause sub-aerial mass flows that could generate tsunamis within the lakes, this would have a devastating impact on the 15,453 residents (2006 Census) who occupy these lake towns, not only in the potential losses of life and property, but the damage to the booming tourism industry would take years to rebuild.

The Otago Regional Council, responsible for the area, has recognised that in such an event, tsunamis could occur in both lakes but have yet to learn any more about it. This is interesting as if an event was to happen in peak seasons such as summer around Christmas, or in the snow season when the population of these areas nearly double, it would pose a huge management issue. The reason for this huge management issue is the volume of people in these areas would be unknown and supplies and aid would be insufficient. In summer a lot of temporary structures such as tents are put up on the lake shore, these tents provide no protection from a tsunami wave. This is why it is so important to investigate what would happen in such an event so that people can be educated in order to reduce vulnerability in these areas.

Volcanogenic processes

In this article the focus is on tsunamis generated in lakes by volcanogenic processes in terms of gas build up causing violent lake over turns, with other processes such as pyroclastic flows not accounted for, as it requires more complex modelling . Lake overturns can be incredibly dangerous and occur when gas trapped at the bottom of the lake is heated by rising magma causing an explosion and lake overturn, an Example of this is Lake Kivu.

Lake Kivu

Lake Kivu as seen in Figure 2 of Africa's great lakes, it lies on the border between the Democratic Republic of the Congo and Rwanda as shown in Figure 2, and is part of the Great Rift Valley. Being part of the Great Rift Valley means it is affected by volcanic activity beneath the lake, this has led to a build up of methane and carbon dioxide at the bottom of the lake, this build up can lead to violent lake overturns.

Lake over turns are due to volcanic interaction with the water at the bottom of the lake that has high gas concentrations, this leads to heating of the lake and this rapid rise in temperature would spark a methane explosion displacing a large amount of water, followed nearly

Figure 2: Satellite image of Lake Kivu in Africa.

simultaneously by a release of carbon dioxide. This carbon dioxide would suffocate large numbers of people, with a possible tsunami generated from water displaced by the gas explosion effecting all of the 2 million people who occupy the shores of Lake Kivu.[5] This is incredibly important as the warning times for an event such as a lake overturn is incredibly short in the order of minutes and the event itself may not even be noticed. Education of locals and preparation is crucial in this case and a lot of research in this area has been done in order to try to understand what is happening within the lake, in order to try to reduce the effects when this phenomenon does happen.

A lake turn-over in Lake Kivu occurs from one of two scenarios. Either (1) up to another hundred years of gas accumulation leads to gas saturation in the lake, resulting in a spontaneous outburst of gas originating at the depth at which gas saturation has exceeded 100%, or (2) a volcanic or even seismic event triggers a turn-over. In either case a strong vertical lift of a large body of water results in a plume of gas bubbles and water rising up to and through the water surface. As the bubbling water column draws in fresh gas-laden water, the bubbling water column widens and becomes more energetic as a virtual "chain reaction" occurs which would look like a watery volcano. Very large volumes of water are displaced, vertically at first, then horizontally away from the centre at surface and horizontally inwards to the bottom of the bubbling water column, feeding in fresh gas-laden water. The speed of the rising column of water increases until it has the potential to rise 25m or more in the centre above lake level. The water column has the potential to widen to well in excess of a kilometre, in a violent disturbance of the whole lake. The watery volcano may take as much as a day to fully develop while it releases upwards of 400 billion cubic metres of gas (~12tcf). Some of these parameters are uncertain, particularly the time taken to release the gas and the height to which the water column can rise. As a secondary effect, particularly if the water column behaves irregularly with a series of surges, the lake surface will both rise by up to several metres and create a series of tsunamis or waves radiating away from the epicentre of the eruption. Surface waters may simultaneously race away from the epicentre at speeds as high as 20-40m/second, slowing as distances from the centre increase. The size of the waves created is unpredictable. Wave heights will be highest if the water column surges periodically, resulting in wave heights is great as 10-20m. This is caused by the ever-shifting pathway that the vertical column takes to the surface. No reliable model exists to predict this overall turnover behaviour. For tsunami precautions it will be necessary for people to move to high ground, at least 20m above lake level. A worse situation may pertain in the Ruzizi River where a surge in lake level would cause flash-flooding of the steeply sloping river valley dropping 700m to Lake Tanganyika, where it is possible that a wall of water from 20-50m high may race down the gorge. Water is not the only problem for residents of the Kivu basin; the more than 400 billion cubic metres of gas released creates a denser-than-air cloud which may blanket the whole valley to a depth of 300m or more. The presence of this opaque gas cloud, which would suffocate any living creatures with its mixture of carbon dioxide and methane laced with hydrogen sulphide, would cause the majority of casualties. Residents would be advised to climb to at least 400m above the lake level to ensure their safety. Strangely the risk of a gas explosion is not great as the gas cloud is only about 20% methane in carbon dioxide, a mixture that is difficult to ignite.

Hazard mitigation

Hazard mitigation for tsunamis in lakes is immensely important in the preservation of life, infrastructure and property. In order for hazard management of tsunamis in lakes to function at full capacity there are four aspects that need to be balanced and interacted with each other, these are:

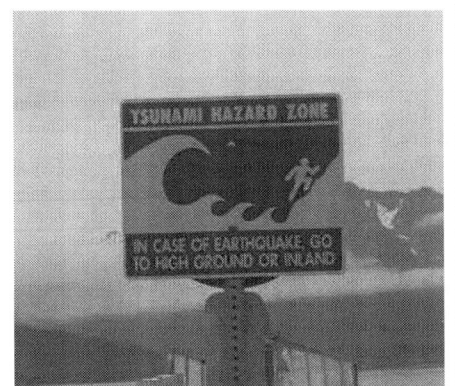

Figure 3: photo of a Tsunami Hazard Zone warning sign in Bamfield.

- **Readiness** (preparedness for a tsunami in the lake)

  - Evacuation plans
  - Making sure equipment and supplies are on standby in case of a tsunami
  - Education of locals on what hazard is posed to them and what they need to do in the event of a tsunami in the lake such as seen in Figure 3.

- **Response** to the tsunami event in the lake

  - Rescue operations
  - Getting aid into the area such as food and medical equipment
  - Providing temporary housing for people who have been displaced.

- **Recovery** from the tsunami

  - Re-establishing damaged road networks and infrastructure
  - Re-building and/or relocation for damaged buildings
  - Clean up of debris and flooded areas of land.

- **Reduction** (plans to reduce the effects of the next tsunami)

  - Putting in place land use zoning to provide a buffer for tsunami run ups, meaning that buildings cannot be built right on the lake shore.

When all these aspects are taken into consideration and continually managed and maintained, the vulnerability of an area to a tsunami within the lake decreases. This is not because the hazard its self has decreased but the awareness of the people who would be affected makes them more prepared to deal with the situation when it does occur. This reduces recovery and response times for an area, decreasing the amount of disruption and in turn the effect the disaster has on the community.

Future research

Investigation into the phenomena of tsunamis in lakes for this article was restricted by certain limitations. Internationally there has been a fair amount of research into certain lakes but not all lakes that can be affected by the phenomenon have been covered. This is especially true for New Zealand with the possible occurrence of tsunamis in our major lakes recognised as a hazard, but with no further research completed.

The reports found from international examples were extremely useful as individual case studies, but due to different definitions for lake tsunamis depending on generation source and different equations for predictions. This made it hard to correlate the different events to see if some general rules can be obtained in terms of wave dynamics and propagation. It is increasingly important that further knowledge is gained on tsunamis in lakes, not only for scientific purposes but also to relay this information to the people who would be affected if a lake tsunami was to occur. The hazard of tsunamis and associated seiches will not stop increasing, more and more people are making themselves vulnerable to this hazard, and due to lack of knowledge and growing populations the devastation when one does occur will be incomprehendable. Increasing knowledge of tsunamis in lakes and what to do in an event of a tsunami will not only makes us more prepared, it will save lives.

Footnotes

[1] Ichinose .G.A, et al; 2000
[2] Freundt Armin et al. 2007
[3] Ichinose .G.A, et al; 2000
[4] Walder J.S, et al; 2003
[5] Volcano Facts (http://www.volcanolive.com/news16.htm)

References

* Walder J.S, et al; 2003; Tsunamis generated by subaerial mass flows; JOURNAL OF GEOPHYSICAL RESEARCH, VOL. 108, NO. B5, 2236, doi:10.1029/2001JB000707

* Ichinose G.A, et al; 2000; The potential hazard from tsunami and seiche waves generated by large earthquakes within Lake Tahoe, California-Nevada; GEOPHYSICAL RESEARCH LETTERS, VOL XX, NO. X, PAGES XXXX-XXXX

* Freundt Armin et al. 2007; Volcanogenic tsunamis in lakes : Examples from Nicaragua and general implications; Pure and Applied Geophysics; ISSN 0033-4553,CODEN PAGYAV, Springer, Basel, SUISSE (1964) (Revue)

Risk

Risk is the potential that a chosen action or activity (including the choice of inaction) will lead to a loss (an undesirable outcome). The notion implies that a choice having an influence on the outcome exists (or existed). Potential losses themselves may also be called "risks". Almost any human endeavour carries some risk, but some are much more risky than others.

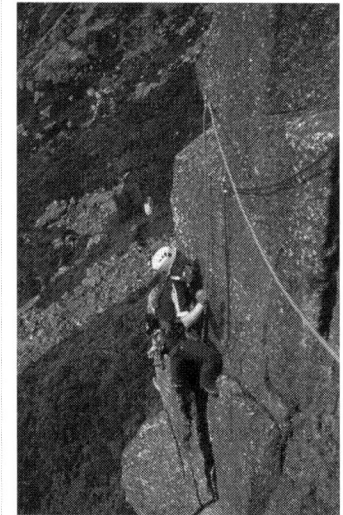

In activities such as rock climbing, participants are consciously taking risk.

Historical background

The Oxford English Dictionary cites the earliest use of the word in English (in the spelling of *risque*) as from 1621, and the spelling as *risk* from 1655. It defines *risk* as:

> (Exposure to) the possibility of loss, injury, or other adverse or unwelcome circumstance; a chance or situation involving such a possibility.[1]

For the sociologist Niklas Luhmann the term 'risk' is a neologism that appeared with the transition from traditional to modern society.[2] "In the Middle Ages the term *risicum* was used in highly specific contexts, above all sea trade and its ensuing legal problems of loss and damage."[2] [3] In the vernacular languages of the 16th century the words *rischio* and *riezgo* were used.[2] This was introduced to continental Europe, through interaction with Middle Eastern and North African Arab traders. In the English language the term *risk* appeared only in the 17th century, and "seems to be imported from continental Europe."[2] When the terminology of *risk* took ground, it replaced the older notion that thought "in terms of good and bad fortune."[2] Niklas Luhmann (1996) seeks to explain this transition: "Perhaps, this was simply a loss of plausibility of the old rhetorics of *Fortuna* as an allegorical figure of religious content and of *prudentia* as a (noble) virtue in the emerging commercial society."[4]

Scenario analysis matured during Cold War confrontations between major powers, notably the United States and the Soviet Union. It became widespread in insurance circles in the 1970s when major oil tanker disasters forced a more comprehensive foresight. The scientific approach to risk entered finance in the 1960s with the advent of the capital asset pricing model and became increasingly important in the 1980s when financial derivatives proliferated. It reached general professions in the 1990s when the power of personal computing allowed for widespread data collection and numbers crunching.

Governments are using it, for example, to set standards for environmental regulation, e.g. "pathway analysis" as practiced by the United States Environmental Protection Agency.

Definitions of risk

The many inconsistent and ambiguous meanings attached to "risk" lead to widespread confusion and also mean that very different approaches to risk management are taken in different fields.[5] For example:

> The ISO 31000 (2009) /ISO Guide 73 definition of risk is the 'effect of uncertainty on objectives'. In this definition, uncertainties include events (which may or not happen) and uncertainties caused by a lack of information or ambiguity. This definition also includes both negative and positive impacts on objectives.

> Another definition is that risks are future problems that can be avoided or mitigated, rather than current ones that must be immediately addressed.[6]

Risk can be seen as relating to the Probability of uncertain future events.[7] . For example, according to Factor Analysis of Information Risk, risk is:[7] the probable frequency and probable magnitude of future loss. In computer science this definition is used by The Open Group.[8]

OHSAS (Occupational Health & Safety Advisory Services) defines risk as the product of the probability of a hazard resulting in an adverse event, times the severity of the event.[9]

In information security risk is defined as "the potential that a given threat will exploit vulnerabilities of an asset or group of assets and thereby cause harm to the organization",[10]

Financial risk is often defined as the unexpected variability or volatility of returns and thus includes both potential worse-than-expected as well as better-than-expected returns. References to negative risk below should be read as applying to positive impacts or opportunity (e.g., for "loss" read "loss or gain") unless the context precludes this interpretation.

The related term "hazard" is used to mean something that could cause harm.

As risk carries so many different meanings there are many formal methods used to assess or to "measure" risk. Some of the quantitative definitions of risk are well-grounded in statistics theory and lead naturally to statistical estimates, but some are more subjective. For example in many cases a critical factor is human decision making.

Even when statistical estimates are available, in many cases risk is associated with rare failures of some kind, and data may be sparse. Often, the probability of a negative event is estimated by using the frequency of past similar events or by event tree methods, but probabilities for rare failures may be difficult to estimate if an event tree cannot be formulated. This makes risk assessment difficult in hazardous industries (for example nuclear energy) where the frequency of failures is rare and harmful consequences of failure are very high.

Statistical methods may also require the use of a Cost function, which in turn often requires the calculation of the cost of the loss of human life, a difficult problem. One approach is to ask what people are willing to pay to insure against death,[11] and radiological release (e.g., GBq of radio-iodine), but as the answers depend very strongly on the circumstances it is not clear that this approach is effective.

Mathematical formulations

In statistics, the notion of risk is often modelled as the expected value of some outcome seen as undesirable. This combines the probabilities of various possible events and some assessment of the corresponding harms into a single value. (See also Expected utility.) In a formula that can be used in the simple case of a binary possibility (accident or no accident), risk is then:

$$\text{Risk} = (\text{probability of the accident occurring}) \times (\text{expected loss in case of the accident})$$

For example: if activity X may suffer an accident of A at a probability of 0.01 with a loss of 1000, the total risk is a loss of 10, since that is the product of 0.01 and 1 000.

In case of there being several possible accidents, risk is the sum of the all risks for the different accidents, provided that the outcomes are comparable:

$$\text{Risk} = \sum^{\textit{Accidents}} ((\text{probability of the accident occurring}) \times (\text{expected loss in case of the accident}))$$

For example: if activity X may suffer an accident of A at a probability of 0.01 with a loss of 1000, and an accident of type B at probability of 0.000 001 at a loss of 2 000 000, the total risk is a loss of 12, that is 10 from accident of types A and 2 from accidents of type B.

One of the first major uses of this concept was at the planning of the Delta Works in 1953, a flood protection program in the Netherlands, with the aid of the mathematician David van Dantzig.[12] The kind of risk analysis pioneered here has become common today in fields like nuclear power, aerospace and the chemical industry.

In statistical decision theory, the risk function is defined as the expected value of a given loss function as a function of the decision rule used to make decisions in the face of uncertainty.

Risk versus uncertainty

Risk: Combination of the likelihood of an occurrence of a hazardous event or exposure(s) and the severity of injury or ill health that can be caused by the event or exposure(s)

In his seminal work *Risk, Uncertainty, and Profit*, Frank Knight (1921) established the distinction between risk and uncertainty.

> " ". Uncertainty must be taken in a sense radically distinct from the familiar notion of Risk, from which it has never been properly separated. The term "risk," as loosely used in everyday speech and in economic discussion, really covers two things which, functionally at least, in their causal relations to the phenomena of economic organization, are categorically different. ... The essential fact is that "risk" means in some cases a quantity susceptible of measurement, while at other times it is something distinctly not of this character; and there are far-reaching and crucial differences in the bearings of the phenomenon depending on which of the two is really present and operating. ... It will appear that a measurable uncertainty, or "risk" proper, as we shall use the term, is so far different from an unmeasurable one that it is not in effect an uncertainty at all. We ... accordingly restrict the term "uncertainty" to cases of the non-quantitive type.:[13]

Thus, Knightian uncertainty is immeasurable, not possible to calculate, while in the Knightian sense risk is measurable.

Another distinction between risk and uncertainty is proposed in *How to Measure Anything: Finding the Value of Intangibles in Business* and *The Failure of Risk Management: Why It's Broken and How to Fix It* by Doug Hubbard:[14] [15]

> **Uncertainty**: The lack of complete certainty, that is, the existence of more than one possibility. The "true" outcome/state/result/value is not known.

> **Measurement of uncertainty**: A set of probabilities assigned to a set of possibilities. Example: "There is a 60% chance this market will double in five years"

> **Risk**: A state of uncertainty where some of the possibilities involve a loss, catastrophe, or other undesirable outcome.

> **Measurement of risk**: A set of possibilities each with quantified probabilities and quantified losses. Example: "There is a 40% chance the proposed oil well will be dry with a loss of $12 million in exploratory drilling costs".

In this sense, Hubbard uses the terms so that one may have uncertainty without risk but not risk without uncertainty. We can be uncertain about the winner of a contest, but unless we have some personal stake in it, we have no risk. If we bet money on the outcome of the contest, then we have a risk. In both cases there are more than one outcome. The measure of uncertainty refers only to the probabilities assigned to outcomes, while the measure of risk requires both probabilities for outcomes and losses quantified for outcomes.

Risk as a vector quantity

Hubbard also argues that defining risk as the product of impact and probability presumes (probably incorrectly) that the decision makers are risk neutral.[15] Only for a risk neutral person is the "certain monetary equivalent" exactly equal to the probability of the loss times the amount of the loss. For example, a risk neutral person would consider 20% chance of winning $1 million exactly equal to $200,000 (or a 20% chance of losing $1 million to be exactly equal to losing $200,000). However, most decision makers are not actually risk neutral and would not consider these equivalent choices. This gave rise to Prospect theory and Cumulative prospect theory. Hubbard proposes instead that risk is a kind of "vector quantity" that does not collapse the probability and magnitude of a risk by presuming anything about the risk tolerance of the decision maker. Risks are simply described as a set or function of possible loss amounts each associated with specific probabilities. How this array is collapsed into a single value cannot be done until the risk tolerance of the decision maker is quantified.

Risk can be both negative and positive, but it tends to be the negative side that people focus on. This is because some things can be dangerous, such as putting their own or someone else's life at risk. Risks concern people as they think that they will have a negative effect on their future.

Insurance and health risk

Insurance is a risk-reducing investment in which the buyer pays a small fixed amount to be protected from a potential large loss. Gambling is a risk-increasing investment, wherein money on hand is risked for a possible large return, but with the possibility of losing it all. Purchasing a lottery ticket is a very risky investment with a high chance of no return and a small chance of a very high return. In contrast, putting money in a bank at a defined rate of interest is a risk-averse action that gives a guaranteed return of a small gain and precludes other investments with possibly higher gain.

Risks in personal health may be reduced by primary prevention actions that decrease early causes of illness or by secondary prevention actions after a person has clearly measured clinical signs or symptoms recognized as risk factors. Tertiary prevention reduces the negative impact of an already established disease by restoring function and reducing disease-related complications. Ethical medical practice requires careful discussion of risk factors with individual patients to obtain informed consent for secondary and tertiary prevention efforts, whereas public health efforts in primary prevention require education of the entire population at risk. In each case, careful communication about risk factors, likely outcomes and certainty must distinguish between causal events that must be decreased and associated events that may be merely consequences rather than causes.

Information technology risk

Information technology risk, or **IT risk**, **IT-related risk**, is a risk related to information technology. This relatively new term due to an increasing awareness that information security is simply one facet of a multitude of risks that are relevant to IT and the real world processes it supports.

The increasing dependencies of modern society on information and computers networks (both in private and public sectors, including military)[16] [17] [18] has led to a new terms like IT risk and Cyberwarfare.

Information security risk

Information security means protecting information and information systems from unauthorized access, use, disclosure, disruption, modification, perusal, inspection, recording or destruction.[19]

Information security grew out of practices and procedures of computer security.

Information security has grown to **information assurance (IA)** i.e. is the practice of managing risks related to the use, processing, storage, and transmission of information or data and the systems and processes used for those purposes.

While focused dominantly on information in digital form, the full range of IA encompasses not only digital but also analog or physical form.

Information assurance is interdisciplinary and draws from multiple fields, including accounting, fraud examination, forensic science, management science, systems engineering, security engineering, and criminology, in addition to computer science.

So, *IT risk* is narrowly focused on computer security, while *information security* extends on risks related to other forms of information (paper, microfilm). *Information assurance* risks include the ones related to the consistency of the business information stored in IT systems and the one stored on other means and the relevant business consequences.

Economic risk

Economic risks can be manifested in lower incomes or higher expenditures than expected. The causes can be many, for instance, the hike in the price for raw materials, the lapsing of deadlines for construction of a new operating facility, disruptions in a production process, emergence of a serious competitor on the market, the loss of key personnel, the change of a political regime, or natural disasters.[20] Reference class forecasting was developed to eliminate or reduce economic risk.[21]

In business

Means of assessing risk vary widely between professions. Indeed, they may define these professions; for example, a doctor manages medical risk, while a civil engineer manages risk of structural failure. A professional code of ethics is usually focused on risk assessment and mitigation (by the professional on behalf of client, public, society or life in general).

In the workplace, incidental and inherent risks exist. Incidental risks are those that occur naturally in the business but are not part of the core of the business. Inherent risks have a negative effect on the operating profit of the business.

Risk-sensitive industries

Some industries manage risk in a highly quantified and enumerated way. These include the nuclear power and aircraft industries, where the possible failure of a complex series of engineered systems could result in highly undesirable outcomes. The usual measure of risk for a class of events is then:

R = probability of the event × C

The total risk is then the product of the individual class-risks.

In the nuclear industry, consequence is often measured in terms of off-site radiological release, and this is often banded into five or six decade-wide bands.

The risks are evaluated using fault tree/event tree techniques (see safety engineering). Where these risks are low, they are normally considered to be "Broadly Acceptable". A higher level of risk (typically up to 10 to 100 times what is considered Broadly Acceptable) has to be justified against the costs of reducing it further and the possible benefits that make it tolerable—these risks are described as "Tolerable if ALARP". Risks beyond this level are classified as "Intolerable".

The level of risk deemed Broadly Acceptable has been considered by regulatory bodies in various countries—an early attempt by UK government regulator and academic F. R. Farmer used the example of hill-walking and similar activities, which have definable risks that people appear to find acceptable. This resulted in the so-called Farmer Curve of acceptable probability of an event versus its consequence.

The technique as a whole is usually referred to as Probabilistic Risk Assessment (PRA) (or Probabilistic Safety Assessment, PSA). See WASH-1400 for an example of this approach.

In finance

In finance, risk is the probability that an investment's actual return will be different than expected. This includes the possibility of losing some or all of the original investment. In a view advocated by Damodaran, risk includes not only "downside risk" but also "upside risk" (returns that exceed expectations).[22] Some regard a calculation of the standard deviation of the historical returns or average returns of a specific investment as providing some historical measure of risk; see modern portfolio theory. Financial risk may be market-dependent, determined by numerous market factors, or operational, resulting from fraudulent behavior (e.g. Bernard Madoff). Recent studies suggest that testosterone level plays a major role in risk taking during financial decisions.[23] [24]

In finance, *risk* has no one definition, but some theorists, notably Ron Dembo, have defined quite general methods to assess risk as an expected after-the-fact level of regret. Such methods have been uniquely successful in limiting interest rate risk in financial markets. Financial markets are considered to be a proving ground for general methods of risk assessment. However, these methods are also hard to understand. The mathematical difficulties interfere with other social goods such as disclosure, valuation and transparency. In particular, it is not always obvious if such financial instruments are "hedging" (purchasing/selling a financial instrument specifically to reduce or cancel out the risk in another investment) or "speculation" (increasing measurable risk and exposing the investor to catastrophic loss in pursuit of very high windfalls that increase expected value).

As regret measures rarely reflect actual human risk-aversion, it is difficult to determine if the outcomes of such transactions will be satisfactory. Risk seeking describes an individual whose utility function's second derivative is positive. Such an individual would willingly (actually pay a premium to) assume all risk in the economy and is hence not likely to exist.

In financial markets, one may need to measure credit risk, information timing and source risk, probability model risk, and legal risk if there are regulatory or civil actions taken as a result of some "investor's regret". Knowing one's risk appetite in conjunction with one's financial well-being are most crucial.

A fundamental idea in finance is the relationship between risk and return (see modern portfolio theory). The greater the potential return one might seek, the greater the risk that one generally assumes. A free market reflects this principle in the pricing of an instrument: strong demand for a safer instrument drives its price higher (and its return proportionately lower), while weak demand for a riskier instrument drives its price lower (and its potential return thereby higher).

"For example, a US Treasury bond is considered to be one of the safest investments and, when compared to a corporate bond, provides a lower rate of return. The reason for this is that a corporation is much more likely to go bankrupt than the U.S. government. Because the risk of investing in a corporate bond is higher, investors are offered a higher rate of return."

The most popular, and also the most vilified lately risk measurement is Value-at-Risk (VaR). There are different types of VaR - Long Term VaR, Marginal VaR, Factor VaR and Shock VaR[25] The latter is used in measuring risk during the extreme market stress conditions.

In public works

In a peer reviewed study of risk in public works projects located in twenty nations on five continents, Flyvbjerg, Holm, and Buhl (2002, 2005) documented high risks for such ventures for both costs[26] and demand.[27] Actual costs of projects were typically higher than estimated costs; cost overruns of 50% were common, overruns above 100% not uncommon. Actual demand was often lower than estimated; demand shortfalls of 25% were common, of 50% not uncommon.

Due to such cost and demand risks, cost-benefit analyses of public works projects have proved to be highly uncertain.

The main causes of cost and demand risks were found to be optimism bias and strategic misrepresentation. Measures identified to mitigate this type of risk are better governance through incentive alignment and the use of reference class forecasting.[28]

In human services

Huge ethical and political issues arise when human beings themselves are seen or treated as 'risks', or when the risk decision making of people who use human services might have an impact on that service. The experience of many people who rely on human services for support is that 'risk' is often used as a reason to prevent them from gaining further independence or fully accessing the community, and that these services are often unnecessarily risk averse.[29]

Risk in psychology

Regret

In decision theory, regret (and anticipation of regret) can play a significant part in decision-making, distinct from risk aversion (preferring the status quo in case one becomes worse off).

Framing

Framing[30] is a fundamental problem with all forms of risk assessment. In particular, because of bounded rationality (our brains get overloaded, so we take mental shortcuts), the risk of extreme events is discounted because the probability is too low to evaluate intuitively. As an example, one of the leading causes of death is road accidents caused by drunk driving—partly because any given driver frames the problem by largely or totally ignoring the risk of a serious or fatal accident.

For instance, an extremely disturbing event (an attack by hijacking, or moral hazards) may be ignored in analysis despite the fact it has occurred and has a nonzero probability. Or, an event that everyone agrees is inevitable may be ruled out of analysis due to greed or an unwillingness to admit that it is believed to be inevitable. These human tendencies for error and wishful thinking often affect even the most rigorous applications of the scientific method and are a major concern of the philosophy of science.

All decision-making under uncertainty must consider cognitive bias, cultural bias, and notational bias: No group of people assessing risk is immune to "groupthink": acceptance of obviously wrong answers simply because it is socially painful to disagree, where there are conflicts of interest. One effective way to solve framing problems in risk assessment or measurement (although some argue that risk cannot be measured, only assessed) is to raise others' fears or personal ideals by way of completeness.

Neurobiology of framing

Framing involves other information that affects the outcome of a risky decision. The right prefrontal cortex has been shown to take a more global perspective[31] while greater left prefrontal activity relates to local or focal processing[32]

From the Theory of Leaky Modules[33] McElroy and Seta proposed that they could predictably alter the framing effect by the selective manipulation of regional prefrontal activity with finger tapping or monaural listening.[34] The result was as expected. Rightward tapping or listening had the effect of narrowing attention such that the frame was ignored. This is a practical way of manipulating regional cortical activation to affect risky decisions, especially because directed tapping or listening is easily done.

Fear as intuitive risk assessment

For the time being, people rely on their fear and hesitation to keep them out of the most profoundly unknown circumstances.

In *The Gift of Fear*, Gavin de Becker argues that "True fear is a gift. It is a survival signal that sounds only in the presence of danger. Yet unwarranted fear has assumed a power over us that it holds over no other creature on Earth. It need not be this way."

Risk could be said to be the way we collectively measure and share this "true fear"—a fusion of rational doubt, irrational fear, and a set of unquantified biases from our own experience.

The field of behavioral finance focuses on human risk-aversion, asymmetric regret, and other ways that human financial behavior varies from what analysts call "rational". Risk in that case is the degree of uncertainty associated with a return on an asset.

Recognizing and respecting the irrational influences on human decision making may do much to reduce disasters caused by naive risk assessments that pretend to rationality but in fact merely fuse many shared biases together.

Risk assessment and management

Because planned actions are subject to large cost and benefit risks, proper risk assessment and risk management for such actions are crucial to making them successful.[35]

Since risk assessment and management is essential in security management, both are tightly related. Security assessment methodologies like CRAMM contain risk assessment modules as an important part of the first steps of the methodology. On the other hand, risk assessment methodologies like Mehari evolved to become security assessment methodologies. A ISO standard on risk management (Principles and guidelines on implementation) was published under code ISO 31000 on 13 November 2009.

Risk and size

In the book *Megaprojects and Risk*, Professor Bent Flyvbjerg (with Nils Bruzelius and Werner Rothengatter) demonstrates that big ventures (big construction projects, big capital investments, etc.) are highly risky. For instance, such ventures typically have high cost overruns, benefit shortfalls, and schedule delays, plus negative and unanticipated social and environmental impacts.[36]

Risk in auditing

The audit risk model expresses the risk of an auditor providing an inappropriate opinion of a commercial entity's financial statements. It can be analytically expressed as:

$$AR = IR \times CR \times DR$$

Where AR is *audit risk*, IR is *inherent risk*, CR is *control risk* and DR is *detection risk*.

References

[1] Oxford English Dictionary

[2] Luhmann 1996:3.

[3] James Franklin, 2001: *The Science of Conjecture: Evidence and Probability Before Pascal*, Baltimore: Johns Hopkins University Press, 274.

[4] Luhmann 1996:4.

[5] Douglas Hubbard *The Failure of Risk Management: Why It's Broken and How to Fix It*, John Wiley & Sons, 2009.

[6] E.g. "Risk is the unwanted subset of a set of uncertain outcomes." (Cornelius Keating).

[7] "An Introduction to Factor Analysis of Information Risk (FAIR)", Risk Management Insight LLC, November 2006 (http://www.riskmanagementinsight.com/media/docs/FAIR_introduction.pdf);.

[8] Technical Standard Risk Taxonomy ISBN 1-931624-77-1 Document Number: C081 Published by The Open Group, January 2009.

[9] "Risk is a combination of the likelihood of an occurrence of a hazardous event or exposure(s) and the severity of injury or ill health that can be caused by the event or exposure(s)" (OHSAS 18001:2007).

[10] ISO/IEC 27005:2008.

[11] Landsburg, Steven (2003-03-03). "Is your life worth $10 million?" (http://www.slate.com/id/2079475/). *Everyday Economics* (Slate). . Retrieved 2008-03-17.

[12] Wired Magazine, Before the levees break (http://www.wired.com/science/planetearth/magazine/17-01/ff_dutch_delta?currentPage=3), page 3.

[13] Frank Hyneman Knight "Risk, uncertainty and profit" pg. 19, Hart, Schaffner, and Marx Prize Essays, no. 31. Boston and New York: Houghton Mifflin. 1921.

[14] Douglas Hubbard "How to Measure Anything: Finding the Value of Intangibles in Business" pg. 46, John Wiley & Sons, 2007.

[15] Douglas Hubbard "The Failure of Risk Management: Why It's Broken and How to Fix It, John Wiley & Sons, 2009.

[16] Cortada, James W. (2003-12-04) *The Digital Hand: How Computers Changed the Work of American Manufacturing, Transportation, and Retail Industries* USA: Oxford University Press pp. 512 ISBN 0195165888 .

[17] Cortada, James W. (2005-11-03) *The Digital Hand: Volume II: How Computers Changed the Work of American Financial, Telecommunicati ons, Media, and Entertainment Industries* USA: Oxford University Press ISBN 978-0195165876 .

[18] Cortada, James W. (2007-11-06) *The Digital Hand, Vol 3: How Computers Changed the Work of American Public Sector Industries* USA: Oxford University Press pp. 496 ISBN 978-0195165869 .

[19] 44 U.S.C. § 3542 (http://www.law.cornell.edu/uscode/44/3542.html)(b)(1).

[20] (http://ssrn.com/abstract=1012812).

[21] Flyvbjerg, B., 2008, "Curbing Optimism Bias and Strategic Misrepresentation in Planning: Reference Class Forecasting in Practice." European Planning Studies, vol. 16, no. 1, January, pp. 3-21 (http://www.sbs.ox.ac.uk/centres/bt/Documents/Curbing Optimism Bias and Strategic Misrepresentation.pdf).

[22] Damodaran, Aswath (2003). *Investment Philosophies: Successful Investment Philosophies and the Greatest Investors Who Made Them Work*. Wiley. p. 15. ISBN 0-471-34503-2.

[23] Sapienza P., Zingales L. and Maestripieri D. 2009. Gender differences in financial risk aversion and career choices are affected by testosterone. Proceedings of the National Academy of Sciences.

[24] Apicella C. L. and all. Testosterone and financial risk preferences. Evolution and Human Behavior. Vol 29. Issue 6. 384-390. abstract (http://www.ehbonline.org/article/S1090-5138(08)00067-6/abstract).

[25] Value at risk.

[26] http://flyvbjerg.plan.aau.dk/JAPAASPUBLISHED.pdf.

[27] http://flyvbjerg.plan.aau.dk/Traffic91PRINTJAPA.pdf.

[28] http://flyvbjerg.plan.aau.dk/0406DfT-UK%20OptBiasASPUBL.pdf.

[29] A Positive Approach To Risk Requires Person Centred Thinking, Neill et al, Tizard Learning Disability Review http://pierprofessional.metapress.com/content/vr700311x66j0125/

[30] Amos Tversky / Daniel Kahneman, 1981. "The Framing of Decisions and the Psychology of Choice."

[31] Schatz, J., Craft, S., Koby, M., & DeBaun, M. R. (2004). Asymmetries in visual-spatial processing following childhood stroke. Neuropsychology, 18, 340-352.

[32] Volberg, G., & Hubner, R. (2004). On the role of response conflicts and stimulus position for hemispheric differences in global/local processing: An ERP study. Neuropsychologia, 42, 1805-1813.

[33] Drake, R. A. (2004). Selective potentiation of proximal processes: Neurobiological mechanisms for spread of activation. Medical Science Monitor, 10, 231-234.

[34] McElroy, T., & Seta, J. J. (2004). On the other hand am I rational? Hemisphere activation and the framing effect. Brain and Cognition, 55, 572-580.

[35] Flyvbjerg 2006.

[36] Bent Flyvbjerg, Nils Bruzelius, and Werner Rothengatter, 2003, *Megaprojects and Risk: An Anatomy of Ambition* (Cambridge University Press) (http://www.amazon.co.uk/dp/0521009464).

Bibliography

Referred literature

- Bent Flyvbjerg, 2006: *From Nobel Prize to Project Management: Getting Risks Right.* Project Management Journal, vol. 37, no. 3, August, pp. 5–15. Available at homepage of author (http://flyvbjerg.plan.aau.dk/Publications2006/Nobel-PMJ2006.pdf).
- James Franklin, 2001: *The Science of Conjecture: Evidence and Probability Before Pascal*, Baltimore: Johns Hopkins University Press.
- Niklas Luhmann, 1996: *Modern Society Shocked by its Risks* (= University of Hong Kong, Department of Sociology Occasional Papers 17), Hong Kong, available via HKU Scholars HUB (http://hub.hku.hk/handle/123456789/38822).

Books

- Historian David A. Moss's book *When All Else Fails* (http://www.hup.harvard.edu/catalog/MOSWHE.html) explains the U.S. government's historical role as risk manager of last resort.
- Peter L. Bernstein. *Against the Gods* ISBN 0-471-29563-9. Risk explained and its appreciation by man traced from earliest times through all the major figures of their ages in mathematical circles.
- Rescher, Nicholas (1983). *A Philosophical Introduction to the Theory of Risk Evaluation and Measurement.* University Press of America.
- Porteous, Bruce T.; Pradip Tapadar (December 2005). *Economic Capital and Financial Risk Management for Financial Services Firms and Conglomerates.* Palgrave Macmillan. ISBN 1-4039-3608-0.
- Tom Kendrick (2003). *Identifying and Managing Project Risk: Essential Tools for Failure-Proofing Your Project.* AMACOM/American Management Association. ISBN 978-0814407615.
- Flyvbjerg, Bent, Nils Bruzelius, and Werner Rothengatter, 2003. *Megaprojects and Risk: An Anatomy of Ambition* (Cambridge: Cambridge University Press). (http://books.google.com/books?vid=ISBN0521009464&id=RAV5P-50UjEC&printsec=frontcover).
- David Hillson (2007). *Practical Project Risk Management: The Atom Methodology.* Management Concepts. ISBN 978-1567262025.
- Kim Heldman (2005). *Project Manager's Spotlight on Risk Management.* Jossey-Bass. ISBN 978-0782144116.
- Dirk Proske (2008). *Catalogue of risks - Natural, Technical, Social and Health Risks.* Springer. ISBN 978-3540795544.
- Gardner, Dan, *Risk: The Science and Politics of Fear* (http://books.google.com/books?id=5j_8xF8vUlAC&printsec=frontcover), Random House, Inc., 2008. ISBN 0771032994.

Articles and papers

- Clark, L., Manes, F., Antoun, N., Sahakian, B. J., & Robbins, T. W. (2003). "The contributions of lesion laterality and lesion volume to decision-making impairment following frontal lobe damage." *Neuropsychologia*, 41, 1474-1483.
- Drake, R. A. (1985). "Decision making and risk taking: Neurological manipulation with a proposed consistency mediation." *Contemporary Social Psychology*, 11, 149-152.
- Drake, R. A. (1985). "Lateral asymmetry of risky recommendations." *Personality and Social Psychology Bulletin*, 11, 409-417.
- Gregory, Kent J., Bibbo, Giovanni and Pattison, John E. (2005), "A Standard Approach to Measurement Uncertainties for Scientists and Engineers in Medicine", *Australasian Physical and Engineering Sciences in Medicine* **28**(2):131-139.

- Hansson, Sven Ove. (2007). "Risk" (http://plato.stanford.edu/entries/risk/), *The Stanford Encyclopedia of Philosophy* (Summer 2007 Edition), Edward N. Zalta (ed.), forthcoming (http://plato.stanford.edu/archives/sum2007/entries/risk/).
- Holton, Glyn A. (2004). "Defining Risk" (http://www.riskexpertise.com/papers/risk.pdf), *Financial Analysts Journal*, 60 (6), 19–25. A paper exploring the foundations of risk. (PDF file).
- Knight, F. H. (1921) *Risk, Uncertainty and Profit*, Chicago: Houghton Mifflin Company. (Cited at: (http://www.econlib.org/library/Knight/knRUP1.html), § I.I.26.).
- Kruger, Daniel J., Wang, X.T., & Wilke, Andreas (2007) "Towards the development of an evolutionarily valid domain-specific risk-taking scale" (http://www.epjournal.net/filestore/ep05555568.pdf) *Evolutionary Psychology* (PDF file).
- Metzner-Szigeth, A. (2009). "Contradictory Approaches? – On Realism and Constructivism in the Social Sciences Research on Risk, Technology and the Environment." *Futures*, Vol. 41, No. 2, March 2009, pp. 156–170 (fulltext journal: (http://www.sciencedirect.com/science?_ob=ArticleURL&_udi=B6V65-4TGS7JY-1&_user=10&_coverDate=04/30/2009&_rdoc=1&_fmt=high&_orig=search&_sort=d&_docanchor=&view=c&_acct=C000050221&_version=1&_urlVersion=0&_userid=10&md5=054fec1f03e9ec784596add85197d2a8)) (free preprint: (http://egora.uni-muenster.de/ifs/personen/bindata/metznerszigeth_contradictory_approaches_preprint.PDF)).
- Miller, L. (1985). "Cognitive risk taking after frontal or temporal lobectomy I. The synthesis of fragmented visual information." *Neuropsychologia*, 23, 359 369.
- Miller, L., & Milner, B. (1985). "Cognitive risk taking after frontal or temporal lobectomy II. The synthesis of phonemic and semantic information." *Neuropsychologia*, 23, 371 379.
- Neill, M. Allen, J. Woodhead, N. Reid, S. Irwin, L. Sanderson, H. 2008 "A Positive Approach to Risk Requires Person Centred Thinking" London, CSIP Personalisation Network, Department of Health. Available from: http://networks.csip.org.uk/Personalisation/Topics/Browse/Risk/[Accessed 21 July 2008].

External links

- Risk (http://plato.stanford.edu/entries/risk/) - The entry of the Stanford Encyclopedia of Philosophy
- *Risk Management* magazine (http://www.rmmag.com/), a publication of the Risk and Insurance Management Society.
- The Institute of Risk Management (IRM) (http://www.theirm.org/index.html) is risk management's leading international professional education and training body
- *Risk and Insurance* (http://www.riskandinsurance.com/)
- *StrategicRISK, a risk management journal* (http://www.strategicrisk.co.uk/)
- "Risk preference and religiosity" (http://ibcsr.org/index.php?option=com_content&view=article&id=149:risk-preference-and-religiosity&catid=25:research-news&Itemid=59) article from the Institute for the Biocultural Study of Religion (http://ibcsr.org/index.php)

100-year flood

A **one-hundred-year flood** is calculated to be the level of flood water expected to be equaled or exceeded every 100 years on average. The 100-year flood is more accurately referred to as the 1% annual exceedance probability flood, since it is a flood that has a 1% chance of being equaled or exceeded in any single year.[1] Similarly, a flood level expected to be equaled or exceeded every 10 years on average is known as a **ten-year flood**. Based on the expected flood water level, a predicted area of inundation can be mapped out. This floodplain map figures very importantly in building permits, environmental regulations, and flood insurance.

Probability

A 100-year flood has approximately a 63.4% chance of occurring in any 100-year period, not a 100 percent chance of occurring. The probability P_e that a certain-size flood occurring during any period will exceed the 100-yr flood threshold can be expressed as

$$P_e = 1 - \left[1 - \left(\frac{1}{T}\right)\right]^n$$

where **T** is the return period of a given storm threshold (e.g. 100-yr, 50-yr, 25-yr, and so forth), and **n** is the number of years. The exceedance probability P_e is also described as the natural, inherent, or hydrologic risk of failure.[2] [3]

Ten-year floods have a 10% chance of occurring in any given year (P_e =0.10); 500-year have a 0.2% chance of occurring in any given year (P_e =0.002); etc. The percent chance of an X-year flood occurring in a single year can be calculated by dividing 100 by X.

The field of extreme value theory was created to model rare events such as 100-year floods for the purposes of civil engineering. This theory is most commonly applied to the maximum or minimum observed stream flows of a given river. In desert areas where there are only ephemeral washes, this method is applied to the maximum observed rainfall over a given period of time (24-hours, 6-hours, or 3-hours). The extreme value analysis only considers the most extreme event observed in a given year. So, between the large spring runoff and a heavy summer rain storm, whichever resulted in more runoff would be considered the extreme event, while the smaller event would be ignored in the analysis (even though both may have been capable of causing terrible flooding in their own right).

Statistical assumptions

There are a number of assumptions which are made to complete the analysis which determines the 100-year flood. First, the extreme events observed in each year, must be independent from year-to-year. In other words the maximum river flow rate from 1984, can not be found to be significantly correlated with the observed flow rate in 1985. 1985 can not be correlated with 1986, and so forth. The second assumption is that the observed extreme events must come from the same probability distribution function. The third assumption is that the probability distribution relates to the largest storm (rainfall or river flow rate measurement) that occurs in any one year. The fourth assumption is that the probability distribution function is stationary, meaning that the mean (average), standard deviation and max/min values are not increasing or decreasing over time. This concept is referred to as stationarity.[3] [4]

The first assumption has a very low chance of being valid in all places. Studies have shown that extreme events in certain watersheds in the U.S. *are not* significantly correlated, but this must be determined on a case by case basis. The second assumption is often valid if the extreme events are observed under similar climate conditions. For example, if the extreme events on record all come from late summer thunder storms (as is the case in the southwest U.S.), or from snow pack melting (as is the case in north-central U.S.), then this assumption should be valid. If, however, there are some extreme events taken from thunder storms, others from snow pack melting, and others from hurricanes, then this assumption is most likely not valid. The third assumption is only a problem if you are trying to forecast a low, but maximum flow event (say, you are tying to find the max event for the 1-year storm event). Since this is not typically a goal in extreme analysis, or in civil engineering design, then the situation rarely presents itself. The final assumption about stationarity has come into question in light of the research being done on climate change. In short, the argument being made is that if temperatures are changing and precipitation cycles are being altered, then there is compelling evidence that the probability distribution is also changing.[5] The simplest implication of this is that not all of the historical data are, or can be, considered valid as input into the extreme event analysis.

Probability uncertainty

When these assumptions are violated there is an *unknown* amount of uncertainty introduced into the reported value of what the 100-year flood means in terms of rainfall intensity, or river flood depth. When all of the inputs are known the uncertainty can be measured in the form of a confidence interval. For example, one might say there is a 95% chance that the 100-year flood is greater than X, but less than Y.[1] Without analyzing the statistical uncertainty of a given 100-year flood, scientists and engineers can decrease the uncertainty by using two practical rules. First, forecast an extreme event which is no more than double your observation years (e.g. you have 27 observed river measurements, so you can determine a 50-year event since 27×2=54, but not a 100-yr event). The second way to decrease the uncertainty of the extreme event is to forecast a value which is less than the maximum observed value (e.g. the maximum rainfall event on record is 5.25 inches/hour, so the 100-year storm event should be less than this).

Upslope factors

The amount, location, and timing of water reaching a drainage channel from natural precipitation and controlled or uncontrolled reservoir releases determines the flow at downstream locations. Some precipitation evaporates, some slowly percolates through soil, some may be temporarily sequestered as snow or ice, and some may produce rapid runoff from surfaces including rock, pavement, roofs, and saturated or frozen ground. The fraction of incident precipitation promptly reaching a drainage channel has been observed from nil for light rain on dry, level ground to as high as 170 percent for warm rain on accumulated snow.[6]

Most precipitation records are based on a measured depth of water received within a fixed time interval. *Frequency* of a precipitation threshold of interest may be determined from the number of measurements exceeding that threshold value within the total time period for which observations are available. Individual data points are converted to *intensity* by dividing each measured depth by the period of time between observations. This intensity will be less than the actual peak intensity if the *duration* of the rainfall event was less than the fixed time interval for which measurements are reported. Convective precipitation events (thunderstorms) tend to produce shorter duration storm events than orographic precipitation. Duration, intensity, and frequency of rainfall events are important to flood prediction. Short duration precipitation is more significant to flooding within small drainage basins.[7]

The most important upslope factor in determining flood magnitude is the land area of the watershed upstream of the area of interest. Rainfall intensity is the second most important factor for watersheds of less than approximately 30 square miles or 80 km². The main channel slope is the second most important factor for larger watersheds. Channel slope and rainfall intensity become the third most important factors for small and large watersheds, respectively.[8]

Downslope factors

Water flowing downhill ultimately encounters downstream conditions slowing movement. The final limitation is often the ocean or a natural or artificial lake. Elevation changes such as tidal fluctuations are significant determinants of coastal and estuarine flooding. Less predictable events like tsunamis and storm surges may also cause elevation changes in large bodies of water. Elevation of flowing water is controlled by the geometry of the flow channel.[8] Flow channel restrictions like bridges and canyons tend to control water elevation above the restriction. The actual control point for any given reach of the drainage may change with changing water elevation, so a closer point may control for lower water levels until a more distant point controls at higher water levels.

Effective flood channel geometry may be changed by growth of vegetation, accumulation of ice or debris, or construction of bridges, buildings, or levees within the flood channel.

Prediction

Statistical analysis requires all data in a series be gathered under similar conditions. A simple prediction model might be based upon observed flows within a fixed channel geometry.[9] Alternatively, prediction may rely upon assumed channel geometry and runoff patterns using historical precipitation records. The rational method has been used for drainage basins small enough that observed rainfall intensities may be assumed to occur uniformly over the entire basin. Time of Concentration is the time required for runoff from the most distant point of the upstream drainage area to reach the point of the drainage channel controlling flooding of the area of interest. The time of concentration defines the critical duration of peak rainfall for the area of interest.[10] The critical duration of intense rainfall might be only a few minutes for roof and parking lot drainage structures, while cumulative rainfall over several days would be critical for river basins.

Extreme flood events often result from coincidence such as unusually intense, warm rainfall melting heavy snow pack, producing channel obstructions from floating ice, and releasing small impoundments like beaver dams.[11] Coincident events may cause flooding outside the statistical distribution anticipated by simplistic prediction models.[12] Debris modification of channel geometry is common when heavy flows move uprooted woody vegetation and flood-damaged structures and vehicles, including boats and railway equipment.

References

[1] Holmes, R.R., Jr., and Dinicola, K. (2010) *100-Year flood—it's all about chance* U.S. Geological Survey General Information Product 106 (http://pubs.usgs.gov/gip/106/)

[2] Mays, L.W (2005) *Water Resources Engineering* Hoboken: J. Wiley & Sons

[3] Maidment,D.R. ed.(1993) *Handbook of Hydrology* New York:Mcraw-Hill

[4] Water Resources Council Bulletin 17B Water Resources Council Bulletin 17B (http://water.usgs.gov/osw/bulletin17b/dl_flow.pdf) "Guidelines for Determining Flood Flow Frequency,"

[5] See article in Science Magazine: Stationarity is Dead (http://sciencemag.org/cgi/content/full/319/5863/573)

[6] Babbitt, Harold E. and Doland, James J., *Water Supply Engineering*, McGraw-Hill Book Company, 1949

[7] Simon, Andrew L., *Basic Hydraulics*, John Wiley & Sons, 1981, ISBN 0-471-07965-0

[8] Simon, Andrew L., *Practical Hydraulics*, John Wiley & Sons, 1981, ISBN 0-471-05381-3

[9] Linsley, Ray K. and Franzini, Joseph B., *Water-Resources Engineering*, McGraw-Hill Book Company, 1972

[10] Urquhart, Leonard Church , *Civil Engineering Handbook*, McGraw-Hill Book Company, 1959

[11] Abbett, Robert W., *American Civil Engineering Practice*, John Wiley & Sons, 1956

[12] United States Department of the Interior, Bureau of Reclamation, *Design of Small Dams*, United States Government Printing Office, 1973

External links

* " What is a 100 year flood? (http://bcn.boulder.co.us/basin/watershed/flood.html)". Boulder Area Sustainability Information Network (BASIN). URL accessed 2006-06-16.

Absolute probability judgement

Absolute probability judgement is a technique used in the field of human reliability assessment (HRA), for the purposes of evaluating the probability of a human error occurring throughout the completion of a specific task. From such analyses measures can then be taken to reduce the likelihood of errors occurring within a system and therefore lead to an improvement in the overall levels of safety. There exist three primary reasons for conducting an HRA; error identification, error quantification and error reduction. As there exist a number of techniques used for such purposes, they can be split into one of two classifications; first generation techniques and second generation techniques. First generation techniques work on the basis of the simple dichotomy of 'fits/doesn't fit' in the matching of the error situation in context with related error identification and quantification and second generation techniques are more theory based in their assessment and quantification of errors. 'HRA techniques have been utilised in a range of industries including healthcare, engineering, nuclear, transportation and business sector; each technique has varying uses within different disciplines.

Absolute probability judgement, which is also known as *direct numerical estimation* [1], is based on the quantification of human error probabilities (HEPs). It is grounded on the premise that people cannot recall or are unable to estimate with certainty, the probability of a given event occurring. Expert judgement is typically desirable for utilisation in the technique when there is little or no data with which to calculate HEPs, or when the data is unsuitable or difficult to understand. In theory, qualitative knowledge built through the experts' experience can be translated into quantitative data such as HEPs.

Required of the experts is a good level of both substantive experience (i.e. the expert must have a suitable level of knowledge of the problem domain) and normative experience (i.e. it must be possible for the expert, perhaps with the aid of a facilitator, to translate this knowledge explicitly into probabilities). If experts possess the required substantive knowledge but lack knowledge which is normative in nature, the experts may be trained or assisted in ensuring that the knowledge and expertise requiring to be captured is translated into the correct probabilities i.e. to ensure that it is an accurate representation of the experts' judgements.

Background

Absolute probability judgement is an expert judgement-based approach which involves using the beliefs of experts (e.g. front-line staff, process engineers etc.) to estimate HEPs. There are two primary forms of the technique; Group Methods and Single Expert Methods i.e. it can be done either as a group or as an individual exercise. Group methods tend to be the more popular and widely used as they are more robust and are less subject to bias. Moreover, within the context of use, it is unusual for a single individual to possess all the required information and expertise to be able to solely estimate, in an accurate manner, the human reliability in question. In the group approach, the outcome of aggregating individual knowledge and opinions is more reliable.

Absolute probability judgement methodologies

There are 4 main group methods by which absolute probability judgement can be conducted.

Aggregated individual method

Utilising this method, experts make their estimates individually without actually meeting or discussing the task. The estimates are then aggregated by taking the geometric mean of the individual experts' estimates for each task. The major drawback to this method is that there is no shared expertise through the group; however a positive of this is that due to the individuality of the process, any conflict such as dominating personalities or conflicting personalities is avoided and the results are therefore free of any bias.

Delphi method

Developed by Dalkey [2] [3], the Delphi method method is very similar to the Aggregated Individual Method in that experts make their initial estimates in isolation. However following this stage, the experts are then shown the outcome that all other participants have arrived at and are then able to re-consider the estimates which they initially made. The re-estimates are then aggregated using the geometric mean. This allows for some information sharing, whilst avoiding most group-led biases; however there still remains the problem of a lack of discussion.

Nominal group technique (NGT)

This technique takes the Delphi method and introduces limited discussion/consultation between the experts. By this means, information-sharing is superior, and group domination is mitigated by having the experts separately come to their own conclusion before aggregating the HEP scores.

Consensus group method

This is the most group-centred approach and requires that the group must come to a consensus on the HEP estimates through discussion and mutual agreement. This method maximises knowledge sharing and the exchange of ideas and also promotes equal opportunity to participate in discussion. However, it can also prove to be logistically awkward to co-ordinate as it requires that all experts be together in the same location in order for the discussion to take place. Due to this technicality, personalities and other biasing mechanisms such as overconfidence, recent availability and anchoring may become a factor, thus increasing the potential for the results to be skewed. If the circumstance arises in which there is a deadlock or breakdown in group dynamics, it then becomes necessary to revert to one of the other group absolute probability judgement methods.

Absolute probability judgement procedure

1. Select subject matter experts

The chosen experts must have a good working knowledge of the tasks which require to be assessed. The correct number of experts is dependent upon what seems most practicable, while considering any constraints such as spatial and financial availability. However, it should be noted that the larger the group the more likely problems are to arise.

2. Prepare task statement

Task statements are a necessary component of the method; tasks are specified in detail. The more fuller the explanation of the task within the statement, the less likely it will be that the experts will resort to making individual guesses about the tasks. The statement should also ensure that any assumptions are clearly stated in an interpretable format for all experts to understand. The optimal level of detail will be governed by the nature of the task under consideration and the required use of the final HEP estimation.

3. Prepare response booklet These booklets detail the task statement and design of the scale to use in assessing error probability and by which experts can indicate their judgements.[1] . The scale must be one which allows differences to be made apparent. The booklet also includes instructions, assumptions and sample items.

4. Develop instructions for subjects

Instructions are required to specify to the experts the reasons for the session, otherwise they may guess such reasons which may cause bias in the resultant estimates of human reliability.

5. Obtain judgements

Experts are required to reveal their judgements on each of the tasks; this can be done in a group or individually. If done by the former means, a facilitator is often used to prevent any bias and help overcome any problems.

6. Calculate inter-judge consistency

This is a method by which the differences in the HEP estimates of individual experts can be compared; a statistical formulation is used for such purposes.

7. Aggregate individual estimates

Where group consensus methods are not used, it is necessary to compute an aggregate for each of the individual estimates for each HEP.

8. Uncertainty bound estimation Calculated by using statistical approaches involving confidence ranges.

Worked example

Context

In this example, absolute probability judgement was utilised by Eurocontrol, at the experimental centre in Bretigny Paris, using a group consensus methodology.

Required inputs

Each of the grades of staff included in the session took turns to provide estimates of the error probabilities, including ground staff, pilots and controllers. Prior to the beginning of the session, an introductory exercise was conducted to allow the participants to feel more comfortable with use of the technique; this involved an explanation to the background of the method and provided an overview of what the session would entail of. To increase familiarity of the method, exemplary templates were used to show how errors are estimated.

Method

- Initial task statements of the project were created leaving space for individual opinion of task estimates and additional assumptions the group may have collectively foregone.
- A session was held in which the individual scenarios and tasks were accurately detailed to the experts
- Experts, with this knowledge, were then able to enter individual estimations for all tasks under consideration
- Discussion followed in which all participants were provided with the opportunity to express their opinion to the rest of the group
- Facilitation was then used in order to reach a group consensus on the estimate values. Further discussion and amendment took place when necessary.

During the duration of the session it was revealed that the ease with which the experts were able to arrive at a consensus was low with regards to the differing estimates of the various HEP values. Discussions often changed individuals' thinking e.g. in the light of new information or interpretations, but this did not ease reaching an agreement. Due to this difficulty, it was therefore necessary to aggregate the individual estimates in order to calculate a geometric mean of these. The following table displays a sample of the results obtained.

Table: Pilot absolute probability judgement Session—extract of results

Potential Error (Code in Risk Model)	Maximum	Minimum	Range	Geometric Mean
C1a	1.1E-03	2.0E-05	55	2.1E-04
C1b	2.5E-04	1.0E-05	25	3.5E-05
D1	1.0E-03	1.0E-04	10	4.3E-04
F1a	4.0E-04	1.0E-05	40	6.9E-05
F1b	1.0E-03	1.0E-04	10	4.0E-04
F1c	1.0E-03	1.0E-04	10	4.6E-04

In various cases, the range of figures separating the maximum and minimum values proved to be too large to allow to aggregated value to be accepted with confidence These values are the events in the risk model which require to be quantified. There are 3 primary errors in the model that may occur:

- C1: Capturing false information about final approach path
- D1: Failure to maintain a/c on final approach path
- F1: Selecting wrong runway

There were various reasons which can explain the reasons why there was such a large difference in the estimates provided by the group: the group of experts was largely diverse and the experience of the individuals differed. Experience with Ground Based Augmentation System (GBAS) also showed differences. This process was a new experience for all of the experts participating in the process and there was only a single day, in which the session was taking place, to become familiar with its use and use it correctly. Of most significance was the fact that the detail of the assessments was very fine, which the staff were not used to. Experts also became confused about the way in which the assessment took place; errors were not considered on their own and were analysed as a group. This meant that the values estimated represented a contribution of the error on a system failure as opposed to a single contribution to system failure.

Results/outcomes

- Controllers and pilots provided good estimates for the errors and these have been used in some safety cases
- Participants highlighted their understanding of the importance of their participation in the process to provide expertise, as opposed to using external safety analysts instead i.e. their understood their role in carrying out a Human Reliability Assessment of the system
- The experts were provided with a realistic representation of human performance within the system and therefore further safety requirements required to improve the safety and reduce the likelihood of the identified errors. This is particularly beneficial; for the future GBAS.

Lessons from the study

- Time is required to familiarise with the methodology and to understand what is needed to be done in the given context
- Experts are required to understand the circumstances in which HEPs are conditional
- There is a need for true experts to be included in the process and in significant number to allow for the necessary information to be gathered.
- The use of existing information in the process is always helpful for the purposes of standardisation

Advantages of absolute probability judgement

* The method is relatively quick and straightforward to employ. With a greater degree of group discussion in use of the technique, there is more qualitative data that is produced; this can be considered as a useful by-product of the assessment.[1]
* Absolute probability judgement is not restricted to or specialised for use in a particular field; it is easily applicable to an HRA on any industrial sector thus making it a generic technique for use in a wide range of potential applications.[5]
* Useful suggestions may result from discussion as to ways in which a reduction in errors can be achieved[4]

Disadvantages of absolute probability judgement

* Absolute probability judgement is prone to certain biases and group conflicts or problems. Selection of the correct group methodology or high-quality group facilitation may decrease the effect of these biases and increase the validity of the results.[1]
* Locating suitable experts for the absolute probability judgement exercise is a difficult stage of the process, more so due to the ambiguity with which the term 'expert' can be defined [5]
* Because there may be little or no empirical and/or quantitative reasoning underpinning the experts' estimates, it is difficult to be certain of the validity of the final HEPs i.e. there is no means by which guesses can be validated [1]

References

[1] Humphreys, P., (1995) Human Reliability Assessor's Guide. Human Factors in Reliability Group.

[2] Dalkey, N. & Helmer, O. (1963) An experimental application of the Delphi method to the use of experts. Management Science. 9(3) 458-467.

[3] Linstone, H.A. & Turoff, M. (1978) The Delphi Method: Techniques and Applications. Addison-Wesley, London.

[4] Kirwan, Practical Guide to Human Reliability Assessment, CPC Press, 1994

[5] 2004. Eurocontrol Experimental Centre; Review of Techniques to Support the EATMP Safety Assessment Methodology. EuroControl, Vol 1

Acceptable loss

An **acceptable loss** is a sacrifice that is deemed an acceptable cost of doing business. For instance, a church may deem the loss of members who disagree with an evangelical shift to be acceptable if the alternative is to forgo other goals.[1] Anticipated casualties in a military campaign may be held to be acceptable losses as well.[2] A terrorist group may consider the loss of its own members in suicide attacks to be acceptable losses needed to accomplish the mission.[3] The implications of the term may be summed up as "What are we willing to lose to achieve a goal?"[4] During military battles, field commanders are prepared to accept the loss of up to 33% of their troops during combat.[5]

References

[1] http://ctlibrary.com/le/1998/summer/8l3038.html
[2] http://telephonyonline.com/software/commentary/revenue_leak_losses_091307/
[3] http://www.ralphmag.org/AZ/letters.html
[4] http://www.toandfroproductions.com/acceptabledev1.htm
[5] http://cms.firehouse.com/print/Leadership-and-Command/Acceptable-Losses/5$405

Accident-proneness

Accident-proneness, also known as **clumsiness**, is the conception that some people might have predisposition, or that they might be more likely to suffer accidents, such as car crashes and industrial injuries, than other people. It may be used as a reason to deny any insurance on such individuals.

Early work

The early work on this subject dates back to 1919, in a study by Greenwood and Woods, who studied workers at a British munitions factory and found that accidents were unevenly distributed among workers, with a relatively small proportion of workers accounting for most of the accidents. [1] Further work on accident-proneness was carried out in the 1930s and 1940s.

Present study

The subject is still being studied actively. Research into accident-proneness is of great interest in safety engineering, where human factors such as pilot error, or errors by nuclear plant operators, can have massive effects on the reliability and safety of a system. One of the areas of most interest and more profound research is the Aeronautical area, where accidents have been reviewed from psychological and human factors, to mechanical and technical failures. There has been many conclusive studies, that present that human factor has great influence on the results of those occurrences.

Statistical evidence

Statistical evidence clearly demonstrates that different individuals can have different rates of accidents from one another; for example, young male drivers are the group at highest risk for being involved in car accidents. There also seems to be substantial variation in personal accident rates between individuals.

Doubt

However, a number of studies have cast doubt on whether accident-proneness actually exists as a *distinct, persistent and independently verifiable* physiological or psychological syndrome. Although substantial research has been devoted to this subject, there still seems to be no conclusive evidence either for or against the existence of accident proneness in this sense.

Nature and causes

The exact nature and causes of accident-proneness, assuming that it exists as a distinct entity, are unknown. Factors which have been considered as associated with accident-proneness have included absent-mindedness, carelessness, impulsivity, predisposition to risk-taking, and unconscious desires to create accidents as a way of achieving secondary gains.

References

[1] Greenwood, M. and Woods, H.M. (1919) The incidence of industrial accidents upon individuals with special reference to multiple accidents. *Industrial Fatigue Research Board, Medical Research Committee*, Report No. 4. Her Majesty's Stationery Office, London.

Sources

Note: this article is partly based on public domain text from the U.S. government public domain document "Accident Proneness: A Research Review"

External links

- Rodgers, Mark D. and Blanchard, Robert E. *Accident Proneness: A Research Review*. Federal Civil Aeromedical Institute Report DOT/FAA/AM-93-9, March 2003. (http://stinet.dtic.mil/oai/oai?&verb=getRecord& metadataPrefix=html&identifier=ADA266032)
- Arnold J. Rawson. Accident Proneness. *Psychosomatic Medicine* 6:88-94 (1944) (http://www. psychosomaticmedicine.org/cgi/content/abstract/6/1/88)
- W. L. Cresswell and P. Frogatt. Accident Proneness, or Variable Accident Tendency? Dublin: *Journal of the Statistical and Social Inquiry Society of Ireland*, Vol. XX, Part V, 1961/1962, pp152-171 (http://www.tara.tcd. ie/bitstream/2262/4638/1/jssisiVolXXPart5_152171.pdf)
- Accident Statistics and the Concept of Accident-Proneness (http://links.jstor.org/ sici?sici=0006-341X(195112)7:4<340:ASATCO>2.0.CO;2-K)
- Accident Theories and Their Implications for Research (http://www.iprr.org/papers/aaam.html)

Actuary

Actuary

Damage from Hurricane Katrina. Actuaries need to estimate long-term averages of such damage in order to accurately price property insurance.

Occupation	
Names	Actuary
Type	Profession
Activity sectors	Insurance, Reinsurance, Pension plans, Social welfare programs
Description	
Competencies	Mathematics, analytical skills, business knowledge
Education required	See Credentialing and exams
Fields of employment	Insurance companies, consulting firms, government
Related jobs	Underwriter

An **actuary** is a business professional who deals with the financial impact of risk and uncertainty. Actuaries provide expert assessments of financial security systems, with a focus on their complexity, their mathematics, and their mechanisms (Trowbridge 1989, p. 7).

Actuaries mathematically evaluate the likelihood of events and quantify the contingent outcomes in order to minimize losses, both emotional and financial, associated with uncertain undesirable events. Since many events, such as death, cannot be avoided, it is helpful to take measures to minimize their financial impact when they occur. These risks can affect both sides of the balance sheet, and require asset management, liability management, and valuation skills. Analytical skills, business knowledge and understanding of human behavior and the vagaries of information systems are required to design and manage programs that control risk (BeAnActuary 2005a).

In 2010, a study published by job search website CareerCast ranked actuary as the #1 job in the United States (Needleman 2010). The study used five key criteria to rank jobs: environment, income, employment outlook, physical demands and stress. A similar study by *U.S. News & World Report* in 2006 included actuaries among the 25 Best Professions that it expects will be in great demand in the future (Nemko 2006).

Disciplines

Actuaries' insurance disciplines may be classified as life; health; pensions, annuities, and asset management; social welfare programs; property; casualty; general insurance; and reinsurance. Life, health, and pension actuaries deal with mortality risk, morbidity, and consumer choice regarding the ongoing utilization of drugs and medical services risk, and investment risk. Products prominent in their work include life insurance, annuities, pensions, mortgage and credit insurance, short and long term disability, and medical, dental, health savings accounts and long term care insurance. In addition to these risks, social insurance programs are greatly influenced by public opinion, politics, budget constraints, changing demographics and other factors such as medical technology, inflation and cost of living considerations (Bureau of Labor Statistics 2008).

Casualty actuaries, also known as non-life or general insurance actuaries, deal with catastrophic, unnatural risks that can occur to people or property. Products prominent in their work include auto insurance, homeowners insurance, commercial property insurance, workers' compensation, title insurance, malpractice insurance, products liability insurance, directors and officers liability insurance, environmental and marine insurance, terrorism insurance and other types of liability insurance. Reinsurance products have to accommodate all of the previously mentioned products, and in addition have to reflect properly the increasing long term risks associated with climate change, cultural litigiousness, acts of war, terrorism and politics (Bureau of Labor Statistics 2008).

History

Need for insurance

The basic requirements of communal interests gave rise to risk sharing since the dawn of civilization. For example, people who lived their entire lives in a camp had the risk of fire, which would leave their band or family without shelter. After basic exchange came into existence, more complex forms developed beyond a basic barter economy, and new forms of risk manifested. Merchants embarking on trade journeys bore the risk of losing goods entrusted to them, their own possessions, or even their lives. Intermediaries developed to warehouse and trade goods, and they often suffered from financial risk. The primary providers in any extended families or household always ran the risk of premature death, disability or infirmity, leaving their dependents to starve. Credit procurement was difficult if the lender worried about repayment in the event of the borrower's death or infirmity. Alternatively, people sometimes lived too long, exhausting their savings, if any, or becoming a burden on others in the extended family or society (Faculty and Institute of Actuaries 2004).

Early attempts

In the ancient world there was not always room for the sick, suffering, disabled, aged, or the poor—these were often not part of the cultural consciousness of societies (Perkins 1995). Early methods of protection, aside from the normal support of the extended family, involved charity; religious organizations or neighbors would collect for the destitute and needy. By the middle of the 3rd century, 1,500 suffering people were being supported by charitable operations in Rome (Perkins 1995). Charitable protection is still an active form of support to this very day (Tong 2006). However, receiving charity is uncertain and is often accompanied by social stigma. Elementary mutual aid agreements and pensions did arise in antiquity (Thucydides). Early in the Roman empire, associations were formed to meet the expenses of burial, cremation, and monuments—precursors to burial insurance and friendly societies. A small sum was paid into a communal fund on a weekly basis, and upon the death of a member, the fund would cover the expenses of rites and burial. These societies sometimes sold shares in the building of columbāria, or burial vaults, owned by the fund—the precursor to mutual insurance companies (Johnston 1903, §475–§476). Other early examples of mutual surety and assurance pacts can be traced back to various forms of fellowship within the Saxon clans of England and their Germanic forbears, and to Celtic society (Loan 1992). However, many of these earlier forms of surety and aid would fail due to lack of understanding and knowledge (Faculty and Institute of Actuaries

2004).

Development of theory

The 17th century was a period of extraordinary advances in mathematics in Germany, France, and England. At the same time there was a rapidly growing desire and need to place the valuation of personal risk on a more scientific basis. Independently from each other, compound interest was studied and probability theory emerged as a well understood mathematical discipline. Another important advance came in 1662 from a London draper named John Graunt, who showed that there were predictable patterns of longevity and death in a defined group, or cohort, of people, despite the uncertainty about the future longevity or mortality of any one individual person. This study became the basis for the original life table. It was now possible to set up an insurance scheme to provide life insurance or pensions for a group of people, and to calculate with some degree of accuracy how much each person in the group should contribute to a common fund assumed to earn a fixed rate of interest. The first person to demonstrate publicly how this could be done was Edmond Halley. In addition to constructing his own life table, Halley demonstrated a method of using his life table to calculate the premium someone of a given age should pay to purchase a life-annuity (Halley 1693).

2003 US mortality (life) table, Table 1, Page 1

Early actuaries

James Dodson's pioneering work on the level premium system led to the formation of the Society for Equitable Assurances on Lives and Survivorship (now commonly known as Equitable Life) in London in 1762. This was the first life insurance company to use premium rates which were calculated scientifically for long-term life policies, using Dodson's work. The company still exists, though it has run into difficulties recently. After Dodson's death in 1757, Edward Rowe Mores took over the leadership of the group that eventually became the Society for Equitable Assurances in 1762. It was he who specified that the chief official should be called an 'actuary' (Ogborn 1956). Previously, the use of the term had been restricted to an official who recorded the decisions, or 'acts', of ecclesiastical courts, in ancient times originally the secretary of the Roman senate, responsible for compiling the Acta Senatus (Faculty and Institute of Actuaries 2004). Other companies which did not originally use such mathematical and scientific methods most often failed or were forced to adopt the methods pioneered by Equitable (Bühlmann 1997, p. 166).

Development of the modern profession

In the 18th and 19th centuries, computational complexity was limited to manual calculations. The actual calculations required to compute fair insurance premiums are rather complex. The actuaries of that time developed methods to construct easily-used tables, using sophisticated approximations called commutation functions, to facilitate timely, accurate, manual calculations of premiums (Slud 2006). Over time, actuarial organizations were founded to support and further both actuaries and actuarial science, and to protect the public interest by ensuring competency and ethical standards (Hickman 2004, p. 4). However, calculations remained cumbersome, and actuarial shortcuts were commonplace. Non-life actuaries followed in the footsteps of their life compatriots in the early 20th century. In the United States, the 1920 revision to workers' compensation rates took over two months of around-the-clock work by day and night teams of actuaries (Michelbacher 1920, pp. 224, 230). In the 1930s and 1940s, however, rigorous mathematical foundations for stochastic processes were developed (Bühlmann 1997, p. 168). Actuaries could now begin to forecast losses using models of random events instead of deterministic methods. Computers further revolutionized the actuarial profession. From pencil-and-paper to punchcards to microcomputers, the modeling and forecasting ability of the actuary has grown exponentially (MacGinnitie 1980, pp. 50–51).

Another modern development is the convergence of modern financial theory with actuarial science (Bühlmann 1997, pp. 169–171). In the early 20th century, actuaries were developing many techniques that can be found in modern financial theory, but for various historical reasons, these developments did not achieve much recognition (Whelan 2002). However, in the late 1980s and early 1990s, there was a distinct effort for actuaries to combine financial theory and stochastic methods into their established models (D'arcy 1989). Today, the profession, both in practice and in the educational syllabi of many actuarial organizations, combines tables, loss models, stochastic methods, and financial theory (Feldblum 2001, pp. 8–9), but is still not completely aligned with modern financial economics (Bader & Gold 2003).

Responsibilities

Actuaries use skills in mathematics, economics, computer science, finance, probability and statistics, and business to help businesses assess the risk of certain events occurring and to formulate policies that minimize the cost of that risk. For this reason, actuaries are essential to the insurance and reinsurance industry, either as staff employees or as consultants; to other businesses, including sponsors of pension plans; and to government agencies such as the Government Actuary's Department in the UK or the Social Security Administration in the US. Actuaries assemble and analyze data to estimate the probability and likely cost of the occurrence of an event such as death, sickness, injury, disability, or loss of property. Actuaries also address financial questions, including those involving the level of pension contributions required to produce a certain retirement income and the way in which a company should invest resources to maximize its return on investments in light of potential risk. Using their broad knowledge, actuaries help design and price insurance policies, pension plans, and other financial strategies in a manner which will help ensure that the plans are maintained on a sound financial basis (Bureau of Labor Statistics 2008).

Traditional employment

On both the life and casualty sides, the classical function of actuaries is to calculate premiums and reserves for insurance policies covering various risks. Premiums are the amount of money the insurer needs to collect from the policyholder in order to cover the expected losses, expenses, and a provision for profit. Reserves are provisions for future liabilities and indicate how much money should be set aside now to reasonably provide for future payouts. If you inspect the balance sheet of an insurance company, you will find that the liability side consists mainly of reserves.

On the casualty side, this analysis often involves quantifying the probability of a loss event, called the frequency, and the size of that loss event, called the severity. Further, the amount of time that occurs before the loss event is also important, as the insurer will not have to pay anything until after the event has occurred. On the life side, the analysis often involves quantifying how much a potential sum of money or a financial liability will be worth at different points in the future. Since neither of these kinds of analysis are purely deterministic processes, stochastic models are often used to determine frequency and severity distributions and the parameters of these distributions. Forecasting interest yields and currency movements also plays a role in determining future costs, especially on the life side.

Actuaries do not always attempt to predict aggregate future events. Often, their work may relate to determining the cost of financial liabilities that have already occurred, called retrospective reinsurance, or the development or re-pricing of new products.

Actuaries also design and maintain products and systems. They are involved in financial reporting of companies' assets and liabilities. They must communicate complex concepts to clients who may not share their language or depth of knowledge. Actuaries work under a strict code of ethics that covers their communications and work products, but their clients may not adhere to those same standards when interpreting the data or using it within different kinds of businesses.

Non-traditional employment

Many actuaries are general business managers or financial officers. They analyze business prospects with their financial skills in valuing or discounting risky future cash flows, and many apply their pricing expertise from insurance to other lines of business. Some actuaries act as expert witnesses by applying their analysis in court trials to estimate the economic value of losses such as lost profits or lost wages.

There has been a recent widening of the scope of the actuarial field to include investment advice and asset management. Further, there has been a convergence from the financial fields of risk management and quantitative analysis with actuarial science. Now, actuaries also work as risk managers, quantitative analysts, or investment specialists. Even actuaries in traditional roles are now studying and using the tools and data previously in the domain of finance (Feldblum 2001, p. 8). One of the latest developments in the industry, insurance securitization, requires both the actuarial and finance skills (Krutov 2006).

Another field in which actuaries are becoming more prominent is that of Enterprise Risk Management, for both financial and non-financial corporations (D'arcy 2005). For example, the Basel II accord for financial institutions, and its analogue, the Solvency II accord for insurance companies, requires such institutions to account for operational risk separately and in addition to credit, reserve, asset, and insolvency risk. Actuarial skills are well suited to this environment because of their training in analyzing various forms of risk, and judging the potential for upside gain, as well as downside loss associated with these forms of risk (D'arcy 2005).

Remuneration

The credentialing and examination procedure for becoming a fully qualified actuary can be intensely demanding. Consequently, the profession remains very small throughout the world. As a result, actuaries are in high demand, and they are highly paid for the services they render (Simpson 2006). In the UK, where there are approximately 9,000 fully qualified actuaries, typical post-university starting salaries range between GBP £25,300 and £35,000 (approx. US$50,100–US$69,300 c. January 2008) and newly qualified actuaries in insurance companies typically earn somewhere between £60,000 and £75,000 (approx. US$93,100–US$116,900 c. January 2010) per year. Many successful actuaries earn over £100,000 a year (approx. US$198,000 c. January 2008). These reflect nationwide salaries and numbers are likely to be higher in London or in the South East of England (Lomas 2009).

Credentialing and exams

Becoming a fully credentialed actuary requires passing a rigorous series of exams, usually taking several years. In some countries, such as France, most study takes place in a university setting. In others, such as the U.S. and the UK, most study takes place during employment.

Australia

The education system in Australia is divided into three components: an exam-based curriculum; a professionalism course; and work experience (IAA-Ed 2006). The system is governed by the Institute of Actuaries of Australia.

The exam-based curriculum is in three parts. Part I relies on exemptions from an accredited under-graduate degree from either Macquarie University, University of New South Wales, University of Melbourne, Australian National University or Curtin University (IAA-Part I 2006). The courses cover subjects including finance, financial mathematics, economics, contingencies, demography, models, probability and statistics. Students may also gain exemptions by passing the exams of the Institute of Actuaries in London (IAA-Part I 2006). Part II is the Actuarial control cycle and is offered by the first four universities above (IAA-Part II 2006). Part III consists of four half-year courses of which two are compulsory and the other two allow specialization (IAA-Part III 2006).

To become an Associate, one needs to complete Part I and Part II of the accreditation process, perform 3 years of recognized work experience, and complete a professionalism course.

To become a Fellow, Part I, II, III need to be all completed, and a professionalism course. Work experience is not required however, as the Institute deems that those who've successfully completed Part III have shown enough level of professionalism.

Canada

The Canadian Institute of Actuaries (the CIA) recognizes fellows of both the Society of Actuaries and the Casualty Actuary Society, provided that they have specialized study in Canadian actuarial practice. For fellows of the SOA, this is fulfilled by taking the CIA's Practice Education Course (PEC). For fellows of the Casualty Actuarial Society, this is fulfilled by taking the nation specific Exam 6-Canada, instead of Exam 6-United States.[1] Unlike their American counterparts, the CIA only has one class of actuary: Fellow. Further, the CIA requires three years of actuarial practice within the previous decade, and 18 months of Canadian actuarial practice within the last three years, to become a fellow (CIA 2004). The CIA also offers an associate designation however this offered without any voting rights and associates are not permitted to add this designation to their signature.

Denmark

In Denmark it normally takes five years of study at the University of Copenhagen to become an actuary with no professional experience requirement. There is a focus on statistics and probability theory, and a requirement for a master's thesis (Norberg 1990). By Danish law, responsibility for the practise of any life insurance business must be taken by a formally acknowledged and approved actuary. In order to be approved as a formally responsible actuary, three to five years of professional experience is required (Haastrup & Nielsen 2007).

Germany

The current rules for the German Actuarial Society require an actuary to pass more than 13 exams (DAV 2006).

Greece

In Greece the only specialized school of actuaries is the Department of Statistics and Actuary-Finance Mathematics of the University of the Aegean, in Samos. The duration of studies is four years, with a practice period included, and the certificate given is a Bachelor's Degree. The Diploma of Actuary is given by the Actuaries Union of Greece, after successful exams within the Union. Other schools that offer actuary directions can be found throughout the rest departments of Statistics in the various universities of the country, most notably that of the Athens University of Economics and Business (OPA/ASOEE), which is also the top economic university of Greece.

India

The Actuarial Society of India (now converted into Institute of Actuaries of India) offers both associateship and fellowship classes of membership. However, prospective candidates must be admitted to the society as students before they achieve associateship or fellowship. The exam sequence is similar to the British model, with Core and Specialty technical and application exams. The exams are conducted twice a year during the months of May–June and October–November (ASI 2006).

Mexico

Unlike in the United States, in Mexico actuarial training consists of a full four or five-year licenciatura (bachelor) degree course. Only a few universities in the country offer the degree; some of them are the National Autonomous University of Mexico (UNAM), Universidad de las Americas Puebla (UDLAP), Universidad Anahuac, Autonomous Technological Institute of Mexico (ITAM), Autonomous University of Guadalajara (UAG), and Autonomous University of Nuevo León (UANL).

Norway

In Norway the education to become an actuary takes five years. The education usually consists of a bachelors degree (three years) and a masters degree (two years). The bachelors degree needs to contain a specific amount of courses in mathematics and statistics. The masters degree usually consists of one year of courses and one year writing a masters degree about a topic related to the actuarial profession. The University of Bergen and The University of Oslo offers the education to become an actuary in Norway (University of Bergen 2011). In order to become an international qualified actuary a person with an Norwegian actuarial education also need to take two courses in economics (macroeconomics and accounting) and a course in ethics. The course in ethics lasts a day and is offered by the Norwegian Society of Actuaries (Norwegian Society of Actuaries 2011).

Portugal

In Portugal the only school offering a degree in actuarial science is ISEG at the Technical University of Lisbon. It is a 2 years Master degree, fully integrated into the Bologna regimen. If the student does sufficiently well in the programme, as determined by an examiner appointed by the Institute and Faculty of Actuaries, he/she will be exempt from some of the UK professional actuarial examinations.

South Africa

Actuaries in South Africa are served by the Actuarial Society of South Africa (ASSA). Until recently the requirement to qualify as an actuary in South Africa was to pass the exams hosted by the UK bodies. Starting in 2010, a South African actuarial qualification hosted by ASSA has replaced this arrangement (ASSA's website [2]). Key changes include exam syllabuses based on South African specific content. The UK actuarial professional bodies however still supports Actuaries qualification through the UK. Students may receive exemption from part of the examinations for qualification from approved universities. The South Africa qualification does have mutual recognition with many of the international actuarial bodies as well as approval of the syllabus from the International Actuarial Association.

Sweden

Actuarial training in Sweden takes place at Stockholm University. The four-year master's program covers the subjects mathematics, mathematical statistics, insurance mathematics, financial mathematics, insurance law and insurance economics. The program operates under the Division of Mathematical Statistics (Stockholm University 2006).

UK and Republic of Ireland

Qualification in the United Kingdom and the Republic of Ireland consists of a combination of exams and courses provided by the professional bodies: the Institute of Actuaries based in London, England, and the Faculty of Actuaries based in Edinburgh, Scotland — separate but coinciding bodies. No geographic limitations exist for these bodies. Students and actuaries in any part of the UK or the Republic of Ireland may be a member of either or both bodies. The exams may only be taken upon having officially joined the body, unlike many other countries where exams may be taken earlier. However, a candidate may offer proof of having previously covered topics, usually while at university, in order to be exempt from taking certain subjects. The exams themselves are now split into four sections: Core Technical (CT), Core Applications (CA), Specialist Technical (ST), and Specialist Applications (SA). For students who joined the Profession after June 2004, a further requirement that the student carry out a "Work-based skills" exercise has been brought into effect. This involves the student submitting a series of essays to the Profession detailing the work that he or she has performed. In addition to exams, essays and courses, it is required that the candidate have at least three years' experience of actuarial work under supervision of a recognized actuary in order to qualify as a Fellow of the Institute of Actuaries (FIA) or of the Faculty of Actuaries (FFA) (Faculty and Institute of Actuaries 2006).

Actuaries can also gain partial credit towards Fellowship of either the Faculty or Institute of Actuaries by following an actuarial science degree at an accredited university. At the undergraduate level the only locally accredited programmes are currently at University College Dublin, Queen's University Belfast, Heriot-Watt University, University of Edinburgh, the London School of Economics, University of Southampton, City University, London and the University of Kent. Full-time accredited masters programmes are provided only by the University of Kent, Heriot-Watt University and City University; part-time accredited masters degrees are offered by Imperial College London and the University of Leicester. Actuarial programmes that offer the possibility of exemption from individual professional exams are also available at City University, London, Heriot-Watt University, the London School of Economics, the University of Southampton, Swansea University, the University of Manchester, the University of Kent and the University of Warwick. In the Republic of Ireland exemptions are offered by National University of Ireland, Galway, Dublin City University, University College Cork. Some South African universities are also accredited by the Faculty and Institute of Actuaries. These universities include the University of Pretoria, University of Cape Town, Stellenbosch University, University of the Free State and the University of the Witwatersrand. ISEG [3] in Lisbon, Portugal, offers the possibility of exemption from some professional exams of the Faculty and Institute of Actuaries.

United States

In the U.S., for life, health, and pension actuaries, exams are given by the Society of Actuaries, while for property and casualty actuaries the exams are administered by the Casualty Actuarial Society. The Society of Actuaries' requirements for Associateship include passing five preliminary examinations, demonstrating educational experience in economics, corporate finance and applied statistics—called validation by educational experience (VEE), completing an eight-module self-learning series, and taking a course on professionalism. For Fellowship, four other modules, two exams, and a special fellowship admission course is added (SOA 2010). The Casualty Actuarial Society requires the successful completion of seven examinations, two modules and VEE for Associateship and three additional exams for Fellowship. In addition to these requirements, casualty actuarial candidates must also complete professionalism education and be recommended for membership by existing members (CAS 2011).

In order to sign statements of actuarial opinion, however, American actuaries must be members of the American Academy of Actuaries. Academy membership requirements include membership in one of the recognized actuarial societies, at least three years of full-time equivalent experience in responsible actuarial work, and either residency in the United States for at least three years or a non-resident or new resident who meets certain requirements (AAA 2010). Continuing education is required after certification for all actuaries who sign statements of actuarial opinion (AAA 2008).

In the pension area, American actuaries must pass three examinations to become an Enrolled Actuary. Some pension-related filings to the Internal Revenue Service and the Pension Benefit Guaranty Corporation require the signature of an Enrolled Actuary. Many Enrolled Actuaries belong to the Conference of Consulting Actuaries or the American Society of Pension Professionals and Actuaries.

Other countries

Many other countries pattern their requirements after the larger societies of the US or UK. In general, the websites of these organizations are often the easiest source for finding out about membership requirements and resources.

Exam support

As these qualifying exams are rigorous, support is usually available to people progressing through the exams. Often, employers provide paid on-the-job study time and paid attendance at seminars designed for the exams (BeAnActuary 2005b). Also, many companies which employ actuaries have automatic pay raises or promotions when exams are passed. As a result, actuarial students have strong incentives for devoting adequate study time during off-work hours. A common rule of thumb for exam students is that roughly 400 hours of study time are necessary for each four-hour exam (Sieger 1998). Thus, thousands of hours of study time should be anticipated over several years, assuming no failures (Feldblum 2001, p. 6). In practice, as the historical passing percentages remain below 50% for these exams, the "travel time" to credentialing is extended and more study time is needed. This process resembles formal schooling, so that actuaries who are sitting for exams are still called "students" or "candidates" despite holding important positions with substantial responsibilities.

Notable actuaries

Harald Cramér

Swedish actuary and probabilist notable for his contributions in the area mathematical statistics, such as the Cramér–Rao inequality (Cramér 1946). Professor Cramér was an Honorary President of the Swedish Actuarial Society (Kendall 1983).

James Dodson

Head of the Royal Mathematical School, and Stone's School, Dodson built on the statistical mortality tables developed by Edmund Halley in 1693 (Faculty and Institute of Actuaries 2004).

Edmond Halley

While Halley actually predated much of what is now considered the start of the actuarial profession, he was the first to mathematically and statistically rigorously calculate premiums for a life insurance policy (Halley 1693).

James C. Hickman

Notable actuarial educator, researcher, and author (Chaptman 2006).

David X. Li

a Canadian qualified actuary who in the first decade of the 21st century pioneered the use of Gaussian copula models for the pricing of collateralized debt obligations (CDOs). The Financial Times called him "the world's most influential actuary," while in the aftermath of the Global financial crisis of 2008–2009, to which Li's model has been credited partly to blame, his model has been called a "recipe for disaster".

Edward Rowe Mores

First person to use the title 'actuary' with respect to a business position (Ogborn 1956).

William Morgan

Morgan was the appointed Actuary of the Society for Equitable Assurances in 1775. He expanded on Mores's and Dodson's work, and may be rightly considered the father of the actuarial profession in that his title became applied to the field as a whole.(Ogborn 1973).

Anette Norberg

Skip for the Swedish Women's Curling Team at the 2010 Winter Olympics. Norberg has won gold medals at the 2010 Winter Olympics, the 2006 Winter Olympics, seven European Curling Championships, and two World Curling Championships.

Maurice Princet

French actuary and close associate of artist Pablo Picasso. Princet is considered "Le Mathématicien du Cubisme" ("The Mathematician of Cubism") for his "critical influence on Picasso's development as an artist at the birth of cubism" (Boyle 2002).

Frank Redington

Developed the Redington Immunization Theory

Isaac M. Rubinow

Founder and first president of the Casualty Actuarial Society (CASF 2008).

Elizur Wright

American actuary and abolitionist, professor of mathematics at Western Reserve College (Ohio). He campaigned for laws that required life insurance companies to hold sufficient reserves to guarantee that policies would be paid (Stearns 1905).

Fictional actuaries

Due to the low public-profile of the job, some of the most recognizable actuaries to the general public happen to be characters in movies. Many actuaries were unhappy with the stereotypical portrayals of these actuaries as unhappy, math-obsessed and socially inept people; others have claimed that the portrayals are close to home, if a bit exaggerated. (Coleman 2003).

References

- "Continuing Education Requirement" [4] (PDF). *Qualification Standards for Actuaries Issuing Statements of Actuarial Opinion in the United States* (Washington, D.C.: American Academy of Actuaries): 5–7. 2008. Retrieved January 4, 2010.
- "Membership requirements" [5]. Washington, D.C.: American Academy of Actuaries. 2010. Retrieved January 4, 2010.
- "Actuarial Society of India" [6]. Archived from the original [7] on August 23, 2007. Retrieved 2007-08-31.
- Bader, Lawrence N.; Gold, Jeremy (2003). "Reinventing Pension Actuarial Science" [8] (PDF). *Pension Forum* **14** (2): pp. 1–39. Retrieved 2008-09-14.
- "What is an Actuary?" [9]. BeAnActuary. 2005a. Retrieved 2006-06-11.
- "About Actuarial Examinations" [10]. BeAnActuary. 2005b. Retrieved 2006-08-21.
- "Careers" [11]. Bimaonline.com. 2003. Retrieved 2006-06-06.
- Boyle, Phelim (September 2002). "The actuary and the artist" [12] (PDF). *The Actuary*: 32. Retrieved 2007-03-15.
- Bühlmann, Hans (November 1997). "The actuary: The role and limitations of the profession since the mid-19th century" [13] (PDF). *ASTIN Bulletin* **27** (2): 165–171. ISSN 0515-0361. Retrieved 2006-06-28.
- "Actuaries" [14]. *Occupational Outlook Handbook 2008–09 Edition*. U.S. Department of Labor, Bureau of Labor Statistics. 2007-12-18. Retrieved 2008-09-14.
- "2011 CAS Basic Education Summary" [15] (PDF). *Syllabus of Basic Education*. Casualty Actuarial Society. 2011. Retrieved 2011-01-19.
- "History" [16]. *CAS Overview*. Casualty Actuarial Society. 2008. Retrieved 2008-09-14.

- Chaptman, Dennis (2006-09-13). "James C. Hickman, former business school dean, dies" [17]. *News*. University of Wisconsin–Madison. Retrieved 2008-01-11.

- "Membership & Education: Canadian Enrollment Information" [18]. Canadian Institute of Actuaries. October 2004. Retrieved 2006-06-11.

- Coleman, Lynn G. (Spring 2003). "Was "About Schmidt" about actuaries?" [19]. *The Future Actuary* **12** (1). Retrieved 2006-08-29.

- Cramér, Harald (1946). *Mathematical Methods of Statistics*. Princeton, NJ: Princeton Univ. Press. ISBN 0-691-08004-6. OCLC 185436716.

- D'arcy, Stephen P. (May 1989). "On Becoming An Actuary of the Third Kind" [20] (PDF). *Proceedings of the Casualty Actuarial Society* **LXXVI** (145): 45–76. Retrieved 2006-06-28.

- D'arcy, Stephen P. (November 2005). "On Becoming An Actuary of the Fourth Kind" [21] (PDF). *Proceedings of the Casualty Actuarial Society* **XCII** (177): 745–754. Retrieved 2007-07-05.

- "Inhalte der Ausbildung zum/zur Aktuar/in DAV" [22] (in (German) see here [23] for Google translation). German Actuarial Society. 2006. Retrieved 2008-09-28.

- "Actuary Salary Survey" [24]. D. W. Simpson & Company. 2006. Retrieved 2006-06-11.

- Feldblum, Sholom (2001) [1990]. "Introduction". In Robert F. Lowe (ed.). *Foundations of Casualty Actuarial Science* (4th ed.). Arlington, Virginia: Casualty Actuarial Society. ISBN 0-9624762-2-6 LCCN 2001-88378.

- "History of the actuarial profession" [25]. Faculty and Institute of Actuaries. 2004-01-13. Archived from the original [26] on 2008-04-04. Retrieved 2010-09-26.

- "How do I become a student?" [27]. *Actuarial Profession*. Faculty and Institute of Actuaries. 2006. Archived from the original [28] on 2008-05-26. Retrieved 2010-09-26.

- Haastrup, Svend; Jens Perch, Nielsen (2007) (PDF). *The historical perspective of the Danish actuarial profession* [29]. Retrieved 2006-12-14.

- Halley, Edmond (1693). "An Estimate of the Degrees of the Mortality of Mankind, Drawn from Curious Tables of the Births and Funerals at the City of Breslaw; With an Attempt to Ascertain the Price of Annuities upon Lives" [30] (PDF). *Philosophical Transactions of the Royal Society of London* **17**: 596–610. doi:10.1098/rstl.1693.0007. ISSN 0260-7085. Retrieved 2006-06-21.

- Hickman, James (2004). "History of Actuarial Profession" [31] (PDF). *Encyclopedia of Actuarial Science*. John Wiley & Sons, Ltd.. p. 4. Archived from the original [32] on August 4, 2004. Retrieved 2006-06-28.

- "Education" [33]. Institute of Actuaries of Australia. 2006. Archived from the original [34] on February 8, 2007. Retrieved 2007-05-01.

- "Part I" [35]. *Courses*. Institute of Actuaries of Australia. 2006. Archived from the original [36] on April 20, 2007. Retrieved 2007-05-01.

- "Part II (Actuarial Control Cycle)" [37]. *Courses*. Institute of Actuaries of Australia. 2006. Archived from the original [38] on March 15, 2007. Retrieved 2007-05-01.

- "Part III" [39]. *Courses*. Institute of Actuaries of Australia. 2006. Archived from the original [40] on April 3, 2007. Retrieved 2007-05-01.

- Johnston, Harold Whetstone (1932) [1903]. "Burial places and funeral ceremonies" [41]. *The Private Life of the Romans* [42]. Revised by Mary Johnston. Chicago, Atlanta: Scott, Foresman and Company. pp. §475–§476. ISBN 0-8154-0453-0. LCCN 32-7692. Retrieved 2006-06-26. "Early in the Empire, associations were formed for the purpose of meeting the funeral expenses of their members, whether the remains were to be buried or cremated, or for the purpose of building columbāria, or for both....If the members had provided places for the disposal of their bodies after death, they now provided for the necessary funeral expenses by paying into the common fund weekly a small fixed sum, easily within the reach of the poorest of them. When a member died, a stated sum was drawn from the treasury for his funeral .... If the purpose of the society was the building of a columbārium, the cost was first determined and the sum total divided into what we should call shares (sortēs virīlēs), each member taking as many as he could afford and paying their value into the treasury."

- Kendall, David (1983). "A Tribute to Harald Cramer". *Journal of the Royal Statistical Society. Series A (General)* (Oxford, England: Blackwell Publishing) **146** (3): 211–212. ISSN 00359238. JSTOR 2981652.

- Krutov, Alex (2006). "Insurance Linked Securities" [43]. *Financial Engineering News magazine* (48). Retrieved 2006-11-30.

- Loan, Albert (Winter 1991/92). "Institutional Bases of the Spontaneous Order: Surety and Assurance" [44]. *Humane Studies Review* **7** (1). Retrieved 2006-06-26.

- Lomas, Anna (2009-01-23). "Occupational profile: Actuary, consultancy" [45] (PDF). AGCAS. p. 4. Archived from the original [46] on July 28, 2004. Retrieved 2009-01-05.

- MacGinnitie, James (November 1980). "The Actuary and his Profession: Growth, Development, Promise" [47] (PDF). *Proceedings of the Casualty Actuarial Society* **LXVII** (127): 49–56. Retrieved 2006-06-28.

- Michelbacher, Gustav F. (1920). "The Technique of Rate Making as Illustrated by the 1920 National Revision of Workmen's Compensations Insurance Rates" [48] (PDF). *Proceedings of the Casualty Actuarial Society* **VI** (14): 201–249. Retrieved 2006-06-28.

- Needleman, Sarah E. (January 5, 2010). "The Best and Worst Jobs" [49]. *Wall Street Journal*. Retrieved 2010-01-07.

- Nemko, Marty (2006). "Best Careers 2007" [50]. *U.S. News & World Report*. Archived from the original [51] on 2007-12-26. Retrieved 2008-09-14.

- Norberg, Ragnar (1990). "Actuarial Statistics — The European Perspective" [52] (PDF). *International Conference on the Teaching of Statistics 3, Dunedin, New Zealand*. Auckland, New Zealand: International Association for Statistical Education. pp. 405–410. Retrieved 2006-12-14.

- Ogborn, M.E. (December 1956). "The Professional Name of Actuary" [53] (PDF). *Journal of the Institute of Actuaries* (Faculty and Institute of Actuaries) **82**: 233–246. Retrieved April 27, 2011.

- Ogborn, M.E. (July 1973). "Catalogue of an exhibition illustrating the history of actuarial science in the United Kingdom" [54] (PDF). *Journal of the Institute of Actuaries* (Faculty and Institute of Actuaries) **100**: 7–8. Retrieved April 27, 2011.

- Perkins, Judith (1995-08-25). *The Suffering Self; Pain and Narrative Representation in the Early Christian Era*. London, England: Routledge. ISBN 0-415-11363-6. LCCN 94042650.

- Sieger, Richard (March 1998). "What is an Actuary?" [55]. *Future Fellows* **4** (1). Retrieved 2006-06-22.

- "Admission Requirements to the SOA" [56]. *Spring 2008 Basic Education Catalog*. Society of Actuaries. 2008. Archived from the original [57] on December 26, 2007. Retrieved 2008-01-11.

- Slud, Eric V. (2006) [2001]. "6: Commutation Functions, Reserves & Select Mortality" [58] (PDF). *Actuarial Mathematics and Life-Table Statistics* [59]. pp. 149–150. Retrieved 2006-06-28. "The Commutation Functions are a computational device to ensure that net single premiums ... can all be obtained from a single table lookup. Historically, this idea has been very important in saving calculational labor when arriving at premium quotes. Even now...company employees without quantitative training could calculate premiums in a spreadsheet format with the aid of a life table."

- Stearns, Frank Preston (1905). "Elizur Wright" [60] (text). *Cambridge sketches* (1st ed.). Philadelphia, Pennsylvania: J. B. Lippincott Company. LCCN 05-11051. Retrieved 2007-01-15. "This danger could only be averted by placing their rates of insurance on a scientific basis, which should be the same and unalterable for all companies. ... After two or three interviews with Elizur Wright the presidents of the companies came to the conclusion that he was exactly the man that they wanted, and they commissioned him to draw up a revised set of tables and rates which could serve them for a uniform standard."

- "Aktuarieprogrammet" [61] (in (Swedish)). Stockholm University. 2006. Retrieved 2006-09-10.

- Thucydides (c. 431 BCE). "VI — Funeral Oration of Pericles" [62]. *[[The History of the Peloponnesian War* [63]*]]. Translated by Richard Crawley. Greece. ISBN 0-525-26035-8. Retrieved 2006-06-27. "My task is now finished. ... those who are here interred have received part of their honours already, and for the rest, their children will be brought up till manhood at the public expense: the state thus offers a valuable prize, as the garland of victory in this race of valour, for the reward both of those who have fallen and their survivors."*

- Tong, Vinnee (2006-06-19). "Americans' donations to charity near record" [64]. *Chicago Sun-Times* (Digital Chicago Inc.). Retrieved 2006-06-21.

- Trowbridge, Charles L. (1989) (PDF). *Fundamental Concepts of Actuarial Science* [65]. Revised Edition. Actuarial Education and Research Fund. Retrieved 2006-06-28.

- Whelan, Shane (December 2002). "Actuaries' contributions to financial economics" [66] (PDF). *The Actuary* (Staple Inn Actuarial Society): pp. 34–35. Retrieved 2006-06-28.

- "Aktuarstudiet" [67] (in Norwegian). University of Bergen. 2011. Retrieved 2011-03-04.

- "Norwegian Society of Actuaries" [68]. Norwegian Society of Actuaries. 2011. Retrieved 2011-03-04.

[1] http://www.casact.org/admissions/syllabus/
[2] http://www.actuarialsociety.co.za
[3] http://www.iseg.utl.pt
[4] http://www.actuary.org/qualstandards/qual.pdf
[5] http://www.actuary.org/beco.asp#3
[6] http://web.archive.org/web/20070823222851/http://www.actuariesindia.org/index.html
[7] http://www.actuariesindia.org/index.html
[8] http://users.erols.com/jeremygold/reinventingpensionactuarialscience.pdf
[9] http://www.beanactuary.com/about/whatis.cfm
[10] http://www.beanactuary.com/exams/exam_info.cfm
[11] http://www.bimaonline.com/cgi-bin/ind/careersnew/insurancecareers.asp
[12] http://www.the-actuary.org.uk/pdfs/02_09_09.pdf
[13] http://www.casact.org/library/astin/vol27no2/165.pdf
[14] http://www.bls.gov/oco/ocos041.htm
[15] http://www.casact.org/admissions/syllabus/summary.pdf
[16] http://www.casact.org/about/index.cfm?fa=aboutTheCAS
[17] http://www.news.wisc.edu/12874
[18] http://www.actuaries.ca/membership/enrollment_e.cfm
[19] http://www.beanactuary.org/news/futureactuary/2003mar/schmidt.cfm
[20] http://www.casact.org/pubs/proceed/proceed89/89045.pdf
[21] http://www.casact.org/pubs/proceed/proceed05/05755.pdf
[22] http://www.aktuar.de/php/showsite.php?menu=010302&GSAG=4f2539c5ebb3963796a1203ad60192d0
[23] http://translate.google.com/translate?u=http%3A%2F%2Fwww.aktuar.de%2Fphp%2Fshowsite.php%3Fmenu%3D0101&sl=de&tl=en&hl=en&ie=UTF-8
[24] http://www.dwsimpson.com/salary.html
[25] http://web.archive.org/web/20080404072019/http://www.actuaries.org.uk/knowledge/actuarial_history/history_of_profession
[26] http://www.actuaries.org.uk/knowledge/actuarial_history/history_of_profession
[27] http://web.archive.org/web/20080526114844/http://www.actuaries.org.uk/students/getting_started/become_a_student
[28] http://www.actuaries.org.uk/students/getting_started/become_a_student
[29] http://citeseer.ist.psu.edu/cache/papers/cs/16500/http:zSzzSzwww.math.ku.dkzSz~haastrupzSzic2.pdf/the-historical-perspective-of.pdf
[30] http://www.york.ac.uk/depts/maths/histstat/halley.pdf
[31] http://web.archive.org/web/20040804113004/http://www.wiley.co.uk/eoas/pdfs/TAH012-.pdf
[32] http://www.wiley.co.uk/eoas/pdfs/TAH012-.pdf
[33] http://web.archive.org/web/20070208165244/http://www.actuaries.asn.au/Education
[34] http://www.actuaries.asn.au/Education
[35] http://web.archive.org/web/20070420194909/http://www.actuaries.asn.au/Education/Courses/PartOne
[36] http://www.actuaries.asn.au/Education/Courses/PartOne

[37] http://web.archive.org/web/20070315071810/http://www.actuaries.asn.au/Education/Courses/PartTwo

[38] http://www.actuaries.asn.au/Education/Courses/PartTwo

[39] http://web.archive.org/web/20070403154713/http://www.actuaries.asn.au/Education/Courses/PartThree

[40] http://www.actuaries.asn.au/Education/Courses/PartThree

[41] http://www.forumromanum.org/life/johnston_14.html

[42] http://www.forumromanum.org/life/johnston.html

[43] http://www.fenews.com/fen48/one_time_articles/insurance/insurance.html

[44] http://mason.gmu.edu/~ihs/w91essay.html

[45] http://web.archive.org/web/20040728202539/http://www.prospects.ac.uk/downloads/occprofiles/profile_pdfs/
      I1_Actuary,_consultancy.pdf

[46] http://www.prospects.ac.uk/downloads/occprofiles/profile_pdfs/I1_Actuary,_consultancy.pdf

[47] http://www.casact.com/pubs/proceed/proceed80/80049.pdf

[48] http://www.casact.org/pubs/proceed/proceed19/19201.pdf

[49] http://online.wsj.com/article/SB10001424052748703580904574638321841284190.html

[50] http://web.archive.org/web/20071118105300/www.usnews.com/usnews/biztech/best_careers_2007/careertable-njs.htm

[51] http://www.usnews.com/usnews/biztech/best_careers_2007/

[52] http://www.stat.auckland.ac.nz/~iase/publications/18/BOOK2/B7-2.pdf

[53] http://www.actuaries.org.uk/sites/all/files/documents/pdf/0233-0246.pdf

[54] http://www.actuaries.org.uk/sites/all/files/documents/pdf/0005-0014.pdf

[55] http://casact.org/admissions/futfell/mar98/whatis.htm

[56] http://web.archive.org/web/20071226132559/http://www.soa.org/education/course-catalog/spring-exam-session/2008/
      edu-admission-req.aspx

[57] http://www.soa.org/education/course-catalog/spring-exam-session/2008/edu-admission-req.aspx

[58] http://www.math.umd.edu/~evs/s470/BookChaps/Chp6.pdf

[59] http://www.math.umd.edu/~evs/s470/BookChaps/01Book.pdf

[60] http://www.gutenberg.org/dirs/etext05/7camb10.txt

[61] http://www.utbildning.su.se/katalog/Linjer/46.asp

[62] http://classics.mit.edu/Thucydides/pelopwar.2.second.html

[63] http://classics.mit.edu/Thucydides/pelopwar.html

[64] http://www.suntimes.com/output/news/cst-nws-phil19.html

[65] http://www.actuarialfoundation.org/research_edu/fundamental.pdf

[66] http://www.the-actuary.org.uk/pdfs/02_12_08.pdf

[67] http://www.mi.uib.no/adm/grupper/aktuar/aktuar.html

[68] http://www.aktfor.no/organisasjon_english.html

External links

- Actuarial Society of India (http://www.actuariesindia.org/)
- Be An Actuary: The SOA and CAS jointly sponsored web site (http://www.beanactuary.com)
- Institute of Actuaries and Faculty of Actuaries (http://www.actuaries.org.uk/)
- American Society of Pension Professionals & Actuaries (http://www.asppa.org/)
- Global Actuarial Forum, Community and Jobs (http://www.actuaryclub.com/)
- Global actuarial discussion forum (http://www.actuarialoutpost.com/actuarial_discussion_forum/index.php) and actuarial wiki (http://www.actuarialoutpost.com/wiki)
- Actuarial Wiki (http://www.actuarialwiki.org)

ALARP

ALARP stands for "**as low as reasonably practicable**", and is a term often used in the milieu of safety-critical and safety-involved systems. The **ALARP principle** is that *the residual risk shall be as low as reasonably practicable*. It has particular connotations as a route to reduce risks **SFAIRP** (so far as is reasonably practicable) in UK Health and Safety law.

For a risk to be ALARP it must be possible to demonstrate that the cost involved in reducing the risk further would be grossly disproportionate to the benefit gained. The ALARP principle arises from the fact that infinite time, effort and money could be spent on the attempt of reducing a risk to zero. It should not be understood as simply a quantitive measure of benefit against detriment. It is more a best common practice of judgement of the balance of risk and societal benefit.

Factors

In this context, risk is the combination of the frequency and the consequence of a specified hazardous event.

The following factors are likely to be considered when deciding whether or not a risk is *tolerable*.

- Health and safety guidelines
- The specification
- International standards and laws
- Suggestions from advisory bodies
- Comparison with similar hazardous events in other industries

Another factor that comes into the ALARP principle, is the cost of assessing the improvement gained in an attempted risk reduction. In extremely complex systems, this can be very high, and could be the limiting factor in practicability of risk reduction.

Determining that a risk has been reduced to ALARP involves an assessment of the risk to be avoided, of the sacrifice (in money, time and trouble) involved in taking measures to avoid that risk, and a comparison of the two. This is a cost-benefit analysis.

Origin in UK law

The term ALARP arises from UK legislation, particularly the Health and Safety at Work etc. Act 1974, which requires "Provision and maintenance of plant and systems of work that are, so far as is reasonably practicable, safe and without risks to health". The phrase So Far As is Reasonably Practicable (SFARP) in this and similar clauses is interpreted as leading to a requirement that risks must be reduced to a level that is As Low As is Reasonably Practicable (ALARP).

The key question in determining whether a risk is ALARP is the definition of **reasonably practicable**. This term has been enshrined in the UK case law since the case of *Edwards v. National Coal Board* in 1949. The ruling was that the risk must be insignificant in relation to the sacrifice (in terms of money, time or trouble) required to avert it: risks must be averted unless there is a **gross disproportion** between the costs and benefits of doing so.[1]

Including gross disproportion means that an ALARP judgement in the UK is not a simple cost benefit analysis, but is weighted to favour carrying out the safety improvement. However, there is no broad consensus on the precise factor that would be appropriate.

Use outside the UK

Outside the UK the ALARP principle is often not used; instead standards and 'good engineering practice' are adhered to, and legislation tends to require absolute levels of safety.

The term ALARA, or "as low as reasonably achievable" is used interchangeably in the United States of America, almost exclusively in the field of Radiation Protection.

Where the ALARP principle is used, it may not have the same implications as in the UK, as "reasonably practicable" may be interpreted according to the local culture, without introducing the concept of gross disproportionality.

Legal challenge

A 2-year legal battle in the European Court of Justice resulted in the SFAIRP principle being upheld on 18 January 2007.

The European Commission had claimed that the SFAIRP wording in the Health & Safety at Work Act did not fully implement the requirements of the Framework Directive. The Directive gives employers an absolute duty "to ensure the safety and health of workers in every aspect related to the work", whereas the Act qualifies the duty "So Far As is Reasonably Practicable". The court dismissed the action and ordered the Commission to pay the UK's costs.[2] [3]

Had the case been upheld, it would have called into question the proportionate approach to safety risk management embodied in the ALARP principle.

Carrot diagrams

So called carrot diagrams are often used to display risks. They are called carrot diagrams, because they have an elongated triangle in the centre, which looks like a carrot, and indicates the high (normally unacceptable) risks at the top and the low (broadly tolerable) risks at the bottom. The region in between is sometimes called the **ALARP region**; however this is misleading because the ALARP principle applies to all regions. A better name is the 'Tolerable Region', because risks in this region can sometimes be tolerated, if they cannot practically be reduced, in return for the benefits provided by the system or installation that causes the risks.

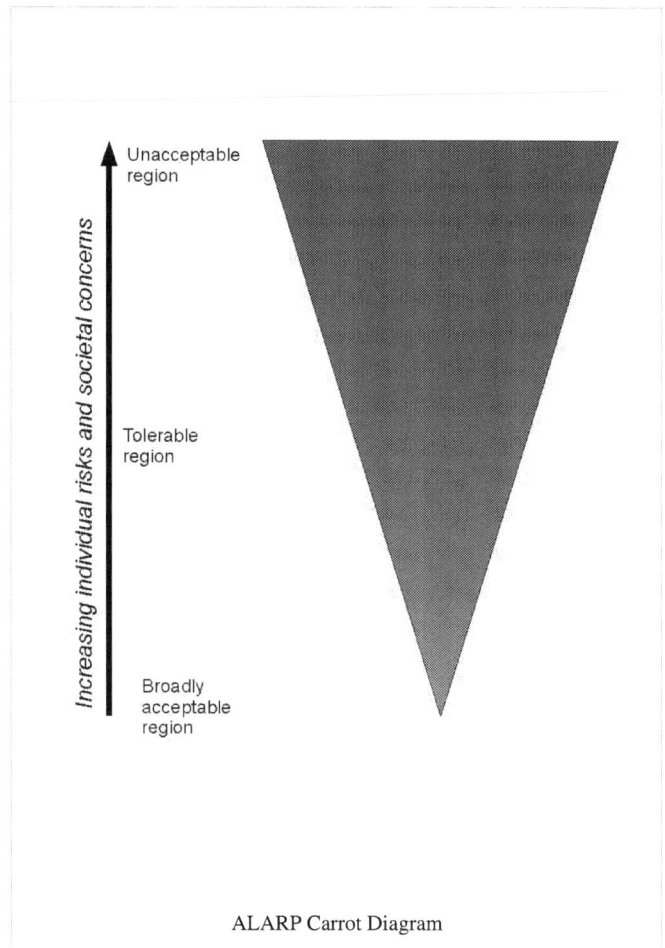

ALARP Carrot Diagram

References

[1] Edwards v. National Coal Board. (http://oxcheps.new.ox. ac.uk/new/casebook/cases/Cases Chapter 25/Edwards v National Coal Board.doc) (1949) All ER 743 (CA)

[2] Judgement of the Court (http://eur-lex.europa.eu/ LexUriServ/LexUriServ. do?uri=CELEX:62005J0127:EN:HTML) on Case C-127/05

[3] Press release (http://www.hse.gov.uk/press/2007/c07007. htm) by the UK Health and Safety Executive

External links

- UK Health and Safety Executive ALARP Guidance (http://www.hse.gov.uk/risk/theory/alarp.htm)

- UK Health and Safety Executive ALARP Cost Benefit Analysis (http://www.hse.gov.uk/risk/theory/alarpcheck.htm)
- UK Defence Standard 00-56 Safety Management Requirements (http://www.dstan.mod.uk/data/00/056/01000400.pdf)

APSYS

APSYS (an abbreviation of **Aérospatiale Protection Systems**), is a subsidiary[1] of Cassidian (an EADS company). APSYS was created in 1985 and specializes in safety and reliability engineering for Life-critical system, using techniques such as ZSA, PRA, FMECA and Fault Tree Analysis.

Markets include Aviation, Defence, Space, Nuclear Energy, Rail, Oil and Gas Industries.[2]

Projects

Some of the notable past and current Apsys projects[3] are as follows:

- Airbus A380
- Airbus A350
- Airbus A400M
- Airbus A340
- French Atomic Commission (CEA)

Software Products

- SIMFIA - A Safety Analysis and Simulation Tool
- SIMLOG - An ILS Tool
- DIAGSYS - A Fault Diagnosis Tool

References

[1] http://www.cassidian.com/cassidian/int/en/our-company/our-locations/Europe/france/elancourt.html
[2] http://www.apsys.eads.net/en/11/Our-Offer
[3] http://eidi.f4e.europa.eu/company_details.php?id=46

External links

- Company Website (http://www.apsys.eads.net/en/5/Home)
- UK Office (http://maps.google.com/maps?q=apsys+uk&um=1&hl=en&biw=1680&bih=935&ie=UTF-8&sa=N&tab=vl)
- APSYS Brochure (http://www.apsys.eads.net/wwwData/files/pdf/Plaquette-APSYS-UK.pdf)

ATHEANA

A Technique for Human Error Analysis (ATHEANA) is a technique used in the field of human reliability assessment (HRA), for the purposes of evaluating the probability of a human error occurring throughout the completion of a specific task. From such analyses measures can then be taken to reduce the likelihood of errors occurring within a system and therefore lead to an improvement in the overall levels of safety. There exist three primary reasons for conducting an HRA; error identification, error quantification and error reduction. As there exist a number of techniques used for such purposes, they can be split into one of two classifications; first generation techniques and second generation techniques. First generation techniques work on the basis of the simple dichotomy of 'fits/doesn't fit' in the matching of the error situation in context with related error identification and quantification and second generation techniques are more theory based in their assessment and quantification of errors. 'HRA techniques have been utilised in a range of industries including healthcare, engineering, nuclear, transportation and business sector; each technique has varying uses within different disciplines.

ATHEANA is used following the occurrence of an incident. The various drivers of an incident and the possible outcomes are categorised into one of the following groupings: organisational influences; performance shaping factors; error mechanisms; unsafe actions; human failure event; unacceptable outcome(s). The resultant model may indicate solutions to improve reliability, however there are no numerical aspects involved in the methodology used to construct the model. Due to this characteristic, the technique is thus not considered to be suitable for use in certain fields such as comparative design work or sensitivity analysis. The methodology of ATHEANA is not predictive but does serve as a diagnostic modelling tool. Furthermore, its lack of Human Error Probability (HEP) as an output is a marked difference of the method compared to first generation HRA methodologies. The outcome provided by ATHEANA identifies various human actions within a system while also eliciting many contextual situations within this system, which influence whether the action will be carried out successfully or will lead to failure.

Background

ATHEANA is a post-incident Human Reliability Assessment (HRA) methodology developed by the US Nuclear Regulatory Commission in 2000. It was developed in the hope that certain types of human behaviour in nuclear plants and industries, which use similar processes, could be represented in a way in which they could be more easily understood. It seeks to provide a robust psychological framework to evaluate and identify Performance Shaping Factors (PSFs) - including organisational/environmental factors - which have driven incidents involving human factors, primarily with the intention of suggesting process improvement.[1]. Essentially it is a method of representing complex accident reports within a standardised structure, which may be easier to understand and communicate.

ATHEANA methodology

There are seven basic steps to the ATHEANA methodology [4]

1. Define and interpret the issue under consideration
2. Detail the required scope of analysis
3. Describe the Base case scenario including the norm of operations within the environment, considering actions and procedures.
4. Define Human Failure Events (HFE's) and/or unsafe actions (UAs) which may affect the task in question
5. Following the identification of the HFEs, they should be further categorised into two primary groups, safe and unsafe actions (UAs). An unsafe action is an action in which the human operator concerned may fail to carry out a task or does so incorrectly and this consequently results in the unsafe operation of the system.
6. Search for deviations from the base case scenario in terms of any probable divergence in the normal environmental operating behaviour in the context of the situational scenario.

7. Preparation for applying ATHEANA

8. In recognition that the environment and the surrounding context may affect the human operator's behaviour, the next stage of the ATHEANA methodology is to take account of what are known as error-forcing contexts (EFCs), which are then combined with performance shaping factors (PSFs), as identified in the figure provided below [2].

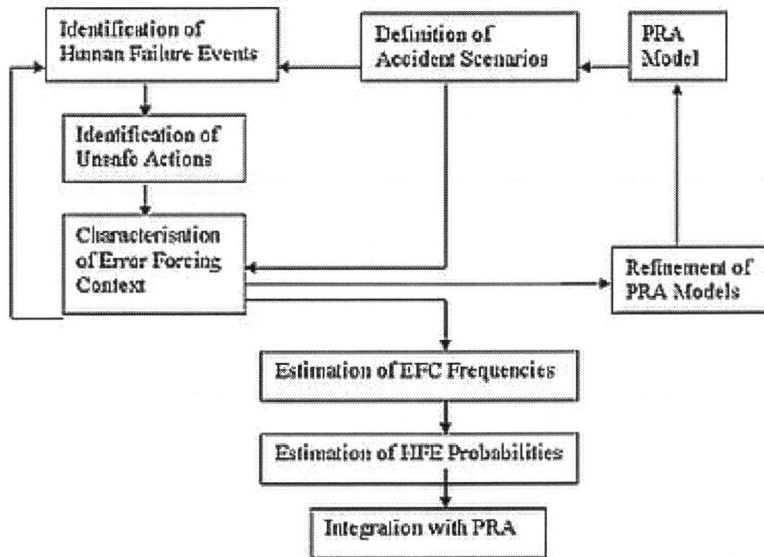

Schematic outline of ATHEANA

The formulation by which ATHEANA quantifies error is as follows [2]:

$$P(HFEijr)= P(EFCi)\ P(UAj|EFCi)\ P(\bar{R}|EFCi|UAj|Eij)$$

where:

- **P(HFEijr)**: the probability of human failure event (HFEijr) occurring
- **P(EFCi):** the probability of error-forcing context
- **P(UAj|EFCi)**: the probability of unsafe action within a specific context or EFC
- **P(¯R|EFCi|UAj|Eij)**: the non-recovery probability in the EFC and given the occurrence of the unsafe action and the existence of additional evidence (Eij) following the unsafe action

Advantages

- The most significant advantage of ATHEANA is that it provides a much richer and more holistic understanding of the context concerning the Human factors known to be the cause of the incident, as compared with most other first generation methods.
- It may also be alleged that carrying out this type of quantitative modelling leads to the enhancement of understanding as it requires stakeholders and decision makers to consider and discuss the contributing aspects as part of the model-building procedure.
- It increases the guarantee that the key risks associated with the Human Failure Events in question have been identified. [3]

- Utilising the ATHEANA methodology, it is possible to estimate Human Error Probabilities considering a variety of differing factors and combinations. [3]
- Compared to many other HRA quantification methods, ATHEANA allows for the consideration of a much wider range of performance shaping factors and also does not require that these be treated as independent. This is important as the method seeks to identify any interactions which affect the weighting of the factors of their influence on a situation

Disadvantages

- The primary shortcoming of the technique is that, from a Probability Risk assessment (PRA) stance, there is no HEP produced. As a result, the ease with which this analysis can be fit into a predictive quantitative risk assessment is reduced.
- Also, while the method is apparent in categorising the human factors contributing to an incident, it fails to prioritise or establish details of the causal relationships between these factors. Thus, further work is required to be performed in order to establish the root cause (s) of an incident from a HRA perspective.
- The outcomes of the human errors under consideration are constrained by previously defined sequences of PSA accidents
- For the purposes of predictive analysis the theoretical foundations on which the ATHEANA methodology is based are considered to be ineffectual

References

[1] Cooper, S.E., Ramey-Smith, A.M. & Wreathall, J., A Technique for Human Error Analysis (ATHEANA). 1996, US Nulcear Regulatory Commission.

[2] Kim, I.S. (2001) Human reliability analysis design review. Annals of Nuclear Energy. 28 1069–1081.

[3] http://www.nrc.gov/reading-rm/doc-collections/nuregs/staff/sr1880/sr1880.pdf

[4] Forster et al. (2004). Expert elicitation approach for performing ATHEANA quantification. Reliability Engineering and Safety System. 83 207-220

[5] Forester J et al. NUREG-1624, (2000), Technical Basis and Implementation Guidelines for A Technique for Human Event Analysis (ATHEANA). Rev. 1

External links

- [1]PDF (709 KB)
- [2]PDF
- [3]PDF
- [4]PDF

References

[1] http://www.nrc.gov/reading-rm/doc-collections/nuregs/staff/sr1880/sr1880.pdf

[2] http://www.sciencedirect.com_science/ob=MImg&_imagekey=B6V4T-49W6R94-1-8&_cdi=5767&_user=875629&_orig=search& _coverDate=02%2F29%2F2004&_sk=999169997&view=c&wchp=dGLbVlb-zSkzV&md5=8f2ef4b7f5e981db31565ad7ca960c0b& ie=_sdarticle.pdf

[3] http://www.sciencedirect.com_science/ob=MImg&_imagekey=B6V4T-40KS1V4-2-1&_cdi=5767&_user=875629&_orig=search& _coverDate=04%2F30%2F1998&_sk=999399998&view=c&wchp=dGLbVlz-zSkzk&md5=2e6c15075427cbecd48bcb21d364c982& ie=_sdarticle.pdf

[4] http://www.osti.gov/energycitations/servlets/purl/249298-QifjaL/webviewable/249298.PDF

Ballpark model

The **ballpark model** is a system under which users of a facility do so at their own risk. The name arises from the fact that visitors to a ballpark bear the risk of getting hit by bats, balls and other objects flying into the stands at high velocities. An example of this type of system is New Hampshire's lack of a requirement that motorists carry liability insurance. The risk of getting hit by a driver who has neither insurance nor the means to pay for damages is borne by other motorists.

It is in contrast to the Disneyland model.

Biosafety

Biosafety: prevention of large-scale loss of biological integrity, focusing both on ecology and human health .

Biosafety is related to several fields:

- In ecology (referring to imported life forms from beyond ecoregion borders),
- In agriculture (reducing the risk of alien viral or transgenic genes, or prions such as BSE/"MadCow", reducing the risk of food bacterial contamination)
- In medicine (referring to organs or tissues from biological origin, or genetic therapy products, virus; levels of lab containment protocols measured as 1, 2, 3, 4 in rising order of danger),
- In chemistry (i.e., nitrates in water, PCB levels affecting fertility) and
- In exobiology (i.e., NASA's policy for containing alien microbes that may exist on space samples - sometimes called "biosafety level 5").

The international Biosafety Protocol deals primarily with the agricultural definition but many advocacy groups seek to expand it to include post-genetic threats: new molecules, artificial life forms, and even robots which may compete directly in the natural food chain.

Biosafety in agriculture, chemistry, medicine, exobiology and beyond will likely require application of the precautionary principle, and a new definition focused on the biological nature of the threatened organism rather than the nature of the threat.

When biological warfare or new, currently hypothetical, threats (i.e., robots, new artificial bacteria) are considered, biosafety precautions are generally not sufficient. The new field of biosecurity addresses these complex threats.

Biosafety level refers to the stringency of biocontainment precautions deemed necessary by the Centers for Disease Control and Prevention (CDC) for laboratory work with infectious materials.

References

- WHO Biosafety Programme [1]
- CDC Biosafety pages [2]
- The Sunshine Project: Nonprofit Laboratory Biosafety Watchdog [3]
- International Centre for Genetic Engineering and Biotechnology (ICGEB): Biosafety pages [4]
- Greenpeace [5] safe trade campaign
- American Biological Safety Association [6]
- Biosafety in Microbiological and Biomedical Laboratories [7]
- Program for Biosafety Systems [8] US-funded program
- Food Security and Ag-Biotech News [9] — balanced global news on biosafety issues in agriculture
- GMO Safety [10] - Information about research projects on the biological safety of genetically modified plants.
- The 2011 International Conference on Biocontainment Facilities [11]

- Karlsruhe Institute of Technology (KIT) - Forschungsstelle für Brandschutztechnik: Research on fire protection and extinguishing systems in microbiological and genetic engineering laboratories. [12]

References

[1] http://www.who.int/csr/labepidemiology/projects/biosafety/en/

[2] http://www.cdc.gov/od/ohs/biosfty/biosfty.htm

[3] http://www.sunshine-project.org

[4] http://www.icgeb.org/biosafety

[5] http://greenpeace.org

[6] http://www.absa.org

[7] http://www.cdc.gov/od/ohs/biosfty/bmbl4/bmbl4toc.htm

[8] http://www.ifpri.org/themes/pbs/pbs.htm

[9] http://www.merid.org/fs-agbiotech/

[10] http://www.gmo-safety.eu/en/

[11] http://www.TradelineInc.com/BIO2011

[12] http://www.ffb.uni-karlsruhe.de/download/IMK_Ber._Nr._149_Kunkelmann_Brandschutz_in_Genlaboren_Teil_1-240.pdf

Biosafety Clearing-House

The **Biosafety Clearing-House** is an international mechanism that exchanges information about the movement of genetically modified organisms, established under the Cartagena Protocol on Biosafety.

Overview of the Biosafety Clearing-House

The Biosafety Clearing-House (BCH) is an information-exchange mechanism established by the Cartagena Protocol on Biosafety to assist Parties to implement its provisions and to facilitate sharing of information on, and experience with, living modified organisms (also known as GMOs). The Biosafety Clearing-House Central Portal [1] is accessible through the Web.

The BCH assists Parties (i.e. governments that have ratified the Protocol) and other stakeholders to make informed decisions regarding the importation or release of living modified organisms. The BCH is a distributed system, and information in it is owned and updated by the users themselves through an authenticated system to ensure timeliness and accuracy.

Mandate of the Biosafety Clearing-House

Article 20, paragraph 1 of the Cartagena Protocol on Biosafety established the BCH as part of the clearing-house mechanism of the Convention on Biological Diversity, in order to:

(a) Facilitate the exchange of scientific, technical, environmental and legal information on, and experience with, living modified organisms; and (b) Assist Parties to implement the Protocol, taking into account the special needs of developing country Parties, in particular the least developed and small island developing States among them, and countries with economies in transition as well as countries that are centres of origin and centres of genetic diversity.

Interoperability and the Central Portal of the BCH

The Biosafety Clearing-House is designed to be interoperable with other databases, so governments may register their information with the central Biosafety Clearing-House database, or with another (interoperable) database of their choice. The location of the information makes no difference to the user, who is able to retrieve all information through the Central Portal of the Biosafety Clearing-House.

To date, a number of relevant databases have been identified and are interoperable with the Central Portal, including national sites such as the United States Regulatory Agencies Unified Biotechnology Website and the Swiss Biosafety Clearing-House, and international databases such as the Organisation for Economic Co-operation and Development (OECD) unique identification database and the International Centre for Genetic Engineering and Biotechnology (ICGEB) biosafety publications database.

First use in international law

The BCH differs from other similar mechanisms established under other international legal agreements because it is in fact essential for the successful implementation of its parent body, the Protocol. It was the first Internet-based information-exchange mechanism created that must be used to fulfil certain international legal obligations - not only do Parties to the Protocol have a legal obligation to provide certain types of information to the BCH within defined time-frames, but certain provisions cannot be implemented without use of the BCH.

For example, under Article 11.1 of the Protocol, a decision taken on domestic use of a GMO that might cross international borders (this includes placing on the market) must be advised to other potentially affected Parties through the BCH within 15 days of making the decision to allow them to assess potential impacts on their own territories. This is in contrast to the Advance Informed Agreement procedure which is a more traditional bilateral discussion between importers and exporters to obtain prior informed consent before releasing GMOs into the environment.

Information in the Biosafety Clearing-House

Categories of information in the BCH

The BCH contains information that must be provided by Parties to the Protocol, such as decisions on release or importation of GMOs, risk assessments, competent national authorities, and national laws; as well as other relevant information and resources, including information on capacity-building, a roster of government-nominated experts in the field, and links to other websites and databases through the Biosafety Information Resource Centre.

Governments that are not Parties to the Protocol are also encouraged to contribute information the BCH, and in fact a large number of the decisions in the BCH have been registered by two non-Party governments (Canada and the United States).

Organisation of information in the BCH

The BCH uses common formats for reporting information from distributed sources, and standardized terminology or "controlled vocabulary" to categorize the information contained within the databases. This allows the many users of the BCH to use the same terms whether they are registering information or searching for it, including synonyms within a language; relationships between terms; and between languages. To enable access to global information, the BCH operates in all six UN languages for both reporting and retrieving data (English, French, Spanish, Russian, Arabic and Chinese).

Capacity Building for participation in the BCH

Recognising the importance of Parties to use and participate in the BCH, the Global Environment Facility approved, in March 2004, a USD $13 million project entitled "Building Capacity for Effective Participation in the Biosafety Clearing House (BCH) of the Cartagena Protocol" to assist eligible Parties of the Protocol. 139 countries are eligible for funding under this project.

External links

- Biosafety Clearing-House Central Portal [2]
- Biosafety Protocol Homepage [3]
- UNEP-GEF Project on Building Capacity for Effective Participation in the Biosafety Clearing House of the Cartagena Protocol [4]

References

Secretariat of the Convention on Biological Diversity (2000) *Cartagena Protocol on Biosafety to the Convention on Biological Diversity: text and annexes*. Montreal, Canada. ISBN 978-92-807-1924-6

Galloway McLean, K (2005): 'Bridging the gap between researchers and policy-makers: International collaboration through the Biosafety Clearing-House [5]' *Environmental Biosafety Research* **4** (2005) 123-126

References

[1] http://bch.biodiv.org
[2] http://bch.cbd.int
[3] http://www.cbd.int/biosafety/
[4] http://www.unep.ch/biosafety/BCH.htm
[5] http://www.edpsciences.org/articles/ebr/pdf/2005/03/ebr0531.pdf

Cartagena Protocol on Biosafety

The **Cartagena Protocol on Biosafety** is an international agreement on biosafety, as a supplement to the Convention on Biological Diversity.

Overview of the Biosafety Protocol

The Biosafety Protocol seeks to protect biological diversity from the potential risks posed by living modified organisms resulting from modern biotechnology.

The Biosafety Protocol makes clear that products from new technologies must be based on the precautionary principle and allow developing nations to balance public health against economic benefits. It will for example let countries ban imports of a living modified organism if they feel there is not enough scientific evidence that the product is safe and requires exporters to label shipments containing genetically altered commodities such as corn or cotton.

The required number of 50 instruments of ratification/accession/approval/acceptance by countries was reached in May 2003. In accordance with the provisions of its Article 37, the Protocol entered into force on 11 September 2003.

Objective of the Protocol

In accordance with the precautionary approach, contained in Principle 15 of the Rio Declaration on Environment and Development, the objective of the Protocol is to contribute to ensuring an adequate level of protection in the field of the safe transfer, handling and use of 'living modified organisms resulting from modern biotechnology' that may have adverse effects on the conservation and sustainable use of biological diversity, taking also into account risks to human health, and specifically focusing on transboundary movements (Article 1 of the Protocol, SCBD 2000).

Living modified organisms (LMOs)

Living modified organisms (known as LMOs) resulting from modern biotechnology are broadly equivalent to genetically modified organisms. The difference between an LMO and a GMO is that a Living Modified Organism is capable of growing, and typically refers to agricultural crops. Genetically Modified Organisms include both LMOs and organisms which are not capable of growing, i.e. are dead. 'Modern biotechnology' is defined in the Protocol to mean the application of in vitro nucleic acid techniques, or fusion of cells beyond the taxonomic family, that overcome natural physiological reproductive or recombination barriers and are not techniques used in traditional breeding and selection.

The Protocol and the Precautionary Approach

One of the outcomes of the United Nations Conference on Environment and Development (also known as the Earth Summit) held in Rio de Janeiro, Brazil, in June 1992, was the adoption of the Rio Declaration on Environment and Development, which contains 27 principles to underpin sustainable development. Commonly known as the precautionary principle, Principle 15 states that "In order to protect the environment, the precautionary approach shall be widely applied by States according to their capabilities. Where there are threats of serious or irreversible damage, lack of full scientific certainty shall not be used as a reason for postponing cost-effective measures to prevent environmental degradation."

Elements of the precautionary approach are reflected in a number of the provisions of the Protocol, such as:

- The preamble, reaffirming "the precautionary approach contained in Principle 15 of the Rio Declaration on environment and Development";

- Article 1, indicating that the objective of the Protocol is "in accordance with the precautionary approach contained in Principle 15 of the Rio Declaration on Environment and Development";
- Article 10.6 and 11.8, which states "Lack of scientific certainty due to insufficient relevant scientific information and knowledge regarding the extent of the potential adverse effects of an LMO on biodiversity, taking into account risks to human health, shall not prevent a Party of import from taking a decision, as appropriate, with regard to the import of the LMO in question, in order to avoid or minimize such potential adverse effects."; and
- Annex III on risk assessment, which notes that "Lack of scientific knowledge or scientific consensus should not necessarily be interpreted as indicating a particular level of risk, an absence of risk, or an acceptable risk."

What does the Protocol cover?

The Protocol applies to the transboundary movement, transit, handling and use of all living modified organisms that may have adverse effects on the conservation and sustainable use of biological diversity, taking also into account risks to human health (Article 4 of the Protocol, SCBD 2000).

Parties and non-Parties to the Protocol

The governing body of the Protocol is called the Conference of the Parties to the Convention serving as the meeting of the Parties to the Protocol (also the COP-MOP). The main function of this body is to review the implementation of the Protocol and make decisions necessary to promote its effective operation. Decisions under the Protocol can only be taken by Parties to the Protocol. Parties to the Convention that are not Parties to the Protocol may only participate as observers in the proceedings of meetings of the COP-MOP.

The Protocol addresses the obligations of Parties in relation to the transboundary movements of LMOs to and from non-Parties to the Protocol. The transboundary movements between Parties and non-Parties must be carried out in a manner that is consistent with the objective of the Protocol. Parties are required to encourage non-Parties to adhere to the Protocol and to contribute information to the Biosafety Clearing-House.

Relationship between the Protocol and the WTO

A number of agreements under the World Trade Organization (WTO), such as the Agreement on the Application of Sanitary and Phytosanitary Measures (SPS Agreement) and the Agreement on Technical Barriers to Trade (TBT Agreement), and the Agreement on Trade-Related Aspects of Intellectual Property Rights (TRIPs), contain provisions that are relevant to the Protocol. The Protocol states in its preamble that parties:

- Recognize that trade and environment agreements should be mutually supportive;
- Emphasize that the Protocol is not interpreted as implying a change in the rights and obligations under any existing agreements; and
- Understand that the above recital is not intended to subordinate the Protocol to other international agreements.

Main features of the Protocol

Overview of features

The Protocol promotes biosafety by establishing rules and procedures for the safe transfer, handling, and use of LMOs, with specific focus on transboundary movements of LMOs. It features a set of procedures including one for LMOs that are to be intentionally introduced into the environment called the advance informed agreement procedure, and one for LMOs that are intended to be used directly as food or feed or for processing. Parties to the Protocol must ensure that LMOs are handled, packaged and transported under conditions of safety. Furthermore, the shipment of LMOs subject to transboundary movement must be accompanied by appropriate documentation specifying, among other things, identity of LMOs and contact point for further information. These procedures and requirements are designed to provide importing Parties with the necessary information needed for making informed decisions about whether or not to accept LMO imports and for handling them in a safe manner.

The Party of import makes its decisions in accordance with scientifically sound risk assessments. The Protocol sets out principles and methodologies on how to conduct a risk assessment. In case of insufficient relevant scientific information and knowledge, the Party of import may use precaution in making their decisions on import. Parties may also take into account, consistent with their international obligations, socio-economic considerations in reaching decisions on import of LMOs.

Parties must also adopt measures for managing any risks identified by the risk assessment, and they must take necessary steps in the event of accidental release of LMOs.

To facilitate its implementation, the Protocol establishes a Biosafety Clearing-House for Parties to exchange information, and contains a number of important provisions, including capacity-building, a financial mechanism, compliance procedures, and requirements for public awareness and participation.

Procedures for moving LMOs across borders

Advance Informed Agreement

The "Advance Informed Agreement" (AIA) procedure applies to the first intentional transboundary movement of LMOs for intentional introduction into the environment of the Party of import. It includes four components: notification by the Party of export or the exporter, acknowledgment of receipt of notification by the Party of import, the decision procedure, and opportunity for review of decisions. The purpose of this procedure is to ensure that importing countries have both the opportunity and the capacity to assess risks that may be associated with the LMO before agreeing to its import. The Party of import must indicate the reasons on which its decisions are based (unless consent is unconditional). A Party of import may, at any time, in light of new scientific information, review and change a decision. A Party of export or a notifier may also request the Party of import to review its decisions.

However, the Protocol's AIA procedure does not apply to certain categories of LMOs:

- LMOs in transit;
- LMOs destined for contained use;
- LMOs intended for direct use as food or feed or for processing

While the Protocol's AIA procedure does not apply to certain categories of LMOs, Parties have the right to regulate the importation on the basis of domestic legislation. There are also allowances in the Protocol to declare certain LMOs exempt from application of the AIA procedure.

LMOs intended for food or feed, or for processing

LMOs intended for direct use as food or feed, or processing (LMOs-FFP) represent a large category of agricultural commodities. The Protocol, instead of using the AIA procedure, establishes a more simplified procedure for the transboundary movement of LMOs-FFP. Under this procedure, A Party must inform other Parties through the Biosafety Clearing-House, within 15 days, of its decision regarding domestic use of LMOs that may be subject to transboundary movement.

Decisions by the Party of import on whether or not to accept the import of LMOs-FFP are taken under its domestic regulatory framework that is consistent with the objective of the Protocol. A developing country Party or a Party with an economy in transition may, in the absence of a domestic regulatory framework, declare through the Biosafety Clearing-House that its decisions on the first import of LMOs-FFP will be taken in accordance with risk assessment as set out in the Protocol and time frame for decision-making.

Handling, Transport, Packaging and Identification

The Protocol provides for practical requirements that are deemed to contribute to the safe movement of LMOs. Parties are required to take measures for the safe handling, packaging and transportation of LMOs that are subject to transboundary movement. The Protocol specifies requirements on identification by setting out what information must be provided in documentation that should accompany transboundary shipments of LMOs. It also leaves room for possible future development of standards for handling, packaging, transport and identification of LMOs by the meeting of the Parties to the Protocol.

Each Party is required to take measures ensuring that LMOs subject to intentional transboundary movement are accompanied by documentation identifying the LMOs and providing contact details of persons responsible for such movement. The details of these requirements vary according to the intended use of the LMOs, and, in the case of LMOs for food, feed or for processing, they should be further addressed by the governing body of the Protocol. (Article 18 of the Protocol, SCBD 2000).

The first meeting of the Parties adopted decisions outlining identification requirements for different categories of LMOs (Decision BS-I/6, SCBD 2004). However, the second meeting of the Parties failed to reach agreement on the detailed requirements to identify LMOs intended for direct use as food, feed or for processing and will need to reconsider this issue at its third meeting in March 2006.

Biosafety Clearing-House

The Protocol established a Biosafety Clearing-House (BCH), in order to facilitate the exchange of scientific, technical, environmental and legal information on, and experience with, living modified organisms; and to assist Parties to implement the Protocol (Article 20 of the Protocol, SCBD 2000). It was established in a phased manner, and the first meeting of the Parties approved the transition from the pilot phase to the fully operational phase, and adopted modalities for its operations (Decision BS-I/3, SCBD 2004).

References

- Secretariat of the Convention on Biological Diversity (2000) *Cartagena Protocol on Biosafety to the Convention on Biological Diversity: text and annexes*. Montreal, Canada. ISBN 92-807-1924-6
- Secretariat of the Convention on Biological Diversity (2004) *Global Biosafety - From concepts to action: Decisions adopted by the first meeting of the Conference of the Parties to the Convention on Biological Diversity serving as the meeting of the Parties to the Cartagena Protocol on Biosafety*. Montreal, Canada.

External links

- Biosafety Protocol Homepage [3]
- Biosafety Clearing-House Central Portal [2]
- Text of the Protocol [1] at the Center for a World in Balance

References

[1] http://www.worldinbalance.net/intagreements/2000-cartagenaprotocol.php

Catastrophe modeling

This article refers to the use of computers to estimate losses caused by disasters. For other meanings of the word catastrophe, including catastrophe theory in mathematics, see catastrophe (disambiguation).

Catastrophe modeling (also known as **cat modeling**) is the process of using computer-assisted calculations to estimate the losses that could be sustained due to a catastrophic event such as a hurricane or earthquake. Cat modeling is especially applicable to analysing risks in the insurance industry and is at the confluence of actuarial science, engineering, meteorology, and seismology.

Perils analysed

Natural catastrophes (sometimes referred to as "nat cat") include:

- hurricane (main peril is wind damage; some models can also include storm surge)
- earthquake (main peril is ground shaking; some models can also include fire following earthquakes and sprinkler leakage damage)
- tornado
- flood
- wind storm/hail
- wildfire

Other catastrophes include:

- terrorism events
- warfare
- Casualty/liability events
- Displacement Crises[1]

Lines of business modeled

- Personal property
- Commercial property
- Forestry
- Workers' compensation
- Automobile physical damage
- Leasehold improvements
- Limited liabilities
- Product liability

Input

The input into a typical cat modelling software package is information on the exposures being analysed that are vulnerable to catastrophe risk. The exposure data can be categorized into three basic groups:

- information on the site locations, referred to as geocoding data (street address, postal code, county/CRESTA zone, et cetera)
- information on the physical characteristics of the exposures (construction, occupation/occupancy, year built, number of stories, number of employees, et cetera)
- information on the financial terms of the insurance coverage (coverage value, limit, deductible, et cetera)

Output

The output is estimates of the losses that the model predicts would be associated with a particular event or set of events. When running a *probabilistic* model, the output is either a probabilistic loss distribution or a set of events that could be used to create a loss distribution; probable maximum losses (PMLs) and average annual losses (AALs) are calculated from the loss distribution. When running a *deterministic* model, losses caused by a specific event are calculated; for example, Hurricane Katrina or "a magnitude 8.0 earthquake in downtown San Francisco" could be analyzed against the portfolio of exposures.

Uses

- Insurers and risk managers use cat modeling to assess the risk in a portfolio of exposures. This might help guide an insurer's underwriting strategy or help them decide how much reinsurance to purchase.
- Some state departments of insurance allow insurers to use cat modelling in their rate filings to help determine how much premium their policyholders are charged in catastrophe-prone areas.
- Insurance rating agencies such as A. M. Best and Standard & Poor's use cat modelling to assess the financial strength of insurers that take on catastrophe risk.
- Reinsurers and reinsurance brokers use cat modelling in the pricing and structuring of reinsurance treaties.
- Likewise, cat bond investors, investment banks, and bond rating agencies use cat modeling in the pricing and structuring of catastrophe bond.

Demand surge

Some cat models allow the user the option of including demand surge in the loss estimates, which is post-event inflation. After a large disaster, construction material and labor can temporarily be in short supply, so construction costs are inflated. The larger the impact of the event on the local economy, the larger the effect of demand surge. For example, an event that causes a $5 billion insurance industry loss might cause demand surge to increase construction costs by 5%, while an event that causes a $40 billion insurance industry loss might cause demand surge to increase construction costs by 25%.

Open catastrophe modeling

Recently, an effort to create and disseminate open multi-hazard cat risk modelling tools was initiated by the Alliance for Global Open Risk Analysis (AGORA) [2].

Additionally, the insurance industry is currently working with the Association for Cooperative Operations Research and Development (ACORD) [3] to develop an industry standard for collecting and sharing exposure data. To date, the industry has been operating on closed, proprietary data formats.

References

Insurance Information Institute, 19 March 2009 [4]

[1] See: Edwards, Scott. *The Chaos of Forced Migration: A Means of Modeling Complexity for Humanitarian Ends*

[2] http://www.risk-agora.org/

[3] http://www.acord.org/

[4] http://www.iii.org/media/hottopics/insurance/catastrophes

External links

- Association for Cooperative Operations Research and Development (ACORD) (http://www.ACORD.org)
- Florida Public Hurricane Loss Model (http://www.cis.fiu.edu/hurricaneloss/)
- The Alliance for Global Open Risk Analysis (AGORA) (http://www.risk-agora.org/)

Certainty effect

Certainty effect refers to the psychological effect resulted from the reduction of probability from certainty to probable (Kahneman & Tversky, 1986)[1]. It is an idea introduced in prospect theory.

Normally a reduction in probability of winning a reward (e.g. reduce from 80% to 20% of chance of winning a reward) creates psychological effect such as displeasure to individuals, which leads to the perception of loss from the original probability thus favoring a risk-aversion decision. However, the same reduction results in larger psychological effect when it is done from certainty than from uncertainty.

Example

Kahneman and Tversky (1986) illustrated the pseudocertainty effect by the following examples.

First, consider this example:

Which of the following options do you prefer?

- A. a sure gain of $30
- B. 80% chance to win $45 and 20% chance to win nothing

In this case, 78% of participants chose option A while only 22% chose option B. This is the typical risk-aversion phenomenon in prospect theory and framing effect.

Now, consider this problem:

Which of the following options do you prefer?

- C. 25% chance to win $30 and 75% chance to win nothing
- D. 20% chance to win $45 and 80% chance to win nothing

In this case, 42% of participants chose option C while 58% chose option D.

Compare to the first problem, both options winning probabilities were quarter of the original (A->C:100%/4=25%, B->D:80%/4=20%) . However, individuals show a greater preference in the second option in the second problem while expected utility remained the same.

External links

- Kahneman, Daniel and Tversky, Amos. *The Framing of Decisions and the Psychology of Choice* Science 211 (1981), pp. 4538, copyright 1981 by the American Association for the Advancement of Science. [2]

Reference

[1] (http://www.cog.brown.edu/courses/cg195/pdf_files/fall07/Kahneman&Tversky1986.pdf), Tversky, A., & Kahneman, D. (1986). Rational Choice and the Framing of Decisions. *The Journal of Business*, **59**, S251-S278.
[2] http://www.cs.umu.se/kurser/TDBC12/HT99/Tversky.html

Consumer's risk

Consumer's risk or **Consumer risk** is a potential risk found in all consumer-oriented products, that a product not meeting quality standards will pass undetected though the manufacturer's quality control system and enter the consumer marketplace.

References

- Hui, Yiu H. (2006). *Handbook of food science, technology, and engineering, Volume 2* (http://books.google. com/books?id=ZxL3KUEzR5AC&pg=SA56-PA15&dq="Consumer+risk"&client=firefox-a& cd=2#v=onepage&q="Consumer risk"&f=false). CRC Press. p. 56-15. ISBN 0849398487.

Cover your ass

Cover Your Ass (**CYA**) or **Cover Your Own Ass** (**CYOA**) describes professional and organizational practices that serve to protect oneself from legal and administrative penalties, criticism, or other punitive measures.

Common practices

- Banking - compliance officers who may know that certain financial transactions are dubious, i.e., that money laundering and terrorist financing will inevitably occur regardless of the amount of regulatory structures put in place,[1] [2] but who comply with all the regulatory requirements, and thus absolve themselves from future liability.
- Journalists - The term's use is also reasonably widespread among journalists[3]

As an example, just before the Space Shuttle Challenger disaster, the final launch approval by Morton Thiokol (the maker of the solid rocket boosters used during the launch) contained the following warning: "Information on this page was prepared to support an oral presentation and cannot be considered complete without the oral discussion". This warning, which was present even though the information was sent by fax, has been labelled as a CYA notice.[4]

Footnotes

[1] The Economist, *Financing terrorism: Looking in the wrong places* (http://economist.com/displaystory.cfm?story_id=5053373). 20 October 2005

[2] Jeffrey Robinson. *Brown's war just doesn't add up: you can't kill terrorists with a calculator* (http://www.timesonline.co.uk/article/0,,1072-2038874,00.html). The Times. 14 February 2006.

[3] Joe Grimm. *Newsroom politics: Cover your ass* (http://www.freep.com/legacy/jobspage/toolkit/cya.htm).

[4] Edward R. Tufte, *Visual Explanations*. Graphics Press, 1997. pp 26–53.

CREAM

CREAM (Cognitive Reliability Error Analysis Method) is a human reliability analysis technique developed by Erik Hollnagel. It is a bi-directional analysis method, meant to be used for both performance prediction and accident analysis. Unlike first generation error analysis methods like THERP, CREAM represents a second generation tool allowing for better analysis by abandoning the hierarchical structure of previous methods and providing better separation between objective and subjective error.

CREAM is a technique used in the field of human reliability assessment (HRA), for the purposes of evaluating the probability of a human error occurring throughout the completion of a specific task. From such analyses measures can then be taken to reduce the likelihood of errors occurring within a system and therefore lead to an improvement in the overall levels of safety. There exist three primary reasons for conducting an HRA; error identification, error quantification and error reduction. As there exist a number of techniques used for such purposes, they can be split into one of two classifications; first generation techniques and second generation techniques. First generation techniques work on the basis of the simple dichotomy of 'fits/doesn't fit' in the matching of the error situation in context with related error identification and quantification and second generation techniques are more theory based in their assessment and quantification of errors. HRA techniques have been utilised in a range of industries including healthcare, engineering, nuclear, transportation and business sector; each technique has varying uses within different disciplines.

CREAM is a second generation HRA method. However compared to many other such methods, it takes a very different approach to modelling human reliability. There are two versions of the technique, the basic and the extended version, both of which have in common two primary features; ability to identify the importance of human performance in a given context and a helpful cognitive model and associated framework, usable for both prospective and retrospective analysis. Prospective analysis allows likely human errors to be identified while retrospective analysis quantifies errors that have already occurred.

The concept of cognition is included in the model through use of four basic 'control modes' which identify differing levels of control that an operator has in a given context and the characteristics which highlight the occurrence of distinct conditions. The control modes which may occur are as follows:

- Scrambled control: the choice of the forthcoming action is unpredictable or haphazard. The situation in question may be portraying rapid alterations in unexpected ways thus eliminating the operator's ability or opportunity to make deductions about the next action required.

- Opportunistic control: the next action is determined by superficial characteristics of the situation, possibly through habit or similarity matching. The situation is characterised by lack of planning and this may possibly be due to the lack of available time.

- Tactical control: performance typically follows planned procedures while some ad hoc deviations are still possible.

- Strategic control: plentiful time is available to consider actions to be taken in the light of wider objectives to be fulfilled and within the given context.

The particular control mode determines the level of reliability that can be expected in a particular setting and this is in turn determined by the collective characteristics of the relevant Common Performance Conditions (CPCs).

Background

CREAM was developed by Eric Hollnagel in 1998 following an analysis of the methods for HRA already in place. It is the most widely utilised second generation HRA technique and is based on 3 primary areas of work; task analysis, opportunities for reducing errors and possibility to consider human performance with regards to overall safety of a system.

The aim of utilising this methodology is to assist an analyst in four main areas:

- identify work, actions or tasks within the system which necessitate or essentially depend on human thinking and which are therefore vulnerable to variations in their level of reliability.
- identify the surrounding conditions in which the cognition of these situations may be reduced and therefore determine what actions may lead to a probable risk
- compile an evaluation from the assessment of the various outcomes of human performance and their effect on system safety – this can then be utilised as part of the probability risk assessment (PRA).
- make suggestions as to how identified error producing conditions may be improved and therefore of how the system's reliability can be enhanced whilst also reducing risk.

Methodology

1. Task analysis

The basic method adopted by the CREAM technique provides an immediate reliability interval based on an assessment of the given control mode, as highlighted by the figures provided in the table below. As can be seen by the contents of the table, each of the specified control modes has an individual reliability level. In the extended CREAM version, the control modes play the role of a weighting factor which scales a nominal failure probability associated to a given cognitive function failure. This version of CREAM is intended to be used for the purposes of a more in depth analysis of human interactions.

Control mode	Reliability interval (probability of action failures)
Strategic	$0.5 \text{ E-5} < p < 1.0 \text{ E-2}$
Tactical	$1.0 \text{ E-3} < p < 1.0 \text{ E-1}$
Opportunistic	$1.0 \text{ E-2} < p < 0.5 \text{ E-0}$
Scrambled	$1.0 \text{ E-1} < p < 1.0 \text{ E-0}$

2. Context description

The intention of the basic CREAM method is to use it as a screening technique with the aim of identifying processes which require a deeper level of analysis; this analysis may then be carried out by the extended CREAM method.

3. Specification of initiating events

When using the basic CREAM method, a task analysis is conducted prior to further assessment. CPCs are assessed according to the descriptors, given in the below Table, in order to judge their expected effect on performance.

CPC name	Level/descriptors	Expected effect on performance reliability
Adequacy of organisation	Very Efficient	Improved
	Efficient	Not Significant
	Inefficient	Reduced
	Deficient	Reduced
Working conditions	Advantageous	Improved
	Compatible	Not significant
	Incompatible	Reduced
Adequacy of MMI and operational support	Supportive	Improved
	Adequate	Not Significant
	Tolerable	Not Significant
	Inappropriate	Reduced
Availability of procedures/ plans	Appropriate	Improved
	Acceptable	Not significant
	Inappropriate	Reduced
Number of simultaneous goals	Fewer than capacity	Not significant
	Matching current capacity	Not significant
	More than capacity	Reduced
Available time	Adequate	Improved
	Temporarily inadequate	Not significant
	Continuously inadequate	Reduced
Time of day (circadian rhythm)	Day-time (adjusted)	Not significant
	Night-time (unadjusted)	Reduced
Adequacy of training and expertise	Adequate, high experience	Improved
	Adequate, limited experience	Not significant
	Inadequate	Reduced
Crew collaboration quality	Very efficient	Improved
	Efficient	Not significant
	Inefficient	Not significant
	Deficient	Reduced

4. Error prediction

The assessments of the CPCs then require to be adjusted according to some specified rules in order to take account of synergistic effects. The matrix above would be considered in the context of the situation under assessment and by this means the previously considered initiating events are reviewed with respect to how they could potentially lead to the occurrence of an error. The rows of the matrix identify the possible outcomes while the columns show the precursors. The analyst then has the task of identifying the columns for which all the rows have been similarly classified into the same group according to the column headings. Predicting the possible outcomes for each of the rows should be done until there are no remaining possible paths. Each of the identified errors requires to be noted along with the causes and the outcomes.

5.

Finally, a simple count is performed of the number of CPCs that are causing an improvement in reliability and those which are reducing it. On the basis of this number the probable control mode is determined, by judging the region given in the graph as depicted below.

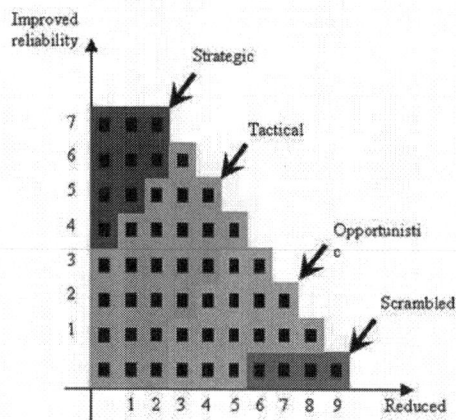

Figure 1   Allocation of probable control modes according to CPCs- each section displays the relation between the CPC score and control modes. The x coordinate represents the number of reduced influence indexes and the y coordinate is the number of improved influence indexes.

6.

The extended version of the CREAM methodology operates in a slightly different manner. Following the initial task analysis, a refinement is then provided in terms of the cognitive activities which are involved in the considered task (classified as co-ordinate, communicate, compare, etc). To these activities a Contextual Control Model (COCOM) function (observation, interpretation, planning and execution) is ascribed (following a table provided) so that a cognitive demand profile may be established.

7.

Following this stage, the probable cognitive function failures are identified, based on a knowledge of the specific tasks, yet following a set of generic cognitive function failures associated to the COCOM functions. Each of these generic failures is associated with a nominal probability which is based on a table given in CREAM. However these probabilities are adjusted depending on the particular control mode. Hence in the extended version of the CREAM methodology the control mode acts in the role of a Performance Shaping Factor with the task of performing adjustments to a nominal probability.

Provided below is a simplified diagrammatic representation of all the stages involved in the complete CREAM methodology.

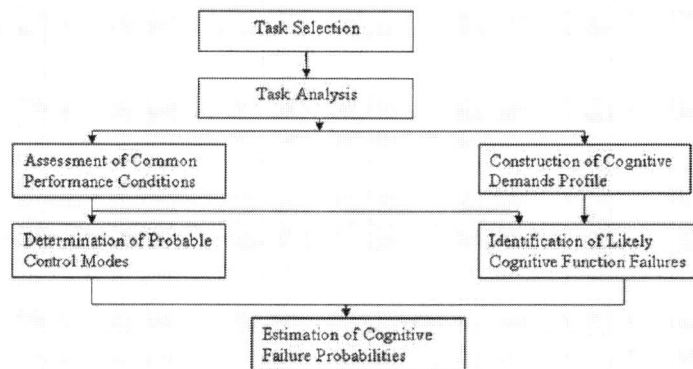

Worked example

Context

The basic example that is provided below concerns the task of 'restarting a furnace following a system trip'. The following figure illustrates the hierarchical task analysis carried out for the task.

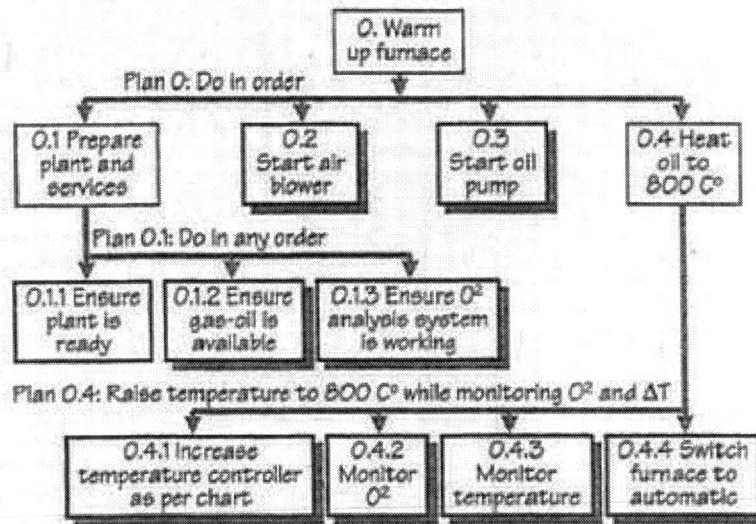

The overall task is made up of four basic tasks, which are further completed by carrying out a number of sub-tasks. First level tasks are required to be performed in the given sequence while the tasks on sub level two can be carried out in any order. Finally the lowest level tasks are conducted as necessary in a repetitive manner.

Assumptions

In this example, a number of assumptions should be noted in order to aid understanding. It is assumed that the warm-up task does not have any procedural support nor is it one that has been trained in detail.

Required inputs

From study of the task analysis, it is then possible to identify the necessary activities of the overall task that must be carried out.

This involves assessing the work conditions under which the task in question is performed. These are judged and rated on a scale as can be seen in the table provided below:

CPC name	Evaluation
Adequacy of Organisation	The quality of the support and resources provided by the organisation for the task or work being performed. This includes communication systems, Safety Management System, support for external activities etc.
Descriptors	*Very efficient/ Efficient/ **Inefficient** / Deficient*
Working conditions	The conditions under which the work takes place, such as ambient lighting, glare on screens, noise from alarms, interruptions from the task etc.
Descriptors	*Advantageous/ **Compatible** /Incompatible*
Adequacy of MMI and operational support	The quality of the MMI and/or specific operational support provided for operators. The MMI includes control panels, workstations, and operational support provided by specifically designed decision aids
Descriptors	*Supportive/ Adequate/ **Tolerable** /Inappropriate*
Availability of procedures/plans	The availability of prepared guidance for the work to be carried out, including operating/ emergency procedures, routines & familiar responses
Descriptors	*Appropriate/ Acceptable/ **Inappropriate***
Number of simultaneous goals	The number of tasks or goals operators must attend to. Since the number of goals is variable, this CPC applies to what is typical/characteristic for a situation.
Descriptors	*Fewer than capacity/ **Matching current capacity** /More than capacity*
Available Time	The time available to complete the work; or the general level of time pressure for the task and the situation type. How well the task is synchronised to the process dynamics.
Descriptors	***Adequate** /Temporarily inadequate /Continuously inadequate*
Time of day (circadian rhythm)	The time at which the task is carried out, in particular whether the person is adjusted to the current time.
Descriptors	***Day-time(adjusted)** /Night-time (unadjusted)*
Adequacy of training and preparation	The level of readiness for the work as provided (by the organisation) through training and prior instruction. Includes familiarisation to new technology, refreshing old skills, etc. as well as the level of operational experience
Descriptors	*Adequate, high experience/ Adequate, limited experience/ **Inadequate***
Crew collaboration quality	The quality of the collaboration between crew members, including the overlap between the official and unofficial structure, the level of trust, and the general social climate among crew members.
Descriptors	*Very efficient/ **Efficient** / Inefficient / Deficient*

Method

In order to calculate the combined CPC score, the assigned ratings of the CPCs are entered in the table as shown in step 3 of the methodology section. Using certain rules [19]an assessment is made as to whether it is necessary to adjust the CPCs. In this example this is not necessary. Therefore the combined CPC score for this example is [3,5,1]. This is interpreted as the CPC's pointing to a reduced performance reliability, 4 CPC's indicate that there is no significant influence and 1 CPC suggests an improved performance reliability.

Result

By determining the most likely control mode for the example, the general action failure probability can also thus be identified. Referring to the graphical display in Figure 1, the result for this example is that the operator is expected to be in an opportunistic control mode. This adequately relates to the assumption provided earlier that the operator under consideration has only slight experience or training for the task and there is insufficient support for the operations involved in the task. It may therefore be suggested that the operator may task a 'try and test' approach, particularly for complicated tasks such as increasing the temperature under controlled conditions.

The last stage of the process is to determine the probability interval for the expected control mode, the opportunistic control mode. Referring to table 1, for this example, the general action failure probability is within the range of 1.0 E-2 < p < 0.5 E-0. As this is not regarded as an acceptable there is no clear and justified reason to continue with the analysis being undertaken.

Advantages

- the technique allows for the direct quantification of human error probability (HEP)
- it also allows the assessor using the CREAM method to specifically tailor the use of the technique to the contextual situation [2]
- the resultant model is highly integrate-able into the primary safety process in use
- the technique uses the same principles for retrospective and predictive analyses [2]
- the approach is very concise, well structured and follows a well laid out system of procedure [2]

Disadvantages

- the technique requires a high level of resource use, including lengthy time periods for completion[2]
- CREAM also requires an initial expertise in the field of human factors (HF) in order to use the technique successfully and may therefore appear rather complex for an inexperienced user[2]
- CREAM does not put forth potential means by which the identified errors can be reduced[2]
- The time required for application is very lengthy

References

[1] Hollnagel, E. (1998). *Cognitive Reliability and Error Analysis Method – CREAM*. Oxford: Elsevier Science.

[2] Salmon, P., Stanton, N.A., & Walker, G. (2003). *Humans Factors Design Methods Review*. Defence Technology Centre.

[3] XuHong, He (2005). "A simplified CREAM prospective quantification process and its application". *Reliability Engineering & Safety System*. 93, 298-306.

[4] Kim, I.S. (2001). "Human reliability analysis design review". *Annals of Nuclear Energy*. 28, 1069-1081.

External links

- CREAM - Cognitive Reliability and Error Analysis Method [1]
- CREAM Navigator - a web-based software tool [2]
- http___www.sciencedirect.com_science__ob=MImg&_imagekey=B6V4T-4N3WYH6-2-V&_cdi=5767&_user=875629&_orig=search&_coverDate=02%2F29%2F2008&_sk=999069997&view=c&wchp=dGLbVlz-zSkzV&md5=6765ccb9f7b272ab27f21d2abfcea6aa&ie=_sdarticle.pdf
- http___www.sciencedirect.com_science__ob=MImg&_imagekey=B6V4T-4FM5CXJ-1-7&_cdi=5767&_user=875629&_orig=search&_coverDate=02%2F28%2F2006&_sk=999089997&view=c&wchp=dGLzVzz-zSkWb&md5=b97868037b541342d6e8f5884dff8914&ie=_sdarticle.pdf

References

[1] http://www.ida.liu.se/~eriho/CREAM_M.htm
[2] http://www.ews.uiuc.edu/~serwy/cream/v0.6beta/

Cultural cognition

The **Cultural cognition of risk**, sometimes called simply **cultural cognition**, refers to the hypothesized tendency of persons to form perceptions of risk and related facts that cohere with their self-defining values. Research examining this phenomenon draws on a variety of social science disciplines including psychology, anthropology, political science, sociology, and communications. The stated objectives of this research are both to understand how values shape political conflict over facts (like whether climate change exists, whether gun control increases crime, whether vaccination of school girls for HPV threatens their health) and to promote effective deliberative strategies for resolving such conflicts consistent with sound empirical data.

Theory and evidence

The *cultural cognition hypothesis* holds that individuals are motivated by a variety of psychological processes to form beliefs about putatively dangerous activities that match their cultural evaluations of them. Persons who subscribe to relatively individualistic values, for example, tend to value commerce and industry and are inclined to disbelieve that such activities pose serious environmental risks. Persons who subscribe to relatively egalitarian and communitarian values, in contrast, readily credit claims of environmental risks, consistent with their moral suspicion of commerce and industry as sources of inequality and symbols of excessive self-seeking.[1] [2]

Scholars have furnished two types of evidence to support the cultural cognition hypothesis. The first consists of general survey data that suggest that individuals' values more strongly predict their risk perceptions than do other characteristics such as race, gender, economic status, and political orientations.[3] [4]

The second type of evidence consists in experiments that identify discrete psychological processes that connect individuals' values to their beliefs about risk and related facts.[5] Such experiments suggest, for example, that individuals selectively credit or dismiss information in a manner that reinforces beliefs congenial to their values.[6] They also show that individuals tend to be more persuaded by policy experts perceived to hold values similar to theirs than by ones perceived to hold values different from theirs.[7] Such processes, the experiments suggest, often result in divisive forms of cultural conflict over facts, but can also be managed in fashions that reduce such disagreement.[8]

Cultural cognition project at Yale Law School

Funded by governmental and private foundation grants, much of the work on cultural cognition has been performed by an interdisciplinary group of scholars affiliated with the Cultural Cognition Project [9]. There are currently over a dozen project members, from a variety of universities. Two members of the project—Dan Kahan and Douglas Kysar—are Yale Law School faculty, although other members (such as Donald Braman of George Washington University Law School and Geoffrey Cohen of the University of Colorado) were previously affiliated with Yale Law School or Yale University.

Significant findings

"White male effect"

Risk-perception researchers have documented that white males are less concerned with a wide variety of risks than are minorities and females, a phenomenon known as the "white male effect" in the risk-perception literature.[10] [11] An article by Kahan, Braman, Gastil, Slovic and Mertz presented evidence that the white male effect is an outgrowth of cultural cognition.[12] The article reports data showing that race and gender differences in risk perception are conditional on cultural values: White males in general appear to be less concerned about risks only because a discrete group of white males who subscribe to hierarchical and individualistic values are extremely skeptical that activities important to their cultural roles (commerce, gun ownership) impose harm on society generally. This finding does not imply, however, that white males or white hierarchical and individualistic males are uniquely prone to form risk perceptions that are congenial to their social values and roles.

Nanotechnology

The Cultural Cognition Project has conducted a series of studies on public perceptions of nanotechnology risks and benefits. Combining survey and experimental methods, the studies present evidence that individuals culturally predisposed to be skeptical of environmental risks are both more likely to seek out information on nanotechnology and more likely to infer from that information that nanotechnology's benefits will outweigh its risks. Individuals culturally predisposed to credit environmental risks construe that same information, when exposed to it in the lab, as implying that nanotechnology's risks will predominate.[13] The studies also present evidence that individuals tend to credit expert information on nanotechnology—regardless of its content—based on whether they share the perceived cultural values of the expert communicator.[14] The studies were issued by the Project on Emerging Nanotechnologies at the Woodrow Wilson International Center for Scholars, one of the research sponsors.

"Scientific Consensus"

The same dynamics that motivate individuals of diverse cultural outlooks to form competing perceptions of risks are likely to cause them to form opposing perceptions of "scientific consensus," cultural cognition researchers have concluded.[15] In an experimental study, the researchers found that subjects were substantially more likely to count a scientist (of elite credentials) as an "expert" in his field of study when the scientist was depicted as taking a position consistent with the one associated with the subjects' cultural predispositions than when that scientist took a contrary position. A related survey showed that members of opposed cultural groups hold highly divergent impressions of what most scientific experts believe on various matters, a finding consistent with the ubiquity of culturally biased recognition of who counts as an "expert." Across a range of diverse risks (including climate change, nuclear waste disposal, and private handgun possession), members of no particular cultural group, the study found, were more likely than any other to hold perceptions of scientific consensus that consistently matched those adopted in "expert consensus reports" issued by the U.S. National Academy of Sciences.

Law

Scholars have also applied the cultural cognition of risk to legal issues. One such study examined how individuals reacted to a videotape of a high-speed police chase. In Scott v. Harris,[16] the U.S. Supreme Court (by a vote of 8-1) had held that "no reasonable jury" could view the tape and fail to find that the driver posed a lethal risk to the public large enough to justify deadly force by the police (namely, ramming the fleeing driver's vehicle, causing it to crash). The majority of study subjects agreed with the Court, but there were significant divisions along cultural lines.[17] Other studies have found that individuals' cultural worldviews influence their perceptions of consent in an acquaintance or date rape scenario,[18] and of the imminence of violence and other facts in self-defense cases involving either battered women or interracial confrontations.[19]

Relationship to other risk perception theories

Cultural cognition is a descendant of two other theories of risk perception. The first is the cultural theory of risk associated with anthropologist Mary Douglas and political scientist Aaron Wildavsky.[20] The cultural cognition hypothesis is derived from Douglas and Wildavsky's claim, advanced most notably in their controversial book *Risk and Culture: An Essay on the Selection of Technical and Environmental Dangers* (1982), that individuals selectively attend to risks in a manner that expresses and reinforces their preferred way of life.

Cultural cognition researchers, along with other scholars who have investigated Douglas and Wildavsky's theory empirically,[21] [22] [23] use attitudinal scales that reflect Douglas's worldview typology. That typology characterizes worldviews, or preferences about how society should be organized, along two cross-cutting dimensions: "group," which refers to how individualistic or group-oriented a society should be; and "grid," which refers to how hierarchical or egalitarian a society should be.[24]

The second theory is the "psychometric paradigm," to which Paul Slovic, a member of the Cultural Cognition Project, has made significant contributions. The psychometric paradigm links risk perceptions to various cognitive and social mechanisms that generally evade simpler, rational choice models associated with economics.[25] [26] Cultural cognition theory posits that these mechanisms mediate between, or connect, individuals' cultural values to their perceptions of risk and other policy-relevant beliefs.

Combing the cultural theory of risk and the psychometric paradigm, cultural cognition, its exponents claim, remedies difficulties with each.[27] The mechanisms featured in the psychometric paradigm (and in social psychology generally) furnish a cogent explanation of why individuals adopt states of mind that fit and promote the aims of groups, including ones featured in Douglas's culture theory. They do so, moreover, in a manner that avoids "functionalism," a criticized form of analysis that identifies group interests, rather than individual ones, as a cause for human action.[28] [29] At the same time cultural theory, by asserting the orienting role of values, explains how the mechanisms featured in the psychometric paradigm can result in differences in risk perception among persons who hold different values. The interrelationship between individual values and perceptions of risk also calls into doubt the depiction of risk perceptions deriving from these mechanisms as products of irrationality or cognitive defect.[30]

Criticisms

Cultural cognition has been subjected to criticisms from a variety of sources. Some rational choice economists[31] as well as some psychologists[32] have suggested that the theory (and ones based on the cultural theory of risk generally) explain only a small fraction of the variation in popular risk perceptions. Some adherents to the cultural theory of risk, including Mary Douglas herself,[33] have criticized cultural cognition for a conception of values that is too tightly modeled on American political disputes and that implicitly disparages the "hierarchical" worldview. Finally, some scholars who emphasize elements of the psychometric paradigm suggest that the influence of cultural values on risk perceptions is best understood as simply an additional source of interference with the rational processing of information.[34]

Notes

[1] Kahan, *Fixing the Communications Failure*.

[2] Kahan, Slovic, Braman & Gastil, *Fear of Democracy*, pp. 1083-84.

[3] Kahan & Braman, *Cultural Cognition and Public Policy*, pp. 155-58.

[4] Kahan, Slovic, Braman & Gastil, *Fear of Democracy*, pp. 1086-87.

[5] Cultural Cognition Project, *Second National Risk and Culture Study*.

[6] Kahan, Braman, Slovic, Cohen & Gastil, *Cultural Cognition of the Risks and Benefits of Nanotechnology*.

[7] Kahan, Braman, Cohen, Slovic & Gastil, *Who Fears the HPV Vaccine?*

[8] Kahan, *The Cognitively Illiberal State*.

[9] http://www.culturalcognition.net

[10] Finucane, Slovic, Mertz & Flynn, *Gender, Race, and Perceived Risk: The "White Male Effect"* (http://www.informaworld.com/smpp/content~db=all~content=a713670162)

[11] Palmer, *Risk Perception: Another Look at the White Male Effect*.

[12] *Culture and Identity-Protective Cognition: Explaining the White-Male Effect in Risk Perception*.

[13] Kahan, Braman, Slovic, Cohen & Gastil, *Cultural Cognition of the Risks and Benefits of Nanotechnology*.

[14] Cultural Cognition Project, *Biased Assimilation, Polarization, and Cultural Credibility*.

[15] Kahan, Jenkins-Smith & Braman, *Cultural Cognition of Scientific Consensus*.

[16] 550 U.S. 372 (2007).

[17] Kahan, Hoffman & Braman, *Whose Eyes Are You Going to Believe?*

[18] Kahan, *Culture, Cognition, and Consent*.

[19] Kahan & Braman, *Self-Defensive Cognition of Self-Defense*.

[20] Rayner, *Cultural Theory and Risk Analysis*.

[21] Dake, *Orienting Dispositions in the Perception of Risk: An Analysis of Contemporary Worldviews and Cultural Biases.*

[22] Jenkins-Smith, *Modeling Stigma.*

[23] Peters & Slovic *The Role of Affect and Worldviews as Orienting Dispositions in the Perception and Acceptance of Nuclear Power.*

[24] Rayner, *Cultural Theory and Risk Analysis,* pp. 87-91.

[25] Slovic, *The Perception of Risk.*

[26] Kahneman, Slovic & Tversky, *Judgment Under Uncertainty: Heuristics and Biases.*

[27] Kahan, *Cultural Cognition as a Conception of the Cultural Theory of Risk.*

[28] Boholm, *Risk Perception: Critique of Cultural Theory,* pp. 68, 79-80.

[29] Kahan & Braman, *Cultural Cognition and Public Policy,* p. 252.

[30] Kahan, Slovic, Braman & Gastil, *Fear of Democracy,* pp. 1088-1106.

[31] Fremling & Lott, *The Surprising Finding That "Cultural Worldviews" Don't Explain People's Views On Gun Control.*

[32] Sjöberg, *World Views, Political Attitudes, and Risk Perception.*

[33] Douglas, *Being Fair to Hierarchists.*

[34] Sunstein, *Misfearing.*

References

Boholm, Å. (1996). Risk perception and social anthropology: critique of cultural theory. *Ethnos*, 68(2), 159-178.

Cultural Cognition Project (2008). Biased Assimilation, Polarization, and Cultural Credibility: An Experimental Study of Nanotechnology Risk Perceptions. *Project on Emerging Nanotechnologies Research Brief No. 3.* (http://www.nanotechproject.org/publications/archive/yale2/)

Cultural Cognition Project (2007). The Second National Risk and Culture Study. (http://papers.ssrn.com/sol3/papers.cfm?abstract_id=1017189)

Dake, K. (1991). Orienting Dispositions in the Perception of Risk: An Analysis of Contemporary Worldviews and Cultural Biases. *Journal of Cross-Cultural Psychology*, 22, 61.

DiMaggio, P. (1997). Culture and Cognition. *Annual Review of Sociology*, 23, 263-287. (http://cogweb.ucla.edu/Abstracts/DiMaggio_97.html)

Douglas, M. (2003). Being Fair to Hierarchists. *University of Pennsylvania Law Review*, 151(4), 1349-1370.

Douglas, M., & Wildavsky, A. B. (1982). *Risk and Culture : An Essay on the Selection of Technical and Environmental Dangers.* Berkeley: University of California Press.

Finucane, M., Slovic, P., Mertz, C. K., Flynn, J., & Satterfield, T. A. (2000). Gender, Race, and Perceived Risk: The "White Male" Effect. *Health, Risk, and Society*, 3(2), 159-172.

Flynn, J., Slovic, P., & Mertz, C. K. (1994). Gender, Race, and Perception of Environmental Health Risk. *Risk Analysis*, 14(6), 1101-1108.

Fremling, G. M., & Lott, J. R. (2003). The Surprising Finding That "Cultural Worldviews" Don't Explain People's Views On Gun Control. *University of Pennsylvania Law Review*, 151(4), 1341-1348.

Jenkins-Smith, H. (2001). Modeling Stigma: An Empirical Analysis of Nuclear Waste Images of Nevada. In J. Flynn, P. Slovic & H. Kunreuther (Eds.), *Risk, Media, and Stigma: Understanding Public Challenges to Modern Science and Technology* (pp. 107-132). London ; Sterling, VA: Earthscan.

Kahan, D. (2007). The Cognitively Illiberal State. *Stanford Law Review*, 60, 115-154. (http://ssrn.com/abstract=963929)

Kahan, D. (2008). Cultural Cognition as a Conception of the Cultural Theory of Risk. *Cultural Cognition Project Working Paper No. 73.* (http://ssrn.com/abstract=1123807)

Kahan, D. (2010). Culture, Cognition, and Consent: Who Perceives What, and Why, in Acquaintance Rape Cases. *University of Pennsylvania Law Review*, 158, 729-812. (http://ssrn.com/abstract=1437742)

Kahan, D. (2010). Fixing the Communications Failure. *Nature*, 463, 296-297. (http://dx.doi.org/10.1038/463296a.)

Kahan, D., & Braman, D. (2008). The Self-defensive Cognition of Self-defense. *American Criminal Law Review*, 45(1), 1-65. (http://papers.ssrn.com/sol3/papers.cfm?abstract_id=1012967)

Kahan, D., & Braman, D. (2006). Cultural Cognition of Public Policy. *Yale Journal of Law and Public Policy*, 24, 147-170 (http://papers.ssrn.com/sol3/papers.cfm?abstract_id=746508).

Kahan, D., Braman, D., Gastil, J., Slovic, P., & Mertz, C. K. (2007). Culture and Identity-Protective Cognition: Explaining the White-Male Effect in Risk Perception. *Journal of Empirical Legal Studies*, 4(3), 465-505. (http://papers.ssrn.com/sol3/papers.cfm?abstract_id=995634)

Kahan, D., Braman, D., Cohen, G., Slovic, P., & Gastil, J., (in press). Who Fears the HPV Vaccine, Who Doesn't, and Why: An Experimental Study of the Mechanisms of Cultural Cognition. *Law and Human Behavior*. (http://papers.ssrn.com/sol3/papers.cfm?abstract_id=1160654)

Kahan, D. M., Jenkins-Smith, H., & Braman, D. (2010). Cultural Cognition of Scientific Consensus. *Journal of Risk Research*. (http://papers.ssrn.com/sol3/papers.cfm?abstract_id=1549444) On-line advance publication at http://dx.doi.org/10.1080/13669877.2010.511246.

Kahan, D., Hoffman, D.A. & Braman, D. (2009). Whose Eyes are You Going to Believe? Scott v. Harris and the Perils of Cognitive Illiberalism. *Harvard Law Review*, 122(3), 837-906. (http://www.harvardlawreview.org/issues/122/jan09/kahan_hoffman_braman.shtml)

Kahan, D., Slovic, P., Braman, D., Cohen G., Gastil, J. (2009). Cultural Cognition of the Risks and Benefits of Nanotechnology. *Nature Nanotechnology*, 4(2), 87-90. (http://dx.doi.org/10.1038/NNANO.2008.341)

Kahan, D., Slovic, P., Braman, D., & Gastil, J. (2006). Fear of Democracy: A Cultural Critique of Sunstein on Risk. *Harvard Law Review*, 119, 1071-1109. (http://www.harvardlawreview.org/issues/119/february06/Book_Review_1637.php)

Kahneman, D., Slovic, P., & Tversky, A. (1982). *Judgment Under Uncertainty: Heuristics and Biases*. Cambridge ; New York: Cambridge University Press.

Palmer, C. (2003). Risk Perception: Another Look at the "White Male Effect." *Health, Risk & Society*, 5(1), 71-83.

Peters, E., & Slovic, P. (1996). The Role of Affect and Worldviews as Orienting Dispositions in the Perception and Acceptance of Nuclear Power. *Journal of Applied Social Psychology*, 26(16), 1427-1453.

Rayner, S. (1992). Cultural Theory and Risk Analysis. In S. Krimsky & D. Golding (Eds.), *Social Theories of Risk* (pp. pp. 83-115). Westport, Conn.: Praeger.

Sjöberg, L. (1998). World Views, Political Attitudes, and Risk Perception. *Risk: Health, Safety and Environment*, 9, 137-152.

Slovic, P. (2000). *The Perception of Risk*. London: Sterling, VA: Earthscan Publications.

Sunstein, C. R. (2006). Misfearing: A Reply. *Harvard Law Review*, 119(4), 1110-1125. (http://www.harvardlawreview.org/issues/119/feb06/sunsteinfeb06.shtml)

Further reading

- Bailey, R. The Culture War on Facts: Are You Entitled to Your Own Truth? *Reasonline*, Oct. 9, 2007. (http://www.reason.com/news/show/122892.html)
- Bailey, R. Everyone Who Knows What They're Talking About Agrees with Me *Reasonline*, Feb. 23, 2010. (http://reason.com/archives/2010/02/23/everyone-who-knows-what-they-a)
- Bond, M. How to Keep Your Head in Scary Situations. *New Scientist*, Aug. 27, 2008. (http://www.newscientist.com/article/mg19926711.500-how-to-keep-your-head-in-scary-situations.html)
- Jones, R. Fearing the Fear of Nanotechnology. *Nature News,* Dec. 9, 2008. (http://www.nature.com/news/2008/081209/full/news.2008.1290.html)

- Joyce, C. Belief In Climate Change Hinges On Worldview. *NPR: All Things Considered,* Feb. 23, 2010. (http://www.npr.org/templates/story/story.php?storyId=124008307)
- National Science Foundation. New Studies Reveal Differing Perceptions of Nature-Altering Science, Dec. 11, 2008. (http://www.nsf.gov/news/news_summ.jsp?cntn_id=112809)
- National Science Foundation. Who's Afraid of the HPV Vaccine? Study Says People's Values Shape Perceptions of HPV Vaccine Risk, Jan. 13, 2010. (http://www.nsf.gov/news/news_summ.jsp?cntn_id=116186)
- National Science Foundation. Why "Scientific Consensus" Fails to Persuade, Sept. 13, 2010. (http://www.nsf.gov/news/news_summ.jsp?cntn_id=117697)
- Ropeik, David. Trains, nukes, marriage, and vaccines (and anything else): Why the facts don't matter. *Scientific American*, Apr. 22, 2011 (http://www.scientificamerican.com/blog/post.cfm?id=trains-nukes-marriage-and-vaccines-2011-04-22)
- Shea, Christopher. The Ninth Annual Year in Ideas: Cognitive Illiberalism. *N.Y. Times Sunday Magazine*, Dec. 10, 2009. (http://www.nytimes.com/projects/magazine/ideas/2009/#c)
- Vedantam, Shankar. Why Voters Play Follow-the-Leader. *Washington Post*, Feb. 4, 2008, A3. (http://www.washingtonpost.com/wp-dyn/content/article/2008/02/03/AR2008020302572.html)
- Weber, Bruce. The Deciders: Umpires v. Judges, *New York Times*, July 12, 2009, WK1. (http://www.nytimes.com/2009/07/12/weekinreview/12weber.html)

External links

- Cultural Cognition Project website (http://culturalcognition.net/)
- Public Lecture on Cultural Cognition by Dan Kahan, University of Florida, Oct. 6, 2009 (http://mediasite.video.ufl.edu/mediasite/Viewer/?peid=e16374d0980344fa911266bf40b60314)

Cultural Theory of risk

The **Cultural Theory of risk**, often referred to simply as Cultural Theory (with capital letters; not to be confused with culture theory), consists of a conceptual framework and an associated body of empirical studies that seek to explain societal conflict over risk. Whereas other theories of risk perception stress economic and cognitive influences, Cultural Theory asserts that structures of social organization endow individuals with perceptions that reinforce those structures in competition against alternative ones. Originating in the work of anthropologist Mary Douglas and political scientist Aaron Wildavsky, Cultural Theory has given rise to a diverse set of research programs that span multiple social science disciplines and that have in recent years been used to analyze policymaking conflicts generally.

Theory and evidence

Risk and blame, group and grid

Two features of Douglas's work inform the basic structure of Cultural Theory. The first of these is a general account of the social function of individual perceptions of societal dangers. Individuals, Douglas maintained, tend to associate societal harms—from sickness to famine to natural catastrophes—with conduct that transgresses societal norms. This tendency, she argued, plays an indispensable role in promoting certain social structures, both by imbuing a society's members with aversions to subversive behavior and by focusing resentment and blame on those who defy such institutions.[1] [2]

The second important feature of Douglas's work is a particular account of the forms that competing structures of social organization assume. Douglas maintained that cultural ways of life and affiliated outlooks can be characterized (within and across all societies at all times) along two dimensions, which she called "group" and "grid."[3] A "high group" way of life exhibits a high degree of collective control, whereas a "low group" one exhibits a much lower one and a resulting emphasis on individual self-sufficiency. A "high grid" way of life is characterized by conspicuous and durable forms of stratification in roles and authority, whereas a "low grid" one reflects a more egalitarian ordering.[4]

Although developed in Douglas's earlier work, these two strands of her thought were first consciously woven together to form the fabric of a theory of risk perception in her and Wildavsky's 1982 book, *Risk and Culture : An Essay on the Selection of Technical and Environmental Dangers*. Focusing largely on political conflict over air pollution and nuclear power in the United States, *Risk and Culture* attributed political conflict over environmental and technological risks to a struggle between adherents of competing ways of life associated with the group-grid scheme: an egalitarian, collectivist ("low grid," "high group") one, which gravitates toward fear of environmental disaster as a justification for restricting commercial behavior productive of inequality; and individualistic ("low group") and hierarchical ("high grid") ones, which resist claims of environmental risk in order to shield private orderings from interference, and to defend established commercial and governmental elites from subversive rebuke.

Later works in Cultural Theory systematized this argument. In these accounts, group-grid gives rise to either four or five discrete ways of life, each of which is associated with a view of nature (as robust, as fragile, as capricious, and so forth) that is congenial to its advancement in competition with the others.[5] [6]

Survey studies

A variety of scholars have presented survey data in support of Cultural Theory. The first of these was Karl Dake, a graduate student of Wildavsky, who correlated perceptions of various societal risks—environmental disaster, external aggression, internal disorder, market breakdown—with subjects' scores on attitudinal scales that he believed reflected the "cultural worldviews" associated with the ways of life in Douglas's group-grid scheme.[7] Later researchers have refined Dake's measures and have applied them to a wide variety of environmental and technological risks.[8] [9] [10] Such studies furnish an indirect form of proof by showing that risk perceptions are distributed across persons in patterns better explained by culture than by other asserted influences.

Case studies

Other scholars have presented more interpretive empirical support for Cultural Theory. Developed in case-study form, their work shows how particular risk-regulation and related controversies can plausibly be understood within a group-grid framework.[11]

Relationship to other risk perception theories

Cultural Theory is an alternative to two other prominent theories of risk perception. The first, which is grounded in rational choice economics, treats risk perceptions as manifesting individuals' implicit weighing of costs and benefits.[12] Douglas and Wildavsky criticized this position in *Risk and Culture*, arguing that it ignores the role of cultural ways of life in determining what states of affairs individuals see as worthy of taking risks to attain.[13] The second prominent theory, which is grounded in social psychology and behavioral economics, asserts that individuals' risk perceptions are pervasively shaped, and often distorted, by heuristics and biases.[14] Douglas maintained that this "psychometric" approach naively attempted to "depoliticize" risk conflicts by attributing to cognitive influences beliefs that reflect individuals' commitments to competing cultural structures.[15]

More recently, some scholars, including Paul Slovic, a pioneer in the development of the psychometric theory, have sought to connect the psychometric and cultural theories. This position, known as the cultural cognition of risk, asserts that the dynamics featured in the psychometric paradigm are the mechanisms through which group-grid worldviews shape risk perception.[16] Anticipating such a program, Douglas herself once suggested that "[i]f we were invited to make a coalition between group-grid theory and psychometrics, it would be like going to heaven."[17]

Application beyond risk perception

Theorists working with Cultural Theory have adapted its basic components, and in particular the group-grid typology, to matters in addition to risk perception. These include political science,[18] public policy,[19] public management and organizational studies,[20] and law.[21]

Criticisms

The Cultural Theory of risk has been subject to a variety of criticisms. Complexities and ambiguities inherent in Douglas's group-grid scheme, and the resulting diversity of conceptualizations among cultural theorists, lead some to believe the theory is fatally opaque.[22] Others object to the theory's embrace of functionalism,[6] [23] a controversial mode of analysis that sees the needs of collective entities (in the case of Cultural Theory, the ways of life defined by group-grid), rather than the decisions of individuals about how to pursue their own ends, as the principal causal force in social relations.[24] Commentators have also critiqued studies that purport to furnish empirical evidence for Cultural Theory, particularly survey studies, which some argue reflect unreliable measures of individual attitudes and in any case explain only a modest amount of the variance in individual perceptions of risk.[25] [26] Finally, some resist Cultural Theory on political grounds owing to Douglas and Wildavsky's harsh denunciation of environmentalists in *Risk and Culture*.[27]

Notes

[1] Douglas (1966).
[2] Douglas (1992).
[3] Douglas (1970), pp. 54-68.
[4] Rayner (1992), p 86.
[5] Mamadouh (1999).
[6] Thompson, Ellis & Wildvasky (1990).
[7] Dake (1991).
[8] Langford, Georgiu, Bateman, Day & Turner (2000).
[9] Peters & Slovic (1996).
[10] Poortinga (2002).
[11] Verweij & Thompson (2006).
[12] Starr (1969).
[13] Douglas & Wildavsky (1982), pp. 194-95.
[14] Kahneman, Slovic & Tversky (1982).
[15] Douglas (1997), pp. 123-26.
[16] Kahan, Slovic, Braman & Gastil (2006), p. 1084.
[17] Douglas (1997), p. 132.
[18] Thompson, Grendstate & Selle (1999).
[19] Swedlow (2002).
[20] Hood (1998).
[21] Kahan, Slovic, Braman & Gastil (2006).
[22] Boholm (2003), p. 66.
[23] Douglas (1986)
[24] Boholm (2003), pp. 68, 79-80.
[25] Marris, Langford, & O'Riordan (1998).
[26] Sjöberg (1998).
[27] Winner (1982).

References

Boholm, Å. (1996). Risk perception and social anthropology: critique of Cultural Theory. *Ethnos*, 68(2), 159-178.

Dake, K. (1991). Orienting dispositions in the perception of risk: An analysis of contemporary worldviews and cultural biases. *Journal of Cross-Cultural Psychology*, 22, 61.

Douglas, M. (1986). *How Institutions Think*. Syracuse, N.Y.: Syracuse University Press.

Douglas, M. (1997). The depoliticization of risk. In R. J. Ellis & M. Thompson (Eds.), *Culture matters: Essays in honor of Aaron Wildavsky* (pp. 121-32). Boulder, Colo.: Westview Press.

Douglas, M. (1970). *Natural Symbols: explorations in cosmology*. New York: Pantheon Books.

Douglas, M. (1966). *Purity and Danger: An analysis of concepts of pollution and taboo*. New York,: Praeger.

Douglas, M. (1992). *Risk and Blame: Essays in Cultural Theory*. London: New York: Routledge.

Douglas, M., & Wildavsky, A. B. (1982). *Risk and Culture: An essay on the selection of technical and environmental dangers*. Berkeley: University of California Press.

Christopher Hood (1998). *The art of the state: Culture, rhetoric, and public management*. Oxford: Clarendon Press.

Kahan, D., Slovic, P., Braman, D., & Gastil, J. (2006). Fear of democracy: A cultural critique of Sunstein on risk. *Harvard Law Review*, 119, 1071-1109. (http:/ / www. harvardlawreview. org/ issues/ 119/ february06/ Book_Review_1637.php)

Kahneman, D., Slovic, P., & Tversky, A. (1982). *Judgment under uncertainty: Heuristics and biases*. Cambridge: New York: Cambridge University Press.

Langford, I. H., Georgiou, S., Bateman, I. J., Day, R. J., & Turner, R. K. (2000). Public perceptions of health risks from polluted coastal bathing waters: A mixed methodological analysis using Cultural Theory. *Risk Analysis*, 20(5), 691-704.

Mamadouh, V. (1999). Grid-Group Cultural Theory: An introduction. *GeoJournal*, 47, 395-409.

Marris, C., Langford, I. H., & O'Riordan, T. (1998). A Quantitative test of the Cultural Theory of risk perceptions: Comparison with the psychometric paradigm. *Risk Analysis*, 18(5), 635-647.

Peters, E., & Slovic, P. (1996). The role of affect and worldviews as orienting dispositions in the perception and acceptance of nuclear power. *Journal of Applied Social Psychology*, 26(16), 1427-1453.

Poortinga, W., Steg, L., & Vlek, C. (2002). Environmental risk concern and preferences for energy-saving measures. *Environment and Behavior*, 34(4), 455-478.

Rayner, S. (1992). Cultural Theory and risk analysis. In S. Krimsky & D. Golding (Eds.), *Social Theories of Risk* (pp. pp. 83-115).

Sjöberg, L. (1998). World views, political attitudes, and risk perception. *Risk: Health, Safety and Environment*, 9, 137-152.

Starr, C. (1969). Social benefit versus technological risk. *Science*, 165(3899), 1232-1238.

Swedlow, B. (2002). Toward cultural analysis in policy analysis: picking up where Aaron Wildavsky left off. *Journal of Comparative Policy Analysis*, 4(2), 267-285.

Thompson, M., Ellis, R., & Wildavsky, A. (1990). *Cultural Theory*. Boulder Colo.: Westview Press: Westport, Conn.: Praeger.

Thompson, M., Grendstad, G., & Selle, P. (1999). *Cultural Theory as political science*. London ; New York: Routledge.

Verweij, M., & Thompson, M. (Eds.). (2006). *Clumsy solutions for a complex world: Governance, politics, and plural perceptions*. Houndmills, Basingstoke, Hampshire ; New York: Palgrave Macmillan.

Winner, L. (1982). Pollution as delusion. *New York Times*, p. BR8 (Aug. 8).

Further reading

- *Organising and Disorganising*, Michael Thompson, Triarchy Press, 2008 (http://www.triarchypress.com/pages/book16.htm)
- Essay by [[Geoff Mulgan (http://www.prospect-magazine.co.uk/article_details.php?id=9600)] in *Prospect* magazine, June 2007]
- Article (http://www.thersa.org/fellowship/journal/features/features/beyond-boom-and-bust) from the RSA journal, 2008
- Video (http://www.thersa.org/fellowship/journal/videos/michael-thompson) discussion between Michael Thompson and Matthew Taylor, *How Cultural Theory can offer a new economic paradigm*, November 2008
- Fourcultures (http://fourcultures.wordpress.com) a blog from a Grid-Group perspective.

Decision theory

Decision theory in economics, psychology, philosophy, mathematics, and statistics is concerned with identifying the values, uncertainties and other issues relevant in a given decision, its rationality, and the resulting optimal decision. It is very closely related to the field of game theory.

Normative and descriptive decision theory

Most of decision theory is normative or prescriptive, *i.e.*, it is concerned with identifying the best decision to take, assuming an ideal decision maker who is fully informed, able to compute with perfect accuracy, and fully rational. The practical application of this prescriptive approach (how people *ought to* make decisions) is called decision analysis, and aimed at finding tools, methodologies and software to help people make better decisions. The most systematic and comprehensive software tools developed in this way are called decision support systems.

Since people usually do not behave in ways consistent with axiomatic rules, often their own, leading to violations of optimality, there is a related area of study, called a positive or descriptive discipline, attempting to describe what people will actually do. Since the normative, optimal decision often creates hypotheses for testing against actual behaviour, the two fields are closely linked. Furthermore it is possible to relax the assumptions of perfect information, rationality and so forth in various ways, and produce a series of different prescriptions or predictions about behaviour, allowing for further tests of the kind of decision-making that occurs in practice.

In recent decades, there has been increasing interest in what is sometimes called 'behavioral decision theory' and this has contributed to a re-evaluation of what rational decision-making requires (see for instance Anand, 1993).

What kinds of decisions need a theory?

Choice under uncertainty

This area represents the heart of decision theory. The procedure now referred to as expected value was known from the 17th century. Blaise Pascal invoked it in his famous wager (see below), which is contained in his *Pensées*, published in 1670. The idea of expected value is that, when faced with a number of actions, each of which could give rise to more than one possible outcome with different probabilities, the rational procedure is to identify all possible outcomes, determine their values (positive or negative) and the probabilities that will result from each course of action, and multiply the two to give an expected value. The action to be chosen should be the one that gives rise to the highest total expected value. In 1738, Daniel Bernoulli published an influential paper entitled *Exposition of a New Theory on the Measurement of Risk*, in which he uses the St. Petersburg paradox to show that expected value theory must be normatively wrong. He also gives an example in which a Dutch merchant is trying to decide whether to insure a cargo being sent from Amsterdam to St Petersburg in winter, when it is known that there is a 5% chance that the ship and cargo will be lost. In his solution, he defines a utility function and computes expected utility rather than expected financial value (see[1] for a review).

In the 20th century, interest was reignited by Abraham Wald's 1939 paper[2] pointing out that the two central procedures of sampling–distribution based statistical-theory, namely hypothesis testing and parameter estimation, are special cases of the general decision problem. Wald's paper renewed and synthesized many concepts of statistical theory, including loss functions, risk functions, admissible decision rules, antecedent distributions, Bayesian procedures, and minimax procedures. The phrase "decision theory" itself was used in 1950 by E. L. Lehmann.[3]

The revival of subjective probability theory, from the work of Frank Ramsey, Bruno de Finetti, Leonard Savage and others, extended the scope of expected utility theory to situations where subjective probabilities can be used. At this time, von Neumann's theory of expected utility proved that expected utility maximization followed from basic postulates about rational behavior.

The work of Maurice Allais and Daniel Ellsberg showed that human behavior has systematic and sometimes important departures from expected-utility maximization. The prospect theory of Daniel Kahneman and Amos Tversky renewed the empirical study of economic behavior with less emphasis on rationality presuppositions. Kahneman and Tversky found three regularities — in actual human decision-making, "losses loom larger than gains"; persons focus more on *changes* in their utility–states than they focus on absolute utilities; and the estimation of subjective probabilities is severely biased by anchoring.

Castagnoli and LiCalzi (1996), Bordley and LiCalzi (2000) recently showed that maximizing expected utility is mathematically equivalent to maximizing the probability that the uncertain consequences of a decision are preferable to an uncertain benchmark (e.g., the probability that a mutual fund strategy outperforms the S&P 500 or that a firm outperforms the uncertain future performance of a major competitor.). This reinterpretation relates to psychological work suggesting that individuals have fuzzy aspiration levels (Lopes & Oden), which may vary from choice context to choice context. Hence it shifts the focus from utility to the individual's uncertain reference point.

Pascal's Wager is a classic example of a choice under uncertainty. The uncertainty, according to Pascal, is whether or not God exists. Belief or non-belief in God is the choice to be made. However, the reward for belief in God if God actually does exist is infinite. Therefore, however small the probability of God's existence, the expected value of belief exceeds that of non-belief, so it is better to believe in God. (There are several criticisms of the argument.)

Intertemporal choice

This area is concerned with the kind of choice where different actions lead to outcomes that are realised at different points in time. If someone received a windfall of several thousand dollars, they could spend it on an expensive holiday, giving them immediate pleasure, or they could invest it in a pension scheme, giving them an income at some time in the future. What is the optimal thing to do? The answer depends partly on factors such as the expected rates of interest and inflation, the person's life expectancy, and their confidence in the pensions industry. However even with all those factors taken into account, human behavior again deviates greatly from the predictions of prescriptive decision theory, leading to alternative models in which, for example, objective interest rates are replaced by subjective discount rates.

Competing decision makers

Some decisions are difficult because of the need to take into account how other people in the situation will respond to the decision that is taken. The analysis of such social decisions is more often treated under the label of game theory, rather than decision theory, though it involves the same mathematical methods. From the standpoint of game theory most of the problems treated in decision theory are one-player games (or the one player is viewed as playing against an impersonal background situation). In the emerging socio-cognitive engineering, the research is especially focused on the different types of distributed decision-making in human organizations, in normal and abnormal/emergency/crisis situations.

Signal detection theory is based on decision theory.

Complex decisions

Other areas of decision theory are concerned with decisions that are difficult simply because of their complexity, or the complexity of the organization that has to make them. In such cases the issue is not the deviation between real and optimal behaviour, but the difficulty of determining the optimal behaviour in the first place. The Club of Rome, for example, developed a model of economic growth and resource usage that helps politicians make real-life decisions in complex situations.

Paradox of choice

Observed in many cases is the paradox that more choices may lead to a poorer decision or a failure to make a decision at all. It is sometimes theorized to be caused by analysis paralysis, real or perceived, or perhaps from rational ignorance. A number of researchers including Sheena S. Iyengar and Mark R. Lepper have published studies on this phenomenon.[4] This analysis was popularized by Barry Schwartz in his 2004 book, *The Paradox of Choice*.

Statistical decision theory

Several statistical tools and methods are available to organize evidence, evaluate risks, and aid in decision making. The risks of Type I and type II errors can be quantified (estimated probability, cost, expected value, etc.) and rational decision making is improved.

One example shows a structure for deciding guilt in a criminal trial:

		Actual condition	
		Guilty	**Not guilty**
Decision	**Verdict of 'guilty'**	True Positive	False Positive (i.e. guilt reported unfairly) **Type I error**
	Verdict of 'not guilty'	False Negative (i.e. guilt not detected) **Type II error**	True Negative |+

|+

Alternatives to decision theory

A highly controversial issue is whether one can replace the use of probability in decision theory by other alternatives.

Probability theory

The Advocates of probability theory point to:

- the work of Richard Threlkeld Cox for justification of the probability axioms,

- the Dutch book paradoxes of Bruno de Finetti as illustrative of the theoretical difficulties that can arise from departures from the probability axioms, and

- the complete class theorems, which show that all admissible decision rules are equivalent to the Bayesian decision rule for some utility function and some prior distribution (or for the limit of a sequence of prior distributions).

Thus, for every decision rule, *either* the rule may be reformulated as a Bayesian procedure, or there is a (perhaps limiting) Bayesian rule that is sometimes better and never worse.

Alternatives to probability theory

The proponents of fuzzy logic, possibility theory, Dempster–Shafer theory and info-gap decision theory maintain that probability is only one of many alternatives and point to many examples where non-standard alternatives have been implemented with apparent success; notably, probabilistic decision theory is sensitive to assumptions about the probabilities of various events, while non-probabilistic rules such as minimax are robust, in that they do not make such assumptions.

General criticism

A general criticism of decision theory based on a fixed universe of possibilities is that it considers the "known unknowns", not the "unknown unknowns": it focuses on expected variations, not on unforeseen events, which some argue (as in black swan theory) have outsized impact and must be considered – significant events may be "outside model". This line of argument, called the ludic fallacy, is that there are inevitable imperfections in modeling the real world by particular models, and that unquestioning reliance on models blinds one to their limits.

For instance, a simple model of daily stock market returns may include extreme moves such as Black Monday (1987), but might not model the market breakdowns following the September 11 attacks.

References

[1] Schoemaker, P. J. H. (1982). "The Expected Utility Model: Its Variants, Purposes, Evidence and Limitations". *Journal of Economic Literature* **20**: 529–563.

[2] Wald, Abraham (1939). "Contributions to the Theory of Statistical Estimation and Testing Hypotheses". *Annals of Mathematical Statistics* **10** (4): 299–326. doi:10.1214/aoms/1177732144. MR932.

[3] Lehmann, E. L. (1950). "Some Principles of the Theory of Testing Hypotheses". *Annals of Mathematical Statistics* **21** (1): 1–26. doi:10.1214/aoms/1177729884. JSTOR 2236552.

[4] Iyengar, Sheena S. and Lepper, Mark R. *When Choice is Demotivating: Can One Desire Too Much of a Good Thing?* (http://www.columbia.edu/~ss957/whenchoice.html). Retrieved 2009-Feb-12.

Further reading

- Akerlof, George A., Yellen, Janet L. (May 1987). *Rational Models of Irrational Behavior.* **77**. pp. 137–142.
- Anand, Paul (1993). *Foundations of Rational Choice Under Risk.* Oxford: Oxford University Press. ISBN 0198233035. (*an overview of the philosophical foundations of key mathematical axioms in subjective expected utility theory – mainly normative*)
- Arthur, W. Brian (May 1991). "Designing Economic Agents that Act like Human Agents: A Behavioral Approach to Bounded Rationality". *The American Economic Review* **81** (2): 353–9.
- Berger, James O. (1985). *Statistical decision theory and Bayesian Analysis* (2nd ed.). New York: Springer-Verlag. ISBN 0-387-96098-8. MR0804611.
- Bernardo, José M.; Smith, Adrian F. M. (1994). *Bayesian Theory.* Wiley. ISBN 0-471-92416-4. MR1274699.
- Clemen, Robert (1996). *Making Hard Decisions: An Introduction to Decision Analysis* (2nd ed.). Belmont CA: Duxbury Press. ISBN 0534260357. (*covers normative decision theory*)
- De Groot, Morris, *Optimal Statistical Decisions.* Wiley Classics Library. 2004. (Originally published 1970.) ISBN 0-471-68029-X.
- Goodwin, Paul and Wright, George (2004). *Decision Analysis for Management Judgment* (3rd ed.). Chichester: Wiley. ISBN 0-470-86108-8. (*covers both normative and descriptive theory*)
- Hansson, Sven Ove. "Decision Theory: A Brief Introduction" (http://www.infra.kth.se/~soh/decisiontheory.pdf) (PDF).

- Khemani , Karan, Ignorance is Bliss: A study on how and why humans depend on recognition heuristics in social relationships, the equity markets and the brand market-place, thereby making successful decisions, 2005.
- Miller L (1985). "Cognitive risk-taking after frontal or temporal lobectomy—I. The synthesis of fragmented visual information". *Neuropsychologia* **23** (3): 359–69. doi:10.1016/0028-3932(85)90022-3. PMID 4022303.
- Miller L, Milner B (1985). "Cognitive risk-taking after frontal or temporal lobectomy—II. The synthesis of phonemic and semantic information". *Neuropsychologia* **23** (3): 371–9. doi:10.1016/0028-3932(85)90023-5. PMID 4022304.
- North, D.W. (1968). "A tutorial introduction to decision theory". *IEEE Transactions on Systems Science and Cybernetics* **4** (3): 200–210. doi:10.1109/TSSC.1968.300114. Reprinted in Shafer & Pearl. *(also about normative decision theory)*
- Peterson, Martin (2009). *An Introduction to Decision Theory*. Cambridge University Press. ISBN 9780521716543.
- Raiffa, Howard (1997). *Decision Analysis: Introductory Readings on Choices Under Uncertainty*. McGraw Hill. ISBN 0-07-052579-X.
- Robert, Christian (2007). *The Bayesian Choice* (2nd ed.). New York: Springer. doi:10.1007/0-387-71599-1. ISBN 0-387-95231-4. MR1835885.
- Shafer, Glenn and Pearl, Judea, ed (1990). *Readings in uncertain reasoning*. San Mateo, CA: Morgan Kaufmann.
- Smith, J.Q. (1988). *Decision Analysis: A Bayesian Approach*. Chapman and Hall. ISBN 0-412-27520-1.
- Charles Sanders Peirce and Joseph Jastrow (1885). "On Small Differences in Sensation" (http://psychclassics. yorku.ca/Peirce/small-diffs.htm). *Memoirs of the National Academy of Sciences* **3**: 73–83. http://psychclassics. yorku.ca/Peirce/small-diffs.htm
- Ramsey, Frank Plumpton; "Truth and Probability" (PDF (http://cepa.newschool.edu/het//texts/ramsey/ ramsess.pdf)), Chapter VII in *The Foundations of Mathematics and other Logical Essays* (1931).
- de Finetti, Bruno (September 1989). "Probabilism: A Critical Essay on the Theory of Probability and on the Value of Science". *Erkenntnis* **31**. (translation of 1931 article)
- de Finetti, Bruno (1937). "La Prévision: ses lois logiques, ses sources subjectives". *Annales de l'Institut Henri Poincaré*.

    de Finetti, Bruno. "Foresight: its Logical Laws, Its Subjective Sources," (translation of the 1937 article (http:// www. numdam. org/ item?id=AIHP_1937__7_1_1_0) in French) in H. E. Kyburg and H. E. Smokler (eds), *Studies in Subjective Probability,* New York: Wiley, 1964.

- de Finetti, Bruno. *Theory of Probability*, (translation by AFM Smith of 1970 book) 2 volumes, New York: Wiley, 1974-5.
- Donald Davidson, Patrick Suppes and Sidney Siegel (1957). *Decision-Making: An Experimental Approach*. Stanford University Press.
- Pfanzagl, J (1967). "Subjective Probability Derived from the Morgenstern-von Neumann Utility Theory". In Martin Shubik. *Essays in Mathematical Economics In Honor of Oskar Morgenstern*. Princeton University Press. pp. 237–251.
- Pfanzagl, J. in cooperation with V. Baumann and H. Huber (1968). "Events, Utility and Subjective Probability". *Theory of Measurement*. Wiley. pp. 195–220.
- Morgenstern, Oskar (1976). "Some Reflections on Utility". In Andrew Schotter. *Selected Economic Writings of Oskar Morgenstern*. New York University Press. pp. 65–70. ISBN 0814777716.

Digital Repository Audit Method Based on Risk Assessment

The **Digital Repository Audit Method Based on Risk Assessment** (**DRAMBORA**) is a methodology and associated software-based toolkit developed by Digital Curation Centre (DCC) and DigitalPreservationEurope (DPE) to support the assessment of digital repositories.

Digital preservation is often defined as a risk management exercise where the aim is to convert the uncertainty about maintaining usability of authentic digital objects into quantifiable risks. The purpose of a digital repository or archive is to do everything it can to mitigate the risks that impede its ability to provide access to authentic digital information across space and time. The term 'digital repository' has a broad range of uses. Some use it for any collections of digital material. Many use it to refer to digital collections (often of ePrints) where the metadata is shared with a particular protocol. A few apply it only to collections of digital material that are intended to survive in an understandable way for very long periods into the future. The measure of success of a repository's work is the 'quality' of information it releases to its users. The DRAMBORA toolkit is intended to facilitate internal audit by providing repository administrators with a means to assess their capabilities, identify their weaknesses, and recognise their strengths.

Digital repositories are still in their infancy and this model is designed to be responsive to the rapidly developing landscape. The development of the toolkit follows a concentrated period of repository pilot audits undertaken by the DCC, conducted at a diverse range of organisations including national libraries, scientific data centres and cultural and heritage data archives. The construction of a toolkit of this kind is a dynamic process and this is the second stage in this process. The DRAMBORA toolkit represents the latest development in an ongoing international effort to conceive criteria, means and methodologies for audit and certification of digital repositories. The intention throughout its development was to build upon, extend and complement existing efforts. A key requirement has been to establish a toolkit that contributes towards a single process for repository assessment. The importance of international cooperation and collaboration, and the potential dangers associated with divergence were acknowledged very early on within the DCC and DPE's work in this area.

Perhaps the most notable efforts to date within this context are those invested within the RLG/NARA Task Force and the nestor working group to develop criteria for audit and certification of trustworthy digital repositories. Further significant work was led by the Center for Research Libraries (CRL [1]). The results of these efforts have been foremost within our considerations throughout the development of this toolkit, and in the DCC-led pilot audits that preceded it. The DCC/DPE working group has engaged with representatives of other groups to agree upon a set of principles, representing the fundamental, objective baseline criteria for preservation repositories, and these and their underlying concepts, are profoundly important within the toolkit. It is anticipated that self-audit based on DRAMBORA can be facilitated if undertaken in association with one or both of the check-lists, and vice versa. The risk-based approach assists efforts to match a repository against these lists of requirements. Only with a clear view of an organisation's business context and its implicit risks can an auditor effectively utilise these requirements. The toolkit contextualises these lists so they can be more effectively applied. In addition to these resources, we have also sought to incorporate and adapt ideas and concepts from an additional, diverse range of sources, including a wide range of international information standards, many with their basis in the risk management industry aiming to broaden ever further the perspectives that our international colleagues have already established.

References

- Andrew McHugh, Perla Innocenti, Seamus Ross (2008). "Assessing risks to digital cultural heritage with DRAMBORA" [2]. *International Documentation Committee of the International Council of Museums (CIDOC) 2008, Athens, Greece, 15–18 September 2008.*

External links

- The Digital Repository Audit Method Based on Risk Assessment (DRAMBORA) [3]

References

[1] http://www.crl.edu/content.asp?l1=13&l2=58&l3=162&l4=91#

[2] http://www.cidoc2008.gr/cidoc/Documents/papers/drfile.2008-06-18.5007058695

[3] http://www.repositoryaudit.eu/

Disappointment

Disappointment the feeling of dissatisfaction that follows the failure of expectations to manifest. Similar to regret, it differs in that the individual feeling regret focuses primarily on the personal choices that contributed to a poor outcome, while the individual feeling disappointment focuses on the outcome itself.[1] It is a source of psychological stress.[2] The study of disappointment—its causes, impact and the degree to which individual decisions are motivated by a desire to avoid it—is a focus in the field of decision analysis,[1] [3] as disappointment is one of two primary emotions involved in decision-making.[4]

Disappointment expressed by a team of American football players commiserating after a defeat.

Disappoint is traced to the Middle English *disappointen* by way of the Old French *desapointer*. In literal meaning, it is to remove from office.[5] Its use in the sense of general frustration traces to the late 15th century, and it first appears recorded in English as an emotional state of dejection in the middle 18th century.[6]

Psychology

Disappointment is a subjective response related to the anticipated rewards.[1] The psychological results of disappointment vary greatly among individuals; while some recover quickly, others mire in frustration or blame or become depressed.[2] A 2003 study of young children with parental background of childhood onset depression found that there may be a genetic predisposition to slow recovery following disappointment.[7] While not every person responds to disappointment by becoming depressed, depression can (in the self psychology school of psychoanalytic theory) almost always be seen as secondary to disappointment/frustration.[8]

Disappointment, and an inability to prepare for it, has also been hypothesized as the source of occasional immune system compromise in optimists.[9] While optimists by and large exhibit better health,[10] they may alternatively exhibit less immunity when under prolonged or uncontrollable stress, a phenomenon which researchers have attributed to the "disappointment effect".[9] The "disappointment effect" posits that optimists do not utilize "emotional cushioning" to prepare for disappointment and hence are less able to deal with it when they experience it.[10] [11] This disappointment effect has been challenged since the mid-1990s by researcher Suzanne C. Segerstrom, who has published, alone and in accord, several articles evaluating its plausibility. Her findings suggest that, rather than being unable to deal with disappointment, optimists are more likely to actively tackle their problems and experience some immunity compromise as a result.[12]

In 1994, psychotherapist Ian Craib published the book *The Importance of Disappointment*, in which he drew on the works of Melanie Klein and Sigmund Freud in advancing the theory that disappointment-avoidant cultures—particularly therapy culture—provides false expectations of perfection in life and prevents people from achieving a healthy self-identity.[13] Craib offered as two examples litigious victims of medical mistakes, who once would have accepted accidents as a course of life, and people suffering grief following the death of a loved one who, he said, are provided a false stage model of recovery that is more designed to comfort bereavement therapists than the bereaved.[14] In a 2004 article, the journal *Psychology Today* recommended handling disappointment through concrete steps including accepting that setbacks are normal, setting realistic goals, planning subsequent moves, thinking about positive role models, seeking support and tackling tasks by stages rather than focusing on the big picture.[2]

Theory

Disappointment theory, pioneered in the mid-1980s by David E. Bell with further development by Graham Loomes and Robert Sugden,[15] revolves around the notion that people contemplating risks are disappointed when the outcome of the risk is not evaluated as positively as the expected outcome.[16] Disappointment theory has been utilized in examining such diverse decision-making processes as return migration, taxpayer compliance and customer willingness to pay.[17]

Disappointed individuals focus on "upward counterfactuals"—alternative outcomes that would have been better than the one actually experienced—to the point that even positive outcomes may result in disappointment.[18] One example, supplied by Bell, concerns a lottery win of $10,000.00, an event which will theoretically be perceived more positively if that amount represents the highest possible win in the lottery than if it represents the lowest.[19] Decision analysts operate on the assumption that individuals will anticipate the potential for disappointment and make decisions that are less likely to lead to the experience of this feeling.[15] Disappointment aversion has been posited as one explanation for the Allais paradox, a problematic response in expected utility theory wherein people prove more likely to choose a sure reward than to risk a higher one while at the same time being willing to attempt a greater reward with lower probability when both options include some risk.[20]

While earlier developers of disappointment theory focused on anticipated outcomes, more recent examinations by Philippe Delquié and Alessandra Cillo of INSEAD have focused on the impact of later disappointment resulting when an actual outcome comes to be regarded negatively based on further development; for example, if a person receives higher than expected gains in the stock market, she may be elated until she discovers a week later that she could have gained much more profit if she had waited a few more days to sell.[15] This experience of disappointment may influence subsequent behavior, and, the analysts state, an incorporation of such variables into disappointment theory may enhance the study of behavioral finance.[15] Disappointment is, along with regret, measured by direct questioning of respondents.[21]

Notes

[1] Bell, David E. (January 1985). "Putting a premium on regret". *Management Science* **31** (1): 117–20. doi:10.1287/mnsc.31.1.117. JSTOR 2631680.

[2] Ma, Lybi. (March 29, 2004). Down But Not Out (http://www.medicinenet.com/script/main/art.asp?articlekey=37951). Originally published in *Psychology Today*. Hosted with permission by medicinenet.com. Retrieved 22/02/08.

[3] Wilco, W. can Dijk, Marcel Zeelenbergb and Joop van der Pligtc (August 2003). "Blessed are those who expect nothing: Lowering expectations as a way of avoiding disappointment". *Journal of Economic Psychology* **24** (4): 505–16. doi:10.1016/S0167-4870(02)00211-8.

[4] Wilco W. van Dijk and Marcel Zeelenberg (December 2002). "Investigating the appraisal patterns of regret and disappointment" (http://www.springerlink.com/content/x4w85n6q1645947m/). *Motivation and Emotion* **26** (4): 321–31. doi:10.1023/A:1022823221146. .

[5] "disappoint". *The American Heritage Dictionary of the English Language, 3rd ed*. Houghton Mifflin Company. 1992. pp. 529.

[6] "disappointment". *The New Shorter Oxford English Dictionary*. **1**. Clarendon Press, Oxford.. 1993. pp. 683. ISBN 0198612710.

[7] Forbes, Erika E., Nathan A. Fox, Jeffrey F. Cohn, Steven F. Galles and Maria Kovacs (March 2006). "Children's affect regulation during a disappointment: Psychophysiological responses and relation to parent history of depression" (http://www.sciencedirect.com/science?_ob=ArticleURL&_udi=B6T4T-4GXVGG5-1&_user=10&_rdoc=1&_fmt=&_orig=search&_sort=d&view=c&_acct=C000050221&_version=1&_urlVersion=0&_userid=10&md5=8e450681748e0dc360ea4bc55111cece). *Biological Psychology* **71** (3): 264–77. doi:10.1016/j.biopsycho.2005.05.004. PMID 16115722. .

[8] Gilbert, Paul (1992). *Depression: The Evolution of Powerlessness*. Guilford Press. p. 315. ISBN 0898628849.

[9] Schwartz, Todd. (Summer 2003) Positive thinking (http://www.lclark.edu/dept/chron/positives03.html) *Chronicle*, Lewis & Clark College. Retrieved 22/02/08.

[10] Neimark, Jill. (May/Jun 2007) The optimism revolution (http://psychologytoday.com/articles/index.php?term=20070424-000004&page=1) *Psychology Today*. Retrieved 22/02/08.

[11] Grohol, John M. (February 4, 2006) Is it best to expect the worst? Psychologists test long-held theory of emotional cushioning (http://psychcentral.com/blog/archives/2006/02/04/is-it-best-to-expect-the-worst-psychologists-test-long-held-theory-of-emotional-cushioning/). pyschcentral.com. Retrieved 22/02/08.

[12] Segerstrom SC (September 2006). "How does optimism suppress immunity? Evaluation of three affective pathways". *Health Psychol* **25** (5): 653–7. doi:10.1037/0278-6133.25.5.653. PMC 1613541. PMID 17014284.. See also Segerstrom SC (May 2005). "Optimism and immunity: do positive thoughts always lead to positive effects?". *Brain Behav. Immun.* **19** (3): 195–200. doi:10.1016/j.bbi.2004.08.003. PMC 1948078. PMID 15797306.

[13] Seale, Clive (2002). *Media and Health*. London: Sage Publications, Inc. pp. 167, 242. ISBN 0761947302.

[14] Seale, p. 167-168.

[15] "Disappointment Without Prior Expectation Cause and Affect" - Understanding emotion in decisions under risk (http://knowledge.insead.edu/abstract.cfm?ct=15268) INSEAD (2005). Retrieved 22/02/08.

[16] Delquié, Philippe and Alessandra Cillo (December 2006). "Disappointment without prior expectation: a unifying perspective on decision under risk" (http://www.springerlink.com/content/8206761u7760120x/). *Journal of Risk and Uncertainty* **33** (3): 197–215. doi:10.1007/s11166-006-0499-4. .

[17] See, for example, Why Do People Go Home Again? Disappointment Theory and Target Saving Theory Revisited (http://ciep.itam.mx/~cuecuecha/Whydopeople2.pdf), David Kelsey, Albert Schepanski (1991). "Regret and disappointment in taxpayer reporting decisions: An experimental study" (http://www3.interscience.wiley.com/cgi-bin/abstract/112770712/ABSTRACT?CRETRY=1&SRETRY=0). *Journal of Behavioral Decision Making* **4** (1): 33–53. doi:10.1002/bdm.3960040104. . and Christian Homburg, Nicole Koschate, Wayne D. Hoyer (April 2005). "Do satisfied customers really pay more? A study of the relationship between customer satisfaction and willingness to pay" (http://www.atypon-link.com/AMA/doi/abs/10.1509/jmkg.69.2.84.60760). *Journal of Marketing* **69** (2): 84–96. doi:10.1509/jmkg.69.2.84.60760. .

[18] Schwartz, Alan (2002). "Expected feelings about risky options". In Moore, Simon. *Emotional Cognition: From Brain to Behavior (Advances in Consciousness Research, 44)*. John Benjamins Publishing Co. pp. 183–96. ISBN 1-58811-224-1.

[19] Bell, David E. (Jan–Feb 1985). "Disappointment in Decision Making under Uncertainty". *Operations Research* **33** (1): 1–27. doi:10.1287/opre.33.1.1. JSTOR 170863.

[20] Jianmin Jia, James S. Dyer and John C. Butler (January 2001). "Generalized disappointment models". *Journal of Risk and Uncertainty* **59** (1): 59–78. and Gul, Faruk (May 1991). "A Theory of Disappointment Aversion" (http://jstor.org/stable/2938223). *Econometrica* **59** (3): 667–86. doi:10.2307/2938223. . For an alternate model of the Allais paradox, see The Allais Paradox (http://www.overcomingbias.com/2008/01/allais-paradox.html) at overcomingbias.com.

[21] Marcatto, Francesco and Donatella Ferrante (January 2008). "The Regret and Disappointment Scale: An instrument for assessing regret and disappointment in decision making" (http://journal.sjdm.org/bb8/bb8.html). *Judgment and Decision Making* **3** (1): 87–99. .

Further reading

- Dealing with disappointment: Parent & child study guides to watching a sports event (http://www.aaasponline. org/files/file/study-guide/10-disappointment.pdf.), Association for Applied Sport Psychology
- Craib, Ian (22 Sep 1994). *The Importance of Disappointment*. Routledge. pp. 216. ISBN 041509383X.
- Loomes, Graham (February 1988). "Further Evidence of the Impact of Regret and Disappointment in Choice under Uncertainty". *Economica* **55** (217): 47–62. doi:10.2307/2554246. JSTOR 2554246.
- Mandel, David R.; Denis J. Hilton and Patrizia Catellani (2005). *The Psychology of Counterfactual Thinking*. Routledge. p. 251. ISBN 0415322413.

Disneyland model

The **Disneyland model** is a proposed system in which users of a service would bear no risk for damage or injuries they sustain that are caused by others, as full liability would be imposed upon the responsible party (and/or their insurers). It is in contrast to the ballpark model, under which people use a service at their own risk. The Disneyland model is frequently advocated as a method by which licensure of motorists and their vehicles could be privatized. Before a person would be granted a license plate, they would need to obtain liability insurance without any caps on coverage amount.[1] The name comes from the fact that at Disneyland, the company is liable for any accidents that befall a customer if they, for instance, ride a ride they were too short for.

References

[1] On the Road: Newsroom: The Independent Institute (http://www.independent.org/newsroom/article.asp?id=2020)

Bill Durodié

Dr **Bill Durodié** is the Senior Fellow coordinating the Health and Human Security research programme in the Centre for Non-Traditional Security (NTS) Studies of the S. Rajaratnam School of International Studies (RSIS), at the Nanyang Technological University (NTU), Singapore, where he teaches a course on 'The Politics of Risk' as part of the Masters programme.

He previously coordinated the Homeland Defence research programme in the Centre of Excellence for National Security (CENS) there, during which time he organised the 3rd Asia-Pacific Programme for Senior National Security Officers (APPSNO), and the conference 'Therapy Culture Revisited: The Impact of the Language of Therapy on Public Policy and Social Resilience', as well as writing policy briefs on various topics pertaining to societal resilience for the Ministry of National Development (MND).

He is an Associate Fellow of the International Security Programme at the Royal Institute of International Affairs (RIIA), Chatham House in London, having also completed three years as Senior Lecturer in Risk and Corporate Security in the Resilience Centre of Cranfield University, part of the Defence Academy of the United Kingdom at Shrivenham. Prior to that he was Director of the International Centre for Security Analysis, and Senior Research Fellow in the International Policy Institute, within the War Studies Group of King's College London.

His main research interest is into the causes and consequences of our contemporary consciousness of risk. He is also interested in examining the erosion of expertise, the demoralisation of élites, the limitations of risk management and the precautionary principle, and the growing demand to engage the public in dialogue and decision-making in relation to science.

Durodié was educated at the Royal College of Science, part of Imperial College London, the London School of Economics, and New College Oxford, one of the constituent colleges of the University of Oxford. In 2007 he was also awarded a PhD by Public Works from Middlesex University.

He is an Honorary Senior Research Fellow in the School of Social Policy, Sociology and Social Research at the University of Kent, and a Fellow of the Royal Society of Arts (FRSA). He has previously been a Member of the Society for Risk Analysis, and an Advisory Forum Member of the Scientific Alliance.

Durodié's work has appeared and been commented on in a wide range of publications, and he is regularly requested to provide expert commentary for television and radio broadcasts. He appeared in the BAFTA award-winning BBC documentary series produced by Adam Curtis: The Power of Nightmares: The Rise of the Politics of Fear.

A transcript of his September 2006 interview with the Australian broadcaster Robyn Williams for 'In Conversation' on ABC Radio National is available from; http://www.abc.net.au/rn/inconversation/stories/2006/1738904.htm

A video podcast of his lecture 'Resilience in the Face of Terrorism' given on 9 March 2007 at the University of Warwick Business School is available from; http://www.wbs.ac.uk/news/features/2007/03/13/Resilience/in/ the

Durodié was one of the founding members of the Manifesto Club (http://www.manifestoclub.com), a network of individuals celebrating human achievement and challenging social, cultural and political pessimism.

External links

- Bill Durodié's homepage [1]
- Chatham House profile [2]

References

[1] http://www.durodie.net/
[2] http://www.chathamhouse.org.uk/about/directory/view/-/id/106/

Economics of security

The **economics of information security** addresses the economic aspects of privacy and computer security. Economics of information security includes models of the strictly rational "homo economicus" as well as behavioral economics. Economics of security addresses individual and organizational decisions and behaviors with respect to security and privacy as market decisions.

Economics of security addresses a core question: why do agents choose technical risks when there exists technical solutions to mitigate security and privacy risks? Economics addresses not only this question, but also inform design decisions in security engineering.

Emergence of economics of security

National security is the canonical public good. The economic status of information security came to the intellectual fore around 2000. As is the case with innovations it arose simultaneously in multiple venues.

In 2000, Ross Anderson wrote, Why Computer Security is Hard [1]. Anderson explained that a significant difficulty in optimal development of security technology is that incentives must be aligned with the technology to enable rational adoption. Thus, economic insights should be integrated into technical design. A security technology should enable the party at risk to invest to limit that risk. Otherwise, the designers are simply counting on altruism for adoption and diffusion. Many consider this publication the birth of economics of security.

Also in 2000 at Harvard, Camp at the School of Government and Wolfram in the Department of Economics argued that security is not a public good but rather each extant vulnerabilities has an associated negative externality value. Vulnerabilities were defined in this work as tradable goods. Six years later, iDEFENSE [2], ZDI [3] and Mozilla [4] have extant markets for vulnerabilities. Vulnerabilities are also known as computer security exploits.

In 2000, the scientists at the Computer Emergency Response Team at Carnegie Mellon University proposed an early mechanism for risk assessment. The Hierarchical Holographic Model provided the first multi-faceted evaluation tool to guide security investments using the science of risk. Since that time, CERT has developed a suite of systematic mechanism for organizations to use in risk evaluations, depending on the size and expertise of the organization: OCTAVE [5]. The study of computer security as an investment in risk avoidance has become standard practice.

In 2001 in an unrelated development, Larry Gordon and Marty Leob published A framework on using information security as a response to competitor analysis systems [6]. These professor of Maryland's Smith School of Business examined the strategic use of security information from a classical business perspective.

The authors came together to develop and expand a series of flagship events under the name Worksop on the Economics of Information Security.

Examples of findings in economics of security

Proof of work is a security technology designed to stop spam by altering the economics. An early paper in economics of information security argued that proof of work cannot work. In fact, the finding was that proof of work cannot work without price discrimination as illustrated by a later paper, Proof of Work can Work [7].

Another finding, one that is critical to an understanding of current American data practices, is that the opposite of privacy is not, in economic terms anonymity, but rather price discrimination. Privacy and price discrimination [8] was authored by Andrew Odlyzko and illustrates that what may appear as information pathology in collection of data is in fact rational organizational behavior.

Hal Varian presented three models of security using the metaphor of the height of walls around a town to show security as a normal good, public good, or good with externalities. Free riding [9] is the end result, in any case.

References

[1] http://www.acsac.org/2001/papers/110.pdf

[2] http://idefense.com/

[3] http://zerodayinitiative.com/

[4] http://www.mozilla.org/security/bug-bounty.html

[5] http://www.cert.org/octave

[6] http://old-www.rhsmith.umd.edu/accounting/mloeb

[7] http://weis2006.econinfosec.org/docs/50.pdf

[8] http://citeseer.ist.psu.edu/odlyzko03privacy.html

[9] http://www.sims.berkeley.edu/resources/affiliates/workshops/econsecurity/econws/49.pdf

External links

- Economics of Information Security (http://infosecon.net/) links to all the past workshops, with the corresponding papers, as well as current conferences and calls for papers.

Centers that study economics of security

- Carnegie Mellon University Heinz School (http://www.heinz.cmu.edu/)
- Carnegie Mellon University Privacy Lab (http://privacy.cs.cmu.edu/)
- Cambridge University Computer Science Laboratory (http://www.cl.cam.ac.uk/research/security/)
- Indiana University School of Informatics (http://informatics.indiana.edu/)
- University of Minnesota (http://www.dtc.umn.edu/)
- University of Michigan School of Information (http://www.si.umich.edu/)
- Harvard University Division of Engineering and Applied Sciences (http://www.eecs.harvard.edu/index/cs/cs_index.php)
- Dartmouth hosts the I3P (http://www.thei3p.org/) which includes the Tuck School as well as the Computer Science Department in studying economics of information security.

Resources in economics of security

- Ross Anderson maintains the Economics of Information Security (http://www.cl.cam.ac.uk/~rja14/econsec.html) page.
- Alessandro Acquisti (http://www.heinz.cmu.edu/~acquisti) has the corresponding Economics of Privacy Resources (http://www.heinz.cmu.edu/~acquisti/economics-privacy.html) page.
- Economics of Information Security (http://infosecon.net/) provides events, books, past workshops, and an annotated bibliography.
- Return on Information Security Investment (http://www.adrianmizzi.com/) provides self assessment questionnaire, papers and links to Information security economics resources.

Emergency

An **emergency** is a situation that poses an *immediate risk* to health, life, property or environment.[1] Most emergencies require urgent intervention to prevent a worsening of the situation, although in some situations, mitigation may not be possible and agencies may only be able to offer palliative care for the aftermath.

While some emergencies are self evident (such as a natural disaster that threatens many lives), many smaller incidents require the subjective opinion of an observer (or affected party) in order to decide whether it qualifies as an emergency.

The precise definition of an emergency, the agencies involved and the procedures used, vary by jurisdiction, and this is usually set by the

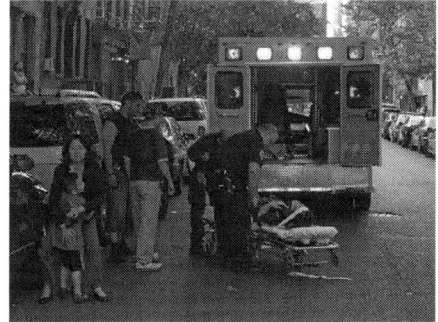

Dangers to life and health are serious enough that emergency response systems are considered vital.

government, whose agencies (emergency services) are responsible for emergency planning and management.

Defining an emergency

In order to be defined as an emergency, the incident should be one of the following:

- Immediately threatening to life, health, property or environment.
- Have already caused loss of life, health detriments, property damage or environmental damage
- Have a high probability of escalating to cause immediate danger to life, health, property or environment

In the United States, it is generally a requirement in most states that a notice be printed in each telephone book requiring that, if a person requests the use of a telephone line (such as a *party line*) because of an emergency, the other person must relinquish use of said line immediately, if their use is not also in the nature of an emergency. An *emergency* is also typically defined by those state statutes as "a condition where life, health or property is in jeopardy, and the prompt summoning of aid is essential."[2]

Whilst most emergency services agree on protecting human health, life and property, the environmental impacts are not considered sufficiently important by some agencies. This also extends to areas such as animal welfare, where some emergency organisations cover this element through the 'property' definition, where animals owned by a person are threatened (although this does not cover wild animals). This means that some agencies will not mount an 'emergency' response where it endangers wild animals or environment, although others will respond to such incidents (such as oil spills at sea that threaten marine life). The attitude of the agencies involved is likely to reflect the predominant opinion of the government of the area.

Types of emergency

Dangers to life

Many emergencies cause an immediate danger to the life of people involved. This can range from emergencies affecting a single person, such as the entire range of medical emergencies including heart attacks, strokes, and trauma, to incidents that affect large numbers of people such as natural disasters including tornadoes, hurricanes, floods, and mudslides.

Most agencies consider these to be the highest priority of emergency, which follows the general school of thought that nothing is more important than human life.[3]

Dangers to health

Some emergencies are not immediately threatening to life, but might have serious implications for the continued health and well-being of a person or persons (although a health emergency can subsequently escalate to be threatening to life).

The causes of a 'health' emergency are often very similar to the causes of an emergency threatening to life, which includes medical emergencies and natural disasters, although the range of incidents that can be categorised here is far greater than those that cause a danger to life (such as broken limbs, which do not usually cause death, but immediate intervention is required if the person is to recover properly)

Dangers to property

Other emergencies do not threaten any people, but do threaten peoples' property. An example of this would be a fire in a warehouse that has been evacuated. The situation is treated as an emergency as the fire may spread to other buildings, or may cause sufficient damage to make the business unable to continue (affecting livelihood of the employees).

Many agencies categorise property emergency as the lowest priority, and may not take as many risks in dealing with it. For instance, firefighters are unlikely to enter a burning building they know to be empty, as the risk is unjustified, but are more likely to enter a building where people are reported as trapped, unless they believe they can stop the spread of the fire, or "save" the building.

Dangers to the environment

Some emergencies do not immediately endanger life, health or property, but do affect the natural environment and creatures living within it. Not all agencies consider this to be a genuine emergency, but it can have far reaching effects on animals and the long term condition of the land. Examples would include forest fires and marine oil spills.

Systems of classifying emergencies

Agencies across the world have different systems for classifying incidents, but all of them serve to help them allocate finite resource, by prioritising between different emergencies.

The first stage in any classification is likely to be defining whether the incident qualifies as an emergency, and consequently if it warrants an emergency response. Some agencies may still respond to non-emergency calls, depending on their remit and availability of resource. An example of this would be a fire department responding to help retrieve a cat from a tree, where no life, health or property is immediately at risk.

Following this, many agencies assign a sub-classification to the emergency, prioritising incidents that have the most potential for risk to life, health or property (in that order). For instance, many ambulance services use a system called the Advanced Medical Priority Dispatch System (AMPDS) or a similar solution.[4] [5] The AMPDS categorises all calls to the ambulance service using it as either 'A' category (immediately life threatening), 'B' Category (immediately health threatening) or 'C' category (non-emergency call that still requires a response). Some services have a fourth category, where they believe that no response is required after clinical questions are asked.

Another system for prioritizing medical calls is known as Emergency Medical Dispatch (EMD).[6] [7] Jurisdictions that use EMD typically assign a code of "alpha" (low priority), "bravo" (medium priority), "charlie" (requiring advanced life support), delta (high priority, requiring advanced life support) or "echo" (maximum possible priority, e.g., witnessed cardiac arrests) to each inbound request for service; these codes are then used to determine the appropriate level of response.[8] [9] [10]

Other systems (especially as regards major incidents) use objective measures to direct resource. Two such systems are SAD CHALET and ETHANE,[11] which are both mnemonics to help emergency services staff classify incidents, and direct resource.[12] Each of these acronyms helps ascertain the number of casualties (usually including the number of dead and number of non-injured people involved), how the incident has occurred, and what emergency services are required.

Agencies involved in dealing with emergencies

Most developed countries have a number of emergency services operating within them, whose purpose is to provide assistance in dealing with any emergency. They are often government operated, paid for from tax revenue as a public service, but in some cases, they may be private companies, responding to emergencies in return for payment, or they may be voluntary organisations, providing the assistance from funds raised from donations.

Most developed countries operate three core emergency services:

- **Police** – who deal with security of person and property, which can cover all three categories of emergency. They may also deal with punishment of those who cause an emergency through their actions.
- **Fire service** – who deal with potentially harmful fires, but also often rescue operations such as dealing with road traffic collisions. Their actions help to prevent loss of life, damage to health and damage to or loss of property.
- **Emergency Medical Service** (Ambulance / Paramedic service) – These services attempt to reduce loss of life or damage to health. This service is likely to be decisive in attempts to prevent loss of life and damage to health. In some areas "Emergency Medical Service" is abbreviated to simply EMS.

In some countries or regions, two or more of these services may be provided by the same agency[13] (e.g. the fire service providing emergency medical cover), and under different conditions (e.g. publicly funded fire service and police, but a private ambulance service)

There may also be a number of secondary emergency services, which may be a part of one of the core agencies, or may be separate entities who assist the main agencies. This can include services providing specialist rescue (such as mountain rescue[14] or mine rescue),[15] bomb disposal[16] or search and rescue.[17] [18] [19]

The Military and the Amateur Radio Emergency Service (ARES) or Radio Amateur Civil Emergency Service (RACES) help in large emergencies such as a disaster or major civil unrest.

Summoning emergency services

Most countries have an emergency telephone number, also known as the universal emergency number, which can be used to summon the emergency services to any incident. This number varies from country to country (and in some cases by region within a country), but in most cases, they are in a short number format, such as 911 (United States),[20] 999 (United Kingdom),[21] [22] 112 (Europe)[23] [24] and 000 (Australia).[25]

The majority of mobile phones will also dial the emergency services, even if the phone keyboard is locked, or if the phone has an expired or missing SIM card, although the provision of this service varies by country and network.[24]

Civil emergency services

In addition to those services provided specifically for emergencies, there may be a number of agencies who provide an emergency service as an incidental part of their normal 'day job' provision. This can include public utility workers, such as in provision of electricity or gas, who may be required to respond quickly, as both utilities have a large potential to cause danger to life, health and property if there is an infrastructure failure.[26] [27]

Emergency action principles (EAP)

Emergency action principles are key 'rules' that guide the actions of rescuers and potential rescuers. Because of the inherent nature of emergencies, no two are likely to be the same, so emergency action principles help to guide rescuers at incidents, by sticking to some basic tenets.

The adherence to (and contents of) the principles by would be rescuers varies widely based on the training the people involved in emergency have received, the support available from emergency services (and the time it will take to arrive) and the emergency itself.

Key emergency principle

The key principle taught in almost all systems is that the rescuer, be they a lay person or a professional, should assess the situation for danger.[28] [29]

The reason that an assessment for danger is given such high priority is that it is core to emergency management that rescuers do not become secondary victims of any incident, as this creates a further emergency that must be dealt with.

A typical assessment for danger would involve observation of the surroundings, starting with the cause of the accident (e.g. a falling object) and expanding outwards to include any situational hazards (e.g. fast moving traffic) and history or secondary information given by witnesses, bystanders or the emergency services (e.g. an attacker still waiting nearby).

Once a primary danger assessment has been complete, this should not end the system of checking for danger, but should inform all other parts of the process.

If at any time the risk from any hazard poses a significant danger (as a factor of likelihood and seriousness) to the rescuer, they should consider whether they should approach the scene (or leave the scene if appropriate).

Managing an emergency

There are many protocols emergency services apply in an emergency, which usually start with planning before an emergency occurs. One commonly used system for demonstrating the phases is shown here on the right.

The planning phase starts at **preparedness**, where the agencies decide on how they will respond to a given incident or set of circumstances. This should ideally include lines of command and control, and division of activities between agencies. This avoids potentially negative situations such as three separate agencies all starting an official rest centre for victims of a disaster.

Following an emergency occurring, the agencies then move to a **response** phase, where they execute their plans, and may end up improvising some areas of their response (due to gaps in the planning phase, which are inevitable due to the individual nature of most incidents).

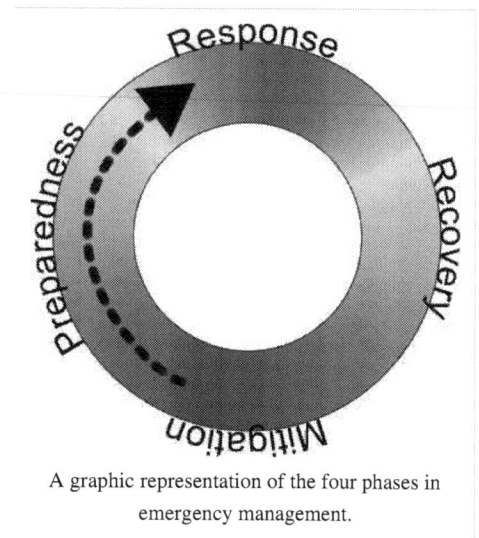

A graphic representation of the four phases in emergency management.

Agencies may then be involved in **recovery** following the incident, where they assist in the clear up from the incident, or help the people involved overcome their mental trauma.

The final phase in the circle is **mitigation**, which involves taking steps to ensure no re-occurrence is possible, or putting additional plans in place to ensure less damage is done. This should feed back in to the preparedness stage, with updated plans in place to deal with future emergencies, thus completing the circle.

State of emergency

In the event of a major incident, such as civil unrest or a major disaster, many governments maintain the right to declare a state of emergency,[30] which gives them extensive powers over the daily lives of their citizens, and may include temporary curtailment on certain civil rights, including the right to trial (for instance to discourage looting of an evacuated area, a shoot on sight policy may be in force)

Personal emergencies

Some people believe they have an emergency in a situation that does not pose a risk to life, physical health, or property. In these instances, some people feel entitled to an emergency response—a view emergencies agencies may not share.

Some of these cases may be genuine emergencies if they threaten the mental health and well-being of the person involved, but many agencies do not recognise this as valid. This is more likely to be dealt with by social services or a physician than by the traditional emergency service agencies.

Links

ERWS - Emergency Rescue World Society : www.erws.org [31]

References

[1] "UK Government Advice on Definition of an Emergency" (http://www.ukresilience.info/upload/assets/www.ukresilience.info/15mayshortguide.pdf) (PDF). . Retrieved 2007-05-30.

[2] Some examples of state statutes defining *emergency* for this purpose: California Penal Code, Sec. 384;

[3] "UK Government document stating that life-saving activity is the highest priority in an emergency" (http://www.ukresilience.info/upload/assets/www.ukresilience.info/emergresponse.pdf) (PDF). . Retrieved 2007-05-30.

[4] "Tampa Fire Department EMS dispatch details" (http://www.tampagov.net/dept_fire/rescue_division/general_info/advanced_medical_priority_dispatch.asp). . Retrieved 2007-05-30.

[5] "London Ambulance Service details of AMPDS use" (http://web.archive.org/web/20070130163345/http://www.londonambulance.nhs.uk/helpweoffer/help1.html). Archived from the original (http://www.londonambulance.nhs.uk/helpweoffer/help1.html) on 2007-01-30. . Retrieved 2007-05-30.

[6] "EMD Resources" (http://www.911dispatch.com/info/emd/index.html). . Retrieved 2007-07-07.

[7] "EMD Training Guide" (http://health.utah.gov/ems/stdseval/training/emd_curriculum_trainee.pdf) (PDF). Utah Bureau of Emergency Medical Services. January 2005. . Retrieved 2007-07-07.

[8] "DEMSOC Annual Report - 2005" (http://www.dhss.delaware.gov/dhss/dph/ems/files/demsocreport2005.txt). Delaware Emergency Medical Services Oversight Council. 2005. . Retrieved 2007-07-08.

[9] Brian Dale. "Using the ECHO Determinant" (http://www.emergencydispatch.org/JOURNAL/articles/UsingECHO.html). . Retrieved 2007-07-08.

[10] Jeff J. Clawson. "EMD: Making the Most of EMS" (http://www.emergencydispatch.org/articles/themostofEMS.htm). . Retrieved 2007-07-08.

[11] "Patient Plus reference to CHALET and ETHANE systems" (http://www.patient.co.uk/showdoc/40001331). . Retrieved 2007-05-30.

[12] "London Emergency planning committee use of CHALET" (http://web.archive.org/web/20070626114729/http://www.leslp.gov.uk/firstoff.htm). Archived from the original (http://www.leslp.gov.uk/firstoff.htm) on 2007-06-26. . Retrieved 2007-05-30.

[13] "New York City Fire Department is the largest combined Fire and EMS service in the United States" (http://www.nyc.gov/html/fdny/html/home2.shtml). . Retrieved 2007-05-30.

[14] "Mountain Rescue Association (US)" (http://www.mra.org/). . Retrieved 2007-05-30.

[15] "United States Mine Rescue Association" (http://www.usmra.com/). . Retrieved 2007-05-30.

[16] "British Army Bomb Disposal Engineer Career Page" (http://www.army.mod.uk/royalengineers/careers/specialist/bombdisposal.htm). . Retrieved 2007-05-30.

[17] "Maritime Search and Rescue Agencies in the UK (at the MCA)" (http://www.mcga.gov.uk/c4mca/mcga-hmcg_rescue/coastguard_operations/maritme_search_and_rescue_assets.htm). . Retrieved 2007-05-30.

[18] "CANIS specialist search dog charity in the UK" (http://www.canis-uk.net/). . Retrieved 2007-05-30.

[19] "Search and Rescue service in Essex, UK" (http://web.archive.org/web/20070929152850/http://essexsearchandrescue.org.uk/modules/news/). Archived from the original (http://essexsearchandrescue.org.uk/modules/news/) on 2007-09-29. . Retrieved 2007-05-30.

[20] "US National Emergency Number Association" (http://www.nena.org/). . Retrieved 2007-05-30.

[21] "History of the 999 System" (http://web.archive.org/web/20070528022735/http://www.fire.org.uk/advice/999history.htm).
      Archived from the original (http://www.fire.org.uk/advice/999history.htm) on 2007-05-28. . Retrieved 2007-05-30.

[22] "Metropolitan Police advice on using 999" (http://web.archive.org/web/20070609160248/http://www.met.police.uk/999/index.
      htm). Archived from the original (http://www.met.police.uk/999/index.htm) on 2007-06-09. . Retrieved 2007-05-30.

[23] "UK government advice on the use of 112 alongside 999" (http://web.archive.org/web/20070403072801/http://www.ofcom.org.uk/
      static/archive/Oftel/publications/ind_guidelines/emer1002.htm). Archived from the original (http://www.ofcom.org.uk/static/archive/
      Oftel/publications/ind_guidelines/emer1002.htm) on 2007-04-03. . Retrieved 2007-05-30.

[24] "European Commission document on the Implementation of the Single 112 emergency number" (http://ec.europa.eu/environment/civil/
      pdfdocs/112surv-2001.pdf) (PDF). . Retrieved 2007-05-30.

[25] "Australian Government Advice on Emergency Calls" (http://emergencycalls.aca.gov.au/). . Retrieved 2007-05-30.

[26] "UK National Gas Emergency Number" (http://www.nationalgrid.com/uk/Gas/Safety/Emergency). . Retrieved 2007-05-30.

[27] "UK Government Gas and Electricity National Emergency Plan" (http://www.dti.gov.uk/files/file33246.pdf) (PDF). . Retrieved
      2007-05-30.

[28] "UK [[Health and Safety Executive (http://www.hse.gov.uk/pubns/indg347.pdf)] publication on dealing with emergencies - Danger
      assessment is the first point"] (PDF). . Retrieved 2007-05-30.

[29] "St John Ambulance UK Primary Assessment guide" (http://www.sja.org.uk/sja/first-aid-advice/life-saving-procedures/
      primary-survey.aspx). . Retrieved 2007-05-30.

[30] "UK Government Civil Contingencies Act, giving powers to declare a state of emergency" (http://www.publications.parliament.uk/pa/
      1d200304/ldbills/077/04077.12-18.html). . Retrieved 2007-05-30.

[31] http://www.erws.org

Fixes that fail

Fixes that fail is a system archetype that in system dynamics is used to describe and analyze a situation, where a fix effective in the short-term creates side effects for the long-term behaviour of the system and may result in the need of even more fixes.[1] This archetype may be also known as fixes that backfire[2] or corrective actions that fail.[3] It resembles the Shifting the burden archetype.[4]

Description

In a "fixes that fail" scenario the encounter of a problem is faced by a corrective action or fix that seems to solve the issue. However, this action leads to some unforeseen consequences. They form then a feedback loop that either worsens the original problem or creates a related one.[2] [3]

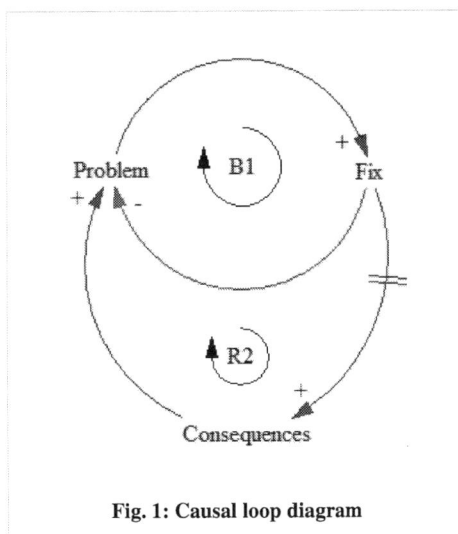

Fig. 1: Causal loop diagram

In system dynamics this is described by a circles of causality (Fig. 1) as a system consisting of two feedback loops. One is the balancing feedback loop B1 of the corrective action, the second is the reinforcing feedback loop R2 of the unintended consequences. These influence the problem with a delay and therefore make it difficult to recognize the source of the new rise of the problem.[1]

Representation of the long-term disadvantages of the scenario can be seen on Fig. 2. Although the symptoms go through a decrease when fixes are applied, the overall crisis threshold rises.[4] [5]

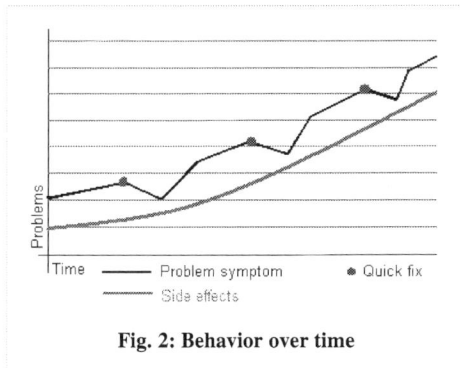

Fig. 2: Behavior over time

A representation with a stock and flow diagram of this archetype is on Fig. 3.

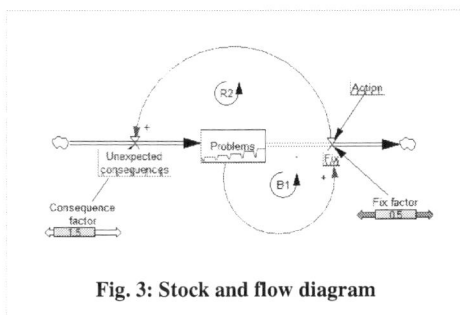

Fig. 3: Stock and flow diagram

The fix influences the amount of problems present in the system proportionally to the fix factor and the problems to be resolved. When activated by the action variable, the fix lowers the problems, thus creating a balancing loop. However, each fix also starts a delayed consequence which adds to the problems proportionally to the consequence factor and the fix applied. Combined, these create a growing amount of problems to be dealt with.

Uses

As an archetype, it helps to gain insight into patterns that are present in the system and thereby also give the tools to change these patterns. In the case of "Fixes that fail", the warning sign is a problem which reappears although fixes were applied. It is crucial to recognize that the fix only adds to the overall deteriorating state and does not solve the problem. To identify this pattern, it is needed to consider a connection between the symptoms and the fixes we apply to solve them, which can be very difficult to do.[4] In management this can be present as a "hero-scapegoat" cycle. While the manager who applied the fix gets promoted for diminishing the problem. A new manager must face the returning problem symptom and may be punished for failing to do his job. Then a new hero is found who temporarily solves the problem symptoms. The delay of the reinforcing loop makes it difficult to recognize the causal relation between the fix applied to the symptoms and the new problems arising. What then seems to be a series of successes in short-term then are steps towards failure on the long-term.[5]

Some typical ways of thinking associated with the pattern are:

- "It always seemed to work before; why isn't it working now?"[1]
- "This is a simple problem and the solution is straightforward."[6]
- "We need to fix this problem now. We can deal with any consequences later." [6]

They can serve as a warning that this archetype is present or will be.

If this pattern is recognized, then there are multiple possibilities how to react, depending on which leverage point is addressed:

- Focus on the long-term and if a fix is inevitably needed, use it only to buy time to work on the long-term remedy.[1]
- Raise awareness of the unintended consequences of the fixes.
- Focus on the underlying problem and not the symptoms.
- Find either a fix without consequences or with limited long-term impact.[2]
- Find a way to measure the intended and also unintended consequences of the solutions by learning also from the past fixes.[4]
- Change the performance review time so that the long-term progress becomes visible.[5]

Examples

A few common examples of the pattern. The situation describes always the starting point to which a fix is applied. This bears then the consequences which are confronted again with a new fix.

- ### Maximizing ROR[1]

    Situation: A manufacturing company becomes successful with high-performance parts, and its CEO wants to maximize the ROR.

    Fix: Refusal of investment in expensive, new production machines.

    Consequences: The product quality drops and therefore the sales of it.

- ### Cutting back maintenance[1]

    Situation: The company needs to save money.

    Fix: Decrease the amount of maintenance.

    Consequences: More breakdowns of the equipment, higher costs and cost-cutting pressure.

- ### Quest for water[6]

    Situation: Farmers are confronted with water shortage.

    Fix: Drilling new wells or making the old ones deeper.

    Consequences: The water table drops.

- ### Cash shortage[5] [6]

    Situation: A person can't pay interest (for example on a credit card).

    Fix: Take up a new loan to pay the interest (a new credit card).

    Consequences: There is more interest to pay next time.

- ### Tax revenue shortage[6]

    Situation: A government is not satisfied with its tax revenues.

    Fix: Increase the cigarette tax to raise more taxes.

    Consequences: Smuggling of cigarettes develops and reduces the amount of taxed cigarettes sold in the country.

References

[1] Senge, Peter M., "The Fifth Discipline" (1990). ISBN 0385260954.

[2] Fixes that backfire (http://www.pegasuscom.com/course_preview/module6/6-05-0-0-fixes.htm) Isee systems, 2006. Retrieved 2011-11-01

[3] Flood, Robert L., "Rethinking The Fifth Discipline: learning within the unknowable" (1999). ISBN 0203028554 p. 19

[4] Braun, William (2002). "System archetypes" (http://www.uni-klu.ac.at/~gossimit/pap/sd/wb_sysarch.pdf) (PDF (298 KB)). . Retrieved 2011-11-01.

[5] Kim, Daniel H., "Fixes that Fail: Why Faster is Slower," *The Systems Thinker Newsletter,* Vol. 10, No. 3 (Apr., 1999)

[6] Fixes That Fail Archetype (http://www.systemswiki.org/index.php?title=Category:Fixes_that_Fail) SystemsWiki, Octobre 2010. Retrieved 2011-11-01

Flood risk assessment

A **flood risk assessment** is an assessment of the risk of flooding, particularly in relation to residential, commercial and industrial land use.

England and Wales

In England and Wales, the Environment Agency requires a Flood Risk Assessment (FRA) to be submitted alongside planning applications in areas that are known to be at risk of flooding (within Flood Zones 2 or 3) and/ or are greater than 1ha in area, planning permission is not usually granted until the FRA has been accepted by the Environment Agency. Flood risk assessments are also relevant to the maintenance and insurance of existing buildings.[1]

PPS 25 - England only

Flood Risk Assessments are required to be completed according to Planning Policy Statement PPS 25: Development and Flood Risk. The initial legislation (PPG25) was introduced in 2001.[2]

PPS 25 was designed to "strengthen and clarify the key role of the planning system in managing flood risk and contributing to adapting to the impacts of climate change."[3] and sets out policies for local authorities to ensure flood risk is taken into account during the planning process to prevent inappropriate development in high risk areas and to direct development away from areas at highest risk.

In its introduction, PPS25 states "flooding threatens life and causes substantial damage to property [and that] although [it] cannot be wholly prevented, its impacts can be avoided and reduced through good planning and management".[4]

Composition of an FRA

For a flood risk assessment to be written information is needed concerning the existing and proposed developments, the Environment Agency modeled flood levels and topographic levels on site. At its most simple (and cheapest) level an FRA can provide an indication of whether a development will be allowed to take place at a site.

An initial idea of the risk of flooding to a local area can be found on the Environment Agency flood map website [5]. However, the Environment Agency use low resolution flood mapping to create this flood map as a cautious estimate of flood risk, and therefore on the more local scale this mapping may not be accurate.[6]

Longer FRAs consist of a detailed analysis of available data to inform the Environment Agency of flood risk at an individual site and also recommend to the developer any mitigation required for a planning application to be submitted. More costly analysis of flood risk can be achieved through detailed flood modelling to challenge the agency's modelled levels and corresponding flood zones.

The FRA takes into account the risk and impact of flooding on the site, and takes into consideration how the development may affect flooding in the local area. It also includes provides recommendations as to how the risk of flooding to the site can be improved or improved following development.

As well as assessing the risk to the site posed by fluvial flooding, FRAs should also consider flooding from other sources including fluvial, groundwater, surface water runoff and sewer flooding.

Other uses

Assessments can also be used to provide insurers with a more detailed assessment of flood risk at a location, and can act as a means of reducing insurance premiums.

Northern Ireland

In 2006, The Department of the Environment, Planning Service published Planning Policy Statement 15 (PPS15): Planning and flood risk.[7] The guidelines are precautionary and advise against development in flood plains and areas subject to historical flooding. In exceptional cases a FRA can be completed to justify development in flood risk areas. Advise on FRA is provided to Planning Service by Rivers Agency.

Republic of Ireland

In 2009, The Department of the Environment, Heritage and Local Government and Office of Public Works published planning guidelines requiring Local Authorities to apply a sequential approach to flood risk management.[8] The guidelines require that proposed development in flood risk areas must undergo a justification test, consisting of a Flood Risk Assessment.[9]

References

[1] Floodrisk Management Research Consortium (http://www.floodrisk.org.uk/)
[2] (http://www.communities.gov.uk/documents/planningandbuilding/pdf/planningpolicystatement25.pdf)
[3] Planning Policy Statement (PPS) 25: Flooding - Corporate - Communities and Local Government (http://www.communities.gov.uk/statements/corporate/planning-policy-flooding)
[4] PPS(25) pdf (http://www.communities.gov.uk/documents/planningandbuilding/pdf/153740)
[5] http://www.environment-agency.gov.uk/subjects/flood/
[6] School of Geographical Sciences, University of Bristol (http://www.ggy.bris.ac.uk/research/hydrology/models/lisflood)
[7] http://www.planningni.gov.uk/index/policy/policy_publications/planning_statements/pps15-flood-risk.pdf
[8] http://www.environ.ie/en/Publications/DevelopmentandHousing/Planning/FileDownLoad,21708,en.pdf
[9] http://www.wre.ie/fra

External links

- US Government: Flooding Assessment in the United States (http://www.floodsmart.gov/prp)

Functional Safety

Functional Safety is the part of the overall safety of a system or piece of equipment that depends on the system or equipment operating correctly in response to its inputs, including the safe management of likely operator errors, hardware failures and environmental changes.

Objective of Functional Safety

The objective of Functional Safety is freedom from unacceptable risk of physical injury or of damage to the health of people either directly or indirectly (through damage to property or to the environment).

Functional Safety is intrinsically end-to-end in scope in that it has to treat the function of a component or subsystem as part of the function of the whole system. This means that whilst Functional Safety standards focus on Electrical, Electronic and Programmable Systems (E/E/PS), the end-to-end scope means that in practice Functional Safety methods have to extend to the non-E/E/PS parts of the system that the E/E/PS actuates, controls or monitors.

Achieving Functional Safety

Functional Safety is achieved when every specified safety function is carried out and the level of performance required of each safety function is met. This is normally achieved by a process that includes the following steps as a minimum:

1. Identifying what the required safety functions are. This means the hazards and safety functions have to be known. A process of function reviews, formal HAZIDs, HAZOPs and Accident Reviews are applied to identify these.

2. Assessment of the risk-reduction required by the safety function. This will involve a Safety Integrity Level (SIL) Assessment. A Safety Integrity Level (SIL) applies to an end-to-end safety function of the safety-related system, not just to a component or part of the system.

3. Ensuring the safety function performs to the design intent, including under conditions of incorrect operator input and failure modes. This will involve having the design and lifecycle managed by qualified and competent engineers carrying out processes to a recognised functional safety standard. In Europe, that standard is IEC EN 61508, or one of the industry specific standards derived from IEC EN 61508.

4. Verification that the system meets the assigned SIL, by determining the Mean Time Between Failures and the Safe Failure Fraction (SFF). The unsafe failure fraction is the probability of the system failing in a dangerous (or critical) state, derived from a Failure Mode and Effects Analysis or (Failure Mode, Effects, and Criticality Analysis) of the system (FMEA or FMECA).

5. Conduct functional safety management audit. The safety lifecycle management audit is a mechanism used to help reduce systematic problems from appearing in the design of a product....the functional safety lifecycle management audit looks at those elements of the manufacturer's process that may impact the quality of the functional safety of the product being produced.[1]

Neither safety nor Functional Safety can be determined without considering the system as a whole and the environment with which it interacts. Functional Safety is inherently end-to-end in scope.

Certifying Functional Safety

Any claim of Functional Safety for a component, subsystem or system should be independently certified to one of the recognised Functional Safety standards. A certified product can then be claimed to be Functionally Safe to a particular Safety Integrity Level or a Performance Level in a specific range of applications: the certificate is provided to the customers with a test report describing the scope and limits of performance.

An important element of functional safety certification is on-going surveillance by the certification agency. This follow-up surveillance ensures that that product, sub-system, or system is still being manufactured in accordance with the what was originally certified for functional safety. Follow-up surveillance may occur as various frequencies depending on the certification agency, but will typically look at the product's hardware, software, as well as the manufacturer's ongoing compliance of functional safety management systems. [2]

The principles underpinning Functional Safety were developed in the military, nuclear and aerospace industries, and then taken up by rail transport, process and control industries developing sector specific standards. Functional Safety standards are applied across all industry sectors dealing with safety critical requirements. Thousands of products and processes meet the standards based on IEC EN 61508: from bathroom showers[3] , automotive safety products, medical devices, sensors, actuators, Process Controllers from ABB[4] , Siemens [5] , and their integration by companies such as Capula [6] to ships, aircraft and major plant.

In Europe, Functional Safety certification is supported by a well-developed infrastructure [7] [8] . The CASS Scheme is the primary method by which products are certified to IEC EN 61508 and related standards, through accredited quality auditors[9] [10] [11] [12] . It is possible to certify both products and processes that manage the lifecycle of the product, (in which case, the company certified would then issue a certificate of conformity to that certification in respect of its relevant products).

The US FAA have similar Functional Safety certification processes, in the form of US RTCA DO-178B for software and DO-254 for hardware [13] [14] , which is applied throughout the aerospace industry.

In the USA, NASA developed an infrastructure for safety critical systems adopted widely by industry, both in North America and elsewhere, with a standard [15] , supported by guidelines [16] . The NASA standard and guidelines are built on ISO 12207, which is a good software practice standard rather than a safety critical standard, hence the extensive nature of the documentation NASA has been obliged to add, compared to using a purpose designed standard such as EN 61508 with the CASS Templates. A certification process for systems developed in accord with the NASA guidelines exists [17] .

Modern E/E/PS medical devices are being certified to 501(k) on the basis of the industry sector specific IEC EN 62304 standard, based on IEC EN 61508 concepts.

MISRA in the automotive industry are moving standards towards IEC EN 61508 in the development of industry specific standards.[18] [19]

Contemporary Functional Safety Standards

The primary Functional Safety standards in current use are listed below:

- IEC EN 61508 Parts 1 to 3 is a core Functional Safety standard, applied widely to all types of safety critical E/E/PS and to systems with a safety function incorporating E/E/PS.
- UK Defence Standard 00-56 Issue 2
- US RTCA DO-178B North American Avionics Software
- US RTCA DO-254 North American Avionics Hardware
- EUROCAE ED-12B European Airborne Flight Safety Systems
- IEC 62304 - Medical Device Software
- IEC 61513, Nuclear power plants – Instrumentation and control for systems important to safety – General requirements for systems, based on EN 61508

- IEC 61511-1, Functional safety – Safety instrumented systems for the process industry sector – Part 1: Framework, definitions, system, hardware and software requirements, , based on EN 61508
- IEC 61511-2, Functional safety – Safety instrumented systems for the process industry sector – Part 2: Guidelines for the application of IEC 61511-1, , based on EN 61508
- IEC 61511-3, Functional safety – Safety instrumented systems for the process industry sector – Part 3: Guidance for the determination of the required safety integrity levels, based on EN 61508
- IEC 62061, Safety of machinery - Functional safety of safety-related electrical, electronic and programmable electronic control systems, based on EN 61508
- EN 50128, Railway Industry Specific
- EN 50129, Railway Industry Specific
- NASA Safety Critical Guidelines
- UL 1998 Software in Programmable Components
- UL 991 Tests for Safety-Related Controls Employing Solid-State Devices
- ISO 13849 Safety of Machinery – Safety-related Parts of Control Systems

References

[1] http://www.ul.com/global/documents/offerings/industries/powerandcontrols/UL%20FS%20Whitepaper%20100803B-rev.pdf

[2] http://www.ul.com/global/documents/offerings/industries/powerandcontrols/UL%20FS%20Whitepaper%20100803B-rev.pdf

[3] TMV2 and TM3 Approval of Kohler- Radacontrols Shower lists EN 61508 compliance, http://www.radacontrols.com/onlinecatalog/pdf/p4639_2.pdf

[4] ABB Industrial IT, EN 61508 compliant. http://www.abb.co.uk/cawp/seitp202/275AC9A14F5C6F69C1256FA90060650B.aspx

[5] TUV Nord EN 61508 Certification of Siemens Integrity VeOSity controller and software, http://www.ghs.com/products/industrial_safety.html

[6] http://www.capula.co.uk/pr-safetysystems.html

[7] The 61508 Association http://www.61508.org

[8] Institution of Engineering and Technology, Safety Zone http://www.theiet.org/

[9] CASS Scheme, Conformity Assessment of Safety Systems, http://www.cass.uk.net/

[10] SIRA Certification http://www.siracertification.com/safety.aspx

[11] 61508 Association, Conformity Assessment http://www.61508.org/ca.htm

[12] TUV Anlagentechnik, Dept ASI, http://www.tüvasi.com/downloads/Certification_Information_2003_05_16.pdf

[13] V. Hilderman, T. Bagha,"Avionics Certification", A Complete Guide to DO-178B and DO-254, ISBN 978-1-885544-25-4

[14] C. Spritzer, "Digital Avionics Handbook, Second Edition - 2 Volume Set (Electrical Engineering Handbook", CRC Press. ISBN: 9780849350085

[15] NASA Software Safety Standard NASA STD 8719.13A

[16] NASA-GB-1740.13-96, NASA Guidebook for Safety Critical Software.

[17] S. Nelson, Certification Processes for Safety-Critical and Mission- Critical Aerospace Software, June 2003, NASA/CR–2003-212806 http://ntrs.nasa.gov/archive/nasa/casi.ntrs.nasa.gov/20040014965_2004000657.pdf

[18] E. Pofahl, "The application of IEC 61508 in the automotive industry", Ford Motor Company http://www.sipi61508.com/ciks/pofahle1.pdf

[19] "Development Guidelines for Vehicle Based Software", MISRA, 1994 (http://www.misra.org.uk/)

External links

- IEC Functional safety zone (http://www.iec.ch/functionalsafety)
- Functional Safety and IEC 61508: A basic guide (http://www.iec.ch/zone/fsafety/pdf_safe/hld.pdf)
- Certified Functional Safety Expert (CFSE) (http://www.cfse.org) - Organization providing certification for Functional Safety professionals
- Inside Functional Safety (http://www.insidefunctionalsafety.com) - Technical magazine focusing on functional safety
- 61508.org The 61508 Association (http://www.61508.org)
- Functional Safety and IEC 61508 (http://www.tuev-nord.de/en/information-technology/Functional_safety_11797_More_electronic_components_mean_new_challenges_11798_ENG_PRODUCTIVE.

htm) TÜV NORD SysTec GmbH

- UL's Functional Safety Certification (http://www.ul.com/functionalsafety)

Global Earthquake Model

The **Global Earthquake Model (GEM)** is a public-private partnership initiated in 2006 by the Global Science Forum of the OECD to develop global, open-source risk assessment software and tools. With committed backing from academia, governments and industry, GEM contributes to achieving profound, lasting reductions in earthquake risk worldwide by following the priorities of the Hyogo Framework for Action.[1] From 2009 to 2013 GEM is constructing its first working global earthquake model and will provide an authoritative standard for calculating and communicating earthquake risk worldwide.

Since March 2009, GEM is a legal entity in the form of a non-profit foundation based in Pavia, Italy. The GEM Secretariat is hosted at the European Centre for Training and Research in Earthquake Engineering (EUCENTRE). The current Secretary General is Rui Pinho.

Mission

Between 2000 and 2010 over half a million people died due to earthquakes and tsunamis,[2] most of these in the developing world, where risks increase due to rapid population growth and urbanization.[3] However in many earthquake-prone regions no risk models exist, and even where models do exist, they are inaccessible. Better risk-awareness can reduce the toll that earthquakes take by leading to better construction, improved emergency response, and greater access to insurance.

GEM will provide a basis for comparing earthquake risks across regions and across borders, and thereby take the necessary first step towards increased awareness and actions that reduce earthquake risk. GEM tools will be usable at the community, national and international level for uniform earthquake risk-evaluation and as a defensible basis for risk-mitigation plans. GEM results will be disseminated all over the world. GEM will build technical capacity and carry out awareness-raising activities.

Scientific Framework

The GEM scientific framework serves as the underlying basis for constructing the global earthquake model, and is organised in three principal integrated modules: Seismic hazard, Seismic risk and Socio-Economic impact.

- The hazard module calculates harmonised probabilities of earthquake occurrence and resulting shaking at any given location.
- The risk module calculates damage and direct losses resulting from this damage such as fatalities, injuries and cost of repair. Damage due to strong ground shaking is calculated by combining building vulnerability, population vulnerability and exposure. GEM will furthermore develop remote-sensing and crowd-data collection techniques to classify, monitor and regularly update building inventory and thus regional vulnerability.
- The socio-economic impact module of GEM will provide tools and indices to both estimate and communicate the impact from earthquakes on the economy and society, concentrating in particular on indirect losses. For example the impact on a company's revenue, on budgets, on poverty. The module will allow for calculations of scenarios which that enable cost/benefit analysis of mitigating actions, such as systematic building strengthening, and facilitate insurance and alternative risk transfer.

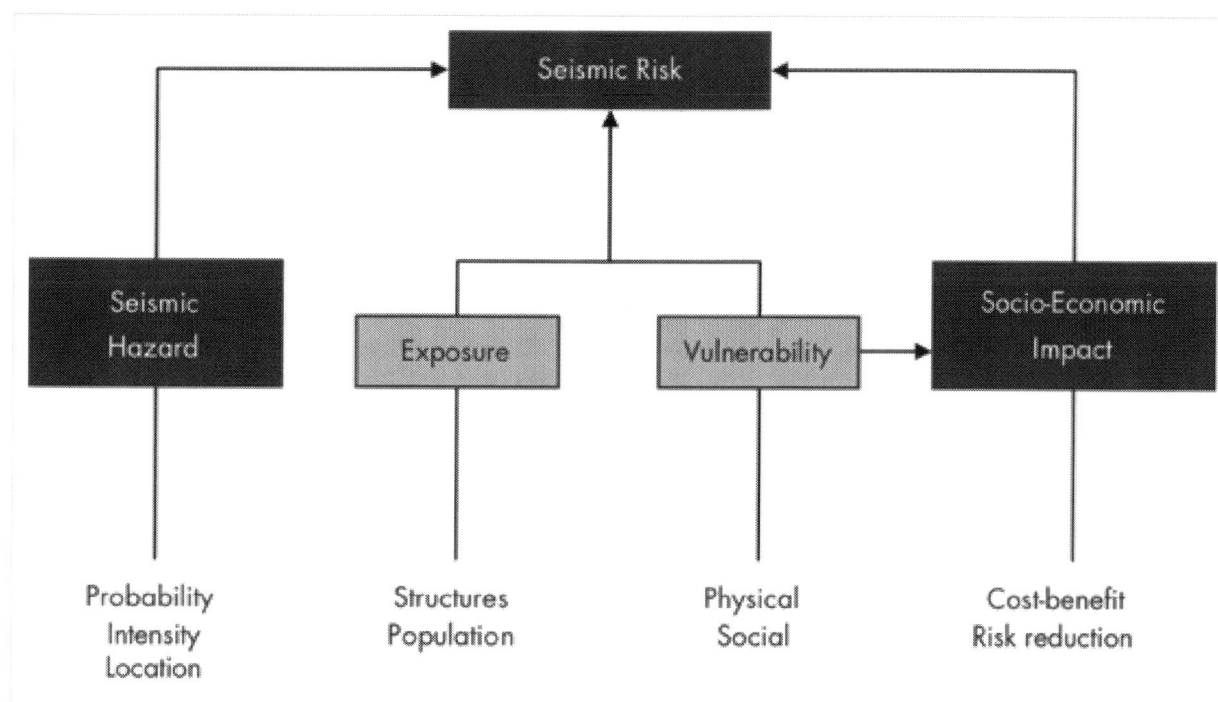

Implementation

It will take five years to build the first working global earthquake model – including corresponding tools, software and datasets. The work started in 2009 and will be finished at the end of 2013. Construction occurs in various stages that are partly overlapping in time. The pilot project GEM1 (January 2009 – March 2010) generates GEM's first products and initial model building infrastructure, Global components will establish a common set of definitions, strategies, standards, quality criteria and formats for the compilation of databases that serve as an input to the global earthquake model. They are addressed by international consortia that respond to calls for proposals on hazard, risk and socio-economic impact. Global components will provide preliminary data on a global scale, but on a local scale, regional and national programmes will provide more detailed and reliable data. Regional Programmes are projects with targeted funding taking place in various regions of the world; currently in the Middle East and Europe programmes have already started. The data produced on a regional and national scale will be carefully quality-controlled and integrated into the global models. The actual development of the model will occur using a common, web-based platform for dynamic sharing of tools and resources, in order to create software and online tools as end-products. The global earthquake model will be tested and evaluated before its official release; the testing procedure will involve the establishment of scientific experiments that are reproducible, transparent, and set up within a controlled environment.

GEM is however more than the creation and release of this first version of the model. GEM strives for continuous improvement of the model and will ensure that results are disseminated, technology is transferred through training and workshops and that awareness raising activities are deployed in order to contribute to risk reduction worldwide.

References

- "Globalizing quake information" [4], Nature Geoscience, December 2008
- "AIR Worldwide Sponsors the Global Earthquake Model (GEM) Project" [5]

External links

- The official GEM website [6]
- GEM on the OECD website [7]

Notes

[1] http://www.unisdr.org/eng/hfa/hfa.htm

[2] http://earthquake.usgs.gov/regional/world/world_deaths.php

[3] see a.o. http://www.geohazards.no/projects/project3_08/project_3_earthq.htm - figure2

[4] http://www.nature.com/ngeo/journal/v1/n12/full/ngeo368.html

[5] http://www.air-worldwide.com/NewsAndEventsItem.aspx?id=16722

[6] http://www.globalquakemodel.org

[7] http://www.oecd.org/document/24/0,3343,en_2649_34319_35997400_1_1_1_1,00.html

GRCM

GRCM refers to the measures, mechanisms and processes in operation within an organisation with the objective of managing Governance, Risk Management and Compliance.

Governance, Risk & Compliance Management

Governance, Risk and Compliance Management (GRCM) represents an emerging management discipline in the cross-functional area of Governance, Risk Management, and Compliance (GRC).

References

IT GRCM Functions Defined [1]

References

[1] http://www.gartner.com/DisplayDocument?id=506100&ref=g_sitelink

Hazard

A **hazard** is a situation that poses a level of threat to life, health, property, or environment. Most hazards are dormant or potential, with only a theoretical risk of harm; however, once a hazard becomes "active", it can create an emergency situation. A hazard does not exist when it is not happening. A hazardous situation that has come to pass is called an incident. Hazard and vulnerability interact together to create risk.

Modes of a hazard

Hazards are sometimes classified into three modes:[1]

- **Dormant** - The situation has the potential to be hazardous, but no people, property, or environment is currently affected by this. For instance, a hillside may be unstable, with the potential for a landslide, but there is nothing below or on the hillside that could be affected.
- **Armed** - People, property, or environment are in potential harm's way.
- **Active** - A harmful incident involving the hazard has actually occurred. Often this is referred to not as an "active hazard" but as an accident, emergency, incident, or disaster.

Wreck on rocks off Orchard Beach, The Bronx during the winter of 2007.

Classifying hazards

By its nature, a hazard involves something that could potentially be harmful to a person's life, health, property, or the environment. One key concept in identifying a hazard is the presence of stored energy that, when released, can cause damage. Stored energy can occur in many forms: chemical, mechanical, thermal, radioactive, electrical, etc. Another class of hazard does not involve release of stored energy, rather it involves the presence of hazardous situations. Examples include confined or limited egress spaces, oxygen-depleted atmospheres, awkward positions, repetitive motions, low-hanging or protruding objects, etc.

There are several methods of classifying a hazard, but most systems use some variation on the factors of "likelihood" of the hazard turning into an incident and the "seriousness" of the incident if it were to occur. (This discussion moved away from hazard to a discussion of risk.)

A common method is to score both likelihood and seriousness on a numerical scale (with the most likely and most serious scoring highest) and multiplying one by the other in order to reach a comparative score.

Risk = Likelihood of Occurrence *x* Seriousness if incident occurred

This score can then be used to identify which hazards may need to be mitigated. A low score on likelihood of occurrence may mean that the hazard is dormant, whereas a high score would indicate that it may be an "active" hazard.

An important component of "seriousness if incident occurred" is "serious to whom?" Different populations may be affected differently by accidents. For example, an explosion will have widely differing effects on different populations depending on the distance from the explosion. These effects can range from death from overpressure or shrapnel to inhalation of noxious gases (for people downwind) to being exposed to a loud noise.

Causes of hazards

There are many causes, but they can broadly be classified as below. See the linked articles for comprehensive lists of each type of hazard.

- Natural hazards include anything that is caused by a natural process, and can include obvious hazards such as volcanoes to smaller scale hazards such as loose rocks on a hillside.
- Man-made hazards are created by humans, whether long-term (such as global warming) or immediate (like the hazards present at a construction site). These include *activity related hazards* (such as flying) where cessation of the activity will negate the risk.
- Deadly force or retribution is that hazard involving any protective and responsive-ready threat of harm or punishment that becomes active in the event of a breach of security, or violation of a boundary or barrier (physical, legal, moral) intended to prevent unauthorized or unsafe access or entry or exposure to a situation, to something, or to someone. This includes the consequences that follow trespass, breach of covenant, outrage or moral panic. (*See* deterrence *and* deterrence theory.)

References

[1] David MacCollum (December 18, 2006). *Construction Safety Engineering Principles: Designing and Managing Safer Job Sites* (http://books.google.com/books?id=IbLrmejZ2UMC&lpg=PA10&ots=yg21-Hs3XK&dq=hazard mode active dormant&pg=PA8#v=onepage&q=hazard mode active dormant&f=false). McGraw-Hill Professional. ISBN 978-0071482448. . Retrieved 2010-07-10.

Health effects of sun exposure

The ultraviolet radiation in sunlight, though a principal source of vitamin D3 compared to diet, is mutagenic.[1] Supplementing diet with vitamin D3 supplies vitamin D without this mutagenic effect[2], but bypasses natural mechanisms that would prevent overdoses of vitamin D generated internally from sunlight. Sunlight is the major source of vitamin D-producing Ultraviolet B radiation, which has a wide range of positive health effects, including possibly inhibiting the growth of some cancers.[3] On the other hand, long-term sunlight exposure is known to be associated with the development of skin cancer, skin aging, immune suppression and eye diseases such as cataracts.[4] Sun exposure has also been associated with the timing of melatonin synthesis and reduced risk of seasonal affective disorder.[5] A number of public health organizations state that there needs to be a balance between the risks of having too much and the risks of having too little sunlight.[6] There is a general consensus that sunburn should always be avoided.

However, not all physicians agree with the assertion that there is an optimal level of sun exposure, with some arguing that it is better to minimize sun exposure at all times and to obtain vitamin D from other sources.[7]

In the United States, serum levels of 25(OH) D_3 are below the recommended levels for a large portion of the general adult population and in most minorities, indicating that Vitamin D deficiency is a common problem in the country.[8]

According to the U.S. National Institutes of Health Office of Dietary Supplements, most people in the United States can meet their vitamin D needs through exposure to sunlight, even though a large portion have serum 25(OH)D_3 levels below recommendations.[2]

Synthesis of vitamin D3

Ultraviolet (UV) B radiation with a wavelength of 290-315 nanometers penetrates uncovered skin and converts cutaneous 7-dehydrocholesterol to previtamin D_3, which in turn becomes vitamin D_3.[9] [10] [11] Season, geographic latitude, time of day, cloud cover, smog, skin melanin content, and sunscreen are among the factors that affect UV radiation exposure and vitamin D synthesis.[11] The UV energy above 42 degrees north latitude (a line approximately between the northern border of California and Boston) is insufficient for cutaneous vitamin D synthesis from November through February;[12] in far northern latitudes, this reduced intensity lasts for up to 6 months. In the United States, latitudes below 34 degrees north (a line between Los Angeles and Columbia, South Carolina) allow for cutaneous production of vitamin D throughout the year.[13]

Complete cloud cover reduces UV energy by 50%; shade (including that produced by severe pollution) reduces it by 60%.[14] UVB radiation does not penetrate glass, so exposure to sunshine indoors through a window does not produce vitamin D.[15] Sunscreens with a sun protection factor of 8 or more appear to block vitamin D-producing UV rays, although in practice people generally do not apply sufficient amounts, cover all sun-exposed skin, or reapply sunscreen regularly.[16] Skin likely synthesizes some vitamin D even when it is protected by sunscreen as typically applied.[2]

The factors that affect UV radiation exposure and research to date on the amount of sun exposure needed to maintain adequate vitamin D levels make it difficult to provide general guidelines. It has been suggested by some vitamin D researchers, for example, that approximately 5–30 minutes of sun exposure between 10 AM and 3 PM at least twice a week to the face, arms, legs, or back without sunscreen usually lead to sufficient vitamin D synthesis and that the moderate use of commercial tanning beds that emit 2%-6% UVB radiation also is effective.[17] [11] Individuals with limited sun exposure need to include good sources of vitamin D in their diet or take a supplement.

Other benefits

There is some evidence that bright light exposure reduces seasonal affective disorder[18] and it is a standard treatment for certain circadian rhythm sleep disorders.

Risks

Despite the importance of the sun to vitamin D synthesis, it is prudent to limit exposure of skin to sunlight[16] and UV radiation from tanning beds.[19] According to the National Toxicology Program Report on Carcinogens from the Department of Health and Human Services, broad-spectrum UV radiation is a carcinogen thought to contribute to most of the estimated 1.5 million skin cancers and the 8,000 deaths due to metastatic melanoma that occur annually in the United States.[16] [20] Lifetime cumulative UV damage to skin is also largely responsible for some age-associated dryness and other cosmetic changes.

Sunbaker, by Max Dupain

It is not known whether a desirable level of regular sun exposure exists that imposes no (or minimal) risk of skin cancer over time. The American Academy of Dermatology advises that photoprotective measures be taken, including the use of sunscreen, whenever one is exposed to the sun.[21]

Safe level of sun exposure

According to a 2007 study submitted by the University of Ottawa to the Department of Health and Human Services in Washington, D.C., there is not enough information to determine a safe level of sun exposure at this time.[12]

There is no consensus on which component of ultraviolet radiation (UVA or UVB or UVC) actually is carcinogenic,[22] and the composition of ultraviolet radiation changes throughout the day: At high noon, ultraviolet radiation reaching ground level is 95% UVA and 5% UVB, while before 10am and after 2pm this percentage changes over time to 99% UVA and 1% UVB.[23] This is caused by the reflection of UVB rays back into space due to sun angle as the earth slowly rotates on its axis. The rate of change is faster the farther the position moves away from the equator (ie more north or south).[24]

On average over a day, 98.7% of the ultraviolet radiation that reaches the Earth's surface is UVA. UVC is almost completely absorbed by the ozone layer and does not penetrate the atmosphere in any appreciable quantities.[25] As a result, only the combination (UVA, UVB, and UVC) known as "ultraviolet radiation" is listed as a carcinogen, the components are only "likely to become" known carcinogens. Solar radiation, also known as "sunlight" is also listed as a carcinogen because it contains ultraviolet radiation. This means also that the UV Index is a measure of total ultraviolet radiation, and not just Vitamin D-producing UVB.[26]

Sunlight is therefore the only listed carcinogen that is known to have health benefits, in the form of helping the human body to make Vitamin D. This makes sunlight unique on the list of known carcinogens.[22]

With new evidence of Vitamin D receptors in all body tissues, experts advise having a balance between Vitamin D from sun exposure and Vitamin D from supplements. The only way to quantify adequate levels of Vitamin D is with a serum 25(OH) D_3 test.[27]

Lifetime sun exposure

There are currently no recommendations on the total safe level of lifetime sun exposure.[12] According to epidemiologist Robyn Lucas at Australian National University,[28] analysis of lifespan versus disease shows that far more lives are lost to diseases caused by lack of sunlight than by those caused by too much.[29] It is inappropriate to recommend total avoidance of sunlight.[30]

Most people receive between 50% and 80% of their lifetime sun exposure before the age of 18[31] . If one is fair skinned, 10 minutes of exposure to sunshine at high noon (in summer) will produce 10,000 IU of Vitamin D; darker skin requires longer exposure.[29] Note that summer peak daily UVB radiation can be one thousand times higher than winter peak daily UVB radiation in temperate regions. For example, in Boston, the summer solstice sun peak altitude is 71 degrees and the corresponding UVB radiation is 73% of max (90 degree sun altitude); the winter solstice sun peak altitude is 24 degrees and the corresponding UVB radiation is 0.03% of max (90 degree sun altitude).[32] [33] The current recommendations for Vitamin D supplementation (between 200 IU and 400 IU[34] are not based on sun exposure levels of Vitamin D production, but on fears of toxicity as each person's Vitamin D status depends on dozens of environmental and nutritional factors.[35] Because of this balance between internal production and external supplementation of Vitamin D, it is up to each individual to be aware of how they feel, and to consider sun exposure and Vitamin D status as part of their overall health.[36]

It has recently been discovered that vitamin D receptors are present in most if not all cells in the body. Additionally, experiments using cultured cells have demonstrated that vitamin D has potent effects on the growth and differentiation of many types of cells. These findings suggest that vitamin D has physiologic effects much broader than a role in mineral homeostasis and bone function. This is an active area of research and a much better understanding of this area will likely be available in the near future.[37]

Sun exposure and survival from malignant melanoma

A study in the February 2, 2005 issue of the Journal of the National Cancer Institute looked at markers of sun exposure in more than 500 people who had recently been diagnosed with malignant melanoma. The researchers found that solar elastosis, or sun damage to the skin, was independently associated with a surprising increased survival from melanoma.[38]

Sunscreen use within the last 10 years or during childhood was not associated with worse survival from melanoma. And all measures of sun exposure (i.e., history of severe sunburn, high levels of intermittent sun exposure, solar elastosis) were associated with improved survival from melanoma. Furthermore, participants who reported high skin awareness, but not those who reported skin examinations, had better survival.[38]

If confirmed, the results of this study suggest that whereas excessive sun exposure leads to the development of melanoma, sun exposure may protect against the progression of melanoma into more fatal disease.

Seasonal variation and sun exposure

There is ample evidence that the death rate in elderly patients increases in winter months. In a recent study of seasonal mortality in terminal cancer patients in the United States, it was found that compared to those patients who died during June, July, and August, the number of deaths of patients increased an average of 20% in January, February, and March. This near-sinusoidal pattern was remarkably consistent over a five year period.[39]

Mortality in the general population declines in the late summer to early fall months. In the Mediterranean countries, the lowest average daily mortality was observed in September. The fewest deaths were in August in Sweden and North America. The fewest deaths in Japan occurred in July. In the southern hemisphere, the lowest mortality in Australia occurred in March and in February for New Zealand.[40]

In Scotland, patients who suffer cardiopulmonary arrest (heart attack) in winter have a significantly lower likelihood of surviving. People who arrested in winter were 19% less likely to survive compared to those who arrested in summer.[41] For Atrial Fibrilation (AF), significantly more hospital admissions occurred in winter compared to summer.[42]

Deaths due to variceal bleeding in France occurred with a clear annual periodicity and peaked in winter (December, January) in the overall population. The distribution of cumulative monthly deaths differed by 24%, with a peak 14% above average in December and a trough 10% below average in July.[43] In the French Three-City study, high blood pressure, defined as a systolic blood pressure of 160 mmHg or higher, or a diastolic blood pressure of 95 mmHg or higher, was detected in 33.4 per cent of participants during winter and 23.8 percent during summer.[44]

UV-B monitoring in the United States

Over the past several years, levels of ultraviolet radiation have been tracked at over 30 sites across North America as part of the UV-B Monitoring and Research Program (UVMRP) at Colorado State University. The below image shows levels of UVB Radiation in June 2008.[45] UVMRP is a data collection and research program of the United States Department of Agriculture (USDA)[46]

UVB Levels in Vitamin D Equivalents:[47]

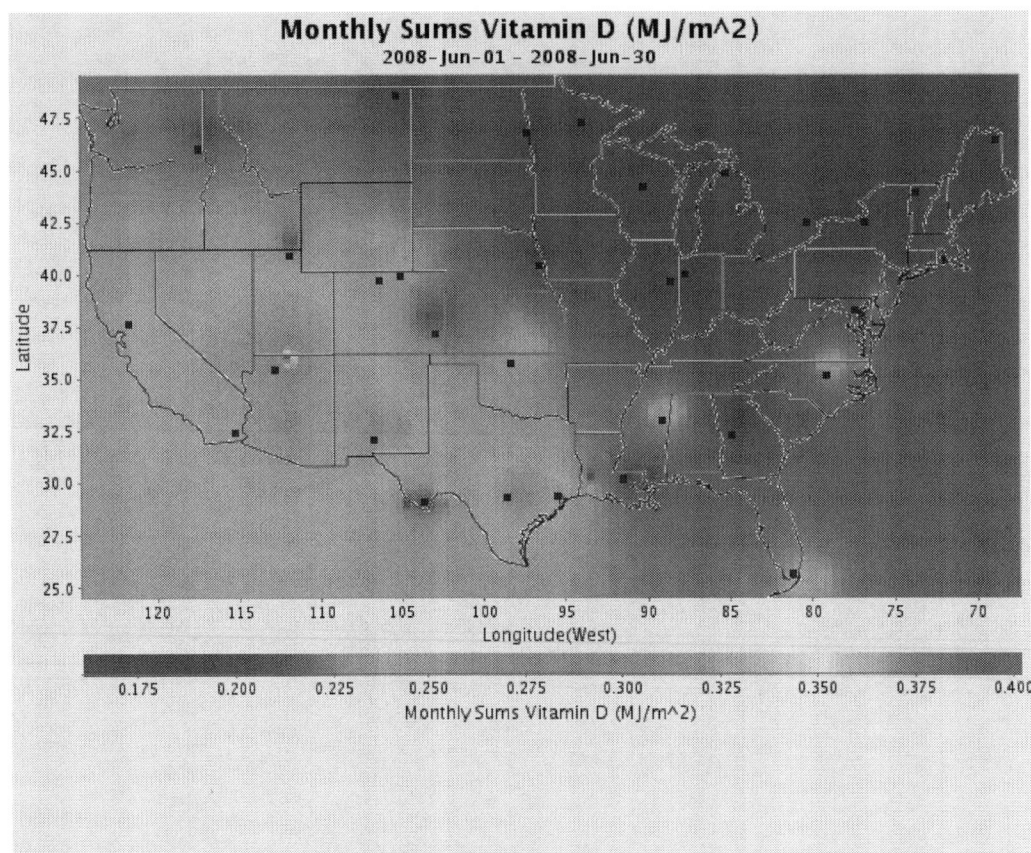

Monthly Sums Vitamin D (MJ/m^2)
2008-Jun-01 – 2008-Jun-30

References

[1] PMID 12174089.

[2] "Dietary Supplement Fact Sheet: Vitamin D" (http://dietary-supplements.info.nih.gov/factsheets/vitamind.asp). Office of Dietary Supplements, National Institutes of Health. .

[3] "Sun 'cuts prostate cancer risk'" (http://news.bbc.co.uk/1/hi/health/4090972.stm). *BBC News*. June 19, 2005. . Retrieved April 1, 2010.

[4] Lucas RM, Repacholi MH, McMichael AJ (June 2006). "Is the current public health message on UV exposure correct?". *Bulletin of the World Health Organization* **84** (6): 485–91. doi:/S0042-96862006000600018. PMC 2627377. PMID 16799733.

[5] Mead MN (April 2008). "Benefits of sunlight: a bright spot for human health" (http://www.ehponline.org/members/2008/116-4/focus.html). *Environmental Health Perspectives* **116** (4): A160–7. PMC 2290997. PMID 18414615. .

[6] "Risks and Benefits" (http://www.cancer.org.au//File/PolicyPublications/PSRisksBenefitsSunExposure03May07.pdf) (PDF). . Retrieved 2010-05-13.

[7] "The Skin Cancer Foundation - The Vitamin D Dilemma | Vitamin D" (http://www.skincancer.org/scf-journal-2008.html). Skincancer.org. . Retrieved 2010-05-13.

[8] Zadshir A, Tareen N, Pan D, Norris K, Martins D (2005). "The prevalence of hypovitaminosis D among US adults: data from the NHANES III". *Ethnicity & Disease* **15** (4 Suppl 5): S5–97–101. PMID 16315387.

[9] Hayes CE, Nashold FE, Spach KM, Pedersen LB (March 2003). "The immunological functions of the vitamin D endocrine system". *Cellular and Molecular Biology* **49** (2): 277–300. PMID 12887108.

[10] Holick MF (October 1994). "McCollum Award Lecture, 1994: vitamin D--new horizons for the 21st century" (http://www.ajcn.org/cgi/pmidlookup?view=long&pmid=8092101). *The American Journal of Clinical Nutrition* **60** (4): 619–30. PMID 8092101. .

[11] Holick, Michael F. (February 2002). "Vitamin D: the underappreciated D-lightful hormone that is important for skeletal and cellular health". *Current Opinion in Endocrinology & Diabetes* **9** (1): 87–98. doi:10.1097/00060793-200202000-00011.

[12] Cranney A, Horsley T, O'Donnell S, *et al.* (August 2007). "Effectiveness and safety of vitamin D in relation to bone health". *Evidence Report/technology Assessment* (158): 1–235. PMID 18088161.

[13] Holick MF (2006). "Vitamin D". In Shike, Moshe; Shils, Maurice Edward. *Modern nutrition in health and disease*. Hagerstwon, MD: Lippincott Williams & Wilkins. ISBN 0-7817-4133-5.

[14] Wharton B, Bishop N (October 2003). "Rickets". *Lancet* **362** (9393): 1389–400. doi:10.1016/S0140-6736(03)14636-3. PMID 14585642.

[15] Holick MF (2005). "Photobiology of vitamin D". In Feldman, David Henry; Glorieux, Francis H.. *Vitamin D*. Amsterdam: Elsevier Academic Press. ISBN 0-12-252687-2.

[16] Wolpowitz D, Gilchrest BA (February 2006). "The vitamin D questions: how much do you need and how should you get it?". *Journal of the American Academy of Dermatology* **54** (2): 301–17. doi:10.1016/j.jaad.2005.11.1057. PMID 16443061.

[17] Holick MF (July 2007). "Vitamin D deficiency". *The New England Journal of Medicine* **357** (3): 266–81. doi:10.1056/NEJMra070553. PMID 17634462.

[18] "Summer sun for winter blues" (http://www.cnn.com/HEALTH/alternative/9907/12/sun.depression/). CNN. July 12, 1999. . Retrieved 2010-03-08.

[19] "The association of use of sunbeds with cutaneous malignant melanoma and other skin cancers: A systematic review". *International Journal of Cancer* **120** (5): 1116–22. March 2007. doi:10.1002/ijc.22453. PMID 17131335.

[20] "Ultraviolet (UV) Radiation, Broad Spectrum and UVA, UVB, and UVC - National Toxicology Program" (http://ntp.niehs.nih.gov/index.cfm?objectid=BD4CD88D-F1F6-975E-792094AC1CE4B062). Ntp.niehs.nih.gov. 2009-01-05. . Retrieved 2010-05-13.

[21] American Academy of Dermatology. Position statement on vitamin D. November 1, 2008. (http://www.aad.org/Forms/Policies/Uploads/PS/PS-Vitamin D.pdf)

[22] "11th Report on Carcinogens" (http://ntp.niehs.nih.gov/ntp/roc/toc11.html). Ntp.niehs.nih.gov. . Retrieved 2010-05-13.

[23] "Ultraviolet (UV) Radiation" (http://www.fda.gov/Radiation-EmittingProducts/RadiationEmittingProductsandProcedures/Tanning/ucm116425.htm). Fda.gov. . Retrieved 2010-05-13.

[24] "Sun Protection Information Sheet, Travellers" (http://www.nathnac.org/travel/misc/travellers_sun.htm). Nathnac. . Retrieved 2010-05-13.

[25] "UVC Radiation" (http://dermatology.about.com/od/glossaryu/g/uvc.htm). Dermatology.about.com. . Retrieved 2010-05-13.

[26] "UV Index Sun Awareness Program" (http://www.hc-sc.gc.ca/hl-vs/sun-sol/uv-prog/index-eng.php). Hc-sc.gc.ca. 2009-09-03. . Retrieved 2010-05-13.

[27] "25-hydroxy vitamin D test: MedlinePlus Medical Encyclopedia" (http://www.nlm.nih.gov/medlineplus/ency/article/003569.htm). Nlm.nih.gov. . Retrieved 2010-05-13.

[28] "ANU - National Centre for Epidemiology and Population Health- NCEPH" (http://nceph.anu.edu.au/Staff_Students/staff_pages/lucas.php). Nceph.anu.edu.au. 2009-12-07. . Retrieved 2010-05-13.

[29] "Time in the Sun: How Much Is Needed for Vitamin D? - US News and World Report" (http://www.usnews.com/health/family-health/articles/2008/06/23/time-in-the-sun-how-much-is-needed-for-vitamin-d.html). Usnews.com. 2008-06-23. . Retrieved 2010-05-13.

[30] http://www.mja.com.au/public/issues/177_11_021202/luc10478_fm.pdf

[31] "Sun Safety" (http://kidshealth.org/parent/firstaid_safe/outdoor/sun_safety.html). Kidshealth.org. . Retrieved 2010-05-13.

[32] "How does UVB intensity vary with solar elevation above horizon? - Yahoo! Answers" (http://answers.yahoo.com/question/index?qid=20080107072603AAfpfSP). Answers.yahoo.com. 2008-01-07. . Retrieved 2010-05-13.

[33] "Sun or Moon Altitude/Azimuth Table" (http://aa.usno.navy.mil/data/docs/AltAz.php). Aa.usno.navy.mil. 2008-09-02. . Retrieved 2010-05-13.

[34] "Vitamin D" (http://www.eatrightontario.ca/en/viewdocument.aspx?id=218). Eatrightontario.ca. . Retrieved 2010-05-13.

[35] "Vitamin D: Vitamin Deficiency, Dependency, and Toxicity: Merck Manual Professional" (http://www.merck.com/mmpe/sec01/ch004/ch004k.html). Merck.com. . Retrieved 2010-05-13.

[36] "Running on Vitamin D at Runner's World" (http://www.runnersworld.com/article/0,7120,s6-242-301--13364-0,00.html). Runnersworld.com. 2008-02-15. . Retrieved 2010-05-13.

[37] "Vitamin D (Cholecalciferol, Calcitriol)" (http://www.vivo.colostate.edu/hbooks/pathphys/endocrine/otherendo/vitamind.html). Vivo.colostate.edu. 2010-04-24. . Retrieved 2010-05-13.

[38] McCoy, Krisha. "Study Suggests History of Sun Exposure May Actually Increase Melanoma Survival Rates" (http://www.mbmc.org/healthgate/GetHGContent.aspx?token=9c315661-83b7-472d-a7ab-bc8582171f86&chunkiid=90212). Mbmc.org. . Retrieved 2010-05-13.

[39] "Seasonal mortality in terminally ill cancer patients." (http://www.asco.org/ASCOv2/Meetings/Abstracts?&vmview=abst_detail_view&confID=65&abstractID=32137). ASCO. . Retrieved 2010-05-13.

[40] "Seasonality of mortality: the September phenomenon in Mediterranean countries - Falagas et al. 181 (8): 484 - Canadian Medical Association Journal" (http://www.cmaj.ca/cgi/content/full/181/8/484). Cmaj.ca. doi:10.1503/cmaj.090694. . Retrieved 2010-05-13.

[41] J P Pella, J Sirelb, A K Marsdenc, S M Cobbeb (1999-07-30). "Seasonal variations in out of hospital cardiopulmonary arrest - Pell et al. 82 (6): 680 - Heart" (http://heart.bmj.com/content/82/6/680.abstract). Heart.bmj.com. . Retrieved 2010-05-13.

[42] "Seasonal variation in morbidity and mortality related to atrial fibrillation" (http://www.biomedexperts.com/Abstract.bme/15458696/Seasonal_variation_in_morbidity_and_mortality_related_to_atrial_fibrillation). BiomedExperts. . Retrieved 2010-05-13.

[43] The American Journal of Gastroenterology (2001-06-01). "Access : Seasonal variations in variceal bleeding mortality and hospitalization in France : The American Journal of Gastroenterology" (http://www.nature.com/ajg/journal/v96/n6/full/ajg2001452a.html). Nature.com. . Retrieved 2010-05-13.

[44] "Seasonal Variation In Blood Pressure" (http://www.medicalnewstoday.com/articles/135805.php). Medicalnewstoday.com. . Retrieved 2010-05-13.

[45] "UV-B Monitoring and Research Program at Colorado State University" (http://uvb.nrel.colostate.edu/UVB/index.jsf). Uvb.nrel.colostate.edu. . Retrieved 2010-05-13.

[46] "UV-B Monitoring and Research Program Monitoring Network at Colorado State University, Overview" (http://uvb.nrel.colostate.edu/UVB/uvb_overview.jsf). Uvb.nrel.colostate.edu. . Retrieved 2010-05-13.

[47] "UV-B Monitoring Project, United States Department of Agriculture; Fort Collins, Colorado" (http://uvb.nrel.colostate.edu/UVB/uvb_network.jsf). Uvb.nrel.colostate.edu. . Retrieved 2010-05-13.

High reliability organization

A **High Reliability Organization (HRO)** is an organization that has succeeded in avoiding catastrophes in an environment where normal accidents can be expected due to risk factors and complexity.

Important case studies in HRO research include the Cuban Missile Crisis, the Three Mile Island nuclear incident, the Challenger explosion, the Bhopal chemical leak, the Tenerife air crash, the Mann Gulch forest fire, the Black Hawk friendly fire incident in Iraq and the Columbia explosion.

History

The roots of HRO theory were built in a stream of theoretical advances by Karlene H. Roberts (UC Berkeley), Herbert Simon, James March, and Karl Weick (University of Michigan) -- who shifted attention away from organizations as rational machines to organizations as arenas in which complex organizational processes occur. The Cuban Missile Crisis was analyzed through this emerging lens by Graham Allison in his 1971 book, *Essence of Decision: Explaining the Cuban Missile Crisis.*

Other important HRO roots -- because they explore the phenomenon of deviation-amplifying loops -- include Cohen, March, and Olson's study of garbage-can decision-making processes, Barry Turner's work on catastrophes, and Barry Staw, Lance Sandelands, and Jane Dutton's research on "threat-rigidity cycles."

The most important early work in HRO research was organizational sociologist Charles Perrow's work on the Three Mile Island nuclear incident in 1979. Perrow's 1984 book [1] included chapters on nuclear incidents, petrochemical plants, aviation accidents, naval accidents, "earth-based system" accidents (dam breaks, earthquakes), and "exotic" accidents (genetic engineering, military operations, and space flight). In rapid succession after the publication of Perrow's book, researchers were confronted with the Chernobyl disaster, the Bhopal chemical leak, and the Challenger explosion.

An initial conference at the University of Texas in April 1987 brought researchers together to focus attention on HROs. Researchers at the University of California, Berkeley, the University of Michigan, the George Washington University and many other universities around the world began to look at organizations in high-risk industries.

At Berkeley, initial research on HROs was done within the Federal Aviation Administration's Air Traffic Control Center, a commercial nuclear power plant, and naval aircraft carriers.

Characteristics

Researchers have found that successful organizations in high-risk industries continually reinvent themselves. For example, when an incident command team realizes what they thought was a garage fire has now changed into a hazardous material incident, they completely restructure their response organization. HRO teams are comfortable and adept at quickly building creative responses to failure. Failure happens, and HRO teams lean on their training, experience and imagination as a reliable means to recover from failure.

There are 5 characteristics of High Reliability Organizations that have been identified [2] as responsible for the "mindfulness" that keeps them working well when facing unexpected situations.

- Preoccupation with failure
- Reluctance to simplify interpretations
- Sensitivity to operations
- Commitment to resilience
- Deference to expertise

Practitioners in High Reliability Organizing (HRO) work in recognized high risk occupations and environments. Wildfires create complex and very dynamic mega-crisis situations across the globe every year. U.S. wildland firefighters, often organized using the Incident Command System into flexible interagency incident management teams, are not only called upon to "bring order to chaos" in today's huge mega-fires, they also are requested on "all-hazard events" like hurricanes, floods and earthquakes. The U.S. Wildland Fire Lessons Learned Center has been providing education and training to the wildland fire community on High Reliability Organizing since 2002. HRO behaviors can be recognized and further developed into high-functioning skills of anticipation and resilience. Learning organizations that strive for high performance in things they can plan for, can become highly reliable organizations that are able to better manage unexpected events that by definition cannot be planned for.

Notes

[1] Perrow, Charles (1999). *Normal Accidents: Living with High-Risk Technologies.* Princeton, NJ, USA: Princeton University Press. ISBN 0-6910-0412-9.

[2] Weick, Karl E.; Kathleen M. Sutcliffe (2001). *Managing the Unexpected - Assuring High Performance in an Age of Complexity.* San Francisco, CA, USA: Jossey-Bass. pp. 10–17. ISBN 0-7879-5627-9.

External links

- High-Reliability.Org website (http://high-reliability.org/)
- High Reliability Management group at LinkedIn.com (http://www.linkedin.com/groups?gid=673677)
- Wildland Fire Lessons Learned Center HRO page (http://www.wildfirelessons.net/HRO.aspx)

Human cognitive reliability correlation

Human Cognitive Reliability Correlation (HCR) is a technique used in the field of Human reliability Assessment (HRA), for the purposes of evaluating the probability of a human error occurring throughout the completion of a specific task. From such analyses measures can then be taken to reduce the likelihood of errors occurring within a system and therefore lead to an improvement in the overall levels of safety. There exist three primary reasons for conducting an HRA; error identification, error quantification and error reduction. As there exist a number of techniques used for such purposes, they can be split into one of two classifications; first generation techniques and second generation techniques. First generation techniques work on the basis of the simple dichotomy of 'fits/doesn't fit' in the matching of the error situation in context with related error identification and quantification and second generation techniques are more theory based in their assessment and quantification of errors. HRA techniques have been utilised in a range of industries including healthcare, engineering, nuclear, transportation and business sector; each technique has varying uses within different disciplines.

HCR is based on the premise that an operator's likelihood of success or failure in a time-critical task is dependent on the cognitive process used to make the critical decisions that determine the outcome. Three Performance Shaping Factors (PSFs) – Operator Experience, Stress Level, and Quality of Operator/Plant Interface - also influence the average (median) time taken to perform the task. Combining these factors enables "response-time" curves to be calibrated and compared to the available time to perform the task. Using these curves, the analyst can then estimate the likelihood that an operator will take the correct action, as required by a given stimulus (e.g. pressure warning signal), within the available time window. The relationship between these normalised times and Human Error Probabilities (HEPs) is based on simulator experimental data.

Background

HCR is a psychology/cognitive modelling approach to HRA developed by Hannaman et al. in 1984. [1] The method uses Rasmussen's idea of rule-based, skill-based, and knowledge-based decision making to determine the likelihood of failing a given task[2] , as well as considering the PSFs of operator experience, stress and interface quality. The database underpinning this methodology was originally developed through the use of nuclear power-plant simulations due to a requirement for a method by which nuclear operating reliability could be quantified.

HCR Methodology

The HCR methodology is broken down into a sequence of steps as given below:

1. The first step is for the analyst to determine the situation in need of a human reliability assessment. It is then determined whether this situation is governed by rule-based, skill-based or knowledge-based decision making.
2. From the relevant literature, the appropriate HCR mathematical model or graphical curve is then selected.
3. The median response time to perform the task in question is thereafter determined. This is commonly done by expert judgement, operator interview or simulator experiment. In much literature, this time is referred to as T1/2 nominal.
4. The median response time, (T1/2), requires to be amended to make it specific to the situational context. This is done by means of the PSF coefficients K1 (Operator Experience), K2 (Stress Level) and K3 (Quality of Operator/Plant Interface) given in the literature and using the following formula:

$$T1/2 = T1/2 \text{ nominal} \times (1 + K1)(1 + K2)(1 + K3)$$

Performance improving PSFs (e.g. worker experience, low stress) will take negative values resulting in quicker times, whilst performance inhibiting PSFs (e.g. poor interface) will increase this adjusted median time.

5. For the action being assessed, the time window (T) should then be calculated, which is the time in which the operator must take action to correctly resolve the situation.

6. To obtain the non-response probability, the time window (T) is divided by T1/2, the median time. This gives the Normalised Time Value. The probability of non-response can then be found by referring to the HCR curve selected earlier. This non-response probability may then be integrated into a fuller HRA; a complete HEP can only be reached in conjunction with other methods as non-response is not the sole source of human error.

Worked example

The following example is taken from Human Factors in Reliability Group[3] in which Hannaman describes analysis of failure to manually SCRAM (perform an ermegency shutdown) in a Westinghouse PWR (Pressurized water reactor, a type of nuclear power reactor).

Context

The example concerns a model in which failures occurs to manually SCRAM in a Westinghouse PWR. The primary task to be carried out involves inserting control rods into the core. This can be further broken down into two sub-tasks which involve namely detection and action, which are in turn based upon recognising and identifying an automatic trip failure.

Assumptions

Given that there exists the assumption that there is simply one option in the procedures and that within training procedures optional actions are disregarded, the likelihood that a reactor trip failure will be incorrectly diagnosed is minimal.

It is also assumed that the behaviour of the operating crew under consideration is skill-based; the reactor trip event which takes place is not part of a routine, however the temporary behaviour adopted by the crew when the event is taking place is nevertheless recognised. Moreover, there are well set procedures which determine how the event should be conducted and these are comprehended and practised to required standards in training sessions.

The average time taken by the crew to complete the task is 25 seconds; there is no documentation as to why this is the case. The average completion times for the respective subtasks are therefore set as 10 seconds for detection of the failure and 15 seconds for taking subsequent action to remedy the situation.

Method

The PSFs (K factor) judged to influence the situation are assessed to be in the following categories: -operator experience is "well trained" -stress level is "potential emergency" -quality of interface is "good" The various K factors are assigned the following values:

- **K1 = 0.0**
- **K2 = 0.28**
- **K3 = 0.0**

Referring to the equation in Step 4 above, the product is therefore equal to the value of 1.28. In response, the average tasks times are altered from 10 and 15 seconds to 12.8 and 19.2 seconds respectively. Given that the PSFs are identical for both of the given subtasks, it is therefore possible to sum the median response times to give a total of 32 seconds, adjusting the figure for stress, compared to a previous total of 25 seconds.

The time window (T) to perform the task as part of the overall system is given as 79 seconds. This time is derived from a study conducted by Westinghouse in which it was discovered that the crew had approximately 79 seconds to complete the task of inserting the control rod to the reactor and then to shut the reactor down in order to inhibit over-pressuring within the main operating system.

Results/Outcome

Consulting the graphical curve central to the technique, the normalised time for the task can thus be established. It is determined by the division of 79 seconds and 32 seconds, giving a result of 2.47 seconds. Identifying this point on the abscissa (the HCR curve model) provides a non response probability of 2.9×10^{-3}; this can also be checked for validation utilising the formula:-

PRT (79) = exp − [(79/32) − 0.7 / 0.407] 1.2 PRT (79) = 2.9 x 10 -3/ demand

Where PRT (T) equals the probability of non success within the system time window T.

Provided below is the graphical solution for the assessment using the HCR technique:

Advantages of HCR

- The approach explicitly models the time-dependent nature of HRA [3]
- It is a fairly quick technique to carry out and has a relative ease of use [3]
- The three modes of decision-making, knowledge-based, skill-based and rule-based are all modelled [3]

Disadvantages of HCR

- The HEP produced by HCR is not complete; it calculates the probability that a system operator will fail to diagnose and process information, make a decision and act within the time available. It does not give any regard to misdiagnoses or rule violations. [3]
- The same probability curves are used to model non-detection and slow response failures. These are very different processes, and it is unlikely that identical curves could model their behaviour. Furthermore, it is uncertain as to whether such curves could be applied to situations in which detection failures or processing difficulties are the primary dominating factors of influence. [3]
- The rules for judging Knowledge-based, Skill-based and Rule-based behaviour are not exhaustive. Assigning the wrong behaviour to a task can mean differences of up to two orders of magnitude in the HEP. [3]
- The method is very sensitive to changes in the estimate of the median time. Therefore, this estimate requires to be very accurate otherwise the estimation in the HEP will suffer as a consequence. [3]
- It is highly resource intensive to collect all the required data for the HCR methodology, particularly due to the necessity of evaluation for all new situations which require an assessment. [3]
- There is no sense of output from the model that indicates in any way of how human reliability could be adjusted to allow for improvement or optimisation to meet required goals of performance. [3]
- Only three PSFs are included in the methodology; there are several other PSF's that could affect performance which are unaccounted for.
- The model is relatively insensitive to PSF changes as opposed to, for example, time parameter changes. [3]
- As the HCR correlation was originally developed for use within the nuclear industry, it is not possible to use the methodology for applications out-with this domain. [3]

References

[1] HANNAMAN, G.W., Spurgin, A.J. & Lukic, Y.D., Human cognitive reliability model for PRA analysis. Draft Report NUS-4531, EPRI Project RP2170-3. 1984, Electric Power and Research Institute: Palo Alto, CA.

[2] Rasmussen, J. (1983) Skills, rules, knowledge; signals, signs and symbols and other distinctions in human performance models. IEEE Transactions on Systems, Man and Cybernetics. SMC-13(3).

[3] Humphreys, P. (1995). Human Reliability Assessor's Guide. Human Factors in Reliability Group.

Human error assessment and reduction technique

Human error assessment and reduction technique (HEART) is a technique used in the field of human reliability assessment (HRA), for the purposes of evaluating the probability of a human error occurring throughout the completion of a specific task. From such analyses measures can then be taken to reduce the likelihood of errors occurring within a system and therefore lead to an improvement in the overall levels of safety. There exist three primary reasons for conducting an HRA; error identification, error quantification and error reduction. As there exist a number of techniques used for such purposes, they can be split into one of two classifications; first generation techniques and second generation techniques. First generation techniques work on the basis of the simple dichotomy of 'fits/doesn't fit' in the matching of the error situation in context with related error identification and quantification and second generation techniques are more theory based in their assessment and quantification of errors. 'HRA techniques have been utilised in a range of industries including healthcare, engineering, nuclear, transportation and business sector; each technique has varying uses within different disciplines.

HEART method is based upon the principle that every time a task is performed there is a possibility of failure and that the probability of this is affected by one or more Error Producing Conditions (EPCs) − for instance: distraction, tiredness, cramped conditions etc. − to varying degrees. Factors which have a significant effect on performance are of greatest interest. These conditions can then be applied to a "best-case-scenario" estimate of the failure probability under ideal conditions to then obtain a final error chance. This figure assists in communication of error chances with the wider risk analysis or safety case. By forcing consideration of the EPCs potentially affecting a given procedure, HEART also has the indirect effect of providing a range of suggestions as to how the reliability may therefore be improved (from an ergonomic standpoint) and hence minimising risk.

Background

HEART was developed by Williams in 1986.[1] It is a first generation HRA technique, yet it is dissimilar to many of its contemporaries in that it remains to be widely used throughout the UK. The method essentially takes into consideration all factors which may negatively affect performance of a task in which human reliability is considered to be dependent, and each of these factors is then independently quantified to obtain an overall Human Error Probability (HEP), the collective product of the factors.

HEART methodology

1. The first stage of the process is to identify the full range of sub-tasks that a system operator would be required to complete within a given task.

2. Once this task description has been constructed a nominal human unreliability score for the particular task is then determined, usually by consulting local experts. Based around this calculated point, a 5th − 95th percentile confidence range is established.

3. The EPCs, which are apparent in the given situation and highly probable to have a negative effect on the outcome, are then considered and the extent to which each EPC applies to the task in question is discussed and agreed, again with local experts. As an EPC should never be considered beneficial to a task, it is calculated using the following formula:

Calculated Effect = ((Max Effect − 1) × Proportion of Effect) + 1

4. A final estimate of the HEP is then calculated, in which the identified EPC's play a large part in the determination of.

Only those EPC's which show much evidence with regards to their affect in the contextual situation should be used by the assessor.[2]

Worked example

Context

A reliability engineer has the task of assessing the probability of a plant operator failing to carry out the task of isolating a plant bypass route as required by procedure. However, the operator is fairly inexperienced in fulfilling this task and therefore typically does not follow the correct procedure; the individual is therefore unaware of the hazards created when the task is carried out

Assumptions

There are various assumptions that should be considered in the context of the situation:

- the operator is working a shift in which he is in his 7th hour.
- there is talk circulating the plant that it is due to close down
- it is possible for the operator's work to be checked at any time
- local management aim to keep the plant open despite a desperate need for re-vamping and maintenance work; if the plant is closed down for a short period, if the problems are unattended, there is a risk that it may remain closed permanently.

Method

A representation of this situation using the HEART methodology would be done as follows:

From the relevant tables it can be established that the type of task in this situation is of the type (F) which is defined as 'Restore or shift a system to original or new state following procedures, with some checking'. This task type has the proposed nominal human unreliability value of 0.003.

Other factors to be included in the calculation are provided in the table below:

Factor	Total HEART Effect	Assessed Proportion of Effect	Assessed Effect
Inexperience	x3	0.4	(3.0-1) x 0.4 + 1 =1.8
Opposite technique	x6	1.0	(6.0-1) x 1.0 + 1 =6.0
Risk Misperception	x4	0.8	(4.0-1) x 0.8 + 1 =3.4
Conflict of Objectives	x2.5	0.8	(2.5-1) x 0.8 + 1 =2.2
Low Morale	x1.2	0.6	(1.2-1) x 0.6 + 1 =1.12

Result

The final calculation for the normal likelihood of failure can therefore be formulated as:

0.003 x 1.8 x 6.0 x 3.4 x 2.2 x 1.12 = 0.27

Advantages

- HEART is very quick and straightforward to use and also has a small demand for resource usage [3]
- The technique provides the user with useful suggestions as to how to reduce the occurrence of errors[4]
- It provides ready linkage between Ergonomics and Process Design, with reliability improvement measures being a direct conclusion which can be drawn from the assessment procedure.
- It allows cost benefit analyses to be conducted
- It is highly flexible and applicable in a wide-range of areas which contributes to the popularity of its use [3]

Disadvantages

- The main criticism of the HEART technique is that the EPC data has never been fully released and it is therefore not possible to fully review the validity of Williams EPC data base. Kirwan has done some empirical validation on HEART and found that it had "a reasonable level of accuracy" but was not necessarily better or worse than the other techniques in the study.[5] [6] [7] Further theoretical validation is thus required.[2]
- HEART relies to a high extent on expert opinion, first in the point probabilities of human error, and also in the assessed proportion of EPC effect. The final HEPs are therefore sensitive to both optimistic and pessimistic assessors
- The interdependence of EPCs is not modelled in this methodology, with the HEPs being multiplied directly. This assumption of independence does not necessarily hold in a real situation.[2]

References

[1] WILLIAMS, J.C. (1985) HEART – A proposed method for achieving high reliability in process operation by means of human factors engineering technology in Proceedings of a Symposium on the Achievement of Reliability in Operating Plant, Safety and Reliability Society. NEC, Birmingham.

[2] Kirwan, B. (1994) A Guide to Practical Human Reliability Assessment. CPC Press.

[3] Humphreys. P. (1995). Human Reliability Assessor's Guide. Human Reliability in Factor's Group.

[4] http://www.hf.faa.gov/Portal/ShowProduct.aspx?ProductID=90

[5] Kirwan, B. (1996) The validation of three human reliability quantification techniques - THERP, HEART, JHEDI: Part I -- technique descriptions and validation issues. Applied Ergonomics. 27(6) 359-373.

[6] Kirwan, B. (1997) The validation of three human reliability quantification techniques - THERP, HEART, JHEDI: Part II - Results of validation exercise. Applied Ergonomics. 28(1) 17-25.

[7] Kirwan, B. (1997) The validation of three human reliability quantification techniques - THERP, HEART, JHEDI: Part III -- practical aspects of the usage of the techniques. Applied Ergonomics. 28(1) 27-39.

Human reliability

Human reliability is related to the field of human factors engineering and ergonomics, and refers to the reliability of humans in fields such as manufacturing, transportation, the military, or medicine. Human performance can be affected by many factors such as age, state of mind, physical health, attitude, emotions, propensity for certain common mistakes, errors and cognitive biases, etc.

Human reliability is very important due to the contributions of humans to the resilience of systems and to possible adverse consequences of human errors or oversights, especially when the human is a crucial part of the large socio-technical systems as is common today. User-centered design and error-tolerant design are just two of many terms used to describe efforts to make technology better suited to operation by humans.

Human reliability analysis techniques

A variety of methods exist for human reliability analysis (HRA).[1] [2] Two general classes of methods are those based on probabilistic risk assessment (PRA) and those based on a cognitive theory of control.

PRA-based techniques

One method for analyzing human reliability is a straightforward extension of probabilistic risk assessment (PRA): in the same way that equipment can fail in a plant, so can a human operator commit errors. In both cases, an analysis (functional decomposition for equipment and task analysis for humans) would articulate a level of detail for which failure or error probabilities can be assigned. This basic idea is behind the Technique for Human Error Rate Prediction (THERP).[3] THERP is intended to generate human error probabilities that would be incorporated into a PRA. The Accident Sequence Evaluation Program (ASEP) human reliability procedure is a simplified form of

THERP; an associated computational tool is Simplified Human Error Analysis Code (SHEAN) [4].[5] More recently, the US Nuclear Regulatory Commission has published the Standardized Plant Analysis Risk (SPAR) human reliability analysis method also because of human error.[6] [7]

Cognitive control based techniques

Erik Hollnagel has developed this line of thought in his work on the Contextual Control Model (COCOM) [8] and the Cognitive Reliability and Error Analysis Method (CREAM).[9] COCOM models human performance as a set of control modes—strategic (based on long-term planning), tactical (based on procedures), opportunistic (based on present context), and scrambled (random) - and proposes a model of how transitions between these control modes occur. This model of control mode transition consists of a number of factors, including the human operator's estimate of the outcome of the action (success or failure), the time remaining to accomplish the action (adequate or inadequate), and the number of simultaneous goals of the human operator at that time. CREAM is a human reliability analysis method that is based on COCOM.

Related techniques

Related techniques in safety engineering and reliability engineering include failure mode and effects analysis, hazop, fault tree, and SAPHIRE: Systems Analysis Programs for Hands-on Integrated Reliability Evaluations.

Human Factors

Since the end of WWII human factors issues have become a paramount concern in aviation safety. It's estimated that anywhere between 90% to 95% of aviation accidents and incidents are caused by human factors. But exactly what is considered a human factor? Human factors is a all encompassing effort to compile data about human capabilities and limitations and apply that data to equipment, systems, software, facilities, procedures, jobs, environments, training, staffing, and personnel management to produce safe comfortable, ergonomic and effective human performance. The FAA is currently making an effort to integrate human factors into all aspects of aviation where safety is a major concern. As a result the FAA issued FAA order 9550.8 which is a human factors policy that states the following:

Human factors shall be systematically integrated into the planning and execution of the functions of all FAA elements and activities associated with system acquisitions and system operations. FAA endeavors shall emphasize human factors considerations to enhance system performance and capitalize upon the relative strengths of people and machines. These considerations shall be integrated at the earliest phases of FAA projects.

The FAA has realized that when most individuals think of a system or project, they usually consider only the tangibles such as hardware, software and equipment. Most individuals fail to think about the end user of the product, the human being. Therefore during systems designing consideration for different aptitudes and abilities are never considered. The FAA's combating this predominant thought pattern by the introduction of what is known as "Total System Performance". Total System Performance is a measure of probability. The probability that the total system will perform correctly, when it is available, is the probability that the hardware/software will perform correctly, times the probability that the operating environment will not degrade the system operation, times the probability that the user will perform will perform correctly. It's been discovered that a system can work perfectly in a test environment, demonstration site or laboratory and then not perform as well once the human being enters the loop as the operator. In order to compensate for this fact, human factors must be accounted for and integrated into new systems. By doing so there will be increased performance accuracy, decreased performance time and enhanced safety. FAA research has indicated that designing systems to improve human performance is cost effective and safe when done early in the developmental stages of a project. Some potential human factors to consider during research and development stages are functional design, safety and health, work space, display and controls, information requirements, display presentation, visual/aural alerts, communications, anthropometrics and environment.

Human error

Human error has been cited as a cause or contributing factor in disasters and accidents in industries as diverse as nuclear power (e.g., Three Mile Island accident), aviation (see pilot error), space exploration (e.g., Space Shuttle Challenger Disaster), and medicine (see medical error). It is also important to stress that "human error" mechanisms are the same as "human performance" mechanisms; performance later categorized as 'error' is done so in hindsight:[10] [11] therefore actions later termed "human error" are actually part of the ordinary spectrum of human behaviour. The study of absent-mindedness in everyday life provides ample documentation and categorization of such aspects of behavior. While human error is firmly entrenched in the classical approaches to accident investigation and risk assessment, it has no role in newer approaches such as resilience engineering.[12]

Categories of human error

There are many ways to categorize human error.[13] [14]

- exogenous versus endogenous (i.e., originating outside versus inside the individual)[15]
- situation assessment versus response planning[16] and related distinctions in

  - errors in problem detection (also see signal detection theory)
  - errors in problem diagnosis (also see problem solving)
  - errors in action planning and execution[17] (for example: slips or errors of execution versus mistakes or errors of intention[18] [19])

- By level of analysis; for example, perceptual (e.g., optical illusions) versus cognitive versus communication versus organizational.

The cognitive study of human error is a very active research field, including work related to limits of memory and attention and also to decision making strategies such as the availability heuristic and other cognitive biases. Such heuristics and biases are strategies that are useful and often correct, but can lead to systematic patterns of error.

Misunderstandings as a topic in human communication have been studied in conversation analysis, such as the examination of violations of the cooperative principle and Gricean maxims.

Organizational studies of error or dysfunction have included studies of safety culture. One technique for organizational analysis is the Management Oversight Risk Tree (MORT).[20] [21]

Human Factors Analysis and Classification System (HFACS)

See Human Factors Analysis and Classification System in Main article: National Fire Fighter Near-Miss Reporting System

The Human Factors Analysis and Classification System (HFACS) was developed initially as a framework to understand "human error" as a cause of aviation accidents.[22] [23] It is based on James Reason's Swiss cheese model of human error in complex systems. HFACS distinguishes between the "active failures" of unsafe acts, and "latent failures" of preconditions for unsafe acts, unsafe supervision, and organizational influences. These categories were developed empirically on the basis of many aviation accident reports.

"Unsafe acts" are performed by the human operator "on the front line" (e.g., the pilot, the air traffic controller, the driver). Unsafe acts can be either errors (in perception, decision making or skill-based performance) or violations (routine or exceptional). The errors here are similar to the above discussion. Violations are the deliberate disregard for rules and procedures. As the name implies, routine violations are those that occur habitually and are usually tolerated by the organization or authority. Exceptional violations are unusual and often extreme. For example, driving 60 mph in a 55-mph zone speed limit is a routine violation, but driving 130 mph in the same zone is exceptional.

There are two types of preconditions for unsafe acts: those that relate to the human operator's internal state and those that relate to the human operator's practices or ways of working. Adverse internal states include those related to physiology (e.g., illness) and mental state (e.g., mentally fatigued, distracted). A third aspect of 'internal state' is really a mismatch between the operator's ability and the task demands; for example, the operator may be unable to make visual judgments or react quickly enough to support the task at hand. Poor operator practices are another type of precondition for unsafe acts. These include poor crew resource management (issues such as leadership and communication) and poor personal readiness practices (e.g., violating the crew rest requirements in aviation).

Four types of unsafe supervision are: inadequate supervision; planned inappropriate operations; failure to correct a known problem; and supervisory violations.

Organizational influences include those related to resources management (e.g., inadequate human or financial resources), organizational climate (structures, policies, and culture), and organizational processes (such as procedures, schedules, oversight).

Controversies

Some researchers have argued that the dichotomy of human actions as "correct" or "incorrect" is a harmful oversimplification of a complex phenomena.[24] [25] A focus on the variability of human performance and how human operators (and organizations) can manage that variability may be a more fruitful approach. Newer approaches such as resilience engineering mentioned above, highlights the positive roles that humans can play in complex systems. In resilience engineering, successes (things that go right) and failures (things that go wrong) are seen as having the same basis, namely human performance variability. A specific account of that is the efficiency–thoroughness trade-off (ETTO) principle,[26] which can be found on all levels of human activity, in individual as well as collective.

Footnotes

[1] Kirwan and Ainsworth, 1992

[2] Kirwan, 1994

[3] Swain & Guttman, 1983

[4] http://www.osti.gov/energycitations/product.biblio.jsp?osti_id=10162198

[5] Wilson, 1993)

[6] SPAR-H (http://www.nrc.gov/reading-rm/doc-collections/nuregs/contract/cr6883/)

[7] Gertman et al., 2005

[8] (Hollnagel, 1993)

[9] (Hollnagel, 1998)

[10] Reason, 1991

[11] Woods, 1990

[12] Hollnagel, E., Woods, D. D. & Leveson, N. G. (2006). Resilience engineering: Concepts and precepts. Aldershot, UK: Ashgate

[13] Jones, 1999

[14] Wallace and Ross, 2006

[15] Senders and Moray, 1991

[16] Roth et al., 1994

[17] Sage, 1992

[18] Norman, 1988

[19] Reason, 1991

[20] (Kirwan and Ainsworth, 1992;

[21] search for MORT on the FAA Human Factors Workbench (http://www2.hf.faa.gov/workbenchtools/)

[22] Shappell and Wiegmann, 2000

[23] Wiegmann and Shappell, 2003

[24] Hollnagel, E. (1983). Human error. (Position Paper for NATO Conference on Human Error, August 1983, Bellagio, Italy)

[25] Hollnagel, E. and Amalberti, R. (2001). The Emperor's New Clothes, or whatever happened to "human error"? Invited keynote presentation at 4th International Workshop on Human Error, Safety and System Development.. Linköping, June 11–12, 2001.

[26] Hollnagel, E. (2009). The ETTO Principle - Efficiency-Thoroughness Trade-Off. Why things that go right sometimes go wrong. Ashgate

References

- Gertman, D. L. and Blackman, H. S. (2001). *Human reliability and safety analysis data handbook*. Wiley.
- Gertman, D., Blackman, H., Marble, J., Byers, J. and Smith, C. (2005). *The SPAR-H human reliability analysis method. NUREG/CR-6883. Idaho National Laboratory, prepared for U. S. Nuclear Regulatory Commission.* (http://www.nrc.gov/reading-rm/doc-collections/nuregs/contract/cr6883/)
- Hollnagel, E. (1993). *Human reliability analysis: Context and control*. Academic Press.
- Hollnagel, E. (1998). *Cognitive reliability and error analysis method: CREAM*. Elsevier.
- Hollnagel, E. and Amalberti, R. (2001). *The Emperor's New Clothes, or whatever happened to "human error"? Invited keynote presentation at 4th International Workshop on Human Error, Safety and System Development.*. Linköping, June 11–12, 2001.
- Hollnagel, E., Woods, D. D., and Leveson, N. (Eds.) (2006). *Resilience engineering: Concepts and precepts*. Ashgate.
- Jones, P. M. (1999). *Human error and its amelioration. In* Handbook of Systems Engineering and Management *(A. P. Sage and W. B. Rouse, eds.), 687-702*. Wiley.
- Kirwan, B. (1994). *A Guide to Practical Human Reliability Assessment*. Taylor & Francis.
- Kirwan, B. and Ainsworth, L. (Eds.) (1992). *A guide to task analysis*. Taylor & Francis.
- Norman, D. (1988). *The psychology of everyday things*. Basic Books.
- Reason, J. (1990). *Human error*. Cambridge University Press.
- Roth, E. et al. (1994). *An empirical investigation of operator performance in cognitive demanding simulated emergencies. NUREG/CR-6208, Westinghouse Science and Technology Center*. Report prepared for Nuclear Regulatory Commission.
- Sage, A. P. (1992). *Systems engineering*. Wiley.
- Senders, J. and Moray, N. (1991). *Human error: Cause, prediction, and reduction*. Lawrence Erlbaum Associates.
- Shappell, S. & Wiegmann, D. (2000). *The human factors analysis and classification system - HFACS. DOT/FAA/AM-00/7, Office of Aviation Medicine, Federal Aviation Administration, Department of Transportation.*. (http://www.nifc.gov/safety_study/accident_invest/humanfactors_class&anly.pdf)
- Swain, A. D., & Guttman, H. E. (1983). *Handbook of human reliability analysis with emphasis on nuclear power plant applications.*. NUREG/CR-1278 (Washington D.C.).
- Wallace, B. and Ross, A. (2006). *Beyond human error*. CRC Press.
- Wiegmann, D. & Shappell, S. (2003). *A human error approach to aviation accident analysis: The human factors analysis and classification system.*. Ashgate.
- Wilson, J.R. (1993). *SHEAN (Simplified Human Error Analysis code) and automated THERP*. United States Department of Energy Technical Report Number WINCO--11908. (http://www.osti.gov/energycitations/product.biblio.jsp?osti_id=10162198)
- Woods, D. D. (1990). *Modeling and predicting human error. In J. Elkind, S. Card, J. Hochberg, and B. Huey (Eds.),* Human performance models for computer-aided engineering *(248-274)*. Academic Press.
- Federal Aviation Administration. 2009 electronic code of regulations. Retrieved September 25, 2009, from http://www.airweb.faa.gov/Regulatory_and_Guidance_Library

Further reading

- Autrey, T.D. (2007). . *Practicing Perfection Institute Mistake-Proofing Six Sigma: How to Minimize Project Scope and Reduce Human Error* (http://www.practicingperfectioninstitute.com/reports/sixsigma.aspx).

- Davies, J.B., Ross, A., Wallace, B. and Wright, L. (2003). *Safety Management: a Qualitative Systems Approach.* Taylor and Francis.

- Dekker, S.W.A., (2005). *Ten Questions About Human Error: a new view of human factors and systems safety]* (http://www.leonardo.lth.se/sidney_dekker/books/ten_questions_about_human_error/). Lawrence Erlbaum Associates.

- Dekker, S.W.A., (2006). *The Field Guide to Understanding Human Error* (http://www.leonardo.lth.se/sidney_dekker/books/the_field_guide_to_understanding_human_error/). Ashgate.

- Dekker, S.W.A., (2007). *Just Culture: Balancing Safety and Accountability* (http://www.leonardo.lth.se/sidney_dekker/books/just_culture/). Ashgate.

- Dismukes, R. K., Berman, B. A., and Loukopoulos, L. D. (2007). *The limits of expertise: Rethinking pilot error and the causes of airline accidents.* Ashgate.

- Forester, J., Kolaczkowski, A., Lois, E., and Kelly, D. (2006). *Evaluation of human reliability analysis methods against good practices. NUREG-1842 Final Report.* U. S. Nuclear Regulatory Commission. (http://www.nrc.gov/reading-rm/doc-collections/nuregs/staff/sr1842/)

- Goodstein, L. P., Andersen, H. B., and Olsen, S. E. (Eds.) (1988). *Tasks, errors, and mental models.* Taylor and Francis.

- Grabowski, M. and Roberts, K. H. (1996). *Human and organizational error in large scale systems (doi:10.1109/3468.477856),* IEEE Transactions on Systems, Man, and Cybernetics, *Volume 26, No. 1, January 1996, 2-16.*

- Greenbaum, J. and Kyng, M. (Eds.) (1991). *Design at work: Cooperative design of computer systems.* Lawrence Erlbaum Associates.

- Harrison, M. (2004). *Human error analysis and reliability assessment.* Workshop on Human Computer Interaction and Dependability, 46th IFIP Working Group 10.4 Meeting, Siena, Italy, July 3–7, 2004. (http://www.laas.fr/IFIPWG/Workshops&Meetings/46/05-Harrison.pdf)

- Hollnagel, E. (1991). *The phenotype of erroneous actions: Implications for HCI design.* In G. W. R. Weir and J. L. Alty (Eds.), Human-computer interaction and complex systems. Academic Press.

- Hutchins, E. (1995). *Cognition in the wild.* MIT Press.

- Kahneman, D., Slovic, P. and Tversky, A. (Eds.) (1982). *Judgment under uncertainty: Heuristics and biases.* Cambridge University Press.

- Leveson, N. (1995). *Safeware: System safety and computers.* Addison-Wesley.

- Morgan, G. (1986). *Images of organization.* Sage.

- Mura, S. S. (1983). *Licensing violations: Legitimate violations of Grice's conversational principle.* In R. Craig and K. Tracy (Eds.), Conversational coherence: Form, structure, and strategy *(101-115).* Sage.

- Perrow, C. (1984). *Normal accidents: Living with high-risk technologies.* Basic Books.

- Rasmussen, J. (1983). *Skills, rules, and knowledge: Signals, signs, and symbols and other distinctions in human performance models.* IEEE Transactions on Systems, Man, and Cybernetics, *SMC-13, 257-267.*

- Rasmussen, J. (1986). *Information processing and human-machine interaction: An approach to cognitive engineering.* Wiley.

- Silverman, B. (1992). *Critiquing human error: A knowledge-based human-computer collaboration approach.* Academic Press.

- Swets, J. (1996). *Signal detection theory and ROC analysis in psychology and diagnostics: Collected papers.* Lawrence Erlbaum Associates.

- Tversky, A. and Kahneman, D. (1974). *Judgment under uncertainty: Heuristics and biases.* Science, *185, 1124-1131.*

- Vaughan, D. (1996). *The Challenger launch decision: Risky technology, culture, and deviance at NASA.* University of Chicago Press.
- Woods, D. D., Johannesen, L., Cook, R., and Sarter, N. (1994). *Behind human error: Cognitive systems, computers, and hindsight. CSERIAC SOAR Report 94-01.* Crew Systems Ergonomics Information Analysis Center, Wright-Patterson Air Force Base, Ohio.
- CCPS, Guidelines for Preventing Human Error. This book explains about qualitative and quantitative methodology for predicting human error. Qualitative methodology called SPEAR: Systems for Predicting Human Error and Recovery, and quantitative methodology also includes THERP, etc.

External links

Standards and guidance documents

- IEEE Standard 1082 (1997): IEEE Guide for Incorporating Human Action Reliability Analysis for Nuclear Power Generating Stations (http://stdsbbs.ieee.org/descr/1082-1997/)

Tools

- Eurocontrol Human Error Tools (http://www.eurocontrol.int/hifa/public/standard_page/Hifa_HifaData_Tools_HumErr.html)
- EPRI HRA Calculator (http://www.epri.com/hra/discuss.html)

Research labs

- Erik Hollnagel (http://erik.hollnagel.googlepages.com/) at the Crisis and Risk Research Centre (http://www.crc.ensmp.fr/) at MINES ParisTech (http://www.mines-paristech.fr/Accueil/)
- Human Reliability Analysis (http://reliability.sandia.gov/Human_Factor_Engineering/Human_Reliability_Analysis/human_reliability_analysis.html) at the US Sandia National Laboratories
- Center for Human Reliability Studies (http://www.orau.gov/chrs/chrs.htm) at the US Oak Ridge National Laboratory
- Flight Cognition Laboratory (http://hsi.arc.nasa.gov/flightcognition/) at NASA Ames Research Center
- David Woods (http://csel.eng.ohio-state.edu/woods/) at the Cognitive Systems Engineering Laboratory (http://csel.eng.ohio-state.edu/) at The Ohio State University
- Sidney Dekker's Leonardo da Vinci Laboratory for Complexity and Systems Thinking, Lund University, Sweden (http://www.leonardo.lth.se)

Media coverage

- "Human Reliability. We break down just like machines" (http://www.iienet.org/magazine/magazinefiles/IENOV2004_outliers_p66.pdf) Industrial Engineer - November 2004, 36(11): 66

Networking

- High Reliability Management group at LinkedIn.com (http://www.linkedin.com/groups?gid=673677)

Influence diagrams approach

Influence Diagrams Approach (IDA) is a technique used in the field of Human reliability Assessment (HRA), for the purposes of evaluating the probability of a human error occurring throughout the completion of a specific task. From such analyses measures can then be taken to reduce the likelihood of errors occurring within a system and therefore lead to an improvement in the overall levels of safety. There exist three primary reasons for conducting an HRA; error identification, error quantification and error reduction. As there exist a number of techniques used for such purposes, they can be split into one of two classifications; first generation techniques and second generation techniques. First generation techniques work on the basis of the simple dichotomy of 'fits/doesn't fit' in the matching of the error situation in context with related error identification and quantification and second generation techniques are more theory based in their assessment and quantification of errors. 'HRA techniques have been utilised in a range of industries including healthcare, engineering, nuclear, transportation and business sector; each technique has varying uses within different disciplines.

An Influence diagram(ID) is essentially a graphical representation of the probabilistic interdependence between Performance Shaping Factors (PSFs), factors which pose a likelihood of influencing the success or failure of the performance of a task. The approach originates from the field of decision analysis and uses expert judgement in its formulations. It is dependent upon the principal of human reliability and results from the combination of factors such as organisational and individual factors, which in turn combine to provide an overall influence. There exists a chain of influences in which each successive level affects the next. The role of the ID is to depict these influences and the nature of the interrelationships in a more comprehensible format. In this way, the diagram may be used to represent the shared beliefs of a group of experts on the outcome of a particular action and the factors that may or may not influence that outcome. For each of the identified influences quantitative values are calculated, which are then used to derive final Human Error Probability (HEP) estimates.

Background

IDA is a decision analysis based framework which is developed through eliciting expert judgement through group workshops. Unlike other first generation HRA, IDA explicitly considers the inter-dependency of operator and organisational PSFs. The IDA approach was first outlined by Howard and Matheson [1], and then developed specifically for the nuclear industry by Embrey et al. [2].

IDA Methodology

The IDA methodology is conducted in a series of 10 steps as follows:

1. *Describe all relevant conditioning events* Experts who have sufficient knowledge of the situation under evaluation form a group; in depth knowledge is essential for the technique to be used to its optimal potential. The chosen individuals include a range of experts - typically those with first hand experience in the operational context under consideration – such as plant supervisors, reliability assessors, human factor specialists and designers. The group collectively assesses and gradually develops a representation of the most significant influences which will affect the success of the situation. The resultant diagram is useful in that it identifies both immediate and underlying influences of the considered factors with regards their effect on the situation under assessment and upon one another.

2. *Refine the target event definition* The event which is the basis of the assessment requires to be defined as tightly as possible.

3. *Balance of Evidence* The next stage is to select a middle-level event in the situation and using each of the bottom level influences, assess the weight of evidence, also known as the 'balance of evidence'; this represents expert analysis of the likelihood that a specific state of influence or combination of the various influences is existent within the considered situation.

4. *Assess the weight of evidence for this middle-level influence, which is conditional on bottom-level influences* 5. Repeat 3 and 4 for the remaining middle-level and bottom-level influences These three steps are conducted in the aim of determining the extent to which the influences exist in the process, alone and in different combinations, and their conditional effects.

6. *Assess probabilities of target event conditional on middle-level influences*

7. *Calculate the unconditional probability of target event and unconditional weight of evidence of middle-level influences* For the various combinations of influences that have been considered, the experts identify direct estimates of the likelihood of either success or failure.

8. *Compare these results to the holistic judgements of HEPs by the assessors. Revise if necessary to reduce discrepancies.* At this stage the probabilities derived from the use of the technique are compared to holistic estimates from the experts, which have been derived through an Absolute Probability Judgement (APJ) process. Discrepancies are discussed and resolved within the group as required.

9. *Repeat above steps until assessors are finished refining their judgements* The above steps are iterated, in which all experts share opinions, highlight new aspects to the problem and revise the initially made assessments of the situation. The process is deemed complete when all participants reach a consensus that any misgivings about the discrepancies are resolved.

10. *Perform sensitivity analyses* If individual experts remain to be unsure of the discrepancies about the assessments which have been made, then sensitivity analysis can be used to determine the extent to which individual influence assessments affect the target event HEP. Conducting a cost-benefit analysis is also possible at this stage of the process.

Example

The diagram below depicts an influence diagram which can be applied to any human reliability assessment [3].

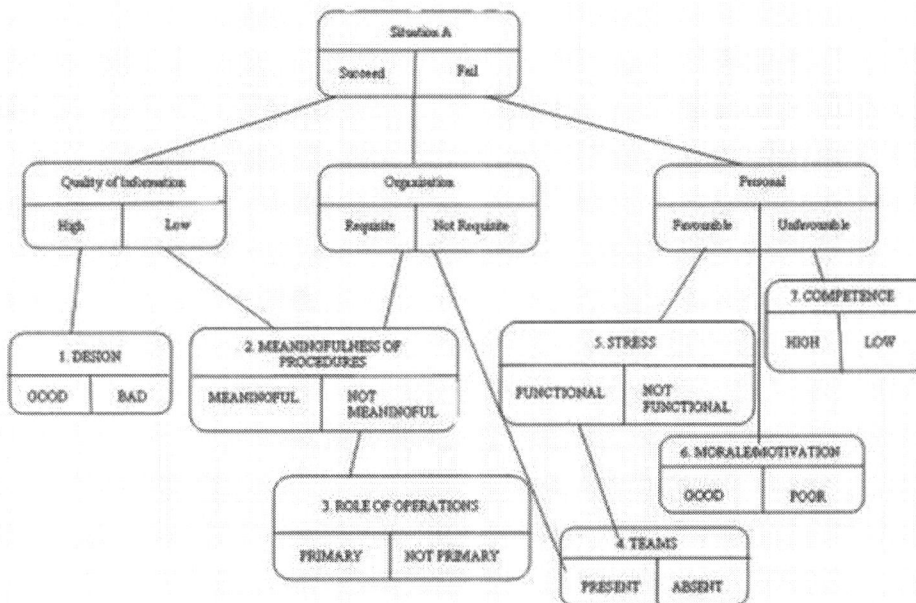

This diagram was originally developed for use in the HRA of a scenario within the settings of a nuclear power situation. The diagram depicts the direct influences of each of the factors on the situation under consideration as well as providing as indication as to the way in which some of the factors affect each other.

There are 7 first level influences on the outcome of the high level task, numbered 1 to 7. Each of these describes an aspect of the task under assessment, which requires to be judged as one of two states.

- The design of the task is judged to be either good or bad
- The meaningfulness of the procedures involved in the completion of the task are simply meaningful or not meaningful
- Operators either possess a role in the task that is of primary importance or that is not considered as a primary role
- For the purposes of completing the considered task, they may or not be a formation of teams of individuals
- the stress levels associated with the task can affect performance and render individuals either functional or not functional
- the surrounding work ethic and environment in which the task takes place will provide either a good level of morale or a poor motivation level
- competence of the individuals who are responsible for carrying out the task is either of a high level or a low level

Differing combinations of these first stage influences affect the state of those on the second level.

- The quality of information, which can either be classed as good or bad, is dependent upon the meaningfulness of the procedures of the task and the task design.
- The organisation, whether it is assessed as either requisite or not requisite, is determined by the role of operations functions in completing the task, the meaningfulness of the procedures and whether or not teams are formed to complete the task
- The personal aspect of the task can be judged as either favourable for successful completion or unfavourable. The way in which this is assessed is dependent on competence level of the concerned individuals, stress levels present, morale/motivation levels of the individuals and whether or not teams are formed to complete the task.

By assessing the state of the second level influences, the quality of information, organisation and personal factors, the overall likelihood of either success or failure of the task can be calculated by means of conditional probability calculations.

Advantages of IDA

- Dependence between PSFs is explicitly acknowledged and modelled [3]
- It can be used at any task "level", i.e. it can be used in a strategic overview or in a very fine breakdown of a task element [3]
- Data requirements are small and no calibration is necessary [3]
- PSFs are precisely defined and their influence is explored in depth [3]
- PSFs and other influence creating error producing conditions are prioritised and if desired, the less significant ones may be ignored
- Sensitivity analysis is possible with use of this technique [3]
- It is possible to generate high amounts of qualitative data through the group discussion process

Disadvantages of IDA

- Building IDAs is highly resource-intensive in terms of organising and supporting an extensive group session involving a suitable range of experts [3]
- Eliciting unbiased HEPs requires further research with regards to their accuracy and justification [3]

References

[1] Howard, R.A. & Matheson, J.E. (2005) Influence diagrams. Decision Analysis. 2(3) 127-143.

[2] EMBREY, D.E. & al, e. (1985) Appendix D: A Socio-Technical Approach to Assessing Human Reliability (STAHR) in Pressurized Thermal Shock Evaluation of the Calvert Cliffs Unit 1, Nuclear Power Plant. Research Report on DOE Contract 105840R21400, Selby, D. (Ed. Oak Ridge National Laboratory, , Oak Ridge, TN.

[3] Humphreys, P. (1995). Human Reliability Assessor's Guide. Human Factors in Reliability Group.

[4] Ainsworth, L.K., & Kirwan, B. (1992). A Guide to Task Analysis. Taylor & Francis.

InfoSTEP

InfoSTEP

Type	Private
Industry	IT Products IT services IT consulting
Founded	1998
Founder(s)	Sagar Anisingaraju Sanjeev Kumar
Headquarters	Santa Clara, California, USA
Key people	**Sagar Anisingaraju** (CEO) **Sanjeev Kumar** (COO)
Services	IT Products IT Services IT Consulting
Website	Infostep.com [1]

InfoSTEP is a company that sells products in the areas of Business Intelligence, Corporate Governance, Risk Management, Data Integration, Data Quality, Data Services, Emerging Technologies, Cloud Computing, Master data management and IT Business Management (ITBM).

InfoSTEP's products include **eLustroHarmony** (Enterprise solution for corporate governance), **eLustroCSA** (Enterprise solution for Control Self Assessments) and **eLustroCEM** (Enterprise solution for managing survey programs).

InfoSTEP Inc. is headquartered in Santa Clara, CA and is an independent subsidiary of MIC Electronics Ltd. InfoSTEP also has offices in India (Mumbai, Hyderabad), Australia and Dubai.

History

InfoSTEP was founded in 1998 by Sagar Anisingaraju and Sanjeev Kumar and is headquartered in Santa Clara, California.

In Nov 2005, InfoSTEP opened a Centre of excellence (COE) for BI and BPM in Hyderabad, India.

MIC Electronics, the leader in Light Emitting Diode (LED) display systems acquired majority stake in InfoSTEP in December 2007. However, InfoSTEP continues to operate as an independent subsidiary of MIC Electronics.

In 2008, InfoSTEP Inc. and Business Objects presented Quote and Proposal management with Business Applications On Demand

In 2009, InfoSTEP launched its Health care and Life Sciences Practice Micro-site.

Saama Technologies, a pure play BI company, acquired majority stake (68.26%) in InfoSTEP from MIC Electronics in January 2011.

Awards & Recognition

"Best Performing New Solution Provider" for 2007 by Business Objects.

"Best SAP Business User Service Provider" in Indian geography for 2009-2010.

"Best Service Partner Award in BU Space" @ SAP Partner excellence council meet.

Products

eLustroHarmony

eLustroHarmony is an application framework built around COSO control model. It enables CEOs, CFOs and process owners to monitor internal controls in real time and manage business risks within the acceptable tolerance levels. eLustroHarmony provides an open framework and operational tools to configure the control catalogs for the chosen methodology of implementation.

eLustroCSA

Control Self-Assessment (CSA) is a process to assure adequacy of internal controls and to identify opportunities for improvement.

eLustroCEM

eLustroCEM is a suite of tools to manage customer and employee feedback throughout their lifecycle. It includes both operational and analytic tools for capture, analysis and integration.

Services

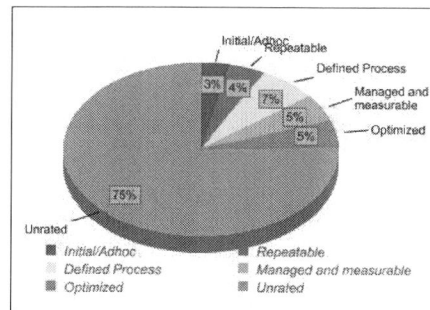

Control health maps across processes

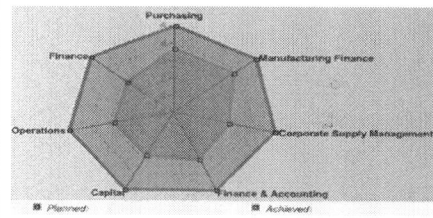

eLustroCSA Executive Dashboard

Business Intelligence

InfoSTEP's solutions in Business Intelligence are geared towards increasing the process efficiencies.

Process Measurement and Improvement

Process Improvement and Measurement forms the actionable part of Business Intelligence. InfoSTEP's approach is based on Six Sigma DMAIC methodology enhanced with pre-defined KPIs specific to the industry and specific business process under consideration.

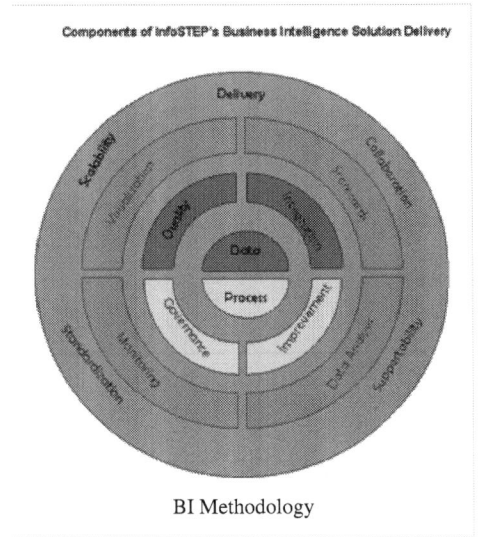

BI Methodology

Enterprise Information Management (EIM)

InfoSTEP's EIM approach involves delivering complete solutions or point solutions, depending on client need.

Business Intelligence Solution Implementation

InfoSTEP's approach in Business Intelligence Solution implementation is based on InfoLEADERSHIP, the methodology that addresses risks and enables proactive management of implementation, enabling highest success rate. As part of the methodology, InfoSTEP also address Change Management related to users by way of training, process flows and prototype reviews.

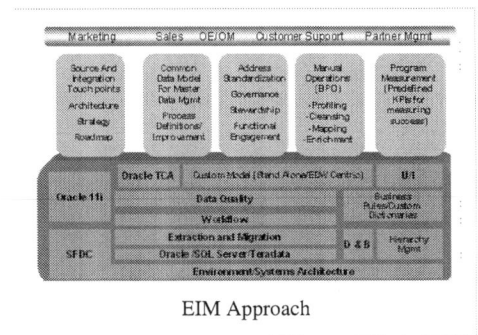

EIM Approach

Platform Migration

InfoSTEP Inc.'s platform migration approach is based on InfoUPGRADE, an upgrade specific methodology that addresses unique challenges associated with migration activities.

Emerging Technologies

InfoSTEP's Emerging Technologies and Information Systems Group (ETIS) offers expertise in helping customers solve complex business problems, implementing business critical IT applications and providing enterprise application integration solutions.

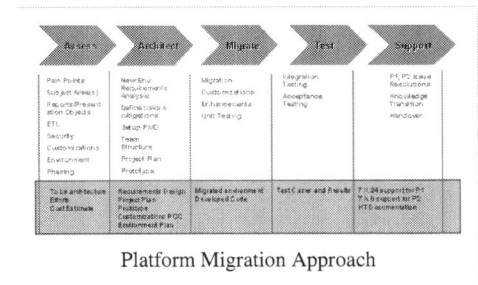

Platform Migration Approach

OnDemand

Elustro On Demand

InfoSTEP's eLustro OnDemand enables connect to customers, partners and users through powerful, scalable and configurable Feedback Collaborative Platform, specially configured to Salesforce.com users.

IT Business Management

InfoSTEP's IT Business Management (ITBM) Practice provides business advisory and implementation services to help customers run their IT as a business.

Partners

InfoSTEP has partnered with leading technology and solution providers. InfoSTEP's list of partners include:

- Aster Data Systems
- BMC Software
  - Consulting Service Partner
  - Enterprise Service Management Solution Partner
- Itko LISA
- Informatica
- Interwoven
- KnowledgeTree
- MicroStrategy
- Oracle Corporation
- SAP
  - Business Objects Migration Specialist
  - Business Objects Authorized Consulting Partner
  - Business Objects Gold Partner
  - Business Objects Solution Provider Partner
- theAppexchange

Customers

InfoSTEP's customer base includes some of the major names like Adobe Systems, Alameda Alliance for Health, American Academy of Ophthalmology, APL, Applied Biosystems, Applied Materials, Asyst, BEA Systems, Bharti AXA General Insurance, BMC Software, Bull Services, Business Objects, Cisco Systems, Citigroup, E-Trade, EA - Electronic Arts, Ebay, HDFC Bank, Hindustan Unilever, I2 Technologies, Informatica, Intuit, Intuitive Surgical, Itko, ITM, Juniper Networks, Kotak Life, Kotak Securities, Linksys, MCI Systemhouse, Meeting Expectations, Nortel, OKI Semiconductors, Oracle Corporation, Pacific Gas and Electric Company, Plantronics, Power Integrations, Reserve Bank of India, Selectica, SGI, Spice Telecom, Stanford School of Medicine, Sun Microsystems, Symantec, Verisign, Veritas Software, Wells Fargo, Winery Exchange, WJ Communications, Yahoo.

Business Intelligence KPI's

InfoSTEP Inc. Center of Excellence conducted frequent surveys among various industries and current InfoSTEP Inc. clients to understand trends, vendor satisfaction, project indicators. These Business Intelligence KPIs are available for free and can be downloaded from their website.

References

[1] http://www.infostep.com

Inherent risk (accounting)

Inherent risk, in auditing, is the risk that the account or section being audited is materially misstated without considering internal controls due to error or fraud. The assessment of inherent risk depends on the professional judgment of the auditor, and it is done after assessing the business environment of the entity being audited.

Range of assessment

Inherent risk is typically assessed using a scale, with assessments being either low, medium, or high. Assessments of medium or high risk will require additional audit work to be performed in order to reduce the audit risk.

Inherent risk is a client risk; since it is outside of the auditor's control the auditor's response is to adjust detection risk.[1]

Factors in assessing inherent risk

Considerations which an auditor may include in assessing inherent risk include:

- complexity of determining the account amount (if it is an estimate or a financial statement disclosure)
- past history (including any audit differences identified)
- the circumstances of the entity's business environment
- management's overall risk awareness

For example, the valuation of accounts receivable would have a higher inherent risk assessment since the amount of allowance is subjective and is an accounting estimate. In contrast, the valuation assertion of cash and cash equivalents would have a lower inherent risk as the amount involves no estimation and is thus less susceptible to manipulation.

References

[1] 1

Jackson & Stent, 2010: Auditing Notes for South African Students (7th Edition)

External links

Discussion of inherent risk (http://www.abrema.net/abrema/IR_g.html)

Insurable risk

An **insurable risk** is a risk that meets the ideal criteria for efficient insurance. The concept of insurable risk underlies nearly all insurance decisions.

For a risk to be insurable, several things need to be true:

- The insurer must be able to charge a premium high enough to cover not only claims expenses, but also to cover the insurer's expenses. In other words, the risk cannot be catastrophic, or so large that no insurer could hope to pay for the loss.

- The nature of the loss must be definite and financially measurable. That is, there should not be room for argument as to whether or not payment is due, nor as to what amount the payment should be.

- The loss should be random in nature, else the insured may engage in adverse selection (antiselection).

Insurance is not effective for risks that are not insurable risks. For example, risks that are too large cannot be insured, or the premiums would be so high as to make purchasing the insurance infeasible. Also, risks that are not measurable, if insured, will be difficult if not impossible for the insurer to quantify, and thus they cannot charge the correct premium. They will need to charge a conservatively high premium in order to mitigate the risk of paying too large a claim. The premium will thus be higher than ideal, and inefficient. Passing of risk involves both party to the contract. The general rule is that unless otherwise agreed, risk passes with title. An agreement to the contrary may be either expressed or implied.

EXCEPTIONS TO THE GENERAL RULE: (A) RISK INCIDENTAL TO TRANSIT: The law provided that where the seller undertakes to make delivery of the goods to the buyer, risk attendant to the system of transportation or voyage contemplated will be borne by the buyer unless the parties agreed to the contrary. This is referred to as insurable risk. (B) RISK ATTRIBUTABLE TO FAULT OF EITHER PARTY: Any damage or loss which arises as a result of the fault or neglect of the seller or the buyer or their respective agents as the case may be shall be borne by that party at fault. (C) GOODS PERISHING: Goods perish not only when they cease to exist physically but also when they cease to exist in a commercial sense, e.g fresh milk gone sour.

International Risk Governance Council

Founded in June 2003 at the initiative of the Swiss government, the **International Risk Governance Council (IRGC)** is an independent and neutral organisation whose purpose is to help improve the understanding and management of potentially global risks that have impacts on human health and safety, the environment, the economy and society at large. This involves working to develop concepts of risk governance, anticipating major risk issues and providing risk governance policy advice for key decision-makers.

IRGC focuses in particular on emerging, systemic risks for which governance deficits exist, and aims to provide recommendations for how policymakers can correct these deficits. Many of these risks are complex, uncertain, or even ambiguous. In most cases, the potential benefits and risks interconnect. By facilitating a better understanding of these risks and their scientific, political, social, and economic contexts, IRGC aims to foster improvements in risk governance that will ultimately optimise risk-related decision-making and maximise public trust in governance processes and structures.

Where important, global risks are concerned, IRGC considers it essential that the principles of integrated risk governance become accepted and implemented at the very highest levels of decision-making. It believes that, by combining forces and strengthening their scientific research agendas, governments, industry, international and large non-governmental organisations can achieve more coherent and better science-based policymaking, regulation and risk communication, resulting in implementation of the best possible options for governing global risks.

External links

- Official Website [1]

References

[1] http://www.irgc.org

ITGC

IT general controls (ITGC) are controls that apply to all systems components, processes, and data for a given organization or information technology (IT) environment. The objectives of ITGCs are to ensure the proper development and implementation of applications, as well as the integrity of programs, data files, and computer operations.

The most common ITGCs:

- Logical access controls over infrastructure, applications, and data.
- System development life cycle controls.
- Program change management controls.
- Data center physical security controls.
- System and data backup and recovery controls.
- Computer operation controls.

General Computer Controls

ITGCs may also be referred to as General Computer Controls which are defined as: Controls, other than application controls, which relate to the environment within which computer-based application systems are developed, maintained and operated, and which are therefore applicable to all applications. The objectives of general controls are to ensure the proper development and implementation of applications, the integrity of program and data files and of computer operations. Like application controls, general controls may be either manual or programmed. Examples of general controls include the development and implementation of an IS strategy and an IS security policy, the organization of IS staff to separate conflicting duties and planning for disaster prevention and recovery.

Global Technology Audit Guide (GTAG)

GTAGs are written in straightforward business language to address a timely issue related to information technology (IT) management, control, and security. To date, The IIA has released GTAGs on the following topics:

- **GTAG 1:** Information Technology Controls
- **GTAG 2:** Change and Patch Management Controls: Critical for Organizational Success
- **GTAG 3:** Continuous Auditing: Implications for Assurance, Monitoring, and Risk Assessment
- **GTAG 4:** Management of IT Auditing
- **GTAG 5:** Managing and Auditing Privacy Risks
- **GTAG 6:** Managing and Auditing IT Vulnerabilities
- **GTAG 7:** Information Technology Outsourcing
- **GTAG 8:** Auditing Application Controls
- **GTAG 9:** Identity and Access Management

References

GTAG 8: Christine Bellino, Jefferson Wells, July 2007 GTAG 8: Steve Hunt, Enterprise Controls Consulting LP, Enterprise Controls Consulting LP, July 2007

- ISACA Glossary of terms [1]

External links

- The Institute of Internal Auditors [2]
- Information Systems Audit and Control Association [3]

References

[1] http://www.isaca.org/glossary.htm

[2] http://www.theiia.org

[3] http://www.isaca.org

Journal of Contingencies and Crisis Management

Journal of Contingencies and Crisis Management	
Abbreviated title (ISO)	*JCCM*
Discipline	International Relations Peace and conflict studies
Language	English
Publication details	
Publisher	Blackwell Publishing
Publication history	1993 - present
Frequency	quarterly
Indexing	
ISSN	0966-0879 [1]
Links	
• [JCCM [2] Journal homepage]	

The **Journal of Contingencies and Crisis Management** (JCCM) is a multi-disciplinary, peer-reviewed academic journal that covers all theoretical and practical aspects relating to crisis management.

JCCM is the leading journal on the subject of crisis management. It was founded in 1993 by Prof. Uriel Rosenthal [3] and Prof. Alexander Kouzmin (University of Plymouth). The current editor is Prof. Ira Helsloot (Vrije Universiteit Amsterdam).

Subject areas include: emergency management, risk management, contingency plans, foreign policies, ecological crisis, financial crisis, international relations, security policies, and conflict resolution.

JCCM is published by Blackwell. Reviews from olderissue are regularly re-published in the Political ReviewNet database.

References

[1] http://www.worldcat.org/issn/0966-0879
[2] http://www.blackwellpublishing.com/journal.asp?ref=0966-0879&site=1
[3] biography of Prof.Dr. Uri Rosenthal (http://www.parlement.com/9291000/bio/02273)

External links

• *Journal of Contingencies and Crisis Management* homepage (http://www.blackwellpublishing.com/journal. asp?ref=0966-0879&site=1)

Knightian uncertainty

In economics, **Knightian uncertainty** is risk that is immeasurable, not possible to calculate.

Knightian uncertainty is named after University of Chicago economist Frank Knight (1885–1972), who distinguished risk and uncertainty in his work *Risk, Uncertainty, and Profit*:[1]

> "Uncertainty must be taken in a sense radically distinct from the familiar notion of Risk, from which it has never been properly separated.... The essential fact is that 'risk' means in some cases a quantity susceptible of measurement, while at other times it is something distinctly not of this character; and there are far-reaching and crucial differences in the bearings of the phenomena depending on which of the two is really present and operating.... It will appear that a measurable uncertainty, or 'risk' proper, as we shall use the term, is so far different from an unmeasurable one that it is not in effect an uncertainty at all."

Related concepts

Common-cause and special-cause

The difference between predictable variation and unpredictable variation is one of the fundamental issues in the philosophy of probability, and different probability interpretations treat predictable and unpredictable variation differently. The distinction and debate has a long history, referred to as and discussed at common-cause and special-cause.

Ellsberg paradox

The Ellsberg paradox is based on the difference between these two types of risk, and the problems it poses for utility theory – one is faced with an urn that contains 30 red balls and 60 balls that are either all yellow or all black, and one then draws a ball from the urn. This poses both *uncertainty* – whether the non-red balls are all yellow or all black – and *probability* – whether the ball is red or non-red, which is ⅓ vs. ⅔. Expressed preferences in choices faced with this situation reveal that people do not treat these risks the same. This is also termed "ambiguity aversion".

Controversy

Nassim Nicholas Taleb has developed the Black swan theory where there is no distinction between any different kinds of uncertainty. In his book *The Black Swan*, in the section subtitled "The uncertainty of the nerd", he writes:

> In real life you do not know the odds; you need to discover them, and the sources of uncertainty are not defined.

> Economists, who do not consider what was found by noneconomists worthwhile, draw an artificial distinction between Knightian risk (which you can compute) and Knightian uncertainty (which you cannot compute), after one Frank Knight, who rediscovered the notion of unknown uncertainty and did a lot of thinking but perhaps never took risks, or perhaps lived in the vicinity of a casino.

> Had he taken financial or economic risk he would have realized that these "computable" risks are largely absent from real life! They are laboratory contraptions.

References

[1] Knight, F.H. (1921) Risk, Uncertainty, and Profit (http://www.archive.org/details/riskuncertaintyp00knigrich). Boston, MA: Hart, Schaffner & Marx; Houghton Mifflin Company

Manufactured risk

Manufactured risks are risks that are produced by the modernization process, particularly by innovative developments in science and technology. They create risk environments that have little historical reference, and are therefore largely unpredictable. Manufactured risk produces a risk society.

References

• Giddens, Anthony (1999) "Risk and Responsibility" Modern Law Review 62(1): 4

Meteorological intelligence

Meteorological intelligence is information measured, gathered, compiled, exploited, analyzed and disseminated by meteorologists, climatologists and hydrologists to characterize the current state and/or predict the future state of the atmosphere at a given location and time. Meteorological intelligence is a subset of environmental intelligence and is synonymous with the term weather intelligence.

The earliest known use of the term "meteorological intelligence" in a written document dates to 1854 on pg. 168 of the Eighth Annual Report of the Board of Regents of the Smithsonian Institution. This report discusses the Smithsonian Institution's initiative to transmit meteorological intelligence via telegraph lines. An early reference to "meteorological intelligence" in England dates an 1866 issue of The Edinburgh Review which was a prominent Scottish journal during the 19th century (Reeve 1866, pg. 75). Another documented, early known use of the term dates to 1874 in a historical compilation entitled, "The American Historical Record" (Lossing 1874, pg. 125). In this book, Lossing uses the term to refer to weather observations transmitted over telegraph lines for the purpose of studying the nature of storms with the ultimate goal of enhancing public safety through the issuance of storm warnings. This mission was carried out by the Army Signal Service starting in the 1870s who was responsible for communication (via telegraph) of technical intelligence for the army as well as "meteorological intelligence" for the general welfare of the country (Ingersoll 1879, pg. 156).

From the viewpoint of the intelligence community, the term meteorological intelligence is more limited in its use referring to the use of clandestine or technical means to learn about environmental conditions over enemy territory (Shulsky and Schmitt 2002). In the military context, weather information is often referred to as meteorological or environmental intelligence (Hinsley 1990, pg. 420; Platt 1957, pg. 14; U.S. Congress, pg. 164).

With regard to private sector meteorology, the term meteorological intelligence is a broad term of art that is primarily associated with observed and forecast weather information provided to decision makers in one of a number of weather sensitive business areas including: Energy, forestry, agriculture, telecommunications, transportation, aviation, entertainment, retail and construction (CMOS 2001, pg. 23) . It is considered a key aspect of weather risk management for the legal and insurance industries.

Notes

References

- Canadian Meteorological and Oceanographic Society (CMOS), 2001: "Baseline Status of Private Meteorological Services Sector in Canada", prepared by Global Change Strategies International
- Dear, I.C.B. and Foot, M.R.D.: "meteorological intelligence." The Oxford Companion to World War II. Oxford University Press. 2001. Encyclopedia.com. (March 10, 2009).
- Hinsley, Francis F., 1990: "British Intelligence in the Second World War: Its Influence on Strategy and Operations". Cambridge University Press
- Ingersoll, Lurton D., 1879: "A History of the War Department of the United States", published by Francis D. Alohun, 613 pages
- Lossing, Benson J., ed., 1874: "The American Historical Record", Vol. III
- Platt, Washington, 1957: "Strategic Intelligence Production: Basic Principles", published by P.A. Praeger, 302 pages
- Reeve, Henry, ed., 1866: "The Edinburgh Review", Vol CXXIV, published by Archibald Constable, London, 600 pages
- Shulsky, Abram N. and Schmitt, Gary J., 2002: "Silent Warfare: Understanding the World of Intelligence", 3rd ed., 285 pages
- Smithsonian Institution, 1854: "Eighth Annual Report of the Board of Regents of the Smithsonian Institution", published by The Institution, U.S. Gov't Print Off., 310 pages
- U.S. Congress, Office of Technology Assessment, New Technology for NATO: Implementing Follow-On Force Attack, OTA-ISC-309 (Washington, D.C.: US Government Printing Office, June 1987)
- Yokoyama, K., 1993: Studies on the utilization of the mesh meteorological intelligence, *Bulletin of the Yamagata Prefectural Agricultural Experiment Station (Japan)*, 31-37

External links

- http://www.1911encyclopedia.org/Smithsonian_Institution
- http://www.cmos.ca/Privatesector/metstrategyappB.pdf
- http://www.cdef.terre.defense.gouv.fr/publications/doctrine/doctrine03/US/doctrine/art8.pdf
- http://www.scotsatwar.co.uk/AZ/dday.htm
- http://books.google.com/books?id=gIzUGFtsExAC&dq=meteorological+intelligence& ei=8my2Sa_jKIHqkwTd3pn9Bg
- http://www.encyclopedia.com/doc/1O129-meteorologicalintelligenc.html

Micromort

A **micromort** is a unit of risk measuring a one-in-a-million probability of death (from micro- and mortality). Micromorts can be used to measure riskiness of various day-to-day activities. A **microprobability** is a one-in-a million chance of some event; thus a micromort is the microprobability of death. The micromort concept was introduced by Ronald A. Howard who pioneered the modern practice of decision analysis.[1]

Human values

Money

An application of micromorts is measuring the value that humans place on risk: for example, one can consider the amount of money one would have to pay a person to get him or her to accept a one-in-a-million chance of death (or conversely the amount that someone might be willing to pay to avoid a one-in-a-million chance of death). When put thus, people claim a high number but when inferred from their day-to-day actions (e.g., how much they are willing to pay for safety features on cars) a typical value is around $50 (in 2009).[2] [3]

Baseline

The average risk of dying per day can be calculated from the average lifetime. Assuming this is 70 years, that means there is one death for every 25,550 days lived (70 x 365 = 25,550).

The number of micromorts per day is one million divided by that number of days; in this case, about 39 micromorts acquired individually every day. The number of micromorts per hour is divided by 24 hours; that is about 1,63 micromorts per hour. This is just an average across an entire population: the number of micromorts per day will vary across different categories of people, such as by age, sex and lifestyle.

An alternative way of getting the same figure is to take the number of people dying each day in the UK (about 2500), and divide it by the total population (60 million). These figures include all deaths. When natural deaths are excluded, the result measures the risk of premature death, which is roughly one micromort per day. In the UK, approximately 50 people die each day, on average, from non-natural causes [4] .

Additional

Activities that increase the death risk by one micromort, and their associated cause of death:

- smoking 1.4 cigarettes (cancer, heart disease)[5]
- drinking 0.5 liter of wine (cirrhosis of the liver)[5]
- spending 1 hour in a coal mine (black lung disease)[5]
- spending 3 hours in a coal mine (accident))[5]
- living 2 days in New York or Boston (air pollution)[5]
- living 2 months in Denver (cancer from cosmic radiation)[5]
- living 2 months with a smoker (cancer, heart disease)[5]
- drinking Miami water for 1 year (cancer from chloroform)[5]
- Living 150 years within 20 miles of a nuclear power plant (cancer from radiation)[5]
- eating 100 charcoal-broiled steaks (cancer from benzopyrene)[5]
- eating 40 tablespoons of peanut butter (liver cancer from Aflatoxin B)[5]
- eating 1000 bananas, (cancer from radioactive 1 kBED of Potassium-40)
- traveling 6 minutes by canoe (accident)[5]
- traveling 6 miles (10 km) by motorbike (accident)[6]
- traveling 230 miles (370 km) by car (accident)[6]

- traveling 6000 miles (9656 km) by train (accident)[6]
- flying 1000 miles (1609 km) by jet (accident)[5]
- flying 6000 miles (9656 km) by jet (cancer from cosmic radiation)[5]
- receiving one 10mrem chest X-ray in a good hospital (cancer from radiation)[7]
- taking 1 ecstasy tablet[6]

Hang gliding involves a risk of eight micromorts per trip while scuba diving involves five and a parachute jump (in the US) is about 17.[6] [8]

References

[1] Howard, R. A. (1980). "On making life and death decisions". In J. Richard, C. Schwing, Walter A. Albers. Societal Risk Assessment: How Safe Is Safe Enough? General Motors Research Laboratories. New York: Plenum Press. ISBN 0306405547.

[2] Howard, R. A. (1989). "Microrisks for Medical Decision Analysis". *International Journal of Technology Assessment in Health Care* **5** (3): 357–370. doi:10.1017/S026646230000742X. PMID 10295520.

[3] Russell, Stuart; Norvig, Peter (2009). *Artificial Intelligence* (3rd ed.). Prentice Hall. p. 616. ISBN 0136042597.

[4] ONS Mortality statistics (http://www.statistics.gov.uk/downloads/theme_health/DR2008/DR_08.pdf), UK *Office of National Statistics* 2009, ISSN 1757–1375, accessed 2010-12-08

[5] * Howard, Ron RIsky Decisions (http://stanford-online.stanford.edu/sdrmda61w/session10b/slides/sld031.htm) (Slide show), Stanford University

 - Wilson, Richard. "Analyzing the Risks of Daily Life" (http://tobaccodocuments.org/lor/03732381-2387.html). *Technology Review*. . Retrieved 2011-03-16.

[6] Spiegelhalter, David (10 February 2009). "230 miles in a car equates to one micromort: The agony and Ecstasy of risk-taking" (http://www.timesonline.co.uk/tol/comment/columnists/guest_contributors/article5696688.ece). *The Times* (London). . Retrieved 19 April 2009.

[7] "Radiation and Risk" (http://www.physics.isu.edu/radinf/risk.htm). Idaho State University. . Retrieved 2011-03-16.

[8] http://www.skydivingmagazine.com/faq.htm

Further reading

- Ronald A. Howard (1984). "On Fates Comparable to Death". *Management Science* **30** (4): 407–422. doi:10.1287/mnsc.30.4.407.

- Center for the Study and Improvement of Regulation. "What is a MicroMort?" (http://micromorts.org/tutorial2.aspx).

Moral hazard

Moral hazard occurs when a party insulated from risk behaves differently than it would behave if it were fully exposed to the risk.

Moral hazard arises because an individual or institution does not take the full consequences and responsibilities of its actions, and therefore has a tendency to act less carefully than it otherwise would, leaving another party to hold some responsibility for the consequences of those actions. For example, a person with insurance against automobile theft may be less cautious about locking his or her car, because the negative consequences of vehicle theft are (partially) the responsibility of the insurance company.

Economists explain moral hazard as a special case of information asymmetry, a situation in which one party in a transaction has more information than another. In particular, moral hazard may occur if a party that is insulated from risk has more information about its actions and intentions than the party paying for the negative consequences of the risk. More broadly, moral hazard occurs when the party with more information about its actions or intentions has a tendency or incentive to behave inappropriately from the perspective of the party with less information.

Moral hazard also arises in a principal-agent problem, where one party, called an agent, acts on behalf of another party, called the principal. The agent usually has more information about his or her actions or intentions than the principal does, because the principal usually cannot completely monitor the agent. The agent may have an incentive to act inappropriately (from the viewpoint of the principal) if the interests of the agent and the principal are not aligned.

Theory

According to contract theory, moral hazard results from a situation in which a *hidden action* occurs.[1] Quoting Bengt Holmström,

> 'It has long been recognized that a problem of moral hazard may arise when individuals engage in risk sharing under conditions such that their privately taken actions affect the probability distribution of the outcome.'[2]

The name 'moral hazard' comes originally from the insurance industry. Insurance companies worried that protecting their clients from risks (like fire, or car accidents) might encourage those clients to behave in riskier ways (like smoking in bed, or not wearing seat belts). This problem may inefficiently discourage those companies from protecting their clients as much as they would like to be protected.

Economists argue that this inefficiency results from asymmetric information. If insurance companies could perfectly observe the actions of their clients, they could deny coverage to clients choosing risky actions (like smoking in bed, or not wearing seat belts), allowing them to provide thorough protection against risk (fire, accidents) without encouraging risky behavior. But since insurance companies cannot perfectly observe their clients' actions, they are discouraged from providing the amount of protection that would be provided in a world with perfect information.

Economists distinguish moral hazard from adverse selection, another problem that arises in the insurance industry, which is caused by *hidden information* rather than *hidden actions*.

The same underlying problem of unobservable actions also affects other contexts, besides the insurance industry. It also arises in banking and finance: if a financial institution knows it is protected by a lender of last resort, it may make riskier investments than it would in the absence of this protection.

Moral hazard problems also occur in employment relationships. When a firm is unable perfectly to observe the actions taken by its employees, it may be impossible to achieve efficient behavior in the workplace—for example, workers' effort may be inefficiently low. This is called the principal-agent problem, which is one possible explanation for the existence of involuntary unemployment.[3] Similar problems may also occur at the managerial level, because owners of firms (shareholders) may be unable to observe the actions of a firm's managers, opening the door to careless or self-serving decision-making.

In insurance

In insurance markets, moral hazard occurs when the behavior of the insured party changes in a way that raises costs for the insurer, since the insured party no longer bears the full costs of that behavior. Because individuals no longer bear the cost of medical services, they have an added incentive to ask for pricier and more elaborate medical service—which would otherwise not be necessary. In these instances, individuals have an incentive to over consume, simply because they no longer bear the full cost of medical services.

Two types of behavior can change. One type is the risky behavior itself, resulting in what is called *ex ante* moral hazard. In this case, insured parties behave in a more risky manner, resulting in more negative consequences that the insurer must pay for. For example, after purchasing automobile insurance, some may tend to be less careful about locking the automobile or choose to drive more, thereby increasing the risk of theft or an accident for the insurer. After purchasing fire insurance, some may tend to be less careful about preventing fires (say, by smoking in bed or neglecting to replace the batteries in fire alarms).

A second type of behavior that may change is the reaction to the negative consequences of risk, once they have occurred and once insurance is provided to cover their costs. This may be called *ex post* moral hazard. In this case, insured parties do not behave in a more risky manner that results in more negative consequences, but they do ask an insurer to pay for more of the negative consequences from risk as insurance coverage increases. For example, without medical insurance, some may forgo medical treatment due to its costs and simply deal with substandard health. But after medical insurance becomes available, some may ask an insurance provider to pay for the cost of medical treatment that would not have occurred otherwise.

Sometimes moral hazard is so severe it makes insurance policies impossible. Coinsurance, co-payments, and deductibles reduce the risk of moral hazard by increasing the out-of-pocket spending of consumers, which decreases their incentive to consume. Thus, the insured have a financial incentive to avoid making a claim.

Moral hazard has been studied by insurers[4] and academics. See works by Kenneth Arrow,[5] [6] [7] Tom Baker,[8] and John Nyman.

John Nyman suggests that two types of moral hazard exist: efficient and inefficient moral hazard. Efficient moral hazard is the viewpoint that the over consumption of medical care brought forth by insurance does not always produce a welfare loss to society. Rather, individuals attain better health through the increased consumption of medial care, making them more productive and netting an overall benefit to societal welfare. Also, Nyman suggests that individuals purchase insurance to obtain an income transfer when they become ill, as opposed to the traditionalist stance that individuals diversify risk via insurance.

Insurance analysts sometimes distinguish moral hazard from a related concept they call morale hazard.

In finance

Economist Paul Krugman described moral hazard as: "...any situation in which one person makes the decision about how much risk to take, while someone else bears the cost if things go badly."[9] Financial bail-outs of lending institutions by governments, central banks or other institutions can encourage risky lending in the future, if those that take the risks come to believe that they will not have to carry the full burden of potential losses. Lending institutions need to take risks by making loans, and usually the most risky loans have the potential for making the highest return. So-called "too big to fail" lending institutions can make risky loans that will pay handsomely if the investment turns out well, while being bailed out by the taxpayer if the investment turns out badly.

Taxpayers, depositors, and other creditors have often had to shoulder at least part of the burden of risky financial decisions made by lending institutions.[10] [11] [12] [13] According to the World Bank, of the nearly 100 banking crises that have occurred internationally during the last twenty-years, all were resolved by bail outs at taxpayer expense.

Economist Mark Zandi of Moody's Analytics described moral hazard as a root cause of the subprime mortgage crisis. He wrote: "...the risks inherent in mortgage lending became so widely dispersed that no one was forced to worry about the quality of any single loan. As shaky mortgages were combined, diluting any problems into a larger pool, the incentive for responsibility was undermined." He also wrote: "Finance companies weren't subject to the same regulatory oversight as banks. Taxpayers weren't on the hook if they went belly up [pre-crisis], only their shareholders and other creditors were. Finance companies thus had little to discourage them from growing as aggressively as possible, even if that meant lowering or winking at traditional lending standards."[14]

Moral hazard can also occur with borrowers. Borrowers may not act prudently (in the view of the lender) when they invest or spend funds recklessly. For example, credit card companies often limit the amount borrowers can spend with their cards, because without such limits borrowers may spend borrowed funds recklessly, leading to default.

Securitization of mortgages in America, beginning in 1983 at Salomon Brothers, was done in such a fashion that the people arranging the mortgage passed all the risk that the mortgage would fail to the next group down the line. With the present mortgage securitization system in the United States, many different debts of many different borrowers are piled together into a great big pool of debt, and then shares in the pool are sold to lots of creditors – which means that there is no one person responsible for verifying that any one particular loan is sound, that the assets securing that one particular loan are worth what they are supposed to be worth, that the borrower responsible for making payments on the loan can read and write the language that the papers that he signed were written in, or even that the paperwork exists and is in good order. Various people suggest that this may have caused 2007–2008 subprime mortgage financial crisis.[15]

In the period 1998-2007 regulators kept and published detailed statistics on the ethnicity and location of those receiving loans, but failed to pay similar attention to their credit worthiness, default rates or vulnerability to a housing downturn. The data that the regulators focused on was more relevant to politically mobilizing voting blocks in particular electorates than to keeping the financial system solvent.

Brokers, who were not lending their own money, pushed risk onto the lenders. Lenders, who sold mortgages soon after underwriting them, pushed risk onto investors. Investment banks bought mortgages and chopped up mortgage-backed securities into slices, some riskier than others. Investors bought securities and hedged against the risk of default and prepayment, pushing those risks further along. In a purely capitalist scenario, the last one holding the risk (like a game of musical chairs) is the one who faces the potential losses. In the 2007–2008 subprime crisis, however, national credit authorities – in the U.S., the Federal Reserve – assumed the ultimate risk on behalf of the citizenry at large.

Others believe that financial bailouts of lending institutions do not encourage risky lending behavior, since there is no guarantee to lending institutions that a bailout will occur. Decreased valuation of a corporation before any bailout will prevent risky, speculative business decisions by executives who conduct due diligence in their business transactions. The risk and burdens of loss became apparent to Lehman Brothers (who did not benefit from a bailout) and other financial institutions and mortgage companies such as Citibank and Countrywide Financial Corporation, whose valuation plunged during the subprime mortgage crisis.[16] [17] [18]

In management

Moral hazard can occur when upper management is shielded from the consequences of poor decision making. This situation can occur in a variety of situations, such as the following:

- When a manager has a secure position from which he or she cannot be readily removed.
- When a manager is protected by someone higher in the corporate structure, such as in cases of nepotism or pet projects.
- When funding and/or managerial status for a project is independent of the project's success.
- When the failure of the project is of minimal overall consequence to the firm, regardless of the local impact on the managed division.

- When a manager may readily lay blame on an innocent subordinate.
- When there is no clear means of determining who is accountable for a given project.

The software development industry has specifically identified this kind of risky behavior as a management anti-pattern, but it can occur in any field.

- When senior management has its own remuneration as its primary motivation for decision making (ex. hitting short term quarterly earnings targets or creating high medium term earnings, without due regard for the medium term effects on, or risks for the business, so that large bonuses can be justified in the current periods). The shielding occurs because any eventual hit to earnings can most likely be explained away, and in the worst case, if an executive is terminated, usually the executive keeps the high salary and bonuses from years past.

- When a numbered company is used for construction projects as a subsidiary of a larger enterprise. For example: a numbered company is incorporated to construct a condominium in Vancouver. It is built to meet the minimum building code requirements, but is not designed for Vancouver's typical weather patterns (mild temperatures, lots of moisture). A few years later, the exterior cladding of the building is disintegrating with mold and rot. The numbered company that built it has no assets, so the condominium owners must suffer a large expense to rebuild it. In this scenario, the senior officers of the numbered company and its shareholders used the protection of a numbered limited liability company in order to take higher risks in the design and construction. Unless the law and the regulators have some effective means to hold those responsible to account, the Moral Hazard would be expected to continue to future building projects.

In extreme cases, moral hazard can lead to or permit control fraud to occur, where actual illegal activities take place.

History of the term

According to research by Dembe and Boden,[19] the term dates back to the 17th century, and was widely used by English insurance companies by the late 19th century. Early usage of the term carried negative connotations, implying fraud or immoral behavior (usually on the part of an insured party). Dembe and Boden point out, however, that prominent mathematicians studying decision making in the 18th century used "moral" to mean "subjective", which may cloud the true ethical significance in the term.[20]

The concept of moral hazard was the subject of renewed study by economists in the 1960s, and at the time did not imply immoral behavior or fraud; rather, economists use the term to describe inefficiencies that can occur when risks are displaced, rather than on the ethics or morals of the involved parties.

References

[1] A. Mas-Colell, M. Whinston, and J. Green (1995), *Microeconomic Theory*. Chapter 14, 'The Principal-Agent Problem', p. 477.

[2] Holmstrom, B. (1979), 'Moral hazard and observability'. *Bell Journal of Economics*, pp. 74-91.

[3] C. Shapiro and J. Stiglitz (1984), 'Equilibrium unemployment as a worker discipline device'. *American Economic Review* 74 (3), pp. 433-444.

[4] Crosby, Everett (1905). "Fire Prevention" (http://jstor.org/stable/1011015). *Annals of the American Academy of Political and Social Science* (American Academy of Political and Social Science) **26** (2): 224–238. doi:10.1177/000271620502600215. . Crosby was one of the founders of the National Fire Protection Association, NFPA.org (http://www.nfpa.org/itemDetail.asp?categoryID=500&itemID=18020& URL=About Us/History)

[5] Arrow, Kenneth (1963). "Uncertainty and the Welfare Economics of Medical Care" (http://jstor.org/stable/1812044). *American Economic Review* (American Economic Association) **53** (5): 941–973. .

[6] Arrow, Kenneth (1965). *Aspects of the Theory of Risk Bearing*. Finland: Yrjö Jahnssonin Säätiö. OCLC 228221660.

[7] Arrow, Kenneth (1971). *Essays in the Theory of Risk- Bearing*. Chicago: Markham. ISBN 0841020019.

[8] Baker, Tom (1996). "On the Genealogy of Moral hazard". *Texas Law Review* **75**: 237. ISSN 00404411.

[9] Krugman, Paul (2009). *The Return of Depression Economics and the Crisis of 2008*. W.W. Norton Company Limited. ISBN 978-0-393-07101-6.

[10] Summers, Lawrence (2007-09-23). "Beware moral hazard fundamentalists" (http://www.ft.com/cms/s/0/5ffd2606-69e8-11dc-a571-0000779fd2ac.html). *Financial Times*. . Retrieved 2008-01-15.

[11] Brown, Bill (2008-11-19). "Uncle Sam as sugar daddy" (http://www.marketwatch.com/news/story/story. aspx?guid={9F4C2252-8BA7-459C-B34E-407DB32921C1}&siteid=rss). MarketWatch. . Retrieved 2008-11-30.

[12] "Common (Stock) Sense about Risk-Shifting and Bank Bailouts" (http://papers.ssrn.com/sol3/papers.cfm?abstract_id=1321666). SSRN.com. December 29, 2009. . Retrieved January 21, 2009.

[13] "Debt Overhang and Bank Bailouts" (http://papers.ssrn.com/sol3/papers.cfm?abstract_id=1336288). SSRN.com. February 2, 2009. . Retrieved February 2, 2009.

[14] Zandi, Mark (2009). *Financial Shock*. FT Press. ISBN 978-0-13-701663-1.

[15] Holden Lewis (2007-04-18). "'Moral hazard' helps shape mortgage mess" (http://www.bankrate.com/brm/news/mortgages/20070418_subprime_mortgage_morality_a1.asp?caret=3c). Bankrate.com. . Retrieved 2007-12-09.

[16] David Wighton (2008-09-24). "'Paulson bailout: seizing moral high ground can be hazardous'" (http://business.timesonline.co.uk/tol/business/columnists/article4813975.ece). TimesOnline. . Retrieved 2009-03-17.

[17] HFM (2009-03-16). "'The SEC Makes Wall Street More Fraudlent'" (http://www.justput.com/forum/showthread.php?t=6820). Justput.com Post # 17-26. . Retrieved 2009-03-17.

[18] Frank Ahrens (2008-03-19). "*Moral Hazard': Why Risk Is Good'*" (http://www.washingtonpost.com/wp-dyn/content/article/2008/03/18/AR2008031802873.html). The Washington Post. . Retrieved 2009-03-17.

[19] Dembe, Allard E. and Boden, Leslie I. (2000). "Moral Hazard: A Question of Morality?" (http://baywood.metapress.com/link.asp?id=1gu8eqn802j62rxk) New Solutions 2000 10(3). 257-279

[20] David Anderson, Ph. D. "The Story of the moral" (http://www.doli.state.mn.us/if02dec1.htm)

- JSTOR.org (http://www.jstor.org/stable/1011015), A working link to the Everett Crosby article "Fire Prevention"

- JSTOR.org (http://www.jstor.org/stable/1812044), A working link to the Kenneth Arrow article "Uncertainty and the Welfare Economics of Medical Care"

External links

- Saintjoe.edu (http://ingrimayne.saintjoe.edu/econ/RiskExclusion/Risk.html), Discussion of moral hazard and insurance by Robert Schenk

- Gladwell.com (http://www.gladwell.com/2005/2005_08_29_a_hazard.html), The Moral Hazard Myth (in Health Care)

- TheBigMoney.com (http://www.thebigmoney.com/articles/moral-hazard/2008/09/19/what-moral-hazard), What is Moral Hazard

- Press.illinois.edu (http://paq.press.illinois.edu/23/1/hale.html), What's so Moral about the Moral Hazard?

- Marketwatch.com (http://www.marketwatch.com/news/story/story.aspx?guid={9F4C2252-8BA7-459C-B34E-407DB32921C1}&siteid=rss), Uncle Sam as sugar daddy; Marketwatch Commentary: The moral hazard problem must not be ignored

- PBS.org (http://www.pbs.org/wgbh/pages/frontline/meltdown/view/), Inside the Meltdown, PBS's Frontline episode uses the idea as a central theme

- Mises.org (http://mises.org/story/2935), A comparison of the conventional views of moral hazard, with that by Austrian economists

National Risk Register

The **National Risk Register** is a report released by the Cabinet Office in August 2008 as part of the British government's National Security Strategy. It provides an official government assessment of significant potential risks to the United Kingdom.

The National Risk Register divides risks into three main categories: natural events, major accidents and malicious attacks. It evaluates a number of risks under each of these headings, rated by relative impact and relative likelihood, and discusses the measures currently in place to deal with each of these.

It also discusses measures that can be put in place by both individuals and organizations to mitigate the effects of civil disuption.

External links

- http://www.cabinetoffice.gov.uk/reports/national_risk_register.aspx

NIBHV

The **Nederlands Instituut voor BedrijfHulpverlening** (**NIBHV**) is an organisation that deals with the training and certification of Emergency Response Officers in The Netherlands.

Most medium to large companies are obliged to have some sort of Emergency Response Team within their organisation to aid in emergency situations.

NIBHV issues standards in The Netherlands for Emergency Response Officers training and certification[1].

External links

- Official Website for NIBHV [2]
- Official Website for RICAS [3]

References

[1] "*BHV opleiding volgens NIBHV*" (http://web.archive.org/web/20071011002407/http://www.brandweerdelft-rijswijk.nl/index. php?id=195). *Official website of Brandweer Delft - Rijswijk*. Brandweer Delft - Rijswijk, NL. 2006. Archived from the original (http://www. brandweerdelft-rijswijk.nl/index.php?id=195) on 2007-10-11. . Retrieved 2007-06-04.
[2] http://www.nibhv.nl
[3] http://www.ricas.nl

Operational risk

Categories of financial risk
Credit risk   Concentration risk
Market risk   Interest rate risk   Currency risk   Equity risk   Commodity risk
Liquidity risk   Refinancing risk
Operational risk   Legal risk   Political risk
Reputational risk
Volatility risk
Settlement risk
Profit risk
Systemic risk

Basel II
Bank for International Settlements   Basel Accords - Basel I   Basel II
Background
Banking   Monetary policy - Central bank   Risk - Risk management   Regulatory capital   Tier 1 - Tier 2
Pillar 1: Regulatory Capital
Credit risk   Standardized - F-IRB - A-IRB   PD - LGD - EAD   Operational risk   Basic - Standardized - AMA   Market risk   Duration - Value at risk
Pillar 2: Supervisory Review

Economic capital
Liquidity risk - Legal risk
Pillar 3: Market Disclosure
Disclosure
Business and Economics Portal

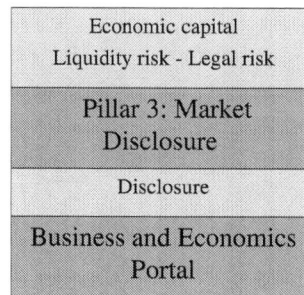

An **operational risk** is, as the name suggests, a risk arising from execution of a company's business functions. It is a very broad concept which focuses on the risks arising from the people, systems and processes through which a company operates. It also includes other categories such as fraud risks, legal risks, physical or environmental risks.

A widely used definition of **operational risk** is the one contained in the Basel II [1] regulations. This definition states that operational risk is the risk of loss resulting from inadequate or failed internal processes, people and systems, or from external events.

The approach to managing operational risk differs from that applied to other types of risk, because it is not used to generate profit. In contrast, credit risk is exploited by lending institutions to create profit, market risk is exploited by traders and fund managers, and insurance risk is exploited by insurers. They all however manage operational risk to keep losses within their risk appetite - the amount of risk they are prepared to accept in pursuit of their objectives. What this means in practical terms is that organisations accept that their people, processes and systems are imperfect, and that losses will arise from errors and ineffective operations. The size of the loss they are prepared to accept, because the cost of correcting the errors or improving the systems is disproportionate to the benefit they will receive, determines their appetite for operational risk.

Determining appetite for operational risk is a discipline which is still in its infancy. Some of the issues and considerations around this process are outlined in this Sound Practice paper published by the Institute for Operational Risk in December 2009.[2]

Background

Since the mid-1990s, the topics of market risk and credit risk have been the subject of much debate and research, with the result that financial institutions have made significant progress in the identification, measurement and management of both these forms of risk. However, it is worth mentioning that the near collapse of the U.S. financial system in September 2008 is a clear indication that our ability to measure market and credit risk is far from perfect.

Globalization and deregulation in financial markets, combined with increased sophistication in financial technology, have introduced more complexities into the activities of banks and therefore their risk profiles. These reasons underscore banks' and supervisors' growing focus upon the identification and measurement of operational risk.

Events such as the September 11 terrorist attacks, rogue trading losses at Société Générale, Barings, AIB and National Australia Bank serve to highlight the fact that the scope of risk management extends beyond merely market and credit risk.

The list of risks (and, more importantly, the scale of these risks) faced by banks today includes fraud, system failures, terrorism and employee compensation claims. These types of risk are generally classified under the term 'operational risk'.

The identification and measurement of operational risk is a real and live issue for modern-day banks, particularly since the decision by the Basel Committee on Banking Supervision (BCBS) to introduce a capital charge for this risk as part of the new capital adequacy framework (Basel II).

Definition

The Basel Committee defines operational risk as:

"The risk of loss resulting from inadequate or failed internal processes, people and systems or from external events."

However, the Basel Committee recognizes that operational risk is a term that has a variety of meanings and therefore, for internal purposes, banks are permitted to adopt their own definitions of operational risk, provided that the minimum elements in the Committee's definition are included.

Scope exclusions

The Basel II definition of operational risk excludes, for example, strategic risk - the risk of a loss arising from a poor strategic business decision.

Other risk terms are seen as potential consequences of operational risk events. For example, reputational risk (damage to an organization through loss of its reputation or standing) can arise as a consequence (or impact) of operational failures - as well as from other events.

Basel II event type categories

The following lists the official Basel II defined event types with some examples for each category:

1. Internal Fraud - misappropriation of assets, tax evasion, intentional mismarking of positions, bribery
2. External Fraud- theft of information, hacking damage, third-party theft and forgery
3. Employment Practices and Workplace Safety - discrimination, workers compensation, employee health and safety
4. Clients, Products, & Business Practice- market manipulation, antitrust, improper trade, product defects, fiduciary breaches, account churning
5. Damage to Physical Assets - natural disasters, terrorism, vandalism
6. Business Disruption & Systems Failures - utility disruptions, software failures, hardware failures
7. Execution, Delivery, & Process Management - data entry errors, accounting errors, failed mandatory reporting, negligent loss of client assets

Difficulties

It is relatively straightforward for an organization to set and observe specific, measurable levels of market risk and credit risk because models exist which attempt to predict the potential impact of market movements, or changes in the cost of credit. It should be noted however that these models are only as good as the underlying assumptions, and a large part of the recent financial crisis arose because the valuations generated by these models for particular types of investments were based on incorrect assumptions.

By contrast it is relatively difficult to identify or assess levels of operational risk and its many sources. Historically organizations have accepted operational risk as an unavoidable cost of doing business. Many now though collect data on operational losses - for example through system failure or fraud - and are using this data to model operational risk and to calculate a capital reserve against future operational losses. In addition to the Basel II requirement for banks, this is now a requirement for European insurance firms who are in the process of implementing Solvency II [3], the equivalent of Basel II for the banking sector.

Methods of operational risk management

Basel II and various Supervisory bodies of the countries have prescribed various soundness standards for Operational Risk Management for Banks and similar Financial Institutions. To complement these standards, Basel II has given guidance to 3 broad methods of Capital calculation for Operational Risk

- Basic Indicator Approach - based on annual revenue of the Financial Institution
- Standardized Approach - based on annual revenue of each of the broad business lines of the Financial Institution
- Advanced Measurement Approaches - based on the internally developed risk measurement framework of the bank adhering to the standards prescribed (methods include IMA, LDA, Scenario-based, Scorecard etc.)

The Operational Risk Management framework should include identification, measurement, monitoring, reporting, control and mitigation frameworks for Operational Risk.

External links

- Operational Risk in the Basel ii framework [4]
- The Institute of Operational Risk [5] The institute provides professional recognition and enables members to maintain competency in the discipline of operational risk.
- OpRisk & Regulation [6] is the home page of the leading educational resource on operational risk, including a magazine, training, conferences, books, etc.
- Revised international capital framework [7] is the text of the new Basel II Accord.
- Operational Risk Blog [8] is a resource for operational risk content.
- Constraints of Consistent Operational Risk Measurement and Regulation: Data Collection and Loss Reporting [9], Andreas A. Jobst, 2007 (Journal of Financial Regulation and Compliance)
- The Credit Crisis and Operational Risk - Implications for Practitioners and Regulators [10], Andreas A. Jobst, 2010 (Journal of Operational Risk, Vol. 5, No. 2)
- The Risk Management Association [11] - leading industry organization for operational risk professionals
- http://bis2information.org: Practical articles, on BIS2 and risk modeling, submitted by professionals to help create an industry standard.
- http://www.bos.frb.org/economic/wp/wp2006/wp0613.htm FRB Boston paper on measurement of operational risk.
- Operational Risk - The Sting is Still in the Tail But the Poison Depends on the Dose [12], Andreas A. Jobst, 2007 (Journal of Operational Risk)
- Convergence of Operational and Credit Risk [13], Tyson Macaulay 2008
- Operational Continuity and Additivity of Operational Risk [14], Tyson Macaulay 2008
- Metrics and Operational Continuity [15], Tyson Macaulay 2008
- Operational Risk Consortium [16] is a consortium that collects and analyzes operational risk loss data for the insurance industry.

References

[1] http://www.bis.org/publ/bcbsca.html

[2] http://www.ior-institute.org/dmdocuments/RiskAppetiteSPGVersion1.pdf

[3] http://ec.europa.eu/internal_market/insurance/solvency/index_en.htm

[4] http://www.bis.org/publ/bcbsca07.pdf

[5] http://www.ior-institute.org/

[6] http://www.opriskandcompliance.com

[7] http://www.bis.org/publ/bcbsca.htm

[8] http://operationalrisk.blogspot.com

[9] http://papers.ssrn.com/sol3/papers.cfm?abstract_id=956214

[10] http://papers.ssrn.com/sol3/papers.cfm?abstract_id=1491193

[11] http://www.rmahq.org/RMA/OperationalRisk/

[12] http://papers.ssrn.com/sol3/papers.cfm?abstract_id=944486

[13] http://www.tysonmacaulay.com/Convergence%20-%20Additivity%20of%20Risk%20-%20Paper%20I%20-%20Feb%202008.pdf

[14] http://www.tysonmacaulay.com/Continuity%20-%20Additivity%20of%20Risk%20-%20Paper%20II%20-%20Feb%202008.pdf

[15] http://www.tysonmacaulay.com/Metrics%20-%20Additivity%20of%20Risk%20-%20Paper%20III%20-%20Feb%202008.pdf

[16] http://www.abioric.com

Outrage factor

In public policy, the **outrage factor** is the portion of public opposition to a policy which does not derive from knowledge of the technical details. While policy analysis by institutional stakeholders may focus on risk-benefit analysis and cost-benefit analysis, popular risk perception is not informed by the same concerns, and so the successful implementation of a policy relying on public support and cooperation will need to address the outrage factor when informing the public about the policy.

Factors

The term "outrage factor" originates from Peter Sandman's 1993 book, *Responding to community outrage: strategies for effective risk communication.*[1] [2] He gives the formula:[3]

> Risk = Hazard + Outrage

Sandman enumerates several sources of outrage:

Voluntary vs. coerced

> People may object to something compulsory which is less dangerous than something else that they do by choice, such as a dangerous sport. [4]

Natural vs. industrial

> A human-made source of risk provides someone to blame for the risk; household radon is less publicly feared than less carcinogenic artificial sources.[5]

Familiar vs. exotic

> [6]

Memorable or not

> Memorableness may derive from personal experience, news reports, fiction, or iconic images or symbols.[7]

Dreaded or not

> Disgust can exaggerate perceived risk[8]

Chronic vs. catastrophic

> people may worry more about continual leakage from a chemical plant than the risk of an explosion[9]

Knowable or not

people take a worst-case approach to uncertainty[10]

Controlled by me vs. others

[11]

Fair or not

[12]

Morally relevant or not

[13]

Can I trust you or not

[14]

Is the process responsive or not

[15]

Issues

The relevance of public outrage has been acknowledged in discussions of various policy debates, including nuclear safety,[16] terrorism,[17] public health,[18] [19] and environmental management.[1] [2]

Addressing outrage

The mass media often frame policy debate by focusing on outrage factors. For proponents of a policy trying to address outrage, Sandman recommends acknowledging and empathising with the underlying sentiment.

References

- Sandman, Peter M. (1993). *Responding to community outrage: strategies for effective risk communication* [20]. American Industrial Hygiene Association. ISBN 093262751X.

Notes

[1] Nebel, Bernard J.; Richard T. Wright (1993). *Environmental science: the way the world works* (http://books.google.com/ books?id=4wjxeUeaRnMC&lpg=PA393&dq="OUTRAGE FACTOR"&pg=PA393#v=onepage&q="OUTRAGE FACTOR"&f=false) (4th ed.). Prentice Hall PTR. pp. 392–3. ISBN 0132854465. .

[2] Hird, John A. (1994). *Superfund: the political economy of environmental risk* (http://books.google.com/books?id=fsTBXJPVmzgC& lpg=PA70&dq="OUTRAGE FACTOR"&pg=PA70#v=onepage&q="OUTRAGE FACTOR"&f=false). JHU Press. p. 70. ISBN 0801848075. .

[3] Sandman, p.1

[4] Sandman, pp.14–17

[5] Sandman, pp.17–19

[6] Sandman, pp.19–23

[7] Sandman, pp.23–27

[8] Sandman, pp.27–29

[9] Sandman, pp.29–33

[10] Sandman, pp.33–37

[11] Sandman, pp.37–41

[12] Sandman, pp.41–44

[13] Sandman, pp.44–49

[14] Sandman, pp.49–62

[15] Sandman, pp.62–73

[16] Williams, David R. (1998). *What is safe?: the risks of living in a nuclear age* (http://books.google.com/books?id=kDIdiej7CEIC& lpg=PA39&dq="OUTRAGE FACTOR"&pg=PA39#v=onepage&q="OUTRAGE FACTOR"&f=false). Royal Society of Chemistry. p. 39. ISBN 0854045694. .

[17] Kayyem, Juliette N.; Robyn L. Pangi (2003). *First to arrive: state and local responses to terrorism* (http://books.google.com/books?id=FHEzLB5dGfQC&lpg=PA68&dq="OUTRAGE FACTOR"&pg=PA68#v=onepage&q="OUTRAGE FACTOR"&f=false). BCSIA studies in international security. MIT Press. p. 68. ISBN 0262611953. .

[18] Milloy, Steven J. (1995). *Science without sense: the risky business of public health research* (http://books.google.com/books?id=rpZKyRI7hocC&lpg=PA8&dq="OUTRAGE FACTOR"&pg=PA8#v=onepage&q="OUTRAGE FACTOR"&f=false). Cato Institute. p. 8. ISBN 1882577345. .

[19] David, Pencheon; David Melzer, Charles Guest, Muir Gray (2006). *Oxford handbook of public health practice* (http://books.google.com/books?id=cYnzLTV7aVEC&lpg=PA221&dq="OUTRAGE FACTOR"&pg=PA221#v=onepage&q="OUTRAGE FACTOR"&f=false). Oxford handbooks (2nd ed.). Oxford University Press. p. 221. ISBN 0198566557. .

[20] http://books.google.com/books?id=M9-bQsx8TnMC

Postcautionary principle

The **postcautionary principle** is a principle of *de facto* environmental management formulated by John Paull in 2007.[1] It is suggested that the postcautionary principle, as the antithesis of the precautionary principle, has guided environmental management, as it is actually practised.

Taking the Rio 1982 formulation of the **pre**cautionary principle as a guide, the **post**cautionary principle has been stated as follows: *"Where there are threats of serious or irreversible damage, the lack of full scientific certainty shall be used as a reason for not implementing cost-effective measures until after the environmental degradation has actually occurred"* [2].

Examples of this principle include: the extinction of the thylacine (Tasmanian tiger), which was, after decades of government bounty hunting (starting in 1888), declared a protected species on 10 July 1936 by the Fauna Board of Tasmania, only weeks before the last one died in captivity (on 7 September 1936); and the 2003 Forestry Tasmania burning of Tasmania's largest tree *El Grande*,[3] a tree protected under legislation, and its subsequent demise, after which "new standard operating procedures" were implemented.[4]

References

[1] Paull, John, Certified Organic Forests & Timber: the Hippocratic Opportunity (http://orgprints.org/11042/), Proceedings ANZSEE Conference 2007, 1-14, 2007

[2] http://orgprints.org/11042

[3] BBC, Forestry officials admit killing biggest tree (http://news.bbc.co.uk/2/hi/asia-pacific/3306655.stm), BBC News, 10 December 2003

[4] FPB, 2004, Derwent 02-03, Forest Practices Board, Hobart, Tasmania, 13 January 2004

Precautionary principle

The **precautionary principle** or precautionary approach states that if an action or policy has a suspected risk of causing harm to the public or to the environment, in the absence of scientific consensus that the action or policy is harmful, the burden of proof that it is *not* harmful falls on those taking the action.

This principle allows policy makers to make discretionary decisions in situations where there is the possibility of harm from taking a particular course or making a certain decision when extensive scientific knowledge on the matter is lacking. The principle implies that there is a social responsibility to protect the public from exposure to harm, when scientific investigation has found a plausible risk. These

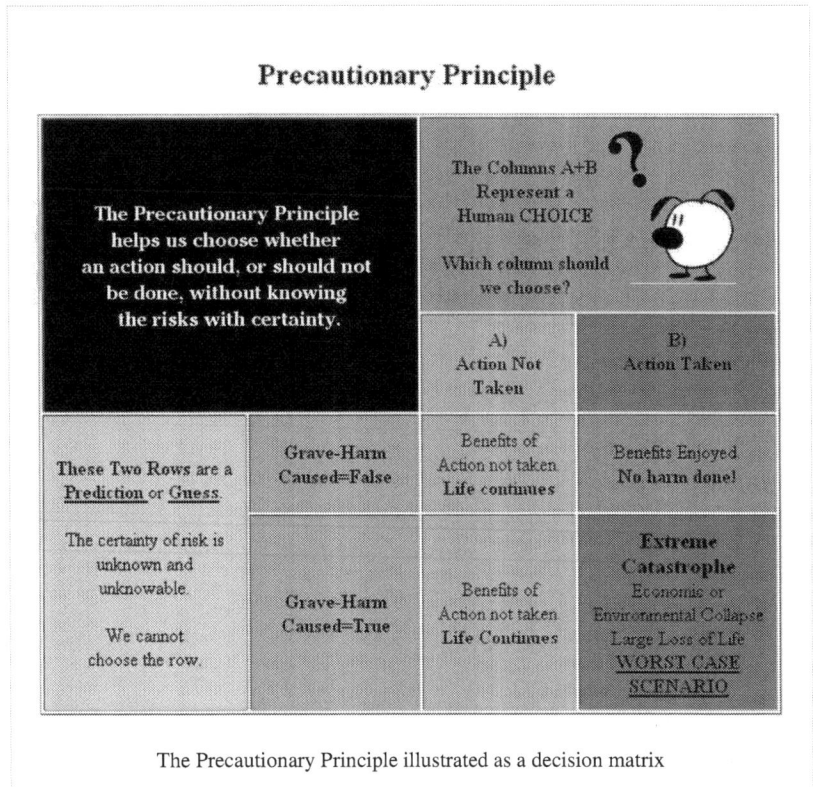

Precautionary Principle

The Precautionary Principle helps us choose whether an action should, or should not be done, without knowing the risks with certainty.

The Columns A+B Represent a Human CHOICE

Which column should we choose?

		A) Action Not Taken	B) Action Taken
These Two Rows are a Prediction or Guess.	Grave-Harm Caused=False	Benefits of Action not taken Life continues	Benefits Enjoyed No harm done!
The certainty of risk is unknown and unknowable. We cannot choose the row.	Grave-Harm Caused=True	Benefits of Action not taken Life Continues	**Extreme Catastrophe** Economic or Environmental Collapse Large Loss of Life WORST CASE SCENARIO

The Precautionary Principle illustrated as a decision matrix

protections can be relaxed only if further scientific findings emerge that provide sound evidence that no harm will result.

In some legal systems, as in the law of the European Union, the application of the precautionary principle has been made a statutory requirement.[1]

Formulations of the precautionary principle

Many definitions of the precautionary principle exist. Precaution may be defined as *"caution in advance,"* *"caution practised in the context of uncertainty,"* or *informed prudence*. All definitions have two key elements.

1. an expression of a need by decision-makers to anticipate harm before it occurs. Within this element lies an implicit reversal of the onus of proof: under the precautionary principle it is the responsibility of an activity proponent to establish that the proposed activity will not (or is very unlikely to) result in significant harm.
2. the establishment of an obligation, if the level of harm may be high, for action to prevent or minimise such harm even when the absence of scientific certainty makes it difficult to predict the likelihood of harm occurring, or the level of harm should it occur. The need for control measures increases with both the level of possible harm and the degree of uncertainty.

One of the primary foundations of the precautionary principle, and globally accepted definitions, results from the work of the Rio Conference, or "Earth Summit" in 1992. Principle #15 of the Rio Declaration notes:

"In order to protect the environment, the precautionary approach shall be widely applied by States according to their capabilities. Where there are threats of serious or irreversible damage, lack of full scientific certainty shall not be used as a reason for postponing cost-effective measures to prevent environmental degradation."[2]

This definition is important for several reasons. First, it explains the idea that scientific uncertainty should not preclude preventative measures to protect the environment. Second, the use of "cost-effective" measures indicates that costs can be considered. This is different from a "no-regrets" approach, which ignores the costs of preventative action.

The 1998 Wingspread Statement on the Precautionary Principle summarizes the principle this way: "When an activity raises threats of harm to human health or the environment, precautionary measures should be taken even if some cause and effect relationships are not fully established scientifically." (The Wingspread Conference on the Precautionary Principle was convened by the Science and Environmental Health Network).

The February 2, 2000 European Commission Communication on the Precautionary Principle notes: "The precautionary principle applies where scientific evidence is insufficient, inconclusive or uncertain and preliminary scientific evaluation indicates that there are reasonable grounds for concern that the potentially dangerous effects on the environment, human, animal or plant health may be inconsistent with the high level of protection chosen by the EU".

The January 29, 2000 Cartagena Protocol on Biosafety says: "Lack of scientific certainty due to insufficient relevant scientific information . . . shall not prevent the Party of import, in order to avoid or minimize such potential adverse effects, from taking a decision, as appropriate, with regard to the import of the living modified organism in question."

It is important to emphasize that, although this principle operates in the context of scientific uncertainty, it is considered by its proponents to be applicable only when, on the basis of the best scientific advice available, there is good reason to believe that harmful effects might occur.

The precautionary principle is most often applied in the context of the impact of human actions on the environment and human health, as both involve complex systems where the consequences of actions may be unpredictable.

As applied to environmental policy, the precautionary principle stipulates that for practices such as the release of radiation or toxins or massive deforestation the burden of proof lies with the advocates. [3] Concerning potential risks to public health, examples of cases in which the precautionary principle has been advocated (but not always accepted) are: the commercialization of genetically modified foods, the use of growth hormones in cattle raising, measures to prevent the "mad cow" disease, health claims linked to phthalates in PVC toys, among many others.

An important element of the precautionary principle is that its most meaningful applications pertain to those that are potentially irreversible, for example where biodiversity may be reduced. With respect to bans on substances like mercury in thermometers, freon in refrigeration, or even carbon dioxide exhaust from automobile engines and power plants, it implies:

> ... a willingness to take action in advance of scientific proof [or] evidence of the need for the proposed action on the grounds that further delay will prove ultimately most costly to society and nature, and, in the longer term, selfish and unfair to future generations.

> − [4]

The concept includes an implicit ethical responsibility towards maintaining the integrity of natural systems, and acknowledges the fallibility of human understanding.

Some environmental commentators take a more stringent interpretation of the precautionary principle, stating that proponents of a new potentially harmful technology must show the new technology is without major harm before the new technology is used.[5] [6]

Origins and theory

The formal concept evolved out of the German socio-legal tradition in the 1930s, centering on the concept of good household management.[7] In German the concept is *Vorsorgeprinzip*, which translates into English as *precaution principle*.

Many of the concepts underpinning the precautionary principle pre-date the term's inception. For example, the essence of the principle is captured in a number of cautionary aphorisms such as "an ounce of prevention is worth a pound of cure", "better safe than sorry", and "look before you leap".[3] The precautionary principle may also be interpreted as the evolution of the ancient medical principle of "first, do no harm" to apply to institutions and institutional decision-making processes rather than individuals.

The precautionary principle is in some ways an expansion of the English common law concept of 'duty of care' originating in the decisions of the judge Lord Esher in the late 1800s. According to Lord Esher: "Whenever one person is by circumstances placed in such a position with regard to another that everyone of ordinary sense who did think, would at once recognise that if he did not use ordinary care and skill in his own conduct with regard to those circumstances, he would cause danger or injury to the person, or property of the other, a duty arises to use ordinary care and skill to avoid such danger". This statement clearly contains elements of foresight and responsibility, but does not refer to a lack of certainty, as the word "would" is used rather than "might", or "could". The other important difference is that the duty of care applies only to people and property, not to the environment.

In economics, the precautionary principle has been analysed in terms of the effect on rational decision-making of the interaction of irreversibility and uncertainty. Authors such as Epstein (1980)[8] and Arrow and Fischer (1974)[9] show that irreversibility of possible future consequences creates a quasi-option effect which should induce a "risk-neutral" society to favor current decisions that allow for more flexibility in the future. Gollier et al. (2000)[10] conclude that "more scientific uncertainty as to the distribution of a future risk— that is, a larger variability of beliefs— should induce Society to take stronger prevention measures today."

Application

The application of the precautionary principle is hampered by both lack of political will, as well as the wide range of interpretations placed on it. One study identified 14 different formulations of the principle in treaties and nontreaty declarations.[11] R.B. Stewart (2002)[12] reduced the precautionary principle to four basic versions:

1. Scientific uncertainty should not automatically preclude regulation of activities that pose a potential risk of significant harm (Non-Preclusion PP).
2. Regulatory controls should incorporate a margin of safety; activities should be limited below the level at which no adverse effect has been observed or predicted (Margin of Safety PP).
3. Activities that present an uncertain potential for significant harm should be subject to best technology available requirements to minimize the risk of harm unless the proponent of the activity shows that they present no appreciable risk of harm (BAT PP).
4. Activities that present an uncertain potential for significant harm should be prohibited unless the proponent of the activity shows that it presents no appreciable risk of harm (Prohibitory PP).

In deciding how to apply the principle, analysis may use a cost-benefit analysis that factors in both the opportunity cost of not acting, and the option value of waiting for further information before acting. One of the difficulties of the application of the principle in modern policy-making is that there is often an irreducible conflict between different interests, so that the debate necessarily involves politics.

Strong vs. weak

Strong precaution holds that regulation is required whenever there is a possible risk to health, safety, or the environment, even if the supporting evidence is speculative and even if the economic costs of regulation are high. In 1982, the United Nations World Charter for Nature gave the first international recognition to the strong version of the principle, suggesting that when "potential adverse effects are not fully understood, the activities should not proceed." The widely publicized Wingspread Declaration, from a meeting of environmentalists in 1998, is another example of the strong version.[13] 'Strong precaution' can also be termed as a "no-regrets" principle, where costs are not considered in preventative action.

Weak precaution holds that lack of scientific evidence does not preclude action if damage would otherwise be serious and irreversible. Humans practice weak precaution every day, and often incur costs, to avoid hazards that are far from certain: we do not walk in moderately dangerous areas at night, we exercise, we buy smoke detectors, we buckle our seatbelts.[13]

According to a publication by the New Zealand Treasury Department,

> The weak version [of the Precautionary Principle] is the least restrictive and allows preventive measures to be taken in the face of uncertainty, but does not require them (eg, Rio Declaration 1992; United Nations Framework Convention of Climate Change 1992). To satisfy the threshold of harm, there must be some evidence relating to both the likelihood of occurrence and the severity of consequences. Some, but not all, require consideration of the costs of precautionary measures. Weak formulations do not preclude weighing benefits against the costs. Factors other than scientific uncertainty, including economic considerations, may provide legitimate grounds for postponing action. Under weak formulations, the requirement to justify the need for action (the burden of proof) generally falls on those advocating precautionary action. No mention is made of assignment of liability for environmental harm.

> Strong versions justify or require precautionary measures and some also establish liability for environmental harm, which is effectively a strong form of "polluter pays". For example, the Earth Charter states: "When knowledge is limited apply a precautionary approach …. Place the burden of proof on those who argue that a proposed activity will not cause significant harm, and make the responsible parties liable for environmental harm." Reversal of proof requires those proposing an activity to prove that the product, process or technology is sufficiently "safe" before approval is granted. Requiring proof of "no environmental harm" before any action proceeds implies the public is not prepared to accept any environmental risk, no matter what economic or social benefits may arise (Peterson, 2006). At the extreme, such a requirement could involve bans and prohibitions on entire classes of potentially threatening activities or substances (Cooney, 2005). Over time, there has been a gradual transformation of the precautionary principle from what appears in the Rio Declaration to a stronger form that arguably acts as restraint on development in the absence of firm evidence that it will do no harm.[14]

International agreements and declarations

The World Charter for Nature, which was adopted by the UN General Assembly in 1982, was the first international endorsement of the precautionary principle. The principle was implemented in an international treaty as early as the 1987 Montreal Protocol, and among other international treaties and declarations [15] is reflected in the 1992 Rio Declaration on Environment and Development (signed at the United Nations Conference on Environment and Development).

"Principle" vs. "approach"

No introduction to the precautionary principle would be complete without brief reference to the difference between the precautionary **principle** and the precautionary **approach**. Principle 15 of the Rio Declaration 1992 states that: "in order to protect the environment, the precautionary approach shall be widely applied by States according to their capabilities. Where there are threats of serious or irreversible damage, lack of full scientific certainty shall be not used as a reason for postponing cost-effective measures to prevent environmental degradation." As Garcia (1995) pointed out, "the wording, largely similar to that of the principle, is subtly different in that: (1) it recognizes that there may be differences in local capabilities to apply the approach, and (2) it calls for cost-effectiveness in applying the approach, e.g., taking economic and social costs into account." The 'approach' is generally considered a softening of the 'principle'.

"As Recuerda has noted, the distinction between the ´precautionary principle` and a ´precautionary approach` is diffuse and, in some contexts, controversial. In the negotiations of international declarations, the United States has opposed the use of the term ´principle` because this term has special connotations in legal language, due to the fact that a ´principle of law` is a source of law. This means that it is compulsory, so a court can quash or confirm a decision through the application of the precautionary principle. In this sense, the precautionary principle is not a simple idea or a desideratum but a source of law. This is the legal status of the precautionary principle in the European Union. On the other hand, an ´approach` usually does not have the same meaning,16 although in some particular cases an approach could be binding. A precautionary approach is a particular ´lens` used to identify risk that every prudent person possesses (Recuerda, 2008)[16]

European Commission

On 2 February 2000, the European Commission issued a Communication on the precautionary principle,[17] in which it adopted a procedure for the application of this concept, but without giving a detailed definition of it. Paragraph 2 of article 191 of the Lisbon Treaty states that

> *"Union policy on the environment shall aim at a high level of protection taking into account the diversity of situations in the various regions of the Union. It shall be based on the precautionary principle and on the principles that preventive action should be taken, that environmental damage should as a priority be rectified at source and that the polluter should pay. "*[18]

After the adoption of the European Commission's Communication on the precautionary principle, the principle has come to inform much EU policy, including that in areas beyond that of environmental policy. It is implemented, for example, in the EU food law and also affects, among others, policies relating to consumer protection, trade and research, and technological development. While a comprehensive definition of the precautionary principle was never formally adopted by the EU, a working definition and implementation strategy for the EU context has been proposed by Rene von Schomberg in Fisher et al. (2006):[19]

"Where, following an assessment of available scientific information, there are reasonable grounds for concern for the possibility of adverse effects but scientific uncertainty persists, provisional risk management measures based on a broad cost/benefit analysis whereby priority will be given to human health and the environment, necessary to ensure the chosen high level of protection in the Community and proportionate to this level of protection, may be adopted, pending further scientific information for a more comprehensive risk assessment, without having to wait until the reality and seriousness of those adverse effects become fully apparent".

USA

On July 18, 2005, the City of San Francisco passed a Precautionary Principle Purchasing ordinance [20], which requires the city to weigh the environmental and health costs of its $600 million in annual purchases – for everything from cleaning supplies to computers. Members of the Bay Area Working Group on the Precautionary Principle including the Breast Cancer Fund, helped bring this to fruition.

Japan

In 1997, Japan tried to use the consideration of the precautionary principle in a WTO SPS Agreement on the Application of Sanitary and Phytosanitary Measures case, as Japan's requirement to test each variety of agricultural products (apples, cherries, peaches, walnuts, apricots, pears, plums and quinces) for the efficacy of treatment against codling moths was challenged.

This moth is a pest that does not occur in Japan, and whose introduction has the potential to cause serious damage. The United States claimed that it was not necessary to test each variety of a fruit for the efficacy of the treatment, and that this varietal testing requirement was unnecessarily burdensome.

Australia

The most important Australian court case so far, due to its exceptionally detailed consideration of the precautionary principle, is Telstra Corporation Limited v Hornsby Shire Council. The case was heard in the New South Wales Land and Environment Court under Justice CJ Preston (24 April 2006).

The Principle was summarised by reference to the NSW *Protection of the Environment Administration Act 1991*, which itself provides a good definition of the principle:

"If there are threats of serious or irreversible environmental damage, lack of full scientific certainty should not be used as a reasoning for postponing measures to prevent environmental degradation. In the application of the principle... decisions should be guided by: (i) careful evaluation to avoid, wherever practicable, serious or irreversible damage to the environment; and (ii) an assessment of risk-weighted consequence of various options".

The most significant points of Justice Preston's decision are the following findings:

1. The principle and accompanying need to take precautionary measures is "triggered" when two prior conditions exist: a threat of serious or irreversible damage, and scientific uncertainty as to the extent of possible damage.
2. Once both are satisfied, "a proportionate precautionary measure may be taken to avert the anticipated threat of environmental damage, but it should be proportionate."
3. The threat of serious or irreversible damage should invoke consideration of five factors: the scale of threat (local, regional etc.); the perceived value of the threatened environment; whether the possible impacts are manageable; the level of public concern, and whether there is a rational or scientific basis for the concern.
4. The consideration of the level of scientific uncertainty should involve factors which may include: what would constitute sufficient evidence; the level and kind of uncertainty; and the potential to reduce uncertainty.
5. The principle shifts the burden of proof. If the principle applies, the burden shifts: "a decision maker must assume the threat of serious or irreversible environmental damage is... a reality [and] the burden of showing this threat... is negligible reverts to the proponent..."
6. The precautionary principle invokes preventative action: "the principle permits the taking of preventative measures without having to wait until the reality and seriousness of the threat become fully known".
7. "The principle should not be used to try to avoid all risks."
8. The precautionary measures appropriate will depend on the combined effect of "the degree of seriousness and irreversibility of the threat and the degree of uncertainty... the more significant and uncertain the threat, the greater...the precaution required". "...measures should be adopted... proportionate to the potential threats".

Corporate

The Body Shop International, a UK-based cosmetics company, recently included the Precautionary Principle in their 2006 Chemicals Strategy. [21]

Environment/health

Fields typically concerned by the precautionary principle are the possibility of:

* Global warming or abrupt climate change in general
* Extinction of species
* Introduction of new and potentially harmful products into the environment, threatening biodiversity (e.g., genetically modified organisms)
* Threats to public health, due to new diseases and techniques (e.g., AIDS transmitted through blood transfusion)
* Persistent or acute pollution (asbestos, endocrine disruptors...)
* Food safety (e.g., Creutzfeldt-Jakob disease)
* Other new biosafety issues (e.g., artificial life, new molecules)

The precautionary principle is often applied to biological fields because changes cannot be easily contained and have the potential of being global. The principle has less relevance to contained fields such as aeronautics, where the few people undergoing risk have given informed consent (e.g., a test pilot). In the case of technological innovation, containment of impact tends to be more difficult if that technology can self-replicate. Bill Joy emphasized the dangers of replicating genetic technology, nanotechnology, and robotic technology in his article in *Wired Magazine*, "Why the future doesn't need us", though he does not specifically cite the precautionary principle. The application of the principle can be seen in the public policy of requiring pharmaceutical companies to carry out clinical trials to show that new medications are safe.

Oxford based philosopher Nick Bostrom discusses the idea of a future powerful superintelligence, and the risks that we/it face should it attempt to gain atomic level control of matter.[22]

Application of the principle modifies the status of innovation and risk assessment: it is not the risk that must be avoided or amended, but a potential risk that must be prevented. Thus, in the case of regulation of scientific research, there is a third party beyond the scientist and the regulator: the consumer.

In an analysis [23] concerning application of the precautionary principle to nanotechnology, Chris Phoenix and Mike Treder posit that there are *two forms* of the principle, which they call the "strict form" and the "active form". The former "requires inaction when action might pose a risk", while the latter means "choosing less risky alternatives when they are available, and [...] taking responsibility for potential risks."The academic Thomas Alured Faunce has argued for stronger application of the precautionary principle by chemical and health technology regulators particularly in relation to TI02 and ZNO nanoparticles in sunscreens, biocidal nanosilver in waterways and products whose manufacture, handling or recycling exposes humans to the risk of inhaling multi-walled carbon nanotubes.[24]

Change of laws controlling societal norms

Associate Justice Martha Sosman's dissent[25] in Goodridge v. Department of Public Health, the decision of the Supreme Judicial Court of Massachusetts that mandated legalization of same sex marriage, is an example of the precautionary principle as applied by analogy to changes in culturally significant social policy. She describes the myriad societal structures that rest on the institution of marriage, and points out the uncertainty of how they will be affected by this re-definition. The disagreement of the majority illustrates the difficulty of reaching agreement on the value of competing perspectives. Although the Goodridge case involved interpreting the state constitution, the substantive canon in Anglo-American jurisprudence that derogations of fundamental societal values should be narrowly construed[26] is analogous to the precautionary principle favoring a statutory interpretation that comports with rather than damages the common law and established norms. See, for example, *Holy Trinity Church v. United States*, 143 U.S. 457 (1892).

Resource management

Several natural resources like fish stocks are now managed by precautionary approach, through Harvest Control Rules (HCR) based upon the precautionary principle. The figure indicates how the principle is implemented in the cod fisheries management proposed by the International Council for the Exploration of the Sea.

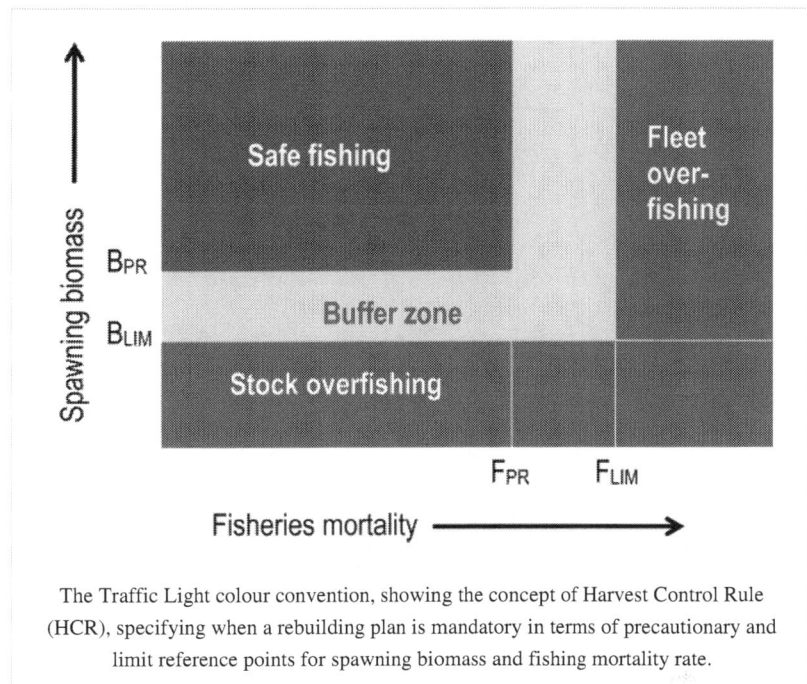

The Traffic Light colour convention, showing the concept of Harvest Control Rule (HCR), specifying when a rebuilding plan is mandatory in terms of precautionary and limit reference points for spawning biomass and fishing mortality rate.

In classifying endangered species, the precautionary principle means that if there is doubt about an animal's or plant's exact conservation status, the one that would cause the strongest protective measures to be realized should be chosen. Thus, a species like the Silvery Pigeon that might exist in considerable numbers and simply be under-recorded or might just as probably be long extinct is not classified as "data deficient" or "extinct" (which both do not require any protective action to be taken), but as "critically endangered" (the conservation status that confers the need for the strongest protection), whereas the increasingly rare, but probably not yet endangered Emerald Starling is classified as "data deficient", because there is urgent need for research to clarify its status rather than for conservation action to save it from extinction.

If, for example, a large ground-water body that many people use for drinking water is contaminated by bacteria (e-coli 0157 H7, campylobacter or leptospirosis) and the source of contamination is strongly suspected to be dairy cows but the exact science is not yet able to provide absolute proof, then the cows should be removed from the environment until they are proved, by the dairy industry, not to be the source or until that industry ensures that such contamination will not recur.

Criticisms

Threshold of plausibility

The Wingspread Statement version of the PP takes the form "When an activity raises threats of harm to human health or the environment, precautionary measures should be taken even if some cause and effect relationships are not fully established scientifically". When applying this principle, it is recommended that society establish a minimal threshold of scientific certainty or plausibility before undertaking precautions. Normally, no minimal threshold of plausibility is specified as a "triggering" condition, so that any indication that a proposed product or activity might harm health or the environment is sufficient to invoke the principle. Often the only precaution taken is a ban on the product or activity.[27]

In Sancho vs. DOE, Helen Gillmor, Senior District Judge, wrote in a dismissal of Wagner's lawsuit which included a popular[28] worry that the LHC could cause "destruction of the earth" by a black hole:

> Injury in fact requires some "credible threat of harm." *Cent. Delta Water Agency v. United States*, 306 F.3d 938, 950 (9th Cir. 2002). At most, Wagner has alleged that experiments at the Large Hadron Collider (the "Collider") have "potential adverse consequences." Speculative fear of future harm does not constitute an

injury in fact sufficient to confer standing. *Mayfield*, 599 F.3d at 970.[29]

Negative consequences of application

The Precautionary Principle may cause resentment, since people are more aware of negative changes than they are positive changes (i.e. a ban is more noted than allowing a proposal to proceed). Because of this effect, a technology which brings advantages may be banned by PP because of its potential for negative impacts, leaving the positive benefits unrealized.[30]

The Hazardous Air Pollutant provisions in the 1990 amendments to the U.S. Clean Air Act are an example of the Precautionary Principle where the onus is now on showing a listed compound is harmless. Under this rule no distinction is made between those air Pollutants that provide a higher or lower risk, so operators tend to choose less-examined agents that are not on the existing list.[31]

A California researcher has pointed out the fallacy of extrapolating possible risk of a proposed product or action, without examining equally closely the possible risks of *not* adopting the proposal. When looking at the proposal, policymakers tend to apply PP to that proposal while assuming the alternative(s) to be risk-free, which places an unfair burden on the proponents of the new product or activity.[32]

Internal Inconsistency

The Precautionary Principle, applied to itself as a policy decision, may rule out its own use depending on the precise definition used; for example, Prohibitory PP as a policy decision would need to demonstrate that no substantial damage would result from the prohibition of products and technologies. For a potential example of this, the uncertain safety and long-term environmental effects of nuclear power led to its disfavor by precautionary groups, which may have resulted in greater carbon emissions through the use of coal power.

Michael Crichton wrote: The "precautionary principle," properly applied, forbids the precautionary principle. It is self-contradictory. The precautionary principle therefore cannot be spoken of in terms that are too harsh.[33]

Perspective

- Critics of the principle argue that it is impractical, since every implementation of a technology carries some risk of negative consequences.[30] For example, when the arrival of amplified music came on the scene, the risk of electrocution and deafness arose. However, this did not prevent it from becoming an artistic and cultural norm.

- A summary of some representative objections to the precautionary principle are described in a Reason article by Ronald Bailey[34] which, using the Wingspread consensus as a starting point, argues the possibilities for misapplication of the principle.

References

[1] Recuerda, Miguel A. (2006). "Risk and Reason in the European Union Law". *European Food and Feed Law Review* **5**.

[2] http://www.unep.org/Documents.multilingual/Default.asp?DocumentID=78&ArticleID=1163

[3] http://www.biotech-info.net/rachels_586.html

[4] http://dieoff.org/page31.htm

[5] European Environmental Bureau. EEB Position on the Precautionary Principle. (http://www.eeb.org/publication/1999/eeb_position_on_the_precautionar.html) December 1999.

[6] Science and Environmental Health Network. The Precautionary Principle: A Common Sense Way to Protect Public Health and the Environment. (http://www.mindfully.org/Precaution/Precautionary-Principle-Common-Sense.htm) January 2000.

[7] http://www.agobservatory.org/library.cfm?refID=30236

[8] Epstein, L.S. (1980). "Decision-making and the temporal resolution of uncertainty" (http://jstor.org/stable/2526180). *International Economic Review* **21** (2): 269–283. doi:10.2307/2526180. .

[9] Arrow, K.J. and Fischer, A.C. (1974). "Environmental preservation, uncertainty and irreversibility" (http://jstor.org/stable/1883074). *Quarterly Journal of Economics* **88** (2): 312–9. doi:10.2307/1883074. .

[10] Gollier, Christian, Bruno Jullien & Nicolas Treich (2000). "Scientific Progress and Irreversibility: An Economic Interpretation of the 'Precautionary Principle'". *Journal of Public Economics* **75** (2): 229–253. doi:10.1016/S0047-2727(99)00052-3.

[11] http://www.biotech-info.net/science_and_PP.html

[12] Stewart, R.B. (2002). "Environmental Regulatory Decision Making Under Uncertainty". *Research in Law and Economics* **20**: 76.

[13] "The paralyzing principle: Does the precautionary principle point us in any helpful direction?" Goliath Business Knowledge on Demand. December 2002. http://goliath.ecnext.com/coms2/gi_0199-2593495/The-paralyzing-principle-does-the.html

[14] "Precautionary Principle: Origins, definitions, and interpretations." Treasury Publication, Government of New Zealand. 2006. http://www.treasury.govt.nz/publications/research-policy/ppp/2006/06-06/05.htm

[15] http://www.biotech-info.net/treaties_and_agreements.html

[16] Recuerda, M. A. (2008). "Dangerous interpretations of the precautionary principle and the foundational values of the European Union Food Law: Risk versus Risk". *Journal of Food Law & Policy* **4** (1).

[17] Communication from the Commission on the precautionary principle, COM(2000) 1 (http://eur-lex.europa.eu/LexUriServ/LexUriServ.do?uri=CELEX:52000DC0001:EN:NOT)

[18] Consolidated Version of the Treaty on the Functioning of the European Union (http://eur-lex.europa.eu/LexUriServ/LexUriServ.do?uri=OJ:C:2010:083:0047:0200:EN:PDF) article 191, paragraph 2

[19] Fisher, Elizabeth, Judith Jones & Rene von Schomberg (eds). *Implementing the Precautionary Principle: Perspectives and Prospects*, Cheltenham, UK and Northampton, MA, US: Edward Elgar (2006)

[20] http://www.municode.com/Resources/gateway.asp?pid=14134&sid=5

[21] http://www.thebodyshopinternational.com/NR/rdonlyres/D7F2A9D1-416A-47B8-8BC3-1E858A37F81C/0/BSI_Chemicals_Strategy.pdf.

[22] Nick Bostrom 2003 Ethical Issues in Advanced Artificial Intelligence - section 2

[23] http://www.crnano.org/precautionary.htm

[24] Faunce TA, *et al.* (2008). "Sunscreen Safety: The Precautionary Principle, The Australian Therapeutic Goods Administration and Nanoparticles in Sunscreens" (http://law.anu.edu.au/StaffUploads/236-Nanoethics Sunscreens 2008.pdf) (PDF). *Nanoethics* **2**: 231–240. doi:10.1007/s11569-008-0041-z. .

[25] http://jurist.law.pitt.edu/same-sex.htm

[26] http://books.google.com/books?id=Cls8AAAAIAAJ&pg=PA389

[27] van den Belt H (July 2003). "Debating the precautionary principle: "guilty until proven innocent" or "innocent until proven guilty"?" (http://www.plantphysiol.org/cgi/pmidlookup?view=long&pmid=12857792). *Plant Physiol.* **132** (3): 1122–6. doi:10.1104/pp.103.023531. PMC 526264. PMID 12857792. .

[28] http://www.wnd.com/?pageId=74461

[29] http://networkedblogs.com/7erBW

[30] Sunstein, Cass R. The Paralyzing Principle: Does the Precautionary Principle Point us in any Helpful Direction? (http://www.cato.org/pubs/regulation/regv25n4/v25n4-9.pdf) Regulation, Winter 2002-2003, The Cato Institute.

[31] Goldstein BD, Carruth RS (2004). "Implications of the Precautionary Principle: is it a threat to science?". *Int J Occup Med Environ Health* **17** (1): 153–61. PMID 15212219.

[32] Sherry Seethaler, *Lies, Damned Lies, and Science: How to Sort through the Noise around Global Warming, the Latest Health Claims, and Other Scientific Controversies* (FT Press, 2009),

[33] Crichton, Michael (2004). *State of Fear*. HarperCollins. p. 571. ISBN 0-06-621413-0.

[34] Bailey, Ronald. Precautionary Tale (http://www.reason.com/news/show/30977.html). Reason. April, 1999

Other publications

- Arrow, K.J., *et al.* (1996). "Is There a Role for Cost-Benefit Analysis in Environmental, Health, and Safety Regulation?". *Science* **272**.

- Andorno, Roberto (2004). "The Precautionary Principle: A New Legal Standard for a Technological Age" (http://www.ethik.uzh.ch/ibme/team/mitarbeitende/andorno/precautionaryprinciple.pdf) (PDF). *Journal of International Biotechnology Law* **1**: 11–19. doi:10.1515/jibl.2004.1.1.11.

- Communication from the European Commission on the precautionary principle Brusells (2000) (http://eur-lex.europa.eu/LexUriServ/LexUriServ.do?uri=CELEX:52000DC0001:EN:NOT)

- European Union (2002), European Union consolidated versions of the treaty on European Union and of the treaty establishing the European community, Official Journal of the European Union, C325, 24 December 2002, Title XIX, article 174, paragraph 2 and 3.

- Greenpeace, "Safe trade in the 21 Century, Greenpeace comprehensive proposals and recommendations for the 4th Ministerial Conference of the World Trade Organisation" pp. 8–9 (http://archive.greenpeace.org/politics/wto/doha_report.pdf)

- Harremoës, Poul, David Gee, Malcolm MacGarvin, Andy Stirling, Jane Keys, Brian Wynne, Sofia Guedes Vaz (October 2002). "The Precautionary Principle in the 20th Century: Late Lessons from Early Warnings — Earthscan, 2002. Review". *Nature* **419**: 433.
- O'Riordan, T. and Cameron, J. (1995), *Interpreting the Precautionary Principle*, London: Earthscan Publications
- Raffensberger C, Tickner J (eds.) (1999) Protecting Public Health and the Environment: Implementing the Precautionary Principle. Island Press, Washington, DC.
- Recuerda Girela, M.A., (2006), Seguridad Alimentaria y Nuevos Alimentos, Régimen jurídico-administrativo. Thomson-Aranzadi, Cizur Menor.
- Recuerda Girela, M.A., (2006), "Risk and Reason in the European Union Law", European Food and Feed Law Review, 5.
- Ricci PF, Rice D, Ziagos J, Cox LA (April 2003). "Precaution, uncertainty and causation in environmental decisions" (http://linkinghub.elsevier.com/retrieve/pii/S0160-4120(02)00191-5). *Environ Int* **29** (1): 1–19. doi:10.1016/S0160-4120(02)00191-5. PMID 12605931.
- Sandin, P. "Better Safe than Sorry: Applying Philosophical Methods to the Debate on Risk and the Precautionary Principle," (2004).
- Stewart, R.B. "Environmental Regulatory Decision making under Uncertainty". In An Introduction to the Law and Economics of Environmental Policy: Issues in Institutional Design, Volume 20: 71-126 (2002).
- Sunstein, Cass R. (2005), *Laws of Fear: Beyond the Precautionary Principle*. New York: Cambridge University Press

External links

- A Small Dose of Toxicology (http://www.asmalldoseof.org/)
- Bay Area Working Group on the Precautionary Principle (http://www.takingprecaution.org)
- Roberto Andorno, "The Precautionary Principle: A New Legal Standard for a Technological Age", *Journal of International Biotechnology Law,* 2004, 1, p. 11-19 (http://www.ethik.uzh.ch/ibme/team/andorno/precautionaryprinciple.pdf)
- Report by the UK Interdepartmental Liaison Group on Risk Assessment, 2002. "The Precautionary Principle: Policy and Application" (http://www.hse.gov.uk/aboutus/meetings/ilgra/pppa.pdf)
- David Appell, *Scientific American*, January 2001: "The New Uncertainty Principle" (http://www.biotech-info.net/uncertainty.html)
- *The Times*, July 27, 2007, Only a reckless mind could believe in safety first (http://www.timesonline.co.uk/tol/comment/columnists/guest_contributors/article2148188.ece)
- *The Times*, January 15, 2005, "What is . . . the Precautionary Principle?" (http://www.timesonline.co.uk/article/0,,1072-1440820,00.html)
- Mismanaging risk - Adam Smith Institute Blog (http://www.adamsmith.org/blog-archive/000995.php)
- Bill Durodié, *Spiked*, March 16, 2004: The precautionary principle assumes that prevention is better than cure (http://www.durodie.net/articles/spiked/20040316precautionaryprinciple.htm)
- European Environment Agency (2001), Late lessons from early warnings: the precautionary principle 1896–2000 (http://reports.eea.eu.int/environmental_issue_report_2001_22/en/Issue_Report_No_22.pdf)
- Applying the Precautionary Principle to Nanotechnology (http://www.crnano.org/precautionary.htm), *Center for Responsible Nanotechnology* 2004
- 1998 *Wingspread Statement on the Precautionary Principle* (http://www.sehn.org/wing.html)
- Science and Environmental Health Network, The Precautionary Principle in Action - a Handbook (http://www.biotech-info.net/handbook.pdf)
- Gary E. Marchant, Kenneth L. Mossman: *Arbitrary and Capricious: The Precautionary Principle in the European Union Courts*. American Enterprise Institute Press 2004, ISBN 0-8447-4189-2; free online PDF (http://www.policynetwork.net/uploaded/pdf/Arbitrary-web.pdf)

- Umberto Izzo, La precauzione nella responsabilità civile. Analisi di un concetto sul tema del danno da contagio per via trasfusionale (e-book reprint) [The Idea of Precaution in Tort Law. Analysis of a Concept against the Backdrop of the Tainted- Blood Litigation], UNITN e-prints, 2007, first edition Padua, Cedam 2004. free online PDF (http://eprints.biblio.unitn.it/archive/00001253/)
- The Precautionary Principle Project: Sustainable Development, Natural Resource Management and Biodiversity Conservation (http://www.pprinciple.net)
- Better Safe than Sorry: Applying Philosophical Methods to the Debate on Risk and the Precautionary Principle (http://www.infra.kth.se/~sandin/dissintro.pdf)
- Communication from the European Commission on the precautionary principle (http://eur-lex.europa.eu/LexUriServ/LexUriServ.do?uri=CELEX:52000DC0001:EN:NOT)
- UK Interdepartmental Liaison Group on Risk Assessment (ILGRA): The Precautionary Principle: Policy and Application (http://www.hse.gov.uk/aboutus/meetings/ilgra/pppa.htm)
- Report of UNESCO's group of experts on the Precautionary Principle (2005) (http://portal.unesco.org/shs/en/ev.php-URL_ID=8050&URL_DO=DO_TOPIC&URL_SECTION=201.html)
- Max More (2010), The Perils Of Precaution (http://www.maxmore.com/perils.htm)

Prudent avoidance principle

Prudent avoidance is a precautionary principle in risk management, stating that reasonable efforts to minimise potential risks should be taken when the actual magnitude of the risks is unknown. The principle was proposed by Prof. Granger Morgan of Carnegie Mellon University in 1989 in the context of electromagnetic radiation safety (in particular, fields produced by power lines).

A report for the Office of Technology Assessment of the US Congress described prudent avoidance of power line fields as:

> "looking systematically for strategies which can keep people out of 60 Hz fields arising from all sources but only adopt those which look to be "prudent" investments given their cost and our current level of scientific understanding about possible risks."

The principle has been adopted in a number of countries, for example Sweden, Denmark, Norway, Australia and New Zealand. While not adopted by any regulatory body at the national level in the USA, the principle has been adopted in some form by a number of local regulatory bodies, for example the public utility commissions in California, Colorado, Connecticut and Hawaii. The Colorado Public Commission states:

> "The utility shall include the concept of prudent avoidance with respect to planning, siting, construction, and operation of transmission facilities. Prudent avoidance shall mean the striking of a reasonable balance between the potential health effects of exposure to magnetic fields and the cost of impacts of mitigation of such exposure, by taking steps to reduce the exposure at reasonable or modest cost. Such steps might include, but are not limited to 1) design alternatives considering the spatial arrangement of phasing of conductors; 2) routing lines to limit exposures to areas of concentrated population and group facilities such as schools and hospitals; 3) installing higher structures; 4) widening right of way corridors; and 5) burial of lines."

The prudent avoidance principle is seen as a better alternative than other proposed approaches to risk management such as ALARA because it makes reasonable efforts to reduce possible risk without creating a specific numeric standard which is not supported by strong scientific evidence.

References

- Nair I, Morgan MG, Florig HK. Biologic effects of power frequency electric and magnetic fields. Office of Technology Assessment Report OTA-BP-E-53. Washington, DC:U.S. Office of Technology Assessment, 1989.
- Jack Sahl and Michael Dolan (1996) An Evaluation of Precaution-based Approaches As EMF Policy Tools in Community Environments [1]. Environmental Health Perspectives Volume 104, Number 9, September 1996
- Colorado Public Commission (CPUC). Statement of adoption in the matter of the rules for electric utilities of the Colorado Public Utilities Commission. Code of Colorado Regulation-723-3 concerning electric and magnetic fields. Denver, CO:Colorado Public Commission, 1992.

References

[1] http://ehp.niehs.nih.gov/members/1996/104-9/sahl.html

Pseudocertainty effect

The **pseudocertainty effect** is a concept from prospect theory. It refers to people's tendency to perceive an outcome as certain while in fact it is uncertain (Kahneman & Tversky, 1986)[1] . It is observed in multi-stage decisions, in which evaluation of outcomes in previous decision stage is discarded when making an option in subsequent stages.

Example

Kahneman and Tversky (1986) illustrated the pseudocertainty effect by the following examples.

First, consider this problem:

Which of the following options do you prefer?

- C. 25% chance to win $30 and 75% chance to win nothing
- D. 20% chance to win $45 and 80% chance to win nothing

In this case, 42% of participants chose option C while 58% chose option D.

Now, consider this problem:

Consider the following two stage game. In the first stage, there is a 75% chance to end the game without winning anything, and a 25% chance to move into the second stage. If you reach the second stage you have a choice between:

- E. a sure win of $30
- F. 80% chance to win $45 and 20% chance to win nothing

Your choice must be made before the outcome of the first stage is known.

This time,74% of participants chose option E while only 26% chose option F.

In fact, the actual probability of winning money in option E (25% x 100% = 25%) and option F (25% x 80% = 20%) is the same as the probability of winning money in option C (25%) and option D (20%) respectively. In the second problem, since individuals have no choice on options in the first stage, individuals tend to discard the first option when evaluating the overall probability of winning money, but just to consider the options in the second stage that individuals have a choice on. This is also known as cancellation, meaning that possible options are yielding to the same outcome thus ignoring decision process in that stage.

External links

- Kahneman, Daniel and Tversky, Amos. *The Framing of Decisions and the Psychology of Choice* Science 211 (1981), pp. 4538, copyright 1981 by the American Association for the Advancement of Science. [2]

Reference

[1] (http://www.cog.brown.edu/courses/cg195/pdf_files/fall07/Kahneman&Tversky1986.pdf), Tversky, A., & Kahneman, D. (1986). Rational Choice and the Framing of Decisions. *The Journal of Business*, **59**, S251-S278.

Residual risk

The **residual risk** is the risk or danger of an action or an event, a method or a (technical) process that, although being abreast with science, still conceives these dangers, even if all theoretically possible safety measures would be applied (scientifically conceivable measures).

The formula to calculate residual risk is (inherent risk) x (control risk) where inherent risk is (threats × vulnerability).

In the economic context, residual means "the quantity left over at the end of a process; a remainder" (dictionary.com).

In the property rights model it is the shareholder that holds the residual risk and therefore the residual profit.

External links

- Economist.com [1]
- Euronuclear.org [2]

References

[1] http://www.economist.com/research/Economics/alphabetic.cfm?LETTER=R#RESIDUAL%20RISK
[2] http://www.euronuclear.org/info/encyclopedia/r/residual-risk.htm

Risk analysis (engineering)

Risk analysis is the science of risks and their probability and evaluation.

Probabilistic risk assessment is one analysis strategy usually employed in science and engineering.

Risk analysis and the risk workshop

Risk analysis should be performed as part of the risk management process for each project. The data of which would be based on risk discussion workshops to identify potential issues and risks ahead of time before these were to pose cost and/ or schedule negative impacts (see the article on Cost contingency for a discussion of the estimation of cost impacts).

The risk workshops should be chaired by a large group ideally between 6 to 10 individuals from the various departmental functions (e.g. project manager, construction manager, site superintendent, and representatives from operations, procurement, [project] controls, etc.) so as to cover every risk element from different perspectives.

The outcome of the risk analysis would be the creation or review of the risk register to identify and quantify risk elements to the project and their potential impact.

Given that risk management is a continuous and iterative process, the risk workshop members would regroup on at regular intervals and project milestones to review the risk register mitigation plans, make changes to it as appropriate and following those changes re-run the risk model. By constantly monitoring risks these can be successfully mitigated resulting in a cost and schedule savings with a positive impact on the project.

Risk analysis and Information security

The risk evaluation of the Information technology environment has been the subject of some methodologies; Information security is a science that based itself on the evaluation and management of security risk, regarding the information used by organization to pursue their business objectives. Standardization bodies like ISO, NIST, The Open Group, Information Security Forum had published different standards in this field. International organizations such ENISA, ISACA had published many papers about it.

External links

- European Institute of risk management [1] (**French**)
- Harvard Center for Risk Analysis [2]
- Center for Risk Management of Engineering Systems, University of Virginia [3]
- RiskBrain - Risk Analysis Using Artificial Intelligence Techniques [4]

References

[1] http://www.cindynics.org
[2] http://www.hcra.harvard.edu/
[3] http://www.sys.virginia.edu/risk/
[4] http://www.riskbrain.com/

Risk aversion

Risk aversion is a concept in psychology, economics, and finance, based on the behavior of humans (especially consumers and investors) whilst exposed to uncertainty.

Risk aversion is the reluctance of a person to accept a bargain with an uncertain payoff rather than another bargain with a more certain, but possibly lower, expected payoff. For example, a risk-averse investor might choose to put his or her money into a bank account with a low but guaranteed interest rate, rather than into a stock that may have high returns, but also has a chance of becoming worthless.

Outside the rather mathematical fields of economics and finance, people have to make choices about how they face risks every day. Some have become very cautious, preferring to minimize risks even when the potential benefit of an action is large.

Example

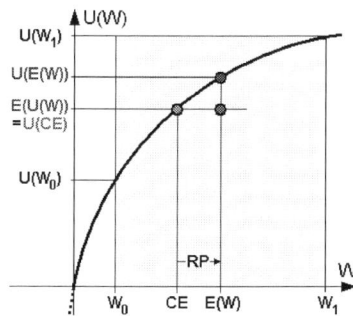

Utility function of a risk-averse (risk-avoiding) individual.

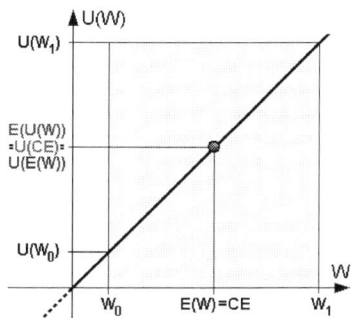

Utility funtion of a risk-neutral individual.

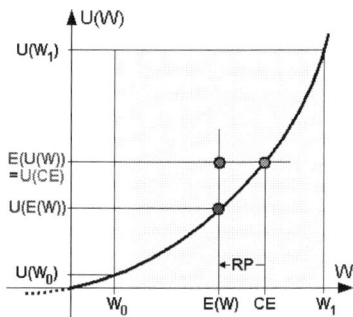

Utility function of a risk-affine (risk-seeking) individual.

A person is given the choice between two scenarios, one with a guaranteed payoff and one without. In the guaranteed scenario, the person receives $50. In the uncertain scenario, a coin is flipped to decide whether the person receives $100 or nothing. The expected payoff for both scenarios is $50, meaning that an individual who was insensitive to risk would not care whether they took the guaranteed payment or the gamble. However, individuals may have different **risk attitudes**. A person is:

- **risk-averse** (or **risk-avoiding**) - if he or she would accept a certain payment (certainty equivalent) of less than $50 (for example, $40), rather than taking the gamble and possibly receiving nothing.
- **risk-neutral** - if he or she is indifferent between the bet and a certain $50 payment.
- **risk-loving** (or **risk-seeking**) - if the guaranteed payment must be more than $50 (for example, $60) to induce him or her to take the guaranteed option, rather than taking the gamble and possibly winning $100.

The average payoff of the gamble, known as its expected value, is $50. The dollar amount that the individual would accept instead of the bet is called the certainty equivalent, and the difference between the expected value and the certainty equivalent is called the risk premium. For risk-averse individuals, it becomes positive, for risk-neutral persons it is zero, and for risk-loving individuals their risk premium becomes negative.

Utility of money

In expected utility theory, an agent has a utility function $u(x)$ where x represents the value that he might receive in money or goods (in the above example x could be 0 or 100).

Time does not come into this calculation, so inflation does not appear. (The utility function $u(x)$ is defined only up to linear transformation - in other words a constant factor could be added to the value of $u(x)$ for all x, and/or $u(x)$ could be multiplied by a positive constant factor, without affecting the conclusions.) An agent possesses risk aversion if and only if the utility function is concave. For instance $u(0)$ could be 0, $u(100)$ might be 10, $u(40)$ might be 5, and for comparison $u(50)$ might be 6.

The expected utility of the above bet (with a 50% chance of receiving 100 and a 50% chance of receiving 0) is,

$$E(u) = (u(0) + u(100))/2,$$

and if the person has the utility function with $u(0)=0$, $u(40)=5$, and $u(100)=10$ then the expected utility of the bet equals 5, which is the same as the known utility of the amount 40. Hence the certainty equivalent is 40.

The risk premium is ($50 minus $40)=$10, or in proportional terms

$$(\$50 - \$40)/\$40$$

or 25% (where $50 is the expected value of the risky bet: ($\frac{1}{2}0 + \frac{1}{2}100$). This risk premium means that the person would be willing to sacrifice as much as $10 in expected value in order to achieve perfect certainty about how much money will be received. In other words, the person would be indifferent between the bet and a guarantee of $40, and would prefer anything over $40 to the bet.

In the case of a wealthier individual, the risk of losing $100 would be less significant, and for such small amounts his utility function would be likely to be almost linear, for instance if u(0) = 0 and u(100) = 10, then u(40) might be 4.0001 and u(50) might be 5.0001.

The utility function for perceived gains has two key properties: an upward slope, and concavity. (i) The upward slope implies that the person feels that more is better: a larger amount received yields greater utility, and for risky bets the person would prefer a bet which is first-order stochastically dominant over an alternative bet (that is, if the probability mass of the second bet is pushed to the right to form the first bet, then the first bet is preferred). (ii) The concavity of the utility function implies that the person is risk averse: a sure amount would always be preferred over a risky bet having the same expected value; moreover, for risky bets the person would prefer a bet which is a mean-preserving contraction of an alternative bet (that is, if some of the probability mass of the first bet is spread out without altering the mean to form the second bet, then the first bet is preferred).

The above is an introduction to the mathematics of risk aversion. However it assumes that the individual concerned will act entirely rationally and will not factor into his decision non-monetary, psychological considerations such as regret at having made the wrong decision. Often an individual may come to a different decision depending on how the proposition is presented, even though there may be no mathematical difference.

Measures of risk aversion

Absolute risk aversion

The higher the curvature of $u(c)$, the higher the risk aversion. However, since expected utility functions are not uniquely defined (are defined only up to affine transformations), a measure that stays constant with respect to these transformations is needed. One such measure is the **Arrow-Pratt measure of absolute risk-aversion** (ARA), after the economists Kenneth Arrow and John W. Pratt,[1] [2] also known as the *coefficient of absolute risk aversion*, defined as

$$A(c) = -\frac{u''(c)}{u'(c)}.$$

The following expressions relate to this term:

- Exponential utility of the form $u(c) = 1 - e^{-\alpha c}$ is unique in exhibiting *constant absolute risk aversion* (CARA): $A(c) = \alpha$ is constant with respect to c.
- Hyperbolic absolute risk aversion (HARA) is the most general class of utility functions that are usually used in practice (specifically, CRRA (constant relative risk aversion, see below), CARA (constant absolute risk aversion), and quadratic utility all exhibit HARA and are often used because of their mathematical tractability). A utility function exhibits HARA if its absolute risk aversion is a hyperbolic function, namely

$$A(c) = -\frac{u''(c)}{u'(c)} = \frac{1}{ac + b}.$$

The solution to this differential equation (omitting additive and multiplicative constant terms, which do not affect the behavior implied by the utility function) is:

$$u(c) = \frac{(c - c_s)^{1-R}}{1 - R}$$

where $R = 1/a$ and $c_s = -b/a$. Note that when $a = 0$, this is CARA, as $A(c) = 1/b = const$, and when $b = 0$, this is CRRA (see below), as $cA(c) = 1/a = const$. See [3]

- *Decreasing/increasing absolute risk aversion* (DARA/IARA) if $A(c)$ is decreasing/increasing. An example of a DARA utility function is $u(c) = \log(c)$, with $A(c) = 1/c$, while $u(c) = c - \alpha c^2$, $\alpha > 0$, with $A(c) = 2\alpha/(1 - 2\alpha c)$ would represent a quadratic utility function exhibiting IARA.
- Experimental and empirical evidence is mostly consistent with decreasing absolute risk aversion.[4]
- Contrary to what several empirical studies have assumed, wealth is not a good proxy for risk aversion when studying risk sharing in a principal-agent setting. Although $A(c) = -\frac{u''(c)}{u'(c)}$ is monotonic in wealth under either DARA or IARA and constant in wealth under CARA, tests of contractual risk sharing relying on wealth as a proxy for absolute risk aversion are usually not identified.[5]

Relative risk aversion

The *Arrow-Pratt measure of relative risk-aversion* (RRA) or *coefficient of relative risk aversion* is defined as

$$R(c) = cA(c) = \frac{-cu''(c)}{u'(c)}.$$

Like for absolute risk aversion, the corresponding terms *constant relative risk aversion* (CRRA) and *decreasing/increasing relative risk aversion* (DRRA/IRRA) are used. This measure has the advantage that it is still a valid measure of risk aversion, even if the utility function changes from risk-averse to risk-loving as c varies, i.e. utility is not strictly convex/concave over all c. A constant RRA implies a decreasing ARA, but the reverse is not always true. As a specific example, the expected utility function $u(c) = \log(c)$ implies RRA = 1.

In intertemporal choice problems, the elasticity of intertemporal substitution is often unable to be disentangled from the coefficient of relative risk aversion. The isoelastic utility function

$$u(c) = \frac{c^{1-\rho}}{1-\rho}$$

exhibits constant relative risk aversion with $R(c) = \rho$ and the elasticity of intertemporal substitution $\varepsilon_{u(c)} = 1/\rho$. When $\rho = 1$ and one is subtracted in the numerator (facilitating the use of l'Hôpital's rule), this simplifies to the case of *log utility,* and the income effect and substitution effect on saving exactly offset.

Implications of increasing/decreasing absolute and relative risk aversion

The most straightforward implications of increasing or decreasing absolute or relative risk aversion, and the ones that motivate a focus on these concepts, occur in the context of forming a portfolio with one risky asset and one risk-free asset.[1] [2] If the person experiences an increase in wealth, he/she will choose to increase (or keep unchanged, or decrease) the *number of dollars* of the risky asset held in the portfolio if *absolute* risk aversion is decreasing (or constant, or increasing). Thus economists avoid using utility functions, such as the quadratic, which exhibit increasing absolute risk aversion, because they have an unrealistic behavioral implication.

Similarly, if the person experiences an increase in wealth, he/she will choose to increase (or keep unchanged, or decrease) the *fraction* of the portfolio held in the risky asset if *relative* risk aversion is decreasing (or constant, or increasing).

Portfolio theory

In modern portfolio theory, risk aversion is measured as the additional marginal reward an investor requires to accept additional risk. In modern portfolio theory, risk is being measured as standard deviation of the return on investment, i.e. the square root of its variance. In advanced portfolio theory, different kinds of risk are taken into consideration. They are being measured as the n-th radical of the n-th central moment. The symbol used for risk aversion is A or A_n.

$$A = \frac{dE(r)}{d\sigma}$$

$$A_n = \frac{dE(r)}{d\sqrt[n]{\mu_n}} = \frac{1}{n}\frac{dE(r)}{d\mu_n}$$

Limitations

The notion of (constant) risk aversion has come under criticism from behavioral economics. According to Matthew Rabin of UC Berkeley, a consumer who,

from any initial wealth level [...] turns down gambles where he loses $100 or gains $110, each with 50% probability [...] will turn down 50-50 bets of losing $1,000 or gaining any sum of money.

The point is that if we calculate the constant relative risk aversion (CRRA) from the first small-stakes gamble it will be so great that the same CRRA, applied to gambles with larger stakes, will lead to absurd predictions. The bottom line is that we cannot infer a CRRA from one gamble and expect it to scale up to larger gambles.

It is noteworthy that Rabin's Economist article went on to criticize the whole field of expected utility and not just constant relative risk aversion. This has led to some confusion in the field. One solution to the problem observed by Rabin is that proposed by prospect theory and cumulative prospect theory, where outcomes are considered relative to a reference point (usually the status quo), rather than to consider only the final wealth.

Risk aversion in the brain

Attitudes towards risk have attracted the interest of the field of neuroeconomics. A study by researchers at the University of Cambridge [6] suggested that the activity of a specific brain area (right inferior frontal gyrus) correlates with risk aversion, with more risk averse participants (i.e. those having higher risk premia) also having higher responses to safer options. This result coincides with other studies,[7] [8] that show that neuromodulation of the same area results in participants making more or less risk averse choices, depending on whether the modulation increases or decreases the activity of the target area.

Public understanding and risk in social activities

In the real world, many government agencies, e.g. Health and Safety Executive, are fundamentally risk-averse in their mandate. This often means that they demand (with the power of legal enforcement) that risks be minimized, even at the cost of losing the utility of the risky activity. It is important to consider the opportunity cost when mitigating a risk; the cost of not taking the risky action. Writing laws focused on the risk without the balance of the utility may misrepresent society's goals. The public understanding of risk, which influences political decisions, is an area which has recently been recognised as deserving focus. David Spiegelhalter is the Winton Professor of the Public Understanding of Risk at Cambridge University; a role he describes as "outreach".[9]

Children's services such as schools and playgrounds have become the focus of much risk-averse planning, meaning that children are often prevented from benefiting from activities that they would otherwise have had. Many playgrounds have been fitted with impact-absorbing matting surfaces. However, these are only designed to save children from death in the case of direct falls on their heads and do not achieve their main goals.[10] They are expensive, meaning that less resources are available to benefit users in other ways (such as building a playground closer to the child's home, reducing the risk of a road traffic accident on the way to it), and children are likely to attempt more dangerous acts, with confidence in the artificial surface. They grow up with a poorer understanding of risk management. Shiela Sage, an early years school advisor, observes "Children who are only ever kept in very safe places, are not the ones who are able to solve problems for themselves. Children need to have a certain amount of risk taking ... so they'll know how to get out of situations."[11] There are also classroom courses in risk taking, for example from a business perspective.[12]

A vaccine to protect children against the three common diseases measles, mumps and rubella was developed and recommended for all children in several countries including the UK. However, a controversy arose around allegations that it caused autism. This alleged causal link was thoroughly disproved,[13] and the doctor who made the claims was expelled from the General Medical Council. Even years after the claims were disproved, some parents wanted to avert the risk of causing autism in their own children. They chose to spend significant amounts of their own money on alternatives from private doctors. These alternatives carried their own risks which were not balanced fairly; most often that the children were not properly immunised against the more common diseases of measles, mumps and rubella.

Similarly, mobile phones may carry some small[14] [15] health risk. While most people would accept that unproven risk to gain the benefit of improved communication, others remain so risk averse that they do not. The COSMOS cohort study continues to study the actual risks of mobile phones.

Risk aversion theory can be applied to many aspects of life and its challenges, for example:

- Bribery and corruption - whether the risk of being implicated or caught outweighs the potential personal or professional rewards
- Drugs - whether the risk of having a bad trip outweighs the benefits of possible transformative one; whether the risk of defying social bans is worth the experience of alteration. See "Harm Reduction".
- Sex - judgement whether an experience that goes against social convention, ethical mores or common health prescriptions is worth the risk.
- Extreme sports - having the ability to go against biological predepositions like the fear of height.
- Play by children in playgrounds or beyond the reach of their parents.

External links

- More thorough introduction [16]
- Paper about problems with risk aversion [17]
- Economist article on monkey experiments showing behaviours resembling risk aversion [18] (requires a paid subscription to economist.com)
- Arrow-Pratt Measure on About.com:Economics [19]
- Risk Aversion of Individuals vs Risk Aversion of the Whole Economy [20]

References

[1] Arrow, K.J.,1965, "The theory of risk aversion," in Aspects of the Theory of Risk Bearing, by Yrjo Jahnssonin Saatio, Helsinki. Reprinted in: Essays in the Theory of Risk Bearing, Markham Publ. Co., Chicago, 1971, 90-109.

[2] Pratt, J. W., "Risk aversion in the small and in the large," Econometrica 32, January–April 1964, 122-136.

[3] Zender's lecture notes (http://leeds-faculty.colorado.edu/zender/Fin7330/1-RiskAversion.doc)

[4] Friend, Irwin and Blume, Marshall (1975), *The Demand for Risky Assets*, The American Economic Review.

[5] Bellemare, Marc F. and Zachary S. Brown, *On the (Mis)Use of Wealth as a Proxy for Risk Aversion* (http://papers.ssrn.com/sol3/papers. cfm?abstract_id=1140668), Working Paper, Duke University.

[6] Christopoulos GI; Tobler PN; Bossaerts P; Dolan RJ; Schultz W (2009). "Neural Correlates of Value, Risk, and Risk Aversion Contributing to Decision Making under Risk.". *J Neurosci* **26** (24): 6469–6472. doi:10.1523/JNEUROSCI.0804-06.2006. PMID 16775134.

[7] Knoch D, Gianotti LR, Pascual-Leone A, Treyer V, Regard M, Hohmann M, Brugger P (2006). "Disruption of right prefrontal cortex by low-frequency repetitive transcranial magnetic stimulation induces risk-taking behavior.". *J Neurosci* **26** (24): 6469–6472. doi:10.1523/JNEUROSCI.0804-06.2006. PMID 16775134.

[8] Fecteau S, Pascual-Leone A, Zald DH, Liguori P, Théoret H, Boggio PS, Fregni F (2007). "Activation of prefrontal cortex by transcranial direct current stimulation reduces appetite for risk during ambiguous decision making.". *J Neurosci* **27** (23): 6212–6218. doi:10.1523/JNEUROSCI.0314-07.2007. PMID 17553993.

[9] Spiegelhalter, David (Michaelmas 2009). "Don's Diary" (http://www.alumni.cam.ac.uk/uploads/File/CAM58/CAM58.pdf#page=5). *CAM*. **58**. Cambridge University Alumni Association. p. 3. .

[10] Gill, Tim (2007). *No fear: Growing up in a Risk Averse society* (http://www.gulbenkian.org.uk/media/item/1266/223/No-fear-19.12. 07.pdf#page=28). Calouste Gulbenkian Foundation. p. 81. ISBN 9781903080085. .

[11] Sue Durant, Sheila Sage. (10 January 2006). *Early Years - The Outdoor Environment* (http://www.teachers.tv/video/214). Teachers TV. .

[12] Wetton, Noreen; Wilson, John (February 2007). *Confident to Earn* (http://www.ea.e-renfrew.sch.uk/curriculinks/Links/Teachers/ ConfidentToEarn.pdf). Scottish Executive Education Department.

[13] Madsen KM, Hviid A, Vestergaard M *et al.* (2002). "A population-based study of measles, mumps, and rubella vaccination and autism". *N Engl J Med* **347** (19): 1477–82. doi:10.1056/NEJMoa021134. PMID 12421889.

[14] "What are the health risks associated with mobile phones and their base stations?" (http://www.who.int/features/qa/30/en). *Online Q&A*. World Health Organization. 2005-12-05. . Retrieved 2008-01-19.

[15] "Electromagnetic fields and public health: mobile telephones and their base stations" (http://www.who.int/mediacentre/factsheets/fs193/en). *Fact sheet N°193*. World Health Organization. June 2000. . Retrieved 2008-01-19.

[16] http://cepa.newschool.edu/het/essays/uncert/aversion.htm#pratt

[17] http://repositories.cdlib.org/cgi/viewcontent.cgi?article=1025&context=iber/econ

[18] http://www.economist.com/science/displayStory.cfm?story_id=4102350

[19] http://economics.about.com/cs/economicsglossary/g/arrow_pratt.htm

[20] http://ssrn.com/abstract=941126

Risk breakdown structure

Risk Breakdown Structure (RBS) - A hierarchically organised depiction of the identified project risks arranged by category.[1] [2]

An Introduction to the Risk Breakdown Structure

When planning a project to meet targets for cost, schedule, or quality, it is useful to identify likely risks to the success of the project. A risk is any possible situation that is not planned for, but that, if it occurs, is likely to divert the project from its planned result. For example, an established project team plans for the work to be done by its staff, but there is the risk that an employee may unexpectedly leave the team.

In Project Management, the *Risk Management Process* has the objectives of identifying, assessing, and managing risks, both positive and negative. All too often, project managers focus only on negative risk, however, good things can happen in a project, "things" that were foreseen, but not expressly planned.

The objective of Risk Management is to predict risks, assess their likelihood and impact, and to actively plan what should be done ahead of time to best deal with situations when they occur.

The risk management process usually occurs in five distinct steps: risk management planning, risk identification, risk analysis, risk response planning, and risk monitoring and control. The central point of risk identification and assessment in risk management is understanding the risk. However, this is also where project managers and risk subject matter experts (SMEs) get the least help from recognized references, best practices, or work standards.

Currently, the Project Management Institute (PMI^r) has a team of SMEs working on a Practice Standard for Risk Management. This team has identified one very good tool: the **Risk Breakdown Structure (RBS)**. The RBS helps the project manager, the risk manager, and almost any stakeholder to understand, and therefore be able to identify and assess risk.

What is a "Risk Breakdown Structure?"

The RBS will prove extremely valuable to better grasp when a project needs to receive special scrutiny, in other words, when risk might happen. The RBS can also help the project manager and the risk manager to better understand recurring risks and concentrations of risk that could lead to issues that affect the status of the project.

Following the concept of the Work Breakdown Structure (WBS), the Risk Breakdown Structure provides a means for the project manager and risk manager to structure the risks being addressed or tracked. Just as PMI defines the Work Breakdown Structure as a "deliverable-oriented grouping of project elements that organizes and defines the total work scope of the project..." the RBS could be considered as a "[sic] a hierarchically organized depiction of the identified project risks arranged by risk category."[3]

Many project managers and risk managers currently use "home-grown" methods for listing, identifying, assessing, and tracking risks in their projects. These methods include: spreadsheets, listing, generic risk taxonomy, based somewhat loosely on various standards and guidelines. [4] [5] [6]

An approach that simply places the risks in a list, a simple table, or even in a database does not provide the strength of using a structured, organized method similar to a Work Breakdown Structure. To fully understand the risks and better identify and assess the risk, a "deep-dive" into each risk, recording as many levels of identification as necessary, may be required. The project value of placing risks in a structure such as this lies in the ability of the project manager and risk manager to then quickly and easily identify and assess the risk, identify the potential risk triggers, and develop a more robust risk response plan [7]. If all risks are placed in a hierarchical structure as they are identified, and the structure is organized by source, the total risk exposure to the project can be more easily understood, and planning for the risk more easily accomplished.

Templates for creating a Risk Breakdown Structure

The concept of the RBS is new. The PMBoK (2004), barely references its use; however, the PMI Standards team has incorporated the RBS in the *Practice Standard for Risk Management* (draft for release in 2009). The PMBoK provides an example graphic of the RBS in Chapter 11, Figure 11.4. This reference has as major topics: Technical, External, Organizational, and Project Management. Another source [8] provides the following major topics: Technical, Management, Organizational, External, and Project Management. Dr. David Hillson, in the proceedings of the Project Management Institute Annual Seminars and Symposium, on Oct. 3-10, 2002,[9] provided several different RBS Structure examples, with topics similar to those already shown. Dr. Hillson broke out two different examples, an RBS for Software Development, which had the following major topics: Product Engineering, Development Environment, Program Constraints; and an RBS for Construction Design, which has these major topics: Environment, Industry, Client, Project.

Each RBS is broken into "levels", with each level providing a more in-depth "view" of the identified risk. As an example, in creating a RBS for software development, Level 1 of the RBS might be Technical, followed by Level 2, Requirements, followed by Level 3, Functional Requirements, Informational Requirements, Non-functional Requirements, etc. If desired, Level 3 can be further refined with Level 4, Stability, Completeness, Functionality, Interfaces, Testability, etc., Level 5, etc.

Once the project team has created its RBS, then individual risks can be identified. Several different techniques for defining the individual risks are available, including brain-storming, surveys, workshops, etc. Each identified risk needs to be categorized, and placed in the RBS under a specific topic (or topics if the risk spans two or more topics, such as a risk in gathering requirements might span Technical, organizational and project management.

NOTE: the RBS will be different between projects, even projects within the same project area, e.g., construction, information technology, environmental remediation, etc.

After the RBS has completed its first "pass" in the creation phase, it can then become an input to qualitative risk analysis, where probabilities, priorities, and impacts are determined.

Using the Risk Breakdown Structure

The RBS serves as more than just a "database" for identifying risks to the project. When created, the RBS provides a vehicle for risk analysis and reporting, and risk comparison across projects. Most importantly, the RBS is "the" tool for risk identification.

Risk Identification

Risk identification will be the first step in determining which risks may affect a project. Identification also provides documentation of the risk characteristics. The first level (Level 1) of the RBS can be used as a sanity check to make certain that all topics that might include risk are covered during the risk identification process. Using the RBS, an iterative process can be initiated that will persist throughout the project life-cycle. The frequency and applicability of this iterative process will be different in each phase of the life-cycle[10]

Using a risk identification checklist that is focused on the RBS, using Levels 2, 3 and below, assists in identifying specific and generic risks. This checklist can then become a part of the project managers' and risk managers' tool set for future projects.

Risk identification leads to quantitative risk analysis, conducted by the Project Risk Manager. Interestingly, sometimes merely identifying the risk will suggest the proper response, which can be entered into the Risk Response Plan.

Risk Analysis (Qualitative Risk Analysis)

Risk analysis is more easily achieved if, after identification, the risks are placed in proper perspective within the RBS by categorizing the risks in the various levels. Risk analysis (quantitative risk analysis) involves the use of techniques for prioritizing the risk, determining the probability of the risk, and calculating the impact of the risk. At no point should the project manager or risk manager decide that the total number of identified risks should cause the cancellation of the project. The total number does not take into account the probability with which the risk will occur, nor the impact to the project, should the risk occur. A few risks, with high probabilities and high impact, are far more critical to the overall success of the project than a large number of risks with low probability and minimal impact. Using the RBS, the project manager and the risk manager should create a "risk score" based on the priority, probability and impact of each risk, and with each "group" of risks (according to the appropriate Level of the RBS).

Using the RBS also offers other valuable understanding into the analysis of the identified risks. Some of these new understandings are:

- Risk exposure type
- Dependencies between risks
- Root causality of risks
- Most significant and least significant risks
- Correlations between risks [11]

Another benefit of the RBS is the ability to focus risk responses to the high probability, high impact, high priority risks using the risk topic groupings.

Summary

Effective risk management demands that the project manager and risk manager fully understand the risks of a project. A successful risk management process would also require a good knowledge and understanding of the business objectives of the project. During risk identification, a large volume of risks can be identified. Simply listing these risks or putting them in a spreadsheet or database does not provide the in-depth understanding of the identified risks necessary to allow a solid risk response planning task. The RBS provides the tool necessary to assist in identifying risks, analyzing risks, and creating a successful risk response plan, and it provides a vehicle for "deep-dives" into the complexity of the risk. Using a hierarchical RBS, similar in its design to the WBS, allows the project and risk managers the opportunity to carefully align the risks in proper categories, using as deep an analysis as time and resources would permit [12] .

References

[1] PMBoK-Project Management Book of Knowledge

[2] PMI *Practice Standard for Risk Management* - currently under development

[3] PMI PMBOK, 3rd Edition, Chapter 11, <u>Risk Management</u>

[4] NIST *Risk Management Guide for Information Technology Systems* http://csrc.nist.gov/publications/nistpubs/800-30/sp800-30.pdf

[5] NASA Procedural Requirements 8000.4: Risk Management Procedural Requirements http://nodis3.gsfc.nasa.gov/displayDir.cfm?t=NPR&c=8000&s=4

[6] PMI PMBOK[r] Chapter 11, Risk Management http://www.pmi.org/Marketplace/Pages/ProductDetail.aspx?GMProduct=00100035801

[7] IEC 62198:2001 *Project Risk Management - Application Guidelines* International Electrotechnical Communication, Geneva Switzerland

[8] http://certifedpmp.wordpress.com/2008/10/11/risk-breakdown-structure-rbs/

[9] http://www.risk-doctor.com/pdf-files/rbs1002.pdf

[10] *Continuous Risk Management Gudidebook*, Richard L. Murphy, *et al.*, SIE/Carnegie-Mellon University press.

[11] *op cit* Hillson,

[12] Project Management Institute, Risk Management Special Interest Group (SIG), http://www.risksig.com/

Risk factor

In epidemiology, a **risk factor** is a variable associated with an increased risk of disease or infection. Sometimes, **determinant** is also used, being a variable associated with either increased or decreased risk. Risk factors or determinants are correlational and not necessarily causal, because correlation does not imply causation. For example, being young cannot be said to cause measles, but young people are more at risk as they are less likely to have developed immunity during a previous epidemic.

Relation to risk

Risk factors are evaluated by comparing the risk of those exposed to the potential risk factor to those not exposed. Let's say that at a wedding, 74 people ate the chicken and 22 of them were ill, while of the 35 people who had the fish or vegetarian meal only 2 were ill. Did the chicken make the people ill?

$$Risk = \frac{\text{number of persons experiencing event (food poisoning)}}{\text{number of persons exposed to risk factor (food)}}$$

So the chicken eaters' risk = 22/74 = 0.297

And non-chicken eaters' risk = 2/35 = 0.057.

Those who ate the chicken had a risk over five times as high as those who did not, suggesting that eating chicken was the cause of the illness. Note, however, that this is *not* proof. Statistical methods would be used in a less clear cut case to decide what level of risk the risk factor would have to present to be able to say the risk factor is linked to the disease (for example in a study of the link between smoking and lung cancer). Even then, no amount of statistical analysis could prove that the risk factor *causes* the disease; this could only be proven using direct methods such as a medical explanation of the disease's roots.

General determinants

The risk of an outcome usually depends on an interplay between multiple determinants. When performing epidemiological studies to evaluate one or more determinants for a specific outcome, the other determinants may act as confounding factors, and need to be controlled for, e.g. by stratification. The potentially confounding determinants varies with what outcome is studied, but the following general determinants are common to most epidemiological associations, and are the determinants most commonly controlled for in epidemiological studies:

- Age
- Sex or gender
- Geographic location

- Ethnicity
- Genetic predisposition
- Occupation
- Social status
- Level of chronic stress
- Diet
- Level of physical exercise
- Alcohol consumption and tobacco smoking
- Other diseases and conditions, commonly diabetes mellitus
- Other social determinants of health

Risk marker

A *risk marker* is a variable that is quantitatively associated with a disease or other outcome, but direct alteration of the risk marker does not necessarily alter the risk of the outcome.

History

The term "risk factor" was first coined by heart researcher Dr. Thomas R. Dawber in a landmark scientific paper in 1961, where he attributed heart disease to specific conditions (blood pressure, cholesterol, smoking).

References

- Case, S.P. and Haines, K.R. (2009) Understanding Youth Offending: Risk Factor Research, Policy and Practice. Cullompton: Willan. http://www.willanpublishing.co.uk/cgi-bin/indexer?product=9781843923411

Risk Management Programme

Risk Management is a research programme set up by the Geneva Association, also known as the International Association for the Study of Insurance Economics. The focus of this programme is manifold and address the following issues: fostering the use of the tools of risk assessment and risk management in new fields of application such as policy making; providing a platform between the insurance community, the engineering and academic communities and policy makers to discuss risk issues; promoting the concept of the insurability of risks as the natural borderline between State legislation and the market economy; identifying new opportunities for insurers in the emerging sustainability concept in order to enlarge the field of insurable risks.[1]

Selected Key Issues

- What are the vulnerabilities in our industrial and services value-added processes?
- Where are the mechanisms for understanding, managing and mitigating these risks?
- How can insurance cope with a more complex and demanding risk scenario?
- What is the new risk environment that has been created in recent years?
- What about technologies being a new source of vulnerability?

Publications

- ***Risk Management***, Geneva Association Information Newsletter, The Geneva Association [2]
- ***Etudes et Dossiers***, Working Paper Series, The Geneva Association [3]
- ***The Geneva Risk and Insurance Review***, formerly The Geneva Papers on Risk and Insurance Theory (until March 2005), The Geneva Association [4] & Springer [5]
- ***Pensions and Life Insurance*** and ***Risk Management/M.O.R.E***, The Geneva Papers on Risk and Insurance - Issues and Practice, Vol.29 - No.3 / July 2004, Palgrave Macmillan [6]
- ***Special Issue on Risk Management***, The Geneva Papers on Risk and Insurance - Issues and Practice, Vol.27 - No.2 / April 2002, Palgrave Macmillan [7]
- ***Strategic Issues in Risk Management and Insurance***, The Geneva Papers on Risk and Insurance - Issues and Practice, Vol.24 - No.3 / July 1999, Palgrave Macmillan [8]
- ***Issues in Risk Management and Insurance***, The Geneva Papers on Risk and Insurance - Issues and Practice, Vol.24 - No.2 / April 1999, Palgrave Macmillan [9]
- ***Risk Management Strategies***, The Geneva Papers on Risk and Insurance - Issues and Practice, No.80 / July 1996
- ***Risk Management Issues***, The Geneva Papers on Risk and Insurance - Issues and Practice, No.76 / July 1995
- ***1973-1993 Twenty Years of Initiatives and Research on the Economic Role of Insurance and Risk Management in Modern Society***, The Geneva Papers on Risk and Insurance - Issues and Practice, No.68 / July 1993
- ***Risk Management Studies***, The Geneva Papers on Risk and Insurance - Issues and Practice, No.64 / July 1992
- ***Hazardous Waste Management***, The Geneva Papers on Risk and Insurance - Issues and Practice, No.51 / April 1989
- ***Risk and Society***, ***The Discount Rate*** and ***Risk and Insurance Issues***, The Geneva Papers on Risk and Insurance - Issues and Practice, No.48 / July 1988
- ***Risk and Insurance Issues***, The Geneva Papers on Risk and Insurance - Issues and Practice, No.44 / July 1987

External links

- The Geneva Association website [10] (known as the International Association for the Study of Insurance Economics)
- The GA M.O.R.E Programme web page [11], Management of Risk in Engineering
- The Risk Institute website [12]
- The ARIA website [13], the American Risk and Insurance Association

References

[1] "Risk Management Research Programme Page" (http://web.archive.org/web/20070611173249/http://www.genevaassociation.org/risk_management.htm). The Geneva Association. Archived from the original (http://www.genevaassociation.org/risk_management.htm) on 2007-06-11. . Retrieved 2007-06-27.

[2] http://www.genevaassociation.org/risk_management.htm

[3] http://www.genevaassociation.org/Etudes&Dossier.htm

[4] http://www.genevaassociation.org/gptheory.htm

[5] http://www.springer.com/east/home/business/journals?SGWID=5-40528-70-35612997-0

[6] http://www.palgrave-journals.com/gpp/journal/v29/n3/index.html

[7] http://www.palgrave-journals.com/gpp/journal/v27/n2/index.html

[8] http://www.palgrave-journals.com/gpp/journal/v24/n3/index.html

[9] http://www.palgrave-journals.com/gpp/journal/v24/n2/index.html

[10] http://www.genevaassociation.org

[11] http://www.genevaassociation.org/More.htm

[12] http://eng.newwelfare.org/?page_id=2

[13] http://www.aria.org/

Risk neutral

In economics and finance, **risk neutral** behavior is between risk aversion and risk seeking. If offered either €50 or a 50% chance of each of €100 and nothing, a risk neutral person would have no preference between the two options. In contrast, a risk averse person presented with these options would accept some amount less than €50 in preference to the risky option, while a risk seeking person would accept a less than 50% chance of €100 in preference to the sure €50.

Theory of the firm

In the context of the theory of the firm, a risk neutral firm facing risk about the market price of its product, and caring only about profit, would maximize the expected value of its profit (with respect to its choices of labor input usage, output produced, etc.). But a risk averse firm in the same environment would typically take a more cautious approach.[1]

Portfolio theory

In portfolio choice,[2] [3] [4] a risk neutral investor able to choose any combination of an array of risky assets (various companies' stocks, various companies' bonds, etc.) would invest exclusively in the asset with the highest expected yield, ignoring its risk features relative to those of other assets, and would even sell short the asset with the lowest expected yield as much as is permitted in order to invest the proceeds in the highest expected-yield asset. In contrast, a risk averse investor would diversify among a variety of assets, taking account of their risk features, even though doing so would lower the expected return on the overall portfolio. The risk neutral investor's portfolio would have a higher expected return, but also a greater variance of possible returns.

The risk neutral utility function

Choice under uncertainty is often characterized as the maximization of expected utility. Utility is often assumed to be a function of profit or final portfolio wealth, with a positive first derivative. The utility function whose expected value is maximized is concave for a risk averse agent, convex for a risk lover, and linear for a risk neutral agent. Thus in the risk neutral case, expected utility of wealth is simply equal to a linear function of expected wealth, and maximizing it is equivalent to maximizing expected wealth itself.

References

[1] Sandmo, Agnar. "On the theory of the competitive firm under price uncertainty," *American Economic Review* 61, March 1971, 65-73.

[2] Edwin J. Elton and Martin J. Gruber, "Modern portfolio theory, 1950 to date", *Journal of Banking and Finance* 21, 1997, 1743-1759.

[3] Markowitz, H.M. *Portfolio Selection: Efficient Diversification of Investments*, 1959. New York: John Wiley & Sons. http://cowles.econ. yale.edu/P/cm/m16/index.htm.(reprinted by Yale University Press, 1970, ISBN 978-0-300-01372-6; 2nd ed. Basil Blackwell, 1991, ISBN 978-1-55786-108-5)

[4] Merton, Robert. "An analytic derivation of the efficient portfolio frontier," *Journal of Financial and Quantitative Analysis* 7, September 1972, 1851-1872.

Risk perception

Risk perception is the subjective judgment that people make about the characteristics and severity of a risk. The phrase is most commonly used in reference to natural hazards and threats to the environment or health, such as nuclear power. Several theories have been proposed to explain why different people make different estimates of the dangerousness of risks. Three major families of theory have been developed: psychology approaches (heuristics and cognitive), anthropology/sociology approaches (cultural theory) and interdisciplinary approaches (social amplification of risk framework).

Early theories

The study of risk perception arose out of the observation that experts and lay people often disagreed about how risky various technologies and natural hazards were.

The mid 1960's saw the rapid rise of nuclear technologies and the promise for clean and safe energy. However, public perception shifted against this new technology. Fears of both longitudinal dangers to the environment as well as immediate disasters creating radioactive wastelands turned the public against this new technology. The scientific and governmental communities asked why public perception was against the use of nuclear energy when all of the scientific experts were declaring how safe it really was. The problem, from the perspectives of the experts, was a difference between scientific facts and an exaggerated public perception of the dangers [1].

A key early paper was written in 1969 by Chauncey Starr.[2] Starr used a revealed preference approach to find out what risks are considered acceptable by society. He assumed that society had reached equilibrium in its judgment of risks, so whatever risk levels actually existed in society were acceptable. His major finding was that people will accept risks 1,000 greater if they are voluntary (e.g. driving a car) than if they are involuntary (e.g. a nuclear disaster).

This early approach assumed that individuals behave in a rational manner, weighing information before making a decision. Individuals have exaggerated fears due to inadequate or incorrect information. Implied in this assumption is that additional information can help people understand true risk and hence lessen their opinion of danger [3]. While researchers in the engineering school did pioneer research in risk perception, by adapting theories from economics, it has little use in a practical setting. Numerous studies have rejected the belief that additional information, alone, will shift perceptions [4].

Psychology approach

The psychology approach began with research in trying to understand how people process information. These early works maintain that people use cognitive heuristics in sorting and simplifying information which lead to biases in comprehension. Later work built on this foundation and became the **psychometric paradigm**. This approach identifies numerous factors responsible for influencing individual perceptions of risk, including dread, newness, stigma, and other factors [5].

Heuristics and biases

The earliest psychometric research was done by psychologists Daniel Kahneman and Amos Tversky, who performed a series of gambling experiments to see how people evaluated probabilities. Their major finding was that people use a number of heuristics to evaluate information. These heuristics are usually useful shortcuts for thinking, but they may lead to inaccurate judgments in some situations — in which case they become cognitive biases.

- **Representativeness**: is usually employed when people are asked to judge the probability that an object or event belongs to a class / processes by its similarity:

- insensitivity to prior probability
- insensitivity to sample size
- misconception of chance (gambler fallacy)
- insensitivity to predictability
- illusion of validity
- misconception of regression

- **Availability heuristic:** events that can be more easily brought to mind or imagined are judged to be more likely than events that could not easily be imagined:

- biases due to retrievability of instances
- biases due to the effectivenss of research set
- biases of imaginability
- illusiory correlation

- **Anchoring and Adjustment heuristic**: people will often start with one piece of known information and then adjust it to create an estimate of an unknown risk — but the adjustment will usually not be big enough:

- insufficient adjustment
- biases in the evaluation of conjunctive and disjunctive event
- anchoring in the assessment of subjective probability distributions

- Asymmetry between gains and losses: People are risk averse with respect to gains, preferring a sure thing over a gamble with a higher expected utility but which presents the possibility of getting nothing. On the other hand, people will be risk-seeking about losses, preferring to hope for the chance of losing nothing rather than taking a sure, but smaller, loss (e.g. insurance).
- Threshold effects: People prefer to move from uncertainty to certainty over making a similar gain in certainty that does not lead to full certainty. For example, most people would choose a vaccine that reduces the incidence of disease A from 10% to 0% over one that reduces the incidence of disease B from 20% to 10%.

Another key finding was that the experts are not necessarily any better at estimating probabilities than lay people. Experts were often overconfident in the exactness of their estimates, and put too much stock in small samples of data[6].

Cognitive Psychology

The majority of people in the general public express a greater concern for problems which appear to possess an immediate effect on everyday life such as hazardous waste or pesticide-use than for long-term problems that may affect future generations such as climate change or population growth [7] . People greatly rely on the scientific community to assess the threat of environmental problems because they usually do not directly experience the effects of phenomena such as climate change. The exposure most people have to climate change has been impersonal; most people only have virtual experience though documentaries and news media in what may seem like a "remote" area of the world. [8] However, coupled with the population's wait-and-see attitude, people do not understand the importance of changing environmentally destructive behaviors even when experts provide detailed and clear risks caused by climate change. [9]

Psychometric paradigm

Research within the psychometric paradigm turned to focus on the roles of affect, emotion, and stigma in influencing risk perception. Melissa Finucane and Paul Slovic have been among the key researchers here. These researchers first challenged Starr's article by examining expressed preference – how much risk people say they are willing to accept. They found that, contrary to Starr's basic assumption, people generally saw most risks in society as being unacceptably high. They also found that the gap between voluntary and involuntary risks was not nearly as great as Starr claimed.

Slovic and team found that perceived risk is quantifiable and predictable. People tend to view current risk levels as unacceptably high for most activities[10] . All things being equal, the greater people perceived a benefit, the greater the tolerance for a risk[11] . If a person derived pleasure from using a product, people tended to judge its benefits as high and its risks as low. If the activity was disliked, the judgments were opposite[12] . Research in psychometrics has proven that risk perception is highly dependent on intuition, experiential thinking, and emotions.

Psychometric research identified a broad domain of characteristics that may be condensed into three high order factors: 1) the degree to which a risk is understood, 2) the degree to which it evokes a feeling of dread, and 3) the number of people exposed to the risk. A dread risk elicits visceral feelings of terror, uncontrollable, catastrophe, inequality, and uncontrolled. An unknown risk is new and unknown to science. The more a person dreads an activity, the higher its perceived risk and the more that person wants the risk reduced [13] .

Anthropology/sociology approach

The anthropology/sociology approach posits risk perceptions as produced by and supporting social institutions [14] . In this view, perceptions are socially constructed by institutions, cultural values, and ways of life.

Cultural theory

"The Cultural Theory of risk" (with capital C and T). Cultural Theory is based on the work of anthropologist Mary Douglas and political scientist Aaron Wildavsky first published in 1982[15] .

In Cultural Theory, Douglas and Wildavsky outline four "ways of life" in a grid/group arrangement. Each way of life corresponds to a specific social structure and a particular outlook on risk. Grid categorizes the degree to which people are constrained and circumscribed in their social role. The tighter binding of social constraints limits individual negotiation. Group refers to the extent to which individuals are bounded by feelings of belonging or solidarity. The greater the bonds, the less individual choice are subject to personal control[16] . Four ways of life include: Hierarchical, Individualist, Egalitarian, and Fatalist.

Risk perception researchers have not widely accepted Cultural theory. Even Douglas says that the theory is controversial; it poses a danger of moving out of the favored paradigm of individual rational choice of which many researchers are comfortable[17] .

Interdisciplinary approach

Social amplification of risk framework

The Social Amplification of Risk Framework (SARF), combines research in psychology, sociology, anthropology, and communications theory. SARF outlines how communications of risk events pass from the sender through intermediate stations to a receiver and in the process serve to amplify or attenuate perceptions of risk. All links in the communication chain, individuals, groups, media, etc., contain filters through which information is sorted and understood.

The framework attempts to explain the process by which risks are amplified, receiving public attention, or attenuated, receiving less public attention. The framework may be used to compare responses from different groups in a single event, or analyze the same risk issue in multiple events. In a single risk event, some groups may amplify their perception of risks while other groups may attenuate, or decrease, their perceptions of risk.

The main thesis of SARF states that risk events interact with individual psychological, social and other cultural factors in ways that either increase or decrease public perceptions of risk. Behaviors of individuals and groups then generate secondary social or economic impacts while also increasing or decreasing the physical risk itself [18].

These **ripple effects** caused by the amplification of risk include enduring mental perceptions, impacts on business sales, and change in residential property values, changes in training and education, or social disorder. These secondary changes are perceived and reacted to by individuals and groups resulting in third-order impacts. As each higher-order impacts are reacted to, they may ripple to other parties and locations. Traditional risk analyses neglect these ripple effect impacts and thus greatly underestimate the adverse effects from certain risk events. Public distortion of risk signals provides a corrective mechanism by which society assesses a fuller determination of the risk and its impacts to such things not traditionally factored into a risk analysis [19].

External links

- "Fear of Crime and Perceived Risk." Oxford Bibliographies Online: Criminology. [20]

References

[1] Douglas, Mary. Risk Acceptability According to the Social Sciences. Russell Sage Foundation, 1985.

[2] "Social Benefits versus Technological Risks" in *Science* Vol. 165, No. 3899. (Sep. 19, 1969), pp. 1232–1238

[3] Douglas, Mary. Risk Acceptability According to the Social Sciences. Russell Sage Foundation, 1985.

[4] [Freudenburg, William R., "Risk and Recreancy: Weber, the Division of Labor, and the Rationality of Risk Perceptions." Social Forces 71(4), (June 1993): 909–932.]

[5] Tversky, Amos and Daniel Kahneman. "Judgment under Uncertainty: Heuristics and Biases." Science 185(4157) (September 1974): 1124–1131.

[6] Slovic, Paul, Baruch Fischhoff, Sarah Lichtenstein. "Why Study Risk Perception?" Risk Analysis 2(2) (1982): 83–93.

[7] "Slimak & Dietz, 2006Koger" cited in Susan M., and Deborah Du Nann. Winter. The Psychology of Environmental Problems: Psychology for Sustainability. 3rd ed. New York: Psychology, 2010. 216-217

[8] Swim, Janet, Susan Clayton, Thomas Doherty, Robert Gifford, George Howard, Joseph Reser, Paul Stern, and Elke Weber. Psychology & Global Climate Change. Publication. American Psychological Association, 2010. Web. 10 Dec. 2010. <http://www.apa.org/science/about/publications/climate-change-booklet.pdf>.

[9] "Sterman, 2008" cited in Koger, Susan M., and Deborah Du Nann. Winter. The Psychology of Environmental Problems: Psychology for Sustainability. 3rd ed. New York: Psychology, 2010. 219

[10] Slovic, Paul, ed. The Perception of Risk. Earthscan, Virginia. 2000.

[11] Slovic, Paul, Baruch Fischhoff, Sarah Lichtenstein. "Why Study Risk Perception?" Risk Analysis 2(2) (1982): 83–93.

[12] Gregory, Robin & Robert Mendelsohn. "Perceived Risk, Dread, and Benefits." Risk Analysis 13(3) (1993): 259–264

[13] Slovic, Paul, Baruch Fischhoff, Sarah Lichtenstein. "Why Study Risk Perception?" Risk Analysis 2(2) (1982): 83–93

[14] Wildavsky, Aaron and Karl Dake. "Theories of Risk Perception: Who Fears What and Why?" American Academy of Arts and Sciences (Daedalus) 119(4) (1990): 41–60.

[15] Douglas, Mary and Aaron Wildavsky. Risk and Culture. University of California Press, 1982.

[16] Thompson, Michael, Richard Ellis, Aaron Wildavsky. Cultural theory. Westview Press, Boulder, Colorado, 1990.

[17] Douglas, Mary. Risk and Blame: Essays in Cultural theory. New York: Routledge, 1992.

[18] Kasperson, Roger E., Ortwin Renn, Paul Slovic, Halina Brown, Jacque Emel, Robert Goble, Jeanne Kasperson, Samuel Ratick. "The Social Amplification of Risk: A Conceptual Framework." Risk Analysis 8(2) (1988): 177–187.

[19] Kasperson, Jeanne X., Roger E. Kasperson. The Social Contours of Risk. Volumne I: Publics, Risk Communication & the Social Amplification of Risk. Earthscan, Virginia. 2005

[20] http://oxfordbibliographiesonline.com/display/id/obo-9780195396607-0051

Risk society

"Risk society" is a term that emerged during the 1990s to describe the manner in which modern society organises in response to risk. The term is closely associated with several key writers on modernity, in particular Anthony Giddens and Ulrich Beck. The term's popularity during the 1990s was both as a consequence of its links to trends in thinking about wider modernity, and also to its links to popular discourse, in particular the growing environmental concerns during the period.[1]

Definition

According to sociologist Anthony Giddens, a risk society is "a society increasingly preoccupied with the future (and also with safety), which generates the notion of risk,"[2] whilst the German sociologist Ulrich Beck defines it as a systematic way of dealing with hazards and insecurities induced and introduced by modernisation itself.[3]

Background

Both authors approach this phenomenon firmly from the perspective of modernity, "a shorthand term for modern society or industrial civilization... modernity is vastly more dynamic than any previous type of social order. It is a society... which unlike any preceding culture lives in the future rather than the past." [4] They also draw heavily on the concept of reflexivity, the idea that as a society examines itself, it in turn changes itself in the process.

Implications

These authors argue that whilst humans have always been subjected to a level of risk - such as natural disasters - these have usually been perceived as produced by non-human forces. Modern societies, however, are exposed to risks such as pollution, newly discovered illnesses, crime, that are the result of the modernization process itself. Giddens defines these two types of risks as external risks and manufactured risks.[5] Manufactured risks are marked by a high level of human agency involved in both producing, and mitigating such risks.

As manufactured risks are the product of human activity, authors like Giddens and Beck argue that it is possible for societies to assess the level of risk that is being produced, or that is about to be produced. This sort of reflexive introspection can in turn alter the planned activities themselves. As an example, disasters such as Chernobyl and the Love Canal Crisis, public faith in the modern project has declined (a claim that has not been independently verified within all population groups) leaving public distrust in industry, government and experts.[6] On the other hand, social concerns have led to the increased regulation of the nuclear power industry and to the abandon of some expansion plans, altering the course of modernization itself. This increased critique of modern industrial practices is said to have resulted in a state of reflexive modernization, illustrated by concepts such as sustainability and the precautionary principle that focus on preventative measures to decrease levels of risk.

There are differing opinions as to how the concept of a risk society interacts with social hierarchies and class distinctions.[7] Most agree that social relations have altered with the introduction of manufactured risks and reflexive modernization. Risks, much like wealth, are distributed unevenly in a population and will influence quality of life.

Beck has argued that older forms of class structure - based mainly on the accumulation of wealth - atrophy in a modern, risk society, in which people occupy social risk positions that are achieved through risk aversion. "In some of their dimensions these follow the inequalities of class and strata positions, but they bring a fundamentally different distribution logic into play"[8] . Beck contends that widespread risks contain a 'boomerang effect', in that individuals producing risks will also be exposed to them. This argument suggests that wealthy individuals whose capital is largely responsible for creating pollution will also have to suffer when, for example, the contaminants seep into the water supply. This argument may seem oversimplified, as wealthy people may have the ability to mitigate risk more easily by, for example, buying bottled water. Beck, however, has argued that the distribution of this sort of risk is the result of knowledge, rather than wealth. Whilst the wealthy person may have access to resources that enable him or her to avert risk, this would not even be an option were the person unaware that the risk even existed.

By contrast, Giddens has argued that older forms of class structure maintain a somewhat stronger role in a risk society, now being partly defined "in terms of differential access to forms of self-actualization and empowerment"[9] . Giddens has also tended to approach the concept of a risk society more positively than Beck, suggesting that there "can be no question of merely taking a negative attitude towards risk. Risk needs to be disciplined, but active risk-taking is a core element of a dynamic economic and an innovative society."[10]

Notes

[1] Caplan, p.7.
[2] Giddens 1999, p.3.
[3] Beck p.21.
[4] Giddens p.94.
[5] Giddens, 1999.
[6] Giddens, 1990.
[7] Caplan, p.6.
[8] Beck, p.23.
[9] Giddens 1991, p. 6.
[10] Giddens, *Runaway World*, 1999, p.29.

References

- Caplan, Pat 'Introduction: Risk Revisited' in Caplan, Pat (ed) 'Risk Revisited', Pluto Press: London (2000).
- Ericson, R.V. & K. Haggerty. 1997. *Policing the Risk Society*. Toronto: University of Toronto Press.
- Giddens, Anthony (1990) *Consequences of Modernity*. Cambridge: Polity Press.
- Giddens, Anthony (1991) Modernity and Self-Identity. Self and Society in the Late Modern Age. Cambridge: Polity (publisher).
- Giddens, Anthony (1998) The Third Way. The Renewal of Social Democracy. Cambridge : Polity (publisher).
- Giddens, Anthony (1999) "Risk and Responsibility" *Modern Law Review* 62(1): 1-10.
- Giddens, Anthony (1999) Runaway World: How Globalization is Reshaping Our Lives. London : Profile.
- Ulrich Beck (1992) *Risk Society: Towards a New Modernity*. New Delhi: Sage. (Translated from the German *Risikogesellschaft* published in 1986.

External links

- Leiss, W. Ulrich Beck, Risk Society, Towards a New Modernity (http://www.ualberta.ca/~cjscopy/articles/ leiss.html). Featured Book Reviews. *Canadian Journal of Sociology,* Online edition.

Risk theory

Risk theory connotes the study usually by actuaries and insurers of the financial impact on a carrier of a portfolio of insurance policies. For example, if the carrier has 100 policies that insures against a total loss of $1000, and if each policy's chance of loss is independent and has a probability of loss of p then the loss can be described by a binomial variable. With a large enough portfolio however, we can use the Poisson function for the frequency of loss variable where λ is used as the mean equal to the number of policies multiplied by p.

External links

- Arcady Novosyolov's Risk Theory site [1]

References

[1] http://risktheory.net/

Risk-based inspection

Risk Based Inspection (**RBI**) is a risk based approach to prioritizing and planning inspection used in engineering industries, and predominant in the oil and gas industries. This type of inspection planning analyses the probability (or likelihood) and consequence of failure of an asset to calculate its risk of failure. The level of risk is used develop a prioritised inspection plan for the asset. It is related to (or sometimes a part of) Risk Based Asset Management (RBAM), Risk Based Integrity Management (RBIM) and Risk Based Management (RBM).

It is used to prioritise inspection, usually by the means of non-destructive testing (NDT), requirements for major oil platforms, refineries and chemical installations around the world. The resulting inspection plan outlines the type and frequency of inspection for the asset. It is used for industrial pipework, process systems, pipelines, structures and many other types of assets in these industries.

Items with high probability and high consequence (i.e. high risk) are given a higher priority for inspection than items that are high probability but for which failure has low consequences. This strategy allows for a rational investment of inspection resources.

Following an explosion in April 2001, the ConocoPhillips-owned Humber Refinery in the United Kingdom was found guilty of failing to appropriately monitor the deterioration of its pipework. An RBI programme has since been employed by the company.[1]

Risk Based Inspection is an inspection planning tool rated under Risk and Reliability Management (RRM).

Objectives

RBI will assist a company to select cost effective and appropriate maintenance and inspection tasks and techniques, to optimize such efforts and cost, to shift from a reactive to a proactive maintenance regime, to produce an auditable system, to give an agreed "operating window", and to implement a risk management tool.

Purposes

The purposes of RBI include:

1. To move away from time based inspection often governed by minimum compliance with rules, regulations and standards for inspection.
2. To apply a strategy of doing what is needed for safeguarding integrity and improving reliability and availability of the asset by planning and executing those inspections that are needed.
3. To provide economic benefits such as fewer inspections, fewer or shorter shutdowns and longer run length.
4. To safeguard integrity.
5. To reduce the risk of failure.

Standards

There are many international engineering standards and recommended practices that outline requirements, methodologies and the implementation of RBI. Included in these are API RP 580[2] & 581.

References

[1] ConocoPhillips Ltd fined (http://www.hse.gov.uk/press/2005/e05089.htm) - Health & Safety Executive website
[2] API Recommended Practice 580 (http://www.api.org/Standards/new/api-rp-580.cfm)

External links

- Health and Safety Executive: Best practice for risk based inspection as a part of plant integrity management (http://www.hse.gov.uk/research/crr_htm/2001/crr01363.htm)

Risk-loving

In economics and finance, a **risk lover** is a person who has a preference for risk. While most investors are considered risk averse, one could view casino goers as risk loving. If offered either €50 or a 50% chance of each of €100 and nothing, a risk seeking person would prefer the gamble even though the gamble and the sure thing both have the same expected value; in fact, the risk lover would be indifferent to accepting a less than 50% chance of €100 versus the sure €50 (how much less would depend on how risk loving the person is). The risk lover would also be indifferent to a 50% chance of each of €X and nothing versus the sure €50, where €X is some amount less than €100 (again, how much less would depend on how risk loving the person is).

The risk loving utility function

Choice under uncertainty is often characterized as the maximization of expected utility. Utility is often assumed to be a function of profit or final portfolio wealth, with a positive first derivative. The utility function whose expected value is maximized is convex for a risk lover, concave for a risk averse agent, and linear for a risk neutral agent. Its convexity in the risk loving case has the effect of causing a mean-preserving spread of any probability distribution of wealth outcomes to be preferred over the unspread distribution.

RISKS Digest

The **RISKS Digest** or **Forum On Risks to the Public in Computers and Related Systems** is an online periodical published since 1985 by the Committee on Computers and Public Policy of the Association for Computing Machinery. The editor is Peter G. Neumann.

It is a moderated forum concerned with the security and safety of computers, software, and technological systems. Security, and risk, here are taken broadly; RISKS is concerned not merely with so-called security holes in software, but with unintended consequences and hazards stemming from the design (or lack thereof) of automated systems. Other recurring subjects include cryptography and the effects of technically ill-considered public policies. RISKS also publishes announcements and Calls for Papers from various technical conferences, and technical book reviews (usually by Rob Slade, though occasionally by others).

Although RISKS is a forum of a computer science association, most contributions are readable and informative to anyone with an interest in the subject. It is heavily read by system administrators, and computer security managers, as well as computer scientists and engineers.

The RISKS Digest is published on a frequent but irregular schedule through the moderated Usenet newsgroup *comp.risks*, which exists solely to carry the Digest.

Summaries of the forum appear as columns edited by Neumann in the ACM SIGSOFT *Software Engineering Notes* (SEN) and the *Communications of the ACM* (CACM).

External links

- [news:///comp.risks RISKS Digest] (Usenet newsgroup *comp.risks*)
- Google groups interface to *comp.risks* [1]
- RISKS Digest web archive [2]
- Mailing List Subscription Web Interface [3]

References

[1] http://groups.google.com/group/comp.risks

[2] http://www.risks.org/

[3] http://lists.csl.sri.com/mailman/listinfo/risks

rNPV

In finance, **rNPV** (risk-adjusted net present value) or **eNPV** (expected NPV) is a method to value risky future cash flows. rNPV modifies the standard NPV calculation of discounted cash flow (DCF) analysis by adjusting (multiplying) each cash flow by the estimated probability that it occurs (the estimated success rate). In the language of probability theory, the rNPV is the expected value

rNPV is the standard valuation method in the drug development industry, where sufficient data exists to estimate success rates for all R&D phases. In finance, a similar technique is used in the probability model of CDS valuation, but in other financial contexts one instead incorporates risk by using a risk premium in the discount rate.

References

- Boris Bogdan and Ralph Villiger, *Valuation in Life Sciences. A Practical Guide*, 2010, third edition, Springer Verlag.
- First published reference: Stewart JJ, Allison PN, Johnson RS. Putting a price on biotechnology. Nat Biotechnol. 2001 Sep;19(9):813-7.

Safety engineering

Safety engineering is an applied science strongly related to systems engineering and the subset System Safety Engineering. Safety engineering assures that a life-critical system behaves as needed even when pieces fail.

Overview

Ideally, safety-engineers take an early design of a system, analyze it to find what faults can occur, and then propose safety requirements in design specifications up front and changes to existing systems to make the system safer. In an early design stage, often a fail-safe system can be made acceptably safe with a few sensors and some software to read them. Probabilistic fault-tolerant systems can often be made by using more, but smaller and less-expensive pieces of equipment.

Far too often, rather than actually influencing the design, safety engineers are assigned to prove that an existing, completed design is safe. If a safety engineer then discovers significant safety problems late in the design process, correcting them can be very expensive. This type of error has the potential to waste large sums of money.

The exception to this conventional approach is the way some large government agencies approach safety engineering from a more proactive and proven process perspective, known as "system safety". The system safety philosophy is to be applied to complex and critical systems, such as commercial airliners, complex weapon systems, spacecraft, rail and transportation systems, air traffic control system and other complex and safety-critical industrial systems. The proven system safety methods and techniques are to prevent, eliminate and control hazards and risks through designed influences by a collaboration of key engineering disciplines and product teams. Software safety is a fast growing field since modern systems functionality are increasingly being put under control of software. The whole concept of system safety and software safety, as a subset of systems engineering, is to influence safety-critical systems designs by conducting several types of hazard analyses to identify risks and to specify design safety features and procedures to strategically mitigate risk to acceptable levels before the system is certified.

Additionally, failure mitigation can go beyond design recommendations, particularly in the area of maintenance. There is an entire realm of safety and reliability engineering known as Reliability Centered Maintenance (RCM), which is a discipline that is a direct result of analyzing potential failures within a system and determining maintenance actions that can mitigate the risk of failure. This methodology is used extensively on aircraft and involves understanding the failure modes of the serviceable replaceable assemblies in addition to the means to detect or predict an impending failure. Every automobile owner is familiar with this concept when they take in their car to have the oil changed or brakes checked. Even filling up one's car with fuel is a simple example of a failure mode (failure due to fuel exhaustion), a means of detection (fuel gauge), and a maintenance action (filling the car's fuel tank).

For large scale complex systems, hundreds if not thousands of maintenance actions can result from the failure analysis. These maintenance actions are based on conditions (e.g., gauge reading or leaky valve), hard conditions (e.g., a component is known to fail after 100 hrs of operation with 95% certainty), or require inspection to determine the maintenance action (e.g., metal fatigue). The RCM concept then analyzes each individual maintenance item for its risk contribution to safety, mission, operational readiness, or cost to repair if a failure does occur. Then the sum total of all the maintenance actions are bundled into maintenance intervals so that maintenance is not occurring around the clock, but rather, at regular intervals. This bundling process introduces further complexity, as it might stretch some maintenance cycles, thereby increasing risk, but reduce others, thereby potentially reducing risk, with the end result being a comprehensive maintenance schedule, purpose built to reduce operational risk and ensure acceptable levels of operational readiness and availability.

Analysis techniques

Analysis techniques can be split into two categories: qualitative and quantitative methods. The both approaches share the goal of finding causal dependencies between an hazard on system level and failures of individual components. Qualitative approaches focus on the question "What must go wrong, such that a system hazard may occur?", while quantitative methods aim at providing estimations about probabilites, rates and/or severity of consequences.

Traditionally, safety analysis techniques rely solely on skill and expertise of the safety engineer. In the last decade model-based approaches have become prominent. In contrast to traditional methods, model-based techniques try to derive relationships between causes and consequences from some sort of model of the system.

Traditional methods for safety analysis

The two most common fault modeling techniques are called failure mode and effects analysis and fault tree analysis. These techniques are just ways of finding problems and of making plans to cope with failures, as in probabilistic risk assessment. One of the earliest complete studies using this technique on a commercial nuclear plant was the WASH-1400 study, also known as the Reactor Safety Study or the Rasmussen Report.

Failure modes and effects analysis

Failure Mode and Effects Analysis (FMEA) is a bottom-up, inductive analytical method which may be performed at either the functional or piece-part level. For functional FMEA, failure modes are identified for each function in a system or equipment item, usually with the help of a functional block diagram. For piece-part FMEA, failure modes are identified for each piece-part component (such as a valve, connector, resistor, or diode). The effects of the failure mode are described, and assigned a probability based on the failure rate and failure mode ratio of the function or component.

Failure modes with identical effects can be combined and summarized in a Failure Mode Effects Summary. When combined with criticality analysis, FMEA is known as Failure Mode, Effects, and Criticality Analysis or FMECA, pronounced "fuh-MEE-kuh".

Fault tree analysis

Fault tree analysis (FTA) is a top-down, deductive analytical method. In FTA, initiating primary events such as component failures, human errors, and external events are traced through Boolean logic gates to an undesired top event such as an aircraft crash or nuclear reactor core melt. The intent is to identify ways to make top events less probable, and verify that safety goals have been achieved.

Fault trees are a logical inverse of success trees, and may be obtained by applying de Morgan's theorem to success trees (which are directly related to reliability block diagrams).

FTA may be qualitative or quantative. When failure and event probabilites are unknown, qualitative fault trees may be analyzed for minimal cut sets. For example, if any minimal cut set contains a single base event, then the top event may be caused by a single failure. Quantitative FTA is used to compute top event probability, and usually requires computer software such as CAFTA from the Electric Power Research Institute or SAPHIRE from the Idaho National Laboratory.

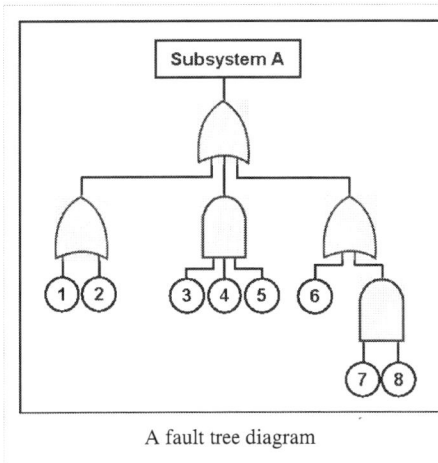

A fault tree diagram

Some industries use both fault trees and event trees. An event tree starts from an undesired initiator (loss of critical supply, component failure etc.) and follows possible further system events through to a series of final consequences. As each new event is considered, a new node on the tree is added with a split of probabilities of taking either branch. The probabilities of a range of "top events" arising from the initial event can then be seen.

Safety certification

Usually a failure in safety-certified systems is acceptable if, on average, less than one life per 10^9 hours of continuous operation is lost to failure. Most Western nuclear reactors, medical equipment, and commercial aircraft are certified to this level. The cost versus loss of lives has been considered appropriate at this level (by FAA for aircraft under Federal Aviation Regulations).

Preventing failure

Probabilistic fault tolerance: adding redundancy to equipment and systems

Once a failure mode is identified, it can usually be prevented entirely by adding extra equipment to the system. For example, nuclear reactors contain dangerous radiation, and nuclear reactions can cause so much heat that no substance might contain them. Therefore reactors have emergency core cooling systems to keep the temperature down, shielding to contain the radiation, and engineered barriers (usually several, nested, surmounted by a containment building) to prevent accidental leakage.

Most biological organisms have a certain amount of redundancy: multiple organs, multiple limbs, etc.

For any given failure, a fail-over or redundancy can almost always be designed and incorporated into a system.

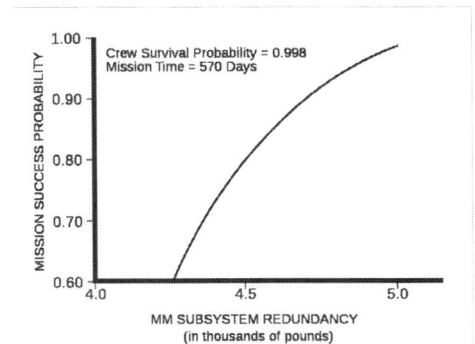

A NASA graph shows the relationship between the survival of a crew of astronauts and the amount of redundant equipment in their spacecraft (the "MM", Mission Module).

When does safety stop, where does reliability begin?

Inherent fail-safe design

When adding equipment is impractical (usually because of expense), then the least expensive form of design is often "inherently fail-safe". The typical approach is to arrange the system so that ordinary single failures cause the mechanism to shut down in a safe way (for nuclear power plants, this is termed a passively safe design, although more than ordinary failures are covered).

One of the most common fail-safe systems is the overflow tube in baths and kitchen sinks. If the valve sticks open, rather than causing an overflow and damage, the tank spills into an overflow.

Another common example is that in an elevator the cable supporting the car keeps spring-loaded brakes open. If the cable breaks, the brakes grab rails, and the elevator cabin does not fall.

Inherent fail-safes are common in medical equipment, traffic and railway signals, communications equipment, and safety equipment.

Containing failure

It is also common practice to plan for the failure of safety systems through containment and isolation methods. The use of isolating valves, also known as the block and bleed manifold, is very common in isolating pumps, tanks, and control valves that may fail or need routine maintenance. In addition, nearly all tanks containing oil or other hazardous chemicals are required to have containment barriers set up around them to contain 100% of the volume of the tank in the event of a catastrophic tank failure. Similarly, in a long pipeline, there are remote-closing valves at regular intervals so that a leak can be isolated. The goal of all containment systems is to provide means of mitigating the consequences of failure.

References

General references

- Lees, Frank (2005). *Loss Prevention in the Process Industries* (3 ed.). Elsevier. ISBN 9780750675550.
- Kletz, Trevor (1984). *Cheaper, safer plants, or wealth and safety at work: notes on inherently safer and simpler plants*. I.Chem.E.. ISBN 0852951671.
- Kletz, Trevor (2001). *An Engineer's View of Human Error* (3 ed.). I.Chem.E.. ISBN 0852954301.
- Kletz, Trevor (1999). *HAZOP and HAZAN* (4 ed.). Taylor & Francis. ISBN 0852954212.
- Lutz, Robyn R. (2000). *Software Engineering for Safety: A Roadmap* (http://www.cs.ucl.ac.uk/staff/A. Finkelstein/fose/finallutz.pdf). The Future of Software Engineering. ACM Press. ISBN 1581132530. Retrieved 31 August 2006.
- Grunske, Lars; Kaiser, Bernhard; Reussner, Ralf H. (2005). *Specification and Evaluation of Safety Properties in a Component-based Software Engineering Process* (http://se.informatik.uni-oldenburg.de/pubdb_files/pdf/ gr06s.pdf). Springer. Retrieved 31 August 2006.
- US DOD (10 February 2000). *Standard Practice for System Safety* (http://www.faa.gov/library/manuals/ aviation/risk_management/ss_handbook/media/app_h_1200.PDF). Washington, DC: US DOD. MIL-STD-882D. Retrieved 31 August 2006.
- US FAA (30 December 2000). *System Safety Handbook* (http://www.faa.gov/library/manuals/aviation/ risk_management/ss_handbook/). Washington, DC: US FAA. Retrieved 31 August 2006.
- NASA (16 December 2008). *Agency Risk Management Procedural Requirements* (http://nodis3.gsfc.nasa.gov/ displayDir.cfm?Internal_ID=N_PR_8000_004A_). NASA. NPR 8000.4A.

External links

- American Society of Safety Engineers (http://www.asse.org) (official website)
- Board of Certified Safety Professionals (http://www.bcsp.org) (official website)
- System Safety Society (http://www.system-safety.org/) (official website)
- The Safety and Reliability Society (http://www.sars.org.uk/)(official website)
- {http://www.csse.org/Canadian Society of Safety Engineering](official website)

Safety instrumented system

A **Safety Instrumented System (SIS)** is a form of process control usually implemented in industrial processes, such as those of a factory or an oil refinery. The SIS performs specified functions to achieve or maintain a safe state of the process when unacceptable or dangerous process conditions are detected. Safety instrumented systems are separate and independent from regular control systems but are composed of similar elements, including sensors, logic solvers, actuators and support systems.

The specified functions, or *safety instrumented functions* (SIF) are implemented as part of an overall risk reduction strategy which is intended to reduce the likelihood of identified hazardous events involving a catastrophic release. The safe state is a state of the process operation where the hazardous event cannot occur. The safe state should be achieved within one-half of the process safety time. Most SIF are focused on preventing catastrophic incidents.

The correct operation of an SIS requires a series of equipment to function properly. It must have sensors capable of detecting abnormal operating conditions, such as high flow, low level, or incorrect valve positioning. A logic solver is required to receive the sensor input signal(s), make appropriate decisions based on the nature of the signal(s), and change its outputs according to user-defined logic. The logic solver may use electrical, electronic or programmable electronic equipment, such as relays, trip amplifiers, or programmable logic controllers. Next, the change of the logic solver output(s) results in the final element(s) taking action on the process (e.g. closing a valve) to bring it to a safe state. Support systems, such as power, instrument air, and communications, are generally required for SIS operation. The support systems should be designed to provide the required integrity and reliability.

International standard IEC 61511 was published in 2003 to provide guidance to end-users on the application of Safety Instrumented Systems in the process industries. This standard is based on IEC 61508, a generic standard for design, construction, and operation of electrical/electronic/programmable electronic systems. Other industry sectors may also have standards that are based on IEC 61508, such as IEC 62061 (machinery systems), IEC 62425 (for railway signaling systems), IEC 61513 (for nuclear systems), and ISO 26262 (for road vehicles, currently a draft international standard).

Other names

Other terms often used in conjunction with and/or to describe safety instrumented systems include:

- Critical control system
- Safety shutdown system
- Protective instrumented system
- Equipment protection system
- Emergency shutdown system
- Safety critical system
- Interlock (engineering)
- Interlocking (railway signalling)

SIS reliability

What a SIS shall do (*the functional requirements*) and how well it must perform (*the safety integrity requirements*) may be determined from Hazard and operability studies (HAZOP), layers of protection analysis (LOPA), risk graphs, and so on. All techniques are mentioned in IEC 61511 and IEC 61508. During SIS design, construction, installation, and operation, it is necessary to verify that these requirements are met. The functional requirements may be verified by design reviews, such as failure modes, effects, and criticality analysis (FMECA) and various types of testing, for example factory acceptance testing, site acceptance testing, and regular functional testing.

The safety integrity requirements may be verified by reliability analysis. For SIS that operates on demand, it is often the probability of failure on demand (PFD) that is calculated. In the design phase, the PFD may be calculated using generic reliability data, for example from OREDA. Later on, the initial PFD estimates may be updated with field experience from the specific plant in question.

It is not possible to address all factors that affect SIS reliability through reliability calculations. It is therefore also necessary to have adequate measures in place (e.g., procedures and competence) to avoid, reveal, and correct SIS related failures.

SIS examples

Safety instrumented systems are most often used in process (i.e., refineries, chemical, nuclear, etc.) facilities to provide protection such as:

- High fuel gas pressure initiates action to close the main fuel gas valve.
- High reactor temperature initiates action to open cooling media valve.
- High distillation column pressure initiates action to open a pressure vent valve.

External links

- ANSI standards [1] Purchase IEC 61511
- ISA Standards [2] Purchase ANSI/ISA 84.00.01-2004
- Center for Chemical Process Safety book, Guidelines for Safe and Reliable Instrumented Protective Systems [3]

References

[1] http://webstore.ansi.org/ansidocstore/find.asp?

[2] http://www.isa.org/Template.cfm?Section=Standards1&template=/Ecommerce/ProductDisplay.cfm&ProductID=7763

[3] http://www.instrumentedprotectivesystems.com/

Safety Integrity Level

Safety Integrity Level (SIL) is defined as a relative level of risk-reduction provided by a safety function, or to specify a target level of risk reduction. In simple terms, SIL is a measurement of performance required for a Safety Instrumented Function (SIF).

The requirements for a given SIL are not consistent among all of the functional safety standards. Within the European Functional Safety standards four SILs are defined, with SIL 4 being the most dependable and SIL 1 being the least. A SIL is determined based on a number of quantitative factors in combination with qualitative factors such as development process and safety life cycle management.

SIL Assignment

There are several methods used to assign a SIL. These are normally used in combination, and may include:

- Risk Matrices
- Risk Graphs
- Layers Of Protection Analysis (LOPA)

The assignment may be tested using both pragmatic and controllability approaches, applying guidance on SIL assignment published by the UK HSE[1] . SIL assignment processes that use the HSE guidance to ratify assignments developed from Risk Matrices have been certified to meet IEC EN 61508

Problems with the use of SIL

There are several problems inherent in the use of Safety Integrity Levels. These can be summarized as follows...

- Poor harmonization of definition across the different standards bodies which utilize SIL
- Process-oriented metrics for derivation of SIL
- Estimation of SIL based on reliability estimates
- System complexity, particularly in software systems, making SIL estimation difficult to impossible

These lead to such erroneous statements as, "This system is a SIL N system because the process adopted during its development was the standard process for the development of a SIL N system", or use of the SIL concept out of context such as, "This is a SIL 3 heat exchanger". According to IEC 61508, the SIL concept must be related to the dangerous failure rate of a system, not just its failure rate. Definition of the dangerous failure modes by safety analysis is intrinsic to the proper determination of the failure rate[2] .

Certification to a Safety Integrity Level

The International Electrotechnical Commission's (IEC) standard IEC 61508, now IEC EN 61508, defines SIL using requirements grouped into two broad categories: hardware safety integrity and systematic safety integrity. A device or system must meet the requirements for *both* categories to achieve a given SIL.

The SIL requirements for hardware safety integrity are based on a probabilistic analysis of the device. To achieve a given SIL, the device must meet targets for the maximum probability of dangerous failure and a minimum Safe Failure Fraction. The concept of 'dangerous failure' must be rigorously defined for the system in question, normally in the form of requirement constraints whose integrity is verified throughout system development. The actual targets required vary depending on the likelihood of a demand, the complexity of the device(s), and types of redundancy used.

PFD (Probability of Failure on Demand) and RRF (Risk Reduction Factor) of low demand operation for different SILs as defined in IEC EN 61508 are as follows:

SIL	PFD	PFD (power)	RRF
1	0.1-0.01	$10^{-1} - 10^{-2}$	10-100
2	0.01-0.001	$10^{-2} - 10^{-3}$	100-1000
3	0.001-0.0001	$10^{-3} - 10^{-4}$	1000-10,000
4	0.0001-0.00001	$10^{-4} - 10^{-5}$	10,000-100,000

For continuous operation, these change to the following.

SIL	PFD	PFD (power)	RRF
1	0.00001-0.000001	$10^{-5} - 10^{-6}$	100,000-1,000,000
2	0.000001-0.0000001	$10^{-6} - 10^{-7}$	1,000,000-10,000,000
3	0.0000001-0.00000001	$10^{-7} - 10^{-8}$	10,000,000-100,000,000
4	0.00000001-0.000000001	$10^{-8} - 10^{-9}$	100,000,000-1,000,000,000

Hazards of a control system must be identified then analysed through risk analysis. Mitigation of these risks continues until their overall contribution to the hazard are considered acceptable. The tolerable level of these risks is specified as a safety requirement in the form of a target 'probability of a dangerous failure' in a given period of time, stated as a discrete SIL level.

Certification schemes are used to establish whether a device meets a particular SIL[3] . The requirements of these schemes can be met either by establishing a rigorous development process, either by establishing that the device has sufficient operating history to argue that it has been proven in use.

Electric and electronic devices can be certified for use in Functional Safety applications according to IEC 61508, providing application developers the evidence required to demonstrate that the application including the device is also compliant. IEC 61511 is an application specific adaptation of IEC 61508 for the Process Industry sector. This standard is used in the petrochemical and hazardous chemical industries, among others.

SIL in Safety Standards

The following standards use SIL as a measure of reliability and/or risk reduction.

- ANSI/ISA S84
- IEC EN 61508 - risk reduction
- IEC 61511
- IEC 62061
- EN 50128
- EN 50129
- MISRA - reliability
- Defence Standard 00-56 Issue 2 - accident consequence

The use of a SIL in specific safety standards may apply different number sequences or definitions to those in IEC EN 61508[4] .

References

[1] M. Charlwood, S Turner and N. Worsell, UK Health and Safety Executive Research Report 216, "A methodology for the assignment of safety integrity levels (SILs) to safety-related control functions implemented by safety-related electrical, electronic and programmable electronic control systems of machines", 2004. ISBN 0 7176 2832 9

[2] F. Redmill, "Understanding the Use, Misuse, and Abuse of SILs" http://www.csr.ncl.ac.uk/FELIX_Web/3A.SILs.pdf with capture date of 11th October 2010

[3] CASS Scheme, Conformity Assessment of Safety Systems, http://www.cass.uk.net/

[4] F. Redmill, "Understanding the Use, Misuse, and Abuse of SILs" http://www.csr.ncl.ac.uk/FELIX_Web/3A.SILs.pdf with capture dates of 9th July 2010 and 11 October 2010

Textbooks

M. Punch, "Functional Safety for the Mining Industry – An Integrated Approach Using AS(IEC)61508, AS(IEC)62061 and AS4024.1." (1st Edition, ISBN 978-0-9807660-0-4, in A4 paperback, 150 pages). www.marcuspunch.com (http://www.marcuspunch.com)

External links

- Safety Users Group (http://www.safetyusersgroup.com) Functional Safety-Information Resources
- Inside Functional Safety (http://www.insidefunctionalsafety.com) Technical magazine focusing on functional safety
- 61508.org (http://www.61508.org) The 61508 Association
- IEC Safety Zone (http://www.iec.ch/functionalsafety) The IEC Functional safety zone
- Functional Safety, A Basic Guide (http://www.ida.liu.se/~snt/teaching/SCRTS/IEC61508_Guide.pdf) Functional Safety and IEC 61508: A basic guide
- Overview of 61508 (http://www2.theiet.org/oncomms/sector/computing/Articles/Object/58D25FCD-6153-46BD-ADAF910D2C4B69D4) Overview of IEC 61508
- SIL Made Simple (http://docs.google.com/viewer?a=v&pid=explorer&chrome=true&srcid=0B5PSPJfG9S5kMzhhZDM4YjMtYjhhMC00NDZhLTgzZTAtNDkzYTk3MGJmNDhh&hl=en_US&authkey=CJqWsYEJ) - White Paper presented at Valve World 2010

Sampling risk

In auditing, sampling is an inevitable means of testing. However, sampling is always associated with **sampling risks** which auditors have to control.

Sampling risk represents the possibility that auditor's conclusion based on a sample is different from that reached if the entire population were subject to audit procedure. The auditor may conclude that material misstatements exist, in fact they do not; or material misstatements do not exist but in fact they do exist. Auditor can lower the sampling risk by increasing the sampling size.

Non-sampling risk includes factors that cause auditors to reach a conclusion other than the sampling size. Misinterpretation of evidence and inappropriate procedures are good examples. Changing of the sampling size would not reduce non-sampling risk.

Scenario analysis

Scenario analysis is a process of analyzing possible future events by considering alternative possible outcomes (scenarios). Thus, the scenario analysis, which is a main method of projections, does not try to show one exact picture of the future. Instead, it presents consciously several alternative future developments. Consequently, a scope of possible future outcomes is observable. Not only are the outcomes observable, also the development paths leading to the outcomes. In contrast to prognoses, the scenario analysis is not using extrapolation of the past. It does not rely on historical data and does not expect past observations to be still valid in the future. Instead, it tries to consider possible developments and turning points, which may only be connected to the past. In short, several scenarios are demonstrated in a scenario analysis to show possible future outcomes. It is useful to generate a combination of an optimistic, a pessimistic, and a most likely scenario. Although highly discussed, experience has shown that around three scenarios are most appropriate for further discussion and selection. More scenarios could make the analysis unclear.[1] [2]

Principle

The analysis is designed to allow improved decision-making by allowing consideration of outcomes and their implications.

Scenario analysis can also be used to illuminate "wild cards." For example, analysis of the possibility of the earth being struck by a large celestial object (a meteor) suggests that whilst the probability is low, the damage inflicted is so high that the event is much more important (threatening) than the low probability (in any one year) alone would suggest. However, this possibility is usually disregarded by organizations using scenario analysis to develop a strategic plan since it has such overarching repercussions.

Financial applications

For example, in economics and finance, a financial institution might attempt to forecast several possible scenarios for the economy (e.g. rapid growth, moderate growth, slow growth) and it might also attempt to forecast financial market returns (for bonds, stocks and cash) in each of those scenarios. It might consider sub-sets of each of the possibilities. It might further seek to determine correlations and assign probabilities to the scenarios (and sub-sets if any). Then it will be in a position to consider how to distribute assets between asset types (i.e. asset allocation); the institution can also calculate the scenario-weighted expected return (which figure will indicate the overall attractiveness of the financial environment). It may also perform stress testing, using adverse scenarios.

Depending on the complexity of the problem scenario analysis can be a demanding exercise. It can be difficult to foresee what the future holds (e.g. the actual future outcome may be entirely unexpected), i.e. to foresee what the scenarios are, and to assign probabilities to them; and this is true of the general forecasts never mind the implied financial market returns. The outcomes can be modeled mathematically/statistically e.g. taking account of possible variability within single scenarios as well as possible relationships between scenarios. In general, one should take care when assigning probabilities to different scenarios as this could invite a tendency to consider only the scenario with the highest probability.[3]

Financial institutions can take the analysis further by relating the asset allocation that the above calculations suggest to the industry or peer group distribution of assets. In so doing the financial institution seeks to control its own business risk rather than the client's risk portfolio.

Geo-political applications

In politics or geo-politics, scenario analysis involves modelling the possible alternative paths of a social or political environment and possibly diplomatic and war risks. For example, in the recent Iraq War, the Pentagon certainly had to model alternative possibilities that might arise in the war situation and had to position materiel and troops accordingly.

Traditional critique

While there is utility in weighting hypotheses and branching potential outcomes from them, reliance on scenario analysis without reporting some parameters of measurement accuracy (standard errors, confidence intervals of estimates, metadata, standardization and coding, weighting for non-response, error in reportage, sample design, case counts, etc.) is a poor second to traditional prediction. Especially in "complex" problems, factors and assumptions do not correlate in lockstep fashion. Once a specific sensitivity is undefined, it may call the entire study into question.

It is faulty logic to think, when arbitrating results, that a better hypothesis will obviate the need for empiricism. In this respect, scenario analysis tries to defer statistical laws (eg., Chebyshev's inequality Law), because the decision rules occur outside a constrained setting. Outcomes are not permitted to "just happen"; rather, they are forced to conform to arbitrary hypotheses ex post, and therefore there is no footing on which to place expected values. In truth, there are no ex ante expected values, only hypotheses, and one is left wondering about the roles of modeling and data decision. In short, comparisons of "scenarios" with outcomes are biased by not deferring to the data; this may be convenient, but it is indefensible.

"Scenario analysis" is no substitute for complete and factual exposure of survey error in economic studies. In traditional prediction, given the data used to model the problem, with a reasoned specification and technique, an analyst can state, within a certain percentage of statistical error, the likelihood of a coefficient being within a certain numerical bound. This exactitude need not come at the expense of very disaggregated statements of hypotheses. R Software, specifically the module "WhatIf,"[4] (in the context, see also Matchit and Zelig) has been developed for causal inference, and to evaluate counterfactuals. These programs have fairly sophisticated treatments for determining model dependence, in order to state with precision how sensitive the results are to models not based on empirical evidence.

References

[1] Aaker, David A. (2001). *Strategic Market Management*. New York: John Wiley & Sons. pp. 108 et seq.. ISBN 0-471-41572-3.

[2] Bea, F.X., Haas, J. (2005). *Strategisches Management*. Stuttgart: Lucius & Lucius. pp. 279 and 287 et seq..

[3] *The Art of the Long View: Paths to Strategic Insight for Yourself and Your Company*, Peter Schwartz, Published by Random House, 1996, ISBN 0385267320 Google book (http://books.google.com/books?id=fILtwg777hsC)

[4] " WhatIf: Software for Evaluating Counterfactuals (http://gking.harvard.edu/bin/windows/contrib/2.6/WhatIf_1.5-4.zip)", H Stoll, G King, L Zeng - Journal of Statistical Software, 2006

- "Learning from the Future: Competitive Foresight Scenarios", Liam Fahey and Robert M. Randall, Published by John Wiley and Sons, 1997, ISBN 0471303526, Google book (http://books.google.com/books?id=KD7VzPqI3S4C)

- "Shirt-sleeve approach to long-range plans.", Linneman, Robert E, Kennell, John D.; Harvard Business Review; Mar/Apr77, Vol. 55 Issue 2, p141

Social risk management

Social risk management (SRM) is a new conceptual framework assigned and designed by the World Bank.[1] The objective of SRM is to extend the traditional framework of social policy to the non-market based social protection of which its three primary strategies include prevention, mitigation, and coping. It is now well understood that social unrest is positively parallel to the poverty. Assisting individuals, households and communities to elevate living standard above the poverty level will harmonize global economy and strengthen the social security.

Strategies

Prevention strategies

Prevention strategies are those implemented to avert a risk. Some typical measures could be:

- In the labor market, SRM intervention targets skill training or job function improvement to reduce the risk of un/under- employment or low wages which are probably man-made.
- In the financial market, SRM emphasize on optimizing macroeconomic policies to reduce the shocks of financial crisis, such as oil price surges, or unpredictable market moves on currencies, indices and blue chip stocks.
- For natural disasters and environment degradation, SRM are gear to deploy a networked warning system or sustainable, renewable and environmental friendly eco-system to minimize the impact of the consequences.
- In health care, SRM focuses on the prevention of pandemic illnesses by implementing vaccination and public health education programs. Setting up rehabilitation centers to help drug addicts.
- In the public social security, establishing a community-based insurance schemes to compensate pensioners, disability or chronic illness person's living expenses. Building up nursing homes for elderlies and setting up public housing for homelesses and orphans.

Mitigation strategies

Mitigation strategies focus on reducing the risk. Common practices are:

- In the financial market, diversifying portfolios or hedging stocks to decrease the exposure of the financial risks.
- Microfinance to the poor or jobless people.

Coping strategies

Coping strategies are designed to relieve the impact of the risk event once it has occurred. The typical examples are

- Issuing government relieve fund or publicly raising money.
- Setting up unemployment benefit schemes.

Source of social risks

The degree of social risks usually vary from idiosyncratic (micro), regional covariant (meso), to nation-wide covariant (macro). The following table lists the source of the risks that are being encompassed

Main Sources of Risks *(adapted from Holzmann and Jorgensen, 2000)*[2]

	Micro (idiosyncratic)	Meso <-------->	Macro (covariate)
Natural		Rainfall Landslides Volcanic eruption	Earthquakes Floods Drought Tornadoes Asteroid impacts
Health	Illness Injury Disability Food poisoning	Pandemics Food poisoning	Pandemics
Life-cycle	Birth Old age Death		
Social	Crimes Domestic violences Drug addiction	Terrorism Gangs	Civil strife War Social upheaval Drug addiction Child abuses
Economic	Unemployment Harvest failure	Unemployment Harvest failure Resettlement	Blue chip company collapsing Financial or currency crisis Market trading shocks
Administrative & Political	Ethnic discrimination	Ethnic conflict Riots Chemical & biological mass destruction Administrative induced accidents & disasters	Political induced malfunction on social programs Coup
Environmental		Pollution Deforestation Nuclear disasters Soil salinities Acid rains	Global warming

References

[1] Holzmann, Robert; Lynne Sherburne-Benz and Emil Tesliuc. "Social Risk Management: The World Bank Approach to Social Protection in a Globalizing World" (http://siteresources.worldbank.org/SOCIALPROTECTION/Publications/20847129/SRMWBApproachtoSP.pdf). World Bank. . Retrieved November 21, 2006.

[2] Holzmann, Robert; Steen Jorgensen (2000). "**Social Risk Management:** A new conceptual framework for Social Protection, and beyond" (http://info.worldbank.org/etools/docs/library/80363/conceptfram.pdf). World Bank. . Retrieved November 21, 2006.

Social vulnerability

In its broadest sense, **social vulnerability** is one dimension of vulnerability to multiple stressors and shocks, including abuse, social exclusion and natural hazards. Social vulnerability refers to the inability of people, organizations, and societies to withstand adverse impacts from multiple stressors to which they are exposed. These impacts are due in part to characteristics inherent in social interactions, institutions, and systems of cultural values.[1]

Because it is most apparent when calamity occurs, many studies of social vulnerability are found in risk management literature (Peacock and Ragsdale 1997; Anderson and Woodrow 1998; Alwang, Siegel et al. 2001; Conway and Norton 2002). However, social vulnerability is a pre-existing condition that affects a society's ability to prepare for and recover from a disruptive event.

Definitions

Vulnerability derives from the Latin word *vulnerare* (to be wounded) and describes the potential to be harmed physically and/or psychologically. Vulnerability is often understood as the counterpart of resilience, and is increasingly studied in linked social-ecological systems. The Yogyakarta Principles, one of the international human rights instruments use the term "vulnerability" as such potential to abuse or social exclusion.[2]

The concept of social vulnerability emerged most recently within the discourse on natural hazards and disasters. To date no one definition has been agreed upon. Similarly, multiple theories of social vulnerability exist (Weichselgartner 2001). Most work conducted so far focuses on empirical observation and conceptual models. Thus current social vulnerability research is a middle range theory and represents an attempt to understand the social conditions that transform a natural hazard (e.g. flood, earthquake, mass movements etc.) into a social disaster. The concept emphasizes two central themes:

1. Both the causes and the phenomenon of disasters are defined by social processes and structures. Thus it is not only a geo- or biophysical hazard, but rather the social context that is taken into account to understand "natural" disasters (Hewitt 1983).

2. Although different groups of a society may share a similar exposure to a natural hazard, the hazard has varying consequences for these groups, since they have diverging capacities and abilities to handle the impact of a hazard.

Taking a structuralist view, Hewitt (1997, p143) defines vulnerability as being:

> ...essentially about the human ecology of endangerment...and is embedded in the social geography of settlements and lands uses, and the space of distribution of influence in communities and political organisation.

this is in contrast to the more socially focused view of Blaikie et al. (1994, p9) who define vulnerability as the:

> ...set of characteristics of a group or individual in terms of their capacity to anticipate, cope with, resist and recover from the impact of a natural hazard. It involves a combination of factors that determine the degree to which someone's life and livelihood is at risk by a discrete and identifiable event in nature or society.

History of the concept

In the 1970s the concept of vulnerability was introduced within the discourse on natural hazards and disaster by O´Keefe, Westgate and Wisner (O´Keefe, Westgate et al. 1976). In "taking the naturalness out of natural disasters" these authors insisted that socio-economic conditions are the causes for natural disasters. The work illustrated by means of empirical data that the occurrence of disasters increased over the last 50 years, paralleled by an increasing loss of life. The work also showed that the greatest losses of life concentrate in underdeveloped countries, where the authors concluded that vulnerability is increasing.

Chambers put these empirical findings on a conceptual level and argued that vulnerability has an external and internal side: People are exposed to specific natural and social risk. At the same time people possess different capacities to deal with their exposure by means of various strategies of action (Chambers 1989). This argument was again refined be Blaikie, Cannon, Davis and Wisner, who went on to developed the Pressure and Release Model (PAR) (see below). Watts and Bohle argued similarly by formalizing the "social space of vulnerability", which is constituted by exposure, capacity and potentiality (Watts and Bohle 1993).

Cutter developed an integrative approach (hazard of place), which tries to consider both multiple geo- and biophysical hazards on the one hand as well as social vulnerabilities on the other hand (Cutter, Mitchell et al. 2000). Recently, Oliver-Smith grasped the nature-culture dichotomy by focusing both on the cultural construction of the people-environment-relationship and on the material production of conditions that define the social vulnerability of people (Oliver-Smith and Hoffman 2002).

Research on social vulnerability to date has stemmed from a variety of fields in the natural and social sciences. Each field has defined the concept differently, manifest in a host of definitions and approaches (Blaikie, Cannon et al. 1994; Henninger 1998; Frankenberger, Drinkwater et al. 2000; Alwang, Siegel et al. 2001; Oliver-Smith 2003; Cannon, Twigg et al. 2005). Yet some common threads run through most of the available work.

Vulnerability within society

Although considerable research attention has examined components of biophysical vulnerability and the vulnerability of the built environment (Mileti, 1999), we currently know the least about the social aspects of vulnerability (Cutter et al., 2003). Socially created vulnerabilities are largely ignored, mainly due to the difficulty in quantifying them. Social vulnerability is created through the interaction of social forces and multiple stressors, and resolved through social (as opposed to individual) means. While individuals within a socially vulnerable context may break through the "vicious cycle," social vulnerability itself can persist because of structural—i.e. social and political—influences that reinforce vulnerability.

Social vulnerability is partially the product of social inequalities—those social factors that influence or shape the susceptibility of various groups to harm and that also govern their ability to respond (Cutter et al., 2003). It is, however, important to note that social vulnerability is not registered by exposure to hazards alone, but also resides in the sensitivity and resilience of the system to prepare, cope and recover from such hazards (Turner et al., 2003). However, it is also important to note, that a focus limited to the stresses associated with a particular vulnerability analysis is also insufficient for understanding the impact on and responses of the affected system or its components (Mileti, 1999; Kaperson et al., 2003; White & Haas, 1974). These issues are often underlined in attempts to model the concept (see Models of Social Vulnerability).

Models of social vulnerability

Two of the principal archetypal reduced-form models of social vulnerability are presented, that have informed vulnerability analysis: the *Risk-Hazard* (RH) model and the *Pressure and Release* model.

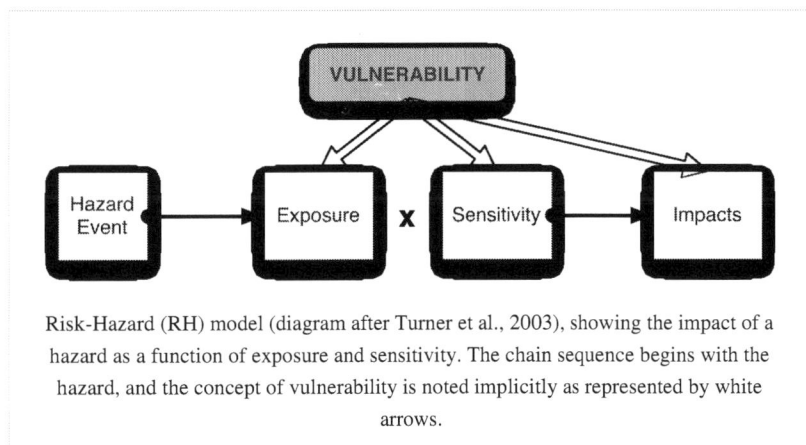

Risk-Hazard (RH) model (diagram after Turner et al., 2003), showing the impact of a hazard as a function of exposure and sensitivity. The chain sequence begins with the hazard, and the concept of vulnerability is noted implicitly as represented by white arrows.

Risk-Hazard (RH) Model

Initial RH models sought to understand the impact of a hazard as a function of exposure to the hazardous event and the sensitivity of the entity exposed (Turner et al., 2003). Applications of this model in in environmental and climate impact assessments generally emphasised exposure and sensitivity to perturbations and stressors (Kates, 1985; Burton et al., 1978) and worked from the hazard to the impacts (Turner et al., 2003). However, several inadequacies became apparent. Principally, it does not treat the ways in which the systems in question amplify or attenuate the impacts of the hazard (Martine & Guzman, 2002). Neither does the model address the distinction among exposed subsystems and components that lead to significant variations in the consequences of the hazards, or the role of political economy in shaping differential exposure and consequences (Blaikie et al., 1994, Hewitt, 1997). This led to the development of the PAR model.

Pressure and Release (PAR) Model

The PAR model understands a disaster as the intersection between socio-economic pressure and physical exposure. Risk is explicitly defined as a function of the perturbation, stressor, or stress and the vulnerability of the exposed unit (Blaikie et al, 1994). In this way, it directs attention to the conditions that make exposure unsafe, leading to vulnerability

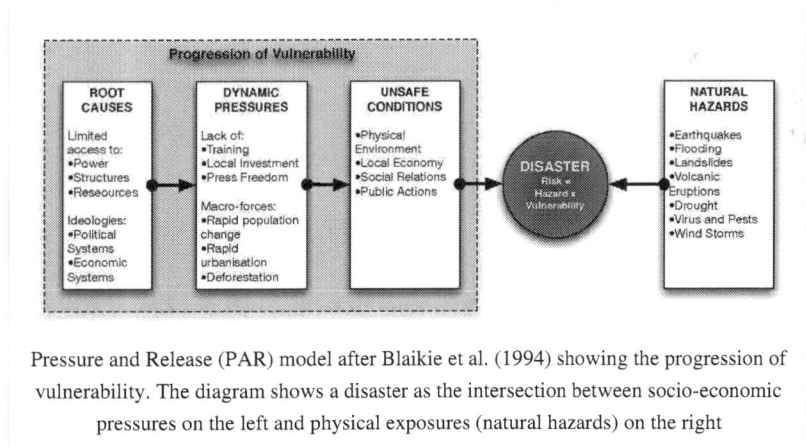

Pressure and Release (PAR) model after Blaikie et al. (1994) showing the progression of vulnerability. The diagram shows a disaster as the intersection between socio-economic pressures on the left and physical exposures (natural hazards) on the right

and to the causes creating these conditions. Used primarily to address social groups facing disaster events, the model emphasises distinctions in vulnerability by different exposure units such as social class and ethnicity. The model distinguishes between three components on the social side: root causes, dynamic pressures and unsafe conditions, and one component on the natural side, the natural hazards itself. Principal root causes include "economic, demographic and political processes", which affect the allocation and distribution of resources between different groups of people. Dynamic Pressures translate economic and political processes in local circumstances (e.g. migration patterns). Unsafe conditions are the specific forms in which vulnerability is expressed in time and space, such as those induced by the physical environment, local economy or social relations (Blaikie, Cannon et al. 1994).

Although explicitly highlighting vulnerability, the PAR model appears insufficiently comprehensive for the broader concerns of sustainability science (Turner et al., 2003). Primarily, it does not address the coupled human environment system in the sense of considering the vulnerability of biophysical subsystems (Kasperson et al, 2003) and it provides little detail on the structure of the hazard's causal sequence. The model also tends to underplay feedback beyond the system of analysis that the integrative RH models included (Kates, 1985).[3]

Criticism of social vulnerability

Some authors criticise the conceptualisation of social vulnerability for overemphasising the social, political and economical processes and structures that lead to vulnerable conditions. Inherent in such a view is the tendency to understand people as passive victims (Hewitt 1997) and to neglect the subjective and intersubjective interpretation and perception of disastrous events. Bankoff criticises the very basis of the concept, since in his view it is shaped by a knowledge system that was developed and formed within the academic environment of western countries and therefore inevitably represents values and principles of that culture. According to Bankoff the ultimate aim underlying this concept is to depict large parts of the world as dangerous and hostile to provide further justification for interference and intervention (Bankoff 2003).

Current and future research

Social vulnerability research has become a deeply interdisciplinary science, rooted in the modern realization that humans are the causal agents of disasters – i.e., disasters are never natural, but a consequence of human behavior. The desire to understand geographic, historic, and socio-economic characteristics of social vulnerability motivates much of the research being conducted around the world today.

Two principal goals are currently driving the field of social vulnerability research:

1. The design of models which explain vulnerability and the root causes which create it, and
2. The development of indicators and indexes which attempt to map vulnerability over time and space (Villágran de León 2006).

The temporal and spatial aspects of vulnerability science are pervasive, particularly in research that attempts to demonstrate the impact of development on social vulnerability. Geographic Information Systems (GIS) are increasingly being used to map vulnerability, and to better understand how various phenomena (hydrological, meteorological, geophysical, social, political and economic) effect human populations.

Researchers have yet to develop reliable models capable of predicting future outcomes based upon existing theories and data. Designing and testing the validity of such models, particularly at the sub-national scale at which vulnerability reduction takes place, is expected to become a major component of social vulnerability research in the future.

An even greater aspiration in social vulnerability research is the search for one, broadly applicable theory, which can be applied systematically at a variety of scales, all over the world. Climate change scientists, building engineers, public health specialists, and many other related professions have already achieved major strides in reaching common approaches. Some social vulnerability scientists argue that it is time for them to do the same, and they are creating a variety of new forums in order to seek a consensus on common frameworks, standards, tools, and research priorities. Many academic, policy, and public/NGO organizations promote a globally applicable approach in social vulnerability science and policy (see section 5 for links to some of these institutions).

Since 2005, the Spanish Red Cross has developed a set of indicators to measure the multi-dimensional aspects of social vulnerability. These indicators are generated through the statistical analysis of more than 500 thousand people who are suffering of economic strain and social vulnerability, and who have a personal record containing 220 variables at the Red Cross database. An Index on Social Vulnerability in Spain is produced annually, both for adults and for children.

Research opportunities and challenges

Research on social vulnerability is expanding rapidly to fill the research and action gaps in this field. This work can be characterized in three major groupings, including research, public awareness, and policy. The following issues have been identified as requiring further attention to understand and reduce social vulnerability (Warner and Loster 2006):

Research

1. Foster a common understanding of social vulnerability – its definition(s), theories, and measurement approaches.

2. Aim for science that produces tangible and applied outcomes.

3. Advance tools and methodologies to reliably measure social vulnerability.

Public awareness

4. Strive for better understanding of nonlinear relationships and interacting systems (environment, social and economic, hazards), and present this understanding coherently to maximize public understanding.

5. Disseminate and present results in a coherent manner for the use of lay audiences. Develop straight forward information and practical education tools.

6. Recognize the potential of the media as a bridging device between science and society.

Policy

7. Involve local communities and stakeholders considered in vulnerability studies.

8. Strengthen people's ability to help themselves, including an (audible) voice in resource allocation decisions.

9. Create partnerships that allow stakeholders from local, national, and international levels to contribute their knowledge.

10. Generate individual and local trust and ownership of vulnerability reduction efforts.

Debate and ongoing discussion surround the causes and possible solutions to social vulnerability. In cooperation with scientists and policy experts worldwide, momentum is gathering around practice-oriented research on social vulnerability. In the future, links will be strengthened between ongoing policy and academic work to solidify the science, consolidate the research agenda, and fill knowledge gaps about causes of and solutions for social vulnerability.

Further reading

Overview

Adger, W. Neil. 2006. Vulnerability. Global Environmental Change 16 (3):268-281.

Cutter, Susan L., Bryan J. Boruff, and W. Lynn Shirley. 2003. Social vulnerability to environmental hazards. Social Science Quarterly 84 (1):242-261.

Gallopín, Gilberto C. 2006. Linkages between vulnerability, resilience, and adaptive capacity. Global Environmental Change 16 (3):293-303.

Oliver-Smith, Anthony. 2004. Theorizing vulnerability in a globalized world: a political ecological perspective. In Mapping vulnerability: disasters, development & people, edited by G. Bankoff, G. Frerks and D. Hilhorst. Sterling, VA: Earthscan, 10-24.

Natural hazards paradigm

Burton, Ian, Robert W. Kates, and Gilbert F. White. 1993. The environment as hazard. 2nd ed. New York: Guildford Press.

Kates, Robert W. 1971. Natural hazard in human ecological perspectives: hypotheses and models. Economic Geography 47 (3):438-451. Mitchell, James K. 2001. What's in a name?: issues of terminology and language in hazards research (Editorial). Environmental Hazards 2:87-88.

Political-ecological tradition

Blaikie, Piers, Terry Cannon, Ian Davis and Ben Wisner. 1994. At risk: natural hazards, people's vulnerability, and disasters. ist ed. London: Routledge. (see below under Wisner for 2nd edition)

Bohle, H. G., T. E. Downing, and M. J. Watts. 1994. Climate change and social vulnerability: the sociology and geography of food insecurity. Global Environmental Change 4:37-48.

Langridge, R.; J. Christian-Smith; and K.A. Lohse. "Access and Resilience: Analyzing the Construction of Social Resilience to the Threat of Water Scarcity" Ecology and Society 11(2): insight section.

O'Brien, P., and Robin Leichenko. 2000. Double exposure: assessing the impacts of climate change within the context of economic globalization. Global Environmental Change 10 (3):221-232.

Quarantelli, E. L. 1989. Conceptualizing disasters from a sociological perspective. International Journal of Mass Emergencies and Disasters 7 (3):243-251.

Sarewitz, Daniel, Roger Pielke, Jr. , and Mojdeh Keykhah. 2003. Vulnerability and risk: some thoughts from a political and policy perspective. Risk Analysis 23 (4):805-810.

Tierney, Kathleen J. 1999. Toward a critical sociology of risk. Sociological Forum 14 (2):215-242.

Wisner, B., Blaikie, Piers, Terry Cannon, Ian Davis. 2004. At risk: natural hazards, people's vulnerability, and disasters. 2nd ed. London: Routledge.

Human-ecological tradition

Brooks, Nick, W. Neil Adger, and P. Mick Kelly. 2005. The determinants of vulnerability and adaptive capacity at the national level and the implications for adaptation. Global Environmental Change 15 (2):151-163.

Comfort, L., Ben Wisner, Susan L. Cutter, R. Pulwarty, Kenneth Hewitt, Anthony Oliver-Smith, J. Wiener, M. Fordham, W. Peacock, and F. Krimgold. 1999. Reframing disaster policy: the global evolution of vulnerable communities. Environmental Hazards 1 (1):39-44. Cutter, Susan L. 1996. Vulnerability to environmental hazards. Progress in Human Geography 20 (4):529-539.

Dow, Kirsten. 1992. Exploring differences in our common future(s): the meaning of vulnerability to global environmental change. Geoforum 23:417-436.

Liverman, Diana. 1990. Vulnerability to global environmental change. In Understanding global environmental change: the contributions of risk analysis and management, edited by R. E. Kasperson, K. Dow, D. Golding and J. X. Kasperson. Worcester, MA: Clark University, 27-44.

Turner, B. L. II, Roger E. Kasperson, Pamela A. Matson, James J. McCarthy, Robert W. Corell, Lindsey Christensen, Noelle Eckley, Jeanne X. Kasperson, Amy Luers, Marybeth L. Martello, Colin Polsky, Alexander Pulsipher, and Andrew Schiller. 2003. A framework for vulnerability analysis in sustainability science. PNAS (Proceedings of the National Academy of Sciences of the United States of America) 100 (14):8074-8079.

Research Needs

Cutter, Susan L. 2001. A research agenda for vulnerability science and environmental hazards [Internet]. International Human Dimensions Programme on Global Environmental Change [cited August 18, 2006]. Available from http://www.ihdp.uni-bonn.de/html/publications/publications.html.

Young, Oran R., Frans Berkhout, Gilberto C. Gallopin, Marco A. Janssen, Elinor Ostrom, and Sander van der Leeuw. 2006. The globalization of socio-ecological systems: an agenda for scientific research. Global Environmental Change 16 (3):304-316.

References

[1] Luis Flores Ballesteros. "What determines a disaster?" 54 Pesos May. 2008:54 Pesos 11 Sep 2008.
  <http://54pesos.org/2008/09/11/what-determines-a-disaster/>

[2] The Yogyakarta Principles, Principle 9, 11 and 15

[3] Wisner, B., P. Blaikie, T. Cannon, and I. Davis. 2004. At Risk. Natural hazards, People's Vulnerability and Disasters. New York: Routledge.

Alwang, J., P. B. Siegel, et al. (2001). Vulnerability: a view from different disciplines. Social Protection Discussion Paper Series No. 0115. Washington, D.C., Social Protection Unit, Human Development Network, The World Bank. Anderson, M. B. and P. J. Woodrow (1998). Rising from the Ashes: Development Strategies in Times of Disaster. London, IT Publications. Bankoff, G. (2003). Cultures of Disaster: Society and natural hazards in the Philippines. London, RoutledgeCurzon.

Blaikie, P., T. Cannon, I. Davis & B. Wisner. (1994). At Risk: Natural hazards, People's vulnerability, and disasters. London, Routledge. Cannon, T., J. Twigg, et al. (2005). Social Vulnerability, Sustainable Livelihoods and Disasters, Report to DFID Conflict and Humanitarian Assistance Department (CHAD) and Sustainable Livelihoods Support Office. London, DFID: 63. Chambers, R. (1989). "Editorial Introduction: Vulnerability, Coping and Policy." IDS Bulletin 20(2): 7. Conway, T. and A. Norton (2002). "Poverty, Risk and Rights: New Directions in Social Protection." Development Policy Review 20(5). Cutter, S. L., J. T. Mitchell, et al. (2000). "Revealing the Vulnerability of People and Places: A Case Study of Georgetown County, South Carolina." Annals of American Geographers 90(4): 713-737. Frankenberger, T. R., M. Drinkwater, et al. (2000). Operationalizing household livelihood security: a holistic approach for addressing poverty and vulnerability. Forum on Operationalising Sustainable Livelihoods Approaches. Pontignano (Siena), FAO. Henninger, N. (1998). Mapping and Geographic Analysis of Human Welfare and Poverty: Review and Assessment. Washington DC, World Resources Institute. Hewitt, K., Ed. (1983). Interpretation of Calamity: From the Viewpoint of Human Ecology. Boston, Allen. Hewitt, K. (1997). Regions of Risk: A Geographical Introduction to Disasters. Essex, Longman. O´Keefe, K. Westgate, et al. (1976). "Taking the naturalness out of natural disasters." Nature 260. Oliver-Smith, A. (2003). Theorizing Vulnerability in a Globalized World: A Political Ecological Perspective. Mapping Vulnerability: Disasters, Development and People. Bankoff, Frerk and Hilhorst. London, Earthscan: 10-24. Oliver-Smith, A. and S. M. Hoffman (2002). Theorizing Disasters: Nature, Power and Culture. Theorizing Disasters: Nature, Power and Culture (Catastrophe and Culture: The Anthropology of Disaster). A. Oliver-Smith. Santa Fe, School of American Research Press. Peacock, W. G. and A. K. Ragsdale (1997). Social Systems, Ecological Networks and Disasters. Hurricane Andrew: Ethnicity, Gender and the Sociology of Disasters. W. G. Peacock, B. H. Morrow and J. Gladwin. New York, NY, Routledge. Villágran de León, J. C. (2006). "Vulnerability Assessment in the Context of Disaster-Risk, a Conceptual and Methodological Review." SOURCE SOURCE No. 4/20. Warner, K. and T. Loster (2006). A research and action agenda for social vulnerability. Bonn, United Nations University Institute of Environment and Human Security. Watts, M. and H. G. Bohle (1993). "The space of vulnerability: the causal structure of hunger and famine." Progress in Human Geography 17(1). Wisner, B,, Blaikie, P., T. Cannon, Davis, I. (2004). At Risk: Natural hazards, people's vulnerability and disasters. 2nd edition, London, Routledge.

Weichselgartner, J. (2001). "Disaster mitigation: the concept of vulnerability revisited." Disaster Prevention and Management 10(2): 85-94.

External links

Social Vulnerability in Spain (applied research based on a set of indicators which cover the muldimensional aspects of social vulnerability, by means of a database specifically designed by the Spanish Red Cross- information in Spanish, executive summaries available also in English language) http://www.sobrevulnerables.es

Hazard Reduction and Recovery Center, Texas A&M University http://archone.tamu.edu/hrrc/

Hazards and Vulnerability Research Institute, University of South Carolina http://webra.cas.sc.edu/hvri/

Livelihoods and Institutions Group, Natural Resources Institute http://www.nri.org/about/0301.htm

Munich Re Foundation http://www.munichre-foundation.org

National University of Colombia, Working Group on Disaster Management http://idea.manizales.unal.edu.co/GTA/GTA.asp?IdGrupo=25

Radical Interpretations of Disaster (RADIX) http://www.radixonline.org

Social protection, International Labour Organisation http://www.ilo.org/public/english/protection/

Social protection, World Bank http://www.worldbank.org/sp

United Nations University's Institute for Environment & Human Security http://www.ehs.unu.edu

Understanding Katrina: Perspectives from the Social Sciences http://understandingkatrina.ssrc.org

Vulnerability Net http://www.vulnerabilitynet.org/latest_news.shtml

Spurious trip level

Spurious Trip Level (STL) is defined as a discrete level for specifying the spurious trip requirements of safety functions to be allocated to safety systems. An STL of 1 means that this safety function has the highest level of spurious trips. The higher the STL level the lower the number of spurious trips caused by the safety system. There is no limit the number of spurious trip levels..

Safety functions and systems are installed to protect people, the environment and for asset protection. A safety function should only activate when a dangerous situation occurs. A safety function that activates without the presence of a dangerous situation (e.g., due to an internal failure) causes economic loss. The spurious trip level concept represents the probability that safety function causes a spurious (unscheduled) trip.

The STL is a metric that is used to specify the performance level of a safety function in terms of the spurious trips it potentially causes. Typical safety systems that benefit from an STL level are defined in standards like IEC 61508[1] IEC 61511[2], IEC 62061[3], ISA S84[4], EN 50204[5] and so on. An STL provides end-users of safety functions with a measurable attribute that helps them define the desired availability of their safety functions. An STL can be specified for a complete safety loop or for individual devices.

For end-users there is always a potential conflict between the cost of safety solutions and the loss of profitability caused by spurious trips of these safety solutions. The STL concept helps the endusers to end this conflict in an a way that safety solutions provide both the desired safety and the desired process availability.

STL determination

The spurious trip level represents asset loss due to an internal failure of the safety function. The more financial damage the safety function can cause due to a spurious trip the higher the STL level of the safety function should be. Each company needs to decide for themselves which level of financial loss they can or are willing to take. This actually depends on many different factors, like the financial situation of the company, the insurance policy, the cost of process shutdown and startup, and so on. All these factors are unique to each company. The table below shows an example of how a company can calibrate its spurious trip levels.

STL	Description
6	Spurious trip costs between 10M and 20M EUR
5	Spurious trip costs between 10M and 20M EUR
4	Spurious trip costs between 5M and 10M EUR
3	Spurious trip costs between 1M and 5M EUR
2	Spurious trip costs between 500k and 1M EUR
1	Spurious trip costs between 100k and 500k EUR
None	Spurious trip costs between 0 and 100k EUR

STL levels

The STL level achieved by a safety function is determined by the probability of fail safe (PFS) of this safety function. The PFS value is determined by internal failures of the safety system that cause the safety function to be executed without a demand from the process. The table below demonstrates the PFS value and spurious trip reduction values of each STL level.

STL level	PFSavg	STR
X	$\geq 10^{-(X+1)}$ to $<10^{-X}$	10^{X}
...	...	...
5	$\geq 10^{-6}$ to $<10^{-5}$	100000
4	$\geq 10^{-5}$ to $<10^{-4}$	10000
3	$\geq 10^{-4}$ to $<10^{-3}$	1000
2	$\geq 10^{-3}$ to $<10^{-2}$	100
1	$\geq 10^{-2}$ to $<10^{-1}$	10

STL vs SIL

Today standards only define the safety integrity level (SIL) for safety functions. Standards do not define STL levels because they do in first instance not represent safety but economic loss. Despite this the STL is also a safety attribute, specially for safety functions in the process, oil & gas, chemical and nuclear industry. In those industries an undesired shutdown of the process leads to dangerous situation as the plant needs to be started up again. Startup and shutdown of a process plant are considered the two most dangerous operational modes of the plant and should be limited to the absolute minimum.

In practice the STL and SIL concepts complement each other. Both factors are attributes of the same safety function. The STL level is determined by the average PFS value of the safety function. The SIL level is determined by the average probability of failure on demand. PFD value of the safety function. The STL level expresses the probability of spurious trips by the safety function, i.e., the safety function is executed without a demand from the process. The SIL level expresses the probability that the safety function does not work upon demand from the process. Both parameters are important to end-users in order to achieve safety and asset protection.

Description	Spurious Trip Level	Safety Integrity Level
Calculated via	Average PFS	Average PFD
Represents	Process availability	Safety availability
Expressed as ...	STL	SIL
Number of levels ...	Unlimited	1 through 4

In order to calculate the PFS or PFD value of a safety loop it is necessary to have a reliability model and reliability data for each component in the safety loop. The best reliability model to use is a Markov model (see Andrey Markov). Typical data required are:

- Lambda safe detected
- Lambda safe undetected
- Lambda dangerous detected
- Lambda dangerous undetected
- Repair rate
- Proof test coverage
- Proof test interval
- Common cause factors

Notes

[1] IEC 61508: Functional safety of electrical/electronic/programmable electronic safety-related systems, IEC, 1998

[2] IEC 61511 - Functional safety - Safety instrumented systems for the process industry sector, IEC, 2003

[3] Safety of machinery - Functional safety of safety-related electrical, electronic and programmable electronic control systems, IEC, 2005

[4] ANSI/ISA-84.00.01-2004 Part 1 (IEC 61511-1 Mod) Functional Safety: Safety Instrumented Systems for the Process Industry Sector

[5] EN 50204 - Electrical apparatus for the detection and measurement of combustible or toxic gases or vapours or of oxygen. Requirements on the functional safety of fixed gas detection systems

External links

- IEC Functional safety zone (http://www.iec.ch/functionalsafety)
- Functional Safety and IEC 61508: A basic guide (http://www.iec.ch/zone/fsafety/pdf_safe/hld.pdf)
- Overview of IEC 61508 (http://www2.theiet.org/oncomms/sector/computing/Articles/Object/ 58D25FCD-6153-46BD-ADAF910D2C4B69D4)
- Safety Users Group (http://www.safetyusersgroup.com) - Functional Safety-Information Resources
- Inside Functional Safety (http://www.insidefunctionalsafety.com) - Technical magazine focusing on functional safety

Square root biased sampling

Square root biased sampling is a sampling method proposed by William H. Press, a professor in the fields of computer sciences and computational biology, for use in airport screenings as a mathematically efficient compromise between simple random sampling and strong profiling.[1] [2]

Using this method, if a group is n times as likely than the average to be a security risk, then persons from that group will be $\sqrt{n}$ times as likely to undergo additional screening.[1] For example, if someone from a profiled group is nine times more likely than the average person to be a security risk, then when using square root biased sampling, people from the profiled group would be screened three times more often than the average person.[3]

Development

Press developed square root biased sampling as a way to sample long sequences of DNA.[3] It had also been developed independently by Ruben Abagyan, a professor at TSRI in La Jolla, California, for use in a different context.[3]

Press later proposed the use of square root biased sampling for use by airport security, in a paper published in Proceedings of the National Academy of Sciences.[1] He argued that this method would be a more efficient use of the limited resources possessed for screening, as compared to the current practice, which can lead to screening the same persons frequently and repeatedly.[2] Use of this method presupposes that those doing the screening have accurate statistical information on who is more likely to be a security risk, which is not necessarily the case.

References

[1] Press, William H. (2008-12-23). "Strong profiling is not mathematically optimal for discovering rare malfeasors" (http://www.pnas.org/content/106/6/1716.full). *Proceedings of the National Academy of Sciences* (University of Texas, Austin, TX) **106**. . Retrieved 2009-11-28.

[2] "Square root bias and airport security screening" (http://homelandsecuritynewswire.com/square-root-bias-and-airport-security-screening). *Homeland Security Newswire*. 2009-02-03. . Retrieved 2009-11-28

[3] "Researcher Proposes Statistical Method to Enhance Secondary Security Screenings" (http://www.utexas.edu/news/2009/02/03/statistical_security/). University of Texas at Austin News. 2009-02-03. . Retrieved 2009-11-28.

Stein's unbiased risk estimate

In statistics, **Stein's unbiased risk estimate (SURE)** is an unbiased estimator of the mean-squared error of a given estimator, in a deterministic estimation scenario. In other words, it provides an indication of the accuracy of a given estimator. This is important since, in deterministic estimation, the true mean-squared error of an estimator generally depends on the value of the unknown parameter, and thus cannot be determined completely.

The technique is named after its discoverer, Charles Stein.[1]

Formal statement

Let $\theta \in \mathbb{R}^n$ be an unknown deterministic parameter and let x be a measurement vector which is distributed normally with mean θ and covariance $\sigma^2 I$. Suppose $h(x)$ is an estimator of θ from x. Then, Stein's unbiased risk estimate is given by

$$\mathrm{SURE}(h) = \|\theta\|^2 + \|h(x)\|^2 + 2\sigma^2 \sum_{i=1}^{n} \frac{\partial h_i}{\partial x_i} - 2\sum_{i=1}^{n} x_i h_i(x)$$

where $h_i(x)$ is the i th component of the estimate, and $\| \cdot \|$ is the Euclidean norm.

The importance of SURE is that it is an unbiased estimate of the mean-squared error (or squared error risk) of $h(x)$, i.e.

$$E\{\mathrm{SURE}(h)\} = \mathrm{MSE}(h).$$

Thus, minimizing SURE can be expected to minimize the MSE. Except for the first term in SURE, which is identical for all estimators, there is no dependence on the unknown parameter θ in the expression for SURE above. Thus, it can be manipulated (e.g., to determine optimal estimation settings) without knowledge of θ.

Applications

A standard application of SURE is to choose a parametric form for an estimator, and then optimize the values of the parameters to minimize the risk estimate. This technique has been applied in several settings. For example, a variant of the James–Stein estimator can be derived by finding the optimal shrinkage estimator.[1] The technique has also been used by Donoho and Johnstone to determine the optimal shrinkage factor in a wavelet denoising setting.[2]

References

[1] Stein, Charles M. (November 1981). "Estimation of the Mean of a Multivariate Normal Distribution". *The Annals of Statistics* **9** (6): 1135–1151. doi:10.1214/aos/1176345632. JSTOR 2240405.

[2] Donoho, David L.; Iain M. Johnstone (December 1995). "Adapting to Unknown Smoothness via Wavelet Shrinkage". *Journal of the American Statistical Association* (Journal of the American Statistical Association, Vol. 90, No. 432) **90** (432): 1200–1244. doi:10.2307/2291512. JSTOR 2291512.

Stunt performer

Stunt performer

Pyrotechnics stunt exhibition by "Giant Auto Rodéo", Ciney, Belgium

Occupation	
Names	Stuntman, stunt performer
Activity sectors	Entertainment
Description	
Competencies	Physical fitness, daring, acting skills
Fields of employment	Film, television, theatre
Related jobs	Stunt double, stunt coordinator, actor, movie star, extra

A **stunt performer**, **stuntman**, or **daredevil** is someone who performs dangerous stunts, often as a career.

These stunts are sometimes rigged so that they look dangerous while still having safety mechanisms, but often they are as dangerous as they appear to be. There is an inherent risk in the performance of all stunt work in film, television and stage work. With more risk in performing stunts in front of a live audience because safety mechanisms cannot be edited out and the audience can see if the performer is genuinely doing what they claim to be doing.

Daredevils are distinct from stunt performers and stunt doubles, as they perform their stunts purely for the sake of the stunt itself, often before an audience for their entertainment and personal monetary gain for the event. While a stunt performer, or stunt double, typically performs stunts intended for use in a motion pictures or dramatized television (although one person could certainly be both, as was the case with Harry Houdini, Jackie Chan, Tony Jaa, Jayan and others). Stunt performers and stunt doubles are generally skilled at performing physical action in character for film and television.

Stunts often seen in films and television include car crashes, falling from great height, dragged behind a horse and being blown up. Film and television stunt performers are often trained in martial arts and stage combat.

Live stunt performers include escape artists, sword swallowers, glass walkers, fire eaters, trapeze artists, and many other sideshow and circus arts. They also include motorcycle display teams and the once popular Wall of Death.

Modern live stunt performers include escape artist and stuntman Roslyn Walker[1] and sideshow veteran Kondini.[2]

Famous stunt performers

- Yakima Canutt, years active 1912-1975
- Yuen Biao
- Jackie Chan
- Dorothy Dietrich[3]
- Helen Gibson
- Harry Houdini[4]
- Sammo Hung
- Tony Jaa
- Jayan
- Evel Knievel
- Robbie Knievel
- Chris Pontius
- Johnny Knoxville
- Kondini[2]
- Akshay Kumar
- Bam Margera
- Steve-O
- Claudio Pacifico
- Travis Pastrana
- Andy Bell
- Sam Patch
- Clem Sohn
- Steve Truglia
- Iko Uwais
- Roslyn Walker[1]
- Donnie Yen

References

[1] Official website for escape artist and stuntman (http://www.roslynwalker.com) Roslyn Walker

[2] http://www.kondini.com

[3] http://www.DorothyDietrich.com

[4] http://www.Houdinni.org Houdini Museum Tour & Magic Show

Substantial equivalence

Substantial equivalence is a concept, developed by OECD in 1991, that maintains that a novel food (for example, genetically modified foods) should be considered the same as and as safe as a conventional food if it demonstrates the same characteristics and composition as the conventional food. Substantial equivalence is important from a regulatory point of view. If a novel food is substantially equivalent to its conventional counterpart, then it could be covered by the same regulatory framework as a conventional food.[1]

The concept is used to determine whether a new food shares similar health and nutritional characteristics with an existing, familiar food with an established history of safe use.

Definition and Controversy

To facilitate rapid approval for genetically modified foods the "substantial equivalence" concept was proposed by the Food and Agriculture Organization (FAO) and World Health Organization in the early 1990s. The stringent testing normally required for new food products can cost millions of dollars and take years of testing before a product gains approval for marketing. Such demands and delays would have made genetically modified foods unprofitable for private companies, substantial equivalence can allow products to get to market within months of their development.

Reasoning about **substantial equivalence** is widely used by national and international agencies - including the Canadian Food Inspection Agency, Japan's Ministry of Health and Welfare and the U.S. Food and Drug Administration, the United Nation's Food and Agriculture Organization, the World Health Organization and the Organisation for Economic Cooperation and Development (hereafter OECD).[2] It has been argued that by invoking the doctrine of substantial equivalence the GMO industry has avoided safety testing, and that forthcoming novel food production technologies may follow this example.[3]

Some other new biochemical concepts that are important for understanding the **substantial equivalence** of a novel food or crop to an existing food or crop are **metabolic profiling** and **protein profiling**. These concepts refer, respectively, to the complete measured biochemical spectrum (total fingerprint) of compounds (metabolites) or of proteins present in a food or crop. Substantially equivalent foods have the same metabolic and protein profiles, or more precisely, **biochemical profiles** of a new food are deemed to be substantially equivalent to an existing food if they fall within the **range of natural variation** already exhibited by **biochemical profiles** of existing foods or crops.

Over the history of its usage the term **substantial equivalence** has been interpreted differently by the various participants in the debate about GM food safety.

The current state of the concept is clarified in several recent food science articles.[2] [4] [5] [6]

> International consensus has been reached on the principles regarding evaluation of the food safety of genetically modified plants. The concept of substantial equivalence has been developed as part of a safety evaluation framework, based on the idea that existing foods can serve as a basis for comparing the properties of genetically modified foods with the appropriate counterpart. Application of the concept is not a safety assessment per se, but helps to identify similarities and differences between the existing food and the new product, which are then subject to further toxicological investigation. Substantial equivalence is a starting point in the safety evaluation, rather than an endpoint of the assessment. (Kuiper and others, 2001)

The utility of the **substantial equivalence** concept is illustrated by the way certain food products - such as processed and purified food components like soybean oil, starch or crystalline sugar - may be considered substantially equivalent even though the varieties from which they were obtained are different.

As a notion **substantial equivalence** was first articulated by the OECD, which hosted discussions that led to a key publication *'Safety Evaluation of Foods Derived by Modern Biotechnology: Concepts and Principles'* (OECD, 1993)[7].

The concept has been criticised, for instance in 1999 by Erik Millstone (University of Sussex) Eric Brunner (UC London) and Sue Mayer (GeneWatch UK)[8] who argued that the concept was pseudo-scientific, and that:

> [T]he biotechnology companies wanted government regulators to help persuade consumers that their products were safe, yet they also wanted the regulatory hurdles to be set as low as possible. Governments wanted an approach to the regulation of GM foods that could be agreed internationally, and that would not inhibit the development of their domestic biotechnology companies.

But **substantial equivalence** recognises the fact that existing foods often contain toxic components (usually called antinutrients) and are still able to be consumed safely - in practice there is some tolerable chemical risk taken with all foods, so a comparative method for assessing safety needs to be adopted. For instance, potatoes and tomatoes can contain toxic levels of respectively, solanine and alpha-tomatine alkaloids.[6] [9]

It also recognised the well supported scientific argument that:

> While rDNA techniques may result in the production of organisms expressing a combination of traits that are not observed in nature, genetic changes from rDNA [recombinant DNA] techniques will often have inherently greater predictability compared to traditional techniques, because of the greater precision that the rDNA technique affords; (and) it is expected that any risks associated with applications of rDNA organisms may be assessed in generally the same way as those associated with non-rDNA organisms.

which was first voiced in 1986 by the OECD Recombinant DNA Safety Considerations. Paris: OECD, 1986, cited by Miller (1999) , and has subsequently re-affirmed in numerous scientific deliberations,[10] and by comprehensive chemical comparisons of recombinant DNA derived crops and their conventional crop counterparts discussed below.

It is for this reason legislators treat a new food by comparison with its nearest existing known counterpart, taking into account natural ranges for variation in metabolic and proteins profiles, and particularly profiles of anti-nutrients. If a GM food was found to be **substantially equivalent** to its nearest existing counterpart by careful compositional analysis ('profiling' or 'fingerprinting') of the full set of chemical compounds in the food, it can be argued that it is at least as safe as that conventional counterpart.

For instance, the US FDA effectively uses **substantial equivalence** as part of their policy:

> The FDA's policy defines certain safety-related characteristics of new foods that, if present, require greater scrutiny by the agency. These include the presence of a substance that is completely new to the food supply, an allergen presented in an unusual or unexpected way (for example, a peanut protein transferred to a potato), changes in the levels of major dietary nutrients, and increased levels of toxins normally found in foods. Additional tests are performed when suggested by the product's composition, characteristics or history of use. For example, potatoes are generally tested for the glycoalkaloid solanine, because this natural toxin has been detected at harmful levels in some new potato varieties that were developed with conventional genetic techniques.[10]

A biotechnology company could establish **substantial equivalence** by comparing food **biochemical profiles** such as protein, carbohydrate, fatty acid levels, nutrients, antinutients and other plant metabolites between the novel food and its traditional counterpart.

Critics have argued that there were no clear and universal guidelines stipulating what to test and how similar the items in question should be. For example, Roundup Ready Soybeans contained a new previously unknown enzyme, *5-enolpyruvyl shikimate-3-phosphate synthetase*. The manufacturer argued that as cooking deactivates the enzyme and people do not eat uncooked Soybeans its presence was irrelevant. Although this argument ignored that the still functional enzyme could be consumed with the meat if the Soybeans were fed to cattle, it was approved by the FDA without testing. Erik Millstone *et al.*[8] state:

> The concept of substantial equivalence has never been properly defined; the degree of difference between a natural food and its GM alternative before its 'substance' ceases to be acceptably 'equivalent'

is not defined anywhere, nor has an exact definition been agreed by legislators. It is exactly this vagueness which makes the concept useful to industry but unacceptable to the consumer.

But the response of the proponents to this criticism was that they were being misrepresented:

> Substantial equivalence is not a substitute for a safety assessment. It is a guiding principle which is a useful tool for regulatory scientists engaged in safety assessments. It stresses that an assessment should show that a GM variety is as safe as its traditional counterparts. In this approach, differences may be identified for further scrutiny, which can involve nutritional, toxicological and immunological testing. The approach allows regulators to focus on the differences in a new variety and therefore on safety concerns of critical importance. Biochemical and toxicological tests are certainly not precluded. Peter Kearns (OECD) Paul Mayers (Health Canada)[11]

The quandary of what to test has been resolved by the concept of testing everything and thus determine the **biochemical profile** of the food, as recently comprehensive biochemical profiling of metabolites and proteins in food have become technically possible. These provide an empirical route for determining if a food is in fact substantially equivalent to an existing food, and this approach, also called metabolomics (for metabolite profiling) or proteomics (protein profiling) has established the equivalence of one strain of GM potato and its conventional counterparts, and also the equivalence of a new GM tomato variety to its existing counterpart.[12] [13] [14]

The range of **biochemical profiles** routinely seen in different conventional varieties of the same crop and under different growing condition[6] [12] [14] provide a natural criterion for defining what constitutes an "equivalent composition". If a new GM food falls within the natural range of existing variation it is equivalent.

Scientists from the United States National Academy of Science, the Royal Society of Canada and the Medical Research Council (UK) have however, pointed out that a genetically engineered food may not only be substantially equivalent, but effectively almost completely identical with its natural counterpart and still contain an unexpected toxic substance not tested for despite passing Substantial Equivalence requirements.[15] A leading pro-GM scientist, Dr Andrew Chesson, admitted that substantial equivalence testing is flawed and that some current safety tests could allow harmful substances to enter the human food chain.[16]

> "Substantial equivalence does not function as a scientific basis for the application of a safety standard, but rather as a decision procedure for facilitating the passage of new products, GE and non-GE, through the regulatory process"—**Royal Society of Canada**[17]

Michael R. Taylor

On the 17th July 1991, Michael R. Taylor was appointed as the FDA's Deputy Commissioner for Policy, the first person to hold this newly created post. Taylor previously worked as a lawyer for Monsanto, where he had great influence on the legalization of the genetically modified bovine growth hormone (BGH). During Taylor's tenure GM seeds were declared to be "substantially equivalent" to non-GM seeds, hence proclaiming proof of the harmlessness of GMs to be unnecessary. After his tenure at the FDA, Taylor became a vice-president of Monsanto. Critics have called for a review of his work at the FDA citing a conflict of interest.

On July 7, 2009, Mr Taylor returned to government as the "senior advisor" to the Commissioner of the US Food and Drug Administration for the Obama administration.[18]

Many commentators see Taylor as the originator of the concept of substantial equivalence.

Vandana Shiva concluded: "a very convenient tool called substantial equivalence principle was cooked up to say 'let's just treated [sic?] genetically engineered organisms like conventional crops'. Of course, they don't say that, when they want to patent these things. At that point, they say these are absolutely "novel", never existed before, not like nature, these are not natural. But when it comes to safety, they say: it's just like nature, exactly as nature made. I sometimes call this ontological schizophrenia." [19]

Bibliography

- Royal Society (2002) *Genetically Modified Plants for Food Use and Human Health* [20].
- Council for Biotechnology Information, March 11, 2001, Substantial Equivalence in Food Safety Assessment [21]
- Millstone, *et al.* (1999) 'Beyond Substantial Equivalence' [22], *Nature* October 7, 1999 [23]
- Henry I. Miller, Hoover Institution, Substantial equivalence: Its uses and abuses Nature Biotechnology 17, 1042 - 1043 (1999)</ref>
- OECD (1993) 'Safety Evaluation of Foods Derived by Modern Biotechnology: Concepts and Principles', Paris: Organisation for Economic Cooperation and Development. [7]
- Kuiper HA, Kleter GA, Noteborn HP, Kok EJ. Assessment of the food safety issues related to genetically modified foods. Plant J. 2001 Sep;27(6):503-28. [24]
- Konig A, Cockburn A, Crevel RW, Debruyne E, Grafstroem R, Hammerling U, Kimber I, Knudsen I, Kuiper HA, Peijnenburg AA, Penninks AH, Poulsen M, Schauzu M, Wal JM. Assessment of the safety of foods derived from genetically modified (GM) crops. Food Chem Toxicol. 2004 Jul;42(7):1047-88. Harvard Center for Risk Analysis, Harvard School of Public Health [25]
- Claire Hope Cummings: Uncertain Peril. Genetic Engineering and the Future of Seeds. Beacon Press, 2008. ISBN 0807085804
- Vandana Shiva: Stolen Harvest: The Hijacking of the Global Food Supply. Zed Books, 2000. ISBN 184277025X, 9781842770252

References

[1] CRS Report for Congress: Agriculture: A Glossary of Terms, Programs, and Laws, 2005 Edition - Order Code 97-905 (http://ncseonline.org/nle/crsreports/05jun/97-905.pdf)

[2] Substantial Equivalence in Food Safety Assessment, Council for Biotechnology Information, March 11, 2001 (http://www.whybiotech.com/index.asp?id=1244)

[3] Paull, J., Beyond Equal: From Same but Different to the Doctrine of Substantial Equivalence (http://dspace.anu.edu.au/bitstream/1885/46994/1/SubstantialEquivalenceMC.pdf,), M/C Journal of Media & Culture, 11(2), 2008.

[4] Assessment of the food safety issues related to genetically modified foods. Kuiper HA, Kleter GA, Noteborn HP, Kok EJ. Plant J. 2001 Sep;27(6):503-28. (http://www.blackwell-synergy.com/doi/abs/10.1046/j.1365-313X.2001.01119.x)

[5] Assessment of the safety of foods derived from genetically modified (GM) crops. Konig A, Cockburn A, Crevel RW, Debruyne E, Grafstroem R, Hammerling U, Kimber I, Knudsen I, Kuiper HA, Peijnenburg AA, Penninks AH, Poulsen M, Schauzu M, Wal JM. Food Chem Toxicol. 2004 Jul;42(7):1047-88. Harvard Center for Risk Analysis, Harvard School of Public Health (http://www.sciencedirect.com/science?_ob=ArticleURL&_udi=B6T6P-4C0TB0F-2&_coverDate=07/31/2004&_alid=467625717&_rdoc=1&_fmt=&_orig=search&_qd=1&_cdi=5036&_sort=d&view=c&_acct=C000050221&_version=1&_urlVersion=0&_userid=10&md5=e427294d0125f467fb9a712cd51340b7)

[6] Substantial equivalence of antinutrients and inherent plant toxins in genetically modified novel foods, Novak, W. K.; Haslberger, A. G.,Food and Chemical Toxicology Volume 38 (6) p.473-483, 2000 (http://www.biotech-info.net/antinutrients.html)

[7] http://www.oecd.org/dataoecd/57/3/1946129.pdf

[8] Beyond 'substantial equivalence'. Nature. 1999 October 7;401(6753):525-6

[9] Agbios commentary on substantial equivalence (http://www.agbios.com/cstudies.php?book=FSA&ev=MON810&chapter=Concepts&lang=)

[10] Substantial equivalence: Its uses and abuses Henry I. Miller, Hoover Institution Nature Biotechnology 17, 1042 - 1043 (1999)

[11] Substantial equivalence is a useful tool Nature. 1999 October 14;401(6754):640-1

[12] Catchpole and others 2005 Hierarchical metabolomics demonstrates substantial compositional similarity between genetically modified and conventional potato crops (http://www.pnas.org/cgi/content/full/102/40/14458)

[13] Corpillo D, Gardini G, Vaira AM, Basso M, Aime S, Accotto GP, Fasano M. Proteomics as a tool to improve investigation of substantial equivalence in genetically modified organisms: the case of a virus-resistant tomato. Proteomics. 2004 Jan;4(1):193-200.

[14] Sirpa O. Kärenlampi and Satu J. Lehesranta 2006 Proteomic profiling (http://www.isb.vt.edu/news/2006/news06.jan.htm#jan0603)

[15] Scientists and scientist organizations rejecting the principle of Substantial Equivalence (http://psrast.org/subeqscireject.htm) Physicians and Scientists for Responsible Application of Science and Technology

[16] UK GM expert calls for tougher tests (http://news.bbc.co.uk/2/hi/uk_news/440352.stm) BBC September 7, 1999

[17] The Royal Society of Canada. Elements of Precaution: Recommendations for the Regulation of Food Biotechnology in Canada, Ottawa, p.182 (April 2001)

[18] http://www.fda.gov/NewsEvents/Newsroom/PressAnnouncements/2009/ucm170842.htm

[19] Fed Up! Genetic Engineering, Industrial Agriculture and Sustainable Alternatives, an Oopen Source Movie, http://www.archive.org/details/Fed_Up_Genetic_Engineering

[20] http://www.icsu.org/1_icsuinscience/GMO/PDF/RoyalSocUK2002.pdf

[21] http://www.whybiotech.com/index.asp?id=1244

[22] http://www.nature.com/nature/journal/v401/n6753/full/401525a0.html

[23] http://www.biotech-info.net/substantial_equivalence.html

[24] http://www.blackwell-synergy.com/doi/abs/10.1046/j.1365-313X.2001.01119.x

[25] http://www.sciencedirect.com/science?_ob=ArticleURL&_udi=B6T6P-4C0TB0F-2&_coverDate=07%2F31%2F2004&_alid=467625717&_rdoc=1&_fmt=&_orig=search&_qd=1&_cdi=5036&_sort=d&view=c&_acct=C000050221&_version=1&_urlVersion=0&_userid=10&md5=e427294d0125f467fb9a712cd51340b7

External links

- GMO Safety (http://www.gmo-safety.eu/archive/432.difference-quality.html) Feedstuff from GM and conventional crops: No difference in quality

Success likelihood index method

Success Likelihood Index Method (SLIM) is a technique used in the field of Human reliability Assessment (HRA), for the purposes of evaluating the probability of a human error occurring throughout the completion of a specific task. From such analyses measures can then be taken to reduce the likelihood of errors occurring within a system and therefore lead to an improvement in the overall levels of safety. There exist three primary reasons for conducting an HRA; error identification, error quantification and error reduction. As there exist a number of techniques used for such purposes, they can be split into one of two classifications; first generation techniques and second generation techniques. First generation techniques work on the basis of the simple dichotomy of 'fits/doesn't fit' in the matching of the error situation in context with related error identification and quantification and second generation techniques are more theory based in their assessment and quantification of errors. 'HRA techniques have been utilised in a range of industries including healthcare, engineering, nuclear, transportation and business sector; each technique has varying uses within different disciplines.

SLIM is a decision-analytic approach to HRA which uses expert judgement to quantify Performance Shaping Factors (PSFs); factors concerning the individuals, environment or task, which have the potential to either positively or negatively effect performance e.g. available task time. Such factors are used to derive a Success Likelihood Index (SLI), a form of preference index, which is calibrated against existing data to derive a final Human Error Probability (HEP). The PSF's which require to be considered are chosen by experts and are namely those factors which are regarded as most significant in relation to the context in question.

The technique consists of two modules: MAUD (multi-attribute utility decomposition) which scales the relative success likelihood in performing a range of tasks, given the PSFs probable to affect human performance; and SARAH (Systematic Approach to the Reliability Assessment of Humans) which calibrates these success scores with tasks with known HEP values, to provide an overall figure.

Background

SLIM was developed by Embrey et al. [1] for use within the US nuclear industry. By use of this method, relative success likelihoods are established for a range of tasks, and then calibrated using a logarithmic transformation.

SLIM Methodology

The SLIM methodology breaks down into ten steps of which steps 1-7 are involved in SLIM-MAUD and 8-10 are SLIM-SARAH.

1. Definition of situations and subsets

Upon selection of a relevant panel of experts who will carry out the assessment, these individuals are provided with as fully detailed a task description as possible with regards to the individual designated to perform each task and further factors which are likely to influence the success of each of these. An in depth description is a critical aspect of the procedure in order to ensure that all members of the assessing group share a common understanding of the given task. This may be further advanced through a group discussion prior to the commencement of the panel session to ascertain of consensus. Following this discussion, the tasks under consideration are then classified into a number of groupings depending upon the homogeneity of the PSF's that have an effect on each. Subsets are thus defined by those tasks which have in common specific PSFs and also by their weighting within a certain sub-group; this weighting is only an approximation at this stage of the process.

2. Elicitation of PSFs

Random sets of 3 tasks are presented to experts from which they are required to compare one against the other two and subsequently identify an aspect in which the highlighted task differs from the remaining two; this dissimilarity should be a characteristic which affects the probability of successful task completion. The experts are then asked to highlight the low and high end-points of the identified PSF i.e. the optimality of the PSF in the context of the given task. For example the PSF may be Time Pressure and therefore the end points of the scale would perhaps be "High level of pressure" to "Low level of pressure". Other possible PSFs may be stress levels, task complexity or degree of teamwork required. The of this stage is to identify those PSF's which are most prevalent in affecting the tasks as opposed to eliciting all the possible influencing factors.

3. Rating the Tasks on the PSFs

The endpoints of each individual PSF, as identified by the expert, are then assigned the values 1 and 9 on a linear scale. Using this scale, the expert is required to assign to each task a rating, between the two end points, which accurately reflects, using their judgement, the conditions occurring in the task in question. It is optimal to consider each factor in turn so that the judgements made are independent from the influence of other factors which otherwise may affect opinion.

4. Ideal Point Elicitation and Scaling Calculations

The "ideal" rating for each PSF is then selected on the scale constructed. The ideal is the point at which the PSF least degrades performance – for instance both low and high time pressure may contribute to increasing the chance of failure. The MAUD software then rescales all other ratings made on the scale in terms of their distance from this ideal point, with the closest being assigned as a 1 and the furthest from this point as a 0. This is done for all PSF's until the experts are agreed that the list of PSF's is exhausted and that all the scale positions identified are correctly positioned.

5. Independence Checks

Using the figures which represent the relative importance of each task and their rating on the relevant scale, these are multiplied to produce a Success Likelihood Index (SLI) figure for each task. To improve the validity of the process it is necessary to confirm that each of the scales in use are independent to ensure no overlap or double counting in the overall calculation of the index. To help carry out this validation task, MAUD software checks for correlations between the experts' scoring on the different scales; if the scale ratings indicate a high correlation, the experts are consulted to reveal whether they agree in their meanings of the ratings on the two scales which are showing similarities. If this situation occurs, the experts are asked to define a new scale which will be a combination of the meaning of the two individually correlated scales. If the correlation is not significant then the scales are treated as independent; in this case, the concerned facilitator is required to make an informed decision as to whether or not the PSFs showing similarities are actually similar and should therefore ensure that a strong justification is explainable for the final decision.

6. Weighting Procedure

This stage of the process concentrates on eliciting the emphasis required to be weighted to each of the PSFs in terms of the influence on the success of a task. This is done by enquiring, with the experts, the likelihood of success between pairs of tasks while considering two previously identified PSFs. By noting where the experts' opinion is changed, the weighting of the effect of each PSF on the task success can thus be inferred. To enhance the accuracy of the outcome, this stage should be carried out in an iterative manner.

7. Calculation of the SLI

The Success Likelihood Index for each task is deduced using the following formula: $SLI_j = (R_{ij}W_i)$ Where

- SLI_j is the SLI for task j
- W_i is the importance weight for the ith PSF
- R_{ij} is the scaled rating of task j on the ith PSF
- x represents the number of PSFs considered.

These SLI's are estimates of the probability with which different types of error may occur.

8. Conversion of SLIs to probabilities

The SLIs previously calculated require to be transformed to HEPs as they are only relative measures of the likelihood of success of each of the considered tasks. The relationship

$$Log\ P = a\ SLI + b$$

is assumed to exist between SLIs and HEPs. P is the probability of success and a and b are constants; a and b are calculated from the SLIs of two tasks where the HEP has already been established.

9. Uncertainty Bound Analysis

Uncertainty bounds can be estimated using expert judgement methods such as Absolute Probability Judgement (APJ).

10. Use of SLIM-SARAH for Cost-Effectiveness Analyses

As SLIM evaluates HEPs as a function of the PSFs, considered to be the major drivers in human reliability, it is possible to perform sensitivity analysis by modifying the scores of the PSFs. By considering the PSFs which may be altered, the degree to which they can be changed and the importance of the PSFs, it is possible to conduct a cost-benefit analysis to determine how worthwhile suggested improvements may be i.e. what-if analysis, the optimal means by which the calculated HEPs can be reduced.

Worked Example

The following example provides a good illustration of how the SLIM methodology is used in practice in the field of HRA.

Context

In this context an operator is responsible for the task of de-coupling a filling hose from a chemical road tanker. There exists the possibility that the operator may forget to close a valve located upstream of the filling hose, which is a crucial part of the procedure; if overlooked, this could result in adverse consequences, of greater effect to the operator in control. The primary human error of concern in this situation is 'failure to close V0204 prior to decoupling filling hose'. The decoupling operation required to be conducted is a fairly easy task to carry out and does not require to be completed in conjunction with any further tasks; therefore is failure occurs it will have a catastrophic impact as opposed to displaying effects in a gradual manner.

Required Inputs

This technique also requires an 'expert panel' to carry out the HRA; the panel would be made up of for example two operators possessing approximately 10 years experience of the system, a human factors analyst and a reliability analyst who has knowledge of the system and possesses a degree of experience of operation. The panel of experts is requested to determine a set of PSFs which are applicable to the task in question within the context of the wider system; of these, the experts are then required to propose those PSFs, of the identified, which are the most important in the circumstances of the scenario. For this example, it is assumed that the panel put forth 5 main PSFs for consideration, which are believed to have the greatest effect on human performance of the task: training, procedures, feedback, perceived risk and time pressure.

Method

PSF Rating

Considering the situation within the context of the task under assessment, the panel are asked to provide further possible human errors which may occur that have the potential of affecting performance e.g. mis-setting or ignoring an alarm. For each of these, the experts are required to establish the degree to which each is either optimal or sub-optimal for the task under assessment, working on a scale from 1 to 9, with the latter being the optimal rating. For the 3 human errors which have been identified, the ratings decided for each are provided below:

Errors	Training	Procedures	Feedback	Perceived Risk	Time
VO2O4 open	6	5	2	9	6
Alarm mis-set	5	3	2	7	4
Alarm ignored	4	5	7	7	2

PSF Weighting

Were each of the identified human errors of equal importance, it would then be possible to obtain the summation of each row of ratings and come to the conclusion that the row with the lowest total rating- in this case it would be alarm mis-set- was the most probable to occur. In this context, as is most often the case, the experts are in agreement that the PSFs given above are not of equal weighting. Perceived risk and feedback are deemed to be of greatest importance, twice as much as training and procedures, which these two are considered to be one and a half times more important than the factor of time. The time factor is of considered of minimal importance in this context as the task is routine and is therefore not limited by time.

The importance of each factor can be observed through the allocated weighting, as provided below. Note that they have been normalised to sum to unity.

PSF	Importance
Perceived Risk	*0.3*
Feedback	*0.3*
Training	*0.15*
Procedures	*0.15*
Time	*0.10*
Sum	*1.0*

Using the figures for the scaled weighting of the PSFs and the weighting of their importance, it is now possible to calculate the Success Likelihood Index (SLI) for the task under assessment.

Weighting	PSF's	V0204	Alarm Mis-set	Alarm Ignored
0.3	*Feedback*	*0.60*	*0.60*	*2.10*
0.3	*Perceived Risk*	*2.70*	*2.10*	*2.10*
0.15	*Training*	*0.90*	*0.75*	*0.60*
0.15	*Procedures*	*0.75*	*0.45*	*0.75*
0.10	*Time*	*0.60*	*0.40*	*0.20*
	SLI (total)	*0.55*	*0.43*	*5.75*

From the results of the calculations, as the SLI for 'alarm mis-set' is the lowest, this suggests that this is the most probable error to occur throughout the completion of the task.

However these SLI figures are not yet in the form of probabilities; they are only indications as to the likelihood by which the various errors may occur. The SLIs determine the order in which the errors are most probable to occur; they do not delineate the absolute probabilities of the PSFs. To convert the SLIs to HEPs, the SLI figures require to first be standardised; this can be done using the following formulation.

$$Log10\ (HEP)\ =\ a.SLI\ +\ b$$

Result

If the two tasks for which the HEPs are known are incorporated in the task set which is undergoing quantification then the equation parameters can be determined by using the method of simultaneous equations; using the result of this the unknown HEP values can thus be quantified. In the example provided, were two additional tasks to be assessed e.g. A and B, which had HEP values of 0.5 and 10 -4 respectively and SLIs respectively of 4.00 and 6.00, respectively, then the formulation would be:

$$Log\ (HEP)\ =\ -1.85SLI\ +\ 7.1$$

The final HEP values would thus be determined as

V0204 = 0.0007 Alarm mis-set = 0.14 Alarm ignored = 0.0003

References

[1] EMBREY, D.E., Humphreys, P.C., rRosa, E.A., Kirwan, B. & Rea, K., SLIM-MAUD: An approach to assessing human error probabilities using structured expert judgement. NUREG/CR-3518. 1984, US Nuclear Regulatory Commission: Washington DC.

[2] Humphreys, P. (1995) Human Reliability Assessor's Guide. Human Factors in Reliability Group.

[3] Kirwan, B. (1994). A Practical Guide to Human Reliability Assessment. CPC Press.

[4] Corlett, E.N., & Wilson, J.R. (1995). Evaluation of Human Work: A Practical Ergonomics Methodology. Taylor & Francis.

Supplier Risk Management

Supplier risk management is an evolving discipline in operations management for manufacturers, retailers, financial services companies and government agencies where the organization is highly dependent on suppliers to achieve business objectives. Outsourcing, globalization, lean supply chain initiatives and supplier rationalization have contributed to a highly fragmented model, where control is often several steps removed from the corporation.

While these models have allowed companies to reduce overall costs and expand quickly into new markets, they are also exposed to the risk of a supplier's suddenly going bankrupt, closing operations or being acquired.

To overcome these challenges, companies mitigate supply chain interruptions and reduce risk with strategies and tactics that address supplier-centric risk at multiple stages in the relationship:

- **On boarding: Bringing suppliers into the operation with registration that includes:**

  - A centralized supplier registration portal
  - Integration of 3rd party performance, financial data and predictive indicators into the supplier profile
- **Monitoring for stability beyond financial data, including:**

  - Criminal and terrorists (i.e. OFAC) ties and operational performance
  - Visibility into potential disruptions caused by geopolitical threats, acts of nature, etc.
- **Cultivating strategic supplier relationships for the long-term:**

  - Leverage supplier scorecards for continuous improvement
  - Establish and use benchmarks for measuring supplier performance
  - Creating a system for collaboration and supplier development
- **Establish control across the extended enterprise:**

  - Create integrated supplier networks
  - Extend performance management benchmarks to 2nd and 3rd tier suppliers

Supplier Risk in Recession and Recovery

In 2008-2009, manufacturers experienced the startling speed at which suppliers can move from stability to shutting down operations. The devastating impact of a crucial supplier failure has moved risk management from add-on service to mission-critical. With a new focus on risk management, manufacturers have seen value whether the economy is stagnant or roaring.

With a transparent, accessible and comprehensive set of supplier information, manufacturers have been able to monitor suppliers for behavioral changes which contribute to overall stability, including:

- Changes in the supplier's management team
- EPA violations
- OSHA incidents

- Quality issues
- Noticeable lags in response time to inquiries
- OFAC violations

Changes in any of these conditions can be defined as parameters for raising an alert. For example, a financially stable supplier may in fact be about to lose it CEO to retirement – which may cause issues within the management team. Early visibility into that change gives the manufacturer time to ensure it doesn't negatively affect customers.

Based on the criticality of the supplier and the nature of the alert received, the manufacturer can then choose to take necessary action, such as calling or visiting the supplier, increase monitoring or move towards terminating the relationship with the supplier and find a replacement.

Benefits

Reducing supplier risk can:

- Give insight to manufacturers to create defensive and offensive strategies that turn risk into a competitive advantage.
- Help determine whether or not it is beneficial for a company to conduct a customer intervention and know in advance what the potential outcomes are for an intervention.
- Improve competitive position in the market.
- Lower supplier costs.
- Position manufacturers to better address customer needs by addressing supplier vulnerabilities before they shut down.

Other References for Supplier Risk

BI: Business Intelligence

MDM: Master Data Management

Risk management

Supplier information management

Supplier performance management

Supply Chain Risk Management

References

- Understanding Risk: Avoiding Supply Chain Disruption, *IndustryWeek*, May 11, 2009 (http://www. industryweek.com/articles/understanding_risk_avoiding_supply_chain_disruption_19096.aspx)

System archetype

System Archetypes are patterns of behavior of a system. Systems expressed by circles of causality have therefore similar structure. Identifying a system archetype and finding the leverage enables efficient changes in a system. The basic system archetypes and possible solutions of the problems are mentioned in #Examples of system archetypes.[1]

Circles of causality

The basic idea of system thinking is that every action triggers a reaction. In system dynamics this reaction is called feedback. There are two types of feedback - reinforcing feedback and balancing feedback. Sometimes a feedback (or a reaction) does not occur immediately - the process contains delays. Any system can be drawn as a diagram set up with circles of causality – including actions, feedbacks and delays.[1]

Reinforcing feedback (+)

Reinforcing feedback (or amplifying feedback) accelerates the given trend of a process. If the trend is ascending, the reinforcing (positive) feedback will accelerate the growth. If the trend is descending, it will accelerate the decline. Falling of an avalanche is an example of the reinforcing feedback process.[1]

Balancing feedback (-)

Balancing feedback (or stabilizing feedback) will work if any goal-state exists. Balancing process intends to reduce a gap between a current state and a desired state. The balancing (negative) feedback adjusts a present state to a desirable target regardless whether the trend is descending or ascending. An example of the balancing feedback process is staying upright on bicycle (when riding).[1]

Delays

Delays in systems cause people to perceive a response to an action incorrectly. This causes an under- or overestimation of the needed action and results in oscillation, instability or even breakdown.[1]

Examples of system archetypes

Balancing process with delay

This archetype explains the system in which the response to action is delayed. If the agents do not perceive the delayed feedback, they might overshoot or underestimate the requisite action in order to reach their goals. This could be avoided by being patient or by accelerating reactions of the system to realized measures. Example: supply chain (The Beer Game)[1]

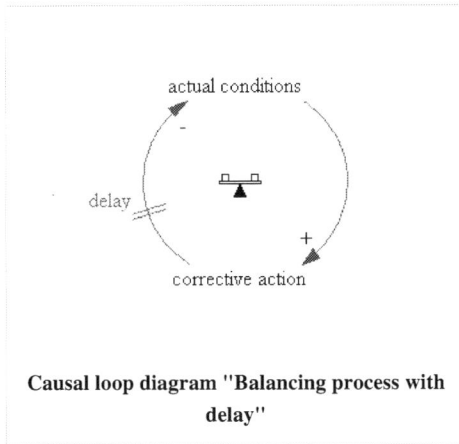

Causal loop diagram "Balancing process with delay"

Limits to growth

The unprecedented growth is produced by a reinforcing feedback process until the system reaches its peak. The halt of this growth is caused by limits inside or outside of the system. However, if the limits are not properly recognized; the former methods are continuously applied, but more and more aggressively. This results in the contrary of the desired state - a decrease of the system. The solution lies in the weakening or elimination of the cause of limitation. Example: dieting, learning foreign languages[1]

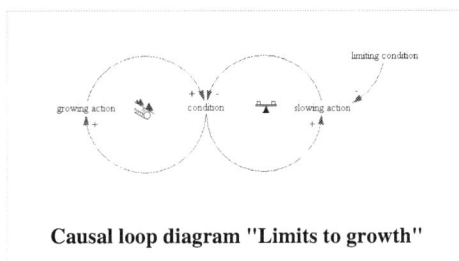

Causal loop diagram "Limits to growth"

Attractiveness Principle is an archetype derived from Limits to Growth. The main difference is that Attractiveness Principle assumes growth is limited with two or more factors.

Shifting the burden

The problem is handled by a simple solution with immediate effect, thereby "healing the symptoms". The primary source of the problem is overlooked, because its remedy is demanding and has no immediate outcome. The origin of the problem should be identified and solved in the long-term run during which the addiction to the symptomatic remedy decreases. Example: drug addiction, paying debts by borrowing[1]

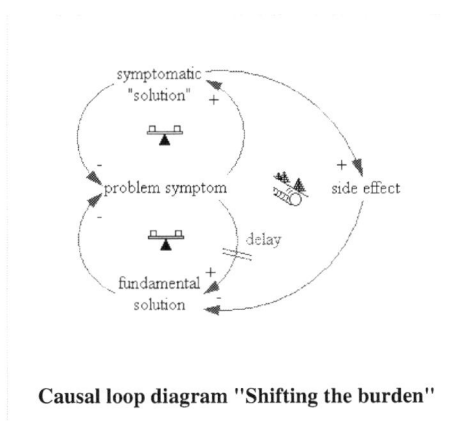

Causal loop diagram "Shifting the burden"

Eroding goals

A kind of shifting the burden archetype. As current problems need to be handled immediately, the long-term goals continuously decline. It can be avoided by sticking to the vision. Example: balancing the public debt, sliding limits of environmental pollution[1]

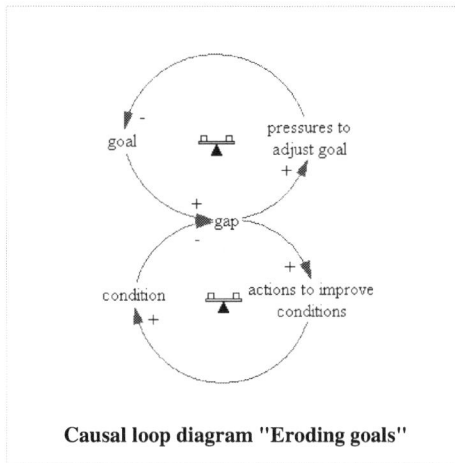

Causal loop diagram "Eroding goals"

Escalation

This archetype could be seen as a non-cooperative game where both players suppose that just one of them can win. They are responding to actions of the other player in order to "defend themselves". The aggression grows and can result in self-destructive behavior. The vicious circle can be broken by one agent stopping to react defensively and turn the game into cooperative one. Example: arms race[1]

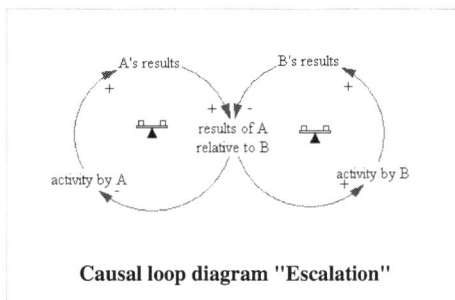

Causal loop diagram "Escalation"

Success to successful

Two people or activities need the same limited resources. As one of them becomes more successful, more resources are assigned to him/it. The second one becomes less and less successful due to lacking resources, and "prove the right decision" to support the first one. Problems occur if the competition is unhealthy and interferes with the goals of the whole system. The two activities or agents might be decoupled or they should receive balanced amount of resources. Examples: two products of one company, work vs. family[1]

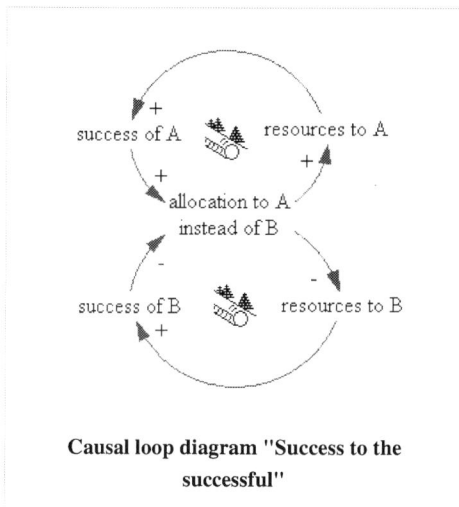

Causal loop diagram "Success to the successful"

Tragedy of the commons

Agents use common limited resource to profit individually. As the use of the resource is not controlled, the agents would like to continuously raise their benefits. The resource is therefore used more and more and the revenues of the agents are decreasing. The agents are intensifying their exploitation until the resource is completely used up or seriously damaged. To protect common resources some form of regulation should be introduced. Example: fish stocks (The Fishing Game)[1]

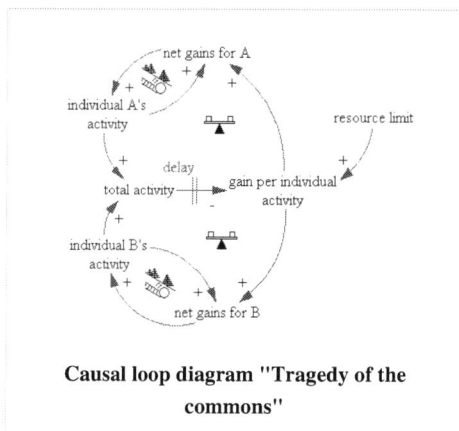

Causal loop diagram "Tragedy of the commons"

Fixes that fail

In the fixes that fail archetype, the problem is solved by some fix (a specific solution) with immediate positive effect. Nonetheless, the "side effects" of this solution turn out in the future. The best remedy seems to apply the same solution. Example: saving costs on maintenance, paying interest by other loans (with other interests)[1]

Causal loop diagram "Fixes that fail"

Growth and underinvestment

The limit to growth is the current production capacity. It can be removed by sufficient investment in new capacities. If the investment is not aggressive enough (or it is too low), the capacities are overloaded, the quality of services declines and the demand decreases. Example: small, but growing company[1]

Causal loop diagram "Growth and underinvestment"

References

[1]

[1] Senge, Peter M. (1990), *The Fifth Discipline* (http://books.google.com/books?id=bVZqAAAAMAAJ), Doubleday/Currency, ISBN 0385260946,

External links

- System Archetypes (http://www.systems-thinking.org/arch/arch.htm)
- System Thinking (http://www.systems-thinking.org/index.htm)

System dynamics

System dynamics is an approach to understanding the behaviour of complex systems over time. It deals with internal feedback loops and time delays that affect the behaviour of the entire system.[1] What makes using system dynamics different from other approaches to studying complex systems is the use of feedback loops and stocks and flows. These elements help describe how even seemingly simple systems display baffling nonlinearity.

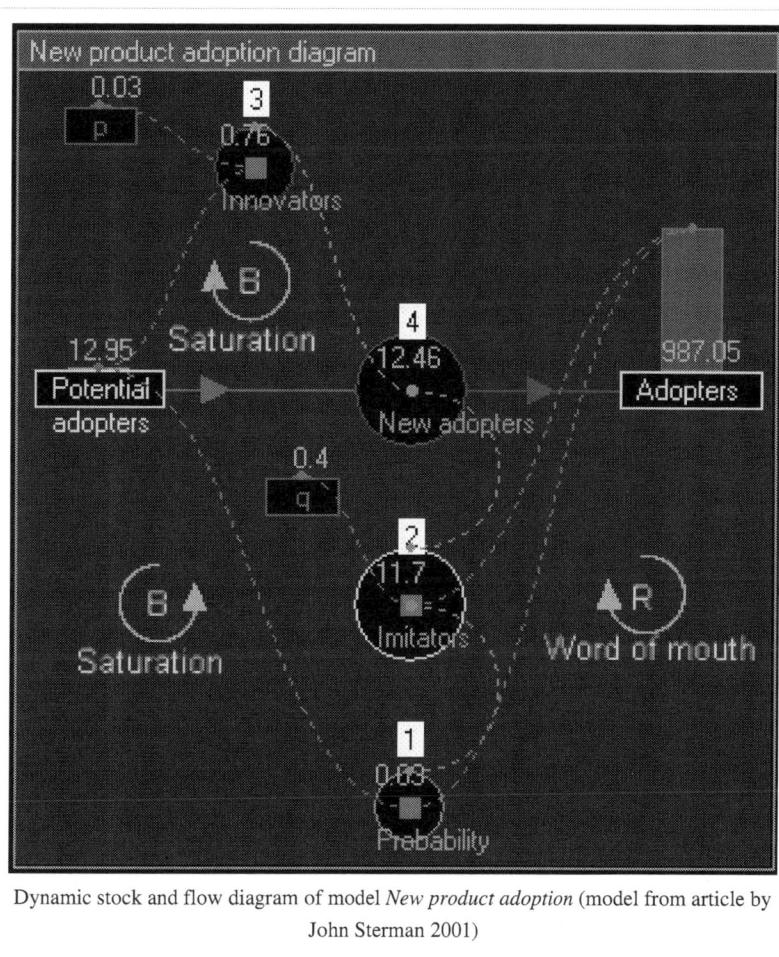

Dynamic stock and flow diagram of model *New product adoption* (model from article by John Sterman 2001)

Overview

System dynamics is a methodology and mathematical modeling technique for framing, understanding, and discussing complex issues and problems. Originally developed in the 1950s to help corporate managers improve their understanding of industrial processes, system dynamics is currently being used throughout the public and private sector for policy analysis and design.[2]

System dynamics is an aspect of systems theory as a method for understanding the dynamic behavior of complex systems. The basis of the method is the recognition that the structure of any system — the many circular, interlocking, sometimes time-delayed relationships among its components — is often just as important in determining its behavior as the individual components themselves. Examples are chaos theory and social dynamics. It is also claimed that because there are often properties-of-the-whole which cannot be found among the properties-of-the-elements, in some cases the behavior of the whole cannot be explained in terms of the behavior of the parts.

History

System dynamics was created during the mid-1950s[3] by Professor Jay Forrester of the Massachusetts Institute of Technology. In 1956, Forrester accepted a professorship in the newly-formed MIT Sloan School of Management. His initial goal was to determine how his background in science and engineering could be brought to bear, in some useful way, on the core issues that determine the success or failure of corporations. Forrester's insights into the common foundations that underlie engineeringt, which led to the creation of system dynamics, were triggered, to a large degree, by his involvement with managers at General Electric (GE) during the mid-1950s. At that time, the managers at GE were perplexed because employment at their appliance plants in Kentucky exhibited a significant three-year cycle. The business cycle was judged to be an insufficient explanation for the employment instability.

From hand simulations (or calculations) of the stock-flow-feedback structure of the GE plants, which included the existing corporate decision-making structure for hiring and layoffs, Forrester was able to show how the instability in GE employment was due to the internal structure of the firm and not to an external force such as the business cycle. These hand simulations were the beginning of the field of system dynamics.[2]

During the late 1950s and early 1960s, Forrester and a team of graduate students moved the emerging field of system dynamics from the hand-simulation stage to the formal computer modeling stage. Richard Bennett created the first system dynamics computer modeling language called SIMPLE (Simulation of Industrial Management Problems with Lots of Equations) in the spring of 1958. In 1959, Phyllis Fox and Alexander Pugh wrote the first version of DYNAMO (DYNAmic MOdels), an improved version of SIMPLE, and the system dynamics language became the industry standard for over thirty years. Forrester published the first, and still classic, book in the field titled Industrial Dynamics in 1961.[2]

From the late 1950s to the late 1960s, system dynamics was applied almost exclusively to corporate/managerial problems. In 1968, however, an unexpected occurrence caused the field to broaden beyond corporate modeling. John Collins, the former mayor of Boston, was appointed a visiting professor of Urban Affairs at MIT. The result of the Collins-Forrester collaboration was a book titled Urban Dynamics. The Urban Dynamics model presented in the book was the first major non-corporate application of system dynamics.[2]

The second major noncorporate application of system dynamics came shortly after the first. In 1970, Jay Forrester was invited by the Club of Rome to a meeting in Bern, Switzerland. The Club of Rome is an organization devoted to solving what its members describe as the "predicament of mankind" -- that is, the global crisis that may appear sometime in the future, due to the demands being placed on the Earth's carrying capacity (its sources of renewable and nonrenewable resources and its sinks for the disposal of pollutants) by the world's exponentially growing population. At the Bern meeting, Forrester was asked if system dynamics could be used to address the predicament of mankind. His answer, of course, was that it could. On the plane back from the Bern meeting, Forrester created the first draft of a system dynamics model of the world's socioeconomic system. He called this model WORLD1. Upon his return to the United States, Forrester refined WORLD1 in preparation for a visit to MIT by members of the Club of Rome. Forrester called the refined version of the model WORLD2. Forrester published WORLD2 in a book titled World Dynamics.[2]

Topics in systems dynamics

The elements of system dynamics diagrams are feedback, accumulation of flows into stocks and time delays.

As an illustration of the use of system dynamics, imagine an organisation that plans to introduce an innovative new durable consumer product. The organisation needs to understand the possible market dynamics in order to design marketing and production plans.

Causal loop diagrams

A causal loop diagram is a visual representation of the feedback loops in a system. The causal loop diagram of the new product introduction may look as follows:

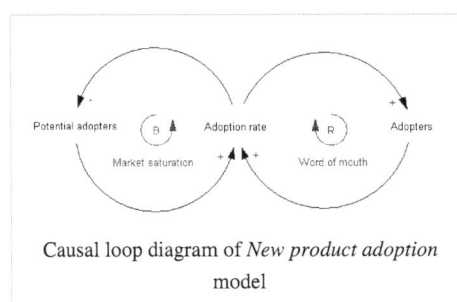

Causal loop diagram of *New product adoption*
model

There are two feedback loops in this diagram. The positive reinforcement (labeled R) loop on the right indicates that the more people have already adopted the new product, the stronger the word-of-mouth impact. There will be more references to the product, more demonstrations, and more reviews. This positive feedback should generate sales that continue to grow.

The second feedback loop on the left is negative reinforcement (or "balancing" and hence labeled B). Clearly growth can not continue forever, because as more and more people adopt, there remain fewer and fewer potential adopters.

Both feedback loops act simultaneously, but at different times they may have different strengths. Thus one would expect growing sales in the initial years, and then declining sales in the later years.

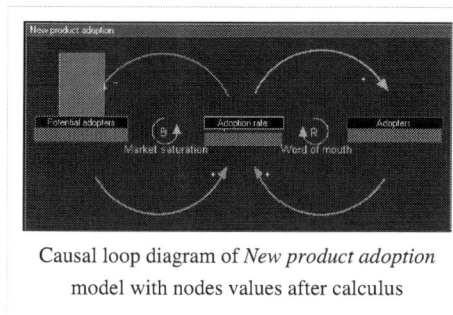

Causal loop diagram of *New product adoption*
model with nodes values after calculus

In this dynamic causal loop diagram :

- step1 : (+) green arrows show that *Adoption rate* is function of *Potential Adopters* and *Adopters*
- step2 : (-) red arrow shows that *Potential adopters* decreases by *Adoption rate*
- step3 : (+) blue arrow shows that *Adopters* increases by *Adoption rate*

Stock and flow diagrams

The next step is to create what is termed a stock and flow diagram. A stock is the term for any entity that accumulates or depletes over time. A flow is the rate of change in a stock.

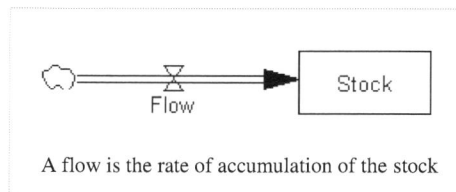

A flow is the rate of accumulation of the stock

In our example, there are two stocks: Potential adopters and Adopters. There is one flow: New adopters. For every new adopter, the stock of potential adopters declines by one, and the stock of adopters increases by one.

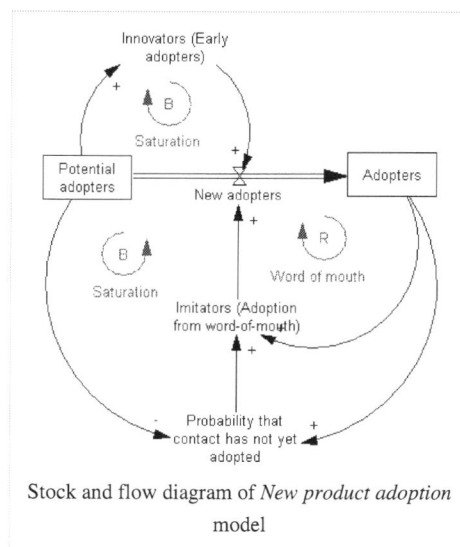

Stock and flow diagram of *New product adoption*
model

Equations

The real power of system dynamics is utilised through simulation. Although it is possible to perform the modeling in a spreadsheet, there are a variety of software packages that have been optimised for this.

The steps involved in a simulation are:

- Define the problem boundary
- Identify the most important stocks and flows that change these stock levels
- Identify sources of information that impact the flows
- Identify the main feedback loops
- Draw a causal loop diagram that links the stocks, flows and sources of information
- Write the equations that determine the flows
- Estimate the parameters and initial conditions. These can be estimated using statistical methods, expert opinion, market research data or other relevant sources of information.[4]
- Simulate the model and analyse results

In this example, the equations that change the two stocks via the flow are:

List of all the equations, in their order of execution in each year, from year 1 to 15:

Dynamic simulation results

The dynamic simulation results show that the behaviour of the system would be to have growth in **Adopters** that follows a classical s-curve shape.

The increase in **Adopters** is very slow initially, then exponential growth for a period, followed ultimately by saturation.

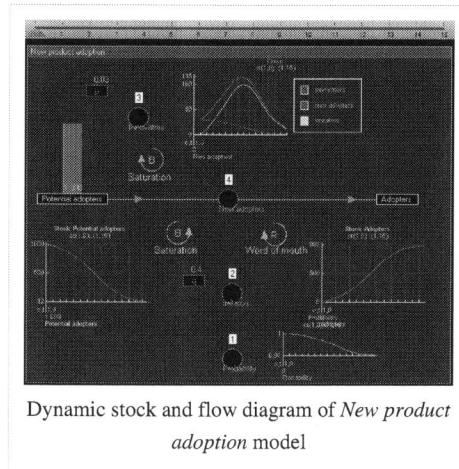

Dynamic stock and flow diagram of *New product adoption* model

Year	Probability	Imitators	Innovators	New adopters	Potential adopters	Adopters
0	0.00	0.00	0.00	0.00	1,000.00	0.00
1	1.00	0.00	30.00	30.00	970.00	30.00
2	0.97	11.64	29.10	40.74	929.26	70.74
3	0.93	26.32	27.88	54.20	875.06	124.94
4	0.88	43.98	26.25	70.23	804.83	195.17
5	0.80	62.45	24.14	86.59	718.24	281.76
6	0.72	81.15	21.55	102.70	615.54	384.46
7	0.62	95.35	18.47	113.82	501.72	498.28
8	0.50	99.66	15.05	114.71	387.01	612.99
9	0.39	95.63	11.61	107.24	279.77	720.23
10	0.28	80.67	8.39	89.06	190.71	809.29
11	0.19	61.51	5.72	67.23	123.48	876.52
12	0.12	42.07	3.70	45.77	77.71	922.29
13	0.08	29.51	2.33	31.84	45.87	954.13
14	0.05	19.08	1.38	20.46	25.41	974.59
15	0.03	11.70	0.76	12.46	12.95	987.05

Stocks and flows values for years = 0 to 15

Application

System dynamics has found application in a wide range of areas, for example population, ecological and economic systems, which usually interact strongly with each other.

System dynamics have various "back of the envelope" management applications. They are a potent tool to:

- Teach system thinking reflexes to persons being coached
- Analyze and compare assumptions and mental models about the way things work
- Gain qualitative insight into the workings of a system or the consequences of a decision
- Recognize archetypes of dysfunctional systems in everyday practice

Computer software is used to simulate a system dynamics model of the situation being studied. Running "what if" simulations to test certain policies on such a model can greatly aid in understanding how the system changes over time. System dynamics is very similar to systems thinking and constructs the same causal loop diagrams of systems with feedback. However, system dynamics typically goes further and utilises simulation to study the behaviour of systems and the impact of alternative policies.[5]

System dynamics has been used to investigate resource dependencies, and resulting problems, in product development.[6] [7]

Example

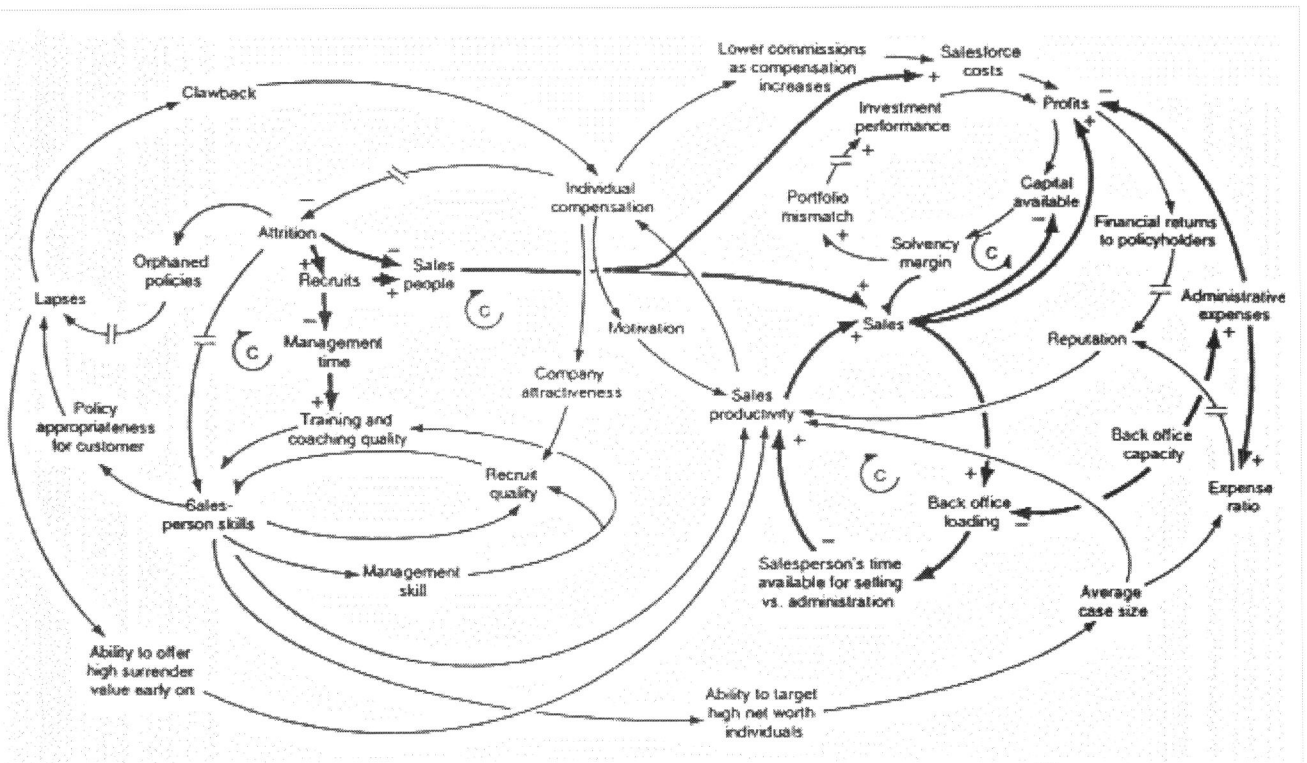

Causal loop diagram of a model examining the growth or decline of a life insurance company.[8]

The figure above is a causal loop diagram of a system dynamics model created to examine forces that may be responsible for the growth or decline of life insurance companies in the United Kingdom. A number of this figure's features are worth mentioning. The first is that the model's negative feedback loops are identified by "C's," which stand for "Counteracting" loops. The second is that double slashes are used to indicate places where there is a significant delay between causes (i.e., variables at the tails of arrows) and effects (i.e., variables at the heads of arrows). This is a common causal loop diagramming convention in system dynamics. Third, is that thicker lines are used to identify the feedback loops and links that author wishes the audience to focus on. This is also a common system dynamics diagramming convention. Last, it is clear that a decision maker would find it impossible to think through the dynamic behavior inherent in the model, from inspection of the figure alone.[8]

Example of piston motion

In this example the crank is driving, we vary both the speed of rotation, its radius and the length of the rod, the piston follows.

Model made with the system dynamics software TRUE.

System dynamics model for Piston Motion
Equations

Variables of the model are assigned to the graphics parameters of the rod and the crank, made with the 3D modeler of TRUE software.

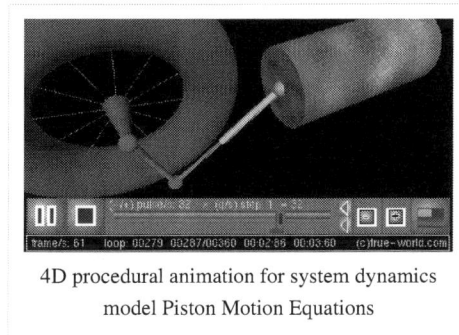

4D procedural animation for system dynamics
model Piston Motion Equations

References

[1] MIT System Dynamics in Education Project (SDEP) (http://sysdyn.clexchange.org)

[2] Michael J. Radzicki and Robert A. Taylor (2008). "Origin of System Dynamics: Jay W. Forrester and the History of System Dynamics" (http://www.systemdynamics.org/DL-IntroSysDyn/start.htm). In: *U.S. Department of Energy's Introduction to System Dynamics*. Retrieved 23 Oktober 2008.

[3] Forrester, Jay (1971). Counterintuitive behavior of social systems. Technology Review 73(3): 52–68

[4] Sterman, John D. (2001). "System dynamics modeling: Tools for learning in a complex world". *California management review* **43** (4): 8–25.

[5] System Dynamics Society (http://www.systemdynamics.org/)

[6] Repenning, Nelson P. (2001). "Understanding fire fighting in new product development". *The Journal of Product Innovation Management* **18** (5): 285–300. doi:10.1016/S0737-6782(01)00099-6.

[7] Nelson P. Repenning (1999). *Resource dependence in product development improvement efforts*, Massachusetts Institute of Technology Sloan School of Management Department of Operations Management/System Dynamics Group, dec 1999.

[8] Michael J. Radzicki and Robert A. Taylor (2008). "Feedback" (http://www.systemdynamics.org/DL-IntroSysDyn/start.htm). In: *U.S. Department of Energy's Introduction to System Dynamics*. Retrieved 23 October 2008.

Further reading

- Forrester, Jay W. (1961). *Industrial Dynamics*. Pegasus Communications. ISBN 1883823366.
- Forrester, Jay W. (1969). *Urban Dynamics*. Pegasus Communications. ISBN 1883823390.
- Meadows, Donella H. (1972). *Limits to Growth*. New York: University books. ISBN 0-87663-165-0.
- Morecroft, John (2007). *Strategic Modelling and Business Dynamics: A Feedback Systems Approach*. John Wiley & Sons. ISBN 0470012862.
- Roberts, Edward B. (1978). *Managerial Applications of System Dynamics*. Cambridge: MIT Press. ISBN 026218088X.
- Randers, Jorgen (1980). *Elements of the System Dynamics Method*. Cambridge: MIT Press. ISBN 0915299399.
- Senge, Peter (1990). *The Fifth Discipline*. Currency. ISBN 0-385-26095-4.
- Sterman, John D. (2000). *Business Dynamics: Systems thinking and modeling for a complex world*. McGraw Hill. ISBN 0-07-231135-5.

External links

- Study Prepared for the U.S. Department of Energy's Introducing System Dynamics - (http://www.systemdynamics.org/DL-IntroSysDyn/)
- Desert Island Dynamics (http://web.mit.edu/jsterman/www/DID.html) "An Annotated Survey of the Essential System Dynamics Literature"

Systems thinking

Systems thinking is the process of understanding how things influence one another within a whole. In nature, systems thinking examples include ecosystems in which various elements such as air, water, movement, plants, and animals work together to survive or perish. In organizations, systems consist of people, structures, and processes that work together to make an organization healthy or unhealthy.

Systems Thinking has been defined as an approach to problem solving, by viewing "problems" as parts of an overall system, rather than reacting to specific part, outcomes or events and potentially contributing to further development of unintended consequences. Systems thinking is not one thing but a set of habits or practices[2] within a framework that is based on the belief that the component parts of a system can best be understood in the context of relationships with each other and with other systems, rather than in isolation. Systems thinking focuses on cyclical rather than linear cause and effect.

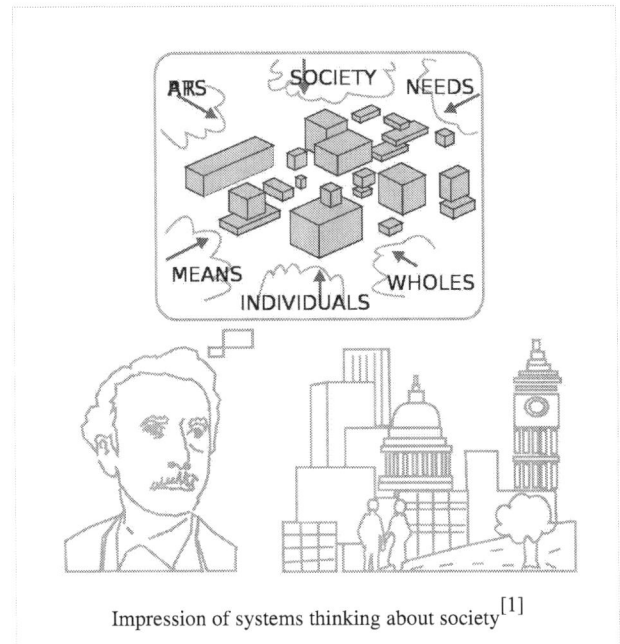

Impression of systems thinking about society[1]

In science systems, it is argued that the only way to fully understand why a problem or element occurs and persists is to understand the parts in relation to the whole.[3] Standing in contrast to Descartes's scientific reductionism and philosophical analysis, it proposes to view systems in a holistic manner. Consistent with systems philosophy, systems thinking concerns an understanding of a system by examining the linkages and interactions between the elements that compose the entirety of the system.

Science systems thinking attempts to illustrate that events are separated by distance and time and that small catalytic events can cause large changes in complex systems. Acknowledging that an improvement in one area of a system can adversely affect another area of the system, it promotes organizational communication at all levels in order to avoid the silo effect. Systems thinking techniques may be used to study any kind of system — natural, scientific, engineered, human, or conceptual.

The concept of a system

Science systems thinkers consider that:

- a system is a dynamic and complex whole, interacting as a structured functional unit;
- energy, material and information flow among the different elements that compose the system;
- a system is a community situated within an environment;
- energy, material and information flow from and to the surrounding environment via semi-permeable membranes or boundaries;
- systems are often composed of entities seeking equilibrium but can exhibit oscillating, chaotic, or exponential behavior.

A holistic system is any set (group) of interdependent or temporally interacting parts. *Parts* are generally systems themselves and are composed of other parts, just as systems are generally parts or *holons* of other systems.

Science systems and the application of science systems thinking has been grouped into three categories based on the techniques used to tackle a system:

- Hard systems — involving simulations, often using computers and the techniques of operations research/management science. Useful for problems that can justifiably be quantified. However it cannot easily take into account unquantifiable variables (opinions, culture, politics, etc.), and may treat people as being passive, rather than having complex motivations.
- Soft systems — For systems that cannot easily be quantified, especially those involving people holding multiple and conflicting frames of reference. Useful for understanding motivations, viewpoints, and interactions and addressing qualitative as well as quantitative dimensions of problem situations. Soft systems are a field that utilizes foundation methodological work developed by Peter Checkland, Brian Wilson and their colleagues at Lancaster University. Morphological analysis is a complementary method for structuring and analysing non-quantifiable problem complexes.
- Evolutionary systems — Béla H. Bánáthy developed a methodology that is applicable to the design of complex social systems. This technique integrates critical systems inquiry with soft systems methodologies. Evolutionary systems, similar to dynamic systems are understood as open, complex systems, but with the capacity to evolve over time. Bánáthy uniquely integrated the interdisciplinary perspectives of systems research (including chaos, complexity, cybernetics), cultural anthropology, evolutionary theory, and others.

The systems approach

The systems thinking approach incorporates several tenets:[4]

- Interdependence of objects and their attributes - independent elements can never constitute a system
- Holism - emergent properties not possible to detect by analysis should be possible to define by a holistic approach
- Goal seeking - systemic interaction must result in some goal or final state
- Inputs and Outputs - in a closed system inputs are determined once and constant; in an open system additional inputs are admitted from the environment
- Transformation of inputs into outputs - this is the process by which the goals are obtained
- Entropy - the amount of disorder or randomness present in any system
- Regulation - a method of feedback is necessary for the system to operate predictably
- Hierarchy - complex wholes are made up of smaller subsystems
- Differentiation - specialized units perform specialized functions
- Equifinality - alternative ways of attaining the same objectives (convergence)
- Multifinality - attaining alternative objectives from the same inputs (divergence)

Some examples:

- Rather than trying to improve the braking system on a car by looking in great detail at the material composition of the brake pads (reductionist), the *boundary* of the braking system may be extended to include the interactions between the:
  - brake disks or drums
  - brake pedal sensors
  - hydraulics
  - driver reaction time
  - tires
  - road conditions
  - weather conditions
  - time of day
- Using the tenet of "Multifinality", a supermarket could be considered to be:
  - a "profit making system" from the perspective of management and owners
  - a "distribution system" from the perspective of the suppliers
  - an "employment system" from the perspective of employees

- a "materials supply system" from the perspective of customers
- an "entertainment system" from the perspective of loiterers
- a "social system" from the perspective of local residents
- a "dating system" from the perspective of single customers

As a result of such thinking, new insights may be gained into how the supermarket works, why it has problems, how it can be improved or how changes made to one component of the system may impact the other components.

Applications

Science systems thinking is increasingly being used to tackle a wide variety of subjects in fields such as computing, engineering, epidemiology, information science, health, manufacture, management, and the environment.

Some examples:

- Science of Team Science
- Organizational architecture
- Job design
- Team Population and Work Unit Design
- Linear and Complex Process Design
- Supply Chain Design
- Business continuity planning with FMEA protocol
- Critical Infrastructure Protection via FBI Infragard
- Delphi method — developed by RAND for USAF
- Futures studies — Thought leadership mentoring
- The public sector including examples at The Systems Thinking Review [5]
- Leadership development
- Oceanography — forecasting complex systems behavior
- Permaculture
- Quality function deployment (QFD)
- Quality management — Hoshin planning [6] methods
- Quality storyboard — StoryTech framework (LeapfrogU-EE)
- Software quality
- Program management
- Project management
- MECE - McKinsey Way
- Sociocracy
- Linear Thinking

Bibliography

- Russell L. Ackoff (1999) *Ackoff's Best: His Classic Writings on Management.* (Wiley) ISBN 0-471-31634-2
- Russell L. Ackoff (2010) *Systems Thinking for Curious Managers* [7]. (Triarchy Press). ISBN 978-0-9562631-5-5
- Béla H. Bánáthy (1996) *Designing Social Systems in a Changing World (Contemporary Systems Thinking).* (Springer) ISBN 0-306-45251-0
- Béla H. Bánáthy (2000) *Guided Evolution of Society: A Systems View (Contemporary Systems Thinking).* (Springer) ISBN 0-306-46382-2
- Ludwig von Bertalanffy (1976 - revised) *General System theory: Foundations, Development, Applications.* (George Braziller) ISBN 0-807-60453-4
- Fritjof Capra (1997) *The Web of Life* (HarperCollins) ISBN 0-00-654751-6
- Peter Checkland (1981) *Systems Thinking, Systems Practice.* (Wiley) ISBN 0-471-27911-0

- Peter Checkland, Jim Scholes (1990) *Soft Systems Methodology in Action*. (Wiley) ISBN 0-471-92768-6
- Peter Checkland, Jim Sue Holwell (1998) *Information, Systems and Information Systems*. (Wiley) ISBN 0-471-95820-4
- Peter Checkland, John Poulter (2006) *Learning for Action*. (Wiley) ISBN 0-470-02554-9
- C. West Churchman (1984 - revised) *The Systems Approach*. (Delacorte Press) ISBN 0-440-38407-9.
- John Gall (2003) *The Systems Bible: The Beginner's Guide to Systems Large and Small*. (General Systemantics Pr/Liberty) ISBN 0-961-82517-0
- Jamshid Gharajedaghi (2005) *Systems Thinking: Managing Chaos and Complexity - A Platform for Designing Business Architecture*. (Butterworth-Heinemann) ISBN 0-750-67973-5
- Charles François (ed) (1997), *International Encyclopedia of Systems and Cybernetics*, München: K. G. Saur.
- Charles L. Hutchins (1996) *Systemic Thinking: Solving Complex Problems* CO:PDS ISBN 1-888017-51-1
- Bradford Keeney (2002 - revised) *Aesthetics of Change*. (Guilford Press) ISBN 1-572-30830-3
- Donella Meadows (2008) *Thinking in Systems - A primer* (Earthscan) ISBN 978-1-84407-726-7
- John Seddon (2008) *Systems Thinking in the Public Sector* [8]. (Triarchy Press). ISBN 978-0-9550081-8-4
- Peter M. Senge (1990) *The Fifth Discipline - The Art & Practice of The Learning Organization*. (Currency Doubleday) ISBN 0-385-26095-4
- Lars Skyttner (2006) *General Systems Theory: Problems, Perspective, Practice* (World Scientific Publishing Company) ISBN 9-812-56467-5
- Frederic Vester (2007) *The Art of interconnected Thinking. Ideas and Tools for tackling with Complexity* (MCB) ISBN 3-939-31405-6
- Gerald M. Weinberg (2001 - revised) *An Introduction to General Systems Thinking*. (Dorset House) ISBN 0-932-63349-8
- Brian Wilson (1990) *Systems: Concepts, Methodologies and Applications, 2nd ed.* (Wiley) ISBN 0-471-92716-3
- Brian Wilson (2001) *Soft Systems Methodology: Conceptual Model Building and its Contribution*. (Wiley) ISBN 0-471-89489-3
- Ludwig von Bertalanffy (1969) *General System Theory*. (George Braziller) ISBN 0-8076-0453-4

References

[1] Illustration is made by Marcel Douwe Dekker (2007) based on an own standard and Pierre Malotaux (1985), "Constructieleer van de mensenlijke samenwerking", in BB5 Collegedictaat TU Delft, pp. 120-147.

[2] http://www.watersfoundation.org/index.cfm?fuseaction=materials.main

[3] Capra, F. (1996) *The web of life: a new scientific understanding of living systems* (1st Anchor Books ed). New York: Anchor Books. p. 30

[4] Skyttner, Lars (2006). *General Systems Theory: Problems, Perspective, Practice*. World Scientific Publishing Company. ISBN 9-812-56467-5.

[5] http://www.thesystemsthinkingreview.co.uk/

[6] http://www.qualitydigest.com/may97/html/hoshin.html

[7] http://triarchypress.com/pages/Systems_Thinking_for_Curious_Managers.htm

[8] http://www.triarchypress.co.uk/pages/book5.htm

External links

- The Systems Thinker newsletter glossary (http://www.thesystemsthinker.com/systemsthinkinglearn.html)
- Dancing With Systems (http://www.projectworldview.org/wvtheme13.htm) from Project Worldview
- Systems-thinking.de (http://www.systems-thinking.de/): systems thinking links displayed as a network
- Systems Thinking Laboratory (http://www.systhink.org/)
- Systems Thinking (http://www.thinking.net/Systems_Thinking/systems_thinking.html)

Technique for Human Error Rate Prediction

Technique for Human Error Rate Prediction (THERP) is a technique used in the field of Human reliability Assessment (HRA), for the purposes of evaluating the probability of a human error occurring throughout the completion of a specific task. From such analyses measures can then be taken to reduce the likelihood of errors occurring within a system and therefore lead to an improvement in the overall levels of safety. There exist three primary reasons for conducting an HRA; error identification, error quantification and error reduction. As there exist a number of techniques used for such purposes, they can be split into one of two classifications; first generation techniques and second generation techniques. First generation techniques work on the basis of the simple dichotomy of 'fits/doesn't fit' in the matching of the error situation in context with related error identification and quantification and second generation techniques are more theory based in their assessment and quantification of errors. 'HRA techniques have been utilised in a range of industries including healthcare, engineering, nuclear, transportation and business sector; each technique has varying uses within different disciplines.

THERP models Human Error Probabilities (HEPs) using a fault-tree approach ,in a similar way to an engineering risk assessment, but also accounts for performance shaping factors (PSFs) that may influence these probabilities. The probabilities for the human reliability analysis event tree (HRAET), which is the primary tool for assessment, are nominally calculated from the database developed by the authors Swain and Guttman; local data e.g. from simulators or accident reports may however be used instead. The resultant tree portrays a step by step account of the stages involved in a task, in a logical order. The technique is known as a total methodology [1] as it simultaneously manages a number of different activities including task analysis, error identification, representation in form of HRAET and HEP quantification.

Background

The Technique for Human Error Rate Prediction (THERP) is a first generation methodology, which means that its procedures follow the way conventional reliability analysis models a machine. [7] The technique was developed in the Sandia Laboratories for the US Nuclear Regulatory Commission [2]. Its primary author is Swain, who developed the THERP methodology gradually over a lengthy period of time. [1]. THERP relies on a large human reliability database that contains HEPs, and is based upon both plant data and expert judgments. The technique was the first approach in HRA to come into broad use and is still widely used in a range of applications even beyond its original nuclear setting.

THERP Methodology

The methodology for the THERP technique is broken down into 5 main stages:

1. *Define the system failures of interest* These failures include functions of the system where human error has a greater likelihood of influencing the probability of a fault, and those of interest to the risk assessor; operations in which there may be no interest include those not operationally critical or those for which there already exist safety counter measures.

2. *List and analyse the related human operations, and identify human errors that can occur and relevant human error recovery modes* This stage of the process necessitates a comprehensive task and human error analysis. The task analysis lists and sequences the discrete elements and information required by task operators. For each step of the task, possible errors are considered by the analyst and precisely defined. The possible errors are then considered by the analyst, for each task step. Such errors can be broken down into the following categories:

- Errors of Omission – leaving out a step of the task or the whole task itself
- Error of Commission – this involves several different types of error:
    - Errors of Selection – error in use of controls or in issuing of commands
    - Errors of Sequence – required action is carried out in the wrong order
    - Errors of Timing – task is executed before or after when required
    - Errors of Quantity – inadequate amount or in excess

The opportunity for error recovery must also be considered as this, if achieved, has the potential to drastically reduce error probability for a task.

The tasks and associated outcomes are input to an HRAET in order to provide a graphical representation of a task's procedure. The trees' compatibility with conventional event-tree methodology i.e. including binary decision points at the end of each node, allows it to be evaluated mathematically. An event tree visually displays all events that occur within a system. It starts off with an initiating event, then branches develop as various consequences of the starting event. These are represented in a number of different paths, each associated with a probability of occurrence. As mentioned previously, the tree works on a binary logic, so each event either succeeds or fails. With the addition of the probabilities for the individual events along each path, i.e., branches, the likelihood of the various outcomes can be found. Below is an example of an event tree that represents a system fire:

Sprinkler System	Call to Fire Dept.	Outcome	Consequence

```
                                        Success
                          Success                      OK              1
                                        Failure
            Fire                                       Partial Damage   2
                                        Success
                          Failure                      Partial Damage   2
                                        Failure
                                                       System Destroyed 3
```

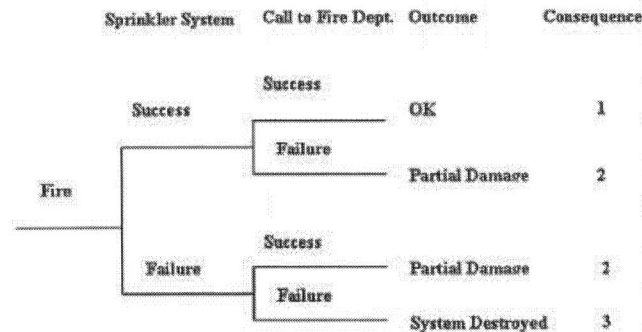

Therefore, under the condition that all of a task's sub-tasks are fully represented within a HRAET, and the failure probability for each sub-task is known, this makes it possible to calculate the final reliability for the task.

3. *Estimate the relevant error probabilities* HEPs for each sub-task are entered into the tree; it is necessary for all failure branches to have a probability otherwise the system will fail to provide a final answer. HRAETs provide the function of breaking down the primary operator tasks into finer steps, which are represented in the form of successes and failures. This tree indicates the order in which the events occur and also considers likely failures that may occur at each of the represented branches. The degree to which each high level task is broken down into lower level tasks is dependent on the availability of HEPs for the successive individual branches. The HEPs may be derived from a range of sources such as: the THERP database; simulation data; historical accident data; expert judgement. PSFs should be incorporated into these HEP calculations; the primary source of guidance for this is the THERP handbook. However the analyst must use their own discretion when deciding the extent to which each of the factors applies to the task

4. *Estimate the effects of human error on the system failure events* With the completion of the HRA the human contribution to failure can then be assessed in comparison with the results of the overall reliability analysis. This can be completed by inserting the HEPs into the full system's fault event tree, which allows human factors to be considered within the context of the full system.

5. *Recommend changes to the system and recalculate the system failure probabilities* Once the human factor contribution is known, sensitivity analysis can be used to identify how certain risks may be improved in the reduction of HEPs. Error recovery paths may be incorporated into the event tree as this will aid the assessor when considering the possible approaches by which the identified errors can be reduced.

Worked Example

Context

The following example illustrates how the THERP methodology can be used in practise in the calculation of Human Error Probabilities (HEPs). It is used to determine the HEP for establishing air based ventilation using emergency purge ventilation equipment on In-Tank Precipitation (ITP) processing tanks 48 and 49 after failure of the nitrogen purge system following a seismic event

Assumptions

In order for the final HEP calculation to be valid, the following assumptions require to be fulfilled:

1. There exists a seismic event initiator that leads to the establishment of air based ventilation on the ITP processing tanks 48 and 49

2. It is assumed that both on and offsite power is unavailable within the context and therefore control actions performed by the operator are done so locally, on the tank top

3. The time available for operations personnel to establish air based ventilation by use of the emergency purge ventilation, following the occurrence of the seismic event, is a duration of 3 days

4. There is a necessity for an ITP Equipment Status Monitoring procedure to be developed to allow for a consistent method to be adopted for the purposes of evaluating the ITP equipment and component status and selected process parameters for the period of an accident condition

5. Assumed response times exist for initial diagnosis of the event and for the placement of emergency purge ventilation equipment on the tank top. The former is 10 hours while the latter is 4 hours.

6. The In-Tank precipitation Process has associated Operational Safety Requirements (OSR) that identify the precise conditions under which the emergency purge ventilation equipment should be hooked up to the riser

7. The "Tank 48 System" Standard Operating Procedure has certain conditions and actions that must be included within for correct completion to be performed (see file for more details)

8. A vital component of the emergency purge ventilation equipment unit is a flow indicator; this is required in the event of the emergency purge ventilation equipment being hooked up incorrectly as it would allow for a recovery action

9. The personnel available to perform the necessary tasks all possess the required skills

10. Throughout the installation of the emergency purge ventilation equipment, carried out by maintenance personnel, a tank operator must be present to monitor this process.

Method

An initial task analysis was carried out on the off normal procedure and standard operating procedure. This allowed for the operator to align and then initiate the emergency purge ventilation equipment given the loss of the ventilation system. Thereafter, each individual task was analysed from which it was then possible to assign error probabilities and error factors to events that represented operator responses.

- A number of the HEPs were adjusted to take account of various identified Performance Shaping Factors (PSFs)
- Upon assessment of characteristics of the task and behaviour of the crew, recovery probabilities were deciphered. Such probabilities are influenced by such factors as task familiarity, alarms and independent checking
- Once error probabilities were decided upon for the individual tasks, event trees were then constructed from which calculation formulations were derived. The probability of failure was obtained through the multiplication of each of the failure probabilities along the path under consideration.

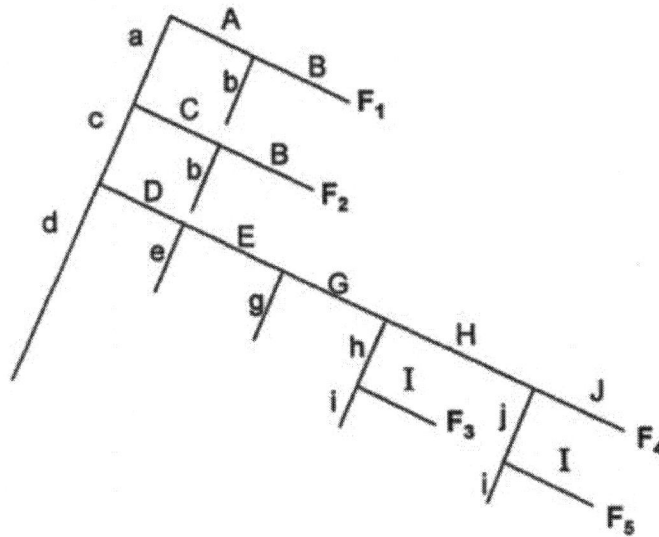

HRA event tree for align and start emergency purge ventilation equipment on In-Tank Precipitation Tank 48 or 49 after a seismic event

The summation of each of the failure path probabilities provided the total failure path probability (FT)

Results

- Task A: Diagnosis, HEP 6.0E-4 EF=30
- Task B: Visual Inspection performed shiftly, recovery factor HEP=0.001 EF=3
- Task C: Initiate standard operating procedure HEP= .003 EF=3
- Task D: Maintainer hook-up emergency purge ventilation equipment HEP=.003 EF=3
- Task E: Maintainer 2 hook-up emergency purge, recovery factor CHEP=0.5 EF=2
- Task G: Tank operator instructing /verifying hook-up, recovery factor CHEP=0.5 Lower bound = .015 Upper bound = 0.15
- Task H: Read Flow Indicator, Recovery Factor CHEP= .15 Lower bound= .04 Upper bound = .5
- Task I: Diagnosis HEP= 1.0E-5 EF=30
- Task J: Analyse LFL Using portable LFL Analyser, Recovery Factor CHEP= 0.5 Lower bound = .015 Upper bound =.15

From the various figures and workings, it can be determined that the HEP for establishing air based ventilation using the emergency purge ventilation equipment on In-tank Precipitation processing tanks 48 and 49 after a failure of the nitrogen purge system following a seismic event is 4.2 E-6. This numerical value is judged to be a median value on the lognormal scale. However, it should be noted that this result is only valid given that all the previously stated assumptions are implemented.

Advantages of THERP

- It is possible to use THERP at all stages of design. Furthermore THERP is not restricted to the assessment of designs already in place and due to the level of detail in the analysis it can be specifically tailored to the requirements of a particular assessment. [3]
- THERP is compatible with Probabilistic Risk Assessments (PRA); the methodology of the technique means that it can be readily integrated with fault tree reliability methodologies. [3]
- The THERP process is transparent, structured and provides a logical review of the human factors considered in a risk assessment; this allows the results to be examined in a straightforward manner and assumptions to be challenged. [3]
- The technique can be utilised within a wide range of differing human reliability domains and has a high degree of face validity. [3]
- It is a unique methodology in the way that it highlights error recovery and it also quantitatively models a dependency relation between the various actions or errors.

Disadvantages of THERP

- THERP analysis is very resource intensive, and may require a large amount of effort to produce reliable HEP values. This can be controlled by ensuring an accurate assessment of the level of work required in the analysis of each stage. [3]
- The technique does not lend itself to system improvement. Compared to some other Human Reliability Assessment tools such as HEART, THERP is a relatively unsophisticated tool as the range of PSFs considered is generally low and the underlying psychological causes of errors are not identified.
- With regards to the consistency of the technique, large discrepancies have been found in practice with regards to different analysts assessment of the risk associated with the same tasks. Such discrepancies may have arisen from either the process mapping of the tasks in question or in the estimation of the HEPs associated with each of the tasks through the use of THERP tables compared to, for example, expert judgement or the application of PSFs. [4, 5, 6].Missing reference 6
- The methodology fails to provide guidance to the assessor in how to model the impact of PSFs and the influence of the situation on the errors being assessed.
- The THERP HRAETs implicitly assume that each sub-task's HEP is independent from all others i.e. the HRAET does not update itself in the event that an operator takes a sub-optimal route through the task path. This is reinforced by the HEP being merely reduced by the chance of recovery from a mistake, rather than by introducing alternative (i.e. sub-optimal) "success" routes into the event-tree, which could allow for Bayesian updating of subsequent HEPs.
- THERP is a "first generation" HRA tool, and in common with other such tools has been criticised for not taking adequate account of context [7]Missing reference

References

[1] Kirwan, B. (1994) A Guide to Practical Human Reliability Assessment. CRC Press.

[2] Swain, A.D. & Guttmann, H.E., Handbook of Human Reliability Analysis with Emphasis on Nuclear Power Plant Applications. 1983, NUREG/CR-1278, USNRC.

[3] Humphreys, P. (1995). Human Reliability Assessor's Guide. Human Factors in Reliability Group.

[4] Kirwan, B. (1996) The validation of three human reliability quantification techniques - THERP, HEART, JHEDI: Part I -- technique descriptions and validation issues. Applied Ergonomics. 27(6) 359-373.

[5] Kirwan, B. (1997) The validation of three human reliability quantification techniques - THERP, HEART, JHEDI: Part II - Results of validation exercise. Applied Ergonomics. 28(1) 17-25.

TESEO

Tecnica Empirica Stima Errori Operatori (TESEO) is a technique in the field of Human reliability Assessment (HRA), that evaluates the probability of a human error occurring throughout the completion of a specific task. From such analyses measures can then be taken to reduce the likelihood of errors occurring within a system and therefore lead to an improvement in the overall levels of safety. There exist three primary reasons for conducting an HRA; error identification, error quantification and error reduction. As there exist a number of techniques used for such purposes, they can be split into one of two classifications; first generation techniques and second generation techniques. First generation techniques work on the basis of the simple dichotomy of 'fits/doesn't fit' in the matching of the error situation in context with related error identification and quantification and second generation techniques are more theory based in their assessment and quantification of errors. 'HRA techniques have been utilised in a range of industries including healthcare, engineering, nuclear, transportation and business sector; each technique has varying uses within different disciplines.

This is a time based model that describes the probability of a system operator's failure as a multiplicative function of 5 main factors. These factors are as follows:

1. **K1**: The type of task to be executed
2. **K2**: The time available to the operator to complete the task
3. **K3**: The operator's level of experience/characteristics
4. **K4**: The operator's state of mind
5. **K5**: The environmental and ergonomic conditions prevalent

Using these figures, an overall Human Error Probability (HEP) can be calculated with the formulation provided below:

K1 x K2 x K3 x K4 x K5

The specific value of each of the above functions can be obtained by consulting standard tables that take account of the method in which the HEP is derived.

Background

Developed in 1980 by Bello and Colombari,[1] TESEO created with the intention of using it for the purpose of conducting HRA of process industries. The methodology is relatively straightforward and is easy to use but is also limited; it is useful for quick overview HRA assessments, as opposed to highly detailed and in-depth assessments. Within the field of HRA, there is a lack of theoretical foundation for the technique, as is widely acknowledged throughout.

TESEO Methodology

When putting this technique into practice, it is necessary for the designated HRA assessor to thoroughly consider the task requiring assessment and therefore also consider the value for Kn that applies in the context. Once this value has been decided upon, the tables, previously mentioned, are then consulted from which a related value for each of the identified factors is found to allow the HEP to be calculated.

Worked Example

Provided below is an example of how TESEO methodology can be used in practice; each of the stages of the process described above are worked through in order.

Context

An operator works on a production transfer line that operates between two tanks. His role is to ensure the correct product is selected for transfer from one tanker to the other by operating remotely located valves. The essential valves must be opened to perform the task.

The operator possesses average experience for this role. The individual is in a control room that has a relatively noisy environment and poor lighting. There is a time window of five minutes for the required task.

Method

The figures for the HEP calculation, obtained from the relevant tables, are given as follows:

- The type of task to be executed: **K1 = 0.01**
- Time available to complete the task: **K2 = 0.5**
- Level of experience: **K3 = 1**
- Operator's state of mind: **K4 = 1**
- Environmental and ergonomic conditions: **K5 = 10**

The calculation for the final HEP figure is therefore calculated as:

```
K1 x K2 x K3 x K4 x K5
=0.01 x 0.5 x 1 x 1 x 10
= 0.05
```

Result

Given the result of this calculation, it can be deduced that were the control room notified of the valves' positions and if the microclimate was better, K5 would be unity, and therefore the HEP would be 0.005, representing an improvement of 1 order of magnitude.

Advantages of TESEO

The technique of TESEO is typically quick and straightforward in comparison to other HRA tools, not only in producing a final result, but also in sensitivity analysis e.g., it is useful in identifying the effects improvements in human factors have on overall human reliability of a task. It is widely applicable to various control room designs or with procedures with varying characteristics.[2]

Disadvantages of TESEO

There is limited work published with regards to the theoretical foundations of this technique, in particular relating to the justification of the five factor methodology.[2] Regardless of the situation, it remains to be assumed that these 5 factors are suffice for an accurate assessment of human performance; as no other factors are considered, this suggests that to solely use these 5 factors to adequately describe the full range of error producing conditions fails to be highly realistic. Further to this, the values of K1-5 are unsubstantiated and the suggested multiplicative relationship has no sufficient theoretical or empirical evidence for justification purposes.

References

[1] Bello, G.C. & Colombari, C. (1980) The human factors in risk analyses of process plants: the control room operator model, TESEO. Reliability Engineering. 1 3-14.

[2] Humphreys, P. (1995) Human Reliability Assessor's Guide. Human Factors in Reliability Group.

Two-moment decision models

Mean-variance analysis redirects here. For mean-variance portfolio theory, see Modern portfolio theory or Mutual fund separation theorem.

In decision theory, economics, and finance, a **two-moment decision model** is a model that describes or prescribes the process of making decisions in a context in which the decision-maker is faced with random variables whose realizations cannot be known in advance, and in which choices are made based on knowledge of two moments of those random variables. The two moments are almost always the mean—that is, the expected value, which is the first moment about zero—and the variance, which is the second moment about the mean (or the standard deviation, which is the square root of the variance).

Two-moment models and expected utility maximization

Suppose that all relevant random variables are in the same location-scale family, meaning that the distribution of every random variable is the same as the distribution of some linear transformation of any other random variable. Then for any von Neumann-Morgenstern utility function, using a mean-variance decision framework is consistent with expected utility maximization,[1] [2] as illustrated in example 1:

Example 1:[3] [4] Let there be one risky asset with random return r, and one riskfree asset with known return r_f, and let an investor's initial wealth be w_0. If the amount q, the choice variable, is to be invested in the risky asset and the amount $w_0 - q$ is to be invested in the safe asset, then contingent on q the investor's random final wealth will be $w=(w_0 - q)r_f + qr$. Then for any choice of q, w is distributed as a location-scale transformation of r. If we define random variable x as equal in distribution to $\frac{w-Ew}{\sigma_w}$, then w is equal in distribution to $(Ew + \sigma_w x)$, where E represents an expected value and σ represents a random variable's standard deviation (the square root of its second moment). Thus we can write expected utility in terms of two moments of w :

$$Eu(w) = \int_{-\infty}^{\infty} u(Ew + \sigma_w x)f(x)dx \equiv v(Ew, \sigma_w),$$

where u is the von Neumann-Morgenstern utility function, f is the density function of x, and v is the derived mean-standard deviation choice function, which depends in form on the density function f. The von Neumann-Morgenstern utility function is assumed to be increasing, implying that more wealth is preferred to less, and it is assumed to be concave, which is the same as assuming that the individual is risk averse.

It can be shown that the partial derivative of v with respect to Ew is positive, and the partial derivative of v with respect to σ_w is negative; thus more expected wealth is always liked, and more risk (as measured by the standard deviation of wealth) is always disliked. A mean-standard deviation indifference curve is defined as the locus of points (σ_w, Ew) with σ_w plotted horizontally, such that $Eu(w)$ has the same value at all points on the locus. Then the derivatives of v imply that every indifference curve is upward sloped: that is, along any indifference curve $dEw / d\sigma_w > 0$. Moreover, it can be shown[3] that all such indifference curves are convex: along any indifference curve, $d^2 Ew / d(\sigma_w)^2 > 0$.

Example 2: The portfolio analysis in example 1 can be generalized. If there are n risky assets instead of just one, and if their returns are jointly elliptically distributed, then[5] [6] all portfolios can be characterized completely by their mean and variance—that is, any two portfolios with identical mean and variance of portfolio return have identical distributions of portfolio return—and all possible portfolios have return distributions that are location-scale-related to each other. Thus portfolio optimization can be implemented using a two-moment decision model.

Example 3: Suppose that a price-taking, risk-averse firm must commit to producing a quantity of output q before observing the market realization p of the product's price.[7] Its decision problem is to choose q so as to maximize the expected utility of profit:

Maximize $Eu(pq - c(q) - g)$,

where E is the expected value operator, u is the firm's utility function, c is its variable cost function, and g is its fixed cost. All possible distributions of the firm's random revenue pq, based on all possible choices of q, are location-scale related; so the decision problem can be framed in terms of the expected value and variance of revenue.

Non-expected-utility decision making

If the decision-maker is not an expected utility maximizer, decision-making can still be framed in terms of the mean and variance of a random variable if all alternative distributions for an unpredictable outcome are location-scale transformations of each other.[8]

References

[1] Mayshar, J., "A note on Feldstein's criticism of mean-variance analysis," *Review of Economic Studies* 45, 1978, 197-199.

[2] Sinn, H.-W., *Economic Decisions under Uncertainty*, second English edition, 1983, North-Holland.

[3] Meyer, Jack. "Two-moment decision models and expected utility maximization," *American Economic Review* 77, June 1987, 421-430.

[4] Tobin, J., "Liquidity preference as behavior towards risk," *Review of Economic Studies* 25(1), February 1958, 65–86. Also in: (1) M. G. Mueller, ed., *Readings in Macroeconomics*, Holt, Rinehart & Winston, Inc., 1966, pp. 65-86; (2) Richard S. Thorn, ed., *Monetary Theory and Policy*, Random House, 1966, pp. 172–191; (3) H. R. Williams and J. D. Huffnagle, eds., *Macroeconomic Theory*, Appleton-Century-Crofts, 1969, pp. 299–324; (4) *Essays in Economics: Macroeconomics, Vol. 1*, chapter 15; (5) J. Tobin and D. Hester, eds., *Risk Aversion and Portfolio Choice*, Cowles Monograph No. 19, John Wiley & Sons, 1967; (6) David Laidler, ed., *The Foundations of Monetary Economics, Vol. 1*, Edward Elgar Publishing Ltd., 1999.

[5] Chamberlain, G., "A characterization of the distributions that imply mean-variance utility functions", *Journal of Economic Theory* 29, 1983, 185-201.

[6] Owen, J., and Rabinovitch, R. "On the class of elliptical distributions and their applications to the theory of portfolio choice", *Journal of Finance* 38, 1983, 745-752.

[7] Sandmo, Agnar. "On the theory of the competitive firm under price uncertainty," *American Economic Review* 61, March 1971, 65-73.

[8] Bar-Shira, Z., and Finkelshtain, I., "Two-moments decision models and utility-representable preferences," *Journal of Economic Behavior and Organization* 38, 1999, 237-244. See also Mitchell, Douglas W., and Gelles, Gregory M., "Two-moments decision models and utility-representable preferences: A comment on Bar-Shira and Finkelshtain, vol. 49, 2002, 423-427.

Vulnerability

For other uses of the word "Vulnerability", please refer to vulnerability (computing) You may also want to refer to natural disaster and vulnerability index.

Vulnerability refers to the susceptibility of a person, group, society or system to physical or emotional injury or attack. The term can also refer to a person who lets their guard down, leaving themselves open to censure or criticism. Vulnerability refers to a person's state of being liable to succumb to manipulation, persuasion, temptation etc.

A **window of vulnerability**, sometimes abbreviated to **wov**, is a time frame within which defensive measures are reduced, compromised or lacking.

Vulnerabilities exploited by psychological manipulators

See Vulnerabilities exploited by manipulators

Common applications

In relation to hazards and disasters, **vulnerability** is a concept that links the relationship that people have with their environment to social forces and institutions and the cultural values that sustain and contest them. "The concept of vulnerability expresses the multidimensionality of disasters by focusing attention on the totality of relationships in a given social situation which constitute a condition that, in combination with environmental forces, produces a disaster".[1]

It's also the extent to which changes could harm a system, or to which a community can be affected by the impact of a hazard.

In global warming, vulnerability is the degree to which a system is susceptible to, or unable to cope with, adverse effects of climate change, including climate variability and extremes.[2]

Emerging research

Vulnerability research covers a complex, multidisciplinary field including development and poverty studies, public health, climate studies, security studies, engineering, geography, political ecology, and disaster and risk management. This research is of particular importance and interest for organizations trying to reduce vulnerability — especially as related to poverty and other Millennium Development Goals. Many institutions are conducting interdisciplinary research on vulnerability. A forum that brings many of the current researchers on vulnerability together is the Expert Working Group (EWG).1 Researchers are currently working to refine definitions of "vulnerability", measurement and assessment methods, and effective communication of research to decision makers (Birkmann et al. 2006).

Major research questions

Within the body of literature related to vulnerability, major research streams include questions of methodology, such as: measuring and assessing vulnerability, including finding appropriate indicators for various aspects of vulnerability, up- and downscaling methods, and participatory methods (Villagran 2006).

A sub-category of vulnerability research is social vulnerability, where increasingly researchers are addressing some of the problems of complex human interactions, vulnerability of specific groups of people, and the impact of shocks from natural hazards, climate change, and other kinds of disruptions upon the human community. The importance of the issue is indicated by the establishment of endowed chairs at university departments to examine social vulnerability.

Military vulnerability

In military terminology, vulnerability is a form of survivability, the others being susceptibility and recoverability. Vulnerability is defined in various ways depending on the nation and service arm concerned, but in general it refers to the near-instantaneous effects of a weapon attack. In some definitions, recoverability (damage control, firefighting, restoration of capability) is included in vulnerability.

A discussion of warship vulnerability can be found here.[3]

Expert Working Group on Vulnerability

The Expert Working Group on Vulnerability is a group of experts brought together by the United Nations University Institute of Environment and Human Security (UNU-EHS). The overall goal of the Expert Working Group is to advance the concept of human security regarding vulnerability of societies to hazards of natural origin. The EWG exchanges ideas about the development of methodologies, approaches and indicators to measure vulnerability. This is a key task to build a bridge between the theoretical conceptualization of vulnerability and its practical application in decision-making processes. The Expert Working Group is an exchange platform for experts and practitioners from various scientific backgrounds and world regions dealing with the identification and measurement of vulnerability. Emphasis is given to the identification of the different features and characteristics of vulnerability, coping capacities and adaptation strategies of different social groups, economic sectors and environmental components.

References

[1] Bankoff et al. 2004: 11
[2] Glossary Climate Change (http://www.global-greenhouse-warming.com/glossary-climate-change.html)
[3] Warship Vulnerability (http://www.ausairpower.net/Warship-Hits.html)

- Bankoff, Greg, George Frerks and Dorothea Hilhorst. 2004. *Mapping Vulnerability*. Sterling: Earthscan.
- Birkmann, Joern (editor). 2006. *Measuring Vulnerability to Natural Hazards – Towards Disaster Resilient Societies*. UNU Press.
- Thywissen, Katharina. 2006. "Components of Risk: A comparative glossary." SOURCE No. 2/2006. Bonn, Germany.
- Villagran, Juan Carlos. ""Vulnerability: A conceptual and methodological review." SOURCE. No. 2/2006. Bonn, Germany.

External links

- BUGTRAQ-VULNERABLE SITE TRACKER (http://bugtraq.totalh.com) (vulnerability kinds)
- United Nations University Institute of Environment and Human Security (http://www.ehs.unu.edu)
- MunichRe Foundation (http://www.munichre-foundation.org)
- Community based vulnerability mapping in Búzi, Mozambique (GIS and Remote Sensing) (http://projects. stefankienberger.at/vulmoz/)
- Satellite Vulnerability (http://www.fas.org/spp/eprint/at_sp.htm)
- Top Computer Vulnerabilities (http://www.sans.org/top20/?utm_source=web-sans&utm_medium=text-ad& utm_content=Free_Resources_Homepage_top20_free_rsrcs_homepage&utm_campaign=Top_20&ref=27974)

Weather risk management

Weather risk management is a type of risk management done by organizations to address potential financial losses caused by unusual weather.

Overview

Energy, agriculture, transportation, construction, municipalities, school districts, travel, food processors, retail sales and real estate are all examples of industries whose operations and profits can be significantly affected by the weather. For example, unusually mild winters diminish consumer demand for heating and erode the profit margins for utility companies. Unexpected weather events can cause significant financial losses. Weather information and forecasts utilized in risk management decision making is often referred to as meteorological intelligence.

The weather risk market makes it possible to manage the financial impact of weather through risk transfer instruments based on a defined weather element, such as temperature, rain, snow, wind, etc. Weather risk management is a way for organizations to limit their financial exposure to disruptive weather events. By making a payment (a "premium") to a separate company that will assume the financial weather risk for them, an organization essentially is buying a type of insurance - the company assuming the risk will pay the buyer a pre-set amount of money which will correspond to the loss or cost increase caused by the disruptive weather.

Catastrophic weather events such as hurricanes are typically managed through traditional insurance contracts that pay based on indemnity loss. Insurance is a heavily regulated industry with specific requirements and qualification criteria. Due to the indemnity nature of insurance, actual loss must be proven to an insurance carrier before the payment can be processed. In contrast, financial loss such as erosion of margin, portfolio loss or increased expenses usually do not qualify for insurance payouts. Financial instruments such as derivative transactions can provide more flexible and customized risk management opportunities than the typical insurance contracts as they are priced and settled on the parameters of measured weather rather than the associated financial loss.

Market participants

A wide range of capital providers make markets in weather risk. To date the weather risk management trading market is primarily made up of dedicated weather trading operations, such as Nephila Capital Ltd, Galileo Weather Risk Management Advisors LCC, Swiss Re, RenRe, and Coriolis Capital, who execute trade orders in weather or weather-contingent commodity trades, the trading desks of financial institutions and utilities, such as Susquahanna Energy and Aquila who hedge their own risk as well as speculative trades for a merchant portfolio, professional commodity traders, such as RJO and hedge and private equity funds such as Tudor Capital. Transactions can be effected over-the-counter (OTC) or on commodity exchanges such as The Chicago Mercantile Exchange (CME). Still other operations, such as Storm Exchange, Inc and WeatherBill, provide corporate and municipal clients with the necessary financial context to gauge the impact of the weather on profit and loss before executing trades either OTC or through the CME.

Regulation

The Commodity Exchange Act ("The Act"), Section 5d establishes weather in a category of market exempt from Commission oversight.

Rule 36.2 defines those commodities that are eligible to trade on an exempt board of trade as commodities having:

1. A nearly inexhaustible deliverable supply;
2. A deliverable supply that is sufficiently large, and a cash market sufficiently liquid, to render any contract traded on the commodity highly unlikely to be susceptible to the threat of manipulation;
3. No cash market.

The CFTC determined that weather indices are eligible to be traded on EBOTs by order dated May 30, 2002 [1].

Tax treatment

Accounting for OTC weather derivatives as a hedge

Companies that are subject to public disclosure to regulators or their shareholders must demonstrate that the purchase or a sale of a derivatives is true and fair hedge, not speculation. SFAS 133 and IAS provide guidelines on the steps that are required. **FAS 133 Accounting for Weather Derivatives**: For U.S. accounting standards, Over-the-Counter (OTC) weather derivative transactions can generally get an exemption under **derivatives & hedging disclosure rules** of Financial Accounting Standard No. 133 [2] (FAS 133 [2]) section 10 for non-exchange contracts settled on climatic variables, although specific structures and applications have to be assessed for each company environment. All written non–exchanged–traded option–based weather derivatives contracts should be carried at fair value with subsequent changes in fair value reported in current earnings.

Accounting for Exchange traded and speculative weather derivatives

When they are standardized and traded on exchanges, weather derivatives will fall within the scope of SFAS 133. EITF Issue No 99–2 "Accounting for weather derivatives" provides guidance on accounting for weather derivatives that are not exchange–traded. Entities that enter into speculatives or trading non–exchange derivatives contracts should apply the intrinsic method.

Further reading

- Considine, G., 2000, "Introduction to Weather Derivatives" [3], Weather Derivatives Group, Aquila Energy.
- Peter Robison, "Funds raise interest in weather futures" [4], *Bloomberg News*, August 2, 2007.
- USA Today (2008), "Weather Derivatives becoming hot commodities" [5], USA Today Online posted 6/9/2008.
- Alice Gomstyn, Rich Blake and Dalia Fahmy, "Want a Weather Forecast? Ask Wall Street" [6] *ABC News*, February 8, 2010.
- Dischel, R. S., Ed. (2002). "Climate Risk and the Weather Market: Financial Risk Management with Weather Hedges" [7], Risk Books.
- Jewson, S., A. Brix and C. Ziehmann (2005). "Weather Derivatives Valuation: The Meteorological, Statistical, Financial and Mathematical Foundations" [8]. Cambridge, Cambridge University Press.
- Golden, L. L., M. Wang and C. C. Yang "Handling Weather Related Risks Through the Financial Markets: Considerations of Credit Risk, Basis Risk, and Hedging." [9] Journal of Risk & Insurance, Vol. 74, No. 2, pp. 319–346, June 2007.
- Myers, R. (2008) "What Every CFO Needs to Know About Weather Risk Management" [10], Storm Exchange, Inc. & CME Group
- Mathews, J. S. (2009) "Dog Days and Degree Days" [11], CME Group

- Tang, K., Ed. (2010). "Weather Risk Management: A guide for Corporations, Hedge Funds and Investors" [12], Risk Books.

External links

- Weather Products at Chicago Mercantile Exchange [13]
- Weather Risk Management Association (WRMA) [14]
- Weather Risk links collection [15]
- Weather Derivatives and Weather Risk Professionals Group [16]
- Weather Risk Management Option with the Meteorology Undergraduate Programme at Penn State [17]
- Weather risk management and risk transfer news and research from Artemis.bm [18]

References

[1] http://www.cftc.gov/stellent/groups/public/@iodtefs/documents/file/deawiebots05-02.pdf

[2] http://www.risklimited.net/fas133-summary.htm

[3] http://www.cme.com/weather/introweather.pdf

[4] http://www.iht.com/articles/2007/08/01/bloomberg/bxfund.php

[5] http://www.usatoday.com/weather/forecast/2008-06-09-weather-derivative_N.htm

[6] http://abcnews.go.com/print?id=9757635

[7] http://riskbooks.com/Energy%20and%20Commodities/Climate-Risk-Weather-Market.php

[8] http://books.google.co.uk/books?id=IV8wh2zme5AC&lpg=PP1&pg=PP1#v=onepage&q=&f=false

[9] http://www.actuaries.org/ASTIN/Colloquia/Manchester/Papers/brockett_paper_final.pdf

[10] http://www.cmegroup.com/trading/weather/files/WeatherRisk_CEO.pdf

[11] http://www.cmegroup.com/trading/weather/files/WT133_Weather_White_Paper_Final.pdf

[12] http://riskbooks.com/Insurance/Weather%20Risk%20Management.php

[13] http://www.cmegroup.com/trading/weather/

[14] http://www.wrma.org

[15] http://wxrisk.wikia.com/

[16] http://www.linkedin.com/groups?gid=64408

[17] http://www.met.psu.edu/academics/undergraduate-studies/options-within-the-major/weather-risk-management

[18] http://www.artemis.bm

Article Sources and Contributors

Operational risk management *Source*: http://en.wikipedia.org/w/index.php?oldid=428921314 *Contributors*: Anon lynx, CodeGeneratR, Corp Vision, Dkeditor, Dmccreary, Dylan Lake, Edlitz36, Epbr123, FranssenM, GESICC, Gaius Cornelius, Hu12, InformationGuy, Jabencarsey, JonHarder, Jzupan, Krakfly, Kuru, Leolaursen, Letmebefell, Materialscientist, Outriggr, Piano non troppo, Pnm, Quaeler, Rbaker22, Rjwilmsi, Sengkang, Storm Rider, TScabbard, Vfp15, Yhkhoo, 53 anonymous edits

Risk management *Source*: http://en.wikipedia.org/w/index.php?oldid=431746325 *Contributors*: 3myazilim, AbsolutDan, Acidtekno, Actuarial disco boy, Actuary, Adang11, Adaveni, Adjusting, Adrius42, Akamad, Aktyagiipr, Alanpc1, Alansohn, Alexius08, Anikasavage, Anna Lincoln, Anon lynx, Anonymous anonymous, Antaeus Feldspar, Antandrus, Antur, Anubhavklal, Ap, Appraiser, Arcadian, ArnoldReinhold, Aschuster, Ash, Astudent, Audrius, Auntof6, Avb, Avraham, Awf206, AxelBoldt, BD2412, BIG4PAPA, Backburner001, Bbkobl, Beland, Biker Biker, Bill Coffin, Bill.albing, Biscuittin, Blanchardb, Blowdart, Bmi232, BoweryBleecker, Bradingrish, Breno, Brodger3, BrotherFlounder, Bryanhall, Btyner, Budgey99, C-M, CQPress, Carry Lesco, Cerebellum, Charles Matthews, Charlesbaldo, Charnwood, Chinsurance, Ck lostsword, Cliff2311, Codetiger, Collinsr, Conversion script, Corp Vision, Cpk, Craigb81, Craigwb, Crazypete101, Cretog8, Cxbrx, DFLovett, DKoenig, Dali1010, Damistmu, DanielDeibler, Dannyl50, Dashdash99, David Smiles, DavidBelew, Davidwikipedia, DeadlyAssassin, Deed89, Diazfrancisca, Dkeditor, Dkutcher, Dmccreary, Dmcq, DocendoDiscimus, Dolly1313, Donmapua, DoriSmith, Dozen, Dpr, Droll, Dukeofwulf, Dvandeventer, EcoMan, EdBever, Edward, Ekotkie, El C, Elizabethkudelasz, Engi08, Epolk, Erie4987, Espoo, Exarion, Excirial, FS riskmgmt, Fastfission, Favonian, Fieldday-sunday, Fijodor, Flyer22, Frankwightman, Frederic Y Bois, Frieda, G. Völcker, GESICC, Gary King, Gatut, Ghaag, Glen, Gogo Dodo, Good Olfactory, Greenmars, Gregalton, Gsaup, Gurch, Gwandoya, Hactuary, Hadal, Hauskalainen, Hcpsyuak1, He Who Is, Heartfocus, Hede2000, Heds 1, Hetar, Hgdastoor, Hogayoga, Hu12, IRP, Ialencar, Icairns, Igfrace, Imroy, Inferno, Lord of Penguins, Itemuk, Itskoolman, IvanLanin, J.delanoy, J04n, J1579, JRaeside, Jaah21, Jaccowiki, Jafcbs, Jcdowney, JennJifsan, Jennnyyyp, Jerryseinfeld, Jessecisneros, John, John Carter, John Fader, Jonhol, Jons63, Jorgewiki, Jtneill, JubalHarshaw, Jvlock, Jwestland, JzG, Karlwiegand, Katapult99, KathrynLybarger, Kbelltrium, Keilana, KeithJonsn, Kenmckinley, Kenstandfield, Khalid, Kokacola, Krakenflies, Krakfly, Ksyrie, Ktlonergan, Kudret abi, Kuru, Kylealanhale, Kyrriana, Laptopjack, Laurabbook, Lawsie, LibLord, Lidram, Light current, Ligulem, Logicmanager, Lucianna8, LyallDNZ, Lyseong, M4gnum0n, MER-C, Makingprogress19, MansonP, Marek69, Mathewstuart, Matt.Chojecki, MattieTK, Mattomoran, Mattsmith86, Maurreen, Mbeychok, Mdd, Mdgarvey, Mdorohovich, MechBrowman, Megadeth186, Michael Hardy, Mikael Häggström, Mkoval, Mohehab, Molly747, MrJones, MrOllie, Ms-grf, Muchness, Mwanner, Myasuda, Mydogategodshat, Möchtegern, Nagle, NawlinWiki, Neo139, Neurolysis, Neutrality, Nicholas Cimini, Nick Green, OAG, Ohnoitsjamie, Olaf, Oleg Alexandrov, Oliverwyman, Onjacktallcuca, Open2universe, Oracleconnect, Overix, P4k, PM Poon, Pakoistinen, Pan Dan, Pastore Italy, Pcb21, PeterBoun, Pgillingwater, Pgreenfinch, Phaydock, Philip Trueman, PhilippeAntras, Phopkin, Piano non troppo, PigFlu Oink, Pm master, Pndt, PolarYukon, PracticalRiskManager, Proman1, Ps07swt, RMAhq, Radak, Rafael.costa.santos, RainbowOfLight, Raymond23, Rbaker22, Regregex, Resolute, Riggwelter, Ringbark, RiskWise101, Riskex, Riskrisk, Rjwilmsi, Rkitko, Robina Fox, Robinh, Ronz, Ryanmcdaniel, SEI Publications, SafetyTempsLimited, Sam Hocevar, Sandymok, Schwijker, Scientizzle, Seth Nimbosa, SevenSigma, Shadow1, Sharkford, Simesa, Simpleblob, Siroxo, Sjakkalle, SlyFrog, Sopoforic, Sox First, SpaceFlight89, Spalding, Srathi, Srich32977, Stankir, Supergreg no1, Sweerek, THEN WHO WAS PHONE?, Taxman, That Guy, From That Show!, The Anome, The undertow, Themfromspace, Theodolite, This lousy T-shirt, ThreeDee912, Thuja, Tilleyg, Tomisti, Topiarydan, Trivialist, Trout Fisher 03, Trusilver, Ulric1313, Urbanette, Utcursch, Versageek, Vina, Viriditas, Visual risk management, Wavelength, White Trillium, Wik, Wikichops, Wikimaguire, Winchelsea, Wizardman, Wmahan, Wmasterj, Wolfram.Tungsten, Woohookitty, Wouldyou, Wtmitchell, Wuhwuzdat, Yaparla qatester, Ytiugibma, Yuriybrisk, ZK 41110, Zodon, 724 anonymous edits

Association of Management Consulting Firms *Source*: http://en.wikipedia.org/w/index.php?oldid=396227527 *Contributors*: AMCForg, Hullaballoo Wolfowitz, Mwtoews, Orangemike, Pberkle, R'n'B, Rettetast, Woohookitty

Peter L. Bernstein *Source*: http://en.wikipedia.org/w/index.php?oldid=426097297 *Contributors*: All Hallow's Wraith, Arthur Rubin, Bongomatic, Bplittle124, Consultright, FeanorStar7, Fjarlq, Gadfium, George Burgess, JDMBAHopeful, Kaisershatner, Kern.scott, Kumioko, Lamro, Lockley, Mfitzger, Michael David, Ninja247, Pearle, Pontificake, Pwaldron, RJFJR, Rjwilmsi, Roman Spinner, Simon12, Splintercellguy, Suckaduck, Todd Vierling, Urbanrenewal, Useight, Versageek, Wikix, 30 anonymous edits

Building Safer Communities. Risk Governance, Spatial Planning and Responses to Natural Hazards *Source*: http://en.wikipedia.org/w/index.php?oldid=425548193 *Contributors*: Gidonb, Lieiro, Malcolma, Rettetast, Woohookitty, Wouldyou

Burn pit *Source*: http://en.wikipedia.org/w/index.php?oldid=431011653 *Contributors*: DASonnenfeld, Davy p, Fred Bauder, Jncraton, Nono64, Rjwilmsi

Cascading Discontinuity Sets *Source*: http://en.wikipedia.org/w/index.php?oldid=390622980 *Contributors*: Bearcat, Desiredfutures, Esoweteric, Malcolma, Ronz, Time Immemorial

Dangerous Goods Safety Advisor *Source*: http://en.wikipedia.org/w/index.php?oldid=415686377 *Contributors*: 3family6, Alton, Amanje, Astrophysicist1975, Autoerrant, Bearcat, Biscuittin, Davbon, Edgar181, FrozenPurpleCube, Groomer, Kjkolb, LilHelpa, Micru, Ncecash, Petenv, Pzavon, Utcursch, White.matthew.09, 8 anonymous edits

Defensive driving *Source*: http://en.wikipedia.org/w/index.php?oldid=431597172 *Contributors*: ALewis109, Adam.J.W.C., Adaminafl, Alexforcefive, Anakata, Andy Marchbanks, Arcadian, Bakilas, BeastRHIT, Beetstra, BlankVerse, BlueH2O, Brandon, Charleswj, Chiggerferocity, Chopperphil, Comic19, Ctbolt, Dancter, Daniel J. Leivick, Defensive Driving Solutions, Emperorbma, FrecklesCat, Fullrabb, GT, GeneGilbreath, Gerovitus, Greglocock, Heroeswithmetaphors, Heron, Hurkyl, Ilovesocks, Indon, Interiot, JayFout, Jeff G., Jeremykemp, John C PI, Jwissick, KADART, Kungfuadam, Kwiksafe, Law, Legionarius, Lincolnite, LocoBurger, Lucien504, Mac, Marek69, Mhoskins, Milkmandan, Mot Adv-NSW, MrOllie, Naff89, NatlSafetyCouncil, Nekura, Neorunner, Neutrality, NigelJ, Pcb21, Pcresham, Peter bertok, Peterson1234, Portgame, Prolog, Roadmr, Robef, Schwarzenneger, Secondss, Shimgray, Spalding, Speed8ump, Spellmaster, Taliswolf, Testmasters, Thisisbossi, Thomas Larsen, Tom.roseberry, Ufwuct, Vaoverland, Vees, Veinor, Vshahid, Wavelength, Wmahan, Woohookitty, WriterListener, XLerate, Zzuuzz, 208 anonymous edits

David Eager *Source*: http://en.wikipedia.org/w/index.php?oldid=417044214 *Contributors*: Epbr123, Katharineamy, Kooka86, Mandarax, Racklever, Vipinhari, 1 anonymous edits

Exposure Factor *Source*: http://en.wikipedia.org/w/index.php?oldid=390029122 *Contributors*: BD2412, Eeekster, Fabrictramp, Katharineamy, Malcolma, Phillip.dt25, Woohookitty

Michael Featherstone *Source*: http://en.wikipedia.org/w/index.php?oldid=405646807 *Contributors*: Capricorn24, Conquistador2k6, Epbr123, Paalappoo, Rmosler2100, Travburch, Wikiwarrior07, Will Beback Auto, 8 anonymous edits

Financial risk management *Source*: http://en.wikipedia.org/w/index.php?oldid=424914497 *Contributors*: Agacademic 2001, Aintneo, Altruism, Antandrus, Avssrs, Barkeep, Btyner, Chunt@euromoney.com, D6, DKoenig, DS1953, Dashdash99, Debresser, DocendoDiscimus, Drewwiki, Dvandeventer, EcoMan, Editor1962, Eximexchange, Fintor, Gregalton, Htournyol, Iratheclimber, Jeff3000, Juzeris, Ksvrando, Kuru, LeadSongDog, Ligulem, Maurreen, Metosa, Outriggr, Pnm, Poppybaobao, Quadell, Regregex, Riskrisk, Struway, StuffOfInterest, Taffenzee, Taxman, That Guy, From That Show!, TheMightyHercules, Veneto, Wombatfrog, Woohookitty, Ypetrachenko, 62 anonymous edits

Fish & Richardson *Source*: http://en.wikipedia.org/w/index.php?oldid=430672234 *Contributors*: Andrew987654321, Appraiser, Arthena, Bhadani, CJLL Wright, Crzrussian, Cs-wolves, Dale Arnett, Duncan fr, ERcheck, Eastlaw, Edcolins, Frankg, GearedBull, Greenshed, GreysAnatomy, Ground Zero, Jlamay1213, Jokestress, Jreferee, Kklargey, Lacanj8, Lamro, Lneal, Lotje, Lredfi, MER-C, Madcoverboy, Niremetal, Nycbl1y, OccamzRazor, Ospalh, Panoptical, Phillipsjc, Plastikspork, Pygora123, Ronhjones, Webmasteratfish, WhisperToMe, Wknight94, Xnatedawgx, Y, 51 anonymous edits

Flood Forecasting Centre *Source*: http://en.wikipedia.org/w/index.php?oldid=432515816 *Contributors*: Yorkshiresky

Hazard prevention *Source*: http://en.wikipedia.org/w/index.php?oldid=400300652 *Contributors*: Altermike, Beland, Bobo192, Mac, Mashgral, Nopetro, SmokeyJoe, William Avery, Winchelsea, Woland37, Woohookitty, Ytiugibma, Zigger, 5 anonymous edits

Institute of Risk Management *Source*: http://en.wikipedia.org/w/index.php?oldid=348124776 *Contributors*: EastTN, Fabrictramp, Geoff Plourde, Irmmarketing, John of Reading, Pigman, 8 anonymous edits

Insurance Certificate Tracking *Source*: http://en.wikipedia.org/w/index.php?oldid=432376815 *Contributors*: Auntof6, Avington2915, Beverita, Cary W. White, Eejay62, Etyler22, Jmoreland, Katharineamy, LTSINC, Maria Llamas, Sara Williams 2116, Tassedethe, 60 anonymous edits

Investment Controlling *Source*: http://en.wikipedia.org/w/index.php?oldid=409685207 *Contributors*: Alarics, Bearcat, Jsfouche, Stefan.illmer, 41 anonymous edits

ISO 31000 *Source*: http://en.wikipedia.org/w/index.php?oldid=427115481 *Contributors*: Auntof6, DPdH, Deltaker, GESICC, Gary King, IvanLanin, Nasa-verve, Spiritia, Supergreg no1, Tcharvin, 13 anonymous edits

List of books about risk *Source*: http://en.wikipedia.org/w/index.php?oldid=429907011 *Contributors*: Jonkerz, Kintetsubuffalo, Melaen, Protonk, Wavelength, Wouldyou, 1 anonymous edits

Master of Science in Risk Management Program for Executives *Source*: http://en.wikipedia.org/w/index.php?oldid=421625459 *Contributors*: Bearcat, Fintor, Kbelltrium, Malcolma, Nolelover, Skier Dude

Moody's Analytics *Source*: http://en.wikipedia.org/w/index.php?oldid=423143033 *Contributors*: Chris the speller, DGG, Edward, GoingBatty, Random User 937494, Redraiders203, Tassedethe, 17 anonymous edits

Occupational safety and health *Source*: http://en.wikipedia.org/w/index.php?oldid=432691194 *Contributors*: A3RO, AJR, Abby, Aksati, Alansohn, Alaughingmind, Allangam, Anghe20, Anna Lincoln, Arcadian, Art LaPella, Atama, Athena.JJ.Bi, B6bloke, Bae2501, Bananus, Barek, Barryofblackburn, Basket of Puppies, Ben Ben, BesselDekker, BeverlyCrusher, Biscuittin, Bj816, Bobo192, Bongomatic, Boothy443, Bristoluk, Brossow, Bultro, C. J. Harrington, C.Fred, CWii, Caltas, Can't sleep, clown will eat me, Capricorn42, Captronnc, Carax, Cburnett, Celeste1983, Charles Matthews, Chaser, Chemical Engineer, Chrissy385, Christyschultz, Ciarondunne, Corti, Corvus cornix, Cotinis, Crigaux, Ctbolt, Culmensis, Cépey, DARTH SIDIOUS 2, DASonnenfeld, Davjoh, Debresser, Diego Grez, Doc Tropics, Doug s, Dublin123, E-pen, EagleFan, Egmontaz, El C, Elmf, Erianna, Erich Schmidt, Escape Orbit, Farquaadhnchmn, Fencingtim, FireMonty, Flowanda, Fordmadoxfraud, Gaius Cornelius, Garpert, Gatorsdc2006, Gerryfmarr, Geschichte, Gfoley4, Ghirlandajo, Glane23, Gmaxwell, Graibeard, Gregfitzy, Grubber, Gurch, Gveret Tered, Hassansadik123, Health4Work, Heinzbeano, Henrywilter, Heracles31, HexaChord, Hgfernan, Hobartimus, Irf5, Isis150, Iss246, Issacomm, Issacommunication, J.delanoy, J04n, JLaTondre, JRI, Jauerback, Jimmckay, Joclimer, John.spamkiller, JohnCD, Johncherrie, Jokestress, Jrdioko, Jsmith86, JuniperisCommunis, Jusdafax, JustAGal, KD888, Keegan, Kerotan, Kill me when i die, KnowledgeOfSelf, Krawi, Kurieeto, Kuru, Kvdveer, Lacort, Lafumaking, Ldbrown, LeaveSleaves, Letheork, LilHelpa, Lionbait, Lowellian, MAPERC Outreach, Marekza, Marky-Son, Martarius, Materialscientist, Matt Fitzpatrick, Mbeychok, MiFeinberg, Micki.baron, Mikael Häggström, MikeRich29, MikeyAdamz, Mlaffs, Mophead23, Mr pand, MrOllie, MrRadioGuy, Mschweigert, Mutinus, Narayanese, Nelson huang2003, Neutrality, Nick Levine, Niteowlneils, Nmarkiewicz, Nodal Plane, Nomad, Nopetro, Oephpest, Old Moonraker, Ollie8557, Omicade, Onslaught 789, Oxymoron83, PIROCKS, Paul foord, Paulburnett, Penbat, PhilKnight, Philip.marshall, Piano non troppo, PigFlu Oink, Pinethicket, Posturite, Pzavon, Quinsareth, Rani Lueder, Reaper Eternal, Reasonable2, Redvers, Rettetast, Ricardovyhmeister, Rich Farmbrough, Rickw1010, Rifleman 82, Rjwilmsi, Robert Weemeyer, Rodneyep, Ronz, S, Samulili, Scartol, Seth Ilys, Sethpn, Shoefly, Signalhead, SimonWade, Smim90, Snalwibma, Solarusdude, Solipsist, Squids and Chips, Srbauer, Subodhsapkota, SunCreator, Sushiflinger, Tamarkot, TanyaMorose, TastyPoutine, Tazmaniacs, Techman224, Terlan, Texture, The Thing That Should Not Be, The Wikipedist, Thebritishippie, Timtregenza, Tobustar, Tony K10, Tortillovsky, TriniSocialist, TurboForce, Twang, UncleDouggie, Usb10, Utcursch, Vanjagenije, Victorhoe, VictorianMutant, VigilancePrime, WOSlinker, Waggers, Wavelength, White Shadows, Wiki-uk, Wizzy, Worksafe, Xyzzyplugh, Zahlie, Zsero, Zzuuzz, 537 anonymous edits

Opasnet *Source*: http://en.wikipedia.org/w/index.php?oldid=411450357 *Contributors*: Jtuom, 1 anonymous edits

Open assessment *Source*: http://en.wikipedia.org/w/index.php?oldid=411450435 *Contributors*: Jtuom, 1 anonymous edits

Profit risk *Source*: http://en.wikipedia.org/w/index.php?oldid=423888034 *Contributors*: Db0527, Pnm, R'n'B, Winter Breeze, Yudomunartono, 4 anonymous edits

Project risk management *Source*: http://en.wikipedia.org/w/index.php?oldid=413634900 *Contributors*: Berek, GoingBatty, Pax85, Ravindraprasad, SBaker43

Ready Georgia *Source*: http://en.wikipedia.org/w/index.php?oldid=396487809 *Contributors*: Ground Zero, Ilyushka88, JohnCD, Leeatcookerly, Miller17CU94, Pauli133, Piledhigheranddeeper, SoWhy, Suzyq527, Wilson172, 4 anonymous edits

Risk assessment *Source*: http://en.wikipedia.org/w/index.php?oldid=429725148 *Contributors*: 1carpediem, Agesworth, Aksi great, Alansohn, Aleenf1, Allstarecho, AndrewRA, Anna Lincoln, ArnoldReinhold, Baiusmc, Bcontins, Ben Harris-Roxas, Bicchi, Bobo192, CambridgeBayWeather, Cenarium, Cheapskate08, ChemGardener, Chemical Engineer, Chillllls, Chris the speller, Ckragrud, ColetteHoch, Cometstyles, CountdownCrispy, DHMan, Dan D. Ric, Danny50, David Shay, DavidBailey, DeadEyeArrow, Deltaker, Deville, Dolly1313, Dostupidthingsfaster, EdBever, Eddiejoe97, El C, El grimley, Epbr123, Erianna, Faradayplank, Femto, Frederic Y Bois, Funandtrvl, GESICC, GRBerry, Ghaag, Gogo Dodo, HG, Hle37, Hu12, Huggle, JennJifsan, Jezsheena, Jimmaths, Jmlk17, Johnqtodd, KVDP, Kaiserb, Kku, Kolbasz, Krakfly, Krawi, Kuebi, Kuru, Lacort, Lalnikveil, Light current, Lotje, Lucianna8, Luna Santin, M4gnum0n, Mac, Mark7211, Materialscientist, Maximus Rex, Melcombe, Michael Hardy, Mikael Häggström, Mnath, Mnent, Monnini1, MrOllie, Murftown, Máirtín, NYScholar, Nelson50, Outriggr, OverlordQ, Paddles, Pastore Italy, Philip Trueman, Piano non troppo, Pinethicket, Pm master, R'n'B, Reconsider the static, Regregex, Riskrisk, Rixs, Rjwilmsi, Rodhullandemu, Ronz, SEI Publications, SMC, Samwaltersdc, SatuSuro, SchnitzelMannGreek, Sciurinæ, Shimeru, Shirulashem, Smallbones, Smalljim, Smeto, SpaceFlight89, Suffusion of Yellow, Supergreg no1, THSlone, Tassieroy, Taxman, Tedickey, The Anome, The Thing That Should Not Be, Therefore, Timtregenza, Trakesht, Urbanette, Vaceituno, Wavelength, Welsh, WookieInHeat, Wotnow, WriterHound, Zaggernaut, Zhenqinli, °¡°, 295 anonymous edits

Risk governance *Source*: http://en.wikipedia.org/w/index.php?oldid=400940317 *Contributors*: Bearian, Lieiro, Malcolma, PamD, Sadads, Wouldyou, 1 anonymous edits

Risk International *Source*: http://en.wikipedia.org/w/index.php?oldid=431177425 *Contributors*: Bearcat, JustAGal, R'n'B, Rjwilmsi, Thepaxtons, 31 anonymous edits

Risk management framework *Source*: http://en.wikipedia.org/w/index.php?oldid=427113612 *Contributors*: Mrmdog, Rich Farmbrough, 1 anonymous edits

Risk management tools *Source*: http://en.wikipedia.org/w/index.php?oldid=430886951 *Contributors*: Akerans, Biscuittin, Dawnseeker2000, Dr.sumeetmalhotra, Egandrews, GESICC, Johncharnes, Johnfos, Kiaorabro, Linexero, Madonna56, MrOllie, Rb208849, RiskOpportunities, Riskrisk, Small Bug, Weavers46, 20 anonymous edits

Risk pool *Source*: http://en.wikipedia.org/w/index.php?oldid=426316014 *Contributors*: Big000000, Busy Stubber, Condem, Dondegroovily, Eiland, Funandtrvl, Hhhggg, IRP, Jcwondrous, John Broughton, Malcolma, Paultt, Pnm, SMcCandlish, Soumyasch, The Squicks, The Thing That Should Not Be, Twas Now, 20 anonymous edits

RiskAoA *Source*: http://en.wikipedia.org/w/index.php?oldid=418340062 *Contributors*: Drbreznjev, GESICC, Giraffedata, Pollinosisss, 14 anonymous edits

Security risk *Source*: http://en.wikipedia.org/w/index.php?oldid=411303091 *Contributors*: Ash, Pastore Italy, Reddi, Sophus Bie, Supergreg no1, 3 anonymous edits

Singapore Mercantile Exchange *Source*: http://en.wikipedia.org/w/index.php?oldid=432330613 *Contributors*: Avicennasis, BD2412, CTZSMX, Cowanthantzin, GoingBatty, Hu12, Kingturtle, Mariope, Mean as custard, Mr. Glengarry Glen Ross, PhilKnight, Pnm, Pontificalibus, R'n'B, Seaphoto, ShelfSkewed, Tassedethe, Woohookitty, 33 anonymous edits

Singapore Workplace Safety and Health Conference *Source*: http://en.wikipedia.org/w/index.php?oldid=404553714 *Contributors*: Auntof6, Diannaa, Funandtrvl, Katharineamy, Mark.chen.sprg, Micru, Santryl

Student Investment Advisory Service (SIAS Fund) *Source*: http://en.wikipedia.org/w/index.php?oldid=422595410 *Contributors*: SaraMoghaddamjo

Julian Talbot (risk management) *Source*: http://en.wikipedia.org/w/index.php?oldid=427724706 *Contributors*: Edoakley, Eeekster, Graeme Bartlett, Jon2777, Kudpung, Riskdude, 7 anonymous edits

Tsunami *Source*: http://en.wikipedia.org/w/index.php?oldid=432928342 *Contributors*: (jarbarf), *drew, -js-, 129.128.164.xxx, 23prootie, 28bytes, 2k8, 3centsoap, 4Leben2, 4r1st0tl3, 5 albert square, 63.192.137.xxx, A Softer Answer, A. di M., A3r0, ACSE, Aaron11193, Aaronbrick, Abstract Idiot, Academic Challenger, Acalamari, Adam Carr, Adam McMaster, Adam1213, AdamJacobMuller, Adambro, Adamsrock, Adashiel, Adhi Nugroho, Aecis, Aeusoes1, Aewadi, Agateller, Ahoerstemeier, Aicchalmers, Ajraddatz, Akamad, Akronym, Alan Pascoe, Alanbly, Alastair Haines, Albrozdude, Aldis90, Ale jrb, Alecl1996, Alessandro57, Alex12345678910, AlexNg, Alexd, AlexiusHoratius, Alexlemon, Alhutch, Ali'i, Ali@gwc.org.uk, Alias Flood, Aliekens, Aliter, Allison Stillwell, Almafeta, Amalthea, Amanbis, Amcfreely, AnAj, Anakixbutt23, Anas Salloum, Anders Torlind, Andonic, Andre Engels, Andrewpmack, Andrewrost3241981, Andthu, Andy, Andy M. Wang, Andy Smith, AndyBQ, Andyd1, Andyjsmith, Anetode, Angry bee, Animum, Ann Stouter, AnnaFrance, AnonGuy, Anonymous Dissident, Anonymous editor, Antandrus, Anthony Appleyard, Antonrojo, Anyeverybody, Aowpr, Arcata1, Arch dude, Archanamiya, Archfalhwyl, Arjun01, Arnfinn Christensen, Arthur Smart, Article7, Arunsingh16, Arwel Parry, Asabbagh, Ashmoo, Asprakash, Astronautics, Atlant, Attarparn, Aude, Autodidactyl, Autoerrant, Avb, Avia, AvicAWB, Avicennais, Avraham, Awien, Axl, Az1568, AzaToth, Azalea pomp, BARLOWG, BME, BNSF1995, Badgernet, Bakanov, Bal00, Balweyn1977, Banes, BanyanTree, Barbara Shack, Barbi6, Barneca, Bart133, BaseballDetective, Bdegfcunbbfv, Bear475, Bearcat, Bedel23, Beland, Belligero, Belovedfreak, Ben Ben, Ben Webber, Bender235, Bendono, Benlembo7, Beno1000, Berek, BerserkerBen, BesigedB, Bevo74, Bhadani, Bhadaur, Bhawani Gautam, Big Bird, Biglovinb, Bigmuggle, Bináris, Black Kite, BlackDragon235, Blainster, Blightsoot, Blouseman, BlueAg09, BlueMoonlet, Blueboy96, Bluesquareapple, Bluethedog01, Bluetooth954, Boa22, Bobblewik, Bobo192, Bonadea, Bongwarrior, Boothy443, Bootluy, Boris Allen, Boris Crépeau, Born2x, Bovineone, Bradleyb2007, Brat32, Brclark12, Brekky, BrianGV, Bridgecross, Broccoli, Bruce1ee, Brucedog3, Brusegadi, BryanG, Bsadowski1, Bubba hotep, Bubblybabs, Bunny-chan, Butros, Buuuu, Bydand, Béka, C'est moi, C4100, CAPS LOCK, CJCurrie, CNRNair, CQJ, Cadwaladr, Calabraxthis, Calmfeet, Caltas, Calton, CambridgeBayWeather, Camelhumps, Cameron Nedland, Can't sleep, clown will eat me, CanOfWorms, Canderson7, CanisRufus, Canterbury Tail, Carcharoth, Casper2k3, Cause of death, Cbustapeck, Ccmonty, Cdc, Cedders, CeilingCrash, Celestianpower, Celestra, Centauri, Centrx, Cerfa, Cessator, Chameleon, Chansonh, Charan094, CharlotteWebb, Chaser, ChongDae, Chovain, Chowbok, Chris 73, ChrisRuvolo, Chrishmt0423, Chrislk02, CiTrusD, Cimon Avaro, Cobaltbluetony, CodeWeasel, Collabi, Comehomeusa, Cometstyles, Commander Keane, Computerjoe, Computerman45, Confession0791, Conversion script, Cool Blue, Cool Nerd, Coolcaesar, Coredesat, Cosmic Latte, CountdownCrispy, Cowman109, Cp111, Craig Pemberton, CrankyScorpion, Cremepuff222, Crowsnest, CryptoDerk, CryptoStorm, Crystallina, Cthompson, Cuchullain, Curps, Cybercobra, Cyberman9997, Cyberpaul, Cygnus78, Cyrius, D, D052, DARTH SIDIOUS 2, DHN, DJ Clayworth, DVD R W, Da Vynci, Daa89563, Daanschr, Dabbler, Dabomb87, Dadude3320, Damian Yerrick, Damoncoffey, Dan Guan, Dan100, Danger, Daniel.Cardenas, Danielaustinhall12, Danny, Dannyc77, Danski14, Dar-Ape, Davesmall52, David Woodward, David0811, DavidNONO, Davidmaxwaterman, Davidsalzberg, Dawnseeker2000, Dbfirs, Dbtfz, Dcflyer, Dd12345, DeadEyeArrow, Deadcorpse, DeadlyAssassin, Dekimasu, Deli nk, Delirium, Delldot,

Deltabeignet, Denelson83, DennisJOBrien@yahoo.com, Deor, DerHexer, Dethme0w, Dezzman1625, Dfrizzellrocks, Dialh, Diberri, Diderot, Digicana, Digitalme, Dipa1965, Discospinster, Djd1219, Doc Tropics, Doc glasgow, DocWatson42, Doctor250, Dod1, Don Ellis, Dori, Dotuniverce, Dr bab, DragonflySixtyseven, Drick, DropDeadGorgias, Drunkenmonkey, Dsmdgold, Dudecon, Durin, Dwheeler, Dyingdreams, Dysepsion, E Wing, EJF, ESkog, Eatsaq, Eazye24, Eclypse, Ed Poor, Ed8r, Edwy, Egg Centric, Egil, Ejrs, El C, Elcocinero, EldKatt, Elen of the Roads, Elfino, Eliz81, Elizabeyth, Emmaskis, Emperorbma, Endofskull, Envirodan, Epicstonemason, Epipelagic, Erebus555, Ereza, ErikHaugen, Erinlynn240, ErrantX, Estel, Etxrge, Eugeneloh, EventHorizon, Evercat, Everton, Everyking, Evil Monkey, Excirial, FF2010, FT2, Fabianhow, Fabullus, Factoflife, Facts707, Fayenatic london, Ferkelparade, Fg2, Fieldmarshal Miyagi, Firstorm, FisherQueen, Fiziker, Flakker, Flockmeal, Flowerpotman, Fly by Night, Flyguy649, Fnfd, Forever Dusk, Fortdj33, Fossiliferous, Fram, Francs2000, Frangibility, Fratrep, Freakofnurture, Fredrik, FreplySpang, Friendly Neighbour, Frymaster, Funnybunny, FutureNJGov, Fuzheado, Fvw, Fys, GHe, GJeffery, GRAHAMUK, Gadfium, Gaff, Gaius Cornelius, Galoubet, Garyms1963, GavinTing, Gdr, Ged UK, Geek84, Gene Nygaard, Geni, GeoGreg, George07, GeorgeOrr, Ghettodude, Ghodgen, Giftlite, Gilgamesh, Gilliam, Gimboid13, Ginger74, Ginsengbomb, Glass Sword, Glen, Glenn, Glenn L, Glrx, Gogo Dodo, Golbez, GorillaWarfare, Goudzovski, Gracenotes, GraemeL, Graham87, Greggreggreg, GregorB, Gregory j, Grm wnr, Grover cleveland, Gruepig, Gryspnik, Gtdp, Gtg204y, Gugilymugily, Guitarkid44, Gun Powder Ma, Gurch, Gurchzilla, Gwen Gale, Gwernol, Gzornenplatz, H.sand01, HXL49, Hadal, Hahaandy1, HalfShadow, Halo3general, Hans Dunkelberg, HarveyHenkelmann, Haukurth, Hdt83, Heartlander, Heds 1, Hello32020, HenkvD, Henry Flower, HenryLi, Henrythe8thIam, Herbee, Heron, HiLo48, Hill466, Himasaram, Hippalus, Hippietrail, Hmains, Hoboday, Hokeman, Hontogaichiban, Hu12, Hut 8.5, I already forgot, I80and, IGeMiNix, Icairns, Icetea8, Iciac, Idwood, Imaglang, Imnotminkus, InShaneee, Indosauros, Ingolfson, Inkling, Insanity Incarnate, Instinct, Intelati, Inter16, Interent, Into The Fray, Invincible Ninja, Ioeth, Ivvan Cain, Ixfd64, J, J.delanoy, JALockhart, JHunterJ, JIMBO WALES, JMPZ, JNW, JRM, JYolkowski, JackSchmidt, Jacobolus, Jacoplane, Jafeluv, JamesAM, JamesBWatson, Jamiesuthzerland, Janadore, Janko, Jantangring, Jareha, Jatlas, Javajunkiewa, JayEsJay, Jayden54, Jbvillarante, Jcmurphy, Jcw69, JePe, Jebba, Jeffq, Jeffrey O. Gustafson, JeremyA, Jespinos, Jess Mars, Jez, Jfiling, Jfrink, Jh51681, Jhi, Jiddisch, Jingjun, Jkl sem, Jklin, Jmateos, Jni, JoanneB, Joaop, JodyB, JoeOnSunset, JoeSmack, Johan1298, Johann Wolfgang, John Fader, John Foley, John254, JohnWittle, Johnbibby, Johnuniq, Johnxxx9, Jon186, Jonathan Hall, Jonny.holbrook, Joseph Solis in Australia, JoshRaspberry, Joshafina, Joshbuddy, Jossi, Joyous!, Jpgordon, Jrdioko, Jredmond, Jreferee, Jsc83, Jtkiefer, JulieADriver, Jun-Dai, Junjk, Jurema Oliveira, Justin Eiler, Juze, Juzeris, Jwihbey, K10wnsta, KJS77, Kablammo, Kajasudhakarababu, Karada, Karimarie, Karmosin, Kasparvp, Kasperd, Katalaveno, Kathar, Kchishol1970, Keilana, Keith Edkins, KeithH, Kelly Martin, Ken l lee, Keristrasza, Kerotan, Kesac, Kesuari, Kevin B12, Khaosworks, Kharoon, Khukri, Khym Chanur, KindGoat, King of Hearts, KingTT, Kiteinthewind, Kittybrewster, Kizor, Kjkolb, Kjnangre, Kk8998982, Kkken, Klaam, Klaser, Klestrob44, Kmort7, Knowledge Seeker, KnowledgeOfSelf, Knulclunk, Knutux, Koavf, Kool danielz, Kotjze, Kotoviski, KrakatoaKatie, Krellis, Kribbeh, Krich, Kubigula, Kukini, Kungfuadam, Kuru, Kurykh, Kwamikagami, KyraVixen, L Kensington, L.vivian.richard, L1A1 FAL, L33tminion, LOL, LSAyear7, Lahiru k, Latka, Leafyplant, Lebron96, Leh.mo, Lelkesa, Lemi4, Leonard G., Leszek Jańczuk, Levineps, Lfstevens, Liam1985, Lifung, Lights, Lil devil, Lilac Soul, Lindblum, LinguistAtLarge, LinuxSneaker, Little Spike, Little jim, LittleOldMe, LittleOldMe old, Livajo, Lkseitz, Llort, Loranchet, Lotje, Lowellian, Luckyherb, Luckyluke, Lucm, Ludahai, Lumos3, Luna Santin, Lupo, M00dimus, MER-C, MMMMMEEEEE, MONGO, MPF, MZMcBride, Mac Davis, Madman, Mafia unit, Magister Mathematicae, Magnus Manske, Mailer diablo, Majoreditor, Majorly, Malerin, Malo, Manamanam, Mandel, Mani1, Manning Bartlett, Marc van Leeuwen, Marcocampo, Mark, MarkBolton, Markaci, Markerqueen, Marshman, Martinp23, Martocticvs, Mary quite contrary, Mary629, Marysunshine, Mathmoclaire, Matt Crypto, Matt Whyndham, Matthuxtable, Mattun0211, Maustrauser, Mav, Mawfive, Maxamegalon2000, Mboverload, Mbz1, Mclay1, Mcpusc, Meaghan, Megan 189, Meggar, Melaen, Meodipt, Merfer, Mets501, MetsFan76, Meursault2004, Mewantcookie, Mexaguil, Mh, Michael A. White, Michael Devore, Michael Hardy, Michaelas10, Michaelbusch, Michalchik, Midgrid, Mike R, Mike Rosoft, MikeLeeds, Mikegrant, Mikenorton, Mikeo, Mikhail Ryazanov, Milkyface, Mimigu, Mimihitam, MindlessXD, Minesweeper, Mini-Geek, Minimac, Minor Contributer, Miraceti, Mistachicken, Mlewan, Mnemeson, MoRsE, Mockiewicz, Modernist, Moeron, Monedula, Monkeybooty, Moondyne, Moonriddengirl, Mooquackwooftweetmeow, Mordemur, Moreschi, Moshe Constantine Hassan Al-Silverburg, Moxy, Mr Adequate, Msgohan, Muhammad Nabil Berri, Mushroom, Mustafaa, Mwparenteau, Myanw, Mythbusters, N-Man, N. Harmonik, NCurse, NHRHS2010, Nahallac Silverwinds, Nakon, Namazu-tron, Nargis 2008, NatureA16, Nauticashades, NawlinWiki, Ncrfgs, Neg, Netjeff, Neutrality, NewEnglandYankee, Newton2, Newtrend19, Ngatimozart, Nick, Nickybutt, Nikhilajain, Nikkigordon, Ninteneo1379, Nishy123, Nivix, Nk, Nkf31, Nns, Noahisnice, Noctibus, Nofeeling, Nohat, Noisy, Nopetro, NormalGoddess, Northumbrian, Notary137, Nposs, Nricardo, Nscheffey, NuclearWarfare, Nv8200p, O1ive, Oarih, Ocatecir, Oda Mari, Off!, Ohms law, Ohnoitsjamie, Omicronpersei8, Ondewelle, Onsly, Opelio, Opusaug, Orangbukit, Orangutan, Orcaborealis, Ouishoebean, Oxymoron83, PRiis, Pabix, Palmleaf, Pamri, Panzuriel, Paolo.dL, Papalew, Paperboy3000, Paranoid, Pascal666, PascalMichelSI, Patriarca12, Patrick, Pattermeister, PaulGarner, Pauldavidgill, Pavel Vozenilek, Pcb21, Pdn, PeaceNT, Pedro, Pegasus1138, Penmachine, Per Honor et Gloria, Peregrine981, Persian Poet Gal, Perspective, Peruvianllama, Peter L, Pevarnj, Pgan002, Pgk, Phenz, Phgao, Philip Trueman, PhilipC, Phoenixrod, Phonemonkey, Pierre.Nakhimov, Pietdesomere, Pigman, Pilotguy, Pinethicket, Pinpoint23, Piotrus, Pippu d'Angelo, Pixel23, PizzaMargherita, Pjvpjv, Platypusmonotreme, Plkrtn, Plop, Plrk, Plumbago, Pmcm, Pne, Poindexter Propellerhead, Pol098, Pollinator, Ponder, Postmortemjapan, Prefect, Prolog, Proteus, PsyMar, Pupster21, Pursey, Pygenot, Qblik, Quasipalm, Quintote, Qwfp, Qworty, Qxz, RG2, RHSydnor, RJBurkhart, RJFJR, RJN, RaCha'ar, Rachel Pearce, Radon210, RagaBhakta, Raghuvamsha, RainbowOfLight, Ramanpotential, Randy Johnston, Ranix, Rannpháirtí anaithnid (old), Raul654, Raven4x4x, Ravenhull, Ravigateway, Ray Van De Walker, Rdsmith4, Red Director, RedWordSmith, Reedy, Relaxation, Retiono Virginian, Rettetast, Revmachine21, Revth, RexNL, Rhion, Riana, Richardrut, Richjkl, RickK, Risker, Rje, Rjstern, Rl, Rmain, Rmhermen, Robchurch, RobertG, Robertoremes, Robertvan1, RockMagnetist, Rocket71048576, RodC, RogueNinja, Roleplayer, Rolypolyman, RonGroth, Ronewolf, Rory096, Rossoxxx, RoyBoy, Royalguard11, Rsduhamel, Ruakh, Rubyrussia, Rumping, RunOrDie, RxS, Rxnd, Ryan Reich, Rydel, Rye1967, Ryry0401, Ryulong, Rzf3, SDC, SJP, SKAZNBOI, SNIyer12, SWAdair, Sagar jina, Salsb, Salvio giuliano, Sam, Sam Korn, Sampi, Samueldevadoss, Sanchom, Sandover, SandyGeorgia, Sango123, Santaduck, Sanya, Saros136, Sasquatch, Sat84, Sceptre, SchmuckyTheCat, Schnolle, Schwede66, SciAndTech, Scientific American, Scientizzle, Scigeek, Scodger4, Scohoust, ScorpO, Scott Sanchez, Sct72, Sd31415, Sean William, Seb az86556, Seddon, Selket, Sengkang, Seraphimblade, Serendipodous, Seth Ilys, Sgkay, Sgstarling, Shadowjams, ShakingSpirit, Shalmanese, Shaneblake, Shanel, Shanes, ShattaAD, Shenme, Shimeru, Shinasu, Shiva's Trident, Shizane, Shizhao, Shoessss, Sholtar, Shopping.f, Shreemurphy, Shustov, Si Gam Acèh, SidP, Signalhead, SimonP, Simonxag, Singhalawap, Sir Nicholas de Mimsy-Porpington, Sixtimes, Sizzlingsteaks, Sj, Sjakkalle, SkerHawx, SkyWalker, Skyrun, Slakr, Slash Angus, Slawojarek, SlimVirgin, Slyder, Smallverm, SmartGuy, Smartsanu, Smeagol1123, SmilesALot, Smithbrotherles, Snjolfur, Soccerproffesor, Someguy1221, Somettime, Songs, Sophia, Sordomudo11, Sottolacqua, Soumyasch, Sowelilitokiemu, SpNeo, Space man, Sparkit, Sparky the Seventh Chaos, Spartan-James, Spartian, Specialegb, Spiffy sperry, Splash, Spliffy, Spoonkymonkey, Sport7, SpuriousQ, Squrtle11, Srikeit, Steel, Stefan teplan, Stephen Compall, Stephenb, Stephenpace, Steve Zissou, SteveHopson, Stevebritgimp, Steven Weston, Steven Zhang, Stevertigo, Stinkychops, Stirling Newberry, Stochata, Stratshaw, Strikesvl, Sue Rangell, Suede, Sundar, Sunray, Superbeecat, Superm401, Sv650madness, Sweet Blue Water, Swlenz, Sylvain Mielot, SyntaxError55, Szyslak, TAMIL81, TFOK123, THF, TJeong123, TParis, TTGL, Ta bu shi da yu, Tachyon01, Tactel, Takarada, Talldave, Tanaats, Tandrasz, Tangotango, Tarafuku10, Tarquin, Tawker, Tbc2, Tbhotch, TedE, Tejastheory, Tempodivalse, Tequendamia, Terence, Teshoma, Tetsuowilliams, TexMurphy, Tez99, The Anome, The Geologist, The High Fin Sperm Whale, The Man in Question, The Obfuscator, The Peacemaker, The Rambling Man, The Shadow-Fighter, The Utahraptor, The snare, The undertow, TheBilly, TheDoctor10, TheHerbalGerbil, TheNewPhobia, TheProject, TheSeer, Theda, Theinsomniac4life, Thelониouszen, Theresa knott, Thingg, Tiddly Tom, Tifoo, Tim Q. Wells, Timetogo, Timneu22, Timothyngim, Tireoghain2, Titoxd, Titus III, Tobogganoggin, Tom harrison, Tomgally, Tonicthebrown, Tony1, Tonyle, Tonym88, Tourdeforcex, Tpbradbury, Tranletuhan, Trevor MacInnis, Triona, TrippyTaka, Trulystand700, TrumanRu, Trumpet marietta 45750, Trusilver, Try0yrt, Tttecumseh, Tupolev154, Tuxide, Tvbrichmond, Twiceuponatime, Twinsday, TwoOneTwo, UFu, UberScienceNerd, Ufundo, UkPaolo, Ukvilly, Ultratomio, Umapathy, Ummm777, UniReb, Uragomo, Ustas, Vaibhavkumarsingh, Vald, VampWillow, Vanis314, Vanished user 03, Vardion, Vc-wp, Verdadero, Verdlanco, Versageek, Veyklevar, Vibsir2, Vidhaug, Vipinhari, Viriditas, Virtualaris, Vishnuvardhan27, Visor, Vivaldi, Vivio Testarossa, Volnturista, Vrenator, Vsmith, WIKIDTW 2010, WJBscribe, WODUP, Waggers, Walton One, WarBaCoN, Warmaster, WarthogDemon, Wavelength, Wayfarer, Wayne Slam, Wayward, Webbbbbbber, Weird Bird, Wenli, Wereldburger758, Wereon, Westendgirl, Whatthefat, Where, WhisperToMe, Whitetigah, Wiki alf, Wiki wonderful, Wiki235, WikiDao, Wikipedia Admin, Willemtijssen, William Avery, William2251, Wilt, Wimt, Wingover, Wizzard2k, Wk muriithi, Wknight94, Wm, Wmahan, Wohlstrom96, WolfmanSF, Wolfsumatra, Woody, Wrkrboob, Wrp103, Wykebjs, X!, X201, X4096, Xdenizen, Xevi, Xevious, Xiahou, Xipirho, Xrharris, Xymmax, Yamamoto Ichiro, Ybbor, Yearofthedragon, YellowMonkey, Yelyos, Yomamaonfire, Yonghokim, Youdabom, Youssefsan, Ypacaraí, Yuckfoo, Yummifruitbat, Zaian, Zantastik, Zap Rowsdower, Zaphod Beeblebrox, Zemlor, Zen-master, Zero0000, ZimZalaBim, Zisky, Zntrip, Zone46, Zootsuits, Zosodada, Zro, Zsinj, Zzuuzz, Τασουλα, □□□ □□□, 4232 anonymous edits

Tsunamis in lakes *Source*: http://en.wikipedia.org/w/index.php?oldid=422220348 *Contributors*: AstroHurricane001, C4100, Drbreznjev, Epicstonemason, George Nowak, JacintaMorgan27, JamesBWatson, LorenzoB, Lowellian, NameIsRon, Schwede66, Twinsday, VernoWhitney, Xtzou, 1 anonymous edits

Risk *Source*: http://en.wikipedia.org/w/index.php?oldid=433006648 *Contributors*: -oo0(GoldTrader)0oo-, 1ForTheMoney, 4twenty42o, 927, A.Ward, Abheid, Actorstudio, AdjustShift, Ahoerstemeier, Aixroot, Al001, Alansohn, Aldaron, Alex S, Algorithme, Allanon97, Altenmann, Ancheta Wis, Andman8, Andycjp, Anon lynx, Apparition11, Arauzo, ArnoldReinhold, Avraham, BBird, Baartmns, Backvoods, Bart133, Beland, BenC7, Bhupinder.Kunwar, Bihco, Bill52270, Billy hentenaar, Bjp716, BlairZajac, Bob Burkhardt, Bonus Onus, Bovineone, Brick Thrower, BrokenSegue, Bruceporteous, Burntsauce, CALR, CDN99, COMPFUNK2, CSWarren, Caissa's DeathAngel, Calliopejen1, CambridgeBayWeather, Capricorn42, CaptainLexicon, Carax, CarolynLMM, Carrp, Caster23, Cate, Charles Matthews, Charles T. Betz, Cheapskate08, Chinsurance, Christian List, Ciphergoth, Clementina, Cobaltbluetony, Coldmember, Colignatus, Commander Keane, Condrs01, Conversion script, Cretog8, CurranH, Cutler, Cyberdog, DCstats, DFLovett, Daguero, David w carraher, Davies69, Dean Armond, Derek Balsam, Dhartung, Dialectric, Dionisiofranca, Dkeditor, Doc Quintana, DocendoDiscimus, DomCleal, DonSiano, Doobliebop, DrWorld, Drivi86, Dsp13, Duoduoduo, Dylan Lake, EPM, ERosa, Editor1962, Eeekster, Eep², Emezei, Emvee, Enchanter, Engi08, Evil Monkey, Fieldday-sunday, Fjejsing, Former user, Freddie Coster, Frederic Y Bois, Fuhghettaboutit, GRF Davos, Gaius Cornelius, Galoubet, Garion96, Geoff Leeming, Geoffr, Giftlite, Glane23, Glinos, Gogo Dodo, Gomm, Gregorford, Gsaup, Gurch, Habiibi, Hairhorn, HalJor, HalfShadow, Hayabusa future, He Who Is, Heiyuu, Helgus, Henrygb, Heron, Hgty, Hobsonlane, Hu12, Hubbardaie, Husond, Iam, Iamaav8r, Iamthesaju, Icewraithuk, Interik, Iranianson, J.delanoy, JForget, JIH3, JRR Trollkien, Jauricchio, Jaxl, Jeff3000, Jeronimo, Jerryseinfeld, Jheald, Jimmaths, Jjeeppyy, John Quiggin, Johnny Pez, Jon Lackow, Jpbowen, Jtneill, Kateshortforbob, Kenmckinley, Kered77, Kintetsubuffalo, Kku, Kpmiyapuram, Krakfly, Kuru, Kvdveer, Kwhitten, Lambiam, Larry V, Lasersniper, LcawteHuggle, LeadSongDog, Lear's Fool, Lee Daniel Crocker, Levineps, LilHelpa, Linuxlad, Lolcakeheads, Lowellian, M-banker-212, MCTales, Maashatra11, Mac, Marco Krohn, Martarius, Martinp, Mason3*, Matthew Blake, Maudonk, Max Neill, Mbc362, Mboverload, Mdgarvey, Melcombe, MementoVivere, Michael Hardy, Miller52, Mirv, Mnath, Monk Bretton, Moonriddengirl, MrOllie, MrQwag, Msngupta, My Cat inn, Myanw, Mynameisrich69, Myrvin, NHRHS2010, Neelix, Nevcao, Nikai, Nsaa, Nurg, Ohnoitsjamie, Oliverwyman, Omegapowers, Osias, Overix, OwenX, Oxymoron83, Pakoistinen, Panybour, Partha lal, Pastore Italy, Patrick, Pgan002, Pgr94, Pgreenfinch, PhilipMW, Piacereina, Pianoman23, Pilgaard, Platothefish, Pm master, Pnm, Pointergrl, R'n'B, RSStockdale, Razimantv, Rd232, Regregex, Requestion, Rescherpa, RevRagnarok, Rgvandewalker, Rhobite, RicCooper, Rich Farmbrough, Rich257, Rimini, Risk Analyst, Riversider2008, Rjwilmsi, Roelzzz, Roni38, Ronz, Ryklin, SAE1962, SDC, Sam Hocevar, Satori Son, Scalene, Scott Sanchez, SebastianHelm, Seffer, Servalo, Severa, Shoefly, SilkTork, Simesa, Simoes, Simon123, Sjforman, Sketchmoose, Snow555, SnowFire, Snowded, Snowmanradio, SocialNeuro, Sonderbro, SpeakerFTD, Spearhead, Spunch, Stemonitis, Stevenjones15, Stijn Vermeeren, Subsolar, Sugarfoot1001, Supergreg no1, Tedickey, Tenmei, Testbed, Texacali3d, The Anome, The Interior, The Thing That Should Not Be, The-dissonance-reports, TheGrappler, Thfmax, Tlroche, Tony Fox, Tonytypoon, Treisijs, Tutmaster321, Tyrol5, UninvitedCompany, Urbanette, Vald, Velho, Visual risk management, WadeLondon, Warpfactor, Wayne Slam, WaysToEscape, Wemlands, Wikiklrsc, Wikomidia, Wood Thrush, Woohookitty, Wordsmith,

Wouldyou, Wtmitchell, Wuhwuzdat, Xyzzyplugh, Yamamoto Ichiro, Yone Fernandes, Z10x, Zaggernaut, Zara1709, Zodon, Zzyzx11, 377 anonymous edits

100-year flood *Source*: http://en.wikipedia.org/w/index.php?oldid=428281650 *Contributors*: Aspects, Avraham, Bfinn, Bobzilla42, Brian0918, Brion VIBBER, Bryan Derksen, Carcharoth, ChrisKil, Darkwind, Embokias, Epbr123, Epolk, Esa 0, Gilliam, Grutness, Gwinva, Hooperbloob, Imzadi1979, J Milburn, Jaknouse, Jaksmata, Jeff R. Frengal, Kwlamb, Lightmouse, Longhair, Lova Falk, Mcwik1925, Melcombe, Merovingian, Michael A. White, Mild Bill Hiccup, MisfitToys, Ms2ger, Nick Dillinger, Pimemorizer, Plastikspork, Prikryl, Qertis, Quinn35, Robertb-dc, The Anome, The Cunctator, Thewellman, Velella, Villy, WTucker, Wik, 36 anonymous edits

Absolute probability judgement *Source*: http://en.wikipedia.org/w/index.php?oldid=413810859 *Contributors*: Bvlax2005, Fabrictramp, Ggd101, Melcombe, Pigman, RHaworth

Acceptable loss *Source*: http://en.wikipedia.org/w/index.php?oldid=393378540 *Contributors*: Akhil 0950, Aldrich Hanssen, Atlantima, Bearcat, Fleebo, Ged UK, Malcolma, Sumsum2010, Woohookitty

Accident-proneness *Source*: http://en.wikipedia.org/w/index.php?oldid=417513417 *Contributors*: 1ForTheMoney, Barbara Shack, Biscuittin, CambridgeBayWeather, Ccacsmss, Diannaa, Doczilla, GregorB, Keilana, LIC Habeeb, Mattisse, PizzaBox, Rich Farmbrough, Sxhpb, The Anome, The Man in Question, West.andrew.g, WhatamIdoing, Wikiain, 26 anonymous edits

Actuary *Source*: http://en.wikipedia.org/w/index.php?oldid=432828819 *Contributors*: (Biatch), 16@r, 2over0, A.bianchini1981, A.j.g.cairns, AKTUER, Acplib, Actreal, Actuarial disco boy, ActuarialFellow, Actuaryclub, Ahmed.pervez, Amitgk, Andy yang, Anlace, Antandrus, AppleJuggler, Artoasis, Ashvidia, Astator, Asyndeton, Avekashgupta, Avraham, Azimout, BC Graham, BD2412, Bakemaster, Barnabypage, Barneca, Bensin, Bernd in Japan, Bobbeuerlein, Bobmack89x, Booyabazooka, Bowl of vindaloo, Brighterorange, Brookie, Bruceporteous, Buchanan-Hermit, CQJ, Caltas, Careercornerstone, Casternpollux, Catchpole, Causa sui, Cedars, Cedrus-Libani, Charles Matthews, Chesterg, Chivista, Chris the speller, Cntras, Comma55, Correogsk, Crystallina, DARTH SIDIOUS 2, DMacks, DVD R W, Daniel Case, David Shay, Deetdeet, Denisarona, Denkertje, Dfarmer, Dmr2, Dolphin51, Dpv, Dudegalea, Dwayne, EamonnPKeane, EdH, Edge3, Edward, Eeekster, El Zoof, Emurphy42, Enchanter, Epeefleche, Erebus555, Ergative rlt, Excirial, FRValkenburg, Feeanor, Femto, Feureau, Fggsgfdsfrv, Finecactuary, Finn-Zoltan, Fjmarais, FlipCockle, Gadfium, Gadget850, Gaius Cornelius, Galen100, Gary King, Giftlite, Girly girl 14, Gobonobo, Gofastfast, GreenislandM, Greenocean1, Harryboyles, Hedgeh0g, Hemmingsen, Hmains, Horselover Frost, Hsep88, II MusLiM HyBRiD II, Icey, ImperfectlyInformed, Info4all, It Is Me Here, Ixfd64, JIW, Jafcbs, JamesBWatson, JamieGillis, Jared Hunt, Javary, Jeff Silvers, Jeffthe3rd, Jivecat, Jkeene, Jlang, John wesley, John.kraemer, JohnCD, Jonverve, JordanSamuels, Josephbrophy, Josh4987, Joshuamaggid, Kazvorpal, Koristka, Kuru, Ladril, LaidOff, Lambolouie, Langhorner, Lightmouse, Lourdescenteno, Luka Krstulović, Lynne Jorgensen, MALLUS, MDBentley, MECU, MER-C, Macheide, Malik Shabazz, Malo, Manop, MarkS, Markus Kuhn, Mathstat, MatthewMain, Mav, Michael Hardy, Michaelrccurtis, MikeTheActuary, MisfitToys, Mohitshah12345, Moonlight Mile, Moverton, Mulaohu, Mygangdu, NIMark, NSH001, NawlinWiki, Netoholic, Nikai, Nishantsah, Novacatz, Nricardo, Nscheffey, NuclearWarfare, Oden, Olivier, Olivierchaussavoine, Omicronpersei8, Orange Suede Sofa, OverInsured, Oxymoron83, PTSE, Pacoworld, Pasajero, Peterxyz, Pinethicket, PoeticVerse, Pol098, Promethean, Quarl, RATM4EVER, RFerreira, Raul654, Redquark, Redrosie, Remurmur, Requestion, RexNL, Reywas92, Rich Farmbrough, Rick S. Calcutta, Rio 001, Rjwilmsi, RobertG, Romanm, SYSS Mouse, Sal196, SandyGeorgia, Sanjiv swarup, Schmock, Sebesta, Sgeureka, Shawnc, Signor Eclectic, SimonP, Slawojarek, Sobaka, Someones life, Spanish landlord, Sphilbrick, Spiritia, Starfallen, Staxringold, Stigmj, Sugarfoot1001, Sygsyg, Systemfan33, TBrsa, Tanyia, Tayana, Tbhotch, Tedgeisel, The wub, TheActuary, TheGerm, TheJC, TheObtuseAngleOfDoom, ThirteenthGreg, Timo Honkasalo, Toddst1, Treisijs, Uncle Dick, Universalcosmos, Unused0015, Usb10, Utopial, Uxejn, VerballyInsane, Victoria1510, WRK, Weiheong, Wikifia, Wikiwikiusername, Willpeavy, Wizardman, Wpedzich, Zeus1233, Zoso Jade, Zubenzenubi, 497 anonymous edits

ALARP *Source*: http://en.wikipedia.org/w/index.php?oldid=420469228 *Contributors*: A bit iffy, Afaber012, Andycjp, Blackhawktch, Dwlegg, Forteblast, Gaius Cornelius, Gaz Man, Gtk123, JRI, JoergenB, JustAGal, MatthewDBA, MinimanDragon32, Poupoune5, SimonP, The Anome, 26 anonymous edits

APSYS *Source*: http://en.wikipedia.org/w/index.php?oldid=415863655 *Contributors*: AvicAWB, Jameswraitih, 12 anonymous edits

ATHEANA *Source*: http://en.wikipedia.org/w/index.php?oldid=413810074 *Contributors*: Fabrictramp, Ggd101, J04n, Liveboy, Michael Hardy, Pdeitiker, Pigman, RHaworth, Stijndon, Tavix, Woohookitty, 2 anonymous edits

Ballpark model *Source*: http://en.wikipedia.org/w/index.php?oldid=412767546 *Contributors*: Aldrich Hanssen, Bearsaresoft, John Quiggin, KathrynLybarger

Biosafety *Source*: http://en.wikipedia.org/w/index.php?oldid=422562675 *Contributors*: 8.218, Anthere, ArnoldReinhold, Beetstra, Dogwood123, Egomaniac, G. Völcker, Guanaco, JRR Trollkien, Johntex, Just Another Dan, Koswac, Leyo, MisterHand, NadiaLala, Nicmila, Optakeover, Pollinosisss, Rcaravana, Rhobite, Sjjupadhyay, Tevildo, Walden, Wallet, Zigger, Zundark, 40 anonymous edits

Biosafety Clearing-House *Source*: http://en.wikipedia.org/w/index.php?oldid=430224331 *Contributors*: Edward, Good Olfactory, Kirsty, LinguistAtLarge, Wavelength, 1 anonymous edits

Cartagena Protocol on Biosafety *Source*: http://en.wikipedia.org/w/index.php?oldid=417308119 *Contributors*: Anthere, ArnoldReinhold, Bolivian Unicyclist, Dar-Ape, Dia^, Dr Oldekop, Drilnoth, Droll, ESkog, Ediacara, Ekotkie, Emperorbma, GB fan, Good Olfactory, Graham87, Johntex, Kirsty, Kofiannansrevenge, Light current, MMc, Marcelcorso, Msh210, NSR, Nicholas Cimini, Nicmila, Pixeltoo, Proofreader, Rhobite, Shadowpsi, Shell Kinney, Sjjupadhyay, Sloman, Sumivec, 22 anonymous edits

Catastrophe modeling *Source*: http://en.wikipedia.org/w/index.php?oldid=420395459 *Contributors*: Amatulic, Anniepoo, AvicAWB, Avraham, Belovedfreak, Bobblehead, CRGreathouse, Cmdrjameson, EQECAT, Glpita, Gogo Dodo, GraemeL, Hu12, ISCM, JIW, Johnread777, Kilmer-san, Koavf, Minatsu, Mminter73, MorgothX, Nick Number, PeterFV, Pgbalachan, Pinkville, Ravensburg13, Rjwilmsi, Ronz, Rxnd, SDC, Samw, SimonPBiggs, Smalljim, Spencerk, Testbed, TheTrucker100, 82 anonymous edits

Certainty effect *Source*: http://en.wikipedia.org/w/index.php?oldid=426764669 *Contributors*: Jodyng888, Malcolmxl5, 2 anonymous edits

Consumer's risk *Source*: http://en.wikipedia.org/w/index.php?oldid=386132341 *Contributors*: Bearcat, Bearian, Djmckee1, EoGuy, Fl, Hoop6464, Jeepday, Mattg82, Pekaje, Uncle G, Valrith, Woohookitty, Xezbeth, 1 anonymous edits

Cover your ass *Source*: http://en.wikipedia.org/w/index.php?oldid=414717148 *Contributors*: Alecclews, Antoin, Badagnani, Bjalring, Captain-tucker, ChriKo, Circeus, Cybercobra, Cyborgxxi, Doulos Christos, Graham87, Jerry Story, JimVC3, Josh3736, Korg, Legis, LegitimateAndEvenCompelling, Longhair, Luk, Medinoc, NawlinWiki, NeonMerlin, Nescio, Phoenixrod, Private Butcher, Rjanag, Rogerborg, Rossami, Sam Korn, Schutz, Scriberius, StaticGull, Steevven1, Surv1v4l1st, Tim1357, Utcursch, Wikip rhyre, Yworo, 33 anonymous edits

CREAM *Source*: http://en.wikipedia.org/w/index.php?oldid=406790219 *Contributors*: BBonds, Drilnoth, Dspdude, Ggd101, Ioeth, Nurg, Skippy le Grand Gourou, 2 anonymous edits

Cultural cognition *Source*: http://en.wikipedia.org/w/index.php?oldid=430300451 *Contributors*: Db wikipedia id, Eiland, Gary King, JaGa, Leszek Jańczuk, Lightsin, Likebirds, Mboverload, 4 anonymous edits

Cultural Theory of risk *Source*: http://en.wikipedia.org/w/index.php?oldid=363020873 *Contributors*: Acsumama, Andreas Philopater, Beeswaxcandle, JaGa, Johnpdeever, Likebirds, Magnusyoung, Meika, Michael Hardy, Michael Rogers, Robofish, Suvinaib, Testbed, Triarchy, 9 anonymous edits

Decision theory *Source*: http://en.wikipedia.org/w/index.php?oldid=430437412 *Contributors*: 3mta3, 7&6=thirteen, Adoniscik, Ados, Alan Dawrst, Alexwl, Andeggs, AndriusKulikauskas, Angela, Anonyhole, Arthur Rubin, Bennose, BillieBC, Billjefferys, Bjoram11@yahoo.co.in, BlaiseFEgan, Bordley, Bracton, CRGreathouse, Cacophony, Canadaduane, ChangChienFu, ChristophDemmer, ComputerGeezer, Cretog8, Curiousli, D6, DRE, Dandv, David Eppstein, Dcljr, DimaDorfman, DoubleBlue, Duoduoduo, Esdaniel, Fennec, Finn Krogstad, Frymaster, Gandalf61, Giac, Giftlite, Gis72, Glumundrung, GoingBatty, Gomm, Goochelaar, Gurchzilla, Gustronico, Hactuary, Helgus, Hubbardaie, INic, Inforom, Ixfd64, J04n, JYOuyang, Jackdavinci, Jamelan, Jeff3000, Jheald, Jimmaths, Jiuguang Wang, Jmath666, John Quiggin, Jon Awbrey, Jwdietrich2, KSchutte, Karada, KenKendall, Kiefer.Wolfowitz, Kpmiyapuram, Kzollman, LeadSongDog, Lucidish, Magmi, Mandarax, Matdrodes, Matt.voroney, Mdd, Melcombe, Michael Hardy, Michael Slone, Miskin, Mmmarilyn, Nbarth, Neelix, NeoJustin, Nesbit, NewEconomist, NoychoH, Nrlsouza, Ohnoitsjamie, Orion88, Othercriteria, Pa68, Paulscrawl, Pbech, Phiwum, Phronetic, Posiebers, RDBrown, RJBurkhart, RJBurkhart3, Rd232, Regregex, Rich Farmbrough, RichardF, Rjwilmsi, Rlsheehan, Robinh, Rodii, Seglea, Shoefly, Slach, Smellyfarts001, Snoyes, Stephensuleeman, Stw, Tassedethe, Taxman, Terra Novus, Tesseract2, Themepark, Themusicgod1, Think Fast, Thomasmeeks, Trade2tradewell, Trialsanderrors, Twins Too!, U89djt, Verne Equinox, Volunteer Marek, WayneToms, WikiWikiWilson, Wile E. Heresiarch, Winterfors, Xyzzyplugh, Zvika, 126 anonymous edits

Digital Repository Audit Method Based on Risk Assessment *Source*: http://en.wikipedia.org/w/index.php?oldid=431658435 *Contributors*: Dancter, Felix Folio Secundus, Jpbowen, Rjwilmsi, SeamusRoss, 8 anonymous edits

Disappointment *Source*: http://en.wikipedia.org/w/index.php?oldid=431069205 *Contributors*: Belovedfreak, BorgQueen, Carabinieri, Ciphers, Daniel2424, EivindJ, GRBerry, Gujuguy, Hadseys, J04n, Justin W Smith, Lemmey, Lightmouse, Magshim, ManiacKilla, Mattisse, Mlwmarsha, Moonriddengirl, Neelix, OnBeyondZebrax, Puffin, Quiddity, RDBrown, Radicalross, Riffic, Rjwilmsi, Staloysius, Stifle, Struthious Bandersnatch, The Thing That Should Not Be, Wavelength, What a rip off Super Bowl 2010, Wragge, Xme, 口口 口口 口口口, 50 anonymous edits

Disneyland model *Source*: http://en.wikipedia.org/w/index.php?oldid=385301028 *Contributors*: Aldrich Hanssen, John Quiggin, PamD, Pokeronskis, Rhebus, 1 anonymous edits

Bill Durodié *Source*: http://en.wikipedia.org/w/index.php?oldid=419539671 *Contributors*: 2over0, AKGhetto, Chasnor15, Durodie, Edward, Jaraalbe, Johnpacklambert, RichardVeryard, RogDel, Simonross99, Studerby, Timrollpickering, Zoicon5, 9 anonymous edits

Economics of security *Source*: http://en.wikipedia.org/w/index.php?oldid=421642359 *Contributors*: Ali K, Beanary, DanielPharos, Editor2020, Elonka, Elwyn.benson, John Quiggin, JonHarder, Ljean, Michael Hardy, MrOllie, Nakedjuice, Neelix, Pansearch, Sensenmann, Tassedethe, TastyPoutine, 19 anonymous edits

Emergency *Source*: http://en.wikipedia.org/w/index.php?oldid=430041398 *Contributors*: 23skidoo, Alansohn, Alex756, Arun, Belovedfreak, Berendale1, Bináris, CDN99, CWenger, Cameron Dewe, Can't sleep, clown will eat me, Cometstyles, DXRAW, David Shankbone, Dep. Garcia, Djegan, Djm1279, Dlyons493, Drdrei, Duffman, Dweller, Eclecticology, Evil saltine, Fr00gi, Geniac, Gilliam, Globalrightpath, Heyyoguy123, Ianblair23, Interiot, Jacob.jose, Jhfireboy, JohnCD, Joseph 098, Kmote, L Kensington, Labfab, Leyo, LilyKitty, Lobstertoes, Lugnuts, Mahanga, Mediatheconflict, Mhym, Minerva, Neelix, Nemesis90, Neum, Neutrality, Nonerds10, Nopetro, Orzetto, Owain.davies, Paiamshadi, Pamri, Paul Erik, QuartierLatin1968, Quiddity, R'n'B, RememberMe?, Reviewgirlerika, Rfc1394, Riddley, Rjwilmsi, Rror, Seabhcan, Shadowjams, Shoessss, SimonP, Skinny McGee, Sortior, Stultiwikia, SuperHamster, The Anome, The Letter J, The Transhumanist, Wasell, WayKurat, Wikiloop, Wikiwonderwomanwashere, Woohookitty, Yakudza, Yidisheryid, ZayZayEM, 94 anonymous edits

Fixes that fail *Source*: http://en.wikipedia.org/w/index.php?oldid=408729488 *Contributors*: Chris the speller, Svarnyp

Flood risk assessment *Source*: http://en.wikipedia.org/w/index.php?oldid=422179148 *Contributors*: Alan Liefting, Bodaonline, CaribDigita, Davidnporter, Dustmagic, Dycedarg, Flowanda, Francescocorsi, Giraffedata, Hmains, Lizstephens, Melcombe, Mmedo, Mortense, Paddy158, RichardVeryard, Spuddery, TFOWR, Velella, 27 anonymous edits

Functional Safety *Source*: http://en.wikipedia.org/w/index.php?oldid=424312149 *Contributors*: Amdo9902, Chris the speller, Cusimanoja, DVdm, Dheenadhayalan, Keith D, Ladybetty, MrOllie, Mrausand, Ree0051, SUG-INFO, UnbiasedHistory, Wolfch, 29 anonymous edits

Global Earthquake Model *Source*: http://en.wikipedia.org/w/index.php?oldid=404395590 *Contributors*: Researcher17int, Welsh, Winterst, 7 anonymous edits

GRCM *Source*: http://en.wikipedia.org/w/index.php?oldid=432110547 *Contributors*: Angus Lepper, Bwpach, Canis Lupus, Corp Vision, Gil Gamesh, ICameToSee, Rjwilmsi, Woohookitty

Hazard *Source*: http://en.wikipedia.org/w/index.php?oldid=430688864 *Contributors*: 10metreh, 16@r, ARUNKUMAR P.R, Alaniaris, Andrijko Z., BRG, BTH, Barneca, Beland, Bongwarrior, Buddy23Lee, Carcharoth, Cedars, ChillDeity, Chris Mason, Chris the speller, Chuckgrigsby, DARTH SIDIOUS 2, DandyDan2007, David Johnson, Deltaker, Drphilharmonic, E Wing, Edgar181, Elpezmuerto, Escherichia coli, Essexmutant, Ftgubyui byu8ib7yuoi9, Gilgamesh, Guitargodharry, Gurch, Hazard2, Hendrecoed, Hermitstudy, Hotpockets1234, Infarom, Insanity Incarnate, Iridescent, J.delanoy, JHunterJ, Jakg, Jauhienij, JimVC3, Joanjoc, Johnbibby, Ka Faraq Gatri, Kingpin13, L Kensington, L33tsrus, LOL, Lanternix, Lateg, Light current, LilHelpa, Luna Santin, Madhero88, Malcolm Farmer, Matthew Yeager, MattieTK, Meegs, Minimac, NuclearFunk, Owain.davies, Oxymoron83, Patrick, Peak, Peoplesyak, Piano non troppo, Pzavon, Qxz, R'n'B, Raul654, Rich Farmbrough, Rodhullandemu, Scott Sanchez, Snowolf, SoWhy, Stwalkerster, Tabletop, Template namespace initialisation script, Tristanb, Ulric1313, Vuo, W!B:, Wavy G, WhiteCrane, WikipedianYknOK, Ylem, □□ □ □□□ □□ □, 132 anonymous edits

Health effects of sun exposure *Source*: http://en.wikipedia.org/w/index.php?oldid=429806875 *Contributors*: 1ForTheMoney, Acalamari, Bigger digger, Cassowary, Chris Capoccia, Chrisminter, Connormah, Cybercobra, Emezei, Gilderien, Gobonobo, Hordaland, Jrennie, Julesd, LilHelpa, Miyagawa, My Core Competency is Competency, Nightsmaiden, Nono64, Pro crast in a tor, Quantumor, R0uge, Rjwilmsi, ShelfSkewed, The Anome, Thumperward, 83 anonymous edits

High reliability organization *Source*: http://en.wikipedia.org/w/index.php?oldid=314755601 *Contributors*: Appleseed, David Christenson, DoorsAjar, JamesDouglasOrton, Johnabrams, Jpbowen, Kappa, Prainog, Skittleys, Tabletop, Trialsanderrors, Zigger, 9 anonymous edits

Human cognitive reliability correlation *Source*: http://en.wikipedia.org/w/index.php?oldid=364732663 *Contributors*: EagleFan, Ggd101, HaeB, RHaworth, Rich Farmbrough, Wwoods, 1 anonymous edits

Human error assessment and reduction technique *Source*: http://en.wikipedia.org/w/index.php?oldid=404675456 *Contributors*: 100110100, Anna Lincoln, Diego Moya, Ggd101, Me Three, RHaworth, Redconfetti, 11 anonymous edits

Human reliability *Source*: http://en.wikipedia.org/w/index.php?oldid=431687733 *Contributors*: Alfpooh, AndrewHowse, Apoc2400, Ballin123!, BazookaJoe, Carlos Porto, Condem, DCDuring, Doodoobutter, Duke Ganote, EamonnPKeane, Gary King, Gavrilov, Ggd101, Grutness, Holek, Hollnagel, Huuhaa, JaGa, Jugendstil, Kku, Kroede, Lordjohan, LouScheffer, Mausy5043, Mdd, MeltBanana, Michael Hardy, MistyMorn, Mj076c, MoodyGroove, Nasnema, NearlyNormal, Nurg, Paranomia, PetterEkhem, Phila 033, Pmjones, Rich Farmbrough, Rjwilmsi, Spalding, Timautrey, Uncle G, Versageek, Wavelength, Xanzzibar, Zundark, 40 anonymous edits

Influence diagrams approach *Source*: http://en.wikipedia.org/w/index.php?oldid=348724529 *Contributors*: Cybercobra, D6, Ggd101, RHaworth, WereSpielChequers

InfoSTEP *Source*: http://en.wikipedia.org/w/index.php?oldid=422076663 *Contributors*: Bhargav.mantha, Cander0000, Colonies Chris, CommonsDelinker, Dlrohrer2003, Fabrictramp, Kku, Martarius, Mean as custard, Muhandes, Pahari Sahib, R'n'B, Scoty6776, Tamariki, VamsiSasidhar, Woohookitty, ∆, 10 anonymous edits

Inherent risk (accounting) *Source*: http://en.wikipedia.org/w/index.php?oldid=430948998 *Contributors*: AccZA, Cburge, Chessy999, Dennis Bratland, Dlrohrer2003, Fraudy, Grafen, JLTurner71, R'n'B, 8 anonymous edits

Insurable risk *Source*: http://en.wikipedia.org/w/index.php?oldid=392104835 *Contributors*: ArnoldReinhold, Avraham, B. Wolterding, Bluemoose, Dozen, Letterwing, Mdwyld, Pearle, Shoefly, THEN WHO WAS PHONE?, Taxman, Timc, 6 anonymous edits

International Risk Governance Council *Source*: http://en.wikipedia.org/w/index.php?oldid=430982744 *Contributors*: ArnoldReinhold, Arthur Rubin, Chrisbunting, GregRobson, IRGC, Jerryseinfeld, Lisatwo, Rich257, 2 anonymous edits

ITGC *Source*: http://en.wikipedia.org/w/index.php?oldid=417748919 *Contributors*: Fabrictramp, Kevinmon, Music Sorter, Pauldemoel, RHaworth, Sadads, Vashtihorvat, 2 anonymous edits

Journal of Contingencies and Crisis Management *Source*: http://en.wikipedia.org/w/index.php?oldid=324613220 *Contributors*: Crusio, Diamondspill, FlowmasterBB, Livefornow34, Non-dropframe, Politicflyer

Knightian uncertainty *Source*: http://en.wikipedia.org/w/index.php?oldid=430262766 *Contributors*: Bluemoose, Brighterorange, Gary King, John Quiggin, Kjetil1001, Maurreen, Melcombe, Michael Hardy, Nbarth, Pearle, Qwfp, Rl, Thomasmeeks, 8 anonymous edits

Manufactured risk *Source*: http://en.wikipedia.org/w/index.php?oldid=408324232 *Contributors*: Dravecky, GregorB, Katy-Anne, Malcolma, Mcfly85, Robofish, Samw, Uncle G, 2 anonymous edits

Meteorological intelligence *Source*: http://en.wikipedia.org/w/index.php?oldid=315887360 *Contributors*: LilHelpa, Rich Farmbrough, Wxhat1, 15 anonymous edits

Micromort *Source*: http://en.wikipedia.org/w/index.php?oldid=423420769 *Contributors*: 3mta3, Aa42john, Bearcat, BrotherE, CBM, CecilPL, Drf5n, EgonWillighagen, Ferdiaob, Goethean, Hairy Dude, Janke, JavaTenor, Jeodesic, John Broughton, MartinPoulter, Maurice Carbonaro, Michael Hardy, NVar, Nick Levine, NuageBleu, PegArmPaul, Pokipsy76, Pro crast in a tor, Rjwilmsi, Rothorpe, Somersetlevels, Starfallen, Stpasha, Tony Sidaway, Twirligig, Weregerbil, Widefox, Zebediah49, 26 anonymous edits

Moral hazard *Source*: http://en.wikipedia.org/w/index.php?oldid=431102258 *Contributors*: 2020Speculator, Afa86, Aiko, Airphloo, Alex1011, Anber, Andycjp, Armeria, Arnyg1, Ary29, Avicennasis, Bellemichelle, Bender235, Bethipedia, BigK HeX, Bracton, CRGreathouse, Calabraxthis, Cameronbeheshti, Camiolo, Caravaca, Carlb, Cburnett, ChýnaDragön, Ciphergoth, Ckatz, Cojoco, Cretog8, Cumulus Clouds, David Eppstein, Dinomite, Dthomsen8, Edward Z. Yang, Ehn, Elockid, Everything counts, Farcaster, Financestudent, Fshrode, Gabefarkas, Glen, GodSaysNoMore, Gregalton, GregorB, GypsyBanksters, HFM, Hadal, Halgin, Hires an editor, Hmains, Ihcoyc, IlluminatiX, ImperfectlyInformed, InnerSpacePilot, Isnow, James A. Donald, Jas The Bass, Jdevine, Jkatzen, John Broughton, John Quiggin, JohnDoe0007, Johnuniq, Jokebox13, Jsavit, Kappa, Karada, Kelson, Korvus, Kwharris, Lacrimosus, Lambiam, Lawrencekhoo, Leibniz, Lotje, Lowellian, Magellan nh, MalevolentParasiticRat-LikeBanksters, MarceloB, Marudubshinki, Mc6809e, Meiguoren16, Miss Madeline, Mitch Ames, Mlittman, Mmortal03, MoraSique, Motmahp, Mr Moribund, Mr magoo, MrDarcy, MrOllie, Mullibok, Mushroom, Nick Number, Nick2588, OilyChernobyl, Or79, OrganLeroy, Ot, Pakaran, Paul Bonneau, Pax:Vobiscum, Peligro, Pgreenfinch, PhilipR, Pjpark, Pseudo-Richard, PtAuAg, Rast, Ravensfire, Rayguest, Redraiders203, Remember, Rememberway, RepublicanJacobite, RichardVeryard, Rinconsoleao, Rjwilmsi, Rvladams, SCFilm29, Schol-R-LEA, Scking73, Sfmammamia, Shippy Underwood, Sidewinder1, SimonP, Smithamurali, Smyth, Syd1435, Taxman, Texnician, ThaddeusB, Thelb4, Tim Starling, TimOertel, Tmh, TomPurdue, Twerges, UnDegree, WatchAndObserve, WeedOutWanderingBanksters, Werdsters, Will Beback, Wilvos91, Wizardman, Worrydream, Wtmitchell, Xprime, Zaak, 211 anonymous edits

National Risk Register *Source*: http://en.wikipedia.org/w/index.php?oldid=246328543 *Contributors*: The Anome, TreasuryTag

NIBHV *Source*: http://en.wikipedia.org/w/index.php?oldid=422863638 *Contributors*: Deepraj, Laeto, Pegship, Rxnd, 1 anonymous edits

Operational risk *Source*: http://en.wikipedia.org/w/index.php?oldid=426009280 *Contributors*: A.Ward, Ahoerstemeier, Armanaziz, ArnoldReinhold, Bellenion, Bunnyhop11, CarrieCalder, ChrisCork, Colonies Chris, Corp Vision, Ctbolt, Culmensis, Dancter, Daniel Dickman, Dmccreary, DomCleal, Esperry, Ginsengbomb, Hedgefundoprisk, Hu12, Irevient, IvanLanin, Jaccowiki, Jen Svensson, Jerryseinfeld, Kuru, LARS, Leirith, Louizehh, Luk, Mennonot, Mpurdy, N2e, Nsaa, Nshuks7, Pnm, Prayukth, RMAhq, Rani silveroak, Rbaker22, Rickycds, Riskbooks, Storm Rider, Taxman, Themfromspace, Tnagelberg, Vfp15, WAvegetarian, Woohookitty, 100 anonymous edits

Outrage factor *Source*: http://en.wikipedia.org/w/index.php?oldid=324535632 *Contributors*: Jnestorius, Rodw

Postcautionary principle *Source*: http://en.wikipedia.org/w/index.php?oldid=422561493 *Contributors*: Evb-wiki, Flex, Kaihsu, Uttaranchal, Wavelength, 9 anonymous edits

Precautionary principle *Source*: http://en.wikipedia.org/w/index.php?oldid=430692130 *Contributors*: "alyosha", A.K.a., AT2663, Aavrakot, Account3915, Ajkr925, Alai, Alfio, Angelbo, Anlace, Anthere, Apathos, Apoc2400, AppleJuggler, Argon233, Argyriou, Arnejohs, ArnoldReinhold, Arnoutf, Arodb, Arthena, Arthur Rubin, Astudent, B4hand, Batmanand, Bbold, Bcasterline, Beherbert, Behun, Ben Harris-Roxas, Bhuston, Bobdobbs1723, Bogdangivaus, Bookandcoffee, Boud, Brownpau, Bryan Derksen, Bsimmons666, Carcharoth, Chaser, Chester Markel, Chris Henniker, Ckatz, Closedmouth, Colonies Chris, Common Man, Corixidae, Crasch, DDima, DanaJayne, Danelosis, Dark Mage, Dartelaar, David Levy, DerekMorr, Digenti, Dj Capricorn, Dmatisoff, Drbreznjev, Dtremenak, Dunsandel, Dysmorodrepanis, Dzsi, Eastlaw, Ed Poor, Eiland, Eloquence, Emcee, Father Goose, Fauncet, Flex, FrankTobia, Freakofnurture, GangofOne, Getf*cked, Gonzeaux, Graham87, Guanaco, Hbent, Heron, Hu12, Infineede, Informed counsel, JRR Trollkien, Japan-man, Jimjamjak, Johnfos, Jon Nevill, Jorfer, Jrtayloriv, Juanita09, Kaihsu, Kazvorpal, Knappster, Kravietz, Krueschan, Lee Daniel Crocker, Mahlum, Mailer diablo, Maurice Carbonaro, Metamagician3000, Mgreenbe, Michael Hardy, Mietchen, Miguelaznar, Mike Treder, Modulatum, Mosquitopsu, Mringgaard, NeonMerlin, Neutrality, Nijhofrene, Nikai, No Guru, Nopetro, Ohnoitsjamie, PWhittle, Palfrey, Parmaestro, Paul Bonneau, Pdelong, Pearle, Pensatrice, Pgreenfinch, PhilHibbs, PhilMacD, Pince Nez, Pnprice, Polly, Populus, Prospect77, Punchi, Pvednes, RDBrown, Ralgara, Raymondwinn, Rd232, Reblf, Reedy, Rich Farmbrough, Richard001, Ricklaman, Ricky81682, Rmauger, Rmhermen, Rob G Weemhoff, Robert Merkel, Rosie.cooney, Sam Hocevar, Samuel Erau, Sardanaphalus, Sasoriza, Scientific29, Sgsg, Skier Dude, Snowolf, Snoyes, Someoneisatthedoor, Spiffy sperry, Sponge, Srleffler, StN, Staalmannen, Tarotcards, Thadius856AWB, The Anome, The Baroness of Morden, Tobias Schmidbauer, Tralala, Tresckow, Ttguy, Unknown, Uttaranchal, Vladimir.frolov, Vortexrealm, WRK, Wavelength, Westendgirl, WhatamIdoing, WhyBeNormal, Wickethewok, Wik, Wild Pansy, Winged Cat, Wknight94, Woffie, Wolfkeeper, Woohookitty, XP1, Ynhockey, °¡°, 210 anonymous edits

Prudent avoidance principle *Source*: http://en.wikipedia.org/w/index.php?oldid=390293120 *Contributors*: Daykart, Devourer09, Dual Freq, EALacey, Emersoni, Jaraalbe, ObsidianOrder, 1 anonymous edits

Pseudocertainty effect *Source*: http://en.wikipedia.org/w/index.php?oldid=427215162 *Contributors*: Aaron Kauppi, Bluemoose, Charles Matthews, Jodyng888, Loudsox, Mattisse, Maurreen, Mostargue, RichardF, Rjwilmsi, Smmurphy, The Anome, 7 anonymous edits

Residual risk *Source*: http://en.wikipedia.org/w/index.php?oldid=333198700 *Contributors*: Bob Castle, Geniac, Kittell, MER-C, Marilyn.hanson, RJHall, SAE1962, Smalltalkman, Timothy Cooper, 13 anonymous edits

Risk analysis (engineering) *Source*: http://en.wikipedia.org/w/index.php?oldid=403118788 *Contributors*: Beland, Carcharoth, Cheapskate08, Dolly1313, EdBever, Ghaag, Jhafner1, Jkhcanoe, John Quiggin, JohnTauxe, Jon186, Jorgewiki, Kku, Krakfly, Melcombe, Metosa, Mhenry@virginia.edu, Nelson50, Neurolysis, Pastore Italy, Pm master, Rl, Rwendland, SebastianHelm, Sfmammamia, Srich32977, Srleffler, Tmonzenet, Uthbrian, Versageek, Walter Görlitz, Wikimaguire, 30 anonymous edits

Risk aversion *Source*: http://en.wikipedia.org/w/index.php?oldid=428502891 *Contributors*: Abdel Hameed Nawar, ArnoldReinhold, Ask123, Avraham, Blaxthos, Bombshell, Brossow, Btyner, C960657, CRGreathouse, Calmarc, Captain economics, Charles Matthews, Chris814, Codetiger, Cretog8, Dcgdeakin, Der gestiefelte kater, Doczilla, DrDeke, Dreftymac, Dreispt, Duoduoduo, Ehrenkater, Engi08, EnumaElish, Galaxiaad, Holon67, Hq3473, Inhumandecency, Isomorphic, IstvanWolf, J heisenberg, Jlpinar83, John Quiggin, Joy, Karada, Kpmiyapuram, Landroni, Lawrencekhoo, Leolaursen, Marknoel, Mattisse, Michael Hardy, Mindmatrix, Nesbit, Netsumdisc, Outriggr, Patrick, Paulck, Pearle, Pete.Hurd, Petrus, Pgreenfinch, Qniemiec, Quiddity, Rdls01, Rieger, Rinconsoleao, Rixs, Rjwilmsi, Salix alba, Samw, Shae, SimonP, Sugarfoot1001, Tobacman, Toh, Wikifmri, Woohookitty, 112 anonymous edits

Risk breakdown structure *Source*: http://en.wikipedia.org/w/index.php?oldid=422077594 *Contributors*: A ataol, Colonies Chris, D6, Fabrictramp, Goodwin816, Katharineamy, Lysy, Malcolma, Mmingoia, PamD, Paulmnguyen, PigFlu Oink, Rich Farmbrough, Skysmith, Ukexpat, Woohookitty, 5 anonymous edits

Risk factor *Source*: http://en.wikipedia.org/w/index.php?oldid=431052150 *Contributors*: Alansohn, Camw, Col tom, Colorado Jeff, DocWatson42, Ed g2s, Faigl.ladislav, Guptan99, Hazard-SJ, Imoen, Jagged 85, Jmarchn, Jxb311, Karl-Henner, Lars Washington, Lomis, Mac, McSly, Melcombe, Mikael Häggström, Neutrality, Osnimf, Pabloes, Qwfp, Smmurphy, Spcase, Sundin1001, Syncategoremata, Taw5000, ThanksForTheFish, Theda, Wayne Slam, WhatamIdoing, Zigger, Zigomer trubahin, Zodon, 口 田 口 口口口, 14 anonymous edits

Risk Management Programme *Source*: http://en.wikipedia.org/w/index.php?oldid=427425845 *Contributors*: Charnwood, Dali1010, Into The Fray, Versageek, 4 anonymous edits

Risk neutral *Source*: http://en.wikipedia.org/w/index.php?oldid=425298118 *Contributors*: Ahoerstemeier, Alsocal, Arsenikk, Bluemoose, Charles Matthews, ClaimJumperBob, Dosai, Duoduoduo, Dupz, Joy, Maurreen, Michael Snow, Mike Storm, Outriggr, Pearle, Personman, Roadrunner, Severo, Tabletop, Tristanreid, Vald, Wongm, Zeycus, Zzuuzz, 15 anonymous edits

Risk perception *Source*: http://en.wikipedia.org/w/index.php?oldid=419437767 *Contributors*: Aboutmovies, Acsumama, Alan Liefting, Andycjp, Arnoutf, Bobblehead, Brainhell, CALR, Chowpj, Decstop, Fnurke, Frankie816, Gary Cziko, HG, Jvaf26, Katach, Melcombe, Michael Hardy, NameIsRon, Optichan, P4k, Requestion, Rousea1224, Testbed, Twodanish, 38 anonymous edits

Risk society *Source*: http://en.wikipedia.org/w/index.php?oldid=427553552 *Contributors*: Amikeco, Binary TSO, Blathnaid, Brighterorange, Christopher Kraus, David Levy, Eiland, Garion96, Ginsengbomb, Gregbard, Hchc2009, Ictlogist, Katy-Anne, Korny O'Near, Lendorien, MacMed, MrRadioGuy, Paisian, Peumel, Piano non troppo, RG2, Struway, Sunray, Xenon chile, 38 anonymous edits

Risk theory *Source*: http://en.wikipedia.org/w/index.php?oldid=330403321 *Contributors*: Avraham, CBM, Jitse Niesen, John wesley, Melcombe, Sanpitch

Risk-based inspection *Source*: http://en.wikipedia.org/w/index.php?oldid=416873244 *Contributors*: Bearian, Ben.c.roberts, Fletcher1957, Frap, John knight, Kauczuk, Logen1980, Mabasara, Materialscientist, Melaen, Pjhirst, Rjwilmsi, TomGreen, Varlaam, Williamborg, Woohookitty, 11 anonymous edits

Risk-loving *Source*: http://en.wikipedia.org/w/index.php?oldid=403739411 *Contributors*: Brian Pearson, Cessator, Duoduoduo, Kjm, Lova Falk, Malcolma

RISKS Digest *Source*: http://en.wikipedia.org/w/index.php?oldid=411259497 *Contributors*: 89020, Betacommand, CesarB, Crusio, Cyrius, Dawynn, Dsp13, Fubar Obfusco, Jidanni, John Darrow, JonHarder, Jpbowen, Martarius, Miym, Ssbohio, Uncle G, 4 anonymous edits

rNPV *Source*: http://en.wikipedia.org/w/index.php?oldid=418093707 *Contributors*: Btyner, Fabrictramp, Gabriel1907, Nbarth, Villigerr, 2 anonymous edits

Safety engineering *Source*: http://en.wikipedia.org/w/index.php?oldid=432092643 *Contributors*: 208.186.187.xxx, 208.187.134.xxx, Abdull, Aeonx, Analogkidr, Anandsince, Appicharlask, Arcadian, Arisepeter, ArnoldReinhold, Arru, Arthur Smart, Atlant, Bananfisk, Beetstra, Bellhalla, Brighterorange, C J Cowie, CatherineMunro, Charles Matthews, Chemical Engineer, Conversion script, Curtlsmith, Cutler, Cyrus Grisham, Daniel.birket, Darklilac, David Biddulph, David Caldwell, DennisDaniels, Derek Ross, Dislocate, Dj245, DoriSmith, Dual Freq, Dwstclair, E mraedarab, Fagreene, Frap, Freakofnurture, Froucoux, Gavrilov, Gobonobo, Grafen, Hanwufu, Hullernuc, Inwind, Itemuk, Itsnotrocketscience, Jaganath, Jameswraith, JeffTan, Jfdwolff, Jkl, Joclimer, Jogloran, John, John of Reading, Johnfos, Johnqtodd, Jpbowen, Kelly Martin, Kl4m, Kuru, Kvng, Lautreamont, Linuxlad, Littenberg, Ludovic Dugué, Marj Tiefert, Mausy5043, Mbeychok, Mdd, Michael Hardy, Musiphil, Mykolas OK, Neuromusic, OrgasGirl, Park Flier, Peterlewis, Petri Krohn, Petter73, Philnik, Pissant, Plugwash, Pmjones, Prolog, Quarl, RedWolf, Rich Baldwin, Rich Farmbrough, Rjwilmsi, Rlsheehan, Rocket000, Ronz, Rrburke, Rwendland, SaRSUK, Sade, Sam Hocevar, Schapelj, Shimgray, Shoefly, Simesa, SimonP, Sonett72, Syd1435, Syncmaster941bw, Systemsafetyskeptic, Tabletop, Talon Artaine, Tangent747, Tenmei, The Anome, The number c, TheKMan, TheSafetyEngineer, Thinking of England, Thseamon, Tiddly Tom, Tom harrison, TreveX, Utcursch, Vanished user 39948282, Versageek, Wavelength, WikHead, Wikichugoku, Willking1979, Wolfsbane2k, Wronkiew, Wyatts, 154 anonymous edits

Safety instrumented system *Source*: http://en.wikipedia.org/w/index.php?oldid=406502009 *Contributors*: Angela summers, Avalon, Bassplr19, Biscuittin, Dharrold, Dmcnair2007, Email4mobile, EmersonsJimCahill, G totya, Inwind, JaGa, Kku, Ladybetty, Lotje, Lundteig, ManojMohamed, Mausy5043, Mchristman, MrOllie, Mrausand, Pip2andahalf, Propaniac, RHaworth, SUG-INFO, Silversol, Worldbookman, 12 anonymous edits

Safety Integrity Level *Source*: http://en.wikipedia.org/w/index.php?oldid=431147121 *Contributors*: Alan Liefting, Aquillion, Brindis, Cubidoo, DagErlingSmørgrav, Eclipsed, Email4mobile, Emilyexida, Frecklefoot, HenkvD, Imsuraar, Jspayne, Littenberg, Lonelydarksky, Maurice.mccarthy, Mbarrieau, Mchristman, Michalgarbowski, MrOllie, Mrausand, Physchim62, Poco a poco, SUG-INFO, Sababu, Shot info, Silversol, Simon Brown HSE, TexasAndroid, The Anome, Tobias Bergemann, Tsool, UnbiasedHistory, Vimalesh28, Whitepaw, Wolfch, Worldbookman, Xobnkaj, 65 anonymous edits

Sampling risk *Source*: http://en.wikipedia.org/w/index.php?oldid=419147141 *Contributors*: C S, Cander0000, Fabrictramp, Jay1279, Melcombe, Michael Hardy, R'n'B, Tassieroy, 1 anonymous edits

Scenario analysis *Source*: http://en.wikipedia.org/w/index.php?oldid=430509353 *Contributors*: Aferistas, Amorymeltzer, Anikasavage, ArnoldReinhold, Chrislenhart, Cremepuff222, Ghaag, Ileshko, Jls29452, JonHarder, King brosby, Kkorpinen, Kuru, Machiatesla, Mcflashgordon, Mdd, Michael Hardy, Mydogategodshat, Nbarth, OStewart, Patrizio2, Philip Trueman, Phoenixrod, Rjwilmsi, Ronniefaron, Ronz, Sam Hocevar, Scheubi84, Tdeloggio, Timchik, VeryVerily, Voudourisv, Walter Görlitz, 42 anonymous edits

Social risk management *Source*: http://en.wikipedia.org/w/index.php?oldid=352906158 *Contributors*: Bobblehead, Clerks, Espoo, FusionNow, Leonard^Bloom, Rich Farmbrough, Rxnd, Seraphimblade, Seth Nimbosa, Shadowjams, Shiftchange, Sinotara, The Famous Movie Director, WODUP, Woohookitty, 66 anonymous edits

Social vulnerability *Source*: http://en.wikipedia.org/w/index.php?oldid=429553112 *Contributors*: AndrewHowse, Anna, Caiaffa, Chris the speller, Gmalgesini, HamburgerRadio, Heds 1, Isholand, John of Reading, Kajervi, Kwarner, LilHelpa, LilyKitty, Mausy5043, Mild Bill Hiccup, Rigadoun, Sk8r890, SlipperyHippo, Sphilbrick, Stimers, Terrycannon, Woohookitty, 17 anonymous edits

Spurious trip level *Source*: http://en.wikipedia.org/w/index.php?oldid=428860175 *Contributors*: Cubidoo, Download, Email4mobile, Jo7hs2, RHaworth, Tassedethe, 7 anonymous edits

Square root biased sampling *Source*: http://en.wikipedia.org/w/index.php?oldid=400848784 *Contributors*: Canglesea, Gyrobo, Sophus Bie, The Anome, 3 anonymous edits

Stein's unbiased risk estimate *Source*: http://en.wikipedia.org/w/index.php?oldid=426377007 *Contributors*: David Eppstein, Michael Hardy, Miracle Pen, Rjwilmsi, Tassedethe, Zvika, 3 anonymous edits

Stunt performer *Source*: http://en.wikipedia.org/w/index.php?oldid=432157072 *Contributors*: 700clubjej, AdySarbus, Alakon, Anonymous101, Araignee, ArtGriggs, Artful Dodger, Arthena, Asfarer, Bdell555, Bigpinkthing, Blayrow, Bluerasberry, Borgx, Bryan Derksen, CZmarlin, Cab88, Can't sleep, clown will eat me, CanisRufus, CarlesMartin, Cecole, Cimon Avaro, Circusandmagicfan, Clarityfiend, Cmr08, CodeMonk, Cometstyles, Dar-Ape, Darius Sinclair, DarkAudit, Dave judge, Deleting Unnecessary Words, Dgiglio1, Die Titanic, Drdisque, Dstraitjacket, E2XGUY, Eekerz, Elenseel, Elonka, Erudnetti, Famousruler, February 2004 in used, Fieldday-sunday, Filip en, Flominator, Foglamps, Franz Liszt, Fruppence, Furrykef, Fyrael, Gareth E Kegg, Geniac, Gilliam, Grm wnr, Gwernol, Hektor, Igno2, InspectorSands, Isotope23, Ixfd64, JHunterJ, Jagged 85, Jehfes, Jerjan33, Jrdioko, Jvhertum, KGasso, Kanġi Oĥanko, Kaskader, Kingpin13, Kizor, Koavf, Kolinthepenguin, Kungfuadam, Lenoxus, Leszek Jańczuk, Liftarn, Locutus Borg, Lviatour, Magicusa, Magicusb, MarkSutton, Mdwh, Michael Snow, Mini-Geek, MisfitToys, Misterx2000, Mtmelendez, NaidNdeso, Neurolysis, Normalsam, Nyttend, Pakaran, Pavium, Phoenixrod, Pilgrim2457, Pinkadelica, Quill, RainbowOfLight, Rawling, Rigadoun, Rklawton, Rror, Ryocharlesyang, SGBailey, ScAvenger lv, Serpens, Shiyu918, Shrum0101, Shswatek, Skysmith, Srikanthdileep, Struway2, Tanthalas39, Ted Wilkes, Teo64x, The Famous Movie Director, The Thing That Should Not Be, Tide rolls, Tujo, Twinsday, Vardan10, Vlad, Wavehunter, WikiLaurent, Youal, 181 anonymous edits

Substantial equivalence *Source*: http://en.wikipedia.org/w/index.php?oldid=429939500 *Contributors*: AAMiller, Agradman, Aircorn, ArnoldReinhold, Bananaclaw, Billy Pilgrim, Biosicherheit, Colincbn, Darth Panda, Detribe, Ediacara, Feneon, Flauto Dolce, G. Völcker, Gaius Cornelius, Geoffreyt, Gregbard, Ifpri, Jrn, Keepcalmandcarryon, Lerna, LilHelpa, Maestlin, Martpol, Micyclebicycle, Nicholas Cimini, Nutriveg, Res2216firestar, Rjwilmsi, Sei Shonagon, Tazmaniacs, The Transhumanist, TimVickers, Timo Honkasalo, Ttguy, WLRoss, 37 anonymous edits

Success likelihood index method *Source*: http://en.wikipedia.org/w/index.php?oldid=294260488 *Contributors*: D6, Ggd101, RHaworth, Rich Farmbrough, Whpq

Supplier Risk Management *Source*: http://en.wikipedia.org/w/index.php?oldid=382051197 *Contributors*: Cameron Scott, Fshenstone, Hmains, IrishG, Jpkara, KLim1284, Ortichi, SupplierPM, Tassedethe, Topbanana, 8 anonymous edits

System archetype *Source*: http://en.wikipedia.org/w/index.php?oldid=410710382 *Contributors*: B Jana, Esowteric, J04n, KaterinaFarska, Koavf, Mr pand, Nono64, R'n'B, ShelfSkewed, Svarnyp

System dynamics *Source*: http://en.wikipedia.org/w/index.php?oldid=432134805 *Contributors*: Andrejskraba, Anerxelda, Anikasavage, Ant133, Apdevries, Arnejohs, Atlant, B Jana, Balbir Thomas, Benwu, Boud, Bskarin, COMPATT, CX, Chairman S., Chuunen Baka, Crbnblu, DeanKeaton, Djjrjr, Dynamoton, EconSD, Emcod, Emilianolince, Erkan Yilmaz, Faraon x, Fenster, Frisbeeralf, Gelderlander1, Hendrik Fuß, Hgfernan, IPSOS, Imrum, JaeDyWolf, Jhargrov, Jheuristic, Jonverve, Jpbowen, Kai neumann, Kenneth M Burke, Kuru, Laklare, Laser813, Lexor, Livingthingdan, Lontjr, MITalum, Marcelo1229, Mark Krueger, Mathmanta, Matilda, Mbonline, Mdd, Michael Hardy, Modify, Mooredr, MrOllie, Nasmtih, Opavlov, Ossimitz, Patrhoue, PilotPrecise, Pjlamberson, PlatonicIdeas, Pmkpmk, RJBurkhart3, RichardVeryard, RobinLovelace, Ronz, Rzaytsev, Scishop, Serinde, Slon02, SoftwareDeveloper, Sprobst76, Thopper, Voyevoda, Wapcaplet, Wayiran, WiKimik, Wikip rhyre, Xilaile, Yakushima, Zennie, 146 anonymous edits

Systems thinking *Source*: http://en.wikipedia.org/w/index.php?oldid=431569870 *Contributors*: Ahoerstemeier, Akella, Ambitus, AndrewCarey, Anikasavage, Apesofgod, Aranda, Architectchao, Begeun, Benking, Bishonen, Bkell, Bookandcoffee, Brunoton, Btphelps, CALR, CX, Canadianshoper, Cassbeth, Ckatz, Cogitoergovigeo, Cp111, Dancter, De728631, Dragon 280, DragonHawk, Drunken Pirate, EagleFan, Earthdenizen, Erkan Yilmaz, Evanreyes, Everyking, Fakk, Fenice, Fixaller, Frap, Fuzzform, George100, Globaleducator, Gmyersnj, Gobonobo, Gogo Dodo, Gondwanabanana, Harshmellow, Hu12, Igni, Ihcoyc, Immunize, Ireneshusband, J.delanoy, J04n, JIP, Jackvinson, Jeff3000, Jmeppley, Joarsolo, Jose Icaza, Jpbowen, Jschlesinger, Kevin Kidd, Kilmer-san, Kingturtle, Kostmo, LaughingMan, Lbeaumont, Len Raymond, Letranova, Lexor, LightAnkh, Lova Falk, M.v.alexander, MarcoLittel, Mariaflags, Marktompsett, Maurreen, Max786, Mbadri, Mdd, Merbst, Metaknight19, MethodicEvolution, Mindmatrix, Mkoval, Mnent, Mufka, Mydogategodshat, NLPepa, Nad, Nentrex, Nick8325, NickRichmond, NoFisch, Nosmo, Paulreali, Phanerozoic, PiaH, Qswitch426, RJBurkhart3, Redsx414, Rherold123, Rich Farmbrough, Ritafelgate, Robin klein, Robina Fox, Ronz, Rtsdteamscience, Ryandwayne, SE SME, Shadowjams, Skittleys, Smalltalkman, Spalding, Ssdd980, Stefanson, Steve Erlank, Summers, Taxisfolder, Tbackstr, The Rambling Man, TheProphetess, TheTito, Themfromspace, Theredteamrocks, Thseamon, Tito Otero, Tomecito, Tothebarricades.tk, Ty580, Underpants, Vincehk, Viriditas, Vsmith, Wavelength, Westlafayette, Will Beback, 187 anonymous edits

Technique for Human Error Rate Prediction *Source*: http://en.wikipedia.org/w/index.php?oldid=424860423 *Contributors*: Fabrictramp, Ggd101, J04n, Mission Fleg, Synergy, Tenmei, 6 anonymous edits

TESEO *Source*: http://en.wikipedia.org/w/index.php?oldid=428446861 *Contributors*: Fabrictramp, Ggd101, Mission Fleg, Pietrow, RHaworth, Synergy, TheAllSeeingEye, 3 anonymous edits

Two-moment decision models *Source*: http://en.wikipedia.org/w/index.php?oldid=429936030 *Contributors*: Duoduoduo, Rich Farmbrough

Vulnerability *Source*: http://en.wikipedia.org/w/index.php?oldid=422257675 *Contributors*: 16@r, Adequate, Alphanis, Andycjp, Anthony, Arthena, Arthur Fonzarelli, Backburner001, Batmanx, Beland, Beware the Unknown, CALR, CardinalDan, Christian75, Correogsk, DMacks, DanielPharos, Dekisugi, Derek farn, Epbr123, Ewawer, Geofferybard, Heds 1, Imark 02, Julia Rossi, KimvdLinde, Kwarner, LiveDiverse, Lova Falk, Mac, Mani1, Mgiganteus1, Mindmatrix, Mriya, Nikai, OSborn, Oli Filth, Penbat, PigFlu Oink, Pigman, Quandaryus, Queenmomcat, Quintote, Ronbo76, Ronz, Scott Sanchez, SkyLined, Spartan-James, TheRedPenOfDoom, Thumperward, VMS Mosaic, WaysToEscape, Wikieditor1988, 68 anonymous edits

Weather risk management *Source*: http://en.wikipedia.org/w/index.php?oldid=426566461 *Contributors*: Bjg3c, Duckwing, Editor2020, GalileoRisk, Giraffedata, John Broughton, Oduntanr, Rosannevdw, Wavelength, Wxhat1, 18 anonymous edits

Image Sources, Licenses and Contributors

License

Made in the USA
Lexington, KY
11 February 2012